Research Methods in Lifespan Development

Gary L. Creasey

Illinois State University

PEARSON

Boston • New York • San Francisco
Mexico City • Montreal Toronto • London • Madrid • Munich
Paris • Hong Kong • Singapore • Tokyo • Cape Town • Sydney

To Pat, my wonderful wife and colleague

Executive Editor: *Karon Bowers*
Series Editorial Assistant: *Deb Hanlon*
Executive Marketing Manager: *Pamela Laskey*
Senior Production Editor: *Karen Mason*
Editorial Production Service: *nSight, Inc.*
Composition Buyer: *Linda Cox*
Manufacturing Buyer: *Megan Cochran*
Electronic Composition: *Laserwords*
Cover Administrator: *Kristina Mose-Libon*

For related titles and support materials, visit our online catalog at www.ablongman.com.

Between the time website information is gathered and then published, it is not unusual for some sites to have closed. Also, the transcription of URLs can result in typographical errors. The publisher would appreciate notification where these errors occur so that they may be corrected in subsequent editions.

Library of Congress Cataloging-in-Publication Data

Creasey, Gary.
    Research methods in lifespan development / Gary L. Creasey.
        p. cm.
    Includes bibliographical references and index.
    ISBN 0-205-35481-5 (alk. paper)
        1. Developmental psychology--Research--Methodology. I. Title.

BF713.C724 2005
155'.072--dc22

                                                                2005048166

Printed in the United States of America

10 9 8 7 6 5 4 3 2 1   10 09 08 07 06 05

Contents

7   *Assessing Child Intellect and Language*   190

8   *Assessing Social Development in Children*   222

Preface

Fifteen years ago, as a new assistant professor, I was assigned to teach a research methods course in lifespan development. Unfortunately, I ran into a big cold front the first day of class. I specifically remember standing outside the classroom, fully expecting that there would be no students in the room because *it was that quiet*. The students were frozen in their seats, you could hear a pin drop, and apprehension was painted all over their faces. I could almost hear them thinking, "This *research* class is going to prevent me from graduating."

That was fifteen years ago, and I still teach this class. Why, might you ask, would I enjoy teaching a class that so many students seem to dread? I like teaching this course because I live and breathe the material and love the moment during the term that I walk into class and hear "the buzz"—that is, hear the animated conversations of the students who were so silent and anxious at the beginning of the term. Of course, the students are probably not talking about the course material, but at the very least, they do not seem scared about coming to class!

What's the magic that converts these students? A cynic would say I'm just too easy and I probably just gloss over the "hard science." "You just sit around and talk about babies, right?" the critic might claim. I'm not sure my students would agree with this position; in fact, students who do not work hard in my class definitely pay the consequences. I believe the students change their impressions mainly because of the material, and it is hoped, partly due to me! A passion for a subject shows up in our teaching behavior. This is an exciting field, and the students love to see connections between all of this science and everyday applications.

However, praying to win the lottery does not do much good if you do not buy a lottery ticket; you must participate to win! The book, in my opinion, is our major enabler; it must support us and take students to new places that instructors do not have the time or expertise to cover. It must be as good, or even more effective than the instructor. However, this objective is a challenge because many students view books in research methods as dry and boring. "Book makes a good pillow" was one of my favorite teaching-evaluation comments. So, instead of complaining about the currently available books, I decided to do something about it and write my own. Let's consider some of the features of this book that will help both student and instructor:

Methods Made "User Friendly" and Relevant

The tone of the book is "down to earth" and "user friendly." I expect that some students will be apprehensive about the class, and the material is meant to be enjoyable and to not intimidate. In some cases, I had students read material that might be viewed as particularly challenging or muddy, and I used their comments to help clarify matters. In any case, the tone of the book is meant to relax the reader. I find that once students are relaxed, they comprehend the material better.

The material is also relevant. I know of numerous examples of experts who have developed creative, yet easy-to-use, methods that can be used by student researchers. I have also catalogued common mistakes that some of the top people in the field have occasionally made. These successes and miscues are liberally peppered throughout the book. In addition, the book addresses common questions that I have heard from students over the years, such as how to locate good measures, identify an important outcome variable, or find a representative study sample. Why is relevance such an important issue? The student researcher needs to know more than how to define the term *representative sample;* that is, they need to be armed with a strategy that would allow them to actually *obtain* such a sample.

A Lifespan Approach

Instructors teach this course in different ways. Some teach this class as a general research-methods class and provide examples from lifespan research on how to design experiments, explain the concept of validity, or critically evaluate research. Although it is tempting to craft a book that primarily covers introductory research methods and experimental psychology, there are lots of fine books that already meet this objective. In reality, many institutions require students to take *two* major methodology classes: one provides coverage of basic or general research methods, whereas the other is meant to provide a presentation of advanced research methods relevant to a discipline, such as personality, biobehavioral, or lifespan-research methods. This book is primarily tailored for the latter class; that is, I assume the student has already had some exposure to basic research methods. Also, I see a difference between a methods course and a statistics course; in short, the text overviews *methods* that are common to the lifespan researcher and is not meant to function as a statistics primer.

Another problem is that instructors differ in the amount of coverage they expend on different stages of the lifespan. I have had more than one instructor tell me that their course title is, "*Developmental Research Methods*" or "*Research Methods in Human Development*," yet they only provide coverage of methods used by infancy or child-development researchers. Of course, if I adopted this approach then I would lose anyone who discusses methodological issues pertaining to the latter part of the lifespan. I believe this book could fit the needs of just about anyone who teaches the class; it is the first one of its kind that provides a *comprehensive lifespan perspective* of research methods and approaches. The amount of coverage instructors devote to each chapter is an individual choice; however, students should still feel buying the book was worthwhile even if the instructor did not assign every chapter.

Organization

How does one go about organizing a developmental book—chronologically or topically? I discussed this issue with students. Most preferred a straightforward approach that first reviews research methods in the book (with a developmental twist) and then exposes the reader to methodological issues and approaches that face researchers across all developmental stages. The excellent reviewers who provided commentary on earlier drafts of the manuscript reinforced this opinion, and this stance was supported via my discussions with other faculty who teach the course. Although I empathize with the instructor who prefers a topical approach, I was simply overwhelmed with the numbers of instructors, students, and reviewers who preferred otherwise. I personally feel we would lose the lifespan flavor if this book were written in a topical format; I think such a book would look like a general research-methods book with lots of lifespan examples.

Application

One of the most exciting facts about lifespan research is that it is both scientific and applied. Incoming students do not always share this perspective, and many believe that professionals in this area "just do research." The book material should alter this stance. The importance of research methods is firmly articulated and, where possible, the book presents links between basic research and applied work. "One hand (research) holds the other (application)" is a major premise reflected throughout the book. In particular, *the boxed material* promotes connections between research and application.

Current Trends

The requirements for an experiment or a longitudinal design have not changed much over the years, which begs the question of whether we need a methods book that reflects "current approaches." I argue that a current approach is critical; for example, does the average reader have any idea of how to conduct experimental research over the Internet? Beyond considering such major technological changes, some research paradigms that were in vogue only a few years ago are now viewed as outdated. For example, we used to assess peer popularity by asking for teacher input; today, everyone asks the peers themselves for such information. In addition, our theories for understanding developmental populations are very fluid. For example, at one time we believed that parents, peers, and schools were primarily responsible for supporting adolescent development; however, newer work suggests that the very neighborhoods they live in may have even stronger effects! Because we use theory to guide the development of our research and ultimate selection of our study variables, it is important that (a) theory have a place in such a book and (b) the theoretical approaches that are represented are as current as possible.

Pedagogy: A Focus on Active Learning

Throughout, the book constantly encourages readers to consider how they would use the material as student researchers. In addition, at the end of most sections, "What Do You Think?" exercises are included to encourage critical thinking and application. At the end of each chapter, the student is encouraged to perform one or more "Research Navigator™" assignments. These activities ask students to read an on-line research article that reflects primary themes in the chapter and then respond to a number of questions. I believe it is very important for students to actually see that researchers in the real world grapple with the very topics presented in this book. This book is available packaged with access to Research Navigator™ (order # ISBN 0-205-47662-7. Please contact your Allyn & Bacon representative for additional information.

In terms of other pedagogical features, most of the chapter introductions are short and to the point and may contain short stories or vignettes that are relevant to the chapter theme. In addition, learning objectives are always included at the end of the introductory material. Chapter summaries are also concise yet encourage students to reflect on important chapter material. The boxed material contains information on recent methodological trends or research that has sparked important applications or explains why a researcher must often adapt methods for special populations or when conducting research in other cultures. Finally, key terms are highlighted throughout the chapters and appear in a glossary at the end of the book.

Acknowledgments

I dedicated the book to my wife, Pat Jarvis, because she was not only my major supporter but also provided invaluable insight and advice regarding certain chapter material and organizational issues. In addition, my departmental colleagues have been incredibly supportive during this process, and almost all, at one time or another, offered suggestions that influenced the content of the book. I would also like to thank the editorial team at Allyn & Bacon for their support, including Karon Bowers, my sponsoring editor, and Lara Torsky, one of the best editorial assistants in the business. I appreciate the feedback from the reviewers of this text: Catherine Bagwell, University of Richmond; David F. Bjorklund, Florida Atlantic University; Jack Demick, University of Massachusetts Medical School; Chryle Elieff, University of Illinois at Urbana Champaign; Roseanne Flores, Hunter College; Rebecca Foushée, Fontbonne University; Kimberly Rynearson, Tarleton State University; Amy Shapiro, University of Massachusetts; David Sobel, Brown University; Anne Watson, Illinois Wesleyan University; Katja Wiemer-Hastings, Northern Illinois University; Bonnie M. Wright, Gardner-Webb University. Thanks to Laura Berk for permission to use photos from her outstanding book, and her gentle support and suggestions throughout this process. Also, thanks to Kate Johnson and Kate Watson for their diligent work in creating the glossary. My sons, Zachary and Alex, were incredibly inspirational and understanding during the writing process; I had to include some of their stories in the book because they are always on my mind. They make parenting a true joy.

Gary L. Creasey

1

General Research Strategies

Isn't it ridiculous for the government to fund research on largely insignificant matters that are best answered by using a little common sense? The problem is that human beings, from infants to seniors can be unpredictable creatures. Thus, basic and applied research is needed to address important societal issues. For example, did you know that premature infants whose limbs are periodically massaged display better weight gain and go home earlier than babies who do not receive such treatment (Field, Hernandez-Reif, & Freedman, 2004)? Did you know that one could observe a newlywed couple for 15 minutes and predict whether they will divorce or not (e.g., Gottman & Notarius, 2002)? If you doubt the importance of the latter research, I encourage you to tally the number of marital counselors in your community.

The primary objective of this book is to help you appreciate the beauty of lifespan-development research in a user-friendly way. Although some of you might want to "jump right into it," it is important to consider that new students often possess very different backgrounds. Some students have had coursework in child development or aging; others have had training in statistics or research design, and still others have had little exposure to these topics.

Because of this concern, it is important to operate from a similar foundation and to develop a knowledge base regarding basic research skills that are applicable to just about any discipline. After reading this introductory material, you should be able to:

- Describe the major themes of the field.
- Discuss how to better plan and design research.
- Identify the strengths and weaknesses of designs that incorporate age as a major study variable.
- Discuss how to select good measures for your research.

There are three major themes to think about as you read this chapter. First, learning the basic terminology is important, because these concepts will be revisited throughout the

1

book. Second, a solid understanding of the introductory material will allow you to better critique existing research. Third, many research problems can be avoided through careful planning.

The Field of Lifespan Development

To gain an understanding of the field, let's overview a number of important themes. First, although there are many experts who study developmental processes in infants and children, there are a growing number of professionals who work with adolescents and adults. There are also a number of experts who study individuals across all phases of development! Thus, this textbook reminds you that our field encompasses the entire *lifespan*.

The field is also *multicontextual.* For example, whereas early theories heavily emphasized the role of the family (particularly mothers) in development (Freud 1940/1963), more modern theories acknowledge that developmental progress can also be affected by other contexts (Erikson, 1950; Bronfenbrenner, 1989). Think of your own development and how different settings (e.g., schools, part-time work experiences, extracurricular activities) and people (parents, siblings, teachers) have influenced your thinking and behavior over time. In a way, these contexts can be viewed as independent laboratories for the study of human development.

Lifespan development, like many scientific disciplines, is fast becoming *collaborative* and *multidisciplinary* in nature. Professionals in this field have found that many complex problems can be best solved using a team of professionals with different backgrounds and training. The image of the lone research scientist, which might discourage some from pursuing research careers, is a stereotypical image. Many developmental specialists routinely collaborate with other professionals in and outside their home institution. For example, developmental experts at over twenty universities are conducting a landmark study to determine the effects of preschool child-care arrangements on intellectual, emotional, and social abilities (e.g., NICHD Early Child Care Research Network, 2003). You will learn more about this exciting study in the Research Navigator™ assignment at the end of the chapter.

Scientific is another theme of this field. Although some specialists have many interesting ideas that have implications for theory, research, and practice, I cannot underscore enough the importance of testing these ideas in a thorough, scientific manner. For instance, for many years we assumed that romantic couples who could not resolve conflicts were at risk for relationship instability and dissolution. However, more recent research has noted that many happily married couples argue about the same topics year after year—that is, they may never completely resolve an issue. What separates these couples from those that divorce is that they argue about contentious issues in a civil manner (Gottman, 1994). If you went to a relationship counselor, would you want a therapist who was trained the "new" or "old" way? Thus, our research findings frequently have *applied value,* and shape scientific and public opinion about major issues facing our society (such as parenting, child care, and adult learning).

Change is another concept frequently associated with lifespan development, and documenting change in and between individuals is a special challenge to our field. However, our job is not complete once we have documented change. We also have to reach some conclusions as to *why* we have documented changes in our sample. Perhaps your own experiences can shed some light on the difficulty of this task. For example, think of some aspect of your own behavior (e.g., sharing, food preferences, trust in others, sexual behavior). It is probably quite simple to think of how your behavior or thinking on the issue has changed over time; yet, pinpointing exactly *why* you have changed is probably a more daunting task.

Pretend for a moment that you are interested in documenting associations between age and use of banking technology. In order to conduct this study, you interview a number of people across several age groups about their use of automatic teller machines (ATM). After collecting your data, you discover that the older participants use ATMs less than the younger participants do. Although you have documented that older and younger people use this form of technology differently, can you explain *why* these differences were present?

Influences on Development

To provide some clues to support your decision, let's consider three types of influence that are thought to spark change within individuals. According to Baltes (1979), change can be facilitated by normative age-graded, normative history-graded, and nonnormative influences. Although these influences are easy to define, *it can be difficult to ascertain which influence is affecting our data.* The three sources of influences are described in Table 1.1.

Developmentalists are primarily interested in documenting **normative age-graded influences**. This type of influence may be biological, cognitive, or social in origin, is experienced by most people, and is highly related to age (Baltes, Reese, & Lipsitt, 1980). Can you think of some common normative age-graded influences? Puberty is a biological event that is experienced by most people, within a fairly common time frame. Puberty sparks predictable mental (e.g., increases in perspective taking) and social (e.g., increased peer involvement) changes within the individual. In Western societies, college graduation, marriage, childrearing, grandparenthood, and retirement are just a few social events that most people experience that are associated with age.

Thus, if we conclude that older individuals are reluctant to use ATMs because people naturally become more resistant to technology as they get older, then we are making the assumption that this change is normal, happens to most people, and is highly tied to age. However, although this conclusion makes sense, there are other factors that can also

TABLE 1.1 *Influences on Development*

Normative Age-Graded	Influences, highly tied to age, that occur to most people in a society. Examples might include puberty, menopause, retirement, and marriage.
Normative History-Graded	Historical events that influence an entire cohort or generation of people within a society. Examples might include major wars, severe economic depression, or major changes in technology.
Nonnormative	Rare events, such as child abuse, that affect a minority of people. Alternatively, these can be fairly common events, such as losing a spouse, that occur at atypical times during our life (e.g., young adulthood).

influence development. For example, older people might shun ATM technology because computer technology was less available to them when they were younger. Throughout our lifespan, major societal events, wars, and major economic change can influence our development. Developmentalists frequently refer to these events as **normative history-graded influences** (Baltes, 1979). Such events may influence an entire cohort, or generation of people, yet not affect subsequent generations. For example, although you might assume that your older relatives are frugal with money because they are getting older, it is also possible that they learned the value of saving money because of their experiences coping with the Great Depression.

Although both normative age-graded and history-graded influences can affect ATM usage, yet another possibility is that more random events might alter such behavior. For example, a major lottery winner might simply hire someone to handle his or her banking affairs! These random life events, referred to as **nonnormative influences**, can affect development and behavior and have little to do with age or historical events. Although many experiences could qualify as nonnormative influences, such events are usually atypical experiences that affect a minority of people or common events that occur at "odd" times in our life, such as becoming a parent at age 13.

Thus, normative age-graded, history-graded, and nonnormative influences all affect our development. The trick is to determine how these influences separately and jointly shape our developmental progress. You will learn how to isolate the developmental effects of these influences later in the chapter.

What Do You Think?

Think carefully about your physical, cognitive, emotional, and social development. List several normative age-graded influences that may have influenced your development. In addition, have any nonnormative influences affected your development? Finally, what historical or societal changes (e.g., September 11, 2001, or 9/11) have influenced your thinking and behavior over time? What changes in society, education, or technology may affect the development of your children but not necessarily yourself?

The Field of Lifespan Development: A Summary

In conclusion, lifespan development experts face important challenges. We must take great strides to ensure that our work is scientifically rigorous, and meet the added challenge of documenting how and why we change over time. In order to introduce you to how we cope with these issues, let us first turn to some basic research methods. Later, I will specify how to document basic developmental processes, and pinpoint the types of influences (i.e., normative age-graded, normative history-graded, nonnormative) that may affect our study results.

General Research Methods

Initial Planning: The Importance of Theory

Planning research does not have to take months or years. The first step is to select an issue or problem that *interests you* and then become a student of the issue. For example, pretend that you are interested in ascertaining the effects of home video-game play on the development of children. Once the general topic is selected, it is important to educate yourself thoroughly about the research problem, theories behind the topic, current issues and trends, as well as major methodological concerns. There are many styles regarding how to tackle this undertaking; however, one method is to organize your literature in a *chronological* fashion. This strategy allows one to observe the unfolding of major theoretical, conceptual, and methodological debates. The following questions should be addressed during the review:

1. What theoretical perspectives have been used to tackle this issue?
2. How do experts define major concepts pertaining to the topic?
3. What are commonly used and generally accepted methods we can use to accurately assess the issue?
4. When summarizing all of the research, what questions remain to be answered?

The utterance "I just want to make sure nobody has done this study before," is the mantra of the novice researcher. Although lightning can strike twice, it is unlikely that your topic has been studied in exactly the way you want to. The important thing is to develop a *theory-based rationale* for your investigation and predictions. Although theory and hypothesis are sometimes viewed as interchangeable terms, they are different concepts. A **theory** is a philosophical assumption about probable associations between different variables or constructs, such as, "Praising children just spoils them." Most lifespan professionals embrace the following theoretical assumptions (Muuss, 1996):

a. *Development follows predictable, often age-related, patterns.* This is the core theoretical assumption of age-normative influence.
b. *These patterns can be assessed.* We can identify contextual variables, such as family support, that may facilitate or inhibit development.
c. *Developmental outcomes are often based on our developmental history.* For instance, an adolescent who bullies others probably has encountered previous events (e.g., child maltreatment) that explain this behavior.
d. *As they mature, people can increasingly shape their own development.*

Theories are used to guide the development of your study hypothesis, or your theory-based prediction of what you expect to find. When formulating hypotheses, Ray (1997) suggests that hypotheses should be *logical* and *concrete*.

Logical Hypotheses. Try to answer the original research question: does home video-game play really affect development? *What are your hypotheses or predictions and exactly what theory are you basing these predictions on?* In the case of our research question, there are theories that explain the effects of media usage on development. For example, *displacement theory* asserts that the addition of one form of entertainment affects or *displaces* child activities that most closely resemble the newly acquired activity. This theory suggests that a newly acquired video-game system would more likely take time away from television use or outdoor play than from school activities. You could make the prediction that home video-games will more likely affect time involvement with other forms of entertainment rather than with school performance. In reality, this is exactly what studies of this kind have found

(Creasey & Myers, 1986). The lesson is that we *do not* use personal assumptions or opinions to justify our hypotheses; rather, we use an established theory to guide the predictions.

Concrete Hypotheses and Study Variables.   In order to make hypotheses concrete, we must provide an **operational definition** for each concept represented in our prediction. Let's suppose you predict that violent video-game play causes increases in children's aggression. In this case, you must define each concept—that is, you must define both violent video-game play and aggression. For example, aggression could be defined as an intentional act meant to injure or harm another person (Berkowitz, 1993). Providing an operational definition for each concept is important in making our hypotheses more concrete, allows others to better understand our work, *and often leads to a logical choice of measures to assess each construct.*

We must also define whether our constructs represent **independent variables** or **dependent variables**. The independent variable represents a construct that you hypothesize will have an influence on a research participant's behavior, thinking, or emotions. The dependent variable is simply your measure of the person's behavior, emotions, thinking; in other words, it is a variable that is influenced by change or variability in the independent variable. Researchers often select several independent and dependent variables when conducting research.

There are two types of independent variables. A *treatment variable* represents a construct that is manipulated by the experimenter. In our study, the treatment variable would be the manipulation of video-game play. You may require the children to play a highly violent, mildly violent, or nonviolent game. A *subject variable* represents a second type of independent variable. We cannot manipulate a subject variable; thus, certain demographic variables, such as age or ethnicity, would represent this type of variable. In addition, there are other variables that are not subject to manipulation, such as parental divorce or retirement.

Like the independent variable, careful consideration should also be made when selecting the dependent variable(s). It is not uncommon for researchers to put tremendous thought into selection and manipulation of a meaningful independent variable and then fall short on this issue when selecting a dependent variable. For example, let's pretend you are interested in describing the achievement outcomes of individuals bullied by peers. Although it may make sense to select grade point average as an achievement variable, does this data adequately measure the construct? In addition, is grade point average a meaningful variable? There are two ways to address such questions. First, operationally defining *all* constructs that will eventually be designated as independent and dependent variables is an important part of the research planning process. Second, selecting sound measures, which will be discussed in more detail later in the chapter, can also ease our concerns regarding this issue.

Research Designs

Things are beginning to take shape. You have formulated research questions, educated yourself about the topic, defined your constructs, identified your independent and dependent

TABLE 1.2 *Research Designs*

Experiment	The researcher manipulates the independent variable in this study. The researcher achieves control over other competing variables that might affect the dependent or outcome measure. Independent variables can be manipulated in the laboratory (*lab experiment*) or the field (*field experiment*). In tightly controlled experimental studies, the researcher can make strong statements about cause and effect.
Randomized Experiment	Same as the experiment except that the researcher maximizes experimental control by randomly assigning participants to experimental conditions.
Quasi-Experiment	Researcher only has partial experimental control in this study. May be able to randomly assign participants to experimental conditions but may also investigate other independent variables, such as sex or marital status, that cannot be manipulated or will not allow for random assignment.
Nonexperimental/Correlational	Researcher cannot randomly assign participants to experimental conditions or manipulate the independent variable. Researcher can only explore relationships or associations between study variables—hence the term *correlation*. Unlike experimental studies, researcher cannot make strong statements regarding causal influences.

variables, and can provide a theoretical rationale for your hypotheses. Another step is to select a research design so you can test your hypotheses. The selection of your research design is dependent on a number of factors; a variety of such designs are described in Table 1.2.

How you state your hypotheses is one factor that influences the selection of a research design. A particularly strong hypothesis states that variations in the independent variable will directly *influence* or *affect* the dependent variable. Another consideration is how to manipulate your independent variable. We can manipulate exposure to violent video-game play in a laboratory setting. However, other variables, such as divorce or losing a spouse, cannot be manipulated. The treatment of the independent variable and how you state your hypotheses are interrelated; *you should not use strong causal language (e.g., effect, cause, influence) in hypotheses in which you cannot manipulate an independent variable.*

Experimental Designs. The chief requirement of the experimental study is that the researcher manipulate the independent variable (or IV) and that all other variables that may influence the dependent variable are minimized or controlled (Kerlinger, 1986). In the *laboratory experiment*, the researcher manipulates the IV in a carefully controlled setting, such as a laboratory. In the *field experiment*, we try to manipulate the IV in a more naturalistic setting, and attempt to achieve as much experimental control as possible. In both cases, the researcher hypothesizes that the manipulation of IV *causes* a resulting change in the dependent variable.

The most optimal experimental control is achieved in laboratory environments. How can we maximize experimental control? Let us revisit our hypothetical video-game study and think about the independent variable. Video-game play is something we can manipulate under controlled conditions. Through manipulation of the IV, we can set up different *experimental levels or conditions*. For example, we can have some children play violent video games (Experimental condition 1), others play nonviolent games (Experimental condition 2), and still others color or draw (Experimental condition 3). Thus, we have addressed one of the central requirements of the experimental design by manipulating the IV.

However, think about other variables that might influence aggressive behavior in children that are unrelated to the independent variable. For example, what if the difficulty level of the violent video game is more advanced than the nonviolent game? Also, consider the different historical experiences the children may bring into the research setting. Some may have experience playing video games; others may not. In addition, what if you have more boys playing the violent video games and more girls engaged in the other activities? Would these factors influence the dependent variable?

Randomized Experimental Designs.   Like the detective, we must *control* for these other variables so we can claim that manipulation of the IV caused a change in the dependent variable. There are many strategies we can use to achieve such control; however, the most rigorous tactic would be to conduct a **randomized experiment**. In this special experimental design, participants are *randomly assigned* to experimental conditions. If we randomly assign our children to the different experimental conditions, we can assume that a number of competing variables (e.g., previous exposure to video games) are randomly distributed across the experimental conditions.

Quasi-Experimental Designs.   While random assignment is highly recommended when conducting experimental research, you can also control for other competing variables by turning potential weakness into strength. If you were really concerned that boys and girls were affected differently by violent video game play, why not simply make the child's sex another independent variable? You would have two independent variables: video-game play (treatment IV) and child sex (subject IV). By the way, because we cannot randomly assign children to their gender, the addition of this particular IV has now altered our design. Instead of an experimental design, we now have a **quasi-experimental design**; that is, we possess an IV that (a) cannot be manipulated; and, (b) participants cannot be randomly assigned to this particular condition (i.e., gender).

It is common for scientists to select several independent variables when conducting research. This strategy provides options for data analysis. After completion of our video-game study, we can examine both experimental main effects and interactions. A **main effect** represents the effect of *one* independent variable on the dependent variable. For example, the association between the child's sex and later aggressive behavior represents one potential main effect. Simply put, the number of main effects is equal to the number of independent variables.

A significant **interaction** between independent variables is far more interesting than a significant main effect. An interaction means that the relationship between one IV and the dependent variable is dependent on the level of another IV. An interaction specifies how two independent variables *work together* to influence the dependent variable (Kerlinger, 1986).

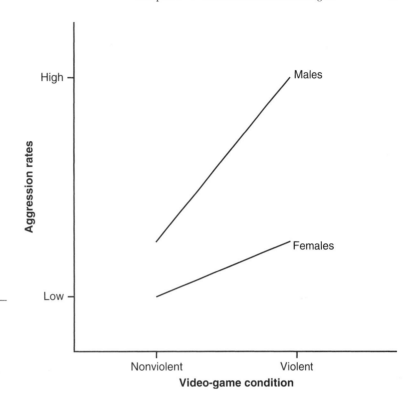

FIGURE 1.1 *The Concept of Interaction*. Note that aggression rates differ between males and females more dramatically in the violent than in the nonviolent video-game condition.

The concept of interaction is often difficult to understand. The data presented in Figure 1.1 perhaps can clarify this term. Note that boys and girls who play the nonviolent video games show low levels of aggression. Further, girls who play the violent video games do not display high levels of aggression, but boys who play them do. Thus, in our study, the effects of violent video-game play on aggression are dependent on the child's sex.

Although the concept of interaction can be difficult to understand, for most research questions, there are rarely simple, main-effect solutions. What if someone told you that divorce was harmful to all children? You probably would say that the relationship between divorce and problems are *dependent* on many things, such as the age of the child or the intensity of fighting between the parents. Also, think of the applied implications when studies yield significant interactions. Documenting that violent video-game play is related to aggressive behavior (a main effect) may not sway parental opinions. However, finding that boys with difficult temperaments were particularly vulnerable to violent video games may persuade parents to be more vigilant regarding this issue.

What Do You Think?

You are interested in identifying variables that predict sharing in children. You document a main effect for child gender and an interaction between child gender and family size. What do these findings suggest?

Nonexperimental/Correlational Designs.   Although the experimental approach represents a powerful way to establish causal relationships between your study variables, there are many issues that cannot be brought under experimental control. In such cases, we must resort to **nonexperimental**, or **correlational**, designs. Nonexperimental designs constitute research in which the investigator does not have direct control over the independent variable because participants have already experienced the condition (e.g., divorce) or the variable simply is impossible to manipulate (e.g., family economic status). Unlike the quasi-experimental approach, these designs do not allow for direct manipulation of any independent variables.

When using the nonexperimental or correlational approach, we are simply examining *relationships or associations* between variables. The causal language used when reporting the results of an experimental study (e.g., words like *effects; influences; caused*) must be considerably softened when using this approach. When conducting correlational research, we evaluate the relationships between our variables through the use of correlation coefficients, which can range from +1 to −1. The following represents a selection of correlation coefficients:

.23   .40   −.67   .01   −.90

Correlation coefficients provide two pieces of information about the associations between our study variables. The numerical coefficient allows one to ascertain the *strength* of association between the two variables. This task is easy to accomplish: *simply ignore the sign* (i.e., positive or negative) and select the most robust coefficient. Thus −.90 represents the strongest association between two study variables in the aforementioned example.

What does this number mean? For example, we find that the correlation between performance on a college entrance exam and later academic performance is .70. To interpret this coefficient, simply square it and multiple the product by 100. Thus .70 × .70 = .49, .49 multiplied by 100 = 49 percent. Thus, about 50 percent of academic performance is accounted for (though not *caused*) by the exam scores. Beyond strength, these statistics provide evidence for the *direction* of associations between the study variables. A positive correlation (e.g., .67; .78) indicates that *high* scores on one measure are related to *higher* scores on another measure (similarly, low scores predict low scores). Conversely, a negative correlation (e.g., −.42; −.68) indicates that *high* scores on one measure are associated with *low* scores on another measure.

For example, suppose a researcher is interested in documenting associations between marital satisfaction and child adjustment. Adjustment is assessed in two ways. The researcher obtains the grade point average of each child, and parents complete a behavior-problem checklist. The researcher then computes the correlation coefficients and documents a positive correlation between marital satisfaction and grade point average, but a negative correlation between satisfaction and child behavior problems. These data are plotted in Figure 1.2. Note that high scores on marital satisfaction are related to higher grade point averages (positive correlation), whereas high satisfaction scores are related to fewer behavior problems (negative correlation).

Correlational research is a valuable tool for demonstrating associations between difficult-to-manipulate variables, such as marital satisfaction or child-care arrangements.

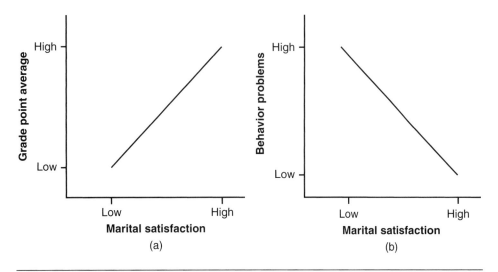

FIGURE 1.2 *Positive and Negative Correlations.* Graph A represents a positive correlation; note that high scores on the marital satisfaction measure are related to high grade point average. Graph B depicts a negative correlation; note that a *high* score on marital satisfaction measure predicts *fewer* child behavior problems.

However, because we have little control over the independent variable, or over other variables that might influence the dependent variable, it is difficult to draw firm conclusions from these studies. It is often difficult to ascertain the direction of effects between the study variables. For example, let's revisit the data presented in Figure 1.2. Although happily married people may simply have well-adjusted children, it is also quite possible that the reverse is true. It is possible that a child who is excelling in school delights her parents, who in turn feel more parental unity and experience more marital harmony! *Thus, it may be difficult to accurately identify the independent and dependent variable when conducting correlational research.*

Another central difficulty rests with how to control for other variables that might influence the dependent variable. For example, if happily married couples are also great parents then it is possible that parenting behaviors, such as school involvement and high achievement expectancies more directly influence academic behavior. In fact, high marital satisfaction, in itself, may have little direct influence on academic behavior. Thus, the association between martial satisfaction and academic behavior can be best explained by an unmeasured third variable. Another way to consider this issue is to think about monthly ice-cream sales and swimming accidents. Although there is certainly a positive correlation between the two variables, their relationship is accounted for by a non-measured variable.

We can improve correlational studies. Some independent variables that are difficult to control can be manipulated under simulated or analog conditions. In this case, you are switching from a correlational to an experimental design. For example, Cummings and colleagues have developed analog procedures to ascertain the effects of interadult conflict on children; the results of this work are contained in Box 1.1. Of course, there are times

BOX 1.1 • *Using Analog Methods to Study Difficult-to-Manipulate Variables*

Sometimes it is tempting to throw up our hands and argue that many interesting phenomena cannot be brought under experimental control. However, with some creative thought, we can use simulated or analog conditions that allow for experimental control over an independent variable that might be impossible to modify in the real world. For example, scholars have known for years that interparent conflict is strongly related to a host of developmental problems in children (e.g., Block, Block, & Gjerde, 1986). Historically, much of the work on this topic has been correlational in nature. A skeptic might raise the chicken-or-egg question— that is, does interparent conflict cause developmental problems, or vice versa.

Of course, there are ways to better tease out this relationship using correlational designs. For example, you might be able to forecast later developmental problems in children by using prenatal assessments of marital conflict. However, what can you conclude if you compute a significant correlation between these two variables? Parents argue and quarrel in different ways. Some shout and yell in front of their children, whereas others do so when their children are not present. Some parents argue about financial issues, and others use their children as a topic for argument. Simply documenting an association between the frequency of interparent

conflict and developmental problems in children sheds little light on this problem. Perhaps from this example you can observe the central weakness of correlational research: *it is very difficult to bring under your control the complexities of your independent variable.*

Mark Cummings's laboratory has shed light on this issue by manipulating interadult conflict under carefully controlled conditions (see Cummings & Davies, 1994 for a review). Cummings trains his research assistants to simulate an argument in front of the child research participant. In some studies he has had research assistants argue directly in front of the child; in other instances, his assistants argue in another room to simulate "arguing behind closed doors." In addition, across several studies he has manipulated the frequency, intensity, and topic of the disagreement.

Perhaps this research also sheds more light on the power of experimental designs. We can more accurately determine under what conditions important variables in our lives facilitate or undermine our development. Of course, observing two strangers engaged in an argument might not have the same impact on children as actual interparent conflict. For example, one might expect that children's reactions would be even stronger in the presence of parents or other attachment figures.

when we must use correlational designs, because there are variables that are not amenable to analog methods. In such cases, these designs can be improved by using established theory to guide us in selecting a *battery* of variables that could potentially influence the dependent variable.

Let's say that you want to identify variables that affect parenting behavior. When reviewing this literature, you will find theories that identify distal and proximal variables that influence this behavior. A **distal variable** represents an event that theoretically took place some time ago, such as interparent conflict exposure during childhood. A **proximal variable** reflects a current, ongoing event, such as marital distress. We can better understand how these variables predict parenting behavior by using a **multivariate correlational design**. In such a design, we first diagram theoretical relationships between all of our study variables, such as those illustrated in Figure 1.3.

What do all of those arrows mean? The arrows represent the theorized direction of effects; for example, it is theoretically assumed that attitudes regarding parenting and parent mental health influence parenting behavior. When designing research of this nature, the insertion of an arrow is *guided by theory*—that is, each arrow must be theoretically justified.

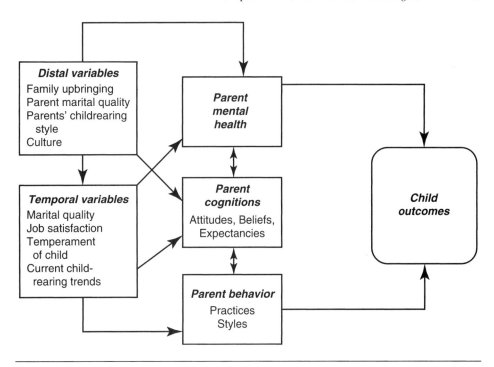

FIGURE 1.3 *Conceptual Framework of Parenting*. This conceptual framework of parenting illustrates how researchers use a multivariate correlational approach to research. Arrows depict hypothesized relationships between variables; each must be theoretically justified.

Using this design allows us to address one of the inherent weaknesses of simple correlational research. That is, other variables that might influence the association between a potential independent (parenting behavior) and dependent (child outcomes) variable are assessed. Once all data has been collected, we can determine the viability of the *entire* diagramed model through a statistical procedure termed **structural equation modeling**. This technique provides more information than a simple correlation statistic because *all* hypothesized relationships between the study variables are assessed simultaneously. In short, the researcher provides statistics regarding how well the data actually fit the hypothesized model and provides an estimate of how well the model "works." This example also illustrates how theory guides hypotheses, study design, and eventual statistical analyses.

Critiquing Designs

When utilizing the most stringent experimental design, we manipulate an independent variable (or a series of independent variables), randomly assign participants to experimental conditions, and control for additional variables that might influence our dependent variable. The advantage of experimental designs is that they possess strong **internal validity**. Internal validity refers to our confidence that the manipulation of the independent variable truly caused a systematic change in the dependent variable.

Experimental designs provide a scientific edge, because strong internal validity allows one to make claims regarding cause and effect. However, high internal validity may have costs. In order to achieve experimental control over the independent variable, the researcher may be forced to create highly artificial environments. For example, a researcher interested in the effects of television violence on children's behavior may expose them to 10 minutes of uninterrupted violence. If children became more violent after watching these television clips, then the researcher can claim that the children became aggressive because they viewed violent programming. Other factors that may influence children's subsequent behavior, such as bad commercials or a lousy plot line, have been effectively eliminated.

However, such experimental control may have drawbacks. How realistic is it for children to watch one violent act after another in the absence of a story plot? How confident is the researcher that the study results will generalize to the "real world"? One thorny issue with experimental designs rests with **external validity**, or one's confidence that the study results will generalize to the broader population residing in the community. A general rule of thumb is that high internal validity compromises external validity (as well as vice versa).

Correlational designs also have advantages and disadvantages. These designs allow us to study important variables, such as divorce, that are difficult to manipulate. Correlational studies may also have practical value. For example, a number of studies suggest that adolescent involvement in extracurricular activities improves school performance and discourages drug use (Mahoney & Cairns, 1997). These findings suggest that encouraging adolescent participation in school clubs and organizations may have beneficial results.

Although correlational studies may achieve high levels of external validity, there is always the danger that internal validity can be seriously compromised. For instance, we cannot randomly assign adolescents to extracurricular activities, and it is difficult to control for other variables that might influence outcome measures. Adolescents who engage in extracurricular activities may have caregivers with high achievement expectancies; thus, increased school performance could naturally occur whether the adolescent was involved in the activity or not.

Controlling Validity Threats

Like the choice of a research design, we should give careful thought to validity threats before study initiation. In terms of achieving strong internal validity, we want to ensure that the independent variable, and *only* the independent variable, is solely responsible for causing some change in the dependent variable. In this section, we will explore some of the more common threats to internal validity; a sampling of these concerns is outlined in Table 1.3.

The Participants: Today's Problems

I once asked a friend in graduate school if it was boring to work with white rats. He responded by saying, "Sometimes, but at least they're predictable." His logic made

TABLE 1.3 *Threats to Internal Validity*

Selection Bias	Subjects drawn from nonequivalent settings. Can be addressed by drawing all subjects from the same setting.
History	Individual differences and experiences between subjects. Can be addressed through random assignment, elimination of the historical effect, matching, or making the historical variable an independent variable.
Statistical Regression	Tendency for high- or low-scoring subjects to score slightly toward the mean during a second round of testing. Can be addressed by using a control group.
Selective Dropout	Nonrandom dropout of subjects. Best addressed through prevention.
Testing Effects	Repeated testing using the same measures may affect subject behavior over time. The use of alternate forms or methods can address this concern.
Time of Measurement Effects	Historical events that occur during the course of a study (e.g., major war). Can be addressed through use of a control group.
Maturation	Naturally occurring changes in subjects because of age or experience. Can be checked through use of a control group.
Instrumentation	Unintended changes in instruments, research settings, or experimenters. Can be addressed through standardization and monitoring.
Reactivity	Unintended changes in subjects, usually resulting from problems with instrumentation. Can be addressed by standardization.

sense because laboratory rats are ordered from the same stock, housed under similar conditions, and have a tremendous respect for science—they will not drop out of your study! Thus it is not surprising that many internal-validity threats rest with the human research participant.

Two sticky issues when working with subjects are **selection bias** and **historical effects** (Cook & Campbell, 1979). **Selection bias** occurs when participants are selected from nonequivalent settings, and represents a special difficulty for lifespan researchers who study different age groups, such as 20-, 40-, and 60-year olds. Might there be a problem if we recruited younger participants from a college campus and older subjects from the community? Documenting that younger subjects were more intelligent may have more to do with the settings the participants were selected from than actual aging processes. Because proper sampling is a central requirement for sound research, we discuss this issue more fully in the next chapter.

Even same-aged participants possess different histories and personal experiences. These different experiences, or **historical effects**, can greatly influence our results. I indicated earlier that overly aggressive children might be more influenced by violent video-game play than less aggressive children. If we only had two study conditions—nonviolent and violent video-game play—our results could be marred if more aggressive children were in the violent condition. Documenting that children were more aggressive after playing violent video games would not be surprising if we had more aggressive children in this condition to start! There are four ways to cope with historical effects (Kirk, 1995):

1. One could simply eliminate a component of the historical effect; for example, one might only include moderately aggressive children in the study. However, one might question how well the results of this study would generalize to the real world.
2. Random assignment of participants to study conditions is another strategy that almost guarantees control over historical validity threats.
3. The researcher could randomly assign equal numbers of highly aggressive and nonaggressive children to each experimental condition. Through such **subject matching**, the researcher is ensured that each experimental group contains equal numbers of subjects regarding the historical effect. Although we have discussed how to match using one variable, some researchers pursue subject matching using multiple variables, such as age, sex, and socioeconomic status.

   Though it is tempting to match highly aggressive and nonaggressive children to our experimental conditions, matching subjects using extreme cutoff scores (e.g., high/low aggression; high/low social class; high/low intelligence) can create another validity threat. Individuals who score extremely high or low on a measure often score slightly more toward the statistical mean over the course of repeated testing, a phenomena known as **statistical regression**. Thus the highly aggressive children may show slightly lower aggression scores after video-game play, whereas the nonaggressive children may appear to become more aggressive.
4. Finally, one could take subject matching one step further by actually analyzing the effect of aggression on the dependent variable. *In this case, the researcher has actually turned the historical variable into an independent variable.* This final strategy represents a powerful, and very interesting, way of controlling historical effects.

The Participants: Tomorrow's Problems

Lifespan researchers frequently study people over time, a technique known as longitudinal research. However, repeated testing can create headaches. For example, **selective dropout** is an additional threat to internal validity. It is normal for people to drop out of a study that covers a lengthy period of time. Geographic mobility is high in our society; thus, when people move they cannot be expected to remain committed to our research. Although *random* dropout can be expected, a chief difficulty arises if such dropout is selective, or *nonrandom*. To check for such random attrition, statistical tests can be conducted to determine whether there is predictability regarding attrition. We can contrast the people who remain in the study to those who drop out on demographic variables, such as socioeconomic status. Exit interviews with people who drop out can also provide us with valuable information. We can rest easier if 10 dropouts provided different reasons for why they dropped out. However, what if almost all of the dropouts indicated that they decided to terminate participation because they "didn't have time" or "your study takes too long to do"?

Why should we be concerned about dropout? Suppose you were interested in how aging affected intelligence over time. In order to address this objective, you obtain a sample of middle-aged adults and administer an intelligence test every five years over the next two decades. At the conclusion of the study, you document that the subjects are brighter than at the first assessment. Although you might argue that wisdom does come with age, it is quite possible that the less intelligent participants simply dropped out of the study.

When studying people over time, there are other validity threats that must be considered. Internal validity can be threatened by **testing effects** in studies that involve repeated trials or measures over time. A participant who takes the same test over and over may base their responses on how they completed the test during the previous assessment. Similarly, a person who undergoes the same experimental condition over time may begin to anticipate certain aspects of the experiment. Although testing effects can be hard to overcome, varying methods or measures over time can offset the difficulty. Some questionnaires and tests have alternate forms that allow us to administer a slightly different version each time.

Another validity threat to longitudinal research rests with ongoing history. Major historical events or societal changes can take place during the course of your study that may alter people's behavior. Similar to history-graded influences, these events could be wars, shifts in political climate, or technological advances. How might these **cohort**, or **time-of-measurement**, **effects**, threaten internal validity? Consider the case of a researcher evaluating an intervention program targeting teen parents. Over time, a television network devotes an entire week of programming that focuses on helping teenagers cope with parenthood. The very next week, the teen parents in the intervention program suddenly report better psychological health and parenting behaviors. What can the researcher conclude? Did they become better parents because of the intervention program or did they simply watch the television special?

Although historical influences primarily affect studies involving repeated assessments over time, randomly assigning participants to a **control group**—which normally contains individuals not exposed to the independent variable—can address this validity threat. Suppose we sampled two groups of teen parents for the intervention. One group would receive the intervention, whereas the other group might be placed in a "waiting list" group to receive the treatment at a later date. If the control group did not show better functioning after the television special, then one could conclude that improvements in parenting behavior resulted from the intervention.

Control groups can also address other validity threats; recall the problems associated with statistical regression toward the mean. Let's pretend that in the teen-parenting study interventions were conducted with parents that scored very high or low on a distress measure. By using this recruitment strategy, we are almost guaranteed to document that the highly distressed teens will show fewer psychological symptoms after the intervention because of statistical regression toward the mean. However, suppose we found that teens in the intervention group showed large declines in psychological distress, yet teens with high levels of psychological distress in the control group showed few declines. If regression to the mean were the only culprit, we would expect very similar levels of declines in both groups.

Maturation is another validity threat that can be potentially checked by inclusion of a control group. For example, do the teen parents show improved health because they were receiving treatment or because they learned coping skills on their own? Over the course of the study, participants can experience naturally occurring intraindividual changes, or *maturation*. A control group addresses this concern. Documenting few changes in the control group and large intervention effects in the treatment group allows us to rule out maturational influences. If maturation were really at work, we would expect the control group to change as well.

Perhaps you can see why random assignment and control groups are viewed as vital components to experimental research. Random assignment disperses differences in historical and educational experiences between people, whereas control groups allow us to ascertain the effects of ongoing historical changes, maturation, and statistical regression toward the mean.

The Experimenter

There are two additional validity threats that are directly controlled by the researcher. **Instrumentation** confounds occur when mistakes occur with our equipment, or even researchers (Cook & Campbell, 1979). For example, if we were timing the duration of parent-infant eye contact, a malfunctioning stopwatch would invalidate our data. However, although equipment and computers can make mistakes, invalid data is more frequently due to human error. For example, a researcher trained to record parent-infant interactions is going to make mistakes if they show up to the experiment tired or ill. The key to accurate data collection is to not only monitor the behavior of a research assistant at the start of an investigation but also to periodically check the reliability of the assistant over time.

I once overheard the remark, "The problem with laboratory research is that the lab is an independent variable." Although this idea may be overstated, the research environment can spark anxieties among research participants. **Subject reactivity** can occur when the research environment causes the subject to behave or think in ways that are not typical. For this reason, researchers often try to make their labs appear as "normal" as possible. Instead of witnessing a room full of computers, electrodes, and wires, a subject may be tested in a lab that resembles a waiting room. Reactivity can also occur in field research. In one study, we had great difficulties videotaping home-based toddler play. The toddlers appeared uncomfortable, and paid more attention to the researchers than to the toys. When queried about this issue, a mother remarked that her toddler was wary because the house was "too quiet." She indicated that her family typically had the television on all of the time. After turning on the television, her toddler immediately began playing with the toys we had brought! Thus subject reactivity can potentially occur in just about any research environment.

Controlling Threats to External Validity

When considering external validity, the researcher must debate how well the study results will generalize to the "real world"; one must consider to what population and setting the results will have application value. In order to address concerns regarding population, astute researchers draw representative samples using **random selection**. The researcher identifies a large potential pool of subjects that represent the demographic makeup of the target population within a particular community, state, or country. Next the researcher randomly selects participants from this subject pool to participate in the study. Because proper sampling represents a common obstacle, we will more fully examine this issue in the next chapter.

The researcher also must consider how well the research results apply to behavior in realistic settings. This issue needs to be addressed when considering both the independent and dependent variables. When we expose participants to independent variables, we should be fairly certain that similar conditions exist in the "real world." In addition, behaviors that are evoked by the independent variable must have *generalizability*. For example, do children who behave aggressively in the laboratory also act in a similar fashion in their own neighborhoods? We will address in more detail how to control for such validity threats in the next chapter.

Summary of Validity Threats

Internal validity refers to the experimenter's confidence that the independent variable truly influenced the dependent variable. *External* validity refers to how well the study results generalize to real people in real settings in the real world. Internal validity threats can result from many factors, but the most common are subject (e.g., maturation, history) or experimenter (e.g., instrumentation) confounds. Control over threats to internal validity can be achieved through careful planning and selection of a research design that has planned controls, such as random assignment and control groups.

What Do You Think?

You are planning to conduct a study with children, adolescents and adults. Luckily, you have three labs, one for each developmental group. How would you design each lab to address concerns regarding the potential artificiality of the lab environment? How might internal and external validity be affected by your lab design?

Developmental Designs

How do normative age-graded, normative history-graded, and nonnormative influences contribute to developmental change? In order to address this issue, lifespan experts incorporate developmental designs in their research studies. In developmental designs, age is treated as an independent subject variable.

Cross-Sectional Designs

The **cross-sectional design** represents one of the most popular developmental designs. As Figure 1.4 shows, people representing different age groups are studied at one time of measurement. For example, to examine the relationship between age and interest in sexual activity, we might recruit groups of 20-, 40-, 60-, and 80-year olds and administer a survey regarding attitudes about sexual activity to each participant.

It is easy to see why this is a popular design. Studies involving cross-sectional designs are quick and inexpensive. Because the participants are studied at one time of measurement, there is no need to worry about attrition or problems associated with repeated testing.

Yet there are drawbacks to cross-sectional research. A central difficulty rests with data interpretation. Recall that a chief task of the lifespan specialist is to tease out the

Cross-sectional design

Age groups	20	40	60	80
Date of birth	1985	1965	1945	1925
Time of measurement		2005		

Longitudinal design

Age	20 → 40 → 60 → 80			
Date of birth	1985			
Time of measurement	2005	2025	2045	2065

FIGURE 1.4 *Traditional Developmental Designs.* In the cross-sectional design, participants representing different age groups are assessed at one time of measurement. Longitudinal designs pertain to the assessment of one sample over time.

relative contribution of normative age-graded, normative history-graded, and nonnormative influences. What can we conclude if a cross-sectional study suggests that older people are less interested in sex than younger participants? Researcher A might conclude that people simply become less interested in sexual activity as they get older (a normative age-graded influence), whereas Researcher B might claim that older people show less interest in sexual activity because of historical differences between the younger and older participants (history-graded influence). For example, Researcher B could suggest that younger people today are more informed and experienced regarding sexuality and that the older participants grew up in a more conventional era. This conclusion would mean that age had little to do with interest in sexual activity and that the older participants in the study had similar attitudes when they were younger.

Differences in historical experiences between age groups in cross-sectional research are termed **cohort differences**. A cohort difference means that one (or more) of our age groups has experienced a major history-graded influence while another has not. For example, older people might be more frugal with their money than younger ones because they grew up during the Great Depression. Thus a chief drawback, or confound, with cross-sectional research is that the effects of age on our dependent variable could be confounded with cohort differences. In other words, it is difficult to discern whether normative age-graded or history-graded influences are affecting our dependent variable. Thus, when using cross-sectional designs, at best the researcher can only conclude that there are *age differences* between the study participants, and will be severely curtailed in making conclusions as to why.

Unlike the design depicted in Figure 1.4, most cross-sectional studies do not contain samples that differ so dramatically in age. Creasey and Kaliher (1994) polled fifth, seventh, and nineth graders regarding their relationships with grandparents. Older adolescents reported more conflict and distancing from their grandparents than the preadolescents. However, reports of love and affection were similar across the age groups, suggesting that the overall relationship quality may not have been dramatically affected.

In this study, important developmental questions about adolescent-grandparent relationships were answered in a short time period. Although the researchers could not completely conclude that the study results resulted from normative age-graded influences, it would be difficult to argue that the results were because of history-graded influences. Given the small, four-year age gap between younger and older participants, it is probable that all participants experienced the same historical events. Thus, cross-sectional designs can be improved if we consider ways to reduce the impact of cohort differences via careful consideration of age groups. This idea is important when studying any issue that is vulnerable to historical or societal change, such as technology, attitudes toward other cultures, sexuality, or perceptions of war and peace.

The influence of history-graded influences is not the only important concern in conducting cross-sectional research. Recall that a minority of our sample could be experiencing changes resulting from nonnormative influences, such as winning the lottery or the untimely death of a spouse. Because these influences affect a minority of the population, one could ignore this influence and assume that the events are not affecting a majority of our participants.

Another possibility would be to poll participants about the occurrence of nonnormative influences over a designated period of time (e.g., six months) and exclude any participant that had experienced such an event. Alternatively, one could tally the number of events and treat nonnormative events as an independent variable *in addition to* the independent variable, age. Potentially, such a study would allow the researcher to examine how age and nonnormative events may interact to predict the dependent variable. In the hypothetical sexuality study, older participants may display less interest in sexual behavior when contrasted to their younger counterparts but only when they are experiencing major nonnormative events.

Longitudinal Designs

Although cross-sectional designs are vulnerable to cohort differences, this potential confound can be eliminated through the use of a **longitudinal design**. When using a longitudinal design, the researcher samples individuals constituting a single age group and then tracks the developmental progress of the participants over time (see Figure 1.4). Because only one age group, or cohort, is utilized, cohort differences are eliminated.

A major advantage of longitudinal designs is that they enable us to document actual changes within a group of people over time. Thus, rather than plotting simple differences between different age groups (i.e., cross-sectional design), we can more realistically conclude that changes over time resulted from age change, or normative age-graded influences.

There are numerous examples of excellent longitudinal research. In one study, adolescents were polled about their involvement in peer crowds (Prinstein & La Greca, 2002). Three primary crowds were identified: "*jocks*" or adolescents who were athletic and on sports teams; "*brains*" or individuals who liked academics and had good grades; and "*burnouts*" or youth who routinely got into trouble in school. The researchers surveyed emotional health during early adolescence (Time 1) as well as middle-late adolescence (ages 15–18) (Time 2). The researchers predicted that crowd membership would affect health changes over time, because identity issues become more important to us during late

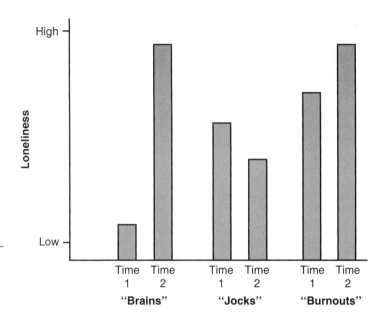

FIGURE 1.5 *Short-Term Longitudinal Design*. Note changes in loneliness as dependent on maturity and crowd affiliation.

adolescence (i.e., an age-normative influence). Because crowd membership somewhat defines one's identity, they expected that adolescents who belonged to crowds that were considered less prestigious in these schools, such as the "brains," would suffer more emotional health problems over time when contrasted to crowds that were held in higher esteem, such as the "jocks." As depicted in Figure 1.5, this particular hypothesis was borne out; that is, the emotional health of the "brains" declined during late adolescence, whereas the health of the "jocks" increased.

Beyond documenting changes brought on by normative age-graded influences, longitudinal research allows for predictions about future behavior. Kupersmidt and Coie (1990) tracked 5th-grade children identified as highly unpopular, or "rejected," by their peers. Years later, the researchers documented that the rejected children were having great difficulty negotiating adolescence, and were at an increased risk for academic problems, truancy, and juvenile crime. Thus, the results of longitudinal research allow us to better predict or "forecast" outcomes for individuals who might possess current behavior profiles. These data have important implications for preventive intervention efforts.

Longitudinal designs also have potential weaknesses. History, or time, of course cannot be held constant. The possibility exists that a major historical or societal event could occur during a longitudinal study. Such a historical event is a *cohort*, or *time-of-measurement* effect (see also p. 17). For example, pretend that you completed a longitudinal study and documented that participants became more empathetic to individuals with sexually transmitted infections. Could you conclude that this change resulted from age or maturity (normative age-graded influence), or from shifts in public opinion regarding the topic?

The confounding of age and time of measurement (i.e., cohort effects) is not the only problem with longitudinal research; it can be time consuming and costly to conduct. Other issues can threaten the integrity of longitudinal research. Internal validity threats, such as subject attrition and the effects of repeated testing, are both problems inherent in longitudinal designs. The external validity of longitudinal research might also be questioned. For example, what type of person participates in a study that spans many years? Are such people typical of the general population?

Despite these difficulties, the longitudinal design is a powerful research tool. With careful thought, a number of its drawbacks can be significantly reduced. For example, although a number of longitudinal studies exist that span across decades, many researchers conduct longitudinal research that is short-term in nature. A longitudinal study tracking changes in adults from age 20 to 25 is much less likely to suffer from time-of-measurement effects than a study that follows participants for 50 years.

Likewise, careful thought about research questions, study variables and measures before the onset of the study can potentially offset problems. For instance, is your study topic going to be equally as important 10 years from now? Will people in the future view your topic and study variables in the same way as people today do? Are there alternative ways to measure your study variables to lessen the impact of repeated testing? How will you achieve a random sample of people, and how will you keep your participants in the study over time? Attention to these questions should always be done before, rather than during, data collection.

What Do You Think?

You want to study how parenting behaviors affect infant social behavior and intelligence during the first two years of life. How might you prevent some of the problems inherent in longitudinal designs, such as testing and subject dropout?

Time-Lag Designs

Thus far, we have considered designs that are strictly developmental in nature and treat "age" as a central independent subject variable. However, there are times when normative history-graded influences have been studied over time. In a **time-lag design**, the researcher holds age constant by assessing people of the *same age group* over time. For example, a researcher might administer a measure to one sample of 18-year-olds, three years later administer the same measure to another group of 18-year-olds, and repeat this assessment for another sample of 18-year-olds three years later. This allows one to track the influence of potential history-graded influences, such as changes in national education policies, over time while holding age constant. Although time-lag designs are very useful as a research method, they can also be used to improve traditional developmental designs.

Modified Developmental Designs

We can improve traditional developmental designs. In the **cross-sectional sequences design**, we complete similar cross-sectional studies over time (Baltes, Cornelius, & Nesselroade, 1979). For example, in one study, identity development in younger (e.g., freshmen)

Cross-sectional sequences design

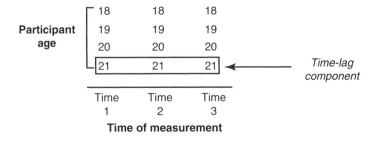

Longitudinal sequences design

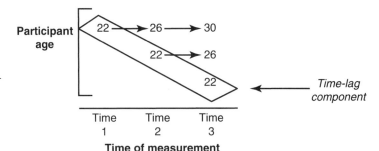

FIGURE 1.6 *Modified Developmental Designs.* Illustrations of cross-sectional sequences and longitudinal-sequences designs. Participants are followed over time in the longitudinal-sequences design.

and older (e.g., seniors) college students was assessed. Ten years later, another group of college students were administered the same measure, which was readministered yet again 10 years later to another group of students (Zuschlag & Whitbourne, 1994).

The design for this study is outlined in Figure 1.6. Can you think of some reasons it has advantages over traditional cross-sectional and longitudinal designs? First, it eliminates problems inherent in traditional longitudinal designs, such as attrition and testing. In addition, using cross-sequential sequences reduce's potential cohort differences, which can plague traditional cross-sectional designs. For instance, at each time of measurement, the researchers documented that older college students were more identity achieved—that is, they had a clearer picture of their career and relationship future than the younger students. Because the same finding was documented at each time, the researcher can make stronger claims about the influence of maturity on identity development.

Finally, the same age groups are represented over time; thus, this design has a built-in time-lag component. The inclusion of time lags allows the researcher to examine historical or time-of-measurement effects. For example, in the identity study, the college seniors showed similar levels of identity achievement across the three times of measurement. If one sample showed much lower achievement than the others, then we could postulate that shifts in societal or educational philosophy might have had an impact. For example, societal pressures to delay serious career or relationship commitments until after college could influence young people to put off important life decisions during the collegiate experience. Thus the cross-sectional sequences design allows us to disentangle normative age-graded and history-graded influences.

The **longitudinal-sequences design** (Schaie, 1994a) is essentially a series of different longitudinal studies. As illustrated in Figure 1.6, the researcher begins the study with an assessment of individuals 18 years of age. Four years later, the researcher reassesses the subjects at age 22, and adds a new group of 18-year-olds. Five years later, the researcher repeats the process, and includes a new group of 18-year-olds. At the conclusion of this study, each wave of subjects has been assessed over different times of measurement.

Like the cross-sectional sequences design, a time-lag component allows one to check for time-of-measurement effects. In addition, notice that a cross-sectional design is built into this design at the final measurement. We could contrast cross-sectional and longitudinal results; similar results would allow for stronger conclusions about potential normative age-graded influences. Finally, in contrast to traditional longitudinal research, the longitudinal comparisons are conducted on samples drawn from several cohorts, rather than just one.

Developmental Designs and Methods

When using developmental designs, the researcher specifies the effects of age and maturation on human behavior, thinking, or socioemotional development. However, some researchers adopt methodological strategies that closely resemble developmental designs, yet do not use age as an independent variable. For example, consider the researcher who tracks changes in adolescent self-esteem during the transition from middle to high school. Is this researcher using a developmental design even though age is not used as a primary variable?

Baltes & Nesselroade (1979) offer useful distinctions between commonly confused terms. In their scheme, a researcher who follows participants over time is using a *longitudinal method.* Using age as a variable is not a central requirement of the longitudinal method; however, all of the potential advantages and pitfalls of longitudinal designs must still be considered. An increasingly popular method of this type is the **microgenetic method**. When using this method, participants are *intensively* observed over a *short period of time* to determine whether behavior, mental activity, or social and emotional functioning display development. For instance, children's behavior during museum trips has been observed to determine whether certain types of parental communication or particular museum exhibits predict changes in the way the children think about science and technology (Crowley & Jacobs, 2002).

The distinction between longitudinal designs and methods can also be applied to cross-sectional research. A researcher collecting all data at one time of measurement is using a cross-sectional method; age may not be a central variable of consideration. The method essentially becomes a developmental design when we decide to treat age as an independent variable.

Summary of Developmental Designs

Through the use of developmental designs, researchers can ascertain how normative age-graded and history-graded influences affect development. Cross-sectional designs, though quick and cost effective, can only confirm the existence of age differences on a study variable. Conclusions can be limited because age may be seriously confounded with generational, or cohort, differences between age groups. In contrast, longitudinal designs allow researchers to more accurately document how normative age-graded influences affect development. Although more informative than cross-sectional designs, longitudinal designs can be time consuming, expensive, and open to a number of validity threats, such as attrition. Both cross-sectional and longitudinal designs can be modified to reduce certain weaknesses inherent in these designs.

Methods of Data Collection

After the researcher has developed the research question and theoretically based hypotheses and designed the study, careful consideration must be made regarding how to assess the study variables. One can pursue either a quantitative or qualitative approach to data collection or some combination of the two. When using the **quantitative approach**, data that is collected to measure thinking, language, or behavior is represented in the form of numbers. For example, a researcher interested in measuring positive emotions in parents may count the number of times they smile at their children in a ten-minute interaction. The quantitative approach is very popular among lifespan professionals because information about people is represented in a precise and standardized manner that can later be analyzed using powerful statistical procedures.

Of course, sometimes it is difficult to understand the meaning or context of a behavior when it's reduced to numbers. For instance, although we generally believe that positive affect is a good thing, what happens if a parent smiles after a child is injured? Thus when using the **qualitative approach** the researcher typically does not reduce human thinking or behavior to numbers. Rather, one adopts a more holistic approach and may note certain global trends in an observation or during an interview. For example, to learn more about parenting in another culture, researcher's may immerse themselves in a particular nonnative community for a period of time and note how parenting practices are similar or different from those in our society.

Interestingly, the most frequent question about research methods that I hear from student researchers is the query, "How do I find a good measure of _____?" Thus, once a decision has been made regarding "how," the researcher must debate whether the measure is a "good" assessment of the study variable. In this next section, you will learn that a good measure should yield consistent (or reliable) and meaningful (or valid) data.

Data-Collection Strategies I: Addressing "How"

Let's first discuss how best to collect our data. How might we measure a construct such as marital harmony? In this section, we will discuss the strengths and weaknesses of questionnaires, interviews, and observational methods. In doing so, we will use marital behavior as the target variable for measurement.

Questionnaires and Interviews. The *survey* or *questionnaire method* represents an economical way to gather data. Questionnaires can be quickly scored, everyone is asked the same questions in a similar manner, and you do not need a skilled person to administer the surveys or score the data. Questionnaire data is easily expressed in numerical form and thus represents the most popular quantitative method. Not surprisingly, there exist innumerable paper-and-pencil questionnaires that assess marital satisfaction and harmony (e.g., Spanier, 1976).

Questionnaires also have drawbacks. Would you trust that the subject is telling the truth or merely producing socially desirable responses? In addition, because individuals are responding to questionnaire items that prompt memories regarding previous emotions, thinking, and behavior, it is entirely possible that the subject's recollection of such events is inaccurate. Questionnaires can also be plagued by **response sets**, in which subjects fall into a pattern of endorsing the same response, such as "Always," for every question. Finally, subjects have very little latitude in terms of how they can respond. For example, documenting that couples "sometimes disagree" when discussing marital problems provides us with little relevant information. What problems do they disagree about? How intense are the disagreements? These questions may not be answered when using standard questionnaires.

To circumvent the latter problem, you could *interview* your couples regarding marital harmony. For example, one could take a commonly used marital satisfaction questionnaire and verbally ask each item. Partners could provide verbal responses and be allowed time to elaborate. Interview data can be very rich and informative if collected by a trained interviewer. For example, consider the data that might be missed when using questionnaire methods:

Interviewer: How would you describe your marital relationship?

Subject: It's great, a perfect marriage. My husband really loves me.

Interviewer: OK, can you provide me an example of when he was recently loving?

Subject: No, he just loves me.

Interviewer: Can you think of one recent story?

Subject: Well, he recently bought me flowers. He told me I was ugly the other day, and I guess he got the flowers because he felt bad.

There is a richness to interview data that is sometimes missing from questionnaires. The participant in the aforementioned example "says" that her husband loves her; she probably would complete a self-report of marital satisfaction in a very positive manner. However, on interview, she "shows" us something different; that is, it appears the relationship is less positive than she is leading us to believe. Perhaps now you can appreciate the beauty of a qualitative approach to data collection; in the above example, the participant provides a context for her thought processes regarding her marriage. Of course, gathering rich interview data requires a skilled interviewer. In addition, interpreting such qualitative interview discourse can be time consuming. Finally, questionnaires and interviews may share a common problem, in that subjects are often asked to recall certain instances of thinking or behavior that may have occurred some time ago.

Observational Methods.   Observational methods represent a final method of data collection. In an **unstructured observation**, we do not manipulate or alter the subject's behavior. The researcher may passively watch children at the playground, or observe romantic couples involved in a dinnertime discussion. Although the term *unstructured* seems antithetical to *scientific*, there is often a rationale for using this approach. Playground behavior or dinnertime conversations represent routine *setting events* in people's lives; that is, these contexts serve as a naturalistic "stimulus" for human interaction. Thus, unstructured observations of naturalistic behavior in routine settings represent an externally valid approach.

In a **structured observation**, we manipulate the context and observe corresponding changes in behavior. In our marital study, we might ask the couple to resolve a conflict or problem. Structured observations allow us to better control the experimental context, and may allow for the observation of events that may be difficult to observe naturalistically.

Of course, one might question the external validity of structured observations. Although the study of marital conflict is difficult to study naturalistically, how "real" is the conflict that we observe when couples are asked to resolve a disagreement in structured settings? To address this concern, Creasey and Ladd (2004) asked young adults to complete a questionnaire regarding how they managed conflict with partners on a daily basis. Next, couples were observed resolving conflict in a laboratory setting. A comparison of the self-report and observational data yielded similar results; that is, individuals who reportedly used positive conflict-management strategies, such as humor, also used the same strategy during the observations. Thus, showing convergence between analog and similar "real-world" methods is one way to address questions about external validity.

Coding Observational Data.   Another important task rests with how to decipher observational data. Field researchers conducting naturalistic observations commonly use one method, the **ethnographic approach**. In order to better understand their subjects, ethnographic researchers conduct careful observations and interviews to provide a running record or description of the behavior of the target sample. This information may be recorded as field notes, or through an audiotaped verbal record. A researcher interested in comparing public romantic relationship behavior across cultures might visit different societies and observe couples interacting in plazas, restaurants, and other public settings. The researcher might take careful notes on their observations and uncover interesting cross-cultural differences in how couples display affection, use nonverbal communication, or even argue in public settings. The ethnographic approach represents a classic qualitative approach to data collection.

Although the ethnographic approach provides rich descriptive data, other methods provide numerical or quantitative data; hence the following methods adhere to the quantitative approach. In **event sampling**, the researcher simply counts the frequency of behaviors or events over a designated period of time (e.g., 15 minutes). In **time sampling**, the researcher counts the frequency of behavior *within* periodic time segments over a designated period of time. For example, instead of counting every behavior that occurs over a 2-hour period, the researcher may count the behavior occurrences for two out of every six minutes. Time sampling is extremely useful when observing the behavior of subjects over a long period of time. For example, a researcher who observes the behavior of children in day care may not want to constantly record every instance of behavior over the entire day. Rather, children may be observed for 10 minutes in the morning, before nap, and on the playground.

Another excellent strategy for studying behavior development is **sequential analysis**, which consists of analyzing behavior sequences between two or more individuals. When using this method, researchers record the occurrence of behavior for each subject over time. They can then conduct **probability estimates** on the likelihood of behavior occurrences by one partner *as a result* of earlier behaviors exhibited by the other partner. In other words, if you say something mean to your romantic partner, what is the probability your partner will (a) hug you; (b) get angry; or (c) become sad? In one such study, Gottman (1994) examined the behaviors that were more likely to anger partners and escalate arguments. He documented that certain behaviors exhibited by husbands were more likely to spark *later* anger in wives than others. In particular, wife anger was predicted by husband inattentiveness during these disagreements.

Sequential analysis is unique, because it can uncover true behavioral development. Using sequential analysis, the researcher can better document which behaviors either escalate, or decrease marital conflict, child tantrums, or altercations between parents and adolescents. These findings would seem to have both important scientific and practical implications.

Data-Collection Strategies II: Addressing "Good"

Once you have decided *how* to measure your study variables, you are next faced with finding a *good* measure. It is very likely that a robust method, whether questionnaire, interview, or observational coding system, has been developed to assess just about any variable that you are interested in measuring. I generally recommend that new researchers *should not* develop their own methods of data collection.

A good measure must have reasonable scientific, or **psychometric properties**. Whenever someone develops a good measure, these psychometric properties are usually established through a series of studies. First, we must ensure that the measure possesses good consistency, or **reliability**. In a **test-retest reliability study**, we ask the same people to complete the measure in two or more trials over a short period of time (e.g., two weeks). The expectancy is that they will complete the measure in a similar fashion over time. In addition, reliable measures should possess good internal consistency. For example, five questionnaire items that supposedly measure "marital satisfaction" should correlate well with one another, and each item should correlate well with our total score of marital satisfaction. The interrelatedness of the items is known as **scale reliability**, whereas the correlation of a particular item with the total score of the construct is known as **item reliability**.

Beyond consistency, we also want to make sure the measure is valid. **Concurrent validity** refers to a significant correlation between the measure (or predictor) and a meaningful outcome measure. For example, we would expect a strong correlation between the results of a marital satisfaction test and couple interactions using observational procedures. The concurrent approach refers to the idea that the measure (marital satisfaction) and outcome variable (behavior observations) are assessed *at the same time of measurement*. **Predictive validity** is achieved if we find a significant correlation between our measure and an outcome measure that is assessed at a *later* date. A marital-satisfaction measure would possess good predictive validity if the measure predicted divorce two years later.

Content validity is the assumption that items on a measure adequately represent the construct. What would you think of a relationship-abuse questionnaire that only contained physical-violence items? Would such a measure represent the construct of relationship abuse, or should the instrument contain additional items representing verbal and emotional abuse?

Finally, **construct validity** refers to your confidence that this measure (e.g., a marital satisfaction survey) truly assesses the hypothetical construct (i.e., marital satisfaction). Presenting a strong argument for the construct validity of a measure takes time. For example, the researcher may conduct a series of studies demonstrating that the measure has good concurrent, predictive, and content validity. In addition, the investigator may show that the measure correlates well with other similar measures but more strongly predicts a meaningful outcome variable than existing instruments. Like the detective, the researcher builds the case using a series of research studies showing that the measure possesses strong construct validity.

Perhaps you can see why I am not in favor of students developing their own measures! Establishing the psychometric properties of an instrument takes time and should be carefully considered when selecting each measure. Generally, published measures have a lengthy psychometric history that should be carefully examined. Selection of measures that have poor psychometric properties may lead to biased results. Thus, significant findings in a study could be diminished by poor instrument selection.

What Do You Think?

You are interested in developing a measure to assess child behavior problems that will be completed by teachers. How would you establish reliability and validity for this measure?

Summary of Data-Collection Methods

Questionnaires, interviews, and observational methods often exist to assess many of the variables of interest to lifespan professionals. Although each method possesses advantages and disadvantages, the psychometric history of the instrument often plays a large role in influencing decisions regarding instrument selection. Thus, one should check the reliability and validity information on a measure before incorporating the instrument in the study.

Chapter Summary

What have you learned after reading this introductory chapter? By now, you may have realized that research scientists possess a number of important skills common to professionals across many important disciplines (e.g., business, medicine, engineering, law). Much like the thinking behind creative marketing schemes or legal-case strategies, research scientists must possess innovative and creative thinking to develop important research questions and ideas. As indicated at the beginning of the chapter, most students, once supplied with background information regarding a research topic, can often generate very interesting research ideas relevant to the field of lifespan development.

Unfortunately, ingenious ideas can become quickly tarnished without a proper research foundation. For this reason, planning and becoming a student of your research idea were recurrent themes throughout this chapter. When planning research, it is imperative that novice researchers become aware of major theoretical, conceptual, methodological issues, and advancements within the research area, and build a careful case (much as a lawyer or detective would) for the eventual study hypotheses. In particular, when developing your hypotheses, it is very important that they are theoretically justified.

The next step is to select a general research design, and if appropriate, a developmental design. The traditional drawbacks to experimental, correlational, cross-sectional, and longitudinal methods *can be addressed through creative thinking on your part.* For example, an ambitious experimental study can be augmented by a small field study to cross-validate research findings and address concerns regarding external validity. Likewise, a modified developmental design can address weaknesses inherent in traditional developmental designs.

In terms of measurement selection, always go with established measures and save instrument development for later in your career. Designing an observational coding system, questionnaire, or interview schedule is not recommended for new researchers. Establishing psychometric properties (i.e., reliability and validity) is a labor-intensive effort, and unless one possesses extensive training in measurement issues, many lifespan experts avoid developing their own measures to assess study variables. Thus, students new to the field should search for commonly used measures that have a history of reliability and validity research.

It is important that you become familiar with the concepts presented in this chapter. At the end of each chapter, you will notice exercises involving the **Research Navigator™** (http://www.researchnavigator.com). A Research Navigator™ guide and your access code should have been packaged with your book. This tool allows you to search for research articles pertaining to lifespan, psychological, sociological, and educational research; it is actually a resource that you can use in all of your classes. Once you have located an array of articles regarding a topic of interest, you can read abstracts or full-length versions of many articles as well as save or print these materials.

Research Navigator™ Exercise 1: Identifying Introductory Terms

Read a research article related to life-span development and answer a series of questions pertaining to the introductory material. Go to Section 2 of the Research Navigator™ homepage, entitled "ContentSelect." First, choose a database to search, such as "Psychology" or "Education." Next, type in a keyword pertaining to a topic that interests you, such as "emotional development." The program will provide you with a list of articles that match your keyword. For this assignment, you will access a full-length research article, read it, and then answer the following questions:

1. What is the purpose of the study, or research questions?
2. What are the hypotheses? Are they well rationalized?

3. What is the research design (i.e., experimental or correlational)? What is the rationale for your answer?
4. What are the independent and dependent variables?
5. Did the study incorporate a developmental design?
6. What methods of measurement were utilized?
7. How were threats to internal and external validity addressed?
8. What reliability and validity information was provided for the study measures in the instrumentation or measures section?
9. How might you improve on this study?

Research Navigator™ Exercise 2: The Scientific, Applied, and Collaborative Nature of the Field

The NICHD Early Child Care Research Network is a group of professionals at over twenty institutions who are investigating the relationship between preschool child-care arrangements and developmental outcomes in children. To better appreciate the scope of this work, conduct a "ContentSelect" search in the *Psychology database* using the term *child-care research*. When reading the brief article descriptions, note that a number of the citations involve studies conducted by this research group, as well as major commentaries on this work (e.g., *Child Development, Vol. 74,* 2003). In addition, there are full-length articles pertaining to the research of this group.

While reading some of these materials, consider the following questions: What are some of the major findings reported by this research team? What are the independent and dependent variables in these studies? Do other researchers agree or disagree with their primary conclusions (*see commentaries*)? What applied or real-world value does this research promise?

2

Participants, Researchers, and Research Settings

Kendra is interested in determining the causes and consequences of relational aggression, or the tendency for some adolescents to use gossiping as a mechanism to ruin the reputations of their peers. She writes a great dissertation proposal, and wins an award from her graduate college to fund the research. Her dissertation committee also applauds her ideas, and the university ethics committee gives her permission to conduct the research.

Kendra then approaches some area middle schools to arrange data-collection times. Although she has had previous success gaining access, this time around, one building principal after another turns down her requests. The reasons for denial vary; one administrator was upset because Kendra failed to consult with her about the project in advance, another felt the risks of the research outweighed the benefits, and yet another principal worried how parents would perceive the project. Distraught, Kendra must abort the dissertation project and return the grant money to the institution; her graduation is delayed by two years.

Unfortunately, this is a true story. Although Kendra developed a brilliant study, she failed to consider some important issues that must be addressed before the first piece of data is collected. In order to conduct research, we must locate our population of interest, consider the ethical ramifications of our work, and identify a research site. In this chapter, you will learn that planning a research study involves more than just reading background material on your topic, developing theoretically based hypotheses and considering different research designs.

After reading this chapter, you should be able to:

- Discuss how to design samples, recruit human subjects, and treat your participants in a humane fashion.
- Consider how your behavior, as a researcher, affects the behavior of research participants.
- Articulate the relative advantages and disadvantages of laboratory and field settings.
- Describe the issues facing researchers who work in school, home-based, and Internet/Web research environments.

Sampling and Recruitment

Although general research strategies were outlined in Chapter 1, there remain other details of designing research that need further elaboration. We must provide an operational definition for the targeted study population and describe how this population will be sampled.

Sampling

There are several steps to creating the **sampling plan**, or a scheme for defining a population of interest and identifying and recruiting people that fit this definition. Chapter 1 described why providing operational definitions for each study variable was a critical step in planning research. In the sampling plan, the first step is to provide an operational definition for our broad, theoretical **target population**. For example, how would you define "retirees," "early adolescents," or "family caregivers?" There are often common standards for defining just about any research population. A researcher interested in sampling "depressed adults" may seek a commonly accepted definition of depression using the Diagnostic and Statistical Manual of Mental Disorders (American Psychiatric Association, 1994).

To further define the target population, it is important to consider whether it represents an area or special population (Gordan, 1999). **Area populations** are defined by geographic area or location, such as the community, state, or nation. For example, educational researchers who study historical shifts in standardized test scores, such as the *Scholastic Aptitude Test*, claim that these results represent the aptitude of adolescents across the entire country. In contrast, **special populations** are defined by subject factors other than geographic locations, and might include people who experience low base rates of a certain behavior (e.g., truancy) or condition (e.g., clinical depression). We must give careful consideration of the type of population to be represented, because it influences our next steps.

Next, we must develop methods to *identify* the **study population**. Identifying this population is based on how we defined the target population. In area population studies, we might gather data on all adults residing in a particular region of the country. In a special population study, we may need more industrious methods to identify the population. To identify "depressed adults," the researcher may have to administer a diagnostic inventory, such as the *Structured Clinical Interview for DSM-IV Axis 1 Disorders* (First, Spitzer, Gibbon & Williams 1995) across different mental health facilities to identify the population. To recap, a target population is really a hypothetical one, yet it has definable labels, such as "preschool children," "college students," or "adolescents with eating disorders." The study population represents *all possible subjects at your disposal* that might make up that target population, such as all college students attending 4-year institutions in the state of California.

Suppose you want to collect data on all college students in California. Because study populations can represent literally millions of potential participants, we must think of ways to identify a **research sample** for participation in our study. This part of the sampling plan is critical, because it affects external validity in two ways. First, we must estimate how well the recruited research sample *represents* the larger population. Second, we must consider how well the study results will *generalize* to the target population of interest.

Probability and nonprobability sampling represent two ways to identify a research sample. In **probability sampling**, we obtain a *sampling frame*, or list of all of the people representing the study population, such as the names of all people living in a community, or all patients diagnosed as depressed in different mental-health facilities (Whitley, 1996). In order to draw the research sample, we then select a sample from this population using some random method (e.g., every fifth name), a process known as **simple random sampling**.

Although simple random sampling is popular, there has been a call in our field for researchers to be more sensitive to demographic factors, such as ethnicity, sex, and social class, when considering sampling methods. In order to capture such diversity, researchers may use a **stratified random sampling method** to ensure representative numbers of demographic subgroups within the study population. For example, consider the hypothetical data presented in Table 2.1, which represents all members of a study population, segregated by gender and ethnicity. The researcher can then randomly select participants from each cell until adequate numbers are drawn to proportionally represent each cell.

Because we may not be able to identify all members of a study population, it can be difficult to meet the criteria for probability sampling. In **nonprobability sampling**, we recruit whomever we can best access (Whitley, 1996). Different methods can be used to access such a sample. For example, one might have access to one particular school, pediatric facility, long-term care unit, or university, which allows for the recruitment of a *convenience sample*. Thus, a researcher interested in working with low-birth-weight infants might collect data on all infants meeting this criterion within a particular pediatric facility.

Many researchers do not have the luxury of a readily convenient sample. In such cases, the researcher may post flyers around the community or buy advertising space in a local newspaper and rely on a *volunteer* or *self-selected* sample. The researcher can also add to their subject pool by using *snowball*, or *chain*, sampling. In such cases, study volunteers are asked to nominate people they know to also participate in the study.

Although nonprobability sampling can lead to fairly quick recruitment and data collection, a chief drawback of this method is that the sample may not reflect the study population. For example, married couples who volunteer for research may not adequately represent all adults involved in marital relationships in the community or state. In addition, those who volunteer for a study may be different from those who do not. For example, volunteers may be more intelligent and better educated than individuals who decline participation (Rosenthal & Rosnow, 1991). Although these drawbacks may not be major enough to block publication of a good study, it is becoming increasingly difficult to publish research in top-tier journals or obtain federal grant support through the use of nonprobability samples.

TABLE 2.1 *Matrix for Sampling by Gender and Ethnicity*

	Males		*Females*	
	Number	*% of Population*	*Number*	*% of Population*
Asian–American	3,000	2%	3,000	2%
African–American	15,000	13%	16,000	13%
Hispanic	8,000	7%	8,020	7%
European American	92,000	78%	92,050	78%

However, there are strategies that can boost the credibility of studies using this method (Gordan, 1999). One technique is to tailor recruitment efforts to ensure that the research sample demographically "mirrors" the potential study population. For example, demographic data may be available at the institutional, community, state, or national level. Although it may not be feasible to obtain a representative sample, a researcher relying on volunteers may block study entry to a particular demographic group of subjects (e.g., white females) once a particular quota has been reached. Recruitment can be continued for individuals who meet other demographic criteria, to eventually select a sample that is demographically similar to the potential study population.

Such mirroring techniques, or **quota sampling**, can be applied to samples that are difficult to identify or obtain. For example, a researcher interested in studying violent men that are court-referred for professional treatment could review the literature to determine a rough profile of the study population. Once determined, the researcher could then limit study enrollment once a particular quota has been reached (e.g., married, middle-class males), and continue enrollment for those whose quotas have not been met (e.g., single, poverty-level males).

We can also use other strategies to bolster the validity of nonrandom samples. One of the best ways to sample a hard-to-locate population is to thoroughly examine the methods of those who have conducted such work in the past. It is possible that well-established techniques exist for sampling even hard-to-locate populations. These methods might include screening procedures, quota sampling methods, snowball sampling methods to obtain matched control groups, or some type of method combination (Gordan, 1999). Again, recent research published in highly respected journals is usually diagnostic of a "good study" that contains sound theory, hypotheses, sampling techniques, and measures. We can learn a lot from modeling the techniques used in such research, similar to those presented in Box 2.1.

What Do You Think?

Suppose you are interested in comparing the intelligence of 25, 45, 65, and 85 year olds using a cross-sectional design within the community. What are some strategies you might use to ensure that your sample is as representative of the community as possible?

Sampling Different Age Groups

Identifying a representative sample of different-aged people represents a thorny issue for lifespan researchers. At first glance, one might conclude that it is as simple as identifying the demographics of a study population *for each age group* in the community and finding ways to recruit samples that closely match these demographics. However, although this strategy represents a powerful way to enhance the external validity of a study, the internal validity of the research might be seriously threatened. For example, it is quite possible that the younger people in the community are better educated than the older adults. If you draw a truly representative sample, then the younger study participants will probably be better educated than the older subjects. How might this influence the data? It is quite possible that resulting age differences in intelligence may result from educational differences than from the effects of the aging process on intellect.

We must consider sample representativeness and internal validity threats in a study involving different age groups. We must first collect as much demographic information on

BOX 2.1 • *Using Multiple Sampling Strategies to Obtain Sample Diversity*

Bradley and colleagues (2000) designed an inventory to assess the quality of the home environment for 10-to-15-year-old adolescents. The Early Adolescent version of the *Home Observation for Measurement of the Environment* (EA-HOME) is an 80-item inventory that is completed by the researcher after a family visit. The assistant interviews family members about parenting practices (e.g., coping with adolescent privacy), household learning materials (e.g., computer access), household safety and rules, and family connectiveness (e.g., parent contact with adolescent peer group). The purpose of developing such an inventory rests with the repeated finding that the quality of one's home environment strongly predicts important child and adolescent developmental outcomes (e.g., Holmbeck, Paikoff, & Brooks-Gunn, 1995).

Although sampling issues are an important consideration for all researchers, such concerns become paramount when developing an actual instrument, such as the EA-HOME. In particular, when developing a home-environment scale, it is important that it be developed on families from all "walks of life." To address this issue, Bradley and colleagues recruited families from different regions of the country (ranging from Little Rock, Arkansas, to Los Angeles, California), cultural (European-, African-, Chinese-, Dominican- and Mexican-Americans), and income groups.

Although purists might voice some objections regarding its sampling procedures, the Bradley et al. (2000) study represents a good example of the multiple methods researchers often use to obtain hard-to-get research samples. For example, the Little Rock researchers primarily recruited their families by randomly calling individuals listed in the local telephone directory. However, because this strategy did not yield representative numbers of low-income families, the researchers next approached families through school,

neighborhood, and community associations located in low-income areas. Approximately 25 percent of the Little Rock sample was recruited in this manner. Conversely, other sites used alternative sampling methods. For example, researchers in New York and San Antonio exclusively used public service announcements and community agencies to recruit large numbers of Mexican- and Dominican-American families. Researchers in Los Angeles used convenience (e.g., church groups) and snowball sampling techniques to recruit Chinese-American families.

The study authors acknowledge various imperfections in their sampling strategy (Bradley et al., 2000). Beyond the fact that different sampling methods were used at different sites, external validity was also compromised because specific research sites (e.g., Los Angeles) oversampled specific cultural groups (e.g., Chinese–American). Do you think that Mexican–American families living in San Antonio adequately represent such families across the country? Beyond these concerns, there have also been objections raised about treating "cultural" or "ethnic" groups as homogenous groups (Gjerde & Onishi, 2000).

There are a number of important learning points that should be gleaned from reviewing the Bradley et al. (2000) study. It is an excellent example of how researchers often use a battery of sampling methods to recruit and oversample hard-to-get populations. Also, this multisite study provides another example of how researchers across the country form collaborative relationships to tackle complex research questions. Although there are valid arguments regarding the external validity of this project, the results of this federally funded study were published in a truly outstanding research journal (*Journal of Research on Adolescence*).

a potential study population as possible, and to make sure that the same data is collected on the study sample. Next, if different age groups are represented, we must give careful consideration to identifying and measuring potential historical variables that may be confounded with cohort or age, such as education, verbal intelligence, gender, and health (Camp, West, & Poon, 1989). This data could be used in different ways. We might consider such historical variables as nuisance variables and simply statistically control for such effects. Alternatively, we may turn one or more of the historical variables into an independent variable (e.g., education), and analyze its effects on the dependent variable in conjunction with age. In such cases, this strategy must also be reflected in the sampling plan, such as sampling equal numbers of college-educated people across age groups.

Once the data are analyzed, the researcher considers how to best report the study results. If the researcher controlled for historical effects, he or she can offer firmer conclusions regarding age comparisons, because threats to internal validity had been addressed. In making comparisons to a larger study population, he or she may also wish to present the data that most accurately reflects the study population. For example, if most of the older adults in the study population are females with a high school education, then we might present data specific to this population.

Recruitment

Recruitment methods operationally define the sampling design of the study. Because many lifespan researchers use nonprobability sampling, they should give careful thought to how subjects will be approached, recruited, and identified. Camp, West and Poon (1989) stipulate that researchers should be sensitive to possible *recruitment site* and *inducement* confounds. We touched on recruitment-site confounds in Chapter 1; that is, data can become highly confounded when subjects are recruited or drawn from nonequivalent settings. For example, recruiting 20-year-old subjects from a college campus and 70-year-old participants from nursing homes threatens both internal and external validity.

Recruitment-site confounds, like many of our research problems, can be best addressed by advance planning. For example, what problems might be encountered if the researcher posts flyers around the community that advertise the study? One immediate issue would be to ensure that flyers were evenly distributed *throughout* the community. Similar issues arise when recruiting subjects using newspaper advertisements, television public service announcements, or random phone calls (e.g., calling every fourth person in the phone book). Consideration must be given to whether most people in the institution, community, or state are at the very least being reached when using these methods.

Beyond the recruitment site, we must also consider how potential subjects may react to our inducement methods. Flyers should be worded in a way that makes the study purpose easily understood by people representing different educational levels. Also, the font size of words contained in a flyer or newspaper advertisement should be readable to individuals across all age brackets.

Although we will explore recruitment issues devoted to specific populations throughout this book, several central concerns will be addressed here. How we induce or attempt to entice subjects to participate in research broaches both methodological and ethical considerations. For example, which of the following flyer headings represents the most effective method for recruiting parents?

"Become a Perfect Parent!"   "Parenting Study"
"Want to Avoid Parenting Mistakes?"   "Parent Study—**$200!**"

Two central issues arise from the flyer headings. The first concern rests with the positive ("Become a Perfect Parent!"), negative ("Want to Avoid Parenting Mistakes?"), or neutral

("Parenting Study") "spin" in the headings. Although flashy positive or negative headings may attract attention and encourage people to volunteer, more pessimistic or anxious people are more likely to partake in studies that involve such recruitment methods (Camp, West & Poon, 1989). Thus, the external validity of research using such methods might be questioned, because the study results will not generalize to a larger study population.

A second consideration rests with monetary payment. Do you think people reluctant to volunteer for a study might change their minds for $200? Interestingly, although people more *quickly* volunteer for behavioral research involving monetary compensation, there are few demographic differences between adults who volunteer for paid research studies and those who volunteer for unpaid studies (Camp, West & Poon, 1989). However, although there may not be differences between those who volunteer or do not volunteer for money, the fact remains that both of these groups are generally better educated and more intelligent than individuals who simply do not volunteer for research at all (Rosenthal & Rosnow, 1991).

The fact that people more quickly volunteer for a study solely because of monetary compensation places the researcher in a delicate situation. There are times when it is simply difficult to recruit a sample that is large enough to satisfy certain design requirements without some form of compensation. However, although it is interesting to hear the phone ring after offering attractive compensation, there remains the underlying ethical concern that these newfound "volunteers" are simply "doing it for the money."

So what can we do to induce a more representative sample of participants while maintaining our ethical integrity? Rosenthal and Rosnow (1975; 1991) recommend the following strategies:

- Communicate to subjects the importance and intellectual stimulation of the research.
- Stress the practical or applied importance of the research.
- Use neutral language in flyers; avoid a threatening or negative tone.
- Offer compensation (money or gifts) that is appropriate for the amount of volunteer effort required.
- Avoid tasks or procedures that could be perceived as stressful.

Summary of Sampling and Recruitment Methods

In this section, various sampling and recruitment methods were described. Although most researchers went to achieve as representative a sample as possible, it is often very difficult to recruit a research sample that is truly representative of the study population. Hopefully, you now have accomplished several important learning objectives. First, like so many issues involving research, sampling and recruitment methods should be given as much thought and weight as hypothesis development, research design, and measurement selection during the research *planning process*. Carefully reviewing the sampling and recruitment methods of other researchers can also stimulate thinking on these issues and allow new researchers to avoid common mistakes. Creativity regarding different sampling and recruitment techniques can also greatly assist researchers in obtaining hard-to-get samples. Finally, obtaining demographic data on the larger study population is an important issue for researchers using nonprobability sampling or other recruitment methods. Demonstrating that a study sample is demographically proportional to the study population allows the researcher to make stronger claims about sample representativeness.

Ethical Issues in Human Development Research

"Federal Government to Suspend all Research Projects at University X"

Increasingly, such unfortunate headlines are appearing in newspapers across the country. Although it is rare for government officials to suspend institutional research or grant funding, such freezes represent a major inconvenience for researchers and unwanted publicity for the institution. Such unwanted publicity can also escalate into intense legal maneuvering in cases in which individual investigators have seriously violated the rights of research participants. Fortunately, serious ethical charges against researchers are rare, and many institutions require researchers to receive intensive training in the federal-government regulations regarding the treatment of human subjects before beginning their studies.

The Institutional Review Board (IRB)

In a training workshop, an instructor well versed in ethics stated, "The ultimate ethical review board is the researcher." This is a very positive statement; it is a safe bet that many researchers go beyond professional ethical guidelines to protect the welfare of their participants, particularly when working with vulnerable populations, such as children.

Unfortunately, simply allowing researchers to identify ethical issues and safeguards is problematic. Although blatantly unscrupulous researchers are quite rare, the careful planning of study details may distract investigators from considering certain ethical issues. In addition, an inexperienced researcher working with a novel but vulnerable population, such as child wards of the state, may be unaware of ethical issues pertaining to this population.

To keep us acutely aware of ethical issues, the federal government has published a number of regulations involving the protection of human subjects (Code of Federal Regulations, 2001). In order to ensure researcher compliance, many institutions have created local **Institutional Review Boards** (IRB) as oversight committees for research involving human and animal populations. IRB oversight is required for institutions that receive federal grant funding and its members are generally composed of researchers and institutional administrators. There are even government regulations for IRB membership. For example, IRB committees are required to have at least five members that have varying backgrounds to allow for adequate review of research commonly conducted at the institution (Code of Federal Regulations, 2001). Thus, an IRB at an academic institution may contain not only faculty and administrators but also a lawyer, physician, and community member.

Although procedures differ across institutions, researchers are normally required to submit a short proposal to a local IRB before they are allowed to recruit subjects or collect data. Although the IRB's chief role is to ensure that investigators comply with federal regulations, it is not uncommon for members to consider the impact of the research from legal and community standpoints as well. Although space limitations prohibit us from fully considering the latter positions (which can get sticky), we will concentrate more attention on general issues that are strongly attended to by the IRB. The primary issues that we will cover include the informed-consent process, research risks and benefits, and participant confidentiality.

Informed Consent

The researcher's plan for securing participant informed consent is highly scrutinized by IRBs. It is not uncommon for researchers to include both oral *and* written components of the informed-consent process. In the oral component, the researcher highlights the subject's rights as a research participant and overviews the language included in the informed consent document. Next, the researcher usually provides the subject an informed-consent document that must be read and signed by the subject. Table 2.2 highlights the information that the informed consent-document must contain, according to federal regulations. In addition, because you may be soon conducting research on your own, Table 2.3 contains an informed-consent template that was approved by an institutional IRB, and deemed compliant with current federal regulations.

There are several caveats to my suggestions regarding informed consent. First, we can ask for a *waiver* of the informed-consent process. For example, a researcher passively observing but not videotaping the behavior of teenagers at a shopping mall could seek relief from the informed-consent process with justification. In this case, the teens are simply not made aware that they are being observed for a study. In addition, consider the case of researchers conducting "on the street" surveys or interviews. Because subject responses are collected in an anonymous fashion, and because such methods usually entail minimal risk, the researcher may use a simple and quick oral-consent process.

TABLE 2.2   *Requirements for Informed Consent (Code of Federal Regulations, 2001)*

Requirement	Important Points to Consider
Purpose and commitment	Subjects should be made aware of the general purpose of the study, study methods and procedures, and time commitment.
Risks	Potential risks must be clearly outlined.
Benefits	Potential benefits to self or others (e.g., the scientific community) shall be clarified.
Alternative treatments	In the case of interventions, other possible treatments that may be effective.
Confidentiality	How will the subject's data be kept confidential? How will the data be stored, analyzed, and ultimately disposed of?
Compensation	If substantial risk is present, how might the subject be compensated if injury were to occur?
Voluntary nature	A statement that the subject's participation is voluntary, and that refusing to participate or discontinue the study will not result in penalty.
Contact people	The name/phone # of the head researcher, should the subject have further questions regarding the purpose of the research. The IRB chairperson should be listed as contact person in case of adverse reactions or injury.

TABLE 2.3 *Sample Informed-Consent Document for Adult Participants*

The policy of this institution is that all research participation is voluntary, and that you have the right to withdraw at any time, without prejudice, should you object to the nature of the research. You will receive compensation for simply reading this consent form. Your responses are confidential. Any report of the data will be in summary form, without identifying individuals. You are entitled to ask questions and receive an explanation of this research after participation. Please read the following statements very carefully.

Study purpose. We are interested in identifying variables that predict success in romantic relationships.

Nature and duration of participation. You will complete several questionnaires about your relationship with your partner. Also, we will interview you about the marital relationship of your parents. This interview will be audiotaped. The study procedures should take about 2 h.

Risks. You will be asked to provide personal information about yourself, partner, and family. The recounting of negative experiences may be personally distressing. In addition, divulging personal information raises concerns regarding privacy.

Benefits. Your participation will help us make a scientific advancement in this area, and eventually assist marital therapists. Because our study is focused on attachment relationships, you may find this experience very enjoyable.

Confidentiality. A code number will be assigned to your questionnaires and audiotape. All data will be kept in a secured laboratory and can only be accessed by the PI and research assistants. All data will be destroyed in seven years.

Opportunities to question and information about results. Technical questions regarding this research should be directed to (*Name/Phone # of Principal Investigator*).

Questions regarding rights as research participant. Any questions regarding your rights as a research participant, or research injuries, should be directed to (*Name/Phone # of IRB Chairperson or other administrative representative*).

I have read the statements above, understand the same, and voluntarily sign this form. I further acknowledge that I have received an offer of a copy of this consent form.

Date: _____

Signature of Participant: _____

Signature of Researcher Obtaining Consent: _____

Institutions, professional organizations, and researchers may establish guidelines regarding the informed-consent process that go beyond federal-government regulations. For example, some institutions require investigators to secure written informed consent for virtually all research studies, even "on the street" surveys. Likewise, some researchers use both oral and written informed-consent procedures for seemingly innocuous research. A rigorous informed-consent process allows the researcher to establish some initial rapport with subjects, and demonstrates to subjects that the researcher is sensitive to their rights as research participants.

What Do You Think?

Investigator A records the behavior of children playing in a local park using a hidden camera, while Investigator B analyzes data from existing hospital records. Both persistently insist that they conduct research that entails "no risk." Do you agree?

Risks and Benefits

Research involving human subjects always includes *potential* risk to the study participants. In the above exercise, consider what might happen if a research assistant who later coded the videotapes of the children happened to be the parent of one of the children. Similarly, consider the case of a research assistant who, upon reviewing existing medical records, discovers that a close friend has cancer. Although these may appear to be extreme cases, lightning can strike in strange places.

It is the obligation of the researcher to outline all foreseeable risks to the IRB and then stipulate how each risk will be minimized. In some cases, risk minimization can be fairly straightforward. For example, consider the risks that might be present in a study that polls college students about contraception use. How would you feel about providing such personal information if you were asked to put your name on this survey or completed the survey sitting closely beside other study participants? In the case of this particular study, asking subjects not to put their names on the surveys, seating participants far apart from one another, and asking participants to drop the surveys in the slot of a large box as they exit the room, could minimize the potential risk of embarrassment.

Although most research involving human subjects involves minimal risk, there are times when researchers request IRB approval for research that may induce temporary stress or discomfort to research participants. The following guidelines should be considered when designing such research:

- *Follow the footsteps of others.* If you are concerned that your method might create discomfort to participants, carefully read the published papers of other researchers that have used similar methods. Journal editors typically ask authors to provide information regarding subject reactions to procedures that seem unusually distressing. Demonstrating to the IRB that other investigators have used similar methods without major problems is a first step.
- *Alternative methods and procedures.* Is there any other way to collect your data without distressing participants? For example, a child asked to complete a series of difficult tasks may experience less discomfort if a parent is present. In fact, the interactions between the child and parent might provide valuable data in itself.
- *Benefits.* What is the benefit/risk ratio of the study? Most IRBs require investigators to clearly outline the potential benefits of the study. For example, stipulating how the study will advance scientific knowledge or how the results will provide important information to the subject, institution, or community are clear benefits. An IRB is unlikely to approve a risky study that does not provide tangible benefits.
- *Who's in charge?* The IRB is often interested in the qualifications of both the head researcher and the research assistants. Because research assistants often have the most direct contact with subjects, the IRB often requires researchers to outline how research assistants will be trained to recognize, and respond to, adverse reactions.
- *Debriefing.* There are several purposes to debriefing. Subjects should be informed of the primary purpose of the study in understandable terms. Of course, full disclosure may do more harm than good. Consider this debriefing statement: "Thank you for participating in this study. We were interested in examining cheating behavior, and

our screening instruments determined that you were likely to cheat, so that's why you were recruited for this study." Thus, researchers can argue for incomplete disclosure in cases in which full debriefing might actually elevate the risk of the study for participants.

Debriefing provides other functions as well. Participants should be allowed to ask questions, and the researcher should ensure that subjects leave the research setting in the same physical and emotional state in which they entered it. Any adverse or unusual reactions should also be recorded.

Confidentiality

Most subjects do not want their data to be viewed or shared by individuals not affiliated with the researcher's laboratory. To ease such concerns, complete *anonymity* can be promised in cases in which data cannot be traced back to the original source. For example, subjects may simply be asked not to put identifying information on surveys. However, complete anonymity is hard to promise when using interview or observational methods.

Although complete anonymity may be difficult to achieve, we can promise that data will be kept private and *confidential*. During the informed-consent process, we must reveal how data will be stored and secured, who will have access to the data, how data will be used, and how it will be eventually disposed or destroyed (Code of Federal Regulations, 2001). Although it is not uncommon for researchers to eventually present actual interview or videotaped data in professional or educational settings, it is mandatory that researchers discuss such plans with potential subjects *before* a consent document is signed.

You may have considered an interesting theme that has arisen from our discussion of research ethics. Treating participants in a humane manner accomplishes more than addressing ethical guidelines. Subjects who see the importance of their participation and feel valued as research participants are probably more likely to volunteer, and be honest in a study than individuals who do not share such perceptions (Rosenthal & Rosnow, 1991).

Vulnerable Populations

Federal-government regulations clearly stipulate that researchers should take special precautions when working with vulnerable populations, such as children, prisoners, pregnant women, mentally disabled persons, or individuals experiencing financial hardship. In particular, they must avoid coercive methods, weigh special risks, and consider important issues involving the informed-consent process.

Coercion. Researchers should be careful not to use methods that pressure or coerce individuals into participating in research. For example, paying financially disadvantaged individuals extravagant amounts of money or offering prisoners reduced sentences in exchange for participating in research raises both ethical and legal questions. In short, compensation for research participation should be logically tied to the time or work commitment involved in the project. To reduce the appearance of coercion, compensation should not be listed as a benefit for participation, and must also be offered to individuals who *decline or terminate* study participation (cf. Kimmel, 1996).

Coercion may have psychological roots as well. A client in a mental-health facility who is asked by a therapist to participate in research may quickly consent to avoid straining the relationship with their therapist. Similarly, children may feel pressure to participate in research if asked by a teacher, as opposed to a novel researcher. Indeed, because even impartial researchers can be viewed as powerful authority figures, care must be taken to adopt a friendly, yet neutral, demeanor during the informed-consent process.

Special Risks.   The researcher must also think about special vulnerabilities that might be unique to their population. For example, most IRBs require researchers working with minors to secure parental permission as well as *minor assent.* In short, the researcher must explain to the parent how the minor will be protected in terms of the informed-consent guidelines shown in Table 2.2, and obtain written permission. The researcher must then explain these same guidelines to the minor, *in understandable terms,* and secure the *oral* permission or assent of the minor. The researcher can proceed only after securing both parental permission and minor assent.

The mental, medical, legal, and developmental status of the participant may present further challenges to the researcher. For example, young children might become more easily aroused by experimental procedures, possess less understanding of the informed-consent process, and react differently to debriefing procedures than would adolescents or adults.

What Do You Think?

A popular yet controversial method of assessing peer reputation is to ask children who they most and least prefer to play with at school (e.g., Asher & Dodge, 1986). What are the advantages and disadvantages of such a method? Consider what ethical issues arise from such research. Box 2.2 describes a fascinating ethical test of this method.

However, Thompson (1990) cautions against concluding that "younger" = "more vulnerable." For example, because adolescence represents a time period marked by self-development, research involving self-concept or self-esteem may present more risk to adolescents than it would to younger children. Similarly, because of maturity in social cognition and perspective taking, adolescents may be particularly sensitive to issues pertaining to confidentiality and data access ("Will my parents see my answers?").

Summary of Ethical Issues

Federal and local regulations regarding the ethical treatment of research participants are often difficult to decipher. In addition, such policies represent the ultimate "moving target," because these guidelines often change with societal and political /agendas. Scrutiny of issues regarding risk minimization, informed consent, confidentiality, and protection of special populations often change with the mood of a country. For example, a major federal case involving wiretapping might provoke changes in federal regulations involving the issue of confidentiality.

Because federal regulations are so fluid, researchers should discuss particularly controversial research ideas with the chairperson of the IRB before submitting a protocol for review. The good news is that research protocols are rarely denied. In fact, IRB members often suggest protocol changes that ultimately benefit both the participants, and the researchers. As stated previously, risk minimization benefits not only the participant but also the researcher. In addition, subjects are more likely to be studied in their natural state, which generally provides more valid study results.

BOX 2.2 • *The Effects of Peer-Reputation Measures*

Think back to the children in your elementary school. You can probably remember some children who everyone liked and some that nobody wanted to be around. Such peer social standing is important for both current and future development. Children who are highly disliked and rejected by their peers are at an increased risk for serious adjustment problems during childhood, adolescence, and adulthood than are children who are well liked (Kupersmidt & Coie, 1990).

In order to assess peer reputation, researchers commonly poll children in schools regarding whom they like and dislike (e.g., Asher & Dodge, 1986). Peer researchers are quite frank that parents, teachers, building principals, and IRB members often voice concerns that such methods might bring harm to children identified as intensely disliked by their peers. For example, children may later compare their responses and tease or taunt more disliked peers.

Although one might persuade an IRB that the benefits of such research might outweigh such risks, this point might not be enough to convince a school principal to allow access. To address such concerns, Hayvren and Hymel (1984) examined the relative impact peer-reputation measures had on interactive behavior. The researchers recorded the interactive behavior of preschool children during free play periods a month before peer-nomination assessments. Next, children were polled regarding the classmates they most and least liked to play with. Immediately after the peer-nomination procedures, the researchers carefully examined whether the children made reference to those procedures or treated the rejected children more poorly. The latter observations were repeated a month after the peer-nomination procedures.

Interestingly, about one-half of the children made some mention of the peer-nomination procedures to their peers. However, these comments were either non-relevant (e.g., "I just played this game with a lady") or positive (e.g., "I picked you as my best friend") in content. In fact, not one child uttered a negative comment, such as, "Did you see the picture of Paul? I told the lady I didn't want to play with him."

The researchers documented no change in behavior toward the children rated as disliked either immediately after, or one month, after the peer-nomination procedures. Although the results may not generalize to adolescent populations, the results of this study indicated that peer-reputation measures have virtually no impact on children. Such data would be valuable information to provide to individuals who express concerns about such procedures.

The Experimenter

One way to think about research is to compare it to an efficient movie production. When making a movie, the producer originates the idea, the actors and technicians actually "make" the movie, and the director ensures that the producer's objectives are addressed. Likewise, many research laboratories contain personnel that have analogous roles. For example, the *principal investigator* (PI) primarily conceptualizes and designs the research protocol. In short, one of the objectives of this book is to train the reader to eventually assume this role. Much like a movie director, the *project director* or coordinator ensures that the PI's research protocol and objectives are consistently addressed. Finally, the *research assistant* or experimenter is generally involved in the "nuts and bolts" of the project. Research assistants, or experimenters, may recruit participants, schedule appointments, run study procedures, and enter or code data.

There may be problems with "doing it all yourself." Assuming all possible roles leaves little time for planning research, and puts the researcher in a conflict of interest. For example, what problems might originate if you code your own videotapes and are aware of the study hypotheses? Although it is rare for researchers to fabricate data, it is possible that awareness of the study hypotheses could unconsciously affect the way we code the data.

Standardization

Because of these concerns, when researchers refer to their "lab," they are usually thinking about more than just equipment and facilities. In order for labs to run efficiently, lab members must all be highly trained in a similar fashion. Achieving uniformity or reliability in lab members across tasks is termed **standardization**. There are a number of ways to achieve standardization. For example, some PIs insist that lab members be standardized across all study tasks (e.g., recruiting subjects, conducting procedures, coding data), other researchers assemble separate teams of assistants that are highly trained for compartmentalized assignments (e.g., running procedures). In the latter case, some research assistants are responsible for recruiting, others may actually collect the data, and still others may code or enter data. There are trade offs to either approach. For example, involvement in all aspects of research can be stimulating, yet it may be difficult to standardize the same research assistants across every study task. Conversely, only allowing highly trained research assistants to focus on one repetitive task could lead to boredom and mistakes.

Although research assistants can be standardized for many aspects of the research protocol (e.g., recruiting subjects, scheduling appointments, coding data), in this section we will primarily examine standardization issues pertaining to study procedures. In short, research assistants should be trained in the same fashion in terms of securing informed consent, administering study methods, and debriefing. Discussing the study protocol with research assistants in lab meetings and providing lab personnel with a written protocol can partly accomplish these objectives. Much like a movie or play, the protocol should contain *scripts* for securing consent, introducing and describing study procedures, and debriefing that each research assistant can role-play. Research assistants can practice the research protocol using a series of practice or pilot subjects. Although role-playing is an acceptable first step to ensuring standardization, piloting procedures using "real" subjects exposes experimenters to the realities of the research environment.

Although some aspects of the research protocol, such as the informed-consent process, can be easily scripted, there are other study procedures that may require extensive training. For example, let's revisit the laboratory of Mark Cummings (e.g., Cummings & Davies, 1994), described in Chapter 1 (Box 1.1). In Cummings's research protocol, a child witnesses the conversation of unfamiliar adults escalating into an argument. The child's reaction to this event is recorded as the dependent variable.

This example strongly highlights the importance of standardization. The adults who model these arguments are confederates or research assistants; and must be trained to argue in the same way in each experimental condition. Because Cummings routinely manipulates variables such as argument topic or anger intensity, the research assistants essentially must become expert "actors" across a variety of experimental conditions.

Although the *intensity* and *duration* of the independent variable must be carefully standardized, there may be reliability issues pertaining to the dependent variable, to consider as well. For example, what would you do if a child started crying after watching an intense argument between two adults? Would you stop the procedures or just assume that this was a natural reaction? Like the manipulation of the independent variable, we must be sure that our research assistants are standardized regarding outcome measures as well. This issue is particularly relevant in studies involving risky procedures; thus, all assistants must be trained to recognize and address potential adverse or atypical reactions in a uniform manner.

Experimenter Bias

Unintentional **experimenter bias** by researchers can occur via unintentional verbal intonations or utterances, facial expressions, or experimenter posture (e.g., Barber & Silver, 1968). Although *subject reactivity* (p. 18) is one possible outcome of experimenter bias, poorly trained experiments may also misjudge subject behavior or make coding or data errors.

Experimenter bias can best be avoided by openly discussing these issues with research assistants, and via observations of experimenters "in action" using pilot subjects. For example, in graduate school, a project coordinator noted experimenter bias and unintended subject reactivity as we videotaped parent-toddler interactions. The toddlers paid more attention to another research assistant and myself than they did to their parents. The project coordinator noted that we had a tendency to stare at the cute toddlers during videotaping. In turn, the toddlers simply stared right back at us! Once we were trained to avoid eye contact with the toddlers, the procedures ran much more smoothly.

An organized research protocol that specifically addresses issues pertaining to experimenter bias may dramatically increase sensitivity to this issue. For example, the *Adult Attachment Interview* (AAI; George, Kaplan & Main, 1996) protocol strongly addresses potential experimenter bias. In this twenty-item interview, subjects are asked probing questions about their relationships with parents during childhood and adolescence. Interviewers are specifically trained to remain emotionally neutral, avoid utterances (such as "Oh, my!") that might reinforce or discourage participant dialogue, and not proceed to a new question until the subject has completely stopped talking. To guard against misinterpreting subject responses, researchers are encouraged to audiotape the interview.

Additional Sources of Subject Reactivity

Experimenter bias is only one source of subject reactivity. In some cases, the experimental setting itself may provoke unintended anxious behavior in our research participants. This may be particularly true for young children and for more senior participants who are not as used to being tested or evaluated. Thus, the subject may respond in socially desirable ways, or attempt to "help" or "hurt" the experimenter by behaving in ways that might either support or deny the study hypotheses.

How might one reduce subject reactivity? Careful consideration of our behavior, the research setting, and experimental procedures can potentially address this problem. In terms of the experimenter's behavior, establishing a professional rapport with the subject at the onset of the study may effectively reduce subject anxiety. For example, a research assistant who asserts, "I just don't like kids," may not be the best person to administer procedures to children. Of course, an overly solicitous demeanor may elicit similar behavior in our subjects; likewise, it is probably wise to use only friends and acquaintances as pilot subjects.

The research setting may also contribute to subject reactivity. A cold, sterile research laboratory may provoke considerable anxiety in young children. For this reason, researchers often adorn laboratories in décor that is appealing to their target population. For example, an adolescent research laboratory may contain posters of popular pop and athletic stars, whereas adults may prefer a simple "waiting room" setting. Because individuals feel more comfortable in more homelike settings, actually testing subjects in their own homes can also decrease subject evaluation apprehension. Of course, there are always trade-offs to consider regarding research settings. Too many posters and decorations might be distracting to children or adolescents, and threats to internal validity are often more persistent when we move our procedures into naturalistic settings.

Our procedures also can affect subject reactivity; for example, I once had a subject nervously state, "I'm not really good at tests; I hope I don't fail!" Because of this concern, introducing procedures as "games" to young children may alleviate subject anxieties. By this point in our discussion, you should have understood why risk-minimization of procedures is important. Beyond our natural ethical concern for subjects, highly stressful procedures may encourage unintended reactions. For this reason, researchers typically introduce less taxing procedures first.

Research Settings

The lab or the field? By now, you can probably articulate the advantages and disadvantages of both laboratory and naturalistic research. In the lab environment, we often achieve more control over our independent variable, as well as over our subjects, and achieve a high level of internal validity. Unfortunately, we may achieve *such* a high degree of internal validity that our results that have little meaning in the real world. Conversely, field studies may possess a "real world" appearance, and produce results that can be generalized to the wider, target population. However, because it is more difficult to achieve experimental control in such settings, internal validity can be compromised when conducting field research.

The distinction between lab and field research often becomes blurred when we move beyond simple textbook descriptions. For example, suppose we have young children play either violent or nonviolent video-games in the lab, and subsequently have teachers observe the playground behavior of these children over the next week. In this instance, the researcher attempts to maintain control over the independent variable, yet assesses the dependent variable in a naturalistic, field environment.

There are four research environments (Parke, 1979). In the traditional laboratory-laboratory (DV) study, the independent variable (IV) is manipulated, and dependent variable (DV) measured, under laboratory conditions. In the traditional field (IV)-field (DV) study, both the independent and dependent variables are considered in the field environment. The aforementioned video-game study would constitute a laboratory (IV)-field (DV) study; the independent variable was manipulated in the lab, and the dependent variable was assessed in the field. Finally, in the field (IV)-laboratory (DV) study, the independent variable is manipulated in the field, whereas the dependent variable is measured in the lab. One might use this design to achieve a more realistic manipulation of the

What Do You Think?

Suppose you are interested in how commercials that target adolescents influence their consumer behavior. Think about how you would change your procedures based on whether you used lab–lab, field–field, lab–field, or field–lab methods.

independent variable in the field, and assess a difficult-to-measure dependent variable in a more controlled environment.

Common Research Settings

Although it is beyond the scope of this book to describe every potential setting available for researchers, we will discuss a number of research environments. In this section, several popular research settings will be described.

Schools.   Researchers who wish to access child and adolescent populations often clamor to obtain access to schools. It is easy to see why: the schools allow lifespan researchers access to a large number of subjects that can be easily tracked over time. Collecting data in a number of schools throughout a district also allows for stronger claims regarding the generalizability of study results. Thus, the advantages schools have to offer, as a research site, do not go unnoticed by researchers. As you might imagine, laboratory schools affiliated with universities, schools in urban areas, and schools located near colleges or universities often get inundated with requests from researchers to use their students for research studies.

Gaining Access.   What are some of the common issues that you may face when attempting to access schools as research sites? Perhaps the first step is to identify a school (or schools) and think carefully about the school context, as well as your role as a researcher. In terms of school context, one might use different approaches when considering entry into university laboratory schools or general, public schools. Because university laboratory schools usually have a specific research mission, school administrators are often quite willing to allow researchers access to their pupils. Although public school administrators may have specific research agendas they would like researchers to pursue, lab-school administrators generally approve just about any type of research that involves no more than minimal risk to the students.

Although it is fairly easy to gain access to lab schools, there are potential drawbacks to this research setting. For example, how well do the demographics of students enrolled in the lab school represent those of the larger community? In addition, I am always concerned with the research savvy of students in lab schools that have heavy "research traffic." In fact, I once had a third grader ask me if he was going to be in the control group!

Public schools are generally more difficult to access than lab schools. For this reason, doing some homework on the school setting is important. Parsons and Meyers (1984) recommend that professionals think carefully about their appearance as an "insider" or "outsider" to school personnel and students. In general, school administrators are much more receptive to the requests of "insiders," or researchers that have an "inside track" for gaining access to the school. These researchers may personally know high-level school administrators or come strongly recommended by parents or teachers.

Because most of us are probably "outsiders," there are strategies we can pursue to look more like an "insider." Identifying the proper individual, or set of individuals, to initially contact regarding the research is an important first step. In many cases, the building principal is the individual who wields the most power regarding student access; however, in more urban areas, the researcher must often gain approval of a school board before they can approach individual building principles (Jacob-Timm, 1995).

Beyond identifying a primary contact person, we should think about the needs of the school. In some states or localities, we might be quickly dismissed if the research protocol does not have implications for education. In urban areas, school administrators may be specifically looking for ways to combat school dropout or violence (Perry, 1995). Lending a careful ear to these concerns represents an important step in making the transition from "outsider" to "insider," particularly if some of these issues are appended to the research protocol for empirical study. Although some researchers may stubbornly pursue their own research agendas, establishing a mutual, collaborative relationship with a school meshes with the multidisciplinary nature of our field, and makes it easier to gain access to the school in the future. This general rule of establishing collaborative relationships with institutional personnel may also apply to other major research settings, such as pediatric facilities, mental health clinics, and retirement communities (Seranno-Garcia, 1990).

Regardless of your "insider" or "outsider" status, a general meeting with the building principal (or members of the school board) will be needed to discuss the research protocol. This meeting is critical; a poorly articulated presentation could doom one's chances of gaining access to the school. The following issues should be addressed during this meeting (cf. Seranno-Garcia, 1990):

- Introduce yourself and state your credentials and affiliation.
- After proper introductions have been made, ask the building principal (or other personnel) to discuss the student demographics of the school, as well as the main strengths and assets of the institution. Next, ask about problems or concerns facing the school or community.
- Outline the specific purpose of your research. Emphasize parallels between your research interests and the school's concerns.
- Indicate applied implications of the research and how the research results might ultimately benefit the institution.
- Describe your methods for obtaining parental permission and student assent.
- Explain the study procedures. Schools are busy places; thus, expect pointed questions regarding teacher involvement, time duration, and space/equipment needs.
- Describe the study risks and benefits.
- Discuss your exit plan. Indicate how results will be shared with school personnel.

Although some of this information might seem more appropriate for a salesperson, the researcher is in basically the same role. It is critical to communicate your interest in working with their population, and to demonstrate a sincere concern regarding major problems that may face the institution. In addition, once a collaborative relationship has been established with the principal, the researcher should next turn to establishing similar relationships with key personnel that work in the institution (Linney, 1989). For example, before one rushes into data collection, initiating small discussion, or **focus groups** with key personnel—or even the students—within the school allows for a firsthand look at issues facing the institution. The focus group input provides rich *qualitative data* regarding the problem, which can be used to augment data collected on the primary research population.

For example, suppose you are interested in investigating how parenting behavior influences adolescent achievement motivation. You distribute questionnaires, which represents use of a *quantitative method*, and find that low parent involvement is positively correlated with low levels of achievement motivation. Consider how the following quote from an adolescent focus group hammers home this finding:

> "Yeah, Mom and Dad don't really care about how much I study; they don't even go to the parent-teacher conferences. Mom told me to watch out, I might lose all my popularity if I do too good at school . . . like, she makes me not even care about school anymore when she talks like that."

Recall in Chapter 1 that I made distinctions between the quantitative and qualitative approaches. I have noticed that many lifespan researchers often line themselves up with one approach or the other, and tend to have strong opinions about people who endorse an opposing position on the matter. Can you see from this example that both approaches can be used? I believe that qualitative data really makes quantitative information "come alive"!

Obtaining Parental Permission

Once we have surmounted school-access hurdles, we next must obtain parental permission to assess the children. Directly mailing permission letters, or having teachers include the letters in student homework or informational packets commonly initiates this goal. In most cases, researchers strive to obtain **active parental consent**. That is, before the child is allowed in the study, we must receive a signed permission letter by at least one parent. Unfortunately, because some schools report that only 10 to 25% of parents even appear to pick up student report cards (Robinson et al., 1993), one can expect that many busy parents will fail to return the permission letters.

Children whose parents grant permission are different than those who do not. Children without parental permission are less liked, more aggressive, more prone to substance abuse, and display more academic problems (Noll et al., 1997). Similar concerns are raised when asking parents to complete and return questionnaires. In one study, minority parents were less likely to return a short survey in a stamped and preaddressed envelope than parents of nonminority children (La Greca & Silverman, 1993). Among nonminority parents, the children whose parents returned the rating scale had better academic skills and fewer peer problems.

Because of these validity concerns, some advocate the use of **passive parental consent**. In this case, parents receive permission letters that instruct them to return the letter only if they *do not* want their child to participate. The researcher assumes that parents who do not return the letter are providing "passive" permission. This strategy can dramatically increase the size of research samples. For example, the use of passive consent strategies can boost student involvement in research as high as 96 percent (Esbensen et al., 1996). This statistic dwarfs response rates using active-consent methods, which are generally between 25 and 50 percent, depending on the school system (Jackson & Warren, 2000).

Do you see any ethical concerns regarding passive parent consent? Sending a consent form home with a young child provides little guarantee that the document will reach a parent. Although mailing the consent form directly to parents with an preaddressed, stamped envelope increases these chances, this strategy does not *guarantee* that a parent will actually read the permission letter. Thus, IRBs rarely grant approval for research protocols containing passive-consent methods.

What if the building principal or school board approves a study using passive-consent methods, yet the researcher's IRB denies such a request? In such cases, some straightforward rules apply. Generally, *whoever demands more restrictions on the researcher wins the debate.* In this case, the researcher's IRB gets the final say. Conversely, personnel at the research site occasionally demand more restrictions than the researcher's IRB. For example, a building principal may require the researcher to also obtain the permission of teachers before experimenters are allowed to use students as research subjects. In such cases, the site personnel always win the debate.

Because most researchers must secure active parental permission, there are techniques we can use to bolster the return rates. For example, Esbensen et al. (1996) achieved a 90 percent parental response rate across four demographically diverse schools using different methods. First, permission slips, accompanied by a letter of support from the assistant superintendent, were handed out in class to students. One week later, this process was repeated for students who had not returned the slip. A letter promising a pizza party for the first class that received all the consent forms accompanied the permission slip. In the following weeks, parents that had not returned the materials were directly mailed the permission slips. The response rate of this study was very encouraging; for example, the return rate of permission slips rose from just over 6 percent to almost 100 percent in five weeks. These data suggest that researchers must be diligent and use multiple methods to ensure return of parental permission slips.

A final caveat should be added to our discussion of school-based research, or research involving just about any community institution. A number of experts strongly suggest that researchers have a clear "exit plan" as data collection nears completion (Brown, Pryzwansky, & Schulte, 1987). Although some may simply pack up and leave, "giving something back" to the school further reinforces our idea of collaborative relationships, strengthens our position as an "insider," and may make it easier to gain access to the facility in the future. For example, researchers may provide free services to the school, deliver short lectures to school personnel on pertinent topics (e.g., school-violence prevention), acknowledge the school in presentations and publications, and share the study results with the school board, principal, teachers, and parents.

Home-Based Research.   It is sometimes very difficult to convince people to come to a research laboratory. Consider the plight of the infancy researcher. The researcher must locate caregivers who are willing to schedule an appointment. Further, caregivers must locate childcare arrangements for other children in the family, pack up the infant and accessories (e.g., bottles, diapers, coats, etc.), commute to the lab, and try to find a free parking place within several blocks of the laboratory. Thus, it is not surprising that lifespan researchers often rely on samples that are more easily at our disposal, and why schools, pediatric facilities, large companies, and retirement communities are often frequented by researchers.

Of course, some of us are simply not fortunate enough to have convenient access to such facilities. The home visit is one solution; I have witnessed many parents, romantic couples, and caregivers of frail elderly utter the phrase, "Well, can't we just do everything at my home?" You can probably think of advantages to this method, however; most notably, the participant is on home territory, which lessens the impact of experimenter effects.

Beyond making life more convenient and comfortable for our subjects, there is an another advantage of home visiting that is very difficult to achieve in traditional laboratory or alternative field (e.g., school) settings. Simply put, the home allows for better assessment of **setting events** (see also p. 28). A setting event refers to specific behaviors or patterns of social interaction that naturally occur within an environment (Howe & Reiss, 1993). For example, family mealtime might be considered a setting event within a home, where as solving math problems might constitute one in a school.

A major advantage of the home visit is that we can observe research participants engaged in naturalistic setting events. For example, we can audiotape family mealtime discussions, videotape children playing with their own toys, or observe an adult child caring for an ill parent. Although these setting events can be simulated in laboratory environments, the external validity of such behavior would be much richer in home environments.

Because a home visit qualifies as field research, the experimental controls that we have over the participant, independent variable, and research setting are not as rigorous as in laboratory research settings. Ringing phones, barking dogs, and the presence of individuals not related to the study can be expected if we do not consider some advance planning. Although it is impossible to prevent every event that might disrupt the study procedures, there are a number of strategies to help home visitors (Patterson, 1982; Wasik, 1993).

- *In advance, establish that all participants will be at the research setting throughout the procedures.* Fully disclose the nature and time duration of the procedures before scheduling the visit. A lengthy Saturday home visit involving a family may conflict with chess tournaments and soccer practices. Such conflict can be prevented if the researcher discusses these concerns with a parent in advance.
- *No guests, no phones, no television.* Gently bring up these concerns when scheduling the home visit with reasonable parameters. A continually ringing phone can be more distracting than a quick response to an incoming phone call.
- *Establish initial rapport, but don't engage in irrelevant discussions or comments during procedures.* This concern can be addressed shortly after our arrival. After general rapport has been established, and informed consent obtained, make it very clear that casual conversation could potentially impede study procedures. For example, when observing the free-play behavior of children, remind the caregiver not to encourage any particular play behavior.
- *Recruit research assistants with strong interpersonal skills and social intelligence.* Although this might seem like an obvious recommendation for any research setting, the unpredictability of home visits often requires the presence of researchers that can "think on their feet." For example, I once witnessed a research assistant effectively calm an estranged spouse who unexpectedly dropped by during a home visit.
- *Take more than one person.* Conventional wisdom would suggest not conducting a home visit alone. Beyond safety concerns, study procedures can often run much more smoothly with more than one researcher. For example, when using a three-person research team, one member can establish rapport and outline and conduct

study procedures, another person may be responsible for videotaping, and the third member may attend to children not directly involved in the study.

- *Get good directions and an area map.* Becoming lost and arriving late for a home visit is not a good way to establish rapport.
- *Pilot, pilot, pilot.* Although research participants are naturally more comfortable in their home environment, the research team is in unfamiliar territory. Piloting all procedures in advance is critical when conducting home visits. In addition, preassembled "packets" containing informed-consent documents, questionnaires, videotapes, and so on should be available to the research team at a moment's notice. Forgetting the videotape for an observational study defeats the primary purpose of the home visit.

You can probably understand why some lifespan researchers avoid home visits. Purists bemoan the lack of experimental control, whereas pragmatics bring up time and expense issues. However, the external validity of home-based research is a major advantage, and threats to internal validity can be offset with some advance planning. Finally, researchers interested in observing research participants in naturalistic settings are not limited to conducting home visits. Box 2.3 describes a fascinating study that focused on identifying sources of neighborhood support for middle-aged children.

What Do You Think?

The study in Box 2.3 highlights a method for identifying sources of support for middle-aged children. How would you modify this method for an adolescent sample? How would this method be superior to gathering data using a support-network questionnaire or interview?

BOX 2.3 • *The Neighborhood Walk*

Bryant (1985) sought to identify sources of support for children, including support figures (e.g., parents, pets, friends), intrapersonal sources (e.g., hobbies), and environmental supports (e.g., clubs). Although this information can be obtained from parents or other support figures, such as teachers (e.g., Achenbach, 1991), Bryant speculated that children themselves could offer a unique perspective. Using children as informants holds important advantages; for example, a parent may not be aware of certain sources of support the child uses when distressed (e.g., sanctuary at the library).

Each child was asked to illustrate their social world by introducing the researcher to friends, secret hiding places, and activities they engaged in during times of duress. Bryant hypothesized that the tour through the neighborhood, or "Neighborhood Walk," would establish rapport and prime young memories better than simple surveys or parental prompting. Bryant theorized that children with robust support networks would be better adjusted than their counterparts who did not.

Bryant's study hypotheses were supported. Intimate contact with grandparents, discussions with pets, and accessibility to structured activities were related to various indices of socioemotional functioning. Beyond establishing these initial validity findings, reliability was also established by repeating the neighborhood tour with a subsample of children. For example, perceptions of support were quite consistent over a two-week time frame. Despite these initial psychometric findings, more reliability and validity research is needed to support the Neighborhood Walk methodology. For example, does the Neighborhood Walk method predict socioemotional adjustment better than the reports of parents or children garnered via questionnaires or interviews? In addition, longitudinal research could better tease out mechanisms of causality. Although Bryant (1985) theorized that robust support networks forecast healthy socioemotional adjustment in children, the reverse could also be true.

Internet Research.   Increasingly, researchers are using the Internet and World Wide Web as an important research tool. We can use these services to access existing data sets, join discussion groups to communicate with other lifespan experts, and collect data from research participants throughout the world. We are no longer limited to collecting data in our community; we can now reach potential research participants throughout our state, country, and world. You can obtain a flavor for the many different types of Internet research by visiting the American Psychological Society Web Site (http://psych.hanover.edu/Research/exponnet.html). This site provides a listing for current Internet studies involving clinical, social, health, and lifespan developmental psychology.

Web-based research holds other advantages. We can collect data more quickly and cheaply; photocopying expenses can be costly when using hard-copy questionnaires. Participants can complete the research anytime at their convenience. The computer medium decreases the odds for experimenter biases and promotes perceptions of anonymity (Davis, 1999). Errors can also be reduced as the participant submits their data. For example, subjects can be reminded of missed questions or out-of-range responses (Epstein et al., 2001).

Web-based methods of data collection can be methodologically robust. The results of Web-based experiments and surveys are similar to those obtained through traditional laboratory or field-based methods (Epstein et al., 2001; McGraw, Tew & Williams, 2000). Unfortunately, almost all of this validity research is based on college-student samples. Can we expect the same findings when using other populations? For example, would a sample of senior citizens complete a survey over the Internet the same way they would in the laboratory? This is the type of question you could answer!

There are strategies we can use to increase the precision of Internet research. Because we have already discussed sampling issues, you are probably wondering how representative Internet-based samples are. Indeed, about one-half of adults do not even own personnel computers (Dillman, 2000), and most Web users are middle-aged, high income men (Krantz & Dalal, 2000). The power of the Internet can help somewhat to offset these problems. First, if we have some idea of the demographics of the study population, then we can recruit extremely large numbers of potential participants and use quota sampling. That is, once a particular segment of our study population has been obtained (e.g., Caucasian males between the ages of 30 and 35), we simply stop collecting data on that segment.

Another strategy would be to recruit individuals that visit Web sites devoted to a particular population. For example, numerous Web sites exist that cater to parents, teachers, adolescents, romantic couples, and senior citizens. These potential participants can be recruited through ongoing discussion groups, chat rooms, or in some cases, by posting your study materials on the Web site (with permission, of course!). I also expect that many readers know how to construct Web sites. A personnel Web-based "research site" can be linked to popular sites devoted to the target population, and located through popular Internet search engines.

Although sampling methods will improve dramatically in the future, conducting the same study procedures on a smaller, local community sample may be another way to quell the concerns of Internet-research skeptics. Demonstrating that responses are similar across different methods (i.e., Internet vs. lab) *within* populations (i.e., young, old, low income, highly educated) constitutes not only a validity check but also a valuable study in itself.

The power of technology can also provide valuable information about subject behavior over the course of the study. We can now identify the Web page that referred the participant to the study, record how long it takes subjects to complete the study materials, and block participants from completing the study procedures more than once (O'Neil & Penrod, 2001). In addition, we can use this technology to track subject dropout, or attrition. In fact, researchers can systematically examine factors related to subject attrition. For example, O'Neil and Penrod (2001) noted that weekend study participants were more likely to complete study procedures than their weekday counterparts.

Of course, the advantages of such technology raise concerns. Computer privacy is an issue throughout the world; thus, the use of tracking software or requiring subjects to provide personal information or e-mail addresses raises major concerns regarding confidentiality. Not surprisingly, when subjects are asked to provide personal information, the chances for study dropout increases (Musch & Reips, 2000; O'Neil & Penrod, 2001). Such statistics are likely to influence our thinking on using monetary payment as a form of subject compensation over the Internet, because participants lose their anonymity if they want to be compensated. For example, although the use of small monetary payments has been shown to increase subject participation in traditional mail surveys (Dillman, 2000), similar methods show very mixed results when used in Web research (Musch & Reips, 2000). In fact, in one Internet study, O'Neil and Penrod (2001) noted that the offer of monetary compensation actually *increased* subject attrition!

In summary, the Internet opens fascinating doors for researchers. Although Internet-based research has its critics, this research context will become increasingly popular over time. In addition, although questionnaires represent the primary data-collection tool, interview data can be conducted using e-mail, instant messaging, and discussion groups. In fact, advances in technology should allow us to eventually conduct real-time interviews with subjects using streaming video and audio. More explicit information regarding Internet research tips are given in Box 2.4.

BOX 2.4 • *Emerging Rules for Internet Research*

Admittedly, today's techniques for Internet research could change or become obsolete in just a few years. However, some very thorough research on this topic should be consulted before one enters this research domain (see Birnbaum, 2000; Dillman, 2000 for excellent reference material). The following issues represent some concerns to think about before using this medium:

• *Be humble.* From a technological standpoint, it is much easier to conduct Web research then it was just five years ago. However, it is hard to be an expert in everything. Quite frankly, many scholars in our field will admit that much of their collegiate computer training involved statistical applications, with less (if any) concentration in Web-based research methods. Because collaboration is an important component in our field, I would suggest working closely with a computer-literate colleague or friend that can help solve the more technical pieces of Web research.

• *Identify the study population.* Try to obtain demographic data, such as gender, income level, and ethnicity on your study population. Because most Web-study participants are North American Caucasian men between the ages of 26 and 35 (Krantz & Dalal, 2000), it is quite possible that the study results may only generalize to a select population. This concern can be addressed by discontinuing subject recruitment once a certain demographic quota has been reached; recruiting could continue for individuals that possess less common demographics.

(*continued*)

BOX 2.4   Continued

- *Monitor validity.* Although the results of Web-based and laboratory studies are quite similar (Birnbaum, 2000), it is a good idea to recruit a smaller, local sample and have these participants complete the study procedures in the lab or field. These results can then be directly compared to the Web results; similar research findings would constitute an important validity check.
- *Pilot procedures.* The functionality of Web sites is often dependent on browser configurations, computer hardware, and system software. Because of this concern, it is advisable to test the Web site using different computers, servers, and search engines. Keep it simple; requiring participants to obtain highly technical "plug ins" or other software creates a barrier and may affect the sample makeup.
- *Create an attractive site.* Web design software has become *much* easier to use, and often contains attractive templates that can be used to construct Web sites. Reips (2000) recommends that researchers should avoid commercial banners, and encourage others to create links to the site.
- *Be careful of compensation and personal-information requirements.* The jury is still out on how subject-compensation and personal-information requirements affect study participation and attrition. The best advice is to pilot procedures with and without compensation and personal information requirements and then compare sample demographics, attrition rates, and study results.
- *Keep "welcome screens" concise and personal.* The first page, or "welcome screen" of the Web site should cover the standard elements of informed consent. Researchers should avoid jargon and highly technical language, offer a convenient mechanism for answering questions, and provide further information about the study (e.g., phone numbers, e-mail address, etc.). Dillman (2000) provides excellent examples of how to construct attractive, easy-to-read welcome screens.
- *Track attrition.* Subject dropout is a major methodological concern among Web researchers. Again, computer software can keep track of how subjects arrive at the Web site, the hour and day subjects complete study procedures, and subject dropout rate.
- *Keep it safe.* Mechanisms to protect subject confidentiality and maintain a secure Web site represent paramount considerations when proposing research using this domain. Not surprisingly, IRBs often require a plan for protecting the privacy of subjects and maintaining data security. Birnbaum (2000) offers a number of important pointers for accomplishing these objectives.
- *Keep up to date on techniques.* There are a growing number of scholars specifically interested in the mechanics of how to design effective Web questionnaires and experiments. There really is an art to these techniques; for example, researchers have documented that individuals are more likely to complete Web studies that begin with easy and interesting tasks (Birnbaum, 2000). Dropout rates decrease if subjects are provided the option of returning study materials via regular mail (Dillman, 2000). Students interested in fascinating questionnaire techniques should consult Baron and Siepmann (2000) and Dillman (2000). In addition, a number of researchers have designed effective experimental methods for the Web context (e.g., Francis, Neath, & Surprenant, 2000).

Summary of Research Settings

Increases in technology and the cleverness of researchers present special challenges to traditional rules regarding research settings. For example, can we always assume that the robust internal validity of a laboratory setting compromises a study's external validity? Consider the family researcher who documents that the conflict-management tactics of family members are similar in laboratory and home settings; the equivalent findings would suggest that the laboratory environment evokes naturalistic behavior. Conversely, is it impossible to achieve internal validity in a field environment? For example, demonstrating that variable manipulations affect behavioral development in schools, households, and Internet environments as potently as lab-based treatments makes a strong validity statement.

Hopefully, an important learning objective has been achieved. Validity skeptics can be effectively silenced when researchers document similar research findings across research settings. Although this may seem like a costly and time-consuming method, the researcher need not collect enormous amounts of data to prove a point (unless documenting equivalent findings across settings is the primary research objective). For example, a researcher using a well-established laboratory method in a field setting (e.g., schools) for the first time may wish to also run the procedures on a small, equivalent sample (e.g., school-aged children) in the laboratory. Demonstrating equivalent findings in this case would make a strong statement regarding the internal validity of the field manipulations.

Chapter Summary

In this chapter, additional considerations for the recruitment and treatment of subjects, experimenter behavior, and research settings were described. All of these issues influence the validity of our research findings. An inadequate sampling plan can seriously limit the generalizability of our findings. At study onset, we must consider how to access a pool of people that will adequately represent a target population. By now, you should be aware that collecting demographic information on the study population and research sample is critical data for addressing criticisms regarding external validity. Also, because recruiting methods can heavily influence the demographic, intellectual, and psychological makeup of our sample, we must monitor the types of individuals who respond to our inducement strategies.

Ethical guidelines for the treatment of human subjects were also described. Although guidelines are forever changing, particular consideration must be given to our informed-consent procedures, risk/benefit ratios, and confidentiality assurances. Although the protection of human subjects is our paramount concern, subjects who are not properly informed of the study procedures and purpose, feel coerced to participate in our research, feel threatened, or perceive their data will not be protected are simply not going to "be themselves" during the study. Thus, sensitivity regarding ethical issues can directly influence the validity of the research.

We also discussed the importance of experimenter and subject behavior during a study and how such behavior can influence the integrity of our results. Chiefly, standardization of the research protocol is a critical step in the research process. A clear step-by-step research protocol, intensive training of research assistants, and piloting of study procedures are common mechanisms used to achieve experimenter standardization. We also considered how our behavior and the experimental setting could influence subject perceptions over the course of the research.

We also described the relative advantages and disadvantages of common research settings. Although it is common to make concrete comparisons regarding validity issues between laboratory and field studies, we pointed out that the research world is much more complex. For example, some researchers manipulate independent variables in the lab, and observe the dependent variable in a field setting (and vice versa).

This chapter discussed three popular research settings. It covered techniques for conducting school-, home-, and Internet-based research. An expert knowledge on how to gain and maintain access to research settings, such as schools, is valuable, because the information can be applied to other research settings, such as companies, long-term care settings, and hospitals. The chapter concluded with a discussion of Internet research. Although there are many potential criticisms of this research domain (chiefly sampling issues), tips were offered to address sampling concerns and data integrity. As with any new research context, cross-validating results with a smaller community sample is a strong methodological check. Because techniques change so drastically, it is recommended that new researchers consult with an experienced professional with an expertise in Internet/computer methods.

Research Navigator™ Exercise: Identifying Sampling, Recruiting, and Consent Procedures

There are two objectives to this assignment. First, you will learn how to conduct a more advanced search for resources using multiple keywords. Second, you will read a research article pertaining to adolescent development and examine how the authors addressed concerns regarding sampling, recruiting, and the informed-consent process.

Go the Research Navigator™ website: http://www.researchnavigator.com. Go to Section 2 of the Research Navigator™ homepage, entitled "ContentSelect" and choose the Psychology database. Next, type in the keyword *early adolescence.* As usual, you will get an array of articles; however, next, click on the Advanced Search box at the top of the paper. Once on this page, type in *early adolescence* by the word *Find,* and then enter a second term directly below, such as *bullying.* Note you can enter as many as three keywords; using this strategy can help you narrow searches. Also note that if the Full Text box is highlighted, your search will be limited to full-text articles—that is, articles that you can read, print, or save from your computer. Although limiting your search to full-text articles is fine for our exercises, you would need to conduct a more expanded search for a term paper or research proposal that includes these articles and abstracts. In the latter cases, you would have to track down the full-length articles at the library.

For this exercise, read one study that uses an adolescent population in the schools. For this assignment, consider the following issues:

- How well was the target population described?
- What were the sampling and recruitment methods?
- Did the author make demographic comparisons between the study population and the research sample?
- What statements were made regarding the representiveness of the sample?
- How was informed consent obtained?
- If minors were involved in the study, how was parental permission and child assent obtained? What percentage of parents declined or did not return consent forms? Did the authors take measures to encourage a higher return rate?
- What precautions were made to minimize risk and ensure confidentiality?
- What methods, if any, were used to train research assistants and ensure standardization?

3

Newborn and Biobehavioral Assessment

A parent was overheard making the remark, "I can't wait for my baby to grow up and actually *do* something; right now she's just a little blob." Although some people believe that infants are not capable of important behavior, infants can do many things. The primary challenge is to design creative methods so that the infant's actual *performance* on a task matches their actual *competence*, or true ability. Thus, although it is difficult to pinpoint who will become a future Nobel Prize winner, it is amazing that certain indices of infant thinking and behavior modestly forecast intellectual and socioemotional competencies during childhood, adolescence, and adulthood (McCall & Carriger, 1993; Waters et al., 2000).

Conversely, it is also true that many competencies are difficult to predict from infant assessments. A fussy, inattentive three month old may not display the same functioning at five years of age. However, it is possible that *present* infant difficulties are important, even if such delays do not forecast later problems. A fussy infant may not necessarily become a fussy teenager, but it is possible that such behavior causes considerable distress for caregivers.

There are a number of issues that we will examine in the present chapter. First, the infant, as a research subject, may cause some to doubt the validity of infancy research. You cannot interview an infant or ask them to complete a questionnaire. However, the reliability of the infant subject is also dependent on the researcher. A researcher poorly trained in infancy research methods, even if armed with strong procedures, is likely to gather data that is not to be trusted. In short, infants can be reliable subjects, *under the right conditions.*

After exploring basic methodological issues facing infancy researchers, we will next turn to ways to assess major infant abilities, such as infant state, arousal, and state regulation. In addition, we will specify methods for assessing basic infant growth and motor development. After reading this chapter, you should be able to:

- Describe major methodological issues facing infancy researchers.
- Discuss basic checklists and behavioral rating scales to assess newborn behavior.
- Illustrate techniques for assessing infant arousal and state regulation.
- Describe methods to assess infant growth and motor development.

Major Methodological Issues

Infancy researchers face a number of methodological hurdles. For example, infants cannot volunteer for a research study! Thus, infancy researchers often resort to creative methods for sampling and recruiting infant populations. Infants are also not very cooperative research participants; they sleep, fuss, and cry. For this reason, we must maximize our chances that each infant research participant is assessed in their most alert, cooperative state.

Advances in medical technology have also led to a plethora of research involving medically challenged infants. For this reason, we will examine special methodological challenges for researchers working with vulnerable infant populations. In addition, because medically challenged infants do not grow up in an environmental vacuum, we will explore different ways to define and assess variables that facilitate or undermine their developmental outcomes.

Sampling and Recruitment

Where do I find infants? The answer to this question depends on a number of factors. Researchers working with newborns often access hospital settings, whereas those who desire older infant samples frequently collaborate with pediatric groups. In addition, infancy researchers may use both facilities; this strategy is often necessary for scientists who seek to chart developmental progress from birth through preschool or beyond.

It is easy to see why infancy researchers seek these facilities as research sites. In terms of recruiting newborns, or *neonates*, a hospital setting allows researchers convenient access to large numbers of parents and infants. The infants are also conveniently at our disposal for neonatal assessments; it's usually a very short walk from the maternity ward to the infant-observation room. Hospital settings also allow researchers to more easily locate and recruit hard-to-find samples (e.g., infants with unusual medical complications), and the newborns in a public facility may reflect the ethnic and socioeconomic demographics of the community.

Many of the aforementioned advantages also hold true regarding pediatric facilities. Also, the fact that infants are routinely brought in for "well-baby visits" (e.g., at 2 weeks, 2 months, 6 months, etc.), allows us a mechanism to reliably follow infants over time. Because the pediatric staff plans patient schedules well in advance, researchers can predict the date for an infant visit. During such a visit, researchers can collect data. For example, caregivers in the waiting room can complete brief questionnaires, and infant assessments can be conducted before the medical checkup in patient rooms. Pediatricians usually allow for brief testing periods before checkups, because this time period is frequently "open" time, and eventual medical testing/procedures (e.g., blood tests, and inoculations) may compromise data collected later.

The chances for obtaining an infant sample that is representative of the community increases when using public health facilities. However, although using multiple hospital/pediatric facilities may increase our odds for a representative sample, this strategy simply may not be feasible for researchers. Many times, we are quite fortunate to gain access to just one hospital or pediatric facility. In such cases, to offset sampling concerns, it is recommended that researchers contrast sample demographics to broader hospital, pediatric facility, or community data.

There are some drawbacks to using these facilities. Chiefly, time is usually not on your side. Hospitals and pediatric facilities are *busy* places! Also, with the advent of "drive-through delivery," many mothers and infants leave the hospital within 24 hours of delivery. In addition, pediatricians and office managers may only allow for brief assessment and testing periods. Finally, there may be concerns with the external validity of certain procedures—that is, how realistic are mother-infant feeding observations that are assessed in a pediatric facility? Infancy researchers with legitimate concerns regarding such validity threats should consider home-based settings for data collection (Seifer, 2001).

Despite these disadvantages, researchers who have access to large public hospital and pediatric facilities are frequently a source of envy. Can you think of some ways to gain access to these facilities? Like experts that conduct school-based research (Chapter 2), one's chances of establishing a recruitment and research site at one of these facilities is greatly enhanced by the researcher's status. For example, a researcher who actually has a job at a hospital or personally knows a key physician or staff member may suddenly gain "insider" status.

For the rest of us, there are strategies that we can use to help us gain access to hospital or pediatric facilities. Like university lab schools, medical facilities with heavy teaching missions typically also have strong research agendas. In such cases, faculty members are often under pressure to train medical students, deliver services, hold administrative appointments, and conduct research. These faculty members often have very innovative ideas that may dovetail nicely with our own research interests. For this reason, researchers interested in gaining access to medical facilities *should initially approach personnel that hold similar research interests.*

Although hospital and pediatric facilities without strong teaching missions (particularly HMOs) are more difficult to access than their medical-school counterparts, there are other bits of advice that can aid infancy researchers that might work in either setting. The facility may require outside researchers to present a short study proposal to a site-approval board. This board is frequently made up of physicians, nurses, and other staff members (e.g., social worker, office manager). Because medical facilities are also businesses, expect challenging questions regarding time pressures on staff and clients, and space requirements. Perhaps a paramount concern rests with the social or medical significance of the research study; any aspect of the research that might have implications for improvements in medical practice should be strongly highlighted.

There are additional considerations. Try to establish working relationships with key medical facility personnel *before* this group meeting; these individuals could become your advocates. Also, when thinking about collaborative relationships, consider the fact that other medical personnel, such as nurses and social workers, can provide valuable input to research-protocol designs. Finally, your "exit plan" will strongly determine your likelihood of gaining access to these facilities in the future. If your relationships with the medical personnel are truly collaborative, plan future meetings to discuss data analytic strategies and eventual dissemination of results (e.g., publications and presentations).

We can use other recruitment tools to access infant samples. Some hospitals publish information regarding new infant deliveries in local newspapers. These "new arrival" pieces may include the infant's name, parent name(s), and even a local street address. Some medical facilities will grant researchers "birth lists" that contain similar information.

In both cases, we can send information regarding the research protocol directly to the infant's home.

Researchers using birth lists from several hospitals can recruit large numbers of infants and families in a short amount of time. Because the eventual sample will be self-selected, we can use *quota sampling* (Chapter 2) to ensure a more representative research sample. That is, once we obtain enough infants that are representative of a certain demographic profile (e.g., white infants from upper–middle-class families), we can end recruitment for these babies and continue collecting data on infants and families that represent the other profiles.

The Importance of Infant State

Newborn infants sleep and cry a lot! This finding is encouraging to researchers who empirically study these phenomena and disheartening to those who wish to work with happy, alert babies. The issue of infant sleep–wake cycles, or **infant state**, is of paramount concern to researchers working with young infants.

For example, a researcher studying infant visual acuity or mother-infant interactions is likely to view infant state as a nuisance variable that must be controlled. This issue becomes magnified for researchers seeking to contrast healthy and vulnerable newborns on such outcome variables. Infants with certain medical difficulties may be less awake and alert than their healthy counterparts, although sometimes the reverse is true. Thus, a researcher insensitive to this issue may document significant differences between groggy, vulnerable infants and their alert, healthy peers on an important outcome variable that has more to do with state disparities than with true developmental differences.

Researchers sensitive to infant-state issues usually employ multiple strategies. Because caregivers are aware of their infant's "best times," assessments may be scheduled during a similar time frame. Researchers working with vulnerable infants may want to keep testing sessions short or schedule multiple assessments over time. Finally, caregivers can be of great assistance in helping researchers cope with infant-state problems. Caregivers are often acutely aware of strategies (e.g., repositioning infant, feeding, burping) that are effective for altering undesirable-state patterns in their own infants.

Some infancy researchers view state as an important variable in its own right. They feel that the amount of time infants remain in specific states (e.g., deep sleep), how well or fluidly they move from one state to another, and how well they regulate their own states are important reflections of central nervous system and biobehavioral development. Because of these concerns, we will explore ways to systematically assess infant state and arousal regulation later in this chapter.

Working with Vulnerable Infants

Advances in medical technology allow us to study developmental processes in infants that may not have even survived in decades past. Infants born at extremely early gestational ages (GAs) or very low birthweights (VLBWs), or who were exposed prenatally to drugs and alcohol have become hot target populations in recent years. However, vulnerable populations are often very difficult to identify, and research can easily succumb to critical methodological problems.

One of the greatest difficulties is the tendency to treat certain target populations (e.g., preterm infants) as a *homogeneous, or highly similar, group.* Do preterm, low birthweight (LBW), and alcohol-exposed infants represent different populations? Because both preterm birth and maternal alcohol consumption are predictors of LBW, it is possible to have the same infant participate in three different studies that supposedly target different populations! Thus, it is very difficult to predict the outcomes of babies born with such vulnerabilities.

The first major step would be to clearly identify a target population (Chapter 2), such as *preterm,* or *small for* **gestational age**, babies. For example, Kleinman (1992) provides useful parameters for identifying preterm infants, routinely identified through gestational age (GA), or age (usually measured in weeks) after conception. Preterm, full-term, and postterm births are defined as follows: Preterm: <37 weeks GA; Full term: 37–42 weeks GA; Postterm: >42 weeks. Information regarding GA is included in an infant's medical chart or may be obtained from the baby's physician.

Another major methodological concern regarding preterm infants rests with the importance of *correcting for prematurity* (Aylward, 2002). It is not fair to compare a newborn infant born at 32 weeks GA (2 months premature!) with a newborn full-term infant born at 40 weeks GA. Rather, preterm-fullterm comparisons should initially be made when preterm babies reach their hypothetical full-term GA (see Dubowitz & Dubowitz, 1981, for a popular GA estimator). Essentially, the researcher treats this hypothetical "due date" (usually calculated by a physician) as the infant's "birthday." In the case of a baby born 32 weeks GA, the researcher would wait approximately 8 weeks to make direct comparisons to newborn, full-term babies. It is recommended that researchers make corrections for prematurity up to 2 years of age (Aylward, 2002).

Like preterm birth, there are commonly accepted definitions for infants possessing different birthweights (Kleinman, 1992). As illustrated in Table 3.1, infants can range from normal to extremely low birthweight (ELBW) (under 2.2 lb.). As you might guess, many preterm infants are also LBW; however, a preterm baby born at 35 week GA *can also be underweight for a normal 35-week GA baby.* This presents a very critical issue. Beyond considering whether a preterm infant is LBW, we must also consider whether the baby is small or underweight for gestational age (SGA). Using these definitions, we can create many different categories or groups of infants that will probably have very different developmental outcomes. For example, a researcher might construct a study using the following infant groups: (a) Full term; (b) Preterm, LBW; (c) Preterm, VLBW; (d) Preterm, LBW, SGA; and (e) Preterm, VLBW, SGA.

TABLE 3.1 *Infant Birthweight Classifications (Kleinman, 1992)*

Classification	Birthweight
Normal birthweight (NWB)	Over 2,500 g (over 5.5 lb.)
Low birthweight (LBW)	1,501 (3.3 lb.) to 2,500 g
Very low birthweight (VLBW)	1,001 to 1,500 g
Extremely low birthweight (ELBW)	Under 1,001 (2.2 lb.)

There are other confounds that can occur when conducting research with these vulnerable infants. For example, some preterm infants develop serious medical complications; others are born healthy. Because our respiratory system is one of the last organ systems to fully develop during the prenatal period, it is not surprising that LBW preterm infants are at risk for serious respiratory distress after birth. However, although over 60% of ELBW preterm infants suffer from severe respiratory distress (resulting in intensive medical intervention), the incidence rate is much lower in more mature, but still premature, infants without birthweight problems (Wyly, 1997). In fact, these statistics would also suggest that about 40% of ELBW preterm infants *do not* have respiratory distress problems. Thus, there is often considerable variability or heterogeneity *within* carefully selected groups of vulnerable infants.

Because the medical condition of preterm infants predicts important developmental outcomes, medical status should be used as a study variable. Although some may view medical status as something that should be eliminated or controlled, many pediatricians are interested in the medical and behavioral outcomes of babies born with certain medical conditions (e.g., Respiratory Distress Syndrome, Intraventricular Hemorrhage). Because medical status, GA, and birthweight are highly intercorrelated variables, it is important that we use strong research designs to disentangle the effects of these variables on later outcome measures. Indeed, these distinctions are very important, because the prognoses for healthy preterm infants are often much better than those of their medically challenged, underweight counterparts (Lester, Freier, & LaGasse, 1995).

There are mechanisms at our disposal to untangle the complexities of research involving vulnerable infant populations. The model presented in Table 3.2 is extremely useful for thinking about important study variables to consider when targeting at-risk populations (ranging from preterm infants to Alzheimer's-disease caregivers). Thus far, we have consistently referred to the internal vulnerabilities (e.g., preterm birth, LBW) of infants. Controlling for, or intensively studying, other

What Do You Think?

Suppose you are interested in the effects of prenatal alcohol exposure on intelligence during the preschool years. Because such exposure is also related to preterm birth and LBW, describe how you would design a study to better determine its effects on later development.

TABLE 3.2 *Definitions Used in Risk Research (Adapted from Seifer, 2001)*

	Effects on Negative Developmental Outcomes	
	Increase	*Decrease*
Locus of Factor **External**	**Risk** e.g., prenatal drug exposure, poverty, maternal depression	**Protection** e.g., good prenatal care, marital harmony, good medical care
Internal	**Vulnerability** e.g., preterm birth, low birth weight, illness	**Resilience** e.g., easy temperament, coping skills

variables in Table 3.2, should increase our accuracy in making predictions about developmental outcome variables.

To illustrate, a researcher interested in tracing the development of VLBW preterm, LBW preterm, and full-term infants should be aware that key external variables (e.g., medical care) might decrease (or increase) the infants' chances for developmental delay. These variables could also be confounded with the infants' birth status. For example, because family socioeconomic status may predict both infant birth status and eventual developmental progress, it would seem imperative that researchers carefully match infant groups on important demographic variables (e.g., family income, ethnicity, parent marital status).

Likewise, a researcher interested in comparing cocaine-exposed babies to nonexposed infants must ensure that the infants are matched on important infant vulnerabilities, such as preterm birth and/or LBW. If the cocaine-exposed infants were more likely LBW (which is often the case), compared with a nonexposed group, it might become very difficult to determine the ultimate causes of developmental delay (e.g., cocaine-exposure or LBW). Because of the potential **risk co-morbidity** or co-occurrence of maternal (and paternal) prenatal drug use (e.g., alcohol and cigarettes), it is not uncommon to ask expectant mothers to complete short surveys regarding prenatal drug use (see Table 3.3). Such information may guide decisions about inclusion (e.g., infants whose mothers solely reported using cocaine) and exclusion (e.g., infants whose mothers smoked, used cocaine, and drank alcohol) of potential research participants.

There are other considerations to ponder when working with vulnerable infants. Beyond proper identification of a target population and the establishment of infant groups matched on important control variables (e.g., family income, parent education), we also must

TABLE 3.3 *Substance-Use Screening Questionnaire (Adapted from Carmichael Olson et al., 1995)*

Have you used the following drugs during your pregnancy?

	Month Before Pregnancy		*During Pregnancy*	
1. Heroin (smack)	YES	NO	YES	NO
If yes, # of times per month	# _____		# _____	
2. Cocaine (crack)	YES	NO	YES	NO
If yes, # of times per month	# _____		# _____	
3. Smoke cigarettes	YES	NO	YES	NO
If yes, # of times per month	# _____		# _____	
4. Alcohol	YES	NO	YES	NO
If yes, # of times per month	# _____		# _____	
5. Methadone	YES	NO	YES	NO
If yes, # of times per month	# _____		# _____	
6. Marijuana (pot, grass)	YES	NO	YES	NO
If yes, # of times per month *etc.*	# _____		# _____	

consider sampling issues. Although it may seem logical to sample infants across several hospital settings, it is possible that differences in medical care could affect our study results. Infants born and treated at regional training hospitals might have better outcomes, because these facilities may have state-of-the-art Neonatal Intensive Care Units, modern technology, and more specialized personnel (Aylward, 2002). In such cases, we must be careful to avoid selection bias—that is, the tendency to draw infant groups from nonequivalent settings.

Finally, identifying variables that *facilitate* development in vulnerable infants, children, adolescents, and adult populations is an important research agenda that has major implications for preventive interventions. Infant resiliency (e.g., easy temperament) and protective environmental variables (e.g., family social support) have been documented to have a positive influence on the development of vulnerable infants (Kopp, 1994). Because many vulnerable infants (even the tiniest and sickest) have positive developmental outcomes, it is important to consider variables that protect or insulate the infant from developmental delay.

Summary of Methodological Issues

In this section, we discussed different ways to recruit samples. Although using hospital and pediatric facilities is an excellent way to recruit substantial numbers of demographically diverse infants, hospital birth lists, newspaper ads, and public service announcements are also acceptable methods for recruiting infants—assuming the researcher is careful to address, and ultimately acknowledge, limitations regarding sample representativeness. Beyond sampling issues, infant-state variability represents a major methodological concern, and becomes paramount when contrasting healthy infants to more vulnerable populations. Finally, we discussed the challenges that face researchers working with risky infant populations.

Neonatal Assessment

Why bother to study **neonates** (first 28 days of life), or newborn infants? This same question was asked years ago by researchers who assumed that assessment of infant neurological development and behavior was a fruitless endeavor because "there was nothing to evaluate" (Lester & Tronick, 2001, p. 363). Today, of course, it's a different story. There are a battery of sophisticated tests and measures to assess neonatal development, and the field of **neonatology** (the study and treatment of newborn infants) represents an exciting medical specialty. My personal respect for the field of neonatology skyrocketed after I witnessed a physician quickly order a newborn to the surgical unit after a routine assessment. Evidently, this specialist noticed an extremity deformity that suggested a major organ system abnormality. This premise was based on the finding that major external features of the newborn (e.g., hands, feet, eyelids) develop at the same time as major organ systems (e.g., cardiovascular system).

There are many *screening* checklists for assessing neonatal neurological, physical, and behavioral development; that is, these measures are frequently used to identify infants who are *potentially* delayed, or at risk for later problems. In this section, some of the more common screening assessments will be described. In addition, there exist very popular neurobehavioral assessment scales that measure a wide range of infant abilities, including early neurological development, reactivity or arousal, and state regulation. In this section, we examine one of the most popular instruments, the Neonatal Behavioral Assessment Scale (NBAS). Finally, we will also discuss popular methods to assess the developmental progress of vulnerable infants.

Common Perinatal Screening Strategies

The time shortly before and after delivery is referred to as the **perinatal period**. There are a number of reasons for perinatal assessment. In terms of clinical applications, early assessment of both infant and mother provides us data important for making predictions about the ultimate health, mortality, and development of the infant. Through early identification or screening, medical interventions can be planned and implemented to reduce the chances of infant mortality, medical complications, and developmental delay (Molfese, 1989).

There are other ways we can use perinatal assessments. We can use these assessments as a dependent variable. A researcher interested in prenatal nicotine exposure may monitor the use of this drug during the prenatal period and use this independent variable to ultimately predict birth complications or early developmental delay in neonates (dependent variable). Alternatively, we can use perinatal assessments as an independent, subject variable. For example, we can classify infants as having either high or low levels of medical complications, and then use this information to make later predictions about health and development.

A listing of the more common screening devices is provided in Table 3.4. From a researcher's perspective, there are several points to consider. First, other than Apgar scores, gestational age, and other routine pieces of infant data (e.g., birthweight; medical status), hospitals are far from standardized regarding the use of perinatal screening instruments. Thus, it is possible to become excited about the reliability and validity of a screening instrument and discover that the hospital research setting does not even use the instrument!

If this is the case, before asking (or begging) physician collaborators to complete perinatal screening assessments, it is important to consider the methodological, conceptual, and theoretical issues of perinatal assessment. These screening inventories were developed to give health-care providers advance insight regarding mothers and infants who might be at medical or developmental risk during the prenatal, delivery, and neonatal periods. In this case these inventories do a good job of assessing that risk. For example, infants who score high on post-natal complication scales (PCS) (e.g., respiratory distress, presence of infections, ventilatory assistance) are also at risk for further medical complications during the neonatal period.

However, these screening inventories were *not* designed to predict the emergence of the next Albert Einstein! These screening inventories do not predict medical or developmental delays past infancy, and at best, such predictions are very modest in nature (Wyly, 1997). Infants do not grow up in an environmental vacuum; there are various risk (poverty) and protective (competent caregiving, medical care) factors that babies face after they leave the hospital. Indeed, with advances in medical care, it is possible that infants who score the lowest on screening devices receive the most intensive medical care. If many of these babies improve through medical interventions, their early perinatal assessment scores would be unrelated to medical or developmental status during later infancy. Thus, although perinatal

TABLE 3.4 *Common Screening Instruments (Adapted from Francis, Self, & Horowitz, 1987)*

Instrument	Description
Apgar System (Apgar, 1953)	This screening test is routinely conducted on all infants minutes after delivery. Zero to 2 ratings are assigned for heart rate, respiratory effort, muscle tone, color, and reflex irritability. Lower scores reflect increased odds for infant mortality and medical complications. *Apgar scores are routinely computed at hospitals in most countries and are kept in the infant's medical records.*
Obstetric Complications Scale (Littman & Parmelee, 1978)	The OCS is a 41-item screening test that contains items that reflect prenatal (e.g., maternal drug use), delivery (e.g., forceps delivery), and nenonatal (e.g., birthweight, Apgar scores) complications. Although the total score can be used, there are many individual items that may be of great use to infancy researchers (e.g., GA, birthweight, Apgar scores).
Postnatal Complications Scale (Littman & Parmelee, 1978)	The PCS is a ten-item scale that reflects postnatal infant complications (e.g., respiratory distress, surgery, convulsions).
Optimal Obstetric Conditions Scale (Prechtl, 1982)	This 62-item scale assesses optimal prenatal, delivery, and postnatal conditions. This scale is very comprehensive, and assesses important background information (e.g., marital state), past obstetrical history, obstetrical complications, delivery complications, and early neonatal condition (e.g., Apgar scores; GA).
Neonatal Perception Inventory (Broussard & Hartner, 1971).	This 6-item inventory assesses neonatal temperament from the caregiver's perspective. This questionnaire contains items that assess perceptions of infant crying, difficulty, feeding, and state regulation. Although neonatal temperament itself can be highly unstable, the caregiver's *perceptions* of this construct can yield useful, clinical information.
Dubowitz Assessment of GA (Dubowitz & Dubowitz, 1981)	This short inventory is completed by pediatricians or neonataloligists to estimate GA. Scoring is heavily based on neurological, reflex, and external criteria (e.g., skin tone, genital development).

assessments are very robust instruments for forecasting present and short-term development over the neonatal period, their use as more long-term predictors should be considered in context. Currently, documenting how later environmental experiences affect associations between neonatal risk and later development represents an exciting research direction.

Neonatal Behavioral Assessment Scale (NBAS)

The *Neonatal Behavioral Assessment Scale* (NBAS; Brazelton, 1973/1984) was developed to assess neonatal competence in a variety of rudimentary activities, such as reflex development, orientation, and state regulation. Although the technical name is NBAS, most infancy researchers use the term *Brazelton*, when referring to this instrument (e.g., "I preformed a Brazelton the other day"). The NBAS is quick to administer (about 30–45 min), does not require the use of technology, and is easy to train newcomers on. A "Brazelton kit" is easy to assemble, requiring only a scoring sheet and everyday items, such as a penlight, bell, and safety pin.

Although the NBAS qualifies as a neonatal assessment device, its conceptual underpinnings are quite different than those of traditional perinatal screening instruments; the latter are traditionally scored by passively observing the infant's behavior and medical difficulties. In contrast, performance on the NBAS is based on behavioral data that is gathered through *examiner interaction* with the infant. Thus, the examiner actively manipulates behavior to assess the baby's best performance on a variety of tasks.

The NBAS taps into a variety of infant abilities that are believed to reflect motor and neurological development (Brazelton, Nugent, & Lester, 1987). In terms of administration, the examiner would ideally like the infant initially *asleep*. Although there are strong methodological reasons for this, the odds are that the examiner will get this wish because sleep is the infant's predominant state! Assuming the infant is asleep, the examiner first briefly flashes the light from a penlight into the infant's eyes a few times.

After a few seconds, most healthy newborns will show some type of behavioral response (e.g., shifting of head, accompanied by gurgles). After the baby settles down (which is an important observation in its own right), the examiner repeats this task repeatedly until the infant's level of response decreases. This response decrement is referred to as *habituation*, or the infant's decreasing responses to redundant visual, auditory, or tactile stimulation (Worobey, 1990). To assess infant habituation to these latter stimuli, the examiner notes responses to the sound of a bell and rattle, as well as a gentle foot prick from a safety pin. Although the examiner primarily records data directly garnered from the habituation tasks (e.g., speed of habituation), he or she also observes other infant behaviors. For example, he or she will note the baby's transformation from sleep to alertness, general skin tone, and motor movements.

After the habituation tasks, the examiner performs several *orientation tasks*. For example, the examiner may pass an object across the infant's field of vision and note visual tracking efforts and small head movements. This process is repeated using auditory stimuli; for example, the examiner may ring a bell or shake a rattle slightly behind the infant's head.

The examination concludes with a series of reflex tests. Many common automatic reflexes, such as the Palmer Grasp—a reflex that is tested by placing one's finger against the infant's palm and noting how well the baby grasps the finger—are elicited. The examiner carefully notes whether the infant's reflexes are hypotonic (underdeveloped), normal, or hypertonic. The final reflex that is tested has a dual purpose. When testing the Moro reflex, the examiner gently pulls the baby to a sitting position and then lets go with a hand behind baby's back to prevent injury! At this juncture most infants startle, begin fussing or crying, and make an "embracing motion" by throwing their arms out, and then bringing them back to the body. This innate reflex is thought to enhance state regulation and facilitate clinging behavior between infant and caregiver.

The NBAS contains 28 behavioral and 18 reflex items. For research purposes, items reflecting common functions can be grouped together to form the seven "clusters" (Lester, Als, & Brazelton, 1982) depicted in Table 3.5. There are many NBAS-based studies that document how prenatal (e.g., maternal substance abuse) and perinatal (e.g., low birth weight, use of obstetric medications) factors influence the neurobehavioral organization of the newborn (Lester & Tronick, 2001). Like perinatal screening assessments, the NBAS is not a strong predictor of emerging competencies past the neonatal period. Perhaps this is a good finding, and suggests that early disorganization in neonatal development can be

TABLE 3.5 *NBAS Behavioral Clusters (Lester, Als, & Brazelton, 1982)*

Cluster	Description
Habituation	Decreasing response rate to redundant visual, auditory, and tactile stimuli.
Orientation	General alertness during NBAS administration and pursuit of the rattle and examiner's face and voice.
Motor	Integrated motor acts and overall muscle tone.
Range of State	Peak state (e.g., alert) and rapidity of state buildup (e.g., from sleep to crying).
State Regulation	Success in maintaining state control.
Autonomic Stability	Tremors, startles, and skin-color changes. These events signify physiological stress.
Reflexes	Summation of deviant reflex scores.

compensated for by infant resiliency (e.g., state-regulation maturation) and protective (e.g., sensitive caregiving) factors (Worobey, 1990).

It is fascinating to witness the wide range of competencies that newborn and preterm infants are capable of displaying. Although preterm infants (particularly medically challenged ones) may display less sophisticated neurobehavioral development (Myers et al., 1992), the fact that these babies display reflexes, track objects, and perform habituation tasks at all suggests that many of these competencies are programmed to develop well before birth. In addition, the social component of the NBAS cannot be ignored; parents are often fascinated to watch their newborns competently execute these tasks. In fact, parents themselves have been trained to conduct NBAS exams on their own infants. It is theorized that such interventions may promote closer relationships between infants and caregivers, and that the NBAS provides a context for parents to "get to know" their infants better. Studies using the NBAS as an intervention are reviewed in Box 3.1.

What Do You Think?

As indicated in Box 3.1, some parents exposed to NBAS training become better parents, whereas others involved in the same intervention program do not. What variables might account for these differences? How would you design a study to better explore these variables?

Additional Behavioral-Assessment Scales

The original intent of the NBAS was to document individual differences in the neonatal behavior of *healthy* infants; thus, it may not be sensitive enough to yield individual differences *within* certain vulnerable populations. In addition, the focus of the NBAS is strictly on the behavior of the newborn; the instrument does not tap important environmental protective and risk factors that might moderate the infant's performance.

To address these concerns, a variety of neurobehavioral assessment tests exist to measure difficulties in vulnerable populations. For example, the *Assessment of Preterm Infant's Behavior* (APIB; Als et al., 1982) and *Neurobehavioral Assessment of the Preterm Infant*

BOX 3.1 • *NBAS Training as an Intervention*

"I can't believe she just did that!" These were the exact words of a parent that slipped up behind us as we were performing an NBAS on a preterm infant; although struggling, the tiny baby was turning her eyes to an object we were passing across her field of vision.

Because the NBAS is such an interactive/social assessment tool, it is not surprising that a number of developmental specialists have used this instrument as an intervention device. Nugent and Steposki (1984) have developed a set of guidelines for using the NBAS as an intervention strategy. Most notably, they recommend that experts train caregivers to administer the NBAS, repeatedly over the first few weeks of the baby's life. They believe that training caregivers to administer this instrument may foster parent-infant interactions, enhance the confidence of caregivers, and serve as a mechanism for parents to "get to know their babies better" (e.g., Worobey & Brazelton, 1986). During NBAS assessment, babies can show parents that they can do more than "eat, sleep, cry, and poop!" (Belsky, 1985, p. 412).

Unfortunately, such intervention studies document mixed results. NBAS-based interventions have only a small to moderate influence on overall parenting quality (Das Eiden & Reifman, 1996). In addition, intervention effects are very weak to modest for enhancing parenting satisfaction and knowledge about infant development (Britt & Myers, 1994; Myers, 1982). Finally, most of the potential beneficial effects of NBAS interventions are temporary.

Why the mixed results? It is very hard to compare NBAS intervention studies, because investigators often use different samples (e.g., healthy versus preterm versus substance exposed), outcome measures (e.g., parent-infant interactions versus infant developmental status), and research designs (e.g., multiple treatment/control groups versus one treatment/no control group). Further, what "counts" as an NBAS-based intervention can vary. For example, some researchers simply allow parents to observe NBAS administration by a trained expert; others intensively train parents to administer the instrument themselves over multiple trials.

There are some promising directions for this area of study. First, vulnerable infants and their families may need more sustained intervention support than a one-time NBAS observation or training. Indeed, infant-parent interventions that provide comprehensive services (e.g., NBAS training plus increasing parent coping skills plus social work services) often have much stronger beneficial effects on infants and families than less holistic treatment efforts (Ramey & Shearer, 1999; Rauh et al., 1988).

In addition, recall our earlier discussions regarding the importance of establishing trust, connectedness, and rapport with study participants. Brazelton (1990), the developer of the NBAS, strongly suspects that the infants and families most in need of intervention services may be the most resistant to treatment. Thus, a resistant or distrusting parent may pay little attention to an NBAS trainer, fail to "practice" NBAS administration with their baby, and be more likely to suffer from subject attrition. Witness the following observation made by Brazelton (1990):

> My researchers would come back from visits to say, "I don't think we're connecting with these people. We can't reach them." The mothers didn't watch us the first time, they gaze-avoided, they talked all the way through. At the second visit, they still gaze-avoided, and they seemed to have their eyes semi-open. By the third visit, they said, "That's what you showed me each time." When you asked them why they seemed not to notice, "We didn't really trust you until you came three times." (p. 1670).

These observations are important, because they highlight how the populations that may be most in need of study and assistance may view us as lifespan researchers and treatment specialists. They also provide a good example of why basic experimental research on seemingly mundane topics (e.g., participant trust and rapport) is so important to us. Discovering strategies that enhance participant trust and receptivity represents an exciting research direction with enormous applied ramifications.

(NAPI; Korner & Thom, 1999) were designed to allow for finer behavioral discriminations in low-birth-weight, medically challenged, preterm infants. Although based on the NBAS, these instruments allow for more flexible administration (to decrease infant stress and optimize performance) and contain items that are relevant to the health and development of preterm infants (e.g., APIB—respiratory functioning). Similar to the NBAS, the items on these instruments can be reduced to scales, or "clusters" of common items. For example, the NAPI contains scales that assess vigor of crying and infant irritability (Korner & Thom, 1999).

The recently developed *NICU Network Neurobehavioral Scale* (NNNS; Lester, 1998) specifies finer discriminations among infants displaying a wide range of vulnerabilities (e.g., preterm; LBW). Although this instrument was designed to compare full-term and preterm infant samples, the scale is particularly sensitive in uncovering behavioral differences in babies exposed to drugs and alcohol. Because different types of drugs or toxins may affect neurological and behavioral development differently, infant reflexes and muscle tone are assessed across a variety of positions. Unfortunately, because some infants exposed to drugs may also be addicted, this instrument contains a Stress/Abstinence scale that contains items (e.g., sweating, abnormal sucking, skin pallor, labored breathing) that allow examiners to make a decision on this issue. The NNNS has shown considerable promise in validity studies. For example, babies exposed to cocaine, alcohol, or a combination of the two substances show unique responses on this instrument. Likewise, it can identify infants exposed to heroin, alcohol, or nicotine (Lester & Tronick, 2001). Thus, the NNNS shows considerable promise as both a clinical/diagnostic and research tool.

Summary of Newborn Assessment

Because newborns are capable of many things, it is not surprising that standard assessment techniques have been developed to provide a general description of infant neurological and biobehavioral development. Although many of the first assessment devices were developed to assess general neonatal abilities and complications, screening tools have recently been developed to better describe the competencies of vulnerable infants. As screening devices, and predictors of short-term medical complications and developmental delay, standard neonatal assessments appear to have modest to excellent validity. However, two important points should be considered. First, the assessments were not designed to make long-range predictions regarding infants. Second, assessment experts using these instruments often make very brief observations to make very important judgments about infant state and arousal regulation, attention, and basic perceptual abilities. Because all of these abilities are important in their own right, it is not surprising that very sophisticated methods have been developed to allow researchers to "go deeper" to assess these constructs. We next turn to assessments that have been designed to intensively assess very specific infant abilities.

State Regulation and Arousal

Many of the items on standard neonatal behavioral assessments measure how well infants regulate states and cope with arousal. These issues are important because infant state and arousal regulation show predictable developmental patterns, and individual differences in these abilities predict skills for emotional and cognitive development. Although it is possible to observe and describe state regulation and arousal using the aforementioned newborn assessments, such assessments are very brief and provide only a general picture of the infant's true abilities. Because state regulation and arousal reflect the biological and behavioral integrity of the infant, there exist more systematic measures to assess these abilities.

Infant State Assessment

Infant state is an important variable in its own right. The development and increasing predictability of infant state reflects maturation of the autonomic nervous system, and common behavioral states (e.g., fussing, crying) can be readily discriminated and attended to by caregivers (Thoman & Whitney, 1990). Individual differences in sleep–wake states differ across infants, and disparities are often documented between high- (e.g., preterm) and low-risk babies. For example, preterm infants are prone to sudden state changes and disruptions in sleep (Ingersoll & Thoman, 1999), as well as increased bouts of crying as they approach term age (Holditch-Davis, 1990). Also, some researchers treat infant state as an independent variable and use state measures to forecast later competencies. For instance, newborn infants experiencing poor state regulation are less mentally advanced at 6 months of age than their counterparts with good state organization (Freudigman & Thoman, 1993).

There are many conceptual and methodological issues that face infant-state researchers. The first step is to classify or operationally define the different infant sleep states, as illustrated in Table 3.6. Although this table represents ten common sleep states, it is not unusual for researchers to collapse classifications to make data coding more feasible. For example, a researcher interested specifically in studying infant sleep states might use the following categories: awake, sleep–awake transition, active sleep, and quiet sleep (Thoman, 2001). Alternatively, coding procedures have been developed to more intensively examine single infant states, such as infant crying (Zeskind & Barr, 1997). Because much work has gone into categorizing and subcategorizing infant states, new researchers should use an established classification system.

Once we have settled on a classification system, the next step is to consider our old friend, *the research setting.* In short, we must consider whether to assess infant state in the hospital, laboratory, or home setting. Population issues may partly guide our decision. Seriously ill infants may have to be assessed in a hospital setting, and healthy babies, because of their short hospital stays, may have to be studied in home or laboratory settings. Likewise, our choice of methods may also guide setting decisions. Research assistants trained to observe infant sleep states might not be welcome in the homes of subjects in the middle of the night! Finally, the purpose of our study might predicate our choice of research setting. A researcher interested in how infants experience shifts in state resulting from stress could effectively conduct such research in a hospital, pediatric, or laboratory setting; however, those with interests in studying infants in their more natural states will probably garner their most valid data in a home-based environment (Sostek & Anders, 1981; Thoman, 2001).

Infancy researchers also have a variety of methods for assessing infant state; selection is often dependent on exactly which phenomena the researcher is interested in recording. For example, a researcher interested in observing natural changes in infant state over a 48-hour period will be unlikely to use human coders to make direct behavior

TABLE 3.6 *Infant State Classifications (Adapted from Thoman, 2001)*

Awake States	
Alert.	Infant's eyes are open, bright, and attentive, or scanning. Motor activity may be high.
Nonalert waking.	Motor activity may be high, yet, eyes are dull and unfocused.
Daze.	Low motor activity. Eyes open and glassy.
Fuss.	Continuous or intermittent fussing.
Cry.	Either single or continuous crying.
Transition States between Sleep and Waking	
Drowsy.	Infant's eyes dull and unfocused, "heavy lidded," or slowly open and close.
Sleep–wake transition.	Infant displays behaviors typical of both wakefulness and sleeping. During period of stirring, infant may emit isolated fussing vocalization.
Sleep States	
Active sleep.	Infant's eyes are closed, respiration is uneven. Rapid eye movements may briefly occur, accompanied by brief eye opening. Other behaviors may include smiling, sucking, or grimacing.
Active-quiet transition sleep.	Periodic regular and irregular respiration, as well as body movements and vocalizations.
Quiet sleep.	Eyes closed, respiration slow and regular. Brief body movements.

observations because of fatigue concerns. The following represent some common methods used by infant-state researchers:

Direct Behavior Observations.   Training raters to observe patterns of infant state regulation represents one of the earliest and most cost-effective methods. Using behavioral cues such as body and eye movements, respiration rate, and muscle tone, raters observe infants over a designated period of time (e.g., five hours) and record behaviors using an event or time-sampling method (See Chapter 1 for a review of observational methods) (Holditch-Davis, 1990). Training raters to use this method is fairly easy, and the results of studies using direct behavior observations have yielded strong, predictable results. For example, Thoman and Whitney (1990) documented that over the course of seven hours of observer recordings, preterm infants sleep less and fuss more than their full-term counterparts.

There are drawbacks to direct behavior observations. Coder fatigue is a concern for lengthy or late-evening data collection, the absence of a taped recording makes it impossible to review previous observations, and the presence of human coders may not be appreciated by other members of a family during an overnight home observation. Because of these concerns, as well as advances in technology, there are alternative methods for assessing infant state.

Video Recording.   Researchers use video recording methods for several reasons. There is no need for a human observer, a close-up and accurate record of the infant's behavior is

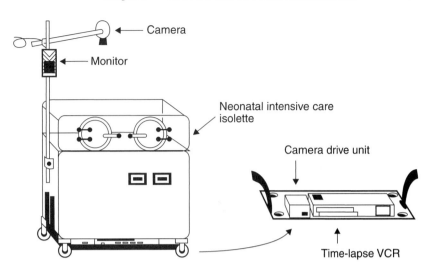

FIGURE 3.1 *Assessing Infant State Using Video Recording.* Note that the recording device is placed under the infant's care isolate.

From Ingersoll, E., & Thoman, E. (1999). Sleep/wake states of preterm infants: Stability, developmental change, diurnal variation, and relation with caregiving activity. Child Development, 70, p. 4. Reprinted with permission of the Society for Research in Child Development.

recorded, and technological features allow us to record behavior in either a continuous or time-lapse mode. A fairly straightforward apparatus is depicted in Figure 3.1; this technology was used to record infant-state changes among a group of hospitalized preterm infants (Ingersoll & Thoman, 1999). Note that much of the equipment is stored under the infant's crib, and a small camera is mounted over the infant to provide an overhead shot of the baby. Thus, data collection is efficient, and the equipment is highly mobile and does not get in the way of busy hospital personnel. In addition, one might imagine that a heavy presence of equipment and wires would represent yet another worry for anxious caregivers highly concerned about the status of their infant which is not the case for this apparatus. Similar technology has been used for home observations involving full-term infants (Sostek & Anders, 1981).

"State Recognition" Methods. Of course, there is a subjective element to coding infant state. An individual interested in specifying shifts in sleep must be trained to document changes in infant behavior, eye movements, and respiration rate. Although the use of time-lapse recording may make this task somewhat easier, state changes in some infants may occur in a very subtle fashion.

However, amazing technological advances now allow infant-state researchers to collect more sound data. Thoman and colleagues (Thoman & Whitney, 1989) have developed a small mattress that can be placed directly under the infant's blanket in a crib. This little device is wired to record subtle changes in infant body movements and respiration rate. The apparatus itself is a fascinating piece of technology; however, the authors have also developed accompanying computer software that automatically tabulates the data and matches it to a database containing infant state "profiles." In other words, the software program assigns a state category based on the match of data from the infant (e.g., slow respiration, low body movements) to the state profile (e.g., quiet sleep)!

Infant state is an important source of study, because its maturation signifies maturity of the nervous system, and infants who possess poor state regulation are at risk for developmental problems. Also, a continually fussy, crying baby exacts a toll on caregivers. Because

BOX 3.2 • *Using the "Breathing Bear" to Assist the State Regulation of Premature Infants*

It is difficult to conduct interventions with medically at-risk premature infants because of their tendency to exhibit poor state regulation and overstimulation (e.g., Field, 1979). To address this problem, Thoman and colleagues have developed a small stuffed bear that is programmed to "breathe" as a source of rhythmic stimulation (Thoman, 1999; Thoman & Graham, 1986). The gently breathing bear is placed near the baby in the infant pram or crib.

This intervention is very unobtrusive. Most notably, the infant can orient toward the bear at its own choosing; thus, the chances for overstimulation are minimized. In addition, the consistent, rhythmic pulsing of the bear is theorized to provide a source of comfort and a model for healthy state regulation. The authors theorize that such an intervention will ultimately facilitate the development of state regulation in these at-risk infants.

To test this premise, the researchers placed "breathing" or inanimate teddy bears in the cribs of premature infants, and recorded infant behavior using time-lapse video recording. Within just a few weeks, the premature infants with the "breathing" bear spent more time in physical contact with it than did the babies with the "nonbreathing" bear. In fact, the results of the time-lapse recording indicated that these little

infants, through body, leg, and arm movements, actually *initiated* physical contact with the "breathing" bear! Over time, these infants also displayed a more even, regular respiratory rate during quiet sleep, slower respiration during active sleep, and less disruptions in sleep patterns, when compared to infants in control groups.

There are many other interventions available for at-risk infants. Massage therapy, parent training, and mechanical ventilation all represent well-established intervention techniques (Field, Hernandez-Reif, & Freedman, 2004). However, the beauty of the "breathing" bear intervention rests with its simplicity and noninvasive nature. The infant is provided a choice for stimulation, allowed to exercise and practice a variety of states through contact with the bear, and provided a warm, gentle model for state regulation (Thoman, 1999). This research also demonstrates the *applied nature of our field* (Chapter 1). These researchers carefully examined an important developmental variable through systematic research (i.e., infant state development), developed robust research methods (e.g., time-lapse video recording to assess state), and then developed a strong intervention program based on their previous theory and methods. Thoman's research program represents a strong exemplar for our field.

of these concerns, infancy researchers have developed interventions to accompany the fascinating methods to assess infant state. One such intervention is described in Box 3.2.

Assessment of Infant Crying

Although we could simply view crying as an annoying infant state, this behavior represents a complex construct. Infant crying is a sign of intense state arousal, and its duration, intensity, and acoustical characteristics can reliably differentiate babies with different developmental histories (e.g., substance-exposed versus nonexposed babies), and make predictions about important outcome variables (e.g., sudden infant death syndrome) (Zeskind, Marshall, & Goff, 1996). Also, crying reflects more than just infant competence. From an evolutionary perspective, infants cry to signal distress and get attention. The way parents perceive and cope with infant crying is important, because such attitudes and behavior influence caregiving behavior.

There are different methods for studying infant crying. With the advent of voice-activated recording methods and wireless microphones, researchers can naturalistically study infant crying simply by leaving a tape recorder in the baby's home. Also, diaries or rating sheets can be given to caregivers in order to rate the frequency, duration, and intensity of crying. Not surprisingly, mothers are quite accurate reporters of infant crying! Although audio recordings provide more precise information about the acoustical nature of infant cries, mothers are accurate recorders of crying frequency and duration (Salisbury et al., 2001).

Infants cry for different reasons. One baby may cry because he or she is hungry, another may be in pain, and yet another may cry for reasons unknown either to the researcher or the baby's frustrated parents. Because there are varying causes for infant crying, researchers often hold this variable constant by *eliciting* this behavior. The most common method involves using a device to snap a rubber band across the infant's foot (e.g., Zeskind, Marshall, & Goff, 1996). The infant's crying bouts are subsequently audiotaped. Although this may seem cruel, the infant is not injured, the cause of the cry is held constant, and parents are rarely disturbed by the resulting behavior. Remember, they hear this all of the time.

Crying frequency, duration, threshold (number of trials it takes to elicit a cry), and latency (time from stimulus, such as rubber band snap, to onset of cry) are common data sources (Zeskind & Lester, 2001). The acoustical features of infant cries are also an important area of study. Infant crying is seldom uniform; the frequency and pitch change over time, perhaps communicating changes in infant distress. Thus, most experts analyze specific acoustical features (e.g., frequency, amplitude, pitch) from the onset to duration of an infant's cry (Green, Gustafson, & McGhie, 1998).

Scientists are increasingly examining the social context of this behavior, such as how adults appraise and respond to infant crying. Although early research examined how adults responded to different "cry types" (e.g., "hunger" versus "pain"), it is believed that there are both common and different acoustical features to infant cries brought upon by different sources (e.g., pain, fatigue, hunger). Because of the occasional *similarities* between cries brought on by different sources, infant crying reflects different degrees of distress rather than a reliable, identifiable cause (e.g., hunger) (Green, Gustafson, & McGhie, 1998).

Methodologically, a number of variables can be manipulated for experimental study involving adult listeners. We can manipulate the acoustical features of infant crying (e.g., low, medium, or high infant distress) as well as its context (Wood & Gustafson, 2001). In terms of the latter, rather than present different "cry types," we can simply inform adult listeners that the different recordings of infant cries reflect different sources (e.g., pain, fatigue). This strategy allows us to manipulate two very important variables (i.e., acoustical features and source). There are other important variables to consider for variable manipulation, such as the listener's relationship with the infant (e.g., parent versus nonparent) (Green & Gustafson, 1983).

What Do You Think?

Suppose you theorize that caregivers who engage in infant maltreatment perceive infant crying differently than caregivers who do not engage in this behavior. How would you design a study to address this issue? What would be your specific independent and dependent variables?

Physiological Indices of Arousal and Regulation

Thus far, we have discussed behavioral strategies for assessing self-regulatory abilities in infants. However, in terms of your own behavior, think of the physiological mechanisms at work when you are startled or upset. Although we can examine the behavioral outcomes of infant arousal and state regulation (e.g., crying and subsequent self-calming), identifying the underlying physiological mechanisms responsible for these subsequent events represents an important line of inquiry.

Heart-Rate Variability and Vagal Tone. When we think of shifts in infant attention, state, or arousal, it is natural to consider corresponding changes in the cardiovascular system. It is safe to assume that our heart rate changes during periods of arousal, which is presumed to reliably reflect corresponding activity in the nervous and respiratory systems. Unfortunately, the association between basic heart rate and nervous system activity *is not consistent.* Because state regulation and arousal reflect nervous-system activity and development, it is important to find assessments that are more directly associated with this activity.

However, there are aspects of cardiovascular behavior that are regulated by neural activity when infants are aroused or attending to stimuli. For example, the *variability* in heart rate (e.g., beat-to-beat variability in heart rate) over time is highly sensitive to neural influences (Porter, 2001). In fact, certain features of heart-rate variability are strongly connected to fluctuations in the autonomic nervous system (Porges, 1991). This is a very important finding because, this component of the nervous system is heavily (and automatically) responsible for mobilizing our defenses (e.g., sharpening attention, increasing metabolism) during times of stress and arousal. To sum up, although basic heart rate is often used as a general marker of fitness and health and is widely studied in psychological research, it is the *patterning of these beats* that best reflects neural influences on the heart and best assesses the integrity of the central nervous system (Porter, 2001).

Heart-rate variability is related to the functioning of the multipurpose *vagus nerve;* thus, this patterning is termed **vagal tone**. During times of low arousal/rest, the autonomic nervous system, through *increased* vagal activity, promotes cellular growth and restoration. However, during times of distress, vagal activity *declines* (or brakes) which mobilize other branches of the nervous system to sharpen attention and increase body metabolism (Porges, Doussard-Roosevelt, & Maiti, 1994).

To measure vagal tone, researchers frequently assess select features of heart-rate variability during times of rest or arousal. The initial step in measuring heart-rate variability is through use of an electrocardiogram, which systematically assesses heart beats, as well as the timing between each beat, or *heart periods.* Through the use of computer software, vagal tone can be calculated through systematic analysis of select features of heart periods, as well as variations of heart periods over time (Porges et al., 1994).

Because vagal tone reflects nervous-system development, it is not surprising that this measure strongly predicts the development of infants. Infants with high vagal tones at rest tend to have better outcomes than their low-tone counterparts. High-vagal-tone infants are often full-term, healthy, possess strong attentional processes, quickly habituate to novel stimuli, are easy to soothe, and have the ability to suppress, or *brake,* vagal tone and heart rate during particularly demanding tasks (Fox, 1989; Huffman et al., 1998; Porges et al., 1994). Not surprisingly, because of their strong attentional and regulatory abilities, high-vagal-tone (at rest) infants also display better mental development than low-vagal-tone babies (Fox & Porges, 1985). Because of these findings, it is not surprising that heart-rate variability research is burgeoning.

Salivary Cortisol. Although collecting sputum, or "spit," samples might seem an inelegant method of data collection, the contents of this substance reveal important information about the arousal and regulatory capabilities of the infant. During times of arousal, our endocrine system produces and regulates important hormones that are dispensed by various organs or glands throughout our body. In particular, the adrenal glands, located above our kidneys, have been identified as important organs that release hormones termed *corticosteroids,* or **cortisol**, during times of arousal. Because cortisol levels can be monitored via blood and saliva sample, the analysis of this hormone has received much attention. In particular, salivary cortisol methods have become very popular, because unlike taking blood samples, saliva samples can be collected painlessly (Lewis & Thomas, 1990)! This is an important issue for researchers that want to monitor the rise and fall of cortisol levels over extended periods of time.

It is easy to obtain saliva samples from infants. Researchers simply swab the infant's tongue, cheeks, and gums with cotton dental rolls (usually containing Kool-Aid crystals) and then analyze the cortisol content of the saliva using a commercially available test kit (Gunnar et al., 1996). To assess arousal responses, we can collect saliva specimens over the course of naturally occurring (e.g., circumcision, inoculations) or structured (e.g., introduction of a strange adult) events that might be distressing (Gunnar et al., 1989; Lewis & Thomas, 1990).

The results of studies using these methods are quite impressive. Older infants secrete less cortisol than young infants, indicating that coping with distress and arousal (e.g., resulting from inoculations or separations) becomes better with age (Gunnar & Nelson, 1994; Lewis & Ramsay, 1995). However, despite these promising results, there are major methodological issues to consider regarding this method. Because cortisol levels naturally rise and fall over the course of the day, base (or initial) cortisol tests are likely to differ between infants because of different sleep–wake cycles, feeding and nap schedules, and sampling times (Gunnar & White, 2001). Beyond controlling or equating infants on these factors, infant cortisol levels are often low when babies are first tested in laboratory environments, quite possibly because of the car ride to the lab (Larson, Gunnar, & Hertsgaard, 1991)! Because this finding reflects the impact of an environmental event, rather than a stable internal state, caregivers should collect a saliva swab from the infant at home (Gunnar & White, 2001). This swab can function as an initial baseline cortisol measure that can be compared to later data collected during arousal manipulations.

Temperament

When asked to describe an infant's temperament, caregivers will often use such words as *active, shy,* or *strong willed.* Although it is fairly easy for us to *describe* temperament, it is quite a chore to actually *define* this construct. **Temperament** has been defined as individual differences in reactivity and self-regulation resulting from heredity, maturational processes, and environmental experience (Rothbart & Derryberry, 1981). In terms of unpacking this concept, we need to consider the terms embedded within the preceding definition. **Reactivity** refers to how the infant responds to different levels of stimulation. Thus, in response to a noise we could measure how long it takes the baby to respond (latency), the amount of noise it takes to get the baby to respond (response threshold), and assess the intensity of the infant's response to the sound. **Self-regulation** involves the baby's attempt to cope with the stimuli

TABLE 3.7 *Hypothetical Model of Reactivity and Self-Regulation (Adapted from Fox, 1989)*

	Regulation	
	High	*Low*
Reactivity **High**	Social Expressive Uninhibited	Hyperactive Uncontrollable
Low	Inhibited Highly controlled Nonexpressive	Social withdrawal Depressed/Fearful

and how well arousal is inhibited. Because infants can score high or low on both dimensions, Table 3.7 illustrates a reorganization of Rothbart's model (Fox, 1989).

Temperament researchers typically use multiple methods to assess this construct. Temperament questionnaires, such as the Infant Temperament Questionnaire (Rothbart, 1981); Infant Characteristic Questionnaire (Bates et al., 1979); or Revised Infant Temperament Questionnaire (Carey & McDevitt, 1978) are particularly accessible instruments for student researchers. On these widely used questionnaires, parents rate such items as "My infant accepts nail cutting without protest" and "My infant is fussy on waking up and going to sleep." Typically, temperament questionnaire items are clustered to form temperament scales or dimensions, such as "Activity Level," "Fearfulness," and "Adaptability."

Temperament questionnaires often contain different items, possess different theoretical underpinnings, target different age groups, and tap different dimensions or facets of temperament. Thus, before using an infant temperament questionnaire, we should carefully read the theoretical orientation of the measure and reliability and validity studies on it. One of the more interesting methodological studies involving infant temperament questionnaires rests with interrater reliability. In such studies, two (usually a parent and a trained expert) or more raters complete a temperament questionnaire, and their responses are subsequently compared. In general, the agreement between raters is modest at best (Rothbart, Chew, & Gartstein, 2001). This finding probably is due to the nature of infant temperament questionnaires; these scales measure *rater perceptions and memories* of infant temperament, as opposed to temperament per se.

Behavior observations represent another way to assess infant temperament. Basically, an observer (e.g., parent, day care provider, trained expert) rates the infant's behavior along important temperament dimensions (e.g., activity, withdrawal) in naturalistic or structured settings. As you might imagine, careful consideration must be given to who is rating the behavior (e.g., parent or researcher), as well as the research setting (home or lab). In addition, the researcher must consider whether to augment behavior ratings with videotape recording.

It is very difficult to make recommendations regarding the best method; the final determination may be driven by the research questions themselves. If you are interested in recording naturally occurring behavior to assess temperament, caregiver reports on the *frequency* of events (e.g., number of times the baby exhibited a fearful response to new events) over a period of days or weeks is superior to having an observer rate the infant's behavior during a short home or laboratory visit. Also, having caregivers report these frequency counts probably yields more reliable data than asking them to provide impressions of broad temperament dimensions (e.g., "Would you say the child was very active this week?") (Rothbart & Derryberry, 1981).

There are some aspects of temperament that are easier to study in a controlled environment, such as the lab. For example, fear and inhibition are difficult to assess in a home setting. In fact, the laboratory itself may increase fearful responses, making it an excellent context in which to study key temperament dimensions. Conversely, this environment may also *suppress* behaviors, such as approach, that might be common in familiar settings (Rothbart et al., 2001). Thus, the choice of our research setting may depend on what aspect of temperament we want to accurately measure.

In terms of behavioral measures, Kagan and colleagues have developed an interesting procedure to assess infant reactivity and self-regulation at relatively young ages (e.g., four months). In this procedure, the infant is placed in a car seat and presented a variety of stimuli (e.g., noises, mobiles, odors, popping of a balloon). Recording the infant's motor movements, fussiness, and tendency to cry provides an assessment of reactivity and self-regulation. Infants who show high frequencies of these behaviors are termed "highly reactive" (defined as babies who show extremely poor self-regulation). In one longitudinal study, Kagan, Snidman, and Arcus (1998) noted fascinating connections between infant reactivity/self-regulation and later social behavior during preschool. The results of this longitudinal study are presented in more detail in Box 3.3.

Because infant temperament has biological roots, researchers also use physiological measures to augment questionnaire data and behavior observations. For example, infants with high vagal tone and heart-rate variability have been shown to display quick reactivity to stimuli and better self-regulation than their counterparts with low vagal tone (Porges et al., 1994). Also, fussier, hard to soothe, babies produce more cortisol compared to infants with good regulatory skills (Gunnar & White, 2001). These physiological measures better allow us to identify the biological underpinnings of temperament.

What Do You Think?

Why might parents and researchers vary in their temperament ratings? Whose ratings are more important in making predictions regarding infant development? What is the rationale for your response?

Summary of State Regulation and Arousal Assessment

How infants react to stimuli and regulate their arousal are important practical and research issues. Infants who display quick reactions to environmental stimuli (or reactivity) and display good arousal control show better developmental outcomes than infants who lack one, or both, of these abilities. Documenting *why* infants display individual differences in these dimensions of temperament and identifying environmental variables that buffer babies with difficult temperaments from adverse outcomes represent exciting research directions.

Although most researchers assess temperament from the parent's perspective using questionnaires, behavioral and physiological strategies are becoming increasingly popular. These methods do not have to be used in isolation from one another. In fact, developing a relatively

BOX 3.3 • *Born Too Shy? A Longitudinal Study of Infant Reactivity*

Jerome Kagan (1994) proposed that highly reactive infants develop fearful responses to new stimuli and will ultimately wind up socially inhibited and shy. Thus, because early infant reactivity is thought to have strong biological underpinnings, his work suggests that social inhibition and shyness are partially programmed by biology. To better examine connections between reactivity, fearful responses, and shyness, Kagan has conducted careful longitudinal work using very impressive methods to assess these study variables.

In one longitudinal study, Kagan and colleagues (1998) assessed infant reactivity by placing 4-month-old babies in car seats and presenting a variety of stimuli (e.g., strong odors, bright mobiles, popping balloons). About 20 percent of the infants were identified as *highly reactive*—that is, they displayed high activity, fussiness, and crying during these presentations.

The infants were assessed over the next four years. At 14 and 21 months of age, fearfulness to unfamiliar events was assessed by exposing the toddlers to somewhat bizarre stimuli, such as an experimenter wearing a gas mask, a clown with a mask, and a mechanical robot. Children were determined to be "fearful" if they showed fearful reactions to the stimuli (e.g., fearful expressions, crying), and low approach behavior to the experimenters and robot. Shyness and social inhibition were next assessed at 4.5 years by noting interactive behavior (e.g., affect, approach behavior) with an experimenter and unfamiliar peer.

What are the odds that a highly reactive infant will be shy during preschool and a low-reactive baby will become a "social butterfly?" Although Kagan, Snidman, and Arcus (1998) documented statistically significant associations between infant reactivity and later fearfulness and inhibited social behavior, only about 25 percent of the highly reactive infants displayed such continuity. Thus, these data suggest that high infant reactivity is a risk factor for the development of shyness and social inhibition but probably exerts an influence only when working in combination with environmental variables. For example, highly reactive infants with cautious, overprotective caregivers display more shyness during later childhood than their counterparts with less-protective parents (Park et al., 1997).

It is somewhat refreshing to not find strong continuity between infant temperament and later developmental outcomes. To do so would suggest that we march in line because of biology and that there is little we can do to overcome social inhibition, fear of public speaking, or wariness of new things. In addition, it would be interesting to look more closely at highly reactive infants who possess multiple risk factors (e.g., highly protective parents) that still do *not* become fearful or socially inhibited. For example, it is possible that some highly reactive infants "grow out of this behavior," even without a supportive environment.

brief questionnaire that corresponds well to behavioral and physiological measures of temperament presents a tempting research agenda for scholars with an eye toward practice. A questionnaire that shows strong correspondence with more "on-line" measures of reactivity and self-regulation could be used as a screening inventory for infant health-care professionals.

Growth and Motor Development

An infant's rate of growth and motor development are strong markers of biological and central-nervous-system development. Like arousal and state regulation, these variables can be used in a number of important ways. For example, we can treat an infant's growth or motor development as a dependent, or outcome, variable. Thus, we can compare infants with different vulnerabilities (e.g., substance-exposed versus nonexposed infants), as well as different environmental circumstances before and after delivery (e.g., prenatal and postnatal nutrition).

We can also treat infant growth and motor development as independent variables and use this data to make predictions about health and development during the preschool or school years.

Physical Growth

Traditionally, we study infant growth processes by assessing weight, height, and head circumference; unusually high or low measurements may signify brain damage or abnormalities. These growth indices are influenced by genetics, prenatal and postnatal nutrition, and nonbiological variables (e.g., physical stimulation, emotional health). Because these variables are such important indicators of growth, infants can be identified as outside normal ranges through the use of standard growth charts (at least when comparing North American infants). Growth charts, such as those presented in Figure 3.2 (National Center for Health Statistics, Centers for Disease Control, 2000), can be used to assess normal length, weight, and head circumference. These statistics are used to operationally define populations with growth disorders, and allow us to make long-term predictions about growth during childhood and adolescence.

Researchers interested in physical growth are currently grappling with different operational definitions for describing certain infant populations. For example, some infants show signs of serious malnutrition (e.g., extremely wasted or thin body structure, serious delays in weight gain), yet live in countries (and households) that are generally well nourished. Although these infants may be somewhat undernourished, their feeding and dietary deficiencies are not serious enough to account for their poor physical growth and weight gain. Thus, in industrialized societies, the development of infants diagnosed with **failure to thrive** (FTT), or seriously impaired growth and weight gain, has become a very hot research topic.

Researchers interested in identifying the antecedents and consequences of FTT are faced with a number of important methodological issues. In terms of diagnosis, it is recommended that researchers use the aforementioned National Center for Health Statistics (NCHS)/CDC growth charts to make this determination. Weight-for-age, height-for-age, and weight-for-height data are used to screen for poor growth; *FTT infants typically fall below the fifth percentile on these measures* (Kessler & Dawson, 1999).

Although FTT infants have disrupted caloric intake, it is difficult to pinpoint the causes of these deficiencies. Because many of these infants have not suffered from major illnesses or other disruptive biological events, it is important to identify potential social and environmental variables that might be responsible. For instance, FTT infants often reside in highly distressed families (Ward, Brazelton, & Wust, 1999), which could disrupt feeding schedules, feedings interactions, and digestion. However, it is very difficult to establish a cause-and-effect relationship from such research. Too often, research on FTT babies is conducted *after* a diagnosis has been made. Although harsh environmental circumstances and insensitive caregiving may have some role in FTT, family distress may be a *result* of having a baby with this syndrome.

What Do You Think?

Suppose you have decided to look for possible roots to FTT. How would you design a study to address this research question? Think carefully about sampling issues, study designs, variable selection, and threats to internal validity (e.g., attrition) in crafting your response.

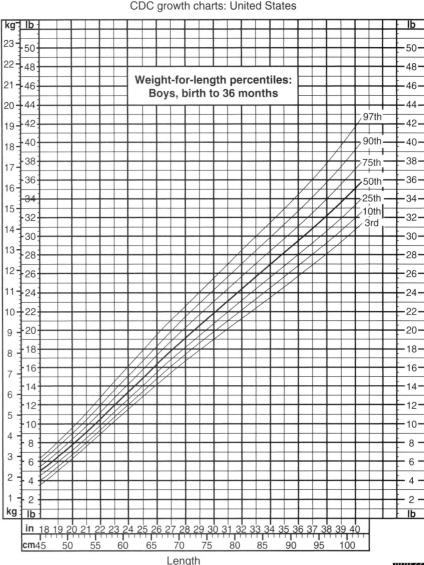

CDC growth charts: United States

**Weight-for-length percentiles:
Boys, birth to 36 months**

FIGURE 3.2   *Standard CDC Growth Chart.* This chart depicts weight-for-length percentiles for boys, from birth to 36 months. Average weight-for-length denoted is by the 50th percentile.

Motor Development

Motor development corresponds directly to development of the central nervous system. Researchers interested in motor development typically assess this construct by examining gross and fine motor abilities. **Gross motor abilities**, which often get the most attention from parents, represent broad motor actions, and include sitting up, crawling, and walking.

Fine motor abilities are more precise actions, involve smaller movements, and include such behaviors as grasping small objects (e.g., an acorn) with a finger and thumb.

There are a number of **standardized scales**, or norm-referenced, measures of motor development. That is, growth and motor data on these scales have been collected on thousands and thousands of babies across different regions of the country, or even the world. The most commonly used motor development scale in the United States is the *Bayley Scales of Infant Development* (BSID; Bayley, 1993). The Bayley Scales can be administered to young children ranging from 2 through 30 months, and contains a Mental and Motor Scale. Because this measure assesses motor and cognitive functioning, more detail regarding its items, administration, and scoring will be presented in the next chapter.

The Motor Scale of the BSID assesses gross and fine motor abilities, muscle control, and coordination. Gross-motor-ability items would include the infant's ability to sit, crawl, or walk; fine abilities would include the ability to pick up a sugar pellet with fingers. The ability to actually put the sugar pellet in a small container would constitute a motor-control and coordination item. Because the BSID is acknowledged as the "gold standard" of standardized infant assessment instruments (Bendersky & Lewis, 2001), it is widely used as a dependent variable, or outcome measure. Infants from a variety of populations (e.g., substance exposed, preterm birth, LBW) have been shown to have differential outcomes on this instrument (Arendt et al., 1999). Although commonly used as an outcome measure, its utility in making long-term predictions has been questioned (Bendersky & Lewis, 2001).

The BSID provides a general, rather than comprehensive, picture of infant motor development. Thus, the BSID works well in differentiating many types of infants on motor abilities. However, a chief difficulty rests with the inability to make extremely fine discriminations *within* certain infant populations. For example, we might note large differences in motor abilities when contrasting full-term infants to preterm infants, yet might be unable to compare infants within the challenged group.

Researchers interested in assessing more severe problems in infant motor abilities, and/or desire to study more in-depth motor-control processes in healthy babies (e.g., posture, muscle tone) should consider measures that are more sensitive to specific types of central nervous system functioning and impairment. The Alberta Infant Motor Scale (AIMS; Piper & Darrah, 1994); Test of Infant Motor Performance (TIMP; Campbell et al., 1994); and, Toddler and Infant Motor Evaluation (TIME; Miller & Roid, 1994) represent strong infant motor assessments. However, these assessments are not interchangeable. The AIMS specifically measures gross (not fine) motor abilities in infants, whereas the TIMP is designed to assess postural control and movement in vulnerable infants. The TIMP is a particularly good measure for assessing motor differences in preterm infants, who often widely differ in muscle control and tone (ranging from normal to an extremely lax, "soupy" feel) (Case-Smith & Bigsby, 2001).

Summary of Growth and Motor Development

Growth and motor development measures have been used to assess outcomes in infants with different medical and developmental histories and to make predictions about future development. Many of these assessments are *norm-referenced,* in the sense that growth and motor data have been collected on thousands and thousands of babies in many counties across the world. Because of all of the previous work on this subject, it has become easier to identify infants who are in need of intervention. Although dietary supplements would seem to be an obvious solution to the infants suffering from severe growth and motor delay, there are nondietary interventions that have been explored to stimulate these abilities. We will explore one of these interventions, infant massage therapy, in more detail in the next chapter.

Chapter Summary

Infants possess a number of important abilities that allow them to react and interact with their new social worlds. Infants show considerable differences in how they react to stimuli (i.e., reactivity or arousal), cope with such stimuli (state regulation), and communicate with their external world (e.g., crying). In this chapter, you were exposed to very discrete methods for assessing each of these abilities, as well as standard assessments to capture functioning *across* these abilities (e.g., Neonatal Assessment Behavior Rating Scale).

In terms of thinking about research, consider that we have reviewed major infant constructs (e.g., arousal), indicated why these activities are important, and reviewed methods for assessing these abilities. Although you should be able to match important methods to the constructs, you should also be able to discuss how all of this information fits into research practice. Perhaps the first step is to consider that all of the major abilities that we have discussed so far can be treated as important independent (predictor) and dependent (outcome) variables. For example, infant reactivity is an ability that may *predict* where the infant is going and *reflects* where the infant has been. At the present time, the latter part of this issue is probably easier for you to deal with than the former. For example, you now know that many infant abilities are governed, or predicted, by important vulnerabilities (medical status), risk (poverty), and protective (high parent education) factors.

On the other hand, perhaps assessing the current status of the infant and specifying factors that influenced this status is our more important job for the moment. Although we would all like to predict who will be a future Nobel Prize Winner, or even who will receive all failing grades in elementary school, it is difficult to make major predictions using infancy data. Perhaps this problem results from our methodological shortcomings in assessment and technology; however, my guess is that some vulnerable infants, based on their own resilient tendencies or because of interventions, overcome their early difficulties and some robust, healthy infants encounter environmental obstacles that end up harming their development. In either case, early infant assessments would not predict these later outcomes.

I am simply using the information presented in Table 3.2 to argue my point. I implore you to etch this table into your mind; it can be used again and again to conceptualize research and enhance our predictive power regarding infant (or child, adolescent, and adult) developmental outcomes. The table also supports my point about the importance of selecting multiple variables for research, particularly when conducting lifespan research.

Research Navigator™ Exercise: Read a Real Sad Study—The Assessment of Infant Crying

The primary objective of this assignment is to learn more about methods used to assess infant crying. Go the Research Navigator™ website: http://www.researchnavigator.com. Next, go to Section 2 of the Research Navigator™ homepage, entitled "ContentSelect," choose the Psychology database, and type *infant crying* as a keyword. After reading a full-length article, try to answer the following questions:

1. Why do the investigators view the study of infant crying as important?
2. What was the purpose of the study, and what were the study hypotheses?
3. Provide a detailed account of how the authors assessed crying. If more than one method was used, what was the rationale for a multimethod approach?
4. What were the primary study findings and conclusions?

4

Assessing Infant Mental Abilities

The assessment of infant mental abilities is a challenge, because they cannot verbally tell you whether they see an object or remember a relative's visit. Fortunately, experts have developed a number of methods for assessing mental activity and development in babies. In this chapter, we will first discuss classic ways to assess infant learning and information processing. Next, we will cover methods to study infant taste, smell, touch, hearing, and vision, and explore how babies come to understand the integrity of objects and develop rules for learning.

Standardized tests have been developed to formally measure infant mental development. We will overview two methods that are used in research and practice settings. Finally, because infant play provides a "window" into cognitive development, we will discuss how to quantify this activity.

After reading this chapter, you should be able to:

- Describe ways to assess basic infant learning and information processing.
- Discuss methodologies of assessing infant sensation and perception.
- Describe ways to measure infant cognitive abilities, such as object concept, categorization, and the baby's understanding of space, time, and number.
- Discuss two commonly used tests to assess infant mental development.
- Describe methods to measure infant free and elicited play.

Assessment of Infant Learning and Information Processing

The **information-processing approach** is a contemporary perspective used to study infant cognitive processes. We can learn a lot about babies as they observe their environment, incorporate stimuli, and retrieve important information. The methodologies that have been developed to assess these abilities are highly quantifiable. We will overview five paradigms to study infant learning and information processing. When working with premobile infants, habituation, instrumental learning, and response expectancy methods are the most contemporary methods. Object-hiding and elicited-information tasks are popular among researchers who work with older infants capable of coordinated reaching and grasping.

Habituation

Habituation refers to the gradual reduction of attentional processes resulting from the repeated or continued presence of a stimulus (see also p. 71). Rather than signifying fatigue or boredom, habituation reflects the infant's increasing knowledge of the stimulus, and thus mirrors an active learning process. It is an *adaptive process* that allows infants to pay less attention to familiar things, and subsequently to attend more to new events in the environment.

Habituation to visual stimuli has received the most scrutiny. Commonly, the infant's visual behaviors, such as fixation and eye movement, are assessed across several trials. Before the trials are conducted, the infant is routinely placed in a comfortable car seat in a visually controlled environment. For example, researchers may place a picture screen in front of the infant, leaving the remainder of the area darkened or enclosed with a curtain. This method is used to ensure that the infant is not distracted by other visual stimuli. To test for habituation, the following trials might be conducted:

1. **Novelty period.** The researcher presents a novel stimulus, such as a picture of a smiling baby, and records the infant's initial **orienting response**, a response used by the infant to maximize attention to the stimulus.
2. **Habituation period.** In this phase, the novel stimulus simply remains (e.g., the picture remains in the infant's field of vision) until the baby looks away, or is flashed over and over at random or predetermined intervals.
3. **Dishabituation period.** In this phase, the researcher introduces a novel stimulus— for example, a bald-headed man. We next pair the new and old stimulus together in the same frame, as depicted in the *paired-comparison procedure* illustrated in Figure 4.1. **Dishabituation** refers to the renewal of the orienting response, or attention, to the new stimulus. As you can guess, the baby attends to the second stimulus, the bald-headed man. The fact that the infant is attending to a new picture indicates that the baby *is not simply tired or bored*; rather, the baby is highly attentive to something new.

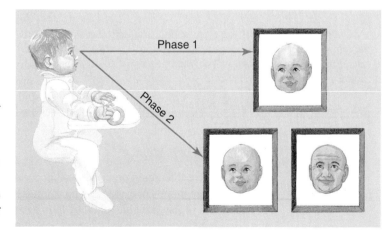

FIGURE 4.1 *Infant Habituation Paired-Comparison Procedure.* In trial two, the baby will stare longer at the bald-headed man, because the picture is novel.

From, Berk, L. (2003). *Child Development*, 6th Ed., p. 136. Reprinted with permission of Allyn & Bacon, Boston, MA.

Pioneering researchers preferred **fixed-trial habituation procedures**, in which the baby was simply shown the same picture repeatedly for a predetermined time period. Perhaps the main difficulty with this procedure is that the infant is not in control of the task, so that some babies may not be given enough time to habituate, and others may habituate quickly and experience a number of trials past their habituation point (Colombo & Mitchell, 1990).

Because of these concerns, experts have increasingly gravitated toward **criterion-based habituation procedures**—that is, *the infant is given control over stimulus presentation.* We can present a picture, wait for an orienting response, and then rate the infant's declining attention by noting the duration of gazes or "looks" over time. Once the baby's visual fixation falls below a predetermined threshold, the next stimulus is presented (Colombo & Mitchell, 1990).

What data are important? Recall that habituation refers to the decline in attention to the continual or repeated presence of a stimulus. We can record the *amount of time* a baby gazes at a familiar picture, or note the *rate at which gazing declines.* We can also collect data during dishabituation. When simultaneously presenting a novel and familiar stimulus, we can record the amount of time the baby gazes at each stimulus (Rose, Feldman, & Wallace, 1988). The fact that most babies stare longer at the novel stimulus is evidence of **recognition memory**—that is, infants stare longer at a new object because they "recognize" that they have seen the old one before.

Because habituation and recognition memory reflect the integrity of the nervous system, physiological responses have also been used to assess these competencies. Because we can study habituation across a number of perceptual modalities, measuring a central physiological variable, such as heart-rate variability, allows researchers the use of a consistent variable that can be studied across all senses. Box 4.1 presents several methods for linking physiological measures to habituation and recognition abilities.

Are the aforementioned habituation methods valid? Infants who rapidly habituate to novel stimuli and show good recognition memory possess strong abilities in terms of encoding, processing, and retrieving information (Colombo, 1995). Also, infants with strong habituation or recognition memory skills score high on intelligence tests during childhood (Fagan & Singer, 1983). Presumably, quick habituation speed is reflective of "quick thinking," an ability that is thought to underlie overall intelligence. However, correlations between the infancy habituation and recognition memory measures and later intelligence measures are modest (e.g., around .35) and dependent on study population (lower correlations for vulnerable populations) (McCall & Carriger, 1993).

What Do You Think?

According to the material presented so far, what happens to infant visual attention, electrical activity in the brain, and heart rate during orienting, habituation, and dishabituation trials? How can we use these responses to assess recognition memory?

Expectancy Formation

There are different learning processes that occur during habituation studies (Fagen & Ohr, 2001). Although infants may stop gazing at familiar stimuli because they have encoded and processed it, it is also possible that they look away because they expect the object to reappear. That infants develop expectancies about future events is an intriguing idea, yet it is

BOX 4.1 • *Physiological Measures to Tap Infant Learning*

If infant habituation reflects the integrity of the central nervous system, then we would expect strong connections between cortical brain activity and infant learning during habituation trials. To test this idea, associations between cortical activity and infant behavior (e.g., gaze preference, sucking rates) have been documented in habituation and recognition memory studies. In particular, **event-related potentials** (ERPs) represent a very exciting method for assessing electrical activity in the brain during infant learning trials. To assess ERPs, researchers typically place small electrodes on the scalps of babies, and assess overall brain activity using an electroencephalogram (EEG). Although the EEG provides a reading of global brain activity, specific ERP readings are typically extracted from the EEG data, because such readings reflect *specific responses in the brain as a result of specific events.*

ERP strength increases when infants are presented novel stimuli and decreases as they habituate. Different experimental presentations of stimuli evoke different types of brain activity. Nelson and Collins (1992) repeatedly presented two pictures to infants over 10 trials. Next, three pictures were flashed repeatedly (and separately) in the following fashion: Familiar Picture #1, 60% of the time; Familiar Picture #2, 20%; Novel Picture, 20%. The infants displayed different ERPs for the novel and familiar stimuli, as well as *between the two familiar stimuli;* the latter findings were theorized to reflect "memory updating" for a familiar stimulus. Similarly, de Haan and Nelson (1997) documented that babies display different EVPs when looking at pictures of mother's and stranger's faces, yet these differences were less pronounced (though significant) when the faces of mothers and strangers were more similar. These researchers theorize that infants use

vastly different neural processes for encoding and processing novel stimuli and more or less recognizable environmental events.

Vagal tone has also been used to assess infant learning. Recall that infant heart-rate variability is a method for assessing infant regulation, and that high vagal tone at rest and vagal suppression (which is theorized to sharpen attentional skills) when aroused, reflect good regulatory skills. In one study, Bornstein and Suess (2000) examined infant gaze fixation to familiar and novel stimuli at 2 and 5 months of age. In addition to habituation measures, they measured infant vagal tone before initial stimulus presentation and then assessed it through a series of habituation trials. The results confirmed that there are close connections between infant regulatory abilities and competent infant learning. Infants who looked at stimuli for brief periods of time during visual attention tasks had higher baseline vagal tones, and were more likely to suppress vagal tone during the habituation tasks. The results suggest that infants with good regulatory abilities pay close attention to novel things, quickly absorb relevant information, adjust, and then move on to new stimuli.

The results of studies using physiological measures highlight mechanisms for development that might be very difficult to uncover through the use of standard infant "looking" habituation and recognition experimental paradigms. The results of cortical activity studies suggest that central nervous system development is important for infant learning and memory. However, connecting physiological self-regulation to cognitive processes in infants is just as important, and may better highlight a variable that mediates associations between environmental events (e.g., interactions with parents) and the development of infant memory.

---

difficult to study expectancy formation using traditional habituation paradigms that rely on simple visual fixation. Thus simple habituation experiments at best illustrate learning processes as the infant *currently* copes with stimuli.

Because "expectancy" refers to the ability to actually *foretell* a future event (Haith & McCarty, 1990), a new methodology was developed to capture this phenomenon. To study expectancy formation, we can create a pattern for stimulus presentation; an object may appear in the left field of vision once, followed by two consecutive trials of right-field presentation. Soon, the baby will glance toward a vision field before the object even appears!

Researchers typically use *anticipation* and *facilitation* speed as important data sources. Anticipation refers to how quickly infants will glance to one side in anticipation of the stimulus. If the infant fails to anticipate an object, facilitation speed is computed by timing how long it takes the baby to look at the object that has suddenly appeared in their field of vision (Canfield & Haith, 1991). You can also use physiological measures to record anticipatory responses in babies. For example, Donohue and Berg (1991) noted that most 7-month-old infants displayed cardiac slowing, or braking, in response to anticipated stimuli.

Keeping track of visual attention as babies glance in different directions is difficult; thus, Haith and colleagues (1988) developed the apparatus depicted in Figure 4.2. Note that the box is enclosed, and only the slide projector provides stimulus input; images are displayed to either the infant's left or right field of vision. The small infrared camera

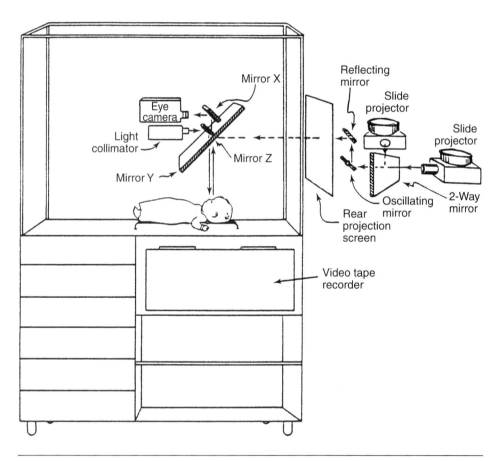

FIGURE 4.2 *Eye-Movement Recording Device.* The slide projector presents the stimulus, and the camera records the side of the screen—left or right—the baby looks toward.

From, Haith, M. et al., (1988). Expectation and anticipation of dynamic visual events by 3.5-month-old babies. *Child Development, 59*, p. 470. Reprinted with permission of the Society for Research in Child Development.

records the infant's exact eye movements and provides the researcher (and computer) information regarding the direction of infant looking.

Researchers have uncovered some interesting findings using visual-expectancy paradigms. Older infants are capable of anticipating more complicated patterns of visual simulation than younger infants (Reznick, Chawarska, & Betts, 2000). Expectancy studies have also been used to make predictions about later competencies. In one study, visual-expectancy measures, and the *Fagan Test of Infant Intelligence* (FTII; Fagan & Shepherd, 1986) were given to 7-to-9-month-old infants (DiLalla et al., 1990). The FTII is composed of habituation speed and recognition-memory items. Despite the inclusion of important variables that underlie intellectual development (e.g., habituation speed, parent education, recognition-memory abilities), expectancy reaction time was the strongest predictor of later intelligence.

Instrumental Conditioning

A **reinforcer** is a stimulus that increases the occurrence of a response. In **instrumental conditioning paradigms**, we present a stimulus, such as a picture of mother's face, that is hypothesized to increase some type of infant behavior, such as sucking or gaze preference. Once a response has been observed, infants are "rewarded" with the reinforcer. The infants will again produce the desired response, hypothetically because they expect that the reward will occur again. Instrumental conditioning and response-expectancy paradigms are close cousins; both experimental procedures value the role of expectancy in the learning process. However, expectancy paradigms place the baby *in a passive position*; the baby's responses do not influence the rate of stimulus presentation.

Rovee-Collier and colleagues (1989) have studied instrumental conditioning using a procedure termed *mobile conjugate reinforcement* via the apparatus depicted in Figure 4.3.

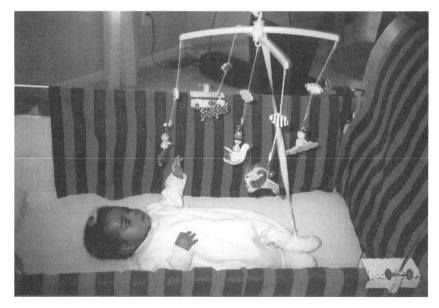

FIGURE 4.3 *Mobile Conjugate Reinforcement Device.* Note that the ribbon is tied to the infant's foot. Any leg kick moves the mobile; the baby learns that it can move the mobile by moving its leg.

From, Rovee-Collier, C., Earley, L., & Stafford, S. (1989). Ontogeny of early event memory: III. Attentional determinants of retrieval at 2 and 3 months. *Infant Behavior and Development, 12*, p. 152. Reprinted with permission of Elsevier Publishers.

In the first trial, or *no reinforcement* baseline phase, the mobile is hung completely out of reach of the baby. In the second trial, or *reinforcement* phase, one end of the mobile is tied to the infant's foot with a ribbon. Any kick causes the brightly colored mobile to move; they learn that leg kicks produce stimulus change. Thus, instrumental-conditioning paradigms are a direct measure of learning that requires active infant participation.

Although the predictive power of infant learning using such procedures is not as impressive as habituation or response-expectancy paradigms (Wyly, 1997), major questions can be addressed using these techniques. Contrasting the learning styles of infants of different ages allows us to better understand the developmental progression of such learning. Manipulating the nature of the stimulus (e.g., mother's versus stranger's face) allows us to determine exactly what is reinforcing to young infants.

Finally, conducting instrumental conditioning procedures and then testing infant memory for these events in the minutes, hours, days, and weeks after the initial administration addresses important questions about infant memory development. For example, consider the infant who learns to move a mobile by kicking a leg and then immediately begins exhibiting this behavior when the apparatus is readministered at a later time. Such behavior provides strong evidence that the infant has learned and retained important information.

What Do You Think?

> Contrast habituation, response expectancy, and instrumental-conditioning paradigms. What do the results of studies using these procedures tell us about current and future mental development? If a parent asked you to perform one of these procedures to "find out how smart my baby will be," what would you recommend?

Object-Hiding and Deferred-Imitation Paradigms

As reaching and grasping become coordinated, we can take advantage of these abilities to assess attention and memory in older babies. In **object-hiding paradigms**, we show the infant an object and then hide it. We can then record the success of subsequent infant search behavior. You can manipulate a number of variables using hiding paradigms—for example, there may be one or more possible hiding places. You will learn more about object-hiding paradigms when we discuss Jean Piaget's cognitive-developmental theory later in the chapter.

Deferred imitation represents another way to document learning and memory in older infants. Although babies can *directly* imitate our actions, with development, they can increasingly imitate behaviors witnessed *at an earlier time*—hence the term *deferred*. For example, a toddler may witness a carpenter hammering boards and then later may bang blocks and other objects with a toy hammer—much to the delight or dismay of caregivers!

In the standard paradigm, the researcher models an action, such as hammering red toy nails in one board, blue nails in another. The researcher provides no instructions, other than to utter phrases to direct the infant's attention, such as "Are you watching me?" After a time period, the infant is given an opportunity to imitate the actions. It is wise not to have parents around, because they might coach the child. In addition, because the teacher's appearance—gender, dress, and eyewear—can influence imitative behavior, novice researchers should consult Meltzoff and Moore (1992) regarding how to better control for these confounds.

In standard deferred-imitation paradigms, the infant observes our action and is given an opportunity to imitate the modeled actions at a later time. However, this paradigm can be modified. First, infants can be allowed to manipulate the objects before the demonstration. Second, they can be given "practice sessions,"; we might ask, "Can you put the red nails in the board like me?" Using such **elicited imitation paradigms**, infants as young as 13 months of age can later imitate the researcher's actions after delays of as long as 8 months (Bauer, Hertsgaard, & Dow, 1994).

Hiding and deferred-imitation methods assess memory processes that are different from the abilities tapped by habituation and instrumental learning paradigms. In a habituation task, the infant is presented a stimulus, and then a short time later the same stimulus is paired with a novel one. A preference for the novel stimulus is taken as evidence that the infant *recognizes* the old stimulus and prefers the new one. However, consider the baby who locates a hidden object or repeats the actions of a model; there are no cues to prompt memory. The only way to correctly imitate the actions is to have a stored *representation* of the modeled behavior. Thus, hiding and deferred-imitation paradigms better tap **recall memory**, or the ability to spontaneously remember something without the presence of cues.

Summary of Infant Learning/Information-Processing Assessment

Habituation, response expectancy, instrumental conditioning, object-hiding, and deferred-imitation methods represent very important paradigms for infancy researchers. The data collected from these procedures give us important information about the development of learning and memory, and in some cases, predicts later competencies during childhood. Because researchers typically use these rudimentary forms of infant learning to study how infants perceive, process, store, and retrieve information, an initial understanding of these methods will make it easier to comprehend much of the material that is to follow.

Infant Sensation and Perception

In this section, you will learn about methods of assessing infant sensation and perception. Sensory capabilities develop well before birth; thus, newborn babies can automatically make certain sensory detections. Because the process is reflexive and fairly passive in nature, we label the initial abilities of the newborn as sensory. In contrast, perception is thought to represent an active process. For example, older infants will visually attend to objects and may organize this information to enhance later retrieval.

Touch

Various stimuli are used to study tactile sensation and perception. Experts interested in light-touch sensation use air puffs or small brushes. Those with interests in temperature reactions present hot and cold objects or liquids (Reisman, 1987). Finally, pain detection is observed during circumcision, inoculation, or blood-drawing procedures. The decision to study responses to light touch, temperature, or pain stimuli is important, because these stimuli excite different areas of the nervous system. Because most of the research focuses on responses to light touch and pain, we will limit discussion to these stimuli.

Light Touch.   Researchers who study light-touch sensation often administer stimuli, such as air puffs to the abdomen. They then observe and assess the infant's responses such as behavioral activity (arm, head, and trunk movements), heart rate, or both. Physiological measures are used in conjunction with behavioral responses, because heart rate is a more sensitive measure of stimulus sensation. For example, even full-term babies sometimes show heart-rate change but no accompanying body movements in response to light touch (Rose, 1990).

Infant state and age predict the direction of heart-rate change in response to light touch. Before 2 months of age, *sleeping* infants show an increase in heart rate in response to novel stimuli; after this age, heart rate decelerates. However, *alert* babies under 2 months show heart-rate deceleration in response to new stimuli. It is possible that heart-rate acceleration reflects the nervous system's attempt to inhibit or block sensory overload, which might be adaptive for sleeping babies. In contrast, deceleration may indicate active interest or an orienting response (Reisman, 1987). In any event, infant state and age represent important study variables, because they predict responses to light touch (as well as other sensory stimuli).

Birth complications and medical status also represent other methodological considerations when assessing touch responses (Rose, 1990). Preterm infants display higher resting heart rates; thus, direct comparisons between preterm and full-term infants should not be based on simple mean differences after stimulus presentation. Rather, we should look at the rate of change in babies over time. Also, preterm infants during the neonatal period require more stimulation to produce a response, and show much slower habituation patterns than full-term babies. *Birth and medical complications can also affect our results when examining chemical, auditory, and visual processes in babies.*

Why is basic research concerning tactile sensation important? Tactile sensation is important in detecting and locating the mother's breast and nipple, and the infant's sucking response is partly based on tactile sensation. Light-touch research also informs interventions with vulnerable babies; the results of some of this work are presented in Box 4.2.

BOX 4.2 • *When's a Touch Too Much? Infant Massage Therapy*

A number of intervention studies have examined the effects of massage therapy and formal handling techniques on vulnerable infants. We assume that gentle stimulation facilitates central nervous system activity and hormone release, which ultimately benefits the infant. Several studies have shown that preterm infants who receive "massage therapy" have better 10-day Neonatal Behavioral Assessment Scale scores, more weight gain, and earlier hospital exits than their nontreated counterparts (Field, 1999; Rausch, 1990). Clearly, these findings represent an exciting research and practice direction.

How do we give a preterm baby a massage? In one study, preterm infants were given Swedish-like massages 45 minutes per day for 10 days. Each session contained three phases. Phases one and three involved moderate massaging that included the neck and shoulders, back, legs, arms, and head and face regions. The middle phase, which included kinesthetic stimulation, involved moving the infant's legs and arms in a bicycling motion. Over time, the babies who received the massage therapy were more alert, gained more weight, and displayed smoother state regulation than their counterparts who received no intervention. The massaged infants spent six fewer days in the hospital than the control babies, resulting in thousands of dollars in savings for these families (Field et al., 1986). This represents yet another instance in which basic research, in this case involving infant sensitivity to touch, has led to creative intervention work.

Pain.　Some routine events, such as circumcision, inoculations, and blood drawings, allow us opportunities to examine pain sensation and perception in human infants. Why would researchers be so interested in pain sensation? I doubt that they conduct such work for the "sake of the science." Monitoring how infants cope with pain sensation provides clues about how to make them more comfortable during routine medical procedures.

How would you monitor pain responses in infants? If you are considering behavioral responses, such as crying, then you have made a good guess. In one system, observers monitor infants as they receive inoculations or blood tests (Worobey & Lewis, 1989). By carefully observing changes in the infant's brow, cheek, and mouth movements, they can rate distress on a 3-point scale (0 = none; 3 = full). Next, coders turn to vocal expressions, making note of the changing nature of infant crying ("full" versus "fussy" crying) during these procedures. The infant is then assigned a vocal-expression score (0 = no sound; 3 = full cry). This seems to be an easy system for newcomers to learn, in that strong interrater reliability is easy to achieve.

Because the field of lifespan development is becoming more biobehavioral, physiological measures are often used *in conjunction* with such simple behavioral measures. For example, Gunnar and colleagues (1995) recorded infant behavioral responses (e.g., crying), vagal tone, and salivary cortisol levels in healthy newborn infants before, during, and after a blood draw. Many infants displayed high levels of crying, large cortisol release, and low vagal tone shortly after this procedure but quickly returned to baseline, suggesting that most healthy newborns have strong neurological organization.

The meaning of pain responses also changes as infants mature. For example, 2-month-old infants who cry more and show greater cortisol levels in response to painful procedures, such as inoculations, cry less and display lower cortisol levels over time to the same procedures (Lewis & Ramsay, 1995). Although strong reactivity to pain during early infancy may reflect robust neurological organization, less reactivity to the same procedures during later infancy represents a sign of developing self-regulatory skills. These data suggest that the developmental status of the infant (as always) is an important study variable.

What Do You Think?

Compare and contrast the behavioral and physiological responses of newborns and older babies to light touch and pain. What is the practical importance of such research?

Chemical Sensation: Olfaction and Taste

Olfactory development is important, because it has strong implications for the development of nursing, self-regulation, food recognition, and the identification of caregivers. Thus, even two-week-old babies can differentiate their own mothers from strangers simply by their sense of smell! How do we assess such perception? Historically, simple head-orientation methods have been used with even neonates. In this basic paradigm, an odor is introduced to one side of the infant and changes in head orientation are noted. By the way, it is important to establish whether the baby has a natural "preference" for one side or another if we position stimuli with different odors on each side of the baby.

Very young babies cannot make smooth, coordinated head turns, so how can olfactory researchers conduct reliable research? In one paradigm, researchers tested babies in bassinets and introduced gauze pads containing different odors. The gauze pads were attached to tubing and placed very close the baby's face, so that a head turn to the left or right would bring the infant's face within 1 to 2 cm (about an inch) of either of the pads. Any slight deviation from midline was defined as infant orientation toward the odor (Makin & Porter, 1989).

Some methodological concerns in this field should be highlighted. When testing for maternal odor preference, it is important to segregate babies by feeding habits (breast- versus bottle-fed), and contrast maternal preference with both unfamiliar nursing and non-nursing mothers. The results of more carefully controlled research have yielded fascinating results, chiefly by two weeks of age; the preference for maternal odors is limited to breast-fed babies (Cernoch & Porter, 1985).

Now, let's turn to taste research. What is your reaction when you bite into incredibly sour candy? If you are like me, you grimace and wrinkle your nose! However, because it is often difficult to evaluate the meaning of gross facial movements, there are coding systems to better capture discrete movements in facial muscles. These analyses are done after introducing stimuli that represent different taste sensations (i.e., sweet, sour, bitter, salty) via a dropper or pacifier. Methodologically, the delivery mechanism—pacifier or dropper—is an important variable to control for because they elicit different senses. That is, the pacifier also elicits tactile sensations.

The *Baby Facial Action Coding System (FACS)* allows raters to score very subtle changes in the shape and position of facial features (Oster & Rosenstein, 1988). Although the infant's facial expressions, depicted in Figure 4.4, are clearly different at a global level, such judgments would be deferred using the Baby FACS until after discrete facial movements (e.g., mouth gaping accompanied by brow movements) had been analyzed. Such a system would seem necessary, because untrained people make serious errors even in global judgments about whether the infant is making a face because of a sour or a sweet taste. The Baby FACS is very valid; for instance, researchers have found significant facial movement differences in most taste sensations (e.g., sour versus bitter) in infants just two hours old (Rosenstein & Oster, 1988)!

Although the Baby FACS is a popular method, most experts use multiple procedures to assess infant taste reactions. These methods might include the measurement of facial expressions, sucking, body movements, crying, and physiological data as infants are exposed to different taste sensations (Barr et al., 1999). One argument for using multiple methods is that taste sensation *does* trigger major behavioral and physiological changes within the baby. These changes are simply not reactions; researchers theorize that subsequent changes in infant biobehavior resulting from taste sensation have important ramifications for health and development.

For example, Blass and Ciaramitaro (1994) examined the impact of odorless, sweet-tasting sucrose on crying and calm babies. Infants prefer sweet substances, perhaps because they are adapted to respond favorably to the sweet-flavored milk of their mothers. The researchers were careful to note changes in crying, body movements, and heart rate after delivering sucrose or ordinary water using a pacifier or dropper. The researchers controlled for both the taste content and delivery mechanisms.

Crying babies supplied sucrose by dropper soon stopped crying, displayed heart rate drops, and repeatedly moved their hands to their mouths (a self-calming activity). *These*

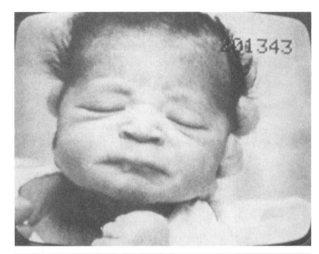

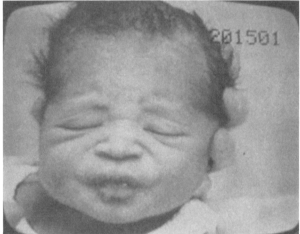

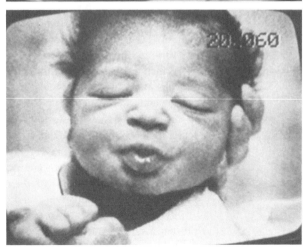

FIGURE 4.4 *Facial-Expression Recordings.*
Sequence of facial expressions elicited from sweet
sensations. Note the look of enjoyment in the last
frame!

From Rosenstein, D., & Oster, H. (1988). Differential facial responses to four basic tastes in newborns. *Child Development,
59*, p. 1562. Reprinted with permission of the Society for Research in Child Development.

findings were long lasting, in the sense that the babies did not return to an agitated state after the sucrose administration by dropper. Although agitated babies given water-filled pacifiers calmed significantly, they became agitated once these pacifiers were removed.

These data suggest that sucking behavior resulting from sucrose ingestion may elicit important self-regulatory skills in infants. The trigger for these skills seems to be sucrose taste stimulation. If the trigger were stimulation of our tactile senses, simply sucking on a pacifier should produce more long-lasting effects. The researchers suggest that sucking responses produced by sucrose ingestion may also trigger the release of opiate like chemicals in the body, which function as a natural painkiller. This may explain the common hospital practice of allowing babies to suck on sucrose-flavored pacifiers during painful procedures.

Like olfaction research, it is important to consider various experimental controls when conducting taste-sensation work. Beyond manipulating taste contents and the delivery system (i.e., dropper or pacifier), controlling for an infant's dietary history is an important consideration in making judgments regarding innate and environmental variables that contribute to taste preference. Harris, Thomas, and Booth (1990) noted that preferences for salty stimuli emerged around 4 months of age in exclusively breast-fed babies. Because exclusively breast-fed infants have no experience with salt, preference to salty substances is initiated by innate forces. However, babies rapidly lose their salt preference if continued exclusively on breast milk, suggesting that a low-sodium diet eventually leads to a preference for low-sodium food. This latter finding has not been replicated for babies exposed to high-sodium diets, strongly suggesting subsequent salt preferences are based on experiential variables.

What Do You Think?

In terms of pain sensation, what are the advantages and disadvantages of finding ways to soothe babies during inoculations and blood drawing? Does tampering with a natural process (i.e., state regulation) have potential negative implications for later development?

Visual Perception

Visual Acuity and Interest.   We can use various methods to assess infant detection (Is an object there?), acuity (What can I see or not see?), and interest (What do I like?). The most common method is to note infant eye movements in response to shapes, objects, or patterns. As with habituation methods, orienting responses and eye-fixation times following various stimuli are recorded.

In the **forced-choice paradigm**, an observer notes the baby's head turn and eye movements to two side-by-side objects or pictures, and calculates the baby's orienting response and interest in each picture or object (e.g., fixation time) (Teller, 1979). The rater is screened from the stimulus presentation by a curtain or partition, and is trained to specifically focus on the infant's behavior; an awareness of the stimulus presentation could bias observer ratings (e.g., "I like brightly colored objects, so the infant must, too.").

Forced-choice methods are used to assess a wide range of infant perceptual abilities, such as pattern/object/color preference and infant visual acuity. **Visual acuity** refers to how accurately we perceive visual information; for example, 20/20 vision refers to our ability to accurately see information at 20 feet. To assess visual acuity in infants, we can present a series of patterns, as depicted in Figure 4.5. In each trial, the black-and-white

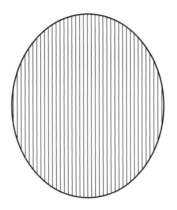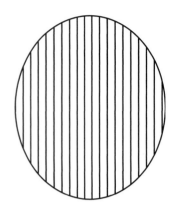

FIGURE 4.5 *Pattern-Discrimination Stimuli.* An infant who shows no preference to the patterns depicted in this figure would be judged to have poorer visual acuity than an infant who prefers one over the other. Across trials, the lines on the right will get progressively closer and gradually appear more like the pattern on the left.

stripes in the right picture get progressively closer, to the point that the infant will show no consistent preference for either image. Infants who display no preference for the two images during early trials have poorer acuity than babies who display a clear preference across more difficult trials.

Although forced-choice methods represent a popular way to assess infant object preference and discrimination, the need for special apparatus and paired stimulus presentations make it cumbersome to use. To overcome this obstacle, Teller and colleagues (1986) developed the *Acuity Card Procedure*, which employs a card set that varies in pattern complexity. Raters simply record the infant's eye movements and fixations; increases in eye movements and briefer fixations indicate the baby is near or past its acuity threshold.

Of course, such procedures do not really tell us exactly what features, edges, boundaries, or contours of the stimuli they find interesting. However, advances in *eye-movement recording technology* allow us to use infrared photography and computer technology to record eye movements, and thus provide a detailed record of exact visual fixations over time. Beyond documenting that an infant prefers a mother's face to a stranger's, we can now determine exactly which features of the mother's face they find interesting. Note in Figure 4.6 that the eye saccades of 1- and 2-month old infants show that the older babies prefer the internal contours of the face—in particular, the eyes and mouth. In fact, even newborns show a preference for shapes or blobs that contain predictable facial features (Simion, Valenza, & Umilta, 1998).

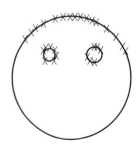

1 month old   **2 month old**

FIGURE 4.6 *Visual Scanning Data.* Computerized output of infant visual scanning data. Note that the older infant scans internal contour of the eyes.

Because habituation researchers have increasingly incorporated physiological measures in their protocols, perception experts have adopted these techniques to study visual perception. Indeed, we have already discussed how infant heart-rate variability can be used to assess infant visual attention (See Box 4.1). Also, because strong cortical evoked potentials are elicited by novel or interesting stimuli, it is common for researchers to assess electrical activity in the brain in order to specify neural mechanisms that underlie visual acuity and pattern discrimination (Salapatek & Nelson, 1985).

Depth Perception.   From a historical perspective, the **visual-cliff paradigm** represents the most recognized method to assess infant depth perception (Gibson & Walk, 1960). As depicted in Figure 4.7, the baby is placed on a table with a glass surface. Directly beneath one side of the glass is a checkered tablecloth; however, under the other side is a space between the glass and checkered pattern, creating the illusion that there is a sudden, steep drop.

Walk and Gibson (1961) noted that almost all infants capable of crawling (6 months or older) readily crossed the shallow side, but when called from the cliff side by their mother, either crawled away or cried in frustration at being unable to get to her. Because this was such a consistent pattern, and because many animals are capable of sophisticated locomotion shortly after birth—an activity that requires depth perception—it was originally concluded that the development of depth perception resulted from innate, biological forces.

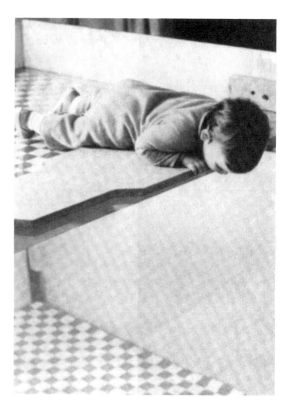

FIGURE 4.7 *Visual-Cliff Paradigm.* A sheet of glass covers the "deep" and "shallow" sides. Infants that do not cross to the "deep" side are assumed to possess depth perception.

From, Bornstein, M., & Lamb, M. (1992). *Development in infancy: An introduction* (p. 184). New York: McGraw Hill. Photo courtesy of R. Walk.

A shortcoming of early visual-cliff research rested with the difficulty of testing pre-crawling babies. However, Campos and colleagues (1970) placed young infants (ages 2 and 3.5 months) on the "deep" side of the visual cliff and monitored changes in heart rate. The older infants showed increases in heart rate, whereas the younger babies showed declines; researchers theorized that increases were caused by fear responses, whereas the declines in younger infants reflected sharpening visual attention and interest. Infants as young as 2 months of age can detect depth; however, they have not learned to fear it. If experience is needed to connect fear with a potential dangerous drop-off, then depth-perception development results from both innate and environmental forces. Indeed, mobile older infants with more crawling experience are less likely to cross onto the deep side than babies with less experience (Bertenthal & Campos, 1990).

Although the visual cliff can determine whether an infant has developed depth perception, it does not provide information regarding aspects of our visual system that allow us to determine depth in the first place. There must be different elements of the visual system that are responsible for depth perception, because it requires us to first detect moving objects, and then to locate and focus on their position.

The visual mechanisms responsible for depth perception are kinetic (motion), binocular, and pictorial depth cues. *Kinetic depth cues* are used to track *motion*. Although babies show quicker orienting responses to moving than unmoving (or static) objects, Bertenthal and colleagues (1987) demonstrated that 3-month-old infants appreciate integrity and coherence of movement. For example, infants exposed to moving dots that represented either a general outline of a person walking, or random, scrambled points of light habituated quicker to the coherent light movements.

Beyond motion detection, we need other cues to make visual adjustments. With eyes uncovered, take a pencil, hold it at arms length and then move it closer to your eyes. Did you notice the position of the pencil changed as you moved it closer? This is because each eye receives a slightly different view of an object, a phenomena termed *retinal disparity*. This disparity becomes greater as an object moves closer, so we use this disparity to gauge depth. *Binocular cues* are responsible for retinal disparity—that is, such disparity is dependent on the functioning of *both eyes*. Binocular cues are also responsible for *visual convergence:* when an object is far away, both eyes appear to stare straight ahead; however, when an object comes closer, the eyes move toward one another to focus on the object.

In order to study the development of binocular cues, we must design methods that control for monocular cues; for example, with a hand over one eye, we can still detect distance and depth. Methods exist that allow one to detect an object only with binocular cues; you can present a picture with series of random dots that represent meaningless dots with one eye covered yet appear to be a moving object with eyes uncovered (Kellman & Banks, 1998). In such studies, with eyes uncovered, 2-month-old infants either do not attend to the dots or may focus on the object with one eye; in neither case does binocular vision appear to be developed—remember, you need both eyes to work together. However, by 3 months, infants will attend longer to the dots; this is about the same time premobile infants show heart rate changes in response to the visual-cliff paradigm.

These cues have implications for other activities that require good depth perception. In one study, infants were allowed to reach for interesting objects, either naturally (binocular) or with one eye covered (monocular vision); infant speed and accuracy in reaching was then recorded. Infant response time and accuracy were much quicker in the binocular condition, indicating that binocular cues also play a role in reaching and grasping (Atkinson, 1998).

Finally, *pictorial depth cues* allow us to perceive depth from flat, two-dimensional objects. Artists appreciate our ability to discern depth from flat objects—consider how paintings provide an illusion of depth in very small, two-dimensional spaces. As with binocular depth cues, the sensitivity of pictorial cues is measured by covering the infant's eye and presenting pictures or objects that vary in size. There are two important assumptions using this paradigm. First, by presenting two identical objects side by side that vary in size, the infant is "fooled" into believing that the larger object is closer. Second, by blocking the vision of one eye, individual differences in infant performance can be attributed to disparities in pictorial rather than binocular depth cues (which have been eliminated by covering the eye). Using such methods, infants engage in preferential reaching of the larger object around 7 months of age (Yonas et al., 1986). Thus, it appears that pictorial cues develop later than kinetic or binocular depth cues.

Auditory Perception

Historically, the **High-Amplitude Sucking** (HAS) *paradigm* (Eimas et al., 1971) was one of the most popular methods for assessing infant auditory perception. In this paradigm the infant is placed in a car seat facing a projection screen in a darkened room. The experimenter places a pacifier nipple in the baby's mouth; any pressure on the nipple is then recorded.

Because infants do not show predictable changes in sucking responses when sounds change, they can be trained to display predictable responses via instrumental conditioning. In the classic HAS paradigm, the infant is trained to increase sucking pressure to trigger the onset of a consonant syllable (/ba/). Only intense (hence the term *high amplitude*) sucking responses will trigger the initial onset of this stimulus. The criterion for triggering the stimulus varies, because infants differ in sucking intensity.

Once this criterion has been set, the initial auditory stimulus is withdrawn for 1 min. Once the infant exhibits a high-amplitude suck, the initial auditory stimulus reappears, which normally triggers an increased sucking response. Once a 20% decline in the sucking response occurs, the criterion for habituation has been reached. Next, infants are assigned to control or experimental groups. Although control babies experience the same auditory stimulus, the infants in the experimental group receive a different sound (/pa/). The theory is that if babies in the experimental group show different sucking rates compared to their control-group counterparts, these infants have detected differences between the two sounds (Jusczyk, 1985). The fact that even 1-month-old infants can discriminate subtle human speech sounds implies that we are biologically programmed not just to make early discriminations in trivial sounds but also to quickly understand subtle differences in *human language.*

An advantage of the HAS sucking techniques is that it can be used with very young infants (e.g., 1–4 months). For many years, this method was a strong fixture in auditory speech-perception research. However, because some infants require substantial time to reach the 20 percent habituation threshold, it is common for them to become fussy during these procedures, and the data for such babies cannot be used. This procedure also seems particularly cumbersome for extremely young or medically challenged infants who have poor sucking responses.

Today, many hearing specialists use conditioned head-turning procedures (Moore, Thompson, & Thompson, 1975), or **visual-reinforcement audiometry** (VRF), to study infant auditory processing. In this procedure, the infant's attention is attracted to a toy after a recorded tone changes. When the infant turns her head to the toy, a darkened box lights up with a noisy, active toy. Picture a toy monkey banging cymbals together. Gradually, upon hearing a tone change, the baby will turn her head to the location of the animated monkey *before* the box lights up.

The VRF is a popular method, because it is less demanding than high-amplitude sucking procedures. Using such procedures, fascinating developmental differences in auditory perception have been identified. Infants can be trained to turn their heads in anticipation of rewards after they hear a subtle tone change; using this technique, we can determine the age at which individual babies can detect these changes. In short, if a baby cannot detect a tone change, they will only turn their head to the clanging monkey *after* the box lights up. Werker (2000) documented that 6-month-old babies turned their heads in anticipation of rewards as they detected subtle sound changes in unfamiliar, nonnative languages. However, infants older than 6 months were unable to make such detections when listening to these unfamiliar speech sounds. This evidence indicates that we are born able to learn any language but gradually lose this ability as we become exposed to our native language.

VRF constitutes a legitimate hearing test for infants older than 5 months, and computer technology exists to analyze infant responses to subtle auditory changes (administered via the computer). The responses are then analyzed and profiled into a hearing-ability category, some of which represent specific types of hearing impairment (Cobo-Lewis & Eilers, 2001).

Because VRF performance is dependent on head turning, it does not work well with very young infants. However, procedures have been developed to study auditory processes in even younger infants. Lynne Olsho and colleagues (1987) developed a procedure in which the baby is exposed to both continuous and changing sounds. During this presentation, an observer notes changes in the infant's behavior, such as eye widening and slight head movements; babies show slight movements as they detect subtle changes in auditory stimuli. The observer is privy only to the infant's behavior and is unaware of the progression of auditory stimuli. This method, termed the **Observer-based Psychoacoustical Procedure**, can be used with infants as young as 2 weeks old (Werner & Bargones, 1992).

Physiological measures, such as heart rate and electrical activity in the brain, can be used to study auditory sensory abilities in both newborns and fetuses in the prenatal period; because fetuses can detect changes in auditory stimuli, integrity to the auditory system must be present before birth. In one study, pregnant women recited a short children's rhyme each day for several weeks. Later, the fetuses were exposed to both the familiar and an unfamiliar rhyme. Amazingly, the heart rates of the fetuses declined as they were read the familiar rhyme; they had "learned" the acoustical features of the stimuli (DeCasper et al., 1994)! Expectant mothers who talk to their unborn babies are not just talking to an empty room, which explains why newborns prefer her voice to that of a stranger (DeCasper & Fifer, 1980).

Cross-Modal Transfer

How would you respond if something slimy were placed in your hand when your eyes were closed? Most people would *visualize* something repellent in their hand, such as a slug. In this case, an object that had stimulated one modality or sense (touch) is perceived by another modality (vision). Such **cross-modal transfer** is thought to represent a complex cognitive process.

Tactile-visual paradigms are frequently used to assess cross-modal transfer; the infant first touches an object without seeing it (Rose & Orlian, 2001), and later, the object is visually presented, along with novel stimuli. Infant preference for the novel stimulus is presumed to reflect tactile visual cross-modal abilities. This ability requires sophisticated cognitive skills. The baby must experience the initial stimuli, transfer the stimuli to another modality, and then recognize he has experienced it before.

There are also methods to assess oral-visual (Meltzoff & Borton, 1979) and auditory-visual (Pickens, 1994) transfer. Although many utilize preferential looking methods to assess cross-modal abilities, physiological measures can be used to identify neural mechanisms that underlie this process. In one study, researchers had 8-month-old infants grasp, touch, and manipulate a small cross. Next, they were shown pictures of the cross, along with a novel stimulus. Throughout the procedures, the researchers monitored electrical activity in the brain, and documented stronger evoked potentials during the presentation of the novel, visual stimulus (Nelson, Henschel, & Collins, 1993).

What Do You Think?

Compare and contrast methods of assessing infant vision, hearing, and cross-modal transfer. What methods seem to be most favored by researchers at the present time?

Summary of Infant Sensation and Perception

In this section we discussed different methods of assessing sensation and perception. Age is very important in such studies; for example, strong behavioral responses to a sensation during the newborn period may reflect a highly developed nervous system. However, a similar reaction at age 1 may indicate poor self-regulation. Increasingly, researchers are using multiple methods to assess infant sensation and perception; for example, we can use behavioral responses and corresponding physiological recordings to make judgment about infant abilities. Although many researchers still study single sensory and perceptual modalities, increasing numbers are researching cross-modal transfer development.

Cognition

It is difficult to discuss infant cognition without first paying homage to the great Swiss theorist Jean Piaget. Piaget is credited with developing a comprehensive four-stage theory of infant/child cognitive development. In the infant **sensorimotor stage** (Stage 1), he stipulated that cognition during infancy develops across the six substages outlined in Table 4.1.

Piaget theorized that the infant's physical experiences with objects leads to an understanding of object integrity—that is, when a toy disappears from the visual field, it is not gone forever. Such competency, according to Piaget, *does not result from simple observation*

TABLE 4.1   *Piaget's Sensorimotor Stage (Birth–2 Years)*

Sensorimotor Substage	Typical Behaviors
1. Reflexes (birth–1 month)	Spontaneous reflexes, such as sucking, grasping, and looking.
2. Primary circular reactions (1–4 months)	Highly focused on self, may repeatedly suck on, or open and close, hands. Knowledge of objects is limited; most objects are mouthed.
3. Secondary circular reactions (4–8 months)	More focus on external world and objects. Will look for objects and engage in simple visually guided object manipulation.
4. Coordination of secondary reactions (8–12 months)	Goal-directed behavior, such as pulling string to obtain a toy. Initial understanding regarding the permanence and purpose of objects (e.g., rings bells or rolls car).
5. Tertiary circular reactions (12–18 months)	Behavior becomes more creative and will engage in behavior to produce effects. Can integrate objects in functional ways—for example, will put a fork on a saucer.
6. Mental combinations and representational thought (18–24 months)	Can mentally represent objects not present. For example, may use a stick as a telephone during pretend play.

but rather from *physical experience with objects.* In addition, as babies become more experienced with objects, they develop rules for the common and uncommon properties of multiple objects, and an understanding of the world, in terms of space, time, and number.

In this next section, common methods for testing Piaget's ideas will be described; you will note that some of the most popular methods were developed by information-processing researchers who study infant attention and perception. This is ironic, because Piaget stipulated that sensory and perceptual processes had little impact on cognitive development, unless coupled with physical, "hands on" experiences with objects.

Object Concept Formation

According to Piaget (1954), in order to develop accurate concepts about objects, infants must understand that objects remain permanent and intact after they leave the visual field—hence the term **object permanence**. Through physical experience, babies come to understand that their actions directly affect objects; for example, pulling the cat's tail makes him run away. In other cases, such actions have no bearing on objects; for example, the cat will not put milk in your bottle, no matter how much you fuss.

Piaget developed simple procedures for assessing object permanence. In his classic object-hiding tasks, the infant was shown an object, which was then moved completely, or partially, out of the baby's visual field. For example, the experimenter might show the baby a stuffed animal, and then make the toy "disappear" by placing it under a napkin. The infant's tendency to "search" for the object, through eye movements, reaching, and grasping were used as markers for object concept knowledge.

Piaget suggested that infants would not search for hidden objects until they had developed purposeful goal-directed behavior (around 8 months). Goal-directed behavior, such as obtaining a toy that is out of reach with a stick, develops through the coordination of multiple ideas: Idea 1—Moving the toy with a stick; Idea 2—Grasping the toy that is now in reaching distance. Piaget noted that infants rarely searched for hidden objects before 8 months, yet by 8 months, most infants will readily search for an object placed under a single napkin.

However, what happens if you take out a second napkin (Location B), place it beside the original napkin (Location A), and then hide the object under the second napkin? Babies between 8 and 12 months will consistently search for the object *under the original hiding place!* Piaget theorized that such **AB search errors** resulted from initial mental constraints on object concept learning, and speculated that objects cease to exist in the baby's mind if *they have not been actually acted upon by the infant.* This finding underscores the essence of his theory—that is, that cognitive development is largely contingent on physical experiences and motor development (hence the term *sensorimotor development*). In the case of the AB search error, the infant looks under the original hiding place, because he trusts his own past experience with the task more than his current visual perception of the experimenter's actions.

Since the development of Piaget's manual search tasks, other methods have been used to mark object concept development. Baillargeon and colleagues (1987, 1991) found that manipulating circumstantial features of hidden objects influences infant visual scanning. Consider the series of events depicted in Figure 4.8. In the habituation task, the infant sees a box rise off the floor, followed by a car going down a ramp, passing behind the box, and emerging on the other side. Next, then are shown "possible" or "impossible" events. In the possible event, a toy that blocks the car's progress is removed before the box is lowered. In the impossible event, the toy remains, the box is lowered, and it appears to the infant that the car traveled right through the object! Baillargeon noted that even 3.5-month-old infants displayed lengthier visual attention to the impossible event, implying

Test events
Possible event

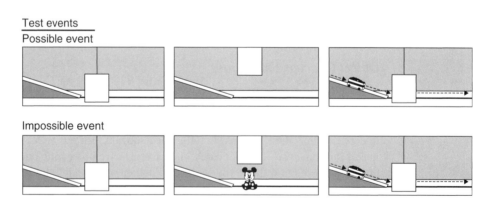

Impossible event

FIGURE 4.8 *Possible/Impossible Barrier Task.* In the possible event, the toy is removed before the box is lowered, but in the impossible event, the toy is not removed, so it appears that the car must pass through the toy to get through the box. Lengthy visual attention to the impossible event would imply that the infant is "surprised" at the series of actions, and must understand the permanence of objects.

Adapted from Baillargeon, R., & DeVos, J. (1991). Object permanence in young infants: Further evidence. *Child Development, 62,* p. 1237. Reprinted with permission of the Society for Research in Child Development.

that the infant's understanding of the rules regarding the integrity of objects develops well before an infant will manually search for hidden objects.

These newer habituation methods allow us to examine visual search/fixation behavior during hiding tasks in infants who are incapable of reaching. Demonstrating that young babies look longer at cars supposedly passing through brick walls than unblocked vehicles suggests that object concept develops well before infants begin reaching for objects and develop goal-oriented behavior. These data contradict Piaget's notion that extensive motor experiences (e.g., reaching and grasping) are required for object concept development. However, does extended infant gaze at such impossible events mean that they really understand the integrity of objects? This question is a concern, because in the standard A-B search paradigm babies who stare for a hidden object in a *correct* location for an extended period of time *subsequently reach in the wrong location* (Hofstadter & Reznick, 1996).

Of course, the looking tasks developed by Baillargeon are similar to response-expectancy methods. In short, babies use visual-recognition memory to anticipate the spatial location of objects. Unfortunately, these methods do not assess what infants know *about their own effect on objects* (Haith & Benson, 1998). In all likelihood, reaching tasks may put more strain and demand on infant information processing. The infant must visually anticipate where a hidden object will be located and keep that image in mind as they initiate reaching behavior. It is possible that different neural mechanisms are responsible for simple visual searching and coordinated visual and reaching behavior (Munakata, 2001). Because the human visual system develops so early, it is possible that coordination between visual and motor activity does not become consolidated until much later in infancy (as originally suggested by Piaget). Thus, babies may be able to anticipate the spatial locations of objects as they come in and out of view but are not able to competently act upon those until they can forecast a connection between their behavior and the outcome of events.

What Do You Think?

How have methodological advances influenced our thinking regarding the development of object concept? Why do more recent findings challenge Piaget's assumptions regarding the role of motor development in cognitive development? Why might babies initially gaze in the correct location for an object yet reach in the incorrect direction?

Categorization

If you were asked to memorize a series of objects—cat, pipe, shoe, dog, cigar, and hat—would you recall the objects in the exact order, or would you categorize the information (e.g., hat-shoe, cat-dog, cigar-pipe) to make it easier to recall? The development of categorization abilities represents an important skill; instead of simply noticing the isolated features of an object, we actively contrast common features across objects or events. Piaget presumed that babies could not develop an understanding of such commonalities until they could acknowledge the existence of objects, and *represent* these objects in memory. Thus, he speculated that categorization abilities were not well developed before 18 months of age.

To test this premise, habituation and paired-comparison paradigms have been used to study categorization skills in young infants (Cohen & Younger, 1984). For example, Quinn, Eimas, and Rosenkrantz (1993) showed 3- and 4-month-old infants pictures of cats until they became familiar with them. Next, they paired pictures of other objects (e.g., dogs, horses) beside cats *represented by other breeds.* Because the babies looked longer at the non-feline pictures, it was deduced that they had categorized relevant features from the original stimuli (e.g., whiskers).

There are growing concerns regarding such habituation and paired-comparison paradigms. As stated earlier, it is hard to discern "what is mentally going on" when an infant stares at one object rather than another. Categorization implies an *active cognitive process* that involves the generalization of behavior to new stimuli (e.g., Persian cat) that share similar features with familiar stimuli (e.g., Calico cat) (Haith & Benson, 1998). Does a loss of attention to the slightly different object accurately reflect this process?

It's possible to study a "more active" categorization process; for example, instrumental conditioning methods have been used to assess infant categorization. In one study, 3-month-old babies were trained to kick a mobile that contained blocks of the same shape (e.g., the letter A). Next, the infants were shown mobiles that contained blocks with similar, yet not exact, shapes (e.g., the letter A in different configurations) or with completely different shapes (e.g., the number 2). Because the infants displayed more kicking behavior in response to mobiles with similar shapes, it was concluded that the babies had categorized the relevant information from the original stimuli (Hayne, Rovee-Collier, & Perris, 1987).

Another method that can be used with older, mobile infants is the **sequential-touching task** (Mandler, Fivush, & Reznick, 1987). In this procedure, the infant is given eight objects; four represent one category (e.g., cars), the other four represent another (e.g., dogs). Infants are deemed to possess categorization skills if they engage in "categorization runs," or the tendency to repeatedly touch the items representing one category rather than the other. Manipulating the objects within sequential-touching tasks allows us to make fine-grained analyses regarding what infants are capable of doing regarding categorization. Mandler and colleagues (1991) found that 18-month-old infants displayed categorization runs when shown animals and vehicles, yet could not exhibit this behavior when presented dogs and rabbits until 24–30 months old.

Deferred imitation represents an additional method of studying infant categorization skills. We can model toys and then observe the infants' behavior as they are exposed to unfamiliar toys that possess similar or dissimilar characteristics as the original stimuli. The fact that infants prefer to play with objects from the previously witnessed categories provides strong evidence that infants use categorization skills to learn and spur recall (Barnat, Klein, & Meltzoff, 1996).

We have described methods of studying categorization skills regarding visual stimuli; however, creative methods have also been developed to assess this competency across other sensory modalities. In conditioned head-turning paradigms, it has been noted that infants less than a year of age can detect subtle similarities and differences in melodies and rhymes (Hayes, Slater, & Brown, 2001; Morrongiello, 1986). Also, studies of preferential listening using high-amplitude sucking methods have shown that newborns can detect similarities and differences in vowel and consonant sounds (Aldridge, Stillman, & Bower, 2001; Shi, Werker, & Morgan, 1999). Young babies

What Do You Think?

A parent asks you to define categorization, as well as how to assess it in young babies. Define and explain the term and give the parent some advice on how she might improve categorization skills in her baby.

can note that "ba" and "bi" contain similar features, indicating that infants very early in the developmental process can organize sounds into meaningful patterns or categories.

What do the results of this research using such creative methods tell us? First, it is apparent that Piaget underestimated the competency of infants regarding categorization skills. In addition, the fact that premobile infants can form categories through perceptual experiences suggests that Piaget also underestimated the importance of basic perceptual functioning and its impact on learning and memory.

Space, Time, and Number

Object experience sets the tone for the development of abstract abilities, such as an understanding of space, time, and number. As infants become interested in combining objects, important learning must take place regarding the spacing and spatial location of objects (in relation to each other, as well as to the baby) the sequencing or timing of events, and the quantity of objects.

Space.   Acredolo (1978) developed an ingenious method of studying spatial orientation and location in infants. In her paradigm, 6-, 11-, and 16-month old infants were seated at a table with a room full of windows. Using a conditioned head-turning paradigm, the infants were trained to look at one particular window. Next, they were positioned on the opposite side of the table; only the older babies looked toward the correct window after being repositioned. Of course, such a task only assesses the infant recall abilities regarding location, because the baby is not given any hints or cues regarding the correct location. In another study, even young infants turned their heads to the correct location when the original window contained blinking lights and bright stripes (Acredolo & Evans, 1980).

One problem is that it takes a long time to get younger babies to look at the right window *during the training period.* It is conceivable that these babies possessed good spatial knowledge, yet were used to looking in a direction because of the large number of training trials. In response to this concern, Bai and Bertenthal (1992) developed the very simple object-hiding procedure depicted in Figure 4.9. In this method, the infant observes a toy hidden under a cup; thus there is no extended training phase. After familiarizing the baby with the task, either the baby or the table is repositioned. Next, the infant is allowed to search for the toy. Why the repositioning of the baby or the table? Simply put, the most robust infant learning occurs in conjunction with both mental and motor experience (a la Piaget). If this premise is true, then more correct responses should occur when the infant's location (as opposed to that of the table) has changed. This was exactly what these researchers documented.

Consider two important theoretical/methodological issues: First, because motor development is tied to spatial knowledge development, locomotor status (precrawling versus crawling) might be a more important study variable than chronological age. Second, landmarks, such as brightly colored lights, can prompt spatial orientation in younger infants, probably because different memory systems are tapped by landmark (recognition) or no landmark (recall) manipulations; free recall is thought to place much more strain on the information-processing system. Thus, when testing memories for location, it is important to define exactly what type of ability—recall or recognition—you wish to assess.

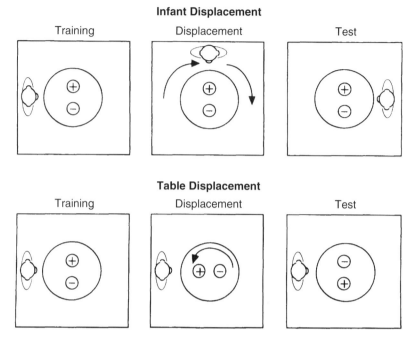

FIGURE 4.9   *Infant/Object Displacement Task.* In the top panel, the infant is repositioned around the table. In the bottom panel, the infant remains in place; however, the table is turned. Infants were more likely to guess correct object placement when they are repositioned (i.e., top panel) because learning is occurring in conjunction with both mental *and* motor experience.

From, Bai, D., & Bertenthal, B. (1992). Locomotor status and the development of spatial search skills. *Child Development, 63*, p. 218. Reprinted with permission of the Society for Research in Child Development.

Time.   When infancy researchers refer to infant time knowledge, they are referring to knowledge about the temporal ordering of events. For example, when an infant raises her arms in the presence of a parent, she is anticipating that an event will occur in time. Likewise, snatching a napkin that conceals an attractive toy requires the infant to initiate behaviors that are co-ordinated with time, as well as order. As infants mature, they gradually become used to the timing and order of events during daily routines (e.g., the bib is put on before supper).

However, although it is one thing to anticipate an event occurrence, it is quite another to *coordinate a series of actions* to produce a desired effect. For example, picture a nice, shiny toy that is resting on the end of a piece of cloth. Unfortunately, there is a barrier blocking the cloth. To get the toy (goal), the infant must *first* knock away the barrier (Action 1), and *second* pull the cloth (Action 2). **Elicited imitation** is a way to demonstrate the infant's ability to temporally order events; for example, we can model a series of actions—such as putting a dress on a doll, and then brushing her hair—encourage the infant to repeat these actions, and then later observe the infant's sequence of behavior.

This approach lends itself to creative manipulations. For example, one can manipulate the number of action sequences; in one condition, the infant may be asked to perform two steps (as depicted in the previous paragraph), in another three steps (e.g., wet the table, wipe the table with a towel, throw the towel away). Also, the infant can be exposed to highly familiar (e.g., bath or feeding sequences) or novel (attaching train cars, putting them on a track, putting a stuffed animal in the first car) events that require temporal sequencing. The results of research using such procedures has demonstrated that infants, as young as 11.5 months, can temporally order simple sequences depicting both novel and familiar events (Bauer & Mandler, 1992).

In summary, there are a variety of methods for assessing infant thinking regarding time. With relatively young infants (e.g., 2–3 months), we can examine simple response expectancies that provide a window into how well babies can anticipate future events. As infants begin to reach and grasp, we can observe the sequence of their problem-solving actions as they strive to meet a desired goal. Finally, we can observe the emergence of script development (i.e., routines that have structure and order) through elicited imitation paradigms.

Number.   Infants less than 6 months of age have rudimentary numerical awareness; for example, in habituation studies, infants show interest shifts when numerical amounts are altered (Starkey, Spelke, & Gelman, 1990). However, this awareness is quite limited. Although young infants can discriminate among small numbers of items (e.g., 11 versus 111), such abilities diminish with exposure to larger units (e.g., 1111 versus 11111).

The results of habituation experiments do not shed light on the process behind numerical awareness. It is unclear whether babies are using a computational process or simply notice that one set of numbers takes up more room than the other (Haith & Benson, 1998). However, this concern can be eliminated using response-expectancy paradigms. For example, consider the case in which a picture is shown in a young infant's left vision field *twice*, followed by a *single* presentation to the right side ($Left_1$, $Left_2$, Right order). This numerical sequence is repeated; however, the timing of the stimulus presentation is altered so that the infant will not simply get used to a cadence or timing pattern. Using such a procedure, even 3-month-old babies quickly look to one side in anticipation of the picture (Canfield & Haith, 1991). In fact, slightly older babies can anticipate the occurrence of the pictures using a more complex numerical series (e.g., $Left_1$, $Left_2$, $Left_3$, Right order); thus young infants can use numerical information to guide behavior (Canfield & Smith, 1996).

Can infants actually calculate math problems? In one study, Wynn (1992) directed the attention of 5-month-old infants to a little stage with a small curtain. In the "addition" condition, an experimenter, concealed behind the stage, introduced a doll, and then lowered the stage curtain. Next, the experimenter behind the stage displayed another doll, and then put the doll behind the curtain—you and I would automatically assume there would be two dolls on stage. In the "correct result" trial, the curtain was raised revealing two dolls, whereas the "incorrect result" trial revealed one doll. A similar set of trails was conducted to simulate a "subtraction condition." Throughout this study, the infant's looking behavior was recorded; infants looked longer at the incorrect results. The researchers concluded that the longer gaze fixation was caused by the infant's "surprise" over the incorrect result, and that such abilities result from innate, or prewired abilities (because they can be assessed so early in life).

Some are skeptical regarding the infant's ability to calculate numerical problems; some children have difficulty calculating very simple math problems until age 3 or 4 (Houde, 1997). Also, one recent study using highly similar methods failed to replicate Wynn's (1992) original findings (Wakeley, Rivera, & Langer, 2000). Although it does appear that even 3-month-old infants are capable of discriminating small sets of objects (e.g., 2 versus 3), the ability of infants to actually calculate math problems is highly debatable.

Summary of Infant Cognition Methods

We have overviewed methodologies that have been used to study the tenets of Piaget's theory of infant cognitive development. Although he developed some fascinating procedures for validating his assertions (e.g., object-hiding tasks), a chief drawback of his methods rests with mobility requirements. Because young infants are not capable of coordinated motor activity, it is virtually impossible to test the competencies of young babies using some of his methods.

As you have learned, the performance of very young infants in habituation, response expectancy, and elicited imitation paradigms suggests that premobile infants are capable of important cognitive abilities well before Piaget theorized they would be. The fact that premobile infants understand the integrity and categorical properties of objects, the spatial location of self in relation to objects, and acquire simple rules regarding time and number, strongly challenges the notion that physical experience is a mandatory requirement for such acquisition.

We have at our disposal a large amount of information regarding what babies can and cannot do. Not surprisingly, infancy experts have developed a number of standardized tests that tap into many of the abilities that we have covered throughout this chapter. We now turn to a sampling of these methods.

Testing Infant Mental Development

In this section, you will learn about two popular, standardized tests of infant mental abilities. My decision to limit our discussion to the *Bayley Scales of Infant Development (BSID)* and the *Battelle Developmental Inventory (BDI)* is multifold. First, these two instruments are widely used for research and have been standardized on large, representative populations; scores yielded by these tests are easy to interpret and can be compared to standard scores. Second, the Bayley and Battelle are easy to learn, provided the student has taken an assessment class, understands the importance of infant state, and is supervised by a trained expert. These tests are widely used in practice settings, and scores are used to screen infants for intervention purposes.

Bayley Scales of Infant Development

The *BSID* (Bayley, 1993) represents one of the most widely used infant assessment instruments. Originally developed in 1933, this instrument has been updated several times. The 1993 edition (BSID-II) was administered to a large number of infants and children (over 1,500) from a diverse sample selected from different regions of the United States, and thus represents the best-standardized infant diagnostic measure. Bayley test results often guide the intervention plans for at-risk infants (e.g., preterms) and may dictate whether a child qualifies for state-funded early intervention (Ross & Lawson, 1997).

The 1993 Bayley manual is very easy to read, and contains explicit administration and scoring instructions, sampling, and psychometric information. A "Bayley Kit" that contains all of the necessary stimulus materials accompanies the manual. The BSID-II contains three major scales; sample items for the mental scale are depicted in Table 4.2. It is rare that we have to administer every Bayley item. When testing a baby for the first time, we generally begin with several items that the infant can easily pass (and omit items that fall below this basal threshold). Once the infant has failed a series of items (3 for mental, 2 for motor), you

TABLE 4.2 *Sample Items from Bayley Mental Development Scale (Bayley, 1993)*

Skill	Item
Habituation	Shake rattle behind baby. Note orienting response, as well as decline in attention after repeated presentation.
Object permanence	Bang a spoon on the table to attract infant's attention. Drop spoon and give credit if baby looks for fallen spoon.
Memory	Determine if baby can remember simple sequences, such as "Pat the table and then touch your nose."
Problem solving	Examiner places toy inside a clear box with one open end. Infant is given credit if she reaches inside box to obtain toy within 20 s.
Language	Note word utterances and baby's use of past tense.
Social problem solving	Ask the child what people do when they go to store. Credit is given if evidence for script development is present ("We get groceries, pay for them, and put them in the car")
Perceptual organization	Child is able to build a simple 2-piece bridge that connects 2 endpoints.

stop the exam, so, there may be a large number of items not administered. Although many items are rated through actual task administration, others can be scored via observation—if the baby walks, you do not have to ask him to walk—or caregiver interview.

Mental Scale. This scale has 178 items that assess language development, object permanence, auditory and visual habituation, problem-solving skills, memory, social problem solving and perceptual organization. Habituation, object permanence, and memory items have been added to the newest version for younger infants. These additions are not surprising; we have already covered research that points to the precocious cognitive abilities of young babies.

Motor Scale. We discussed this scale in the previous chapter. This scale contains 111 items that assess fine and gross motor skills, including the ability to grasp objects, eye-hand-foot coordination, walking, and sitting.

Behavior Rating Scale. This scale measures infant social and biobehavioral functioning, such as attention and arousal (e.g., affect, response to distress), orientation and engagement (e.g., fearfulness), regulatory abilities (e.g., frustration), and motor quality (e.g., tremors). Do the concepts of arousal, engagement, and regulation seem familiar? Recall that such abilities reflect the integrity of the nervous system. This scale is a wonderful addition to the BSID-II; it will be exciting to see whether the scale predicts long-term functioning.

The Behavioral Rating Scale does not require the administration of additional tasks. To complete this inventory, the administrator carefully observes the infant's behavior during the administration of the Mental and Motor Scales. Like the other scales, not every item is scored; rather, the items are grouped at three age levels (1–5 months; 6–12 months; 13–42 months). Every item pertaining to the Attention/Arousal scale is scored for babies between 1 and 5 months; however, such items are not scored for older babies.

For the Mental and Motor Scales, the examiner takes note of the number of passed items and, using the manual, converts these raw scores into standardized Mental Development (MDI) and Psychomotor Index (PDI) scores. The mean for both indexes is 100, with a standard deviation of 15. Scores of 69 or lower on either index would signify delay. Scoring the Behavior Rating Scale is more subjective. Whereas the Mental and Motor Scale items are judged on a pass or fail basis, the BRS items are rated on a 1–5 scale.

The BSID has good short-term test-retest reliability; however, the reliability for the Behavior Rating Scale is not as robust as for the other two scales. This could be because of the subjective nature of the scoring system or because arousal and regulation are less stable over time than mental and motor abilities. The BSID-II, and earlier versions of the Bayley function very well as an outcome, or dependent, measure. A number of vulnerable populations (e.g., medically compromised preterm infants, substance-exposed infants, low-birth-weight babies) are likely to display developmental delays on this instrument (Jacobson & Jacobson, 1995).

Although it is expected that item changes and the addition of the Behavior Rating Scale will increase the predictive power of this instrument, its predictive validity remains an empirical question mark. That is, this instrument has a mediocre track record regarding predictive power. One might wonder whether we will ever develop an instrument that forecasts competence over long periods of time. The nature of what exactly constitutes "competence" changes dramatically over time. Can we really expect a baby who walks at a very young age to also display similar motor prowess at age eight? Also, if infants who score low on the Bayley receive intensive intervention, their mental and motor competence may change.

Battelle Developmental Inventory (BDI)

The 341-item *Battelle Developmental Inventory* (BDI; Newborg et al., 1984) is a standardized instrument that is rated via item administration, interview, and infant observation. The BDI yield scores for five domains: Personal-Social, Adaptive, Motor, Communication, and Cognition. In addition, each of these domains can be subdivided; for example, the Cognitive Domain can be segregated into perceptual discrimination, memory, academic and reasoning skills, and conceptual abilities.

Unlike the Bayley, the Battelle manual offers ways to modify the test for motorically, visually, and hearing-impaired children. Also, the BDI covers the newborn period to age 8. It is not surprising that many agencies devoted to child welfare across the United States use the BDI. It can be administered to individuals with motor and perceptual impairments, and children receiving interventions can be tracked over time using the same instrument.

Because the BDI has not been used for as long as the Bayley has, it possesses a less robust psychometric history; however, it does have good test-retest and interrater reliability. Unlike the original Bayley Scales, the BDI domains modestly correlate with standardized measures of later child intelligence (e.g., .40–.55). This finding could be because the BDI provides a more comprehensive assessment of child competencies than the original Bayley (Gibbs, 1990). Again, with its battery of new items and the Behavioral Rating Scale, it will be interesting to see whether the Bayley Scales of Infant Development-II (1993) possess predictive power similar to that of the BDI. If it does not, I would expect the popularity of the Battelle to rise.

Summary of Infant Tests of Mental Development

What Do You Think?

Will we ever be able to develop a test of infant mental development that strongly forecasts the development of intelligence during childhood? Based on your reading so far, what abilities would you assess if you could assemble such a test?

The BSID and BDI are widely used instruments. Normative data has been established using large representative samples, and users can contrast test results (either in individual or group form) with established norms. Although both tests include scales that assess mental development, the predictive power of infant developmental tests can be enhanced by assessing a broad range of abilities, including motor, language, and social development.

Play Assessment

Because play is theorized to both promote and reflect cognitive competence (Piaget 1954; 1951), researchers have explored ways to assess and quantify this behavior. In the spirit of Piaget's theory, these assessments include strategies for assessing developmental shifts in play behavior and mental functioning that range from (a) random activities involving single objects (e.g., mouthing or banging one object at a time) to (b) behavior that is modified to fit the characteristics of an object (i.e., functional play), such as ringing a bell, to (c) functional play involving the interrelationships between toys or objects (e.g., hammering a peg into a peg board), to (d) pretend or symbolic play, first using single objects (e.g., pretending a stick is a gun) and then involving multiple objects (e.g., pushing a series of blocks like a train) (Bond, Creasey, & Abrams, 1990). These activities dovetail nicely with Piaget's sensorimotor stage.

Methodological Considerations

There are methodological considerations for those who wish to use play assessment as a tool to evaluate infant mental abilities:

- *Not for use with young infants.* Infants under 12 months of age usually do not play with toys in very interesting ways. The manner in which babies mouth and randomly manipulate objects probably predicts little, so I recommend not using play assessments for such young babies.
- *My toys or the infant's?* Using the infant's toys presents methodological concerns. You will have to test infants in their own homes, and the toy sets are not held constant from infant to infant. There is logic to using the toys suggested by the assessment authors. First, infants usually "attack" the toy sets, because they include novel toys. Also, the range of toys—from simple spoons and cups to puzzle boards—is designed to encourage the interest of babies that differ in developmental status.
- *Why does the baby keep showing the parent the toys?* As play becomes more social, older infants are not content to play alone. Often, older infants (e.g., 18 months) will

bring toys to a parent to "see," and it is not uncommon for caregivers to say, for example, "*Why don't you call grandma on the toy phone?.*" If caregivers are present, they must be told to redirect the infant to the play materials, and withhold comments that may encourage higher levels of play (assuming this is not an intent of the assessment).

- *Unstructured (free play) or structured elicitation?* Should we simply observe the infant engaging in free play or attempt to encourage her to play at her top potential? The ultimate decision rests with the nature of your research questions. Unstructured assessments provide a good estimate of the infant's cognitive abilities in isolation from social factors that might moderate this process. In structured elicitation, we either model a set of desired actions with toys or encourage more sophisticated play behavior. Using such assessments, we can observe the infant's competence in response to a modeled task, and note the baby's top potential in play environments.

Infant Free-Play Assessments

There are a number of free-play assessments designed for infants under 2 years (Belsky & Most, 1981; Lowe & Costello, 1988; Morgan, Harmon, & Bennett, 1976; Rubenstein & Howes, 1976). These assessments are easy to administer, require brief testing times, and the authors provide detailed instructions regarding the test kits and coding instructions. To provide a flavor for these assessments, let's overview Belsky and Most's (1981) free-play method. In this assessment, the infant is observed playing with a set of toys for 30 min. The infant's play behaviors are recorded and then coded by noting the infant's most competent play within 10-second intervals; play can be classified as outlined in Table 4.3.

The 12 levels depicted in Table 4.3 can be used individually or grouped into three global ratings: (a) Low-level undifferentiated play (mouthing and simple manipulation); (b) Active transitional or functional play (functional, relational, functional-relational, and enactive naming); and, (c) High-level decontextualized or pretend play. In this respect, the assessment provides comprehensive coverage of Piaget's sensorimotor period, and allows for fine discriminations between levels of play sophistication. For example, rather than viewing pretend play as a global activity for older infants, it captures increasingly complex forms of pretense (Bond, Creasey, & Abrams, 1990).

Are free-play assessments valid? Although 12- to 24-month-old babies who display high levels of complex functional play, such as putting a cup on a saucer, are more cognitively advanced than their counterparts who display less advanced play (Jennings et al., 1979; Power & Radcliffe, 1989), it is debatable whether these play activities hold promise for making more long-term predictions regarding cognitive competence. As one colleague recently noted, "*I do not conduct play assessments until about 16 or 17 months of age; that's when really interesting things begin to happen.*" What does this statement mean? During the latter part of Piaget's sensorimotor period (18–22 months) babies are more adept at representational thought; they can represent objects no longer present. During this representational period, we see *heavy incorporation of symbolic activities* in infant play repertoires.

The aforementioned play assessments trace the development of symbolic play and lower-level functional play in infants. However, increasing interest in individual differences in infant symbolic play has led to the development of assessments that focus more on this ability (McCune-Nicolich, 1983). Westby (2000) has developed a theoretically guided

TABLE 4.3   *Belsky and Most's (1981) Play Categories*

Mouthing	Indiscriminate mouthing of objects.
Simple manipulation of objects	Visually guided manipulation; excludes shaking and banging of objects.
Functional	Manipulation that is appropriate for the object, such as ringing a bell or rolling a car.
Relational	Bringing together two objects in an unrelated manner, such as banging a plate with a stick.
Functional/relational	Bringing together objects in an appropriate manner, such as placing a toy phone on a hook.
Enactive naming	Approximate pretend play; for example, placing the toy phone to ear without making utterances.
Pretend self	Pretense directed toward self, such as feeding self with fork and making chewing sounds.
Pretend other	Pretense directed toward other, such as feeding a doll.
Substitution pretend	Substituting objects; for example, feeding self with stick.
Sequence pretend	Repetition of a single act of pretense, such as drinking from a toy bottle and then giving the doll a drink.
Sequence pretend substitution	Same as previous, except uses object substitution.
Double substitution	For example, treats stick as doll, covers with block, and says, "night, night."

assessment of symbolic play that can be used with children ranging from 8 months to 5 years of age. This system should be used in a lab, because the child should be assessed in "play areas" that include home, kitchen, and store areas. These areas likely encourage the expression of strongly represented scripts—seating dolls around a table, feeding them dinner, and washing dishes—that are reflected in the high-level symbolic play of older children.

Although Westby's system allows for the analysis of functional (e.g., bell ringing) and functional-relational (e.g., placing cup on saucer) play, the strong point of this assessment involves a behavioral checklist that allows raters to ascertain four important play behaviors that reflect advanced cognitive competencies: Representational abilities, script development, play organization, and the involvement of others in play activities. Children who receive high ratings can represent objects that are not present (e.g., using a pencil as a weapon), use highly developed and organized scripts or routines in their play (e.g., bakes cake in oven, feeds doll cake, washes dishes and puts them away), and actively involves others in play (e.g., says to doll, "I'll be the doctor and you be the nurse").

Perhaps now you can appreciate the beauty of free-play assessments. Unlike traditional tests of infant development, one does not need an "examiner." Play is an activity that infants naturally engage in, so you do not have to "pull" the mental activity out of the baby. Free-play assessments are also popular with those who work with infants and children with various impairments (e.g., autism; Down syndrome; speech and hearing difficulties). For example, potential examiner effects and biases are removed, and play assessments offer a robust way to assess the competencies of older children who possess low mental ages.

So, which play assessment is "right" for you? Why not consider several? Assuming infants are supplied a range of play materials and their performances videotaped, it is possible to compare and contrast infant performance across several play-assessment coding systems. It would be interesting to conduct such a study using a longitudinal method and document which assessment best correlates with later measures of cognitive competence.

Elicited-Play Assessments

Unlike infant free-play paradigms, elicited play assessments require the presence of a trained experimenter who models and encourages play behaviors. There are two broad methods that will be discussed: *mastery motivation* and *executive competence* paradigms.

Mastery Motivation Paradigms.   In elicited-imitation or **mastery motivation** paradigms, we model a series of play behaviors across tasks that vary in complexity, such as ringing bells on an activity center or placing pegs in a pegboard. Next, in free play, the child is observed unobtrusively for about three to five minutes across each modeled task. Four general behaviors can be coded: (a) nontask behavior (e.g., inattention to object); (b) visual attention (e.g., looking at object); (c) task-directed behavior (e.g., attempts to use object in appropriate way); and (d) success or solution of task or problem (Morgan & Harmon, 1984).

Thus, when using a mastery motivation paradigm, we focus as much on the process (*how* infants play and use objects) as on the product (*what* infants do with objects) of play behavior. What is so special about mastery motivation? According to White (1959), the roots of infant cognitive competence revolve around an intrinsic desire (or motivation) to directly affect our environment; task accomplishments promote learning as well as positive feelings of accomplishment. What meaningful data can be gathered using mastery motivation paradigms? Motivation assessment includes the infant's *affect* following completion of the activity, as well as *task latency*, or the time it takes the baby to begin the task. Also, noting the amount of time it takes to complete the task can assess infant *persistence*. Thus infant mastery motivation is closely linked to performance speed during task completion.

A great deal of research has gone into establishing the psychometric properties of mastery motivation paradigms. Infants who display high levels of persistence and pleasure over task completion have robust Bayley MDI scores and score high on intelligence tests (Bond, Creasey, & Abrams, 1990). Studies have documented motivational differences between handicapped and nonhandicapped children (MacTurk et al., 1985), and interrater reliability is often high. It is easy to see why reliability is high; you simply time the occurrences of task-directed behavior.

Executive Competence Paradigms.   Whereas Piaget felt that sophisticated infant play resulted from physical experiences with objects, other theorists, such as Vygotsky (1966), felt that social experiences influence the development of play and cognitive competence. According to Vygotsky, advanced cognitive abilities in infants and children do not happen automatically through simple experiences with objects; rather, one's top cognitive potential is achieved through interactions with competent members of one's family or community. Picture an infant who is given a toy car; she may mouth the car, examine its features, and throw it around the room. However, an older sibling may step in and demonstrate how to roll it and make car noises. Shortly, the infant repeats these actions, and demonstrates she possessed this *cognitive potential* all along. It is not surprising that initial pretend play often appears within the context of social interactions with caregivers (Haight & Miller, 1993).

Thus, there is a gap between the types of behaviors infants exhibit in free-play paradigms and what they may be capable of in the presence of a supportive mentor. Belsky and colleagues have developed a two-trial procedure to capture the baby's top cognitive potential, or competence (Belsky, Garduque, & Hrncir, 1984). Simply put, the researcher observes the infant's behavior during a 10-minute free-play procedure. Taking note of the toys that attracted the infant during the first trial, the researcher next attempts to encourage or elicit more competent play behavior by modeling high-level play behaviors during this next trial (e.g., "The baby's thirsty; can you give him a drink?").

Using Belsky and Most's (1981) play coding system (See Table 4.3), three different scores can be computed: (a) *performance*, or highest level of free play; (b) *competence*, or highest level of elicited play; and (c) **executive capacity**, or the difference between performance and competence. In the spirit of mastery motivation paradigms, the brightest and most motivated infants should display little difference between performance and competence during these procedures.

When used strictly as an assessment of cognitive competence, executive-capacity paradigms have yielded disappointing results. In one study, 12- and 18-month executive competence was not significantly correlated with Bayley mental scores (Hrncir, Speller, & West, 1985). However, when considered within a social context, executive-capacity studies have yielded very interesting data. Infants with close emotional relationships or secure attachments with caregivers display smaller discrepancies between performance and competence when contrasted with babies who have anxious or resistant attachment relationships. However, when "stuck" on play materials, these very same secure infants often quickly seek assistance from parents (Teti et al., 1991). Because there is an obvious social component to play as infants mature, we will reconnect with the fascinating construct of play in later chapters.

Summary of Play Assessment

Play assessments are easy to conduct and offer numerous advantages over traditional tests of infant development. All infants across the world like to play, examiner effects are controlled, and the techniques often offer rich data when using handicapped populations. For example, a sample of children with Down syndrome may score very similarly on the Bayley Scale of Mental Development, yet display large individual differences when using a free- or elicited-play assessment (Bond et al., 1990).

What Do You Think?

What are the advantages and disadvantages of standardized tests of infant mental development and play assessments? Why might play assessment represent a culture-free test of mental development?

Chapter Summary

Perhaps now you can better appreciate the major tenets of lifespan development. For example, important learning and memory paradigms, such as habituation and response-expectancy methods, have led to the highly *scientific* study of important infant mental abilities. Through careful manipulation of experimental variables, and through the control of potential confounding variables (e.g., head turn preference), a rigorous scientific process has yielded important information about the nature of infant learning and information processing.

Our field is also *applied*. Although basic research regarding infant perception and cognition is scientifically interesting, one can visualize the practical importance of this work. The earlier we can spot problems, the better. Methodological advances in infant sensation and perception research now allow us to test for delays very early in life. Also, babies can be made more comfortable during painful medical procedures, and we may be able to save the lives of medically challenged infants through the simple act of touch.

Besides reviewing standard paradigms for assessing infant perceptual and cognitive processes, you were also exposed to more formal methods to assess mental abilities. In addition, the popularity of play assessments is rising, and there are a number of research teams working on standardizing popular play tests as you read this chapter. Clearly our field does a good job translating research into practice.

In the spirit of the *lifespan* nature of our discipline, where possible I overviewed important longitudinal work in this chapter. It is interesting that basic information-processing abilities (e.g., habituation speed) are modest predictors of intelligence up to age 11 (Rose & Feldman, 1995). Simple indicators of "quick thinking," are more effective predictors of later intelligence than standardized tests of infant mental development. Although developers of standardized tests of infant mental development are quickly adding items to better capture these infant information-processing abilities, the relationship between infant mental development and later cognitive competency will probably always be slippery in nature. Simply put, the cognitive competencies required for adjustment in young infants may not be the same competencies needed for robust intellect at age 14.

Research Navigator™ Exercise: Object Permanence Methods

The primary objective of this assignment is to learn more about methods used to assess object permanence. Go the Research Navigator™ website http://www.researchnavigator.com. In the "ContentSelect" section, choose the Psychology database, and type *object permanence* as a keyword. After reading a full-length article, try to answer the following questions:

1. What theoretical positions regarding objective permanence were presented?
2. What were the ages of the infants? Why did the author(s) choose this particular age range? How was object permanence assessed?
3. How were infant responses measured?
4. What were the main findings? What theoretical position was supported or not supported in the study?

5

Assessing Infant Socioemotional Development

One-year-old Jana and her mother are in the pediatric waiting room when some nearby construction suddenly starts up. Jana expresses a fearful response and begins crying; however, she immediately calms down after her mother picks her up. Jana survives her well-baby check-up, although she does crawl into her mother's lap after an inoculation.

Jana's emotional maturity is typical for a 1 year old; in fact, babies worldwide learn to express, experience, and regulate fundamental emotions in this fashion. Also, infants develop emotional relationships with their caregivers that are thought to have importance for the development of future attachment relationships, such as friendships, during childhood. The maturity of emotions, emotional regulation, and attachment relationships are also interrelated; Jana's mother provided important emotional support in the above example.

This chapter will describe strategies for assessing such infant emotional and social development. After reading this chapter, you should be able to:

- Identify strategies for assessing basic infant emotions, such as anger and fear.
- Describe ways to measure complex emotions, such as embarrassment and pride.
- Define emotion regulation, discuss how to measure it, and identify potential antecedents for its development, such as caregiver sensitivity.
- Describe strategies for identifying individual differences in attachment relationships.
- Describe the Adult Attachment Interview (AAI), and its classification system.

Capturing Early Emotional Development

"Well, Mom and Dad showed up at my apartment unexpectedly. I was really angry; I was in a bad mood anyway because of final exams. My heart was racing, but I stayed calm. I also felt guilty that my boyfriend was over when they dropped in. I could tell that my Dad was really pissed off because he kept rubbing his face. He doesn't really look mad; he just rubs his face when he is angry. My mom just lost it, she started yelling that my boyfriend and me shouldn't "live together"; she's just jealous."

After reading the vignette, can you see why it can be difficult to study emotional development? Some of her emotions, such as anger, are fundamental; others, such as guilt, are relationship-oriented. Also, there are discrepancies between her **emotional experience**, or subjective emotional impressions ("I'm angry"), **emotional expression** or outward appearance ("I stayed calm"), and **emotional state** ("My heart was really racing") or her physiological responses. Finally, she distinguishes between temporary feelings from this event and her more chronic *mood state*. *Emotions* are triggered via events that occur without warning, and forecast our subsequent behavior (e.g., flight, withdrawal, approach) (Frijda, Kuipers, & ter Schure, 1989). For example, you hear a gunshot (event), become frightened (emotion), and then run (behavior or action). In contrast, moods may be more chronic (e.g., lasting days or weeks), and result from more persisting circumstances. For example, final examinations may put you in a "bad mood."

Having provided some basic definitions, let's first discuss the family of emotions available to infants. Next, we will discuss popular ways to assess emotion regulation.

Assessing Basic Infant Emotions

In order to study emotional development, we need to overview core methodological issues. First, infants can express some basic emotions, such as joy, early in development, whereas others, such as pride, may not become apparent until early childhood. Developmental status, particularly *cognitive maturation*, is one variable to consider in this type of research. In addition, we must consider the nature of **emotional elicitors**, or events that we use to trigger emotional expressions in babies. Finally, once we do something to "move emotions," we must consider how to measure the infant's emotional response.

Cognitive Maturity

When can we reliably study emotions in infants? Some basic emotions, such as joy, have innate origins and are initially reflexive in nature—think of how newborns smile when they have gas (Izard & Ackerman, 2000). However, emotional experiences become cognitively driven over time; for example, adults fear a tax audit, because they can consider its ramifications. Thus, a *cognitive appraisal* ("What's the worst that will happen during this audit process?"), *precedes* the actual emotional experience ("YIKES!").

Thus, if emotional experience is dependent on cognitive maturity, there are constraints on how early we can study certain emotions. Lewis (2000) has developed a framework that describes the development of early emotions, such as anger, that are experienced by all babies across the world. This framework is depicted in Table 5.1. These basic emotions are believed to have innate origins; however, cognitive maturity also influences them. For instance, Cohn and Tronick (1983) documented that 3-month-old babies displayed joy (e.g., smiling) during interactions with mothers; however, they quickly exhibited more sober expressions when mothers were instructed to suddenly adopt "depressed" emotional expressions. The more somber expressions resulted from an expectancy violation; that is, the babies were used to a certain maternal emotional tone—a cognitive appraisal—that was disconfirmed.

TABLE 5.1 *Emotional Development During First Three Years of Life (Adapted from Lewis, 2000)*

Emotions	Cognitive Antecedent	Time
Primary/Basic Emotions		
Anger, sadness, fear, joy, surprise, disgust	Violation or confirmation of expectancy.	First six months
Self-Conscious Emotions		
Envy, empathy, embarrassment	Development of self-recognition self-awareness, and consciousness	Second half of second year
Evaluative Emotions		
Pride, shame, guilt	Acquisition and retention of cultural standards and rules	From 2.5 to 3 years

Although the primary emotions, such as joy, anger, fear, and sadness, emerge during the first 6 months of life, further advances in cognitive development contribute to a sharp upturn in emotional expressions in infants. As babies develop means-end and goal-oriented thinking, the absolute frequency of discrete emotions increases, as infants discover the joys of task accomplishment or anger over failure. Methodologically, we can more reliably study spontaneous emotional expressions as infants become aware that their actions produce consequences. The assessment of spontaneous emotional expressions can be best captured in infants capable of self-produced locomotion (e.g., crawling), which greatly assists them in obtaining objectives (joy over grabbing the remote control box) (Campos, Kermoain, & Zumbahlen, 1992).

The development of self-awareness during the second year of life gives rise to another class of emotions referred to as "self-conscious emotions," such as envy and empathy. We cannot become "green" with envy until we can compare our own status with others; thus, infants cannot show signs of embarrassment until they are capable of self-recognition (Lewis et al., 1989). How can we document that a baby is self-aware? It's pretty easy; all you need is a mirror and some rouge. In the "*rouge test*," you put a dab of rouge on the infant's nose and then hold up a mirror so the baby can see her face. If the baby touches her nose (as opposed to smiling or touching the mirror) it is a safe assumption that she is capable of self-recognition.

The development of moral thinking sets the stage for a new set of emotions. A young child cannot experience pride until he is capable of comparing his behavior to some type of societal standard. Gradually, children increasingly begin looking for the *approval or disapproval of others* as they negotiate important environmental tasks. Methodologically, things become more complex as we grapple with methods of assessing these self-evaluative emotions; instead of just looking at the child's facial expressions and body movements, we now must examine the child's interactions with another person (Stipek, Recchia, & McClintic, 1992).

Cognitive maturity is a prerequisite for more complex emotional development. This is an important consideration when designing research; for example, envy cannot

What Do You Think?

Why is cognitive maturity important to consider when designing research to assess emotional development in infants and children? How might it affect our choice of emotional elicitors and methods of assessing emotional experiences?

be studied until children become self-aware and can make social comparisons. Cognitive maturation is also important to consider when contemplating emotional elicitors and emotional response assessment. For example, a stranger's appearance may elicit differential emotions in different-aged children, and as emotional expressiveness becomes more internalized, we may need to assess a more complex array of variables—facial expressions, body movements, heart rate—to identify emotional experiences.

Emotional Elicitors

It is difficult to study spontaneous infant emotional expressions; most researchers do not want to chase infants around to capture fleeting emotional expressions that have low base rates. For that reason, researchers often contrive situations to "move emotions" in infants.

Eliciting Discrete Emotions.   Although newborns show occasional facial expressions that parallel discrete emotions, most research has focused on babies older than 2 months of age. For example, 2-month-old infants display angry emotional responses to inoculations or expectancy violations (Lewis, Alessandri, & Sullivan, 1990), whereas 4-month-old infants show angry expressions when their arms are restrained (Stenberg, Campos, & Emde, 1983). Likewise, sadness has been observed in 3-month-old babies during inoculations (Izard & Malatesta, 1987), mother–infant interactions, and reward withdrawal (Lewis, 2000). Finally, fear can be elicited in babies as young as 7 months through the presentation of unusual toys, masks, and the visual-cliff paradigm (Campos et al., 1983).

Parents or strangers can elicit emotional expressions. The sudden approach of a stranger reliably elicits fear in older infants, and caregiver separation in unfamiliar environments (e.g., waiting room) has been shown to trigger anger, sadness, or fear in babies as young as 6 to 8 months of age. Likewise, the reappearance of a caregiver after a separation often sparks joy and happiness in babies as young as 8 months of age (Lewis & Michalson, 1983).

Many landmark emotional-development studies involve the assessment of infant emotional expressions in the context of mother–infant interactions (Izard et al., 1995). Caregivers are the infant's natural "emotional partner," and these interactions elicit a wide range of emotions. Caregivers can be instructed to "play as you normally do," "act sad," "take away your baby's favorite toy," or "suddenly leave the room and return." The manipulations are almost limitless, and emotional expression can be put under strict experimental control (robust internal validity) with the baby's primary attachment figure (robust external validity).

Eliciting Self-Conscious Emotions.   How might you elicit self-conscious emotions such as embarrassment, envy, or empathy? Although envy has been largely ignored, embarrassment can be elicited as young as 22 months of age. In one study, toddlers displayed all of the signs of embarrassment (e.g., gaze aversion, hand gestures to face, hair, and other body parts) by viewing themselves in a mirror (Lewis et al., 1989).

Empathy has been documented in young toddlers by observing looks of concern (e.g., "motherly looks") and by physical assistance. In one study, toddler responses to the distress of other children in a day-care setting were observed. For example, when a toddler falls down and starts crying, what do the other toddlers do? Interestingly, the toddlers' expressions of empathy were dependent on socialization experiences. For example, not one toddler who had experienced physical abuse displayed any sign of empathy toward their distressed peers. Instead, the abused toddlers displayed anger or fear. Conversely, toddlers from "nonabusing" families showed concerned responses to these incidents (Main & George, 1985). These data demonstrate that emotional development is not simply governed by cognitive maturation.

Eliciting Self-Evaluative Emotions. When eliciting self-evaluative emotions, such as pride and shame, it is important to adopt a coding system that allows for distinctions between a higher-order emotion, such as pride, and more discrete emotional expressions, such as joy. Also, the developmental status of the child is clearly related to expressions of pride and shame. For example, children under 2 years of age typically show simple joy (e.g., smiling) after successfully completing a task, while slightly older children (2.5 years) will look toward a parent or experimenter for approval (i.e., sign of pride) (Stipek, Recchia, & McClintic, 1992). The emotional elicitation of pride and shame is also clearly affected by task difficulty. Three-year-old children show more pride after completing a difficult task, such as copying a difficult pattern, and more shame after failing an easy task, such as missing an easy basketball shot (Lewis, Alessandri, & Sullivan, 1992).

Like the elicitation of pride and shame, manipulations have been staged to induce guiltlike responses in preschoolers. Researchers interested in guilt often contrive "mishaps," in which children are led to believe that they have made a major mistake. For example, a child may be asked to take care of a doll, but unfortunately, when picked up, the leg falls off the doll! Coders subsequently rate the facial expressions and body movements of the child.

However, guilt in a 2-year-old is different from that in an older preschooler. For example, although toddlers may adopt "guilty" facial expressions after a mishap, older children squirm in their seats and fidget (Kochanska et al., 2002). This tendency for emotions to "leave the face" of older children probably has a lot to do with emotional-regulation maturity. However, cognitive development is not the only variable that influences guilt development; when contrasted to their peers with nondepressed mothers, toddlers with depressed mothers show less tension and frustration after these mishaps (Cole, Barrett, & Zahn-Waxler, 1992). These researchers speculate that such children may reduce their frustrations because they do not want to worry their depressed mothers.

Measuring Emotional Expression and States

Emotion measurement is very controversial; unlike an older child, infants cannot verbalize utterances such as "I'm mad." These utterances are reflections of one's subjective impression of an emotional event, or *emotional experience*. How do we know whether an infant is happy or sad? The material in Table 5.2 could clarify this issue. When assessing emotional experiences in infants, we can analyze facial expressions or physiological responses (e.g., heart rate). Also, we can measure specific actions or behaviors. For example, if emotional

TABLE 5.2 *Characteristics of Emotions (Adapted from Barrett & Campos, 1987; Frijda, 1994)*

Emotion	Adaptive Functions	Facial Expression	Physiological Reaction	Action Tendency
Anger	Attain difficult goals, overcome obstacles, communicate power	Brows lowered and pulled together, lips pulled tightly together	High heart rate and skin temperature, facial flushing	Active forward movement, removal of obstacles
Sadness	Conserve energy; learn which goals are realizable	Corners of mouth pulled downward, inner corner of brows moved upward	Low heart rate, low skin temperature	Disengagement, passive withdrawal
Fear	Avoid danger, both physical and psychological	Brows raised, eyes very wide and tense	High stable heart rate, "gasping" respiration	Flight, active withdrawal
Shame	Maintain social standards, communicate submission	Not documented	Low heart rate, facial blushing	Active or passive withdrawal, avoiding others, hiding self
Pride	Behave appropriately, maintain social standards	Not documented	High heart rate	Outward/upward movement, show accomplishments to others
Guilt	Learn and maintain moral and prosocial behavior	Not documented	High heart rate, irregular respiration	Inclination to make reparation, to inform others, and to punish self

experiences predictably influence actions, we code certain behaviors (e.g., flight) to infer the infant's actual emotional experience. In older subjects, we can examine vocal patterns (e.g., tension), and more complex behavioral sequences (e.g., looking at another person).

Assessing Infant Facial Expressions. The analysis of facial expressions represents a meaningful variable, because there is an innate connectedness between emotional expression and feeling (Izard, 1977). This connectedness is strong until maturational and cultural and socialization experiences influence our tendency to suppress emotions through facial expression. Infant facial expressions, of course, are also important, because they serve a powerful communicative function within the infant-caretaker context, and may reliably forecast important action or behavioral tendencies (e.g., flight) (Frijda & Tcherkassof, 1997).

How do we code infant facial expressions into emotional categories (e.g., anger)? Izard and colleagues have developed two widely used systems, the *Maximally Discriminative Facial Movement Coding System* (MAX; Izard, 1989) and the *System for Identifying Affect Expressions by Holistic Judgments* (Affex, Izard, Dougherty, & Hembree, 1983). As with most facial coding systems, both schemes require sharp close-ups of infant facial expressions. There are advantages to these systems. First, the schemes allow for the coding of *all* the discrete infant emotions, such as anger, sadness, and joy. Second, these systems were developed through careful observations of infant facial expressions across a number of emotion-eliciting contexts; the authors used valid data to guide method development (Izard & Dougherty, 1982).

Let's start with a description of the MAX. The MAX scheme requires coders to rate behaviors within short segments of time (e.g., 5 s). In the first phase of MAX analysis, coders observe each tape segment a minimum of three times. Each time, the coder specifically makes judgments regarding subtle changes in facial behavior across three regions of the face: (a) brows; (b) eyes/nose/cheeks; and (c) mouth/lips/chin. Each appearance change within each facial region is assigned a predetermined number; for example, eye narrowing is Appearance Change 32. After all appearance changes are recorded, particular sequence changes are assigned an emotional expression. For example, in Figure 5.1, the combination of three appearance changes is deemed "sadness."

I would guess that coders must review tape segments more than three times to make accurate judgments; thus, this system can be time consuming (20 to 200 min of coding for each minute of facial behavior; Izard & Dougherty, 1982). However, I expect that changes in technology will encourage more research using the MAX, as well as other facial-expression coding systems. First, videotaping infant facial expressions in digital format will ease coding efforts; real-time coding using computer technology is much easier and more efficient. Also, there will be a day when digital images of infant facial expressions can be readily compared to "profiles" of typical facial expressions

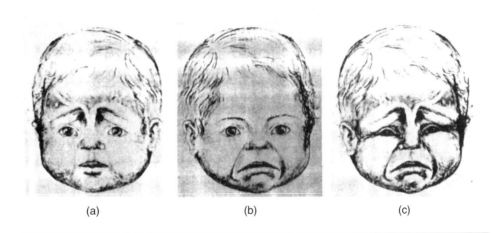

(a)   (b)   (c)

FIGURE 5.1 *Infant Facial Expressions.* Figures represent different appearance changes (AC) captured by MAX system. (A) MAX AC 23; brows raised at inner corners; (B) MAX AC 56; corners of mouth drawn downward and outward; (C) MAX AC 23 + 56 + 33 = sadness.

stored on the computer. This technological advancement will eliminate the potential unreliability of human coders.

Why the need for a second coding system, such as the Affex? Izard and colleagues noted that *untrained raters*, like you and me, could correctly estimate discrete emotions exhibited by babies about 60% of the time! Because untrained raters often look at overall holistic facial features to derive judgments, the researchers developed a system, the Affex, that allows coders to make such global judgments. Instead of carefully rating facial behavior within three regions of the face, the Affex allows coders to study global movement patterns across the entire face and assign direct emotional labels (e.g., sad), without having to assign numbered appearance codes. Thus, the Affex represents a more global, yet more subjective, coding system that allows for quicker ratings of facial expressions.

Much of the earliest infant emotional-development research used the MAX coding system, and found that events designed to elicit emotional expressions (e.g., arm restraint) predicted appropriate MAX codes (e.g., anger). For example, when using the MAX system, babies display joyful facial expressions during interactions with mothers (Malatesta et al., 1986), anger resulting from loss of reward (Lewis, Alessandri, & Sullivan, 1990), sadness and anger caused by caregiver separation (Shiller, Izard, & Hembree, 1986), and pain resulting from inoculation (Izard, Dougherty, & Hembree, 1983). Although these studies provide important validity support, this system may be too time consuming for most.

The Affex has been used with the MAX in more recent work and yields comparable data; that is, predictable emotional expressions, such as sadness, can be coded when infants are exposed to stimuli designed to elicit discrete emotions (e.g., mother instructed to make a sad face; Izard et al., 1995). There are two methodological suggestions offered by its developers. First, one should consider training new coders on the MAX first and then on the Affex. In such cases, coders using the Affex system can use discrete facial expression data to help make global emotional judgments about babies and rely less on "subjective impressions." Also, data derived from the more holistic Affex system can always be augmented with codes obtained from the MAX system. For example, a researcher may code all facial expressions exhibited by babies across all time frames using the Affex and code a portion using the more systematic MAX. Demonstrating that raters derive the same codes from both systems can ease concerns regarding the subjective nature of coding global facial expressions.

Although the MAX and Affex are widely used, these systems have not been immune to criticism. For example, although most experts believe that infants are capable of expressing a number of discrete emotions, it may be too difficult to accurately segregate emotions, such as anger and fear. These emotional expressions share common facial features, and may be blended together; what happens when the baby is both angry and sad? Also, untrained adult observers sometimes are *not good* at judging discrete infant emotions (Oster, Hegley, & Nagel, 1992).

Oster and Rosenstein's (1996) *Baby Facial Action Coding System* (Baby FACS) may have addressed these concerns. The Baby FACS is much like the MAX; coders note distinctive patterns of muscle movements within specific features of the infant's face. However, rather than yielding distinct emotion codes such as joy or sadness, this system yields objective data, such as smiles and frowns. In terms of negative affect, coders do not make decisions regarding whether the baby is mad or sad; rather, they record a combination of facial features communicating distress (e.g., lowered brows, frowning) simply as *negative affect* (Segal et al., 1995). Although this system may seem less complex than the MAX, the intricate rating of facial muscle movements still requires many hours of coding.

Because the Baby FACS focuses on more objective measures of emotions (e.g., simple frowns), this system has become very popular among researchers interested in documenting cross-cultural differences in emotional development. This research provides information regarding how and when socialization processes influence emotional development. Some very interesting cross-cultural research using the Baby FACS is presented in Box 5.1.

Facial movements assessed by these coding systems reflect a state of mind on the part of the infant that has important physiological/cognitive underpinnings, readies the infant for action, and provides important communicative signals for caregivers (Izard & Ackerman, 2000). However, some scholars question the validity of exclusively using facial movements to infer emotional experiences in babies, and suggest that we should examine other variables, such as physiological responses and behavioral movements, in conjunction with such data.

BOX 5.1 • *Facial Expressions in Infants Across Three Cultures*

There is no question that gauging the impact of socialization experiences on infant emotional development is a challenging task. Genetic factors, differences in prenatal care across cultures, ethnic differences in arousal, and cultural differences in parenting behavior could all account for differences (as well as similarities) in emotional expressive behavior and emotion regulation when contrasting infants across different cultures (Fogel, Stevenson, & Messinger, 1992).

Some of the most interesting work in this area pertains to comparisons of European American and Asian infants. Because many Asian nations subscribe to a collectivist culture, infant autonomy and self-expression is favored less than emotional and behavioral restraint. Also, other parenting practices may curb emotional expression in Asian infants. For example, these infants are in closer contact with caregivers, may be carried more, and are more likely to sleep with their caregivers than European American infants. All of these factors may limit the need for overt signaling devices, such as crying and emotional facial expressions.

To explore this issue, the facial expressions of 11-month-old infants from the United States, Japan, and China were compared using the BabyFACS (Camras et al., 1998). All babies were exposed to arm restraints (to elicit angry distress), and a "growing gorilla" (to elicit a fearful response). The researchers ascertained during pilot testing that the stimuli reliably elicited emotional expressions in babies across all cultures. This was an important step; an emotional elicitor in one culture may have no effect on infants reared in another. For example, a baby reared exclusively by two parents may show very different reactions to a stranger than a baby reared in more communal care with familiar and unfamiliar caregivers.

European American and Japanese babies showed few differences in facial expressions during these manipulations (see also Camras et al., 1992). In contrast, Chinese infants were less expressive, and smiled, and cried less. Although Chinese and Japanese infants are reared in collectivist cultures, they display different forms of expressive behavior. Can you think of reasons why? Although in need of empirical testing, perhaps Japanese parents are more exposed to European American values and parenting customs.

Does this research really mean that Chinese infants are less emotionally expressive or reactive than the babies reared in other cultures? Interestingly, one research team noted that 2- to 6-month-old Japanese infants showed more cortisol release shortly after inoculations, when contrasted to European American babies. If such findings were replicated in Chinese infants, the implication would be that these infants are not less reactive than European American babies, but rather just show less reactivity in terms of facial expressions. These speculations also suggest that we need to take a more comprehensive, multimethod approach when measuring emotions in preverbal infants.

Beyond the Face.   Why assess multiple indictors of emotional experience? First, documenting continuity between different modalities of emotional expression would suggest that infant emotions are not poorly organized. Second, additional data, such as behavioral responses, are required to assess more complex emotional expressions, such as pride. Finally, the meaning of simple facial-expression data comes into question when we observe a child initially smile at a stranger and then back away. Although the child's facial expression communicates one thing, the ultimate behavior suggests something different.

The *Infant Regulatory Scoring System* (IRSS) was developed to capture emotional expression across different modalities (Weinberg & Tronick, 1990). It can be used in conjunction with traditional facial-expression coding systems, and measures the different categories of emotional expressions outlined in Table 5.2. In one study, the IRSS was used in conjunction with the Affex facial expression system to code 6-month-old infant emotional expressions during interactions with mothers (Weinberg & Tronick, 1994). After analyzing the interactions, the authors concluded that facial expressions, body movements, and vocalizations co-occur to produce four broad configurations of emotional expressions:

1. *Social engagement.* Facial expression of joy, accompanied by high infant gaze toward the mother, positive vocalizations, low autonomic stress, and low fussiness.
2. *Object engagement.* Facial expression of interest, gaze, and movements directed at object, low escape behavior, vocalizations, low fussing and crying.
3. *Passive withdrawal.* Facial expression of sadness, accompanied by high rates of autonomic stress and fussiness, low levels of activity.
4. *Active protest.* Facial expression of anger, accompanied by high rates of escape, autonomic stress, crying, and gesturing ("Pick me up!").

Documenting connectedness between different emotional expression modalities suggests that emotions are well coordinated in young babies. Also, such connectedness provides emotional *meaning* to the caregiver (and researcher). Place yourself in the position of two caregivers; one focuses solely on facial expressions (e.g., anger), whereas the other uses different modalities (angry expressions, fussy, arms in the air) to assess emotional experience. It is much easier to read the emotional intent of the infant in the latter case.

Although we are likely to see more research on basic infant emotions utilizing multiple assessments of emotional behavior, assessing emotional expressions across multiple modalities becomes mandatory when assessing more complex self-conscious and self-evaluative emotions, such as embarrassment, pride, and guilt. Table 5.3 presents common ways of assessing these emotional expressions in toddlers and preschoolers.

Emotional States.   We often use expressions such as, "He was blinded by jealously" and "She was red with rage" to connect biological states and emotional experiences. Because there may be close connections between infant emotional expressions and physiological states, some have tied the baby's outward emotional behavior to biological antecedents and consequences. Methodologically, it is important to assess emotional behavior and physiological data over time, because events may not occur in synchrony. A heart may not pound until well after a car accident, although a facial expression of fear may have been apparent even *before* the accident. It is also true that physiological behavior is not always a "response" to an emotional elicitor. In some cases, a biological state may help the infant cope with the elicitor.

TABLE 5.3 *Measuring Self-Conscious and Self-Evaluative Emotions*

Emotion	Important Data/Codes
Embarrassment	Smiling facial expression, gaze aversion, hand movements to hair, clothing, face, other body parts (Lewis et al., 1989). Blushing is too inconsistent to use as a code.
Empathy	Concerned facial expression (e.g., sad) or vocal expressions (e.g., "I'm sorry") that may be accompanied by action (e.g., running to a stricken peer). Simple instrumental assistance, not accompanied by concerned facial or vocal expression is deemed "prosocial behavior" (Zahn-Waxler et al., 1992).
Guilt	Gaze aversion, may be accompanied by bodily tension, such as squirming, hanging of head, covering face with hands, etc. (Kochanska et al., 2002).
Pride	Erect posture, joy, smiling, eyes directed at parents or experimenter, pointing to outcome, hand clapping, positive self-evaluation ("Yea!"). Note, simple joy or smiling in isolation of additional behavior is not considered pride. Tendency to look at others for approval may dissipate with maturity (Lewis, Alessandri, & Sullivan, 1992; Stipek, Recchia, & McClintic, 1992).
Shame	Closed or slumped posture, frowning or pouting, looking away from task, negative self-evaluations (e.g., "I'm no good.") (Lewis, Alessandri, Sullivan, 1992; Stipek, Recchia, & McClintic, 1992).

Heart-rate variability, electrical activity in the brain, and cortisol assessments represent three popular ways of linking emotional expressions and physiological states. In terms of heart-rate variability, recall that high resting cardiac vagal tone is associated with strong infant attentional skills and "appropriate" emotional reactivity. For example, babies with high resting vagal tone display more fussing and crying (i.e., signs of anger) during arm-restraint procedures than their counterparts with low vagal tone (Stifter & Fox, 1990), yet display *less* emotional reactivity (e.g., fear, withdrawal) when presented an odd toy (Kagan, Reznick, & Snidman, 1987).

Nervous system integrity, which underlies heart rate variability, plays a major role in our emotional reactivity. Infants with robust nervous system development display anger, sadness, or fear when appropriate! A well-organized infant will become angry when a pacifier is yanked out of its mouth, yet will show more interest than fear when observing an unusual toy. Vagal tone change also indicates more than a physiological response to stimuli. Infants who display quick vagal tone "braking" during arousal show shorter cycles of fussing than infants who display high nonresting heart-rate variability. Thus, cardiac vagal tone plays an important role in infant emotion regulation.

Besides heart-rate variability, researchers have made connections between emotional expressions and electrical activity in the brain. Although some may doubt the existence of "emotional centers" within the cortex, the left frontal region of the brain may involve more pleasurable emotions, such as interest or joy, whereas the right frontal area may be linked to more negative emotions such as sadness. Such theory has been supported by clinical findings, in that damage to left-frontal regions of the brain have been linked to depression, whereas right-frontal damage tends to produce abnormal elation (Cacioppo et al., 2000).

Researchers have linked infant emotional expressions and such activity within these very brain regions. Fox and colleagues (1987; 1991) introduced different manipulations, such as sudden maternal departure or stranger appearance, to elicit a variety of emotions in babies. Infants who displayed more left-frontal activation showed pleasure and joy in situations designed to elicit these emotions, whereas greater right-frontal activation was associated with negative emotional reactions during periods of maternal separation or stranger approach.

Salivary cortisol is another physiological index of emotional state; our adrenal glands release cortisol during times of arousal. Gunnar et al. (1989) demonstrated that babies secrete more cortisol when distressed and secrete less when happy. Cortisol secretion also varies as a function of the baby's maturity and the social context. Babies under 1 year of age show elevated cortisol levels and emotional distress over maternal separation, but over time such separations less reliably predict cortisol changes. Also, the social context can affect the infant's emotional expression and state. Although babies under one year of age often show elevated cortisol levels and emotional distress when suddenly separated from a parent, most infants quickly "stabilize" if a sensitive substitute caregiver is nearby (Gunnar et al., 1992).

Summary of Early Emotional Development

Researchers use infant facial expressions, outward behavior, vocalizations, and physiological assessments to index emotional experiences in babies. Although basic emotions such as joy, fear, and anger may have innate origins, individual differences quickly arise in these emotional responses. Rather than view these individual differences as a nuisance, experts have studied innate and situational variables that account for these disparities. In the next section, we will examine ways to assess individual differences in emotion regulation, and discuss important physiological and societal variables that contribute to its development.

Assessing Emotion Regulation

Outward emotional expressions in babies dissipate as infants learn to regulate emotions; in this section, you will learn how to assess such coping behavior. Also, although physiological mechanisms play some role in the development of emotion regulation, important cognitive and social variables, such as caregiver sensitivity, play a role. We will now discuss how to assess important variables that underlie emotion regulation and regulatory skills.

Definition and Basic Measurement Strategies

Emotion regulation is not simple emotional suppression. Thompson (1994) offers a well-reasoned definition of the concept of emotion regulation:

> Emotion regulation consists of the extrinsic and intrinsic processes responsible for monitoring, evaluating, and modifying emotional reactions, especially their intensive and temporal features, to accomplish one's goals (pp. 27–28).

This definition underscores the adaptive significance of emotion regulation, in that we use it to pursue a goal, such as arousal reduction, or to maintain a positive emotion, such as joy. Thompson's definition also stipulates that emotion regulation is a process, and internal (e.g., vagal tone) and external (e.g., caregiver behavior) factors influence regulatory skills.

Emotion regulation experts frequently structure situations that are designed to elicit different emotions in babies; however, the manipulations must be appropriate for age and culture. For instance, asking a mother to suddenly leave a strange laboratory room may influence 1- and 5-year-olds very differently. In fact, a laboratory setting, in itself, may elicit different emotions and regulatory skills of similarly aged children in different cultures.

After emotional elicitation, the infant's facial expressions, body movements, and vocalizations are monitored, which can yield the following responses (Thompson, 1994):

1. *Response latency.* Time from the onset of the elicitor until the onset or peak of the emotional response.
2. *Rise time.* Time from the onset of the emotional response until the peak intensity of the response.
3. *Persistence or duration.* Total time duration of the emotional response.
4. *Recovery.* Time it takes emotional response to reach baseline level.

How do you assess such abilities? Braungart-Rieker and colleagues (2001) have developed a coding system that captures different infant regulatory behaviors, including escape (e.g., back arching), self-regulation (e.g., thumb sucking), and parent-focused regulation (e.g., gaze at parent). In one study, 4-month-old infants who used considerable amounts of self- and parent-focused regulation were less likely to show sustained bouts of negative affect when contrasted to babies who used less effective strategies. Of course, regulatory behaviors are not confined to observable actions. For example, cardiac vagal braking and cortisol secretion represent internal, physiological mechanisms responsible for regulating arousal.

What Do You Think?

What variables may affect the development of emotional regulatory skills in infants and children? What implications do poor regulatory skills have for compliance and limit setting, peer-group involvement, and behavior in the school context?

Predictors of Emotion Regulation

Emotion-regulation difficulties are associated with achievement, relationship, and mental-health problems (Leventhal & Patrick-Miller, 2000). Thus identifying variables that may affect the development of emotion regulation, such as those outlined in Table 5.4, has important implications for treatment efforts.

When reviewing Table 5.4, note that previously reviewed concepts play an important role in emotion-regulation development; robust nervous-system development, as measured via endocrine activity (i.e., cortisol secretion), heart rate variability or vagal tone, and electrical activity in the brain all influence the infant's reactivity to events, and regulatory processes.

Because we have already discussed how to assess neuroregulatory skills, let's now examine other important variables that affect emotion-regulation development. Three of the most studied variables are social referencing, caregiver sensitivity, and attunement.

Social Referencing.   Even young babies imitate and appropriately react to others' emotions. Gradually, babies use the emotional expressions of caregivers for information regarding how to respond and react to arousing environmental events. Thus you can see why such **social referencing**, is an important aid for the development of emotion-regulation skills.

The visual-cliff, stranger-appearance, and novel-toy procedures represent three basic paradigms for studying social referencing processes (Saarni, Mumme, & Campos, 1998). Recall that in the visual-cliff paradigm, the infant is placed on a table and "fooled" into thinking that crawling to one particular side of the table will result in a sudden fall. In one classic study, mothers coaxed their infants into crawling onto the "deep" side of the table; however, they were trained to exhibit different emotional expressions, such as anger, fear, or joy as their babies social-referenced them. The babies referenced more, showed less distress, and crossed onto the deep end when the mothers displayed happiness but did not in response to negative emotions such as fear (Sorce et al., 1985).

Others have examined how babies use social referencing to cope with a sudden "stranger" appearance (Feinman & Lewis, 1983). Caregivers are instructed to greet either the stranger positively or negatively. Researchers note the infant's referencing behavior, emotional behavior (e.g., distress), and regulatory skills (e.g., smiling at the stranger). Babies display less distress and are more likely to approach the stranger if the mother displays positive emotions.

The *novel-toy procedure* represents the most popular method of assessing social referencing (Saarni, Mumme, & Campos, 1998). In this paradigm, the baby is exposed to a novel whirring robot or crawling toy spider. Caregivers are trained to display certain facial expressions (e.g., fear or joy) and vocalizations (e.g., "Oh my!") upon appearance of the toy. Researchers then record the baby's level of distress, social referencing behavior, and toy approach-or-avoidance behavior. In one study, researchers exposed 12-month-olds to

TABLE 5.4   *Variables that Predict Individual Differences in Emotion Regulation (Adapted from Calkins, 1994)*

Internal Variables	*Examples*
1. Neuroregulatory systems	Endocrine activity (e.g., cortisol release), heart-rate variability/vagal tone, brain electrical activity
2. Temperament/behavioral traits	Attentiveness, arousal or reactivity, soothability, smiling/sociability
3. Cognitive components	Social referencing, expectancies about others and environment, growing awareness regarding need to regulate negative emotions
External Variables	*Examples*
1. Interactive caregiving styles	Responsive to infant/child emotional needs, accepting, accessible, and attentive
2. Explicit training (older children)	Modeling, reinforcement, discipline

different novel toys in the presence of both mothers and fathers. Although some tradition-ally think of mothers as the primary emotional figure in an infant's life, the babies in this study used mothers and fathers equally as social referents and sources of emotional guid-ance (Hirshberg & Svejda, 1990).

Social-referencing paradigms are ripe for different manipulations; it would be in-structive to see how individual differences in infants (e.g., temperament) and caregivers (e.g., mental health) affect study results. For example, babies with high or low vagal tone may show different referencing patterns or use emotional information provided by care-givers differently. Also, babies with caregivers suffering from major affective disturbances, such as depression, may display problematic regulatory behavior in these social-referencing paradigms.

Caregiver Behaviors. Two forms of caregiver behavior have been linked to infant emo-tional development. The first is **caregiver sensitivity**, or the ability to respond appropri-ately to the emotional signals of the infant (DeWolff & van IJzendoorn, 1997). You can see how caregiver sensitivity may affect emotion regulation in infants. For example, what might happen if babies routinely observe parents who display considerable anger when they need assistance or are hurt?

The second important caregiver behavior is **attunement**, or the emotional synchrony between the baby and the caregiver during interactions. Attunement can be witnessed dur-ing playful interactions between the caregiver and infant (e.g., peek-a-boo), and includes behaviors such as mutual eye contact, shared laughter, and coordinated interactions. An in-fant may gaze at her mother, who in turn smiles, and speaks in a high-pitched voice. The baby responds by laughing, which results in mother laughter. In this case, the emotional in-terplay between the mother and infant is coordinated and is a good "match" (Field, 1994).

Caregiver Sensitivity. When considering methods, it's important to consider how experts define caregiver sensitivity, recommendations regarding how to assess it, and coder train-ing requirements. In Western cultures, mothers are viewed as the key target subject for these assessments; other caregivers, such as fathers and siblings are often understudied.

Caregiver sensitivity encompasses 4 components: (a) awareness of infant emotional/communication signals; (b) accurate interpretation of these signals; (c) appropriate re-sponse to signals; and (d) prompt response to these signals (Ainsworth et al., 1974). To as-sess this construct, Ainsworth and colleagues developed a global, 9-point rating scale. Different points on the scale are anchored by lengthy paragraphs, similar to those shown in Table 5.5.

Ainsworth validated these sensitivity scales in both home and laboratory settings; mothers who were rated as highly sensitive to the baby's needs (e.g., crying), had infants who cried less over time, were more compliant, and more securely attached (Ainsworth, Bell, & Stayton, 1971; Bell & Ainsworth, 1972). Unfortunately, these global rating scales may be too unwieldy for most of us; only a highly trained coder familiar with the construct could complete this scale.

Experts have recently assessed caregiver sensitivity by "unpacking" various compo-nents of this construct (e.g., attunement; "appropriate" caregiver response; attention to emo-tional cues) (Braungart-Rieker et al., 2001; Smith & Pederson, 1988), and have developed

TABLE 5.5   *Global Caregiver Sensitivity Scale (samples adapted from Ainsworth et al., 1974)*

Sample Ratings	Description
9 Highly Sensitive	Caregiver is highly attuned to infant's (I's) emotional signals. She is able to see things from I's point of view, and her perceptions are not distorted by her own needs or defenses. She "reads" I's signals and communications swiftly, and knows the meaning of subtle, minimal, and understated cues. She nearly always gives I what he indicates he wants, although perhaps not invariably so.
5 Inconsistently Sensitive	Caregiver's inconsistent sensitivity may occur for any one of several reasons, but the outcome is that she seems to lack warmth in regard to several dealings with the infant. Her awareness of I may be intermittent—often fairly keen, but sometimes lacking . . . What is striking is that a mother who can be as sensitive as she is on so many occasions can be so insensitive on other occasions.
1 Highly Insensitive	Caregiver seems geared exclusively on her own wishes, moods, and activity. That is, caregiver's interventions and initiations of interaction are prompted or shaped largely by signals within herself; if they mesh with infant's signals, this is often no more than coincidence. She does respond if infant's signals are intense enough.

Note: Ratings 3 (Insensitive) and 7 (Sensitive) were omitted. The depicted ratings *do not* include the complete descriptions.

coding systems that systematically rate the different components. Rather than provide a global rating of "caregiver sensitivity," a coder may rate different caregiver behaviors, such as "prompt attention to distress," or "provides positive affect in response to infant smiling."

How do we "elicit" such behavior? Experts often structure infant-caregiver interactions so that caregivers must take note of their babies' emotional cues while engaged in some form of distracter task. This is an externally valid approach. In real life caregivers often must pay bills or prepare dinner with baby nearby. In one study, mothers completed a questionnaire in a room completely devoid of play materials! As you might guess, the typical infant quickly became bored and began making demands while the adult completed the questionnaire. Raters recorded the mother's reactions to infant fussing and established strict criteria for an "appropriate" maternal response, such as picking up and comforting a fussy baby. They noted that the infants with emotionally responsive mothers possessed better emotion regulation than babies with inattentive mothers (Smith & Pederson, 1988).

To make this area more accessible, Pederson and colleagues have developed another method that might be attractive to students. In developing the *Maternal Behavior Q-Set* (Pederson et al., 1990), experts created a large pool of maternal behaviors consistent with Ainsworth's detailed descriptions of maternal sensitivity. Next, they asked other experts in the field to assign different behaviors that would be most and least like the "prototypically" sensitive mother. A sampling of these items is shown in Table 5.6; the entire Q-Set and detailed instructions for administration and scoring are contained in Waters and colleagues (1995).

How does this Maternal Behavior Q-Set procedure work? First, the caregiver's attention is diverted away from the infant by asking the person to complete a questionnaire or some other task (a la Smith & Pederson, 1988). Next, observers take field notes of the caregiver's availability to the infant, her responses to emotional signals, and her monitoring of the baby while engaged in the task (Pederson & Moran, 1995).

TABLE 5.6 *Sample Maternal Behavior Q-Set Items (adapted from Pederson et al., 1990)*

Most Like Prototypically Sensitive Mother

Responds immediately to cries and whimpers.
Arranges her location so that she can perceive infant's signals.
Aware of baby's moods and fluctuations in state.
Waits for infant's response in interactions.
When infant is distressed, mother is able to quickly and accurately identify the source.

Most Unlike Prototypically Sensitive Mother

Mother is unaware of or insensitive to infant's signals of distress.
Teases infant beyond point where infant seems to enjoy it.
Rough or intrusive interactions with infant.
Responds only to frequent, prolonged, or intense signals.
Often appears to "tune out" and not notice distress or bids for attention.

These steps are very similar to other observational coding systems for assessing caregiver sensitivity. However, in the Materal Behavior Q-Set procedure, the rater is next given 90 cards, each containing caregiver behaviors depicted in Table 5.6. The rater then sorts the cards into 9 piles, and 10 cards must go into each pile. Items in pile 1 are considered least characteristic of the caregiver's behavior, whereas items in pile 9 are considered most like her behavior. The sensitivity score is the correlation between the observer's sort and the criterion sort, or the developer's depiction of the ideal, sensitive caregiver.

Materal Behavior Q-Set procedure is easy to use. Raters can review the 90 items ahead of time, and thus know what to look for during the observation. Also, instead of simply recording the simple frequency of a caregiver behavior, observers are forced to make discriminations *across* different behaviors. Thus far, the Maternal behavior Q-Set has been successfully used in a number of studies, and highly sensitive mothers have babies who possess robust emotional development.

Attunement.   Attuned, or synchronous, interactions pertain to how well infants and caregivers regulate and express emotions, and respond to the partner's regulatory needs (Tronick, 1989). Such synchrony is needed for the development of regulatory skills, and major affective disturbances, such as depression, may influence this "emotional dance" (Field, 1995).

How do we assess attunement? Most prefer to videotape infant-caregiver play; the caregiver can be instructed to "play with your baby as you normally do." Certain variables can be manipulated as well. We can contrast interactions across settings (e.g., home versus lab), train caregivers to display different emotional expressions (e.g., joy, depression), or contrast the interactions between caregivers and infants with those of strangers and infants. Caregiver (e.g., mental health functioning), infant (e.g., temperament), and contextual (e.g., culture) variables can be examined to determine whether they predict the interactions.

The nature of caregiver-infant responses across time represents a critical study variable. To capture this process, data-analysis schemes have been developed to record changes in vocal expressions, gaze attention, facial expressions, and body movements exhibited both by the caregiver and infant *across time* (Jaffe et al., 2001; Tronick & Cohn, 1987; Weinberg et al., 1999). Of critical importance is noting the onset and termination of behaviors (e.g., infant smiling), behaviors that antecede these target behaviors (e.g., caregiver vocalization), and concordance between emotional expressions (Field, 1994). Advances in computer technology can help; our main job is entering caregiver and infant codes that are marked by time.

Summary of Emotion-Regulation Assessment

Because emotion regulation sets the tone for the development of emotional coping strategies, identifying the developmental progression and individual differences in regulatory skills is important. In this section, we discussed common ways of assessing this construct. In addition, we discussed methods to measure important antecedents to regulatory skills, such as social referencing skills, caregiver sensitivity, and attunement.

Assessing Infant Attachment

This field peaked my interest some time ago after witnessing the behavior of a toddler in the lab. When I entered the room to discuss the experimental protocol, the little boy immediately crawled under a table. After a few minutes, he motored over to his mother and clung to her throughout my briefing. Soon, the mother suddenly announced that she had to go to the rest room, and as she began to exit the room, the toddler would not let her leave. What amazed me throughout this interaction was that this little boy, whose mother had received a legal conviction for child abuse, *clearly preferred to be around this abusing mother rather than me*. In my mind, there is something deeply fascinating about the attachment process.

In this section, you will learn about contemporary attachment methods. If you find yourself hooked, you should read the *Handbook of Attachment* (Cassidy & Shaver, 1999), or anything written by John Bowlby, Mary Ainsworth, or Mary Main on the subject. Next, we will explore the primary method used to assess attachment relationships between infants and caregivers, the *Strange Situation*. Because classifying infants into attachment categories requires advanced training, we will also discuss other methods used to assess this construct. Also, how the baby's parents think of their own attachment experiences has an influence on caregiver sensitivity, as well as on ultimate attachment outcomes in babies. Our chapter concludes with a discussion on how to assess these adult *generalized attachment representations*.

Definitional and Theoretical Issues

Attachment behaviors are actions the infant directs toward the caregiver, such as clinging, crying, and signaling, that usually result in comfort or reassurance (Bowlby 1969/1982). Without proper context, the presence or absence of these behaviors may not be meaningful. An infant who explores her environment and rarely interacts with her mother in a "stress-free" environment (e.g., family backyard) should not be deemed as possessing "attachment problems," because she is not demonstrating a high level of normal attachment behaviors.

A broader construct is represented by the **attachment relationship**, or affectional tie, between the infant and her caregiver. As articulated by Ainsworth (1989), an attachment relationship or bond must meet the following criteria (see also Cassidy, 1999):

1. Affectional bonds are *persistent* rather than temporary.
2. An affectional bond is directed toward a specific person, who is not interchangeable with another person.
3. The relationship is emotionally significant.
4. The individual wishes to maintain proximity with the person.
5. The individual feels distress when separated or apart from the person.
6. The individual seeks security and comfort in the relationship with the person.

While criteria 1 to 5 encompass many attachment-like, affectional relationships, the last requirement is what ultimately defines an attachment relationship between an infant and her caretaker—that is, the desire to seek contact and comfort from another person, particularly when distressed. Although infant-parent attachment relationships have received the most study, the criteria could apply to other potential attachment figures in the infant's social realm, including grandparents, siblings, and child-care workers.

Bowlby's (1982) ethological attachment theory is the most heavily embraced perspective. Although early psychoanalytic (Freud, 1957) and learning (Sears, Maccoby, & Levin, 1957) theories asserted that attachment relationships between caregivers and infants evolved through primary drive reduction—you feed an infant and the infant associates your presence with food in a pleasurable manner—Bowlby posited that attachment relationships between infants and caregivers were necessary from a survival standpoint. One can imagine a time when proximity to caregivers was mandatory for survival, and wandering from one's community would result in almost certain death.

The gradual development of close, affectional bonds between infants and caregivers is theorized as one major reason our species (as well as other animal species) has become successful (Bowlby, 1988). This premise suggests that if contact between the infant and caregiver is simply allowed, then our biology guarantees infant-caregiver attachments. Indeed, this theory would account for why children of abusive parents, even in the absence of pleasurable parenting behavior, nevertheless become attached to their parents (Cassidy, 1999).

In the spirit of ethological theory, attachment bonds are a phenomenon that should be witnessed across all cultures around the world. Indeed, Bowlby's colleague, Mary Ainsworth, provided support for this premise by documenting that classic signs of infant-caregiver attachment (e.g., proximity seeking, stranger distress, separation anxiety) can be witnessed in other societies (Ainsworth, 1967). However, although Ainsworth's work suggested that almost all infants eventually become attached to primary caregivers, the caregiving environment has been theorized to produce striking differences in the *quality of this attachment*. It is in this area that the methodological work in attachment is strongest. In the next section, we will examine specific ways to assess individual differences in the infant-caregiver attachment relationship.

The Strange Situation

To better capture this diversity, Ainsworth and colleagues developed the **Strange Situation** procedure (Ainsworth et al., 1978). In this methodology, infants are paired with, and separated from, their primary caregiver, as well as a "stranger" over the course of brief observational segments. The exact sequence of these segments is depicted in Table 5.7.

Practical/Methodological Issues.   The Strange Situation procedure is typically conducted in a space of "waiting room" size, adjoined by an observation room with a one-way mirror. The waiting room, which is wired for sound, contains chairs and age-appropriate play materials. Trained personnel are required for this procedure, including the researcher, who must greet the parent and infant, and communicate with the observer in the observation room. The observer times the episodes, communicates with the experimenter regarding who is to enter the room, and signals the parent or stranger for exit via a light knock on the one-way mirror. In addition, the "stranger," is a confederate who responds to, but does not initiate interaction with the baby. The parent is briefed on the nature of this method in advance.

   Why is the Strange Situation viewed as such an ingenious procedure? Chiefly, if the attachment system is activated by stress or alarm, individual differences in attachment relationships could best be assessed under such conditions. There are a number of Strange Situation elements that are thought to activate this system. The novel waiting room, parent separations, and stranger provoke different attachment behaviors, such as exploration and proximity seeking, actions that are thought to underlie the attachment relationship.

   The Strange Situation contains a number of manipulations that address major questions about the infant and caregiver. For example, why might the infant begin crying in segment 6

TABLE 5.7   *Strange Situation Procedure (Adapted from Ainsworth et al., 1978)*

Episode	Participants	Duration	Description/Behavior Highlighted by Episode
1.	Parent, baby, experimenter	30 s–1 min	Introduction to novel room
2.	Parent, baby	3 min	Experimenter leaves room/ exploration of novel room with parent present.
3.	Stranger, parent, baby	3 min	Stranger enters room/ response to stranger with mother present.
4.	Stranger, baby	3 min	Parent leaves room/ response to first separation with stranger present.
5.	Parent, baby	3 min	Parent returns, stranger exits/ response to first reunion
6.	Infant	3 min	Parent exits/response to separation when left alone.
7.	Stranger, baby	3 min	Stranger enters room/response to continuing separation and stranger presence.
8.	Parent, baby	3 min	Parent returns, stranger leaves room /response to second reunion with parent.

Note: Episodes (e.g., 6) may be curtailed if infant becomes highly distressed.

when left alone? Is the baby crying because he misses the caregiver or because he is left alone? The appearance of the stranger in segment seven helps us answer this question. If the baby continues to cry upon the appearance of the stranger, we can infer he misses his mother. However, if he stops crying, then he simply did not want to be left alone.

Let's consider some central methodological issues. This procedure is appropriate for infants between 10 and 24 months of age. Toddlers older than 24 months of age are pretty independent; hence this method may not provoke the distress necessary to trigger the attachment system. It is not recommended to assess an ill infant; however, I doubt if this issue would affect the baby's eventual attachment classification. For example, a sick child may protest more over maternal separation yet still seek comfort with the appearance of the caregiver during the reunion episode (a sign of attachment security). A final concern rests with the appropriateness of this methodology in other cultures. For example, although a "waiting room" laboratory setup may seem like a "strange," but not completely foreign environment to infants in industrialized cultures, babies in developing cultures may have never had exposure to such a context. Please examine how researchers grapple with this important issue in Box 5.2.

Classification System. Ainsworth developed a classification system that identified three *organized* patterns of attachment that can be witnessed in infants across all cultures (Sagi,

BOX 5.2 • *Modifying the Strange Situation*

Ainsworth developed the Strange Situation procedure to identify patterns of attachment in Western infants. However, the contrived "waiting room" setting in some regions of the world may seem "beyond strange" to both the infant and caregiver. Also, babies reared in cultures featuring continual family or communal care—contexts that may feature multiple caregivers and communal sleeping arrangements—may have never been left alone.

Experts often modify the Strange Situation when working with infants and families in other cultures. For instance, True and colleagues (2001) studied mother–infant dyads in the Dogon, a rather isolated ethnic group residing in Mali, West Africa. Mother–infant pairs were studied in remote village and town settings. Although neither context had electricity or running water, the town families were more readily exposed to mass culture, given the researchers' observations of large scale use of radios and VCRs powered by car batteries. In either case, a traditional Strange Situation setting would not seem appropriate.

The researchers collected infant-attachment security and maternal sensitivity data, and tailored the Strange Situation to reflect current living conditions amongst the Dogon people. Most mothers in these polygamous families lived in small compounds consisting of an open courtyard for childrearing, cooking, and socializing, surrounded by small huts generally reserved for sleeping. To simulate this context, the Strange Situation "waiting room" was essentially a small courtyard, set off by hanging mats. The "strangers" were unfamiliar Dogon women who were trained according to Ainsworth's protocol.

The researchers documented that the percentage of secure infants in this study (almost 70%) was very similar to percentages obtained in other cultures, and village and town babies did not differ in terms of attachment security. However, no babies were classified as avoidant! The researchers speculate that, because of the continual presence of many sensitive adults, it may be virtually impossible for an avoidant attachment to develop. In any case, this research provides a good example of how attachment methods must be modified when used in other cultures.

TABLE 5.8 *Strange Situation Classification System (Adapted from Ainsworth et al., 1978; Solomon & George, 1999)*

Group	Sample Description
Secure (B)	Uses mother as secure base for exploration. On separation, shows signs of missing caregiver, especially during the second separation. During reunions, actively greets caregiver with smile, gesture, or vocalizations. If upset, seeks comfort, and once comforted, returns to exploration.
Avoidant (A)	Explores readily, yet displays little affect or secure-base behavior. During separations, responds minimally. During reunions, looks away from, or actively avoids, caregiver. If picked up, may lean away, stiffen, and not "nestle in." Seeks distance from caregiver.
Ambivalent or resistant (C)	Distressed when introduced to room, fails to engage in exploration. Unsettled or distressed upon separation, yet, on reunion, makes bids for caregiver's attention with signs of anger. Fails to be comforted by caregiver.
Disorganized/disoriented (D) (Main & Solomon, 1990)	Behavior appears to lack observable goal, intention, or explanation. For example, may approach caregiver and suddenly back away, display behavioral "freezing," or cover eyes when observing caregiver's presence during reunion. Shows indications of fear/ apprehension of caregiver, confusion, and disorientation. Although may show signs of organized attachment (A, B, C), seems to lack a coherent strategy.

1990). These three organized classifications are depicted in Table 5.8, along with the more recent disorganized/disoriented classification articulated by Main and Solomon (1990). Classification requires formal training from a certified attachment expert, usually outlined in empirical articles that contain research using the Strange Situation procedure.

Secure infants actively explore their environment when not distressed yet seek comfort and proximity from caregivers when upset. Most importantly, a caregiver can readily comfort these babies. *Avoidant* infants distance themselves from caregivers and rely on themselves (or focus on the environment) for comfort. For example, during times of duress, the child may focus on toys rather than the caregiver. *Ambivalent* or *resistant* infants have difficulty with exploration, and often angrily seek contact with caregivers during times of duress, yet cannot be comforted (Ainsworth et al., 1978). The latter two classifications are signs of *attachment insecurity*. Attachment security is considered the modal attachment classification, and is most closely linked with healthy development across cultures.

In Ainsworth's original classification scheme (secure, avoidant, resistant), some infants could not be classified. Upon observing such infants, Main and Solomon (1990) concluded that they did not have an organized attachment system and classified them as *disorganized/disoriented*. Such infants dramatically oscillate between approach and avoidant behavior, and may display bizarre behavior. For example, the infant, upon seeing the parent return to the room, may approach the caregiver and suddenly freeze or put their hands over their eyes, as depicted in Figure 5.2. If the infant is assigned a disorganized classification, the baby should also be assigned a best-fitting organized (i.e., secure, avoidant, ambivalent) classification as well. It is important to pursue this strategy, because

FIGURE 5.2 *Disorganized/Disoriented Infant Behavior.* Note increasing apprehension caused by mother's appearance.

From, Main, M., & J. Solomon, J. (1990). Procedures for identifying infants as disorganized/disoriented during the Ainsworth strange situation. In M. Greenberg, D. Cicchetti, & E. Cummings (Eds.), *Attachment in the preschool years: Theory, research, and intervention* (p. 145). Chicago: University of Chicago Press. Reprinted by permission of University of Chicago Press.

disorganized infants assigned a best-fitting secure classification have better developmental outcomes when contrasted to D (Disorganized) babies that are also insecure (i.e., avoidant or ambivalent/resistant) (Lyons-Ruth & Jacobvitz, 1999).

Reliability/Validity Data.   Infant attachment classifications derived from the Strange Situation are stable over time; however, major changes in infant life circumstances (e.g., sudden loss of parent employment, family stress) have been tied to classification changes over short periods of time (e.g., Waters, 1978). Infant attachment classifications modestly predict important outcomes during childhood and adolescence, such as social competence in the peer group, the ability to cope with stress, psychological health, and school adjustment (Thompson, 1999). The poorest outcomes have been documented for babies classified as disorganized, who tend to develop control-oriented relationships (e.g., may order parent around), behavior problems, and serious difficulties coping with stress (Lyons-Ruth & Jacobvitz, 1999).

Bowlby (1988) suggested that one result of attachment relationships is development of an internal working model of attachment, or a set of expectancies regarding how to treat others and how others should treat you. In one study, 70% of infants classified as secure in the Strange Situation displayed a secure "working model" regarding attachment during late adolescence (Waters et al., 2000). The secure adults could objectively discuss both positive and negative childhood attachment experiences with caregivers, actively valued attachment and attachment relationships, and viewed themselves as worthy attachment figures.

Although attachment insecurity (avoidant, resistant, or disorganized) should be viewed with concern, infant attachment does not automatically predict famine or fortune. I doubt that improvements in methodology will lead to improved predictive power of the Strange Situation. Changes in the caregiver environment, interactions with emerging attachment figures, and ongoing mental reflection regarding previous attachment experiences may either sustain or alter our mental representation of early attachment experiences (Bowlby, 1988).

Attachment Behavior Q-Set

The *Attachment Behavior Q-Set* (AQS Version 3; Waters, 1987) has made attachment research more accessible for those who have not received classification training. Like the Maternal Behavior Q-Set, the AQS consists of 90 statements (you can print the items on individual file cards), that describe the behaviors of infants and toddlers one typically observers during interactions with caregivers. A sampling of items is contained in Table 5.9; all items and scoring instructions can be located in Waters et al., 1995.

Like the Maternal Behavior Q-Set, Waters and colleagues initially asked attachment experts to identify behaviors prototypical of secure and insecure infants. However, unlike the Maternal Behavior Q-Set, the caregiver of the infant (or children up to age five) ordinarily completes the AQS. There are a number of advantages to such an approach. Caregivers witness diverse infant behavior across different contexts. Thus, unlike the brief periods of infant-caregiver behavior witnessed during the Strange Situation, a caregiver can provide a rich account of infant behavior over time. Also, the Q-sort methodology forces caregivers to think objectively about their infants, and make fine discriminations and comparisons in infant behavior.

TABLE 5.9 *Sample Attachment Behavior Q-Set Items (Waters et al., 1995)*

Items Most Like Secure Infant	Child keeps track of mother's location when he plays around the house. Calls to her now and then, notices her go from room to room.
	Child clearly shows a pattern of using mother as a base from which to explore. Moves out to play, returns or plays near her, moves out to play again, etc.
	If held in mother's arms, child stops crying and quickly recovers after being frightened or upset.
	Child follows mother's suggestions readily, even when they are clearly suggestions rather than orders.
	When mother says to follow her, child does so.
	Child puts his arms around mother or puts his hands on her shoulder when she picks him up.
Items Most Like Insecure Infant	Child easily becomes angry at mother.
	When something upsets the child, he stays where he is and cries.
	At home, child gets upset or cries when mother walks out of room.
	Child is demanding and impatient with mother, fusses and persists unless she does what he wants right away.
	When child is upset about mother leaving him, he sits down right where he is and cries, doesn't go after her.
	Child sometimes signals to mother (or gives the impression) that he wants to be put down and then fusses or wants to be picked right back up.

AQS administration is easy; one approach is to initially send caregivers the 90 items about two weeks before the actual sort. With these items in mind, the caregiver can more readily attend to the target behaviors over the two-week period and provide a more accurate sort. After this period, a researcher well versed in the AQS methodology visits the caregiver. The caregiver then sorts the 90 cards into three initial categories (Descriptive, Not Descriptive, and Neither/Cannot Judge), trying to ensure that the number of items per pile is equal. Next, the caregiver makes further discriminations by sorting the cards from the three original to nine categories (9 = Most Descriptive; 1 = Least Descriptive). The researcher can then ask the caregiver to adjust the piles until 10 cards are assigned to each category. Each item in each pile is then given a score, for example, all items in pile 9 are assigned a score of "9."

There are different ways to score the AQS. The AQS items can be combined to form different attachment-security scales, such as proximity, sociability, and positive affect. However, the most popular method is to correlate the caregiver's overall attachment-security rating with the "prototypically secure" child score that has been provided by experts. None of these strategies allow the researcher to "classify" the infant; instead, these methods provide continuous scores of attachment security/insecurity, dependency, or certain facets of attachment security, such as sociability and social perceptiveness.

The AQS is reliable and valid. Observer sorts are consistent over time, and maternal sorts modestly correlate with trained-observer sorts (Waters & Deane, 1985; Teti & McGourty,

What Do You Think?

Suppose you are asked to conduct research to support the contention that the Attachment Behavior Q-Set is a reliable and valid instrument. How might you design the studies to support these points?

1996); however, recent work suggests that observer sorts are more predictive of infant security assessed in the Strange Situation than are maternal sorts (van IJzendoorn et al., 2004). In addition, these correlations, when significant, are only modest. Perhaps the meaning of attachment security differs between the measures. The Strange Situation taps behavior in an environment designed to elicit distress and put strain on the attachment system. Theoretically, it is in these very situations that infants "need" a secure attachment relationship. On the other hand, a careful review of the AQS suggests that many of the items are "home-based," and some items may assess temperamental (as opposed to relationship) characteristics. Thus, these assessments may measure somewhat different, yet overlapping, constructs.

In summary, the AQS is valid, does not require a lot of training, and is easy to score. In addition, the AQS is a fascinating instrument to use when conducting cross-cultural attachment research; the results of some of this research are described in Box 5.3.

Variables that Predict Attachment Security or Insecurity

What predicts the development of attachment relationships between infants and their caregivers? Most of the research focuses on correlating assessments of maternal sensitivity, with either Strange Situation or Attachment Behavior Q-sort security/insecurity ratings. The results of individual studies are mixed; however, when the results of studies are marshaled together using **meta-analyses**, maternal sensitivity is modestly associated with attachment security (DeWolff & van IJzendoorn, 1997). In a meta-analysis procedure, researchers group together studies that contain similar designs, methods, and study populations. Next, they statistically examine the combined effects of the studies on some outcome measure, such as attachment.

Perhaps one of the most exciting research directions has focused on how parental working models of attachment influence caregiver sensitivity and subsequent attachment relationships between infants and caregivers. This is a relatively new line of research, and holds considerable promise for future research, and even practice. We next turn to a popular method of assessing working models of attachment in caregivers.

The Adult Attachment Interview

Theoretically, attachment experiences with caregivers during childhood are internalized as *generalized attachment representation*. These internal working models of attachment are conceptualized as the individual's current state of mind regarding experiences with caregivers, and are theorized to provide the individual a set of rules for the direction of affect, thinking, and behavior in social interactions with attachment figures (Bretherton & Munholland, 1999). The AAI is the most popular method used to assess these attachment representations.

BOX 5.3 • *Is Attachment Security Universally Valued?*

Critics of attachment theory suggest that constructs such as "attachment security" or "maternal sensitivity" might have very different definitions across cultures. For example, many Western theorists feel that infant exploration (during stress-free times), proximity seeking (during times of alarm), and the ability to accept comfort from a caregiver when distressed reflect attachment security. However, in other cultures, such behavior may not be philosophically viewed as a sign of security. In some Eastern cultures (e.g., Japan), infants are encouraged to maintain continual contact with caregivers, whereas exploration and independence are discouraged (Rothbaum et al., 2000). In such cultures, sudden separations would not be routine, may result in overly strong protest, and therefore make it very difficult to calm such infants in a 3-min Strange Situation reunion episode. However, although a Western attachment rater might consider such infants to be ambivalent or resistant, the baby may indeed be secure, given the culture's philosophy regarding attachment and dependence.

The Attachment Behavior Q-Set allows researchers to test exactly what scholars and caregivers view as an ideal infant-caregiver relationship during the first few years of life. Recall that in the development of this instrument, Western attachment experts were asked to sort attachment behaviors into categories that would reflect attachment security. In fact, in terms of identifying attachment security, the following attachment behavior was rated as one of the very most important, which is clearly at odds with the philosophy that dependence and maternal proximity is more desired (Waters et al., 1995):

> Child clearly shows a pattern of using mother as a base from which to explore. Moves out to play; returns or plays near her; moves out to play again, etc.

Why is the Attachment Behavior Q-Set so ingenious? Because Western experts have developed ideal "secure-insecure" criterion sorts, we can ask scholars and caregivers in other cultures to create their own sorts regarding the "ideal" child. If there is disagreement regarding which behaviors the ideal child will display, then the sorts originating from raters in different cultures should be quite different. In perhaps one of the most ambitious studies on this topic, Posada and colleagues asked child-development experts in China, Columbia, Germany, Israel, Japan, Norway, and the United States to provide descriptions, using the AQS, of a "very secure" baby (Posada et al., 1995). In addition, mothers from these cultures were asked to perform the AQS evaluation on their own child and on an "ideal" child.

Interestingly, child-development experts were very similar in their views of which behaviors constitute attachment security. In fact, the correlation between 18 Japanese and 6 United States experts was .90, meaning that experts in these countries view attachment security in much the same way. In addition, the mothers' impressions of which attachment behaviors constitute an "ideal" child were highly correlated with what attachment experts across the world conceptualize as a highly secure child. Thus, although cultures may differ philosophically on what behaviors make up the construct of attachment security, the reality is that child-development experts and parents actually see "eye to eye" regarding which behaviors constitute security and which attachment difficulties. Although more research is needed on this topic, the current study supports the notion that attachment security, and the typical behaviors Western attachment experts ascribes to the construct, are widely held across the world.

Adult Attachment Interview: A Brief Overview

The *Adult Attachment Interview* (AAI; George, Kaplan, & Main, 1996) is a 20-item protocol designed to assess the adult's state of mind regarding attachment experiences. The AAI assesses processing of attachment-relevant information and focuses on violations in linguistic discourse in response to past (e.g., "Provide five adjectives to describe your childhood relationship with your father."), current (e.g., "How do your relationships with your parents affect your current relationships?"), and future (e.g., "What do you hope your children will learn from you?") attachment experiences. The focus of the AAI is the respondent's *present* state of mind regarding emotional relationships, and the interviewer makes no attempts to "recover" past experiences with family members; rather, coders note violations in discourse (e.g., indicating that a parent was supportive and offering no evidence as to why, thought lapses during interview, passive or angry speech); reactions to separation, loss, rejection, and abuse; and perceived value of attachment experiences and how they relate to current development. The AAI has passed numerous reliability and validity tests, and classifications garnered from this interview are largely unrelated to verbal abilities, intelligence, and personality (Hesse, 1999).

As with the Strange Situation, the AAI classification system requires specialized training. The AAI coding scheme yields three organized adult attachment classifications based on the person's state of mind regarding attachment. *Thus it is entirely possible for people who report negative experiences with parents to be rated as secure, given that they are open, objective, accepting, and collaborative regarding these previous experiences.* Further descriptions of these classifications are given in Table 5.10.

Individuals classified as *secure* are coherent and collaborative throughout the interview, and can discuss *both* positive and negative experiences in an objective manner. *Dismissing* adults provide highly positive, generalized representations of attachment experiences, which are unsupported or even contradicted throughout the interview. These individuals are often dismissive of unfavorable attachment experiences ("Mom used to ignore me, but it was for my own good."). *Preoccupied* adults provide excessive discourse when describing attachment experiences and show strong negative (e.g., anger) responses when discussing experiences (Main & Goldwyn, 1994).

After the aforementioned classifications are derived, interviews can be classified as *Unresolved/Disorganized* with respect to past abuse or loss, in which respondents: (a) display major lapses in the monitoring of reasoning surrounding the loss or trauma, such as fears of being taken over mentally by an abusive attachment figure, (b) highly incoherent speech, (c) disbelief that maltreatment or loss has occurred, or, (d) lapses in monitoring of discourse, such as unusual attention to detail of loss or maltreatment, sudden changes of topic, or sudden invasions of other topics or information (Main & Goldwyn, 1994).

Regarding this latter classification, significant childhood loss or repeated physical or sexual abuse experiences *does not* automatically lead to an unresolved attachment classification. There are secure people who have experienced such events yet can speak about them in a coherent manner. *Unresolved* adults *remain* traumatized, as indicated by their peculiar patterns of linguistic discourse during the AAI as they discuss these experiences.

Associations with Infant Attachment and Caregiver Sensitivity

The AAI classifications parallel the infant Strange Situation classifications. Is it possible that infants develop attachment relationships with parents that parallel the way their parents construct relationships with their own caregivers? Amazingly, van IJzendoorn (1995), in a meta-analysis involving 14 studies, noted that about 70% of the time, parents rated as secure or insecure on the AAI had babies with an identical secure-insecure match as assessed via the Strange Situation. For example, a dismissing parent is likely to have an

TABLE 5.10 *Adult Attachment Interview Classifications (adapted from Hesse, 1999)*

Attachment State of Mind	Sample Interview Segment
Secure/Autonomous Coherent and collaborative throughout the Interview. Valuing of attachment, but seems objective regarding any particular event or relationship. Description and evaluation of attachment-related experiences is consistent, whether experiences themselves are favorable or unfavorable.	"Well, mom was always very loving, I can give you a million examples. She used to hug us goodnight, and would let me sleep in her bed if I was sick. Sometimes she would nag us, but she was just looking out for our well being. Do you need any more examples?"
Dismissing Not coherent, dismissing of attachment-related experiences and relationships. Very generalized representations of history that are unsupported or contradicted by autobiographical episodes recounted. Interviews tend to be excessively brief.	"Mom was perfect and loving, but I can't give you any examples to support these adjectives. She was always around, like if I got hurt, quick bandage, "Don't bother me anymore with your little problems." Yea, she was really a loving, perfect mom."
Preoccupied Not coherent. Preoccupied with or by past attachment relationships or experiences. Speaker appears angry, passive, or fearful. Sentences often long, grammatically entangled, or filled with vague usages (e.g., "dadadaddada," "on here"). Transcripts often excessively long.	"Mom was perfect and loving, except when she was thinking of herself, which is all of the time. She must be the most self-absorbed, manipulative woman, you know, "You look so ugly in that dress, it makes you look like a little slut." I, love her, she's crazy, like, 'What's wrong with you, why can't you get good grades like your brother,' yea, and that."
Unresolved/Disorganized During discussions of loss or abuse, individual shows striking lapses in the monitoring of reasoning or discourse. For example, individual may refer to dead person as briefly alive, may lapse into prolonged silences, or lapse into eulogistic speech. *Individual may otherwise fit the other three, organized classifications.*	"Dad has been dead for twenty years. He thinks I should, I mean he thought I should go into business for myself. I feel sometimes he is out there, you know guiding my thoughts and actions, I mean, I see him sometimes briefly in my face in the mirror. When things go right, I just know he is influencing things somehow, you know, steering me in the right direction."

What Do You Think?

A central theory embraced by attachment researchers is that the relationship between parent attachment functioning and the development of infant attachment is explained by parent sensitivity, that is, a parent who is secure will be more sensitive to their infant than an insecure parent. In turn, this sensitivity will affect the development of infant attachment. How would you design a study to validate this theory?

avoidant baby, whereas an unresolved/ disorganized caregiver is more likely to have a disorganized infant. The fact that many of the caregivers in these studies were administered AAIs *before* the birth of their babies makes these results even more compelling.

Adult attachment representations may affect the emotional sensitivity of the caregiver, which in turn predicts infant attachment. However, associations between AAI classification, parent sensitivity, and subsequent infant classifications are only "modest" (Pederson et al., 1998). These modest associations could result from training problems (in such cases, the researcher must be well versed in Strange Situation and AAI classification systems), continued difficulties assessing the slippery construct "caregiver sensitivity," or van IJzendoorn's (1995) *transmission-gap* hypothesis. This latter suggestion simply means that there may be additional variables, such as parental mental health or infant characteristics that help solidify associations between adult and infant attachment.

Frightening or Frightened Caregiver Behavior

Recall that disorganized infants often have a caregiver that is unresolved because of loss or trauma. Adults classified as unresolved/disorganized on the AAI have their own sets of problems, including an increased risk for psychopathology, and control-oriented, violent romantic relationships (Creasey, 2002). Thus, parents of disorganized infants who are unresolved regarding loss or trauma might be prone to very insensitive caregiver behavior. However, when using traditional caregiver sensitivity measures, unresolved/disorganized caregivers are *not* qualitatively different from parents with alternative attachment classifications. This startling finding has led experts to explore other variables that may explain the association between unresolved parent and disorganized infant attachment status.

To begin, scholars have considered what makes an unresolved state of mind regarding attachment different from the other attachment classifications. During the AAI, unresolved adults display startling lapses in the monitoring of reasoning and linguistic processes as they discuss loss or abuse experiences (e.g., "I hided from my father when he used to hit me."). Hesse (1996) suggests that these lapses result from "frightening and/or overwhelming experiences that may momentarily be controlling or altering" linguistic discourser (p. 8). When caregivers are reminded of these experiences, they may momentarily engage in peculiar, frightening, or frightened behavior toward their own infants (Main & Hesse, 1990). Thus, a crying toddler may somehow spark memories in the parent of a time when they were physically abused as a child, resulting in overwhelming feelings of fear or anger in the caregiver that may momentarily lead to somewhat bizarre caregiver behavior.

Main and Hesse (1998) developed a coding system to capture such peculiar parenting behavior, something that simply cannot be captured via traditional caregiver sensitivity paradigms. The coding system, depicted in Table 5.11, consists of six behaviors that encompass two behavioral classes. In the first class, the caregiver exhibits behavior that might be considered frightening to the infant, such as "overwhelming" hide-and-seek games, or temporary dissociative states, in which the parent may still or freeze in midsentence or behavior. For example, as the parent begins to feed a crying baby, the caregiver may adopt a confused, dreamy look, and "freeze" behaviorally for 30 seconds.

The second set of behaviors consists of bizarre conflicts with traditional caregiver behavior, such as extremely timid, deferential (e.g., "Please, please, please drink your milk for your mother, please, please.") or sexualized behavior. In all cases, Main and Hesse (1990) speculate that such bizarre parenting behavior is distinctly frightening or confusing to the infant, suggesting that the caregiver is a major paradox in the infant's life. For example, the infant may not know whether to approach or flee from the caregiver, leading to cases in which babies, when distressed, may experience "fright without solution" (Main & Hesse, 1998).

TABLE 5.11   *Frightening, Frightened, and Disorganized Parenting Behavior (Main & Hesse, 1998)*

Behavioral Typology	Description/Example
Frightening/threatening behavioral patterns	Behavior that is distinctly overwhelming or frightening to a young child. Such as sudden "looming," or "predatory" hunt/chase behavior, where there is no indication of a game.
Frightened behavioral patterns	Caregiver seems "frightened" of infant; for example, may ask infant not to follow, or quickly retreat from the baby.
Direct indices of dissociative state	Caregiver may suddenly still or freeze in mid-action. Often accompanied by glazy, dreamy look.
Timid/deferential behavior	Overly deferential to baby, almost as if role were reversed. May plead submissively with the infant to engage in an action.
Sexualized or spousal behavior	Treats infant almost like a spouse, for example, may kiss infant deeply and repeatedly, or may invite or encourage infant to caress and touch in a sexualized manner.
Other disorganized or disoriented behaviors	Additional unusual, unexplainable caregiver behaviors.

Frightening caregiving behavior may explain the bizarre disorganized infant behaviors witnessed during the Strange Situation. There exist two investigations exploring associations between unresolved adult attachment, frightening or frightened behavior, and infant attachment disorganization (Jacobvitz, Hazen, & Riggs, 1997; Schuengel et al., 1999), and one cross-cultural study (True, Pisani, & Oumar, 2001). In each study caregivers assigned an unresolved AAI classification exhibited high amounts of this bizarre behavior, which in turn predicted infant disorganization.

Summary of Adult Attachment Interview

Although a number of landmark studies have documented amazing relationships between the AAI and infant attachment, there is still much work to be done. Most notable, attachment researchers still have not solved the "transmission gap" problem. That is, caregiver sensitivity, as well as frightening or frightened behavior, does not completely explain the relationship between adult and infant attachment. This finding suggests that there may be other variables, such as the infant's attachment relationship with other potential caregivers (e.g., child-care workers), which also affect infant emotional development.

Chapter Summary

One thing that you may have observed in this chapter is that people often study the development of basic infant emotions, emotion regulation, and attachment in an isolated fashion. That is, researchers tend to have separate "camps," suggesting these constructs represent "different fields of study." However, consider that secure infants are often loaded with positive affect, and they use their caregivers during times of alarm to regulate negative emotions. Thus, there is a need for research that brings these important constructs together.

Also, the role of the caregiver in supporting socioemotional development in infants still remains somewhat unclear. Although most assume that caregivers are an important component of this process, it still seems that just about anything the caregiver does has only a modest effect on infant social and emotional processes. Perhaps improvements in methodologies will change this finding; however, maybe too many of us assume that the caregivers chiefly affect infants, whereas infants contribute little to their own development. However, careful longitudinal work, examining both infant (e.g., biobehavioral variables) and caregiver (e.g., sensitivity) study variables may help us better illuminate this process.

Finally, let me again stress the point that although we seem to know a lot about Caucasian, European American mothers and their infants, we need to better examine the roles of fathers, other relatives, and substitute caregivers in the lives of infants, and consider how these roles may affect the development of infants across other cultures.

Research Navigator™ Exercise: Infant Attachment

The primary objective of this assignment is to learn more about methods used to assess infant attachment. Go the Research Navigator™ website: http://www.researchnavigator.com. In the "ContentSelect" section, choose the Psychology database, and type *infant attachment* as a keyword. After reading a full-length article, try to answer the following questions:

1. What were the primary research questions and hypotheses?
2. How was infant attachment assessed?
3. Was attachment used as an outcome measure or as a predictor of a later competency?
4. What were the primary conclusions?

6

PART III

Research Methods in Child Development

Assessing Cognitive Processes in Children

One day, my 8-year-old son, Alex, told me that his friend had not invited him to a party. I later told my wife that Alex was upset because his friend had "stabbed him in the back." Upon hearing this comment, my son remarked, "Dad, he didn't stab me with a knife!"

In this chapter, you will learn about techniques designed to capture such interesting thinking in children. Recall in Chapter 4 that the cognitive-developmental, information processing, and psychometric approaches represented the major perspectives on human cognition. Experts who embrace these approaches would consider different aspects of Alex's thinking. For example, cognitive-developmental experts, such as Jean Piaget, might compare his reasoning ability with that of older children; older children would understand that initial appearances (stabbed in the back) do not always mesh with reality ("It's a figure of speech").

Information-processing experts are more interested in documenting how children store, process, and retrieve information. These experts might study Alex's memory for the conversation between him and his best friend, and contrast it to how older children remember similar conversations. In this chapter, you will learn about ways to assess storage and retrieval processes, and learn about how to capture strategies children use to remember information.

Psychometric experts are concerned with "what" children have learned. The developers of intelligence tests endorse this perspective; these specialists are interested in documenting individual differences in cognitive abilities. Thus, psychometric researchers are interested in the "product" of cognition, whereas cognitive-developmental and information-processing experts are more interested in the "process." Because process occurs before outcome, we will concentrate our efforts on identifying methodological issues regarding the cognitive-developmental and information-processes approaches in this chapter. In the next chapter, you will learn about ways to capture the "product" of cognition, through the use of intelligence tests.

After reading this chapter, you should be able to:

- Contrast the Piagetian and information-processing perspectives of human cognition.
- Indicate classic Piagetian tasks designed to assess conservation problems, transitivity, class-inclusion errors, and perspective taking.
- Discuss contemporary concerns about Piaget's theory and indicate how researchers assess a child's domain-specific knowledge, "theory of mind," and sociodramatic play.
- Describe how to assess components of the human information-processing system.

Assessing Cognition I: Piagetian Techniques

In this section, you will learn more about Piaget's theory and the simple tasks he created to assess reasoning skills in children; these tasks are reliable and valid. I encourage you to try the tasks with different-aged children. They are easy to administer, and it is hard not to chuckle over the developmental predictability of children's reasoning as they tackle the tasks.

Piaget's Theory: A Brief Overview

Piaget asserted that children advance through the four major stages of cognitive development outlined in Table 6.1. He assumed that children universally progressed through these four stages in an invariant (nonreversible), orderly manner. In addition, Piaget viewed cognitive development as very "child-centered," and theorized that children played an active role in their cognitive development. In developing an understanding of the world, Piaget assumed that children strive to adapt to their surroundings to enhance learning opportunities.

How does such adaptation work? Piaget assumed that children develop increasingly sophisticated mental structures termed **schemes**. A scheme is structured knowledge regarding actions and thoughts that allow us to cope with, and learn about, the environment. To think about how schemes become more sophisticated, consider how schemes regarding a block changes with cognitive maturity. Young infants will put it in their mouth, older infants will throw it across the room or bang it on the table, and preschoolers will place it on top of other blocks to build a tower. Note in this example that increasingly well-organized or coordinated schemes guide both thought and action (behavior). The process of schematic organization is a central tenet of Piaget's theory. For example, an infant presented a stick and an out-of-reach toy may have only two simple, independent schemes in place: knowledge of the stick (scheme one) and the toy (scheme two). As infants cognitively mature, they will integrate these schemes and use the stick to obtain the toy.

How do schemes change and allow children to cope with learning environments? According to Piaget, adaptation occurs as the result of assimilation and accommodation. **Assimilation** is the active integration of new information into previously existing schemes. For example, recently my child picked up a pogo stick and began using it like a machine gun. He assimilated the toy into his existing mental structure regarding a gun (I was not happy with this!). **Accommodation** consists of modifying a scheme based on new experiences that conflicts with the existing scheme. A child may initially call a "cow" a "doggie" or a

TABLE 6.1 *Piaget's Stages of Cognitive Development*

Stage	Description	Assessment Strategies
Sensorimotor (ages birth–2)	Infants come to understand their world primarily from physical experience. Gradually, interest in world shifts from self to objects. Seemingly random interactions with objects become more purposeful and gradually more experimental. By end of 2nd year, can represent objects no longer present through deferred imitation and pretend play.	Can assess infant's understanding regarding integrity of objects by observing the baby manipulating and playing with objects. Goal-directed behavior can be observed via tasks that require 2- or 3-step problem- solving, such as pulling a string to obtain a red ring. Object-hiding tasks allow for assessment of object permanence, and deferred imitation can be used to assess representational skills. *Play assessments also allow for a comprehensive assessment.*
Preoperational (ages 2–7)	Development of sophisticated representational skills and seeds of logical thinking. Constraints on learning are evident; for example, frequently confuses reality with fantasy, may lack perspective taking, and may fail to integrate relevant features of a task. Thus may view a short, wide piece of cake as much bigger than an equivalent-sized thin, long piece. Lack of perspective-taking inhibits teaching efforts by frustrated parents!	Representational skills can be assessed and differentiated from toddler thinking through more complex deferred imitation tasks and pretend-play observations. The prelogical thinking of preschoolers can be assessed using classic Piagetian tasks that routinely uncover problems in perspective-taking, appearance-reality confusions, and tendency to focus on one feature of a task without considering all relevant task features.
Concrete operational (ages 7–11)	Development of consistent, logical thinking across contexts. Thinking becomes less centered and flexible; thus school-aged children are capable of better understanding the perspective of others, and can integrate relevant features of a task. Although good at problem-solving, thinking still is not very abstract or hypothetical in nature. Better at thinking about objects than ideas.	These children frequently solve simple Piagetian tasks that require perspective taking, or the understanding that appearance does not always equate with reality. Capable of tasks that require more complex classification skills; for example, can sort red and blue circles and squares into red circles, red squares, blue circles, and blue squares. Important also to differentiate thinking from formal operational thought.
Formal operational (adolescence)	Thinking can be logical, abstract, and hypothetical. Better scientific and if-then thinking.	Piagetian tasks that assess hypothetical and deductive reasoning. Tasks require manipulation of ideas rather than objects.

stranger "daddy." People around the child will quickly correct her, particularly in the latter case! Gradually, the child adjusts her thinking based on these experiences.

Piaget captured qualitative differences in children's thinking by carefully interviewing children as they reasoned about problems (Piaget, 1929/1979). He noted that age differences in reasoning *went beyond* whether the child correctly solved a task. Rather, he noted that preschoolers, children, and adolescents reasoned very differently when solving problems. This method varies considerably from his work with infants. Much of his theory regarding the sensorimotor period (Stage 1) was based on his naturalistic, home-based, longitudinal observations of his own infants. In contrast, his research on older children involved larger samples that were exposed to tasks designed to elicit thought. In contrast to his infancy work, he used cross-sectional designs to document age differences in the reasoning of older children.

In Chapter 4, I indicated that the sensorimotor period (birth to 2 years) represented only one stage in his theory. Recall that during the latter part of the sensorimotor stage infants acquire the capability to think about events no longer present. Such *representational thought* represents advancement in adaptive thinking, because it allows the child to think beyond the reality of an observed context. For example, a toddler who has a secure representation of her mother can effectively cope with maternal separations because of this particular scheme.

After infants negotiate the sensorimotor period, toddlers enter the preoperational stage (Stage 2; ages 2–6). During the **preoperational stage**, older toddlers and preschoolers continue to represent reality using mental images, language, and solitary pretend play (Piaget & Inhelder, 1969). The development of representational thought represents a major *advancement* in cognitive development. It is apparent from watching young children integrate elaborate sociodramatic themes in play (e.g., "You be Batman and I'll be Spiderman") that preschoolers are capable of advanced representational and occasional logical thinking.

Nevertheless, Piaget believed that there were learning constraints during the preopertational period that precluded the use of the more consistent logical thought exhibited by children in the **concrete operational stage** (Stage 3). He noted that preoperational children were more intuitive in their thinking, and more influenced by the initial appearance in a task than the reality of the situation—think of how preschoolers become frightened of a parent with a mask on. They focus on their one scheme (the mask), without coordinating others ("Mommy has a mask on, but it's still Mommy"). Let's now turn to some simple tasks that Piaget developed to capture differences in schematic organization in younger and older children.

An Introduction to Piagetian Methods

Piaget interviewed children as they completed a variety of simple tasks, and carefully adjusted the interview, depending on the way the child answered his questions and probes. For example, consider a task in which a child is shown two identical balls of clay:

> **Interviewer:** Now watch, I am going to make two sausages out of these balls (Rolls one ball so it is longer and thinner than other). Now do we have the same amount to eat?
>
> **Child (age 5):** No.

Interviewer: What can you do that we'll have the same amount to eat?

Child: (takes about half of the longer sausage): Now we have the same amount to eat.

Interviewer: Do you think so?

Child (looks really carefully): No, you have more, because it's fatter (referring to unchanged sausage).

Interviewer: What can we do so we have the same amount to eat?

Child: I don't know. (adapted from Gallagher & Reid, 1981, p. 88)

Using this technique, Piaget documented that preoperational children repeatedly made errors on **conservation tasks**. In these tasks, Piaget would superficially alter an object's properties, and then ask the child whether or not major features of the object had been changed. Imagine a situation in which a child is presented 5 coins in 2 rows across two trials:

	Trial 1	Trial 2
ROW 1	0 0 0 0 0	0 0 0 0 0
ROW 2	0 0 0 0 0	0 0 0 0 0

In this numerical conversation task, preoperational children made errors in Trial 2 by assuming that Row 2 contained more coins because they took up more space. Thus, preoperational children lack the ability to focus attention on more than one feature of a task, a difficulty known as **centration**. Figure 6.1 contains an example of a Piagetian conservation task. The ability to pass such tests does not appear simultaneously; that is, conservation of number occurs before conversation of mass, which is followed by conservation of weight.

Unlike preoperational children, concrete-operational children avoid centration problems because they possess flexible, coordinated schemata. So, they can mentally picture the coins in Trial 2 (Row 2) spread out, and can picture the coins pushed back into their original place. Similarly, they can understand that if you pour the water back from the tall, thin container into the shorter, wider one the amounts are the same. Thus, concrete-operational children possess the ability to *reverse* mental actions or operations (Inhelder & Piaget, 1964).

Reversibility and centration difficulties can also be witnessed in the preoperational child's classification abilities. In Piaget's **class-inclusion tasks**, preoperational children displayed difficulties understanding the association between a global class (animals) and its subclasses (lions, tigers, and bears). In one such task, the child was questioned about simple class inclusion. For example, consider the following query:

"I have 10 flowers, and most are roses; do I have more roses or more flowers?"

Piaget noted that preschoolers often "centered" on the word "most" and indicated there were more roses! However, a concrete-operational child might say, "There are more roses, but roses are one type of flower. So, roses are the most common flower, but there are more flowers than roses." Most importantly, the concrete-operational child has the ability to go forward and backward in terms of thinking, and considers both sub- (roses) and global (flowers) classes.

In addition to conservation and classification skills, Piaget studied children's understanding of cause and effect. The ability to apply different ideas or schemes to understand

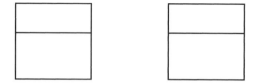

1) Here are 2 glasses. Do they have the same amount of water or does one have more?

2) Next, experimenter pours water from one of the glasses into the tall, thin glass

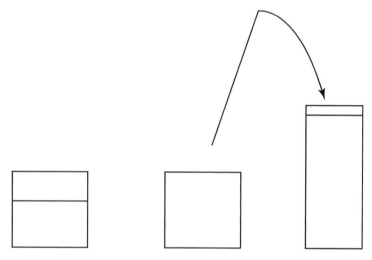

FIGURE 6.1 *Piaget's Liquid-Conservation Task.* Preoperational children will say that the tall, thin glass has more water than the short, wide glass.

3) Is there the same amount of water in the old and new glass, or does one have more? Why?

logical conclusions is termed **transitivity**, and can be understood by viewing the Piagetian task in Figure 6.2. In this task, children are asked what would happen if the first domino were pushed. Preoperational children will understand that pushing the first domino will cause the next one or two to fall, but will claim that the dominos toward the end will not fall because they are too far away. However, concrete-operational children will understand the principle of a chain reaction.

The structure of thought that is captured by this task is relationship transitivity ability. That is, A causes B to fall and B causes C to fall; thus there must be a causative link between A and C (Gallagher & Reid, 1981). An ability to understand the concept of reversibility can also be witnessed in relationship-transitivity exercises. For example, although event A may cause B to occur, B may not necessarily cause event A. However, preoperational children will reason that because A and B are closely connected, one always causes the other. This is an incorrect assumption. For example, I occasionally make a mess

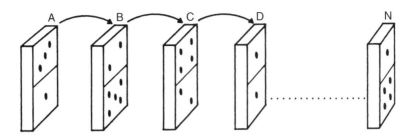

FIGURE 6.2 *Piaget's Domino-Transitivity Task.* Preoperational children will say that domino A will hit B and then C, but will claim that domino N is too far away to be affected by the earlier dominos.

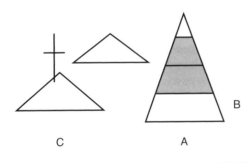

FIGURE 6.3 *Piaget's Three-Mountain Task.* Child, positioned at A, is asked if a doll, positioned behind the mountain at B, can see the steeple, positioned on mountain C. Preoperational children, for the most part, will claim that the doll can see the mountain. To you and me, the doll's position is clearly blocked by the mountain.

in the kitchen; however, a mess in the kitchen does not always mean that I caused it; at least that's my argument to my spouse!

Can we reason with preoperational children so that they can better understand conservation, class inclusion and transitivity tasks? Perhaps one major obstacle is that adultlike logical reasoning does not have much effect on these aforementioned cognitive constraints. Piaget demonstrated this limitation in his *perspective-taking tasks.* In the **three-mountain task**, depicted in Figure 6.3, Piaget documented that preoperational thought is highly *egocentric*; that is, preschoolers often cannot take another person's perspective when presented these tasks.

In this task, the child, seated at position A, is asked if a doll, positioned behind the mountain at B, can see the steeple, positioned on mountain C. Children younger than six indicated that the little doll could see both; however, the steeple is *clearly blocked by the mountain* (Piaget & Inhelder, 1948, 1956). You can move preoperational children around to where the doll is positioned and ask the same question. In such instances, most will say, "No, the doll cannot see the cross," because they realize that they themselves cannot see it. Yet, if you move them back to the original position, they will answer, "Oh yeah, now the little boy can see it." Perhaps this example demonstrates why it is so hard to reason with preoperational children!

Unlike preoperational children, the concrete-operational child can mentally create order and transform objects. This advanced thinking decreases the tendency to center, or focus on the most superficial characteristics of a task. Such thinking allows the child to take the perspective of others and develop more sophisticated classification skills. However, the logical thinking of

What Do You Think?

Describe Piagetian conservation, class-inclusion, transitivity, and perspective-taking tasks and the performance of preoperational and concrete operational children on them.

older children is frequently bound by concrete reality. For example, 6- to 12-year-old children sometimes have difficulties thinking about hypothetical situations and abstract subjects. We will revisit this more advanced, formal operational thinking in Chapter 9.

Summary of Piagetian Theory and Tasks

Whereas Piaget's theoretical rationale for his sensorimotor stage of cognitive developmental was based on repeated, naturalistic observations of his infants, the development of later stages was guided by his observations of larger samples of older children as they negotiated simple tasks that he created. Based on these observations, he noted that toddlers, preschoolers, school-aged children, and adolescents reasoned in qualitatively distinct ways. Further, he suggested that cognitive development occurred in a sudden, stagelike manner.

Methodologically, his simple conservation, class-inclusion, transitivity, and perspective-taking tasks are easy to conduct and replicate when using his protocol. The ease of experimenter training is dependent on the nature of our research question; if you simply want to document age differences in successful task accomplishment, then a highly trained interviewer who probes the reasoning behind children's responses would not be needed. However, there is a concern with such a simple tactic. That is, the reasoning process behind the child's response would not be captured; documenting developmental differences in such reasoning was a central component to his theory. Unfortunately, many subsequent studies using Piagetian tasks—some will be presented in the next section—have relied on this more simplistic method of data gathering.

Piaget's work has made a large impact on the field. His clinical method, carefully probing the reasoning of children during task performance, sharply contrasts with the way we traditionally assess intellect in our society. In conventional intelligence tests, credit is usually given for the response outcome and not the reasoning behind it; the clinical method allows for an assessment of an active cognitive process in motion. Also, his theoretical suggestions have been consistently replicated when using his tasks; preschoolers consistently fail conservation, class-inclusion, appearance-reality, and perspective-taking tasks when using his protocol. His theory has been applied to educational settings; for example, the documentation of certain learning constraints in children probably explains why complex curriculums in science, psychology, and politics are not routinely taught to young children.

Assessing Cognition II: Recent Techniques

Some experts believe Piaget *underestimated* the competencies of children. After slight alterations of some of his original tasks or via task training, children sometimes show more advanced thinking. Also, recall that Piaget felt that cognitive advancement was a child-centered process, and that learning occurred best during solitary learning pursuits. However, some believe that he also *overestimated* the abilities of children, because they do not always show their top cognitive abilities when exposed to solitary learning environments. In this section, we will examine some of this more contemporary work.

Alteration of Task Requirements and Training

Although Piaget's findings have been replicated using his methods (Flavell, 1985), he underestimated children's thinking. This new theory has emerged because of creative modifications to Piagetian tasks that involve adapting the tasks to make them less complex or allowing practice sessions. Let's consider how new methods led to theory modifications regarding the development of conservation, class inclusion, transitivity, and perspective taking.

Conservation/Class Inclusion. Piaget indicated that most children couldn't correctly solve conservation problems until they reached the concrete-operational stage (ages 7–11); their apparent difficulty is caused by centration and their focus on appearance and not reality. For example, when he showed young children (ages 4–7) sugar dissolving in water, they frequently suggested that this substance was "gone forever." Young children could not comprehend the notion that the sugar had dissolved into tiny particles (Piaget & Inhelder, 1941/1974).

However, Rosen and Rozin (1993) documented that young preschoolers (ages 3 to 5) *were* capable of understanding that the sugar had dissolved. These discrepant findings could be because of differences in the experimental context. In the more recent study, children were familiarized to the experimental context and task materials. The young children were first introduced to the stuffed animals Big Bird, and Oscar the Grouch, and allowed to touch, taste, and smell the different substances (soap, sugar, and citric acid) used in the dissolving paradigm. Next, the materials were dissolved, and they were asked to identify the glass of water preferred by the characters (e.g., "Which one for Oscar and which one for Big Bird?").

Most of these children were able to correctly understand the concept of mass or substance. They understood that Oscar preferred the soapy drink because it was "Yucky" and Big Bird liked the sweet drink because it was "Yummy"! The children understood that the sugar was not gone forever (i.e., conserved) because they reasoned that the drink must taste good or bad. When tasks are more familiar, made simpler, or crafted in a "real world" context, even preschoolers can pass Piagetian-like conservation tasks (Gelman & Baillargeon, 1983).

Such findings are not just relevant to conservation tasks; younger preschoolers can correctly understand class inclusion and ignore their intuitive perceptions. In one study, 4-year-olds were shown pictures of a tropical fish, a dolphin, and a shark. The shark was perceptually (or appeared) similar to the dolphin but given the same category label as the tropical fish (both are fish). Next, they were given facts about the different pictures, such as "This one (the shark) breathes differently than this one (the dolphin)." Finally the young children had to decide whether the shark breathed like a tropical fish because both are fish or like a dolphin because they *looked* alike. They consistently ignored the perceptual similarities between the pictures and provided responses that matched with the facts they had been provided (Gelman & Markman, 1986).

Transitivity. Preoperational children can make correct, complex causal links between ideas and objects via training attempts (Holcomb, Stromer, & Mackay, 1997) or by presenting them with relationship-transitivity tasks that involve familiar themes. The child is told, "Child A and Child B are really good friends, and Child B is really good friends with Child C, but not with Child D or Child E. Now, insert people you know into this formula and write down the two most likely to be invited to a party by Child A." This is a simple method with an easily identifiable dependent variable.

If the subject indicates that B and C would be invited, then the child would be rated as possessing correct transitive judgments. Interestingly, although younger children are less likely to get this exercise correct than school-aged children, their performance is enhanced if they are allowed to believe that the children are really good friends versus "just friendly" (Markovits & Dumas, 1999). When tasks are made simpler and relevant, even preoperational children can occasionally pass Piagetian tasks and display more logical thought.

Perspective-Taking Methods.   Experimenters created tasks that demonstrate that preoperational children can engage in perspective taking. For example, preschoolers can consistently draw a line from a character's eyes to an object and indicate what the character is looking at (Yaniv & Shatz, 1990). In addition, young children can consider another's perspective if easily differentiated items are included in tasks similar to the mountain-perspective problem described earlier. In one study, an elaborate display was constructed that required children to drive a Sesame Street character around a setting (i.e., practice session) that included a silo, a farm-house, and farm animals (familiar, easily differentiated objects). When asked to identify animals that only the character could see, even 3-year-old children were able to adopt the other perspective (Borke, 1975).

The way we assess perspective-taking skills as a dependent variable is also an important methodological consideration. For example, preoperational children often fail perspective-taking tasks that require them to select one picture, out of several, that might represent another's perspective from a vantage point that is different from that of the child. However, when this task is made simpler, preoperational children often engage in correct perspective taking. In one study, researchers positioned toys around a table and asked 5-year-olds to sit at different vantage points. Next, the children were instructed to sit at one location at the table, yet were asked to imagine sitting at another (a "pretend" stool). Finally, they were asked to simply identify which toy would be closest to them if they sat at the other location. About 80 percent of the time, the children could adopt the correct perspective; thus, perspective-taking limitations in young children are often task dependent (Newcombe & Huttenlocher, 1992).

In summary, when provided less complex tasks that represent more familiar settings, preschoolers can display occasional logical thought. However, Piaget documented that these children, using his tasks, displayed startling cognitive limitations. Perhaps these discrepant findings could explain why young children do not seem afraid of big rocks, yet are scared of witches. The more experienced the child is with the task or context, the more logical the thinking, which is consistent with Piaget's notion that physical experiences enhance schematic development and organization. Thus, these considerations challenge Piaget's notion that cognitive-development progresses in a global, stagelike manner across all cognitive domains.

What Do You Think?

Consider your thought processes in highly familiar or unfamiliar subjects or domains. Do you display advanced thinking in all domains? How might you design a research study to test the assumption that our thinking is equivalent across different knowledge domains?

Assessing Domain-Specific Knowledge

Neo-Piagetian researchers embrace some of the tenets of Piaget's original theory, yet continue to refine his methodologies to better understand how children's reasoning is affected by task familiarity, complexity, administration, and data-gathering techniques. It also appears that most experts in this area have abandoned his idea of global, rigid, all-or-none stages. These researchers believe that the thinking of preschoolers, children, and adolescents is qualitatively different most, *but not all*, of the time.

For instance, Fischer (1980) proposed that the child and the environment together shape cognitive development. That is, heavy environmental support can lead to cognitive advancement involving certain skills or domains but not others. Thus, rather than accept the notion that there are sudden, global changes in cognitive development, cognitive advancement is most likely to occur in localized cognitive domains or modules. Thinking is assumed to be sharper in domains involving more familiar objects or tasks (Carey & Gelman, 1991). Although Piaget assumed that the scope of cognitive abilities in children is narrow and constrained to cognitive stages, skill or modularity theories assume that the child may show a more broad range of abilities.

Is the latter premise true? In order to test such a theory, researchers frequently assess the skill acquisition of children through training experiences and determine whether such training causes sharp upturns in thinking in localized skills or domains. Alternatively, one can contrast the cognitive development of children who have experience or expertise in certain domains (e.g., chess) to similarly aged children that do not. In one study, researchers controlled for both issues. Chi and colleagues examined skill at sorting toy dinosaurs into different categories, such as size or shape of teeth. These researchers discovered two trends. First, as preschoolers learn more about dinosaurs, they begin sorting and classifying them as concrete-operational children do. Also, "expert" preschoolers who know a lot about dinosaurs are able to sort them into fairly complex categories, such as large dinosaurs with sharp teeth from small ones with dull teeth (Chi & Koeske, 1983; Chi, Hutchinson, & Robin, 1989).

However, not everyone in this field is in complete agreement with this premise and argue that if two equally complex problems are presented to two cognitive domains (e.g., social dilemma versus spatial task) and require similar problem-solving skills, children display highly similar responses across both tasks (Case et al., 1986). Such findings support Piaget's contention that reasoning skills are global in nature rather than confined to specific modules.

Nevertheless, arguments in favor of more skill-specific cognitive development attract a wide following. This new theory may explain why a child demonstrates logical and hypothetical reasoning while playing chess yet shows major limitations in mathematics. Indeed, there has been intensive research identifying cognitive-developmental phases in areas such as music, numerical concepts, scientific reasoning, and spatial abilities (see Case, 1998 for a review). In each case, it is important to examine developmental differences in children's domain-specific thinking, and control for the child's level of expertise regarding a domain module (e.g., chess). Alternatively, level of expertise within a domain can be specifically assessed using pretests, allowing researchers to test important age-by-expertise-level interactions.

Assessing Theory of Mind

Piaget assumed that preoperational children routinely failed his conservation tasks because they had limited insight into their own mental abilities, which explained reality and appearance confusions. That is, to discern between reality and fantasy, we must assemble and organize data (or schemes) and make predictions regarding what is real versus a fantasy, dream, or imagination. Piaget assumed young children were poor at this ability, which explains why young children commonly fear witches more than international terrorism. He theorized that better comprehension regarding mental abilities develops during the concrete-operational period, and is a major force behind more flexible, logical thinking.

An awareness regarding our own thought processes and our beliefs regarding the way the mind operates, has been termed **theory of mind** (ToM) or **metacognitive awareness** (Flavell & Miller, 1998; Wellman & Gelman, 1998). You are aware of factors that influence your attitudes and beliefs, storage and recall of information, and likelihood of engaging in fantasy and imagination. You understand what is real and not real, and can provide a rationale for your reasoning on such issues. ToM research is a hot area, perhaps because recent work demonstrates that it is *during the preschool years* that children show major development, suggesting that Piaget underestimated such cognitive capabilities of young children.

How do you assess theory of mind (ToM) in children? Well, in order not to confuse appearance and reality, the child must be able to mentally theorize, "This looks like X, but I know that it really is Y" (Gopnik & Astington, 1988). To assess such thinking, Flavell and colleagues (1986) developed a simple paradigm in which children are shown tricky or misleading stimuli. For example, the child is shown a sponge that is made to look like a rock, and red objects that appear to change to a black color when placed behind a green filter. Children are asked if the object is "really and truly" a sponge, or if the object has "really and truly" changed color. The dependent variable is the child's response to *both* an appearance and a reality question—for example, in the case of the red object placed behind the green filter:

"When you look at this right now, does it look red or does it look black?" (Appearance)
"What color is this really and truly, red or black?" (Reality)

In most studies, 3-year-olds frequently make errors in such appearance-reality distinctions; however, 4- and 5-year-olds show more adultlike thinking in such tasks (Gopnik & Astington, 1988). Although this suggests that children develop an understanding of their mental abilities earlier than Piaget theorized, it supports his contention that cognitive development occurs in a general stagelike manner. The fact that these age trends have been noted for so many tasks argues against the notion that such thinking occurs in some domains and not in others.

Another component of ToM concerns the child's understanding of the intentions and needs of others. By age 4, children understand that people may have different beliefs and emotions than their own (Gopnik & Astington, 2000). The development of this understanding can be assessed using **false-belief tasks** (Wimmer & Perner, 1983), which represents a second way to assess ToM. In one paradigm, children were shown a box containing dominoes and told that it normally contained these objects. Next, the dominoes were taken out and replaced with a glove. Participants were next asked whether another child would know that the dominoes were no longer in the box; the dependent variable in this case would simply be whether the child gets the task correct or not. Five-year-old children solved this task correctly, whereas 3-year-olds frequently suggested that the novel child would think there was a glove in the closed box (Hogrefe, Wimmer, & Perner, 1986).

The aforementioned paradigm assesses the false belief of *contents*; we can also assess false beliefs regarding the *location* of items or objects. For example, in one paradigm, children were shown a picture of a little boy who had lost his kitten. The experimenter informed the child that the kitten really was in the closet, but that the *little boy believed* the kitten was under the bed. The child was then asked, "Where will he look for the kitten?" and then, "Where is the kitten really?" A correct response on both questions is required for a passing score (Carlson & Moses, 2001). In most studies crafted in this way, 3-year-olds are often incorrect, whereas older children pointed to the bed as the correct location. Note also that this age trend has been apparent in most ToM research presented in this section.

Although the assessment of appearance-reality and false-belief knowledge represents most research involving ToM, other facets of this construct can also be measured. For example, preschoolers gradually learn the art of tricking others, and will swear that daddy's wallet is in the aquarium. Such crafty behavior suggests that the young child believes that her father will think it is in the incorrect location. Thus, paradigms have been created to assess *deception* (Wellman & Bartsch, 1988). In one study, researchers encouraged preschoolers to trick another adult by purposely pointing to the wrong location of an object. The researchers noted that 4-year-olds were much better at this deception than 3-year-olds (Carlson, Moses, & Hix, 1998).

Can you see a pattern to all of these results? The results of appearance-reality, false-belief, and deception research suggest that theory of mind shows rapid development from ages 3 to 5. This development seems to occur sooner than Piaget originally thought, and suggests that even preschoolers are capable of logical thinking. As we will see shortly, information-processing theorists also assess certain elements of ToM. For example, we can interview children about how attention, loud music, or phone conversations can inhibit learning and recall. Again, in such instances, we are truly assessing children's thinking about thinking.

What Do You Think?

What is theory of mind? Describe specific strategies that can be used to assess this construct.

Assessment of Sociodramatic Play

Piaget theorized that advancements in representational thought marked the transition from the sensorimotor to the preoperational period, and that such development is reflected in children's play behavior. He argued that solitary pretend play was a major facilitator of cognitive development and that its function was to allow children to practice schemes for pure pleasure (Piaget, 1951). In Chapter 4, we discussed a number of methods that allow us to assess solitary play. In fact, it is true that such pretend play does become more sophisticated during the preoperational period, and complexity in solitary make-believe play is an important marker of cognitive competence and intelligence (Bond, Creasey, & Abrams, 1990). When considered in this vein, such play may signify more than a pleasurable activity (as Piaget assumed); rather, when preschoolers pretend to feed a doll with a stick, the child is honing skills that are relevant to theory of mind. That is, the child is learning that what one sees (stick, appearance) is not always meshed with reality (Creasey, Jarvis, & Berk, 1998). It would be interesting to document whether advanced play in children contributes to theory-of-mind development.

Researchers who study solitary pretend play complain that it is difficult to get older children to "just play by themselves." For example, even older toddlers will annoy us by continually taking toys to a caregiver when we want them to simply play alone! Of course, we can solve that problem by adhering to solitary-play-assessment protocols. The developers of such assessments often provide instructions on how parents should "behave" during these data-gathering sessions, such as "Do not make any suggestions to your child on how she is to play."

Solitary-pretend-play assessments endorse a standard experimental paradigm that is shared by many who study human cognition—that is, the social environment is viewed as something that should be "held constant," so "true" differences in thinking can be specified. However, some argue that these attempts at experimental control shield us from important, realistic learning environments. For example, sociocultural theorists assert that major advances in cognitive development do not result from solitary engagement with toys; rather, it is high-quality social engagement with others during pretend play or problem-solving tasks that contributes to cognitive and linguistic development (Vygotsky, 1978).

Sociodramatic play may offer a rich opportunity for young children to acquire important cognitive, communicative, and socioemotional skills. The sharing of imaginary objects and ideas between children during play sessions is thought to facilitate cultural rules for interaction and encourage control over thinking and behavior as children integrate mutual, pretend-play themes in an organized, logical manner (Krafft & Berk, 1998). Children who engage in sociodramtic play are expected to develop coordinated thinking as they engage in future environments that are cognitively challenging (Vygotsky, 1978).

What Do You Think?

What is meant by the term *sociodramatic play*? In what types of environments might you "capture" this behavior? How would you measure its quality?

How do you assess sociodramatic play in children? Unlike the analysis of nonsocial pretend play, the child needs a partner. Although some parents may seem delighted to play dolls or "robot wars," most researchers observe play interactions between children and their peers. Although one could examine play with unfamiliar peers, most assess play interactions between a child and a familiar peer(s) in naturalistic research settings, such as day-care centers. In the typical study, researchers observe sociodramatic themes during play interactions, and document how well sophisticated play predicts cognitive or social-developmental outcomes.

When coding sociodramatic play, the researcher must ensure that the behavior is *both* social and involves pretense. For example, researchers who conduct work in this area may code the following behaviors (Smilansky & Shefatya, 1990):

- *Solitary nonpretend play*, such as building a tower of blocks.
- *Solitary pretend play*, such as pushing a car along while making zooming noises.

- *Social nonpretend play*, such as rolling a ball back and forth with a peer.
- *Sociodramatic* or social pretend play, such as "sword fighting" with sticks.

In terms of the social side of this behavior, coders usually document the other child's reaction to play initiation. If the child engages in a behavior that does not attract the attention of another, then the behavior is coded as *solitary*. However, if the other child shows some reaction (e.g., smiles, comments, play behaviors); then the behavior is deemed *social*. If the child does not obtain a response from the child, yet is pretending, then the child is engaged in simple pretend or solitary pretend play. A number of coding systems contain provisions for rating both *solitary and social pretend play*.

Of course, when making such judgments, coders must determine whether the play behavior involves pretense. This determination is usually made when the child assigns imaginary properties to an object, the setting, or a person (Doyle et al., 1992). For example, suddenly announcing that the child-care center has become "Outer Space" *and* provoking a response out of another peer ("I wanna be the captain") would qualify as a sociodramatic theme.

Researchers often assess the sustained quantity of a child's sociodramatic play, as well as its quality (Howes, Unger, & Seidner, 1989; Smilansky & Shefatya, 1990). Perhaps one of the most useful systems for beginners is the *Social Pretend Play Scale* (Howes, Unger, & Seidner, 1989). In this system, the coder makes careful judgments about the maturity of different social pretend behaviors outlined in Table 6.2. In this table, I have also included the *Social Play Scale* (Howes, Unger, & Seidner, 1989) to allow you to make distinctions between the concepts of social play and social pretend play.

The Social Pretend Play Scale is user friendly, has strong theoretical underpinnings, and possesses impressive validity data. For example, Howes and colleagues documented a developmental progression of social pretend play in children; older children routinely engaged in more complex pretend play bouts with their peers. Also, children who engage in high-level sociodramatic play during the preschool years are more likely to display even more complex social pretend play later. These creative players increasingly develop elaborate play scripts that encourage other children to join their imaginary world (Howes & Matheson, 1992).

In the Piagetian tradition, there are qualitative differences in children's pretense. These discrepancies are theorized to reflect important cognitive changes (Bond, Creasey, & Abrams, 1990). However, unlike Piaget, sociodramatic-play researchers assert that there is something *uniquely* adaptive about social pretend play. In other words, although Piaget would argue that solitary pretend play is an important activity for cognitive development, this new breed of experts would assert that sociodramatic play helps children add new skills that may not be acquired through solitary activities (Elias & Berk, 2002; Singer & Singer, 1990).

Conclusions and Piaget's Legacy

Piaget postulated that the primitive representational skills of toddlers mature, become more sophisticated during the preoperational stage (ages 2–7), and eventually evolve into more logical thought during the concrete-operational period (7–12). He crafted ingenious

TABLE 6.2 *Howes' Social Play and Social Pretend Play Levels (Howes, Unger, & Seidner, 1989)*

Level/Approximate Age Ranges	Social Play	Social Pretend Play
I. 12–15 months	Parallel play with eye contact or exchanges in social behavior (A vocalizes; B smiles)	Pretend acts performed proximally and in eye contact with peer elicits no response (A feeds self, B ignores)
II. 15–20 months	Mutual play accompanied by turn-taking social exchanges (while digging in sandbox, A smiles to B, and B vocalizes back).	Performance of similar or identical pretend acts accompanied by eye contact (both push dolls in doll carriages).
III. 20–24 months	Social exchange marked by each partner taking turns at reversing the actions of the other (e.g., rolling ball back and forth).	Similar pretend activities associated with social exchanges (pushing dolls in carriages, A smiles at B, B offers doll to A).
IV. 24–30 months	Joint activity has a common plan and the pair's actions are integrated ("Let's stack these blocks really high").	Children's pretense reflects same theme, but their actions show no integration. For example, while playing "tea party" both pour tea and add sugar to same cup.
V. 30–36 months	Social play activity shows differentiation of leader and follower rules. For example, while building together, A directs construction while B supplies blocks.	Joint pretend activity involves enactment of complementary roles, such as mother-baby or doctor–nurse. For example, A sets table, tells B where to sit, and feeds her. B begins crying as if she were a baby. *Also known as complex pretend play.*

"Piagetian tasks" that consistently demonstrated that the thinking of preschoolers was limited by cognitive constraints. Preschoolers frequently center on the most obvious features of his tasks, and fail to integrate relevant information. He theorized that reasoning with the children was somewhat pointless, given the fact that they are egocentric and cannot take the perspective of another.

With the development of creative methodologies, experts have learned that preschoolers are capable of logical thinking processes and are less handicapped by cognitive constraints *under certain conditions.* Evidence for skill-specific knowledge (e.g., mathematical versus spatial abilities) casts doubt on the idea that global, qualitative cognitive changes occur in the way that Piaget claimed they do. This premise has led some to study stagelike cognitive development within specific domains, and has led others to abandon the idea of a stage-approach altogether. If anything, most experts feel that Piaget underestimated certain competencies of children.

In addition, new research on sociodramatic play challenges Piaget's notion that cognitive development occurs in solitary learning environments, which suggests he also *overestimated* the abilities in children in certain contexts. This idea is not confined to play environments; researchers have also studied how collaborative interactions between children and others advances cognitive development in everyday settings, such as shopping and museum trips. Some of this exciting research is presented in Box 6.1.

BOX 6.1 • *The Museum as a Research Context*

Piaget would endorse self-discovery museums; self-discovery through physical experience was a central premise in his theory. However, some argue that children need the support of adults (e.g., parents, museum personnel) to "get" the purpose of certain exhibits. Children show limited scientific reasoning skills, have problems ascertaining cause and effect and developing hypotheses, and may not "get" the purpose of a scientific task (Klahr, Fay, & Dunbar, 1993; Kuhn et al., 1995). Because of such limitations, it is doubtful that children will generate many "aha" experiences if left to run around museums without any mentoring.

However, simply increasing interactions between children and parents does not automatically translate into learning. In one study, parents and children (8–12 years old) were observed building a small boat. Altering the size, weight, and shape of the boat and making adjustments in water depth represented some of the variables that could affect boat speed. Parents and children were asked to record their observations and delineate modifications they made to make their little boats speedier.

The boat inventions involving parent-child dyads were better than what one would expect from a solitary child. The "teams" made fast boats, and their diaries indicated a clear evolution of scientific reasoning that involved hypothesis generation and testing. Unfortunately, the parents played a heavy role in the creation process. Little cooperative dialogue was observed, which probably means that the children were not involved in hypothesis generation and testing. This is not to say children did not play any role in the discovery process; they often took the lead role in timing its speed. The problem was that children did not contribute much to the scientific reasoning process (Schauble et al., 2002).

In another study, the conversations between children and parents were recorded as they browsed a dinosaur exhibit. Young children (4–6 years olds) correctly identified dinosaur fossils when their parents used simple technical language to endorse a fact (e.g., "This is from a Tyrannosaurs"), or connected a fact with a previous experience (e.g., "These fossils are from Colorado; remember, we went there on vacation last year?"). Such explanations enhanced learning more than technical, scientific language did. Young children recalled more information when parents adjusted their language to "fit" their cognitive level (Crowley & Jacobs, 2002).

If we can identify parent-teaching techniques and communication strategies that result in sudden "aha" experiences in children, then we also must examine what variables moderate this process. Some experts argue that the developmental status of the child is a key variable in understanding how adult-initiated strategies play a role in facilitating scientific learning and strategy acquisition (Kuhn et al., 1995). For instance, Crowley and Jacobs (2002) noted that connecting a learning task to a previous experience (e.g., "Remember when we saw one of these in the book we just read?") increased reasoning in young children but not in preadolescents.

You will learn more about how parent-child communication processes influence cognition and language in our next chapter. Although identifying aspects of parent and child behavior that facilitates thinking is important, we also need to identify contextual variables that may facilitate or inhibit these strategies. For example, certain museum exhibits may facilitate parent-child communication better than others. In addition, certain conditions, such as crowding, may constrain these important learning environments (Schauble et al., 2002).

Piaget's work, of course, has influenced subsequent research methodologies. His careful interviewing techniques, which contained probes adjusted to the child's responses, were a forerunner to the clinical interview techniques used today. Also, experts continue to use (or modify) his tasks in cognitive-developmental research. Finally, Piaget, using small samples of children, carefully analyzed changes in thought processes across a variety of tasks over a period of minutes or hours. This technique foreshadowed the work of contemporary cognitive scientists. Experts today use audiovisual technology, high-speed computers that can lock interview data to real time, and statistical techniques to document actual changes in thinking as children solve Piagetian tasks. This *microgenetic method*, which details the process of how thinking changes over short time periods, was clearly influenced by Piaget (Siegler, 1996).

Assessing Information Processing in Children

Information-processing experts specify how we store, process, and retrieve information (Chapter 4). Theorists who embrace this perspective are united by the computer metaphor; that is, the mind is viewed as similar to the inner workings of the computer. Although Piaget documented how different-aged people reasoned differently, the information-processing perspective explains how we process information. Piagetian and information-processing theories also differ in terms of defining cognitive-developmental progress. Whereas Piaget viewed cognitive development as progressing in an abrupt, stagelike manner, information-processing theorists view cognitive development as a slow, continuous process. Piaget viewed the sophistication of children's reasoning and problem-solving abilities as a meaningful unit of analysis, but information-processing paradigms typically yield more discrete, quantifiable data. For example, processing can be assessed via reaction time, and recall accuracy can be computed by counting the number of words a person correctly remembers in a list-learning experiment.

Although the two perspectives may seem worlds apart, it is interesting that experts who embrace these perspectives often control for social-contextual variables. We rarely see a parent present in Piagetian or information-processing experiments, and observations of children's thinking often take place in highly structured environments. However, there is a social context for cognitive development; we will explore methods for specifying it in the next chapter.

Major Components of the Information-Processing System

Let's first overview standard information-processing terms and definitions; Figure 6.4 contains an adaptation of a popular, multistore, information-processing model (Baddeley & Hitch, 2000). In this model, incoming information is sensed and processed into an **episodic buffer**. The episodic buffer is not really a memory store, because its capacity is very limited, and information is not really "stored here." Rather, this component is a "holding pen" for data, and represents information that is in conscious awareness. *Put simply, whatever you are thinking about right now is in your episodic buffer.*

Sometimes the transfer of information from the episodic buffer to more permanent long-term memory is seemingly automatic. For example, you can probably recall where you were at a various times of the day on 9/11/01. Theoretically, when we are highly aroused or motivated, the information is often stored more effectively. However, often we must manipulate and organize information within the episodic buffer to transfer the information stored into long-term memory accurately. Baddeley (1993) theorizes that a separate component,

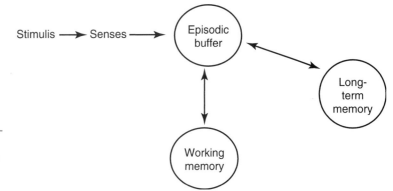

FIGURE 6.4 *Depiction of the Information-Processing System.* This figure depicts major components of the information processing system.

working memory, represents an active system that helps us both store and retrieve information more effectively. For example, we must use cognitive strategies in working memory to enhance both storage and later retrieval. **Control processes** are strategies we use, such as rehearsal, to get information in and out of long-term memory quickly and efficiently.

Although the storage capacity of the episodic buffer is limited and temporary, the capacity of long-term memory is infinite. Different types of memories are contained in long-term storage. First, **explicit memories** (or *declarative* memories) are memories that require conscious recall (Parkin, 1993). Recollecting the name of a fourth-grade teacher, or articulating the meaning of marriage requires you to consciously think about the task. There are two types of explicit (or declarative) memories. **Episodic memories** are *specific* memories regarding past experiences; think about the location of your car keys. Conversely, **semantic memories** refer to broad knowledge regarding important concepts, rules, and general events. Articulating the literary connections between Ernest Hemingway novels or understanding differences between capitalism and communism require a much more integrated, connected form of memory.

Of course, we do not have to consciously think about memories. When you start a car, do you specifically think about pulling out the car key and putting it into the ignition? Some recollections are **implicit memories** (or *nondeclarative*), which require little or no conscious effort. Because our recall of these different memories fluctuates with age, particularly during adulthood, we will revisit these important concepts in later chapters.

Assessing Information-Processing Components and Capabilities

In this section we will overview some techniques that assess information-processing capabilities. As you read about these different methods, be aware of a major controversy: cognitive scientists who use tasks that tap information-processing abilities, as well as more general cognitive development (a la Piaget), have been criticized in the past for a failure to use *consistent* or *meaningful* "yardsticks" to measure cognitive abilities.

This criticism rests on two assumptions. First, certain abilities, such as processing speed, are often assessed differently across studies. Thus, the first concern, which focuses on consistency, pertains to the issue of instrumentation reliability. Second, the meaningfulness of a measure pertains to validity. For example, think of the children who have quick-reaction-time responses to videogames. Is this truly an index of cognitive competence, and does such ability predict other cognitive abilities (e.g., school assignments)? When selecting an information-processing measure, it is important to choose one that has good reliability and validity. This is an important issue, because many of the methods are new and not standardized.

Information-Processing Speed

I encourage you to visit a video-game arcade and observe children rapidly shooting the monsters that predominate in these games. If you believe that these quick-thinking children have fast information-processing speed, then you are in good company (MacLeod, 1991). Also, because tasks on intelligence tests are often timed, there must be an underlying assumption that such quick thinking is a sign of cognitive competence. This idea dovetails strongly with material discussed in Chapter 4 regarding infant habituation speed. Recall that infants who habituated quickly to novel objects often had good intellectual outcomes.

It is interesting that experts who study information-processing speed grapple with the same theoretical issues as neo-Piagetian experts. In particular, researchers are debating how information-processing speed changes with age, and whether or not expertise in a given area influences this speed. That is, expertise may explain both individual and developmental differences in processing speed among children and adolescents.

To address these theoretical issues, complex paradigms have been designed to answer developmental questions about information-processing abilities. In perhaps the best studies, researchers consider both age and expertise as variables that may influence these abilities. For example, in terms of specifying how domain-specific knowledge may influence processing speed, researchers frequently administer tasks that tap into different cognitive domains.

In one study, youth (8–21 years) were administered two processing-speed measures across verbal and spatial domains (Kail, 1986). In one condition, participants were shown slides containing objects that were either similar (e.g., two open umbrellas) or different (an unpeeled and peeled banana). Next, the subjects quickly hit one of two buttons; one button was selected if objects were perceived to be the same, the other if they were different. The computer timed the quickness *and accuracy* of the response—this is a standard method in such research. This particular condition was thought to assess speed of retrieval from semantic memory, and theorized to reflect verbal achievement. Participants were also exposed to a spatial ability task; they viewed slides that contained either identical letters or numbers, or similar stimuli that were rotated at different angles. The subjects had to decide whether the slides contained identical or rotated images by quickly hitting the correct button.

In this study, different-aged participants were assessed to explore developmental differences in processing speed; between ages 8 and 12 processing speed quickly accelerates. The researchers also examined whether information-processing speed varied across domains; they found that speed was not domain specific. Children, adolescents, and adults who speedily processed verbal information quickly also processed spatial information quickly.

Also, *participants of all ages made the same mistakes on these tasks*, which raises questions regarding the development of information-processing speed. One might think that adults process verbal and spatial information more quickly than children do because they have had more practice and have had more years to develop mental strategies for solving problems quickly. However, the fact that children, adolescents, and adults in this study made the *same mistakes* suggests that they actually used similar mental strategies. This finding suggests that expertise or experience is not what explains developmental differences in processing speed.

If quicker processing between young children and adolescents is not due to more efficient processing strategies, then what would account for these age differences? According to some experts, children process slowly because they use more mental effort to focus attention to the task and task requirements. Remember, there is only such much room in the episodic buffer, or conscious thought. If we have to remind ourselves to pay attention, or think about the task requirements, we are using up valuable space, which slows the whole system down. For adults, such attention may occur more automatically, and less conscious thought may be needed to solve the task, which could lead to quicker processing (Case, 1998; Case & Okamoto, 1996).

Recruiting people who are experts or novices regarding a task can also specify the role of expertise on the information-processing system. In one study, adults and children (11-year-olds) who were familiar or unfamiliar with the game of chess were studied. After determining that the chess experts were similar in knowledge of this game, participants were shown chessboards that contained similar or different arrangements of chess pieces. Similar-aged novices processed more slowly than experts. However, the young chess experts took 38 percent longer than the adult experts, and 23 percent longer than the *adult novices* on these tasks. Thus, age differences in processing time could not be explained by domain familiarity. Like Kail's (1986) work, these data suggest that processing speed is more dependent on general developmental processes.

Although most work focuses on visual information-processing speed, there are methods available to assess quick thinking across other modalities. Deary and colleagues developed a procedure to assess processing speed using auditory stimuli. In the standard paradigm, children heard sounds that varied in pitch; for example, each child was exposed to two consecutive low- and high-pitched sounds. The child then simply indicated, as quickly as possible, whether or not the stimulus pairs were high-low or low-high pitches (Deary, Head, & Egan, 1989).

One important aspect of Deary's work concerns its longitudinal nature; because most information-processing research is cross-sectional, it is difficult to ascertain either normative age changes in such abilities or their predictive power. In one study, Deary and colleagues administered the aforementioned auditory-processing procedure and an intelligence test to 11-year-olds. Two years later, the children undertook the same procedures. Assessing speed of processing and intelligence in a longitudinal fashion allowed the researchers to answer a fundamental question: does speed of processing influence the development of intelligence, or do broad intellectual skills affect the development of the information-processing system? In this study, speed of processing predicted the development of broad intellectual abilities over a 2-year period, as opposed to the other way around (Deary, 1995). Fast processing speed may allow children to quickly absorb and learn information across different perceptual modalities, and they can then later master new tasks rapidly and accurately.

Episodic Buffer "Space"

As mentioned earlier, information-processing speed may be constrained in children, because a lack of room or space in the episodic buffer may toss a wrench in the system. Consider this: if you are a performing a task for the first time, such as operating a new computer, are your movements fast or slow? If you have to think about your actions, such as moving a mouse to the correct menu, do your movements slow down? If you are slow, your behavior supports research evidence on information processing. For example, episodic buffer space, or conscious thinking, is extremely limited. Thus multitasking—driving, talking on a cell phone, and lighting a cigarette—can create chaos! In such situations, it may be difficult to free up enough attention to do these activities in a correct, simultaneous manner.

The capacity of this space is traditionally assessed via **memory-span tasks**. Memory span is defined as the number of quickly presented items that the child can repeat in the exact order. Because of the rapidity of item presentation, it is theorized that we do not have the chance to use processing strategies to assist in word recollection. Although words have also been used as stimuli, experts more often use numbers, because people may attempt to group words together to aid recall. In episodic-buffer-capacity studies, we do not want to allow the child to use storage or retrieval strategies but rather to simply estimate how much space is within this hypothetical container. In studies using this technique, researchers simply count the number of digits that children can recall in the correct order. Because 9-year olds are about as accurate as older children, it is believed that our memory span is largely developed by the school years (Dempster, 1981).

Not everyone believes that the episodic buffer gets larger with age; some speculate that the episodic buffer and working memory really share the same space. For example, if we perform a task that requires a lot of attention, operating space is increased. However, this increase pinches the amount of information we can hold in the episodic buffer. Perhaps this explains why some of your professors can deliver flawless lectures without the aid of notes and also notice who falls asleep. Because the lecture is practiced, the professor does not have to pay heavy attention to her thoughts or think about what she may have to say next. This frees up space in the episodic buffer, so she can also monitor the class engagement level as she lectures.

Episodic buffer or memory span may not really get larger with age. Rather, older people may have more space at their disposal, because they do not have to devote as much attention to routine tasks as children do. If this hypothesis is true, then it would suggest that we might need to conduct more research to explain how attention processes and working memory develop. This is precisely the mission of the next section.

Assessing the Efficiency of Working Memory

Much of the data brought into the episodic buffer must be integrated, organized, and processed by working memory to allow for efficient storage. Although storage is seldom a flawless, automatic process, we know from experience that retrieval can also break down if we do not use strategies to help jog our memories. Thus, it comes as no surprise that researchers have documented strategies that we can use to enhance storage *and* retrieval. Let's now consider how researchers study the efficiency of working memory.

Assessing Attention.   Although some might not view attention as a memory strategy, we cannot effectively use these strategies if we are not paying attention to the stimulus! Because the whole system can break down due to attention deficits, it is not surprising that some researchers focus on describing the development of attention in children.

We can measure different aspects of attention. For example, when listening to a lecture, you can attend to the lecture, the weather outside, or the clothing worn by your significant other. Some of this information is important and meaningful for learning, and other information is irrelevant. Thus, our ability to *control* attention is an important research issue. For instance, older children (6 and older) increasingly gain control over attention, because they focus more on the relevant features of tasks. How do we assess this control? Some have studied children's attention control naturalistically. For example, we can instruct children to engage in a task, such as television viewing, and then time how long different-aged children attend to the television screen and remember the primary plot (Anderson & Levin, 1976).

Attention control has been also studied experimentally in laboratory tasks. In the **incidental learning task**, we give the child a task that includes distracting features. For example, the child may be shown a series of cards, each containing an animal and mode of transportation, as depicted in Figure 6.5. The child is next instructed to *memorize the animals* on each card, with the understanding that the cards will be turned over. After the cards are turned over, the child is asked to pick out the card that contained a certain animal, such as the cow. Tabulating *task-relevant* and *incidental learning* assesses attention control. The child's actual task performance, such as correctly identifying cards with different animals, assesses task-relevant learning. Incidental learning assesses the child's recall frequency of task irrelevant features, such as, "By the way, can you show me which card had the plane?". Task-relevant learning rapidly increases after age 6, whereas task-irrelevant or incidental learning decreases.

Thus far we have discussed ways to study attention naturalistically and in the lab; however, some have studied attention by crafting controlled experiments that have a "real world" context. In one study, researchers constructed a model grocery store that contained pictures of different products, such as fruits, vegetables, and frozen foods. Five- and 9-year-old children were then provided a "shopper," and given a grocery list containing pictures of some of the items located in the store. The ordering of the items was not convenient; that is, the shopper had to double back to obtain items if they were collected in the same order as they appeared on the list. The shopping trips of the older children were more organized, and they required less time to shop for the groceries (Gauvain & Rogoff, 1989). This study serves as another example of how well attention becomes organized during middle childhood, a finding that is consistent across different experimental protocols.

Assessing Storage Strategies.   Strategies used to increase the efficiency of storage and retrieval are termed *control processes*. If control processes are internal, then how do we know if a person is using them? Perhaps the most common method is to *infer* the children's use of strategies. We can infer strategy use by observing the patterning of responses during recall. For example, suppose we gave a list of words to a child—dog, dress, cigar, pipe, hat, cat—and the child later recalls the words as dog–cat; cigar–pipe; hat–dress. The reorganization of the words during recall allows us to infer that the child used a memory-enhancing

FIGURE 6.5 *Incidental-Learning Task.* The child is asked to memorize *the animals*, and then the cards are turned over. Task-relevant learning has occurred when the child can correctly point to an overturned card that contains a certain animal, such as the cow. Incidental learning is assessed by asking the child to point to a card (still turned over) that contains a certain mode of transportation, such as the plane. Younger children shower poorer task-relevant learning, because they display incidental learning; that is, they pay attention to an irrelevant feature of the task (the modes of transportation).

strategy, a mnemonic. We can also experimentally manipulate memory strategies by asking some children to use one strategy, and instruct other children to use a different one. Thus, we can either infer memory strategies in children by carefully observing their responses during memory tasks, or we can encourage or induce strategies to achieve more experimental control over the situation.

Information-processing experts claim that there are three important control processes that enhance storage. In **rehearsal**, the individual may simply repeat information embedded within a task until the data is transferred into long-term memory. Of course, although "practice makes perfect" is a good notion, this strategy has a downside if used in isolation from other control processes. For example, reading this chapter over and over may help you learn important terms and definitions, but such rote drilling may not help you apply or organize the information.

Organization refers to organizing pictures or words in the episodic buffer. For instance, rearranging the words—cat, cigar, hat, pipe, dog, dress—to cat–dog; dress–hat, and pipe–cigar, assists the child in organizing the information in more meaningful ways. Finally,

elaboration involves the powerful strategy of using imagery to create associations between related *and unrelated* information. For example, creating mental "pictures" of important ideas can greatly bolster learning. Think about how important concepts in class are easier to store if you can associate the term with a personal event; the concept of *scripts* is easy to store because we can "picture" little children going through bedtime or bath-time rituals. Elaboration also pertains to creating associations between unrelated pieces of information as well. For example, the words *cat*, *apple*, *pipe*, *dog*, *orange*, and *cigar* can be easily stored if we think of a cat smoking a pipe with an apple on its head, and a dog wearing an orange dress smoking a cigar!

We are often consciously aware of these strategies but may not actually use them if we have not learned that they are effective. Similarly, one might master sophisticated storage strategies yet have them rendered ineffective by a loud stereo or roommates. This awareness of what exactly constitutes an effective storage strategy, or what environmental factors may facilitate or impede learning, is termed *metacognitive awareness*. As we mature cognitively, we use more sophisticated storage strategies and become more aware of factors that may impede these strategies (Schneider & Bjorklund, 1998). As we discussed earlier (p. 168), it is largely believed that metacognitive awareness is one additional facet of theory of mind.

Now that we are more familiar with these control processes, let us next turn to assessment strategies. How might you study rehearsal? In some of the earliest work, researchers asked children to wear devices that covered their eyes, but not lips, during list-learning tasks. As the children prepared to recall the items, the researchers would carefully monitor lip movements to determine whether they were using a memory strategy, such as rehearsal. This early work suggested that the use of rehearsal, in particular, increases with age (Flavell, Beach, & Chinsky, 1966).

Other researchers argue that simply repeating ideas or words is only one type of rehearsal. For example, Ornstein and colleagues articulated distinctions between *passive* and *active* rehearsal. The former term equates to rote memorization, whereas active rehearsal refers to using an additional memory aid to boost storage. For example, instead of simply repeating words (e.g., *boy, boy, boy*), the child may use more sophisticated rehearsal, such as repeating the last word they heard (e.g., *bat, grass, boy, boy, boy*), or chunking information into small groups or bits of information (*ball, sea, tree . . . bat, grass, flower*). Because older children are more likely to use active rehearsal, developmental shifts in rehearsal use reflect more the quality than the quantity of this storage aid (Ornstein, Naus, & Liberty, 1975; Ornstein, Baker-Ward, & Naus, 1988).

These results suggest that children use more active rehearsal strategies as they cognitively mature; however, research we have reviewed so far pertains only to studies that infer the *spontaneous* use of storage strategies. Remember, a second methodology pertains to inducing or training children to use a select strategy. In such training studies, even younger children can learn the art of active rehearsal to bolster storage and recall (Naus, Ornstein, & Aivano, 1977).

The assessment of organizational strategies is similar to those used in measuring rehearsal. For example, researchers typically give children word lists that are associated with categories, such as animals, fruits, and modes of transportation. The words, of course, are presented to the child in a random order. Next, the researcher monitors the manner in which the child repeats back the words. If they were repeated back in the exact order, then we would expect that rehearsal was at work. However, if the child presents a different ordering of the words, and the words are grouped into categories, then we could infer the use of organizational strategies. Thus, it is very simple to study how children use both rehearsal and organizational strategies in the same investigation (Cox et al., 1989).

In terms of developmental research, older children are more likely to spontaneously use organizational strategies than their younger counterparts are (Bjorklund & Muir, 1988). However, like active rehearsal, younger children can be trained in organizational strategies to improve storage and recall. As Schneider and Bjorklund (1998) suggest, the fact that third-graders use less sophisticated storage strategies does not necessarily mean that they are not capable of using more advanced aids. Even younger children seem to have "room to operate" a number of storage strategies used by their older counterparts.

This premise may not be true regarding elaboration. Because elaboration requires us to make connections between seemingly unrelated ideas or items, more operating space is required to utilize this strategy. Thus, it is not surprising that adolescents and adults are more likely to use elaboration than children are (Schneider & Pressley, 1997). How might one assess this strategy? Perhaps the most popular method involves presenting participants pairs of nouns (e.g., *car—snow*; *cheeseburger—clown*). In *verbal elaboration* studies, children may be asked to generate a sentence or story containing the nouns (e.g., the car slipped in the snow). However, in *visual* elaboration research the child is asked to generate an image (e.g., "I see a clown eating a big messy cheeseburger"). Elaboration is later assessed by presenting the child the pair of nouns and recording how well the child recalls the sentence or image they had associated with the original stimulus (Schneider & Bjorklund, 1998).

What Do You Think?

What are rehearsal, organization, and elaboration? If you were to conduct a study involving the three storage strategies, how would you assess each construct?

Assessing Storage Strategies: Training Studies.   Inducement, or training, studies have become quite popular for two reasons. First, just because children do not spontaneously use a strategy does not mean they are incapable of generating it. Induction strategies allow for experimental control and standardization of the independent (type of strategy) and dependent (successful use of strategy) variables. Beyond better experimental control, a second consideration rests with application. If younger children can be trained to use these strategies, it translates to better learning; this approach may benefit children with achievement problems.

How might you induce these storage strategies? One method is to use practice sessions in which the child is given a chance to learn about key storage strategies. In the first session, the child is presented a list of words, and their spontaneous use of storage strategies is assessed. Again, to assess spontaneous use, you can either observe the child's pattern of recall, interview the child about how they learned the word list, or both. This first session is important, because it allows one to assess how they naturally use the strategies without experimental constraints.

The actual training session will vary, and hinges on the strategy you want to induce. In one of the best intervention studies, two short training sessions were conducted. In these sessions, third- and sixth-graders were coached on how to use passive *or* active rehearsal, and then encouraged to sort words into meaningless (e.g., *road, coat, boat*) or organized (e.g., *winter, ice, wind*) categories. Some of the children were taught to use more sophisticated strategies (e.g., organization and active rehearsal), some received a strategy mix (e.g., organization and passive rehearsal), and still others were trained in unsophisticated strategies (e.g., unorganized and passive rehearsal).

In the next phase, children were instructed to use the strategies they had learned to remember the words. Third-graders trained to use active rehearsal and organization recalled just as many words as sixth graders, suggesting that they can *use multiple strategies at the same time.* Also, children trained to use organizational strategies did not recall as well if they were also instructed to use passive rehearsal (Cox et al., 1989). Teaching the child a sophisticated storage strategy may not be effective if other strategies the child uses to learn are not considered.

Thus, younger children can be coached to use more effective strategies, which leads to better recall in contrived experimental settings. However, one might question whether these children actually *use* these skills at a later date. Many early training studies yielded disappointing results, and most young children failed to later use the strategies they had learned in these experimental, instructional settings (Brown et al., 1983). However, newer research suggests that children can transfer these skills to new environments, although it is dependent on the instructional procedures used in the training study.

For example, simple knowledge of storage strategies might not help if we do not understand why the strategy is effective. That is, sophisticated storage strategies may work best if coupled with the *metacognitive awareness* that they are effective. Thus, intervention studies may be ineffective if the child does not understand the skills that they have been trained. In one study, researchers trained children to use organizational strategies by encouraging them to group objects into meaningful categories, naming the categories or groups, studying the items in groups for later recall, and then clustering the items during recall. After this coaching session, children were given a metacognitive awareness test (Schneider, 1986). This test contained meaningless and organized word lists, and items pertaining to the usefulness of different strategies (e.g., passive rehearsal, organization). Children were asked to rate the word list that would be the easiest to remember and the viability of the different strategies, and provided options to endorse "do not understand" or "does not make sense" for the different techniques. This assessment documented how well the children understood the strategies they had learned.

The researchers then reevaluated these children, and a control group, at approximately 1 week and 6 months after the training; at every testing session the training group outperformed the control group. However, these findings were strongest among children in the training group who had received higher metacognitive awareness scores. Also, children in the training group performed better if their parents were actively involved in their learning environments. For example, parents who routinely quizzed their children about their learning strategies, assisted them with homework, or involved them in games that required strategic thinking were more likely to have children who benefited from the intervention (Carr et al., 1989). Perhaps these parents further emulated and reinforced the learning strategies modeled in the training program.

The results of this work and others studies indicate that we need to consider important issues when conducting training research. First, this study, and similar research involving preschoolers (Lange & Pierce, 1992), strongly suggest that simply training children to use storage strategies may be rendered ineffective if they do not possess metacognitive understanding of these new skills. Second, we need to demonstrate that a newly acquired skill can be effectively implemented after a training session, and that the effects of a training session show long-term benefits. Finally, the finding that parent behavior may facilitate intervention efforts suggests that we need to consider the learning environments of children outside the training session.

Assessing Retrieval Strategies

How can we distinguish between storage and retrieval deficits in children? Perhaps one way to think about this issue is to again distinguish between the concepts of *recognition* and *recall* (Chapter 4). In a recognition task, the child is shown a series of words or objects, instructed to memorize them, and then later shown the original stimuli in conjunction with irrelevant words or objects. The child simply has to point to the original stimuli. A free-recall task is generally identical to a recognition test; however, the child is required to commit the stimuli to memory and then repeat them back without any aids or primes.

Research suggests that free recall puts much more strain on the information-processing system, and the performance of a child on recall or recognition tasks is dependent on the nature of the task and the child's developmental status. Preschoolers and elementary-aged children perform similarly on recognition tasks, whereas age differences are strongly apparent on recall tasks. In summary, *there is a strong interaction between age and memory task (recall or recognition) on actual performance.*

The fact that even young children perform well on recognition tasks suggests that they are storing the information; thus, the chief problem is that younger children have a hard time retrieving the information from long-term memory. Thus, younger children have more problems retrieving the information from long-term memory during free-recall tasks than do their older counterparts. These findings suggest that we need to understand why children have difficulties getting information "out," and identify strategies that help them with the retrieval process.

How do we assess retrieval strategies? Like the measurement of storage strategies, we can assess the spontaneous use of retrieval techniques. That is, we can infer the use of retrieval strategies through casual observation. For example, Keniston and Flavell (1979) designed a simple paradigm for assessing organizational recall strategies. Different-aged children and adults were presented 20 letters and asked to write each down on separate cards. Next, participants were asked to repeat the letters in a free-recall test. The researchers carefully noted the ordering of letters during the recall test, and coded each letter relevant to its position in the alphabet. Older participants often repeated back letters in a rough alphabetical order, whereas their younger counterparts repeated back the letters in random order. It is doubtful that organizational storage strategies were used, because there was nothing about the task that suggested one should so. Rather, the researchers inferred that the older subjects mentally raced through the alphabet during the recall task, and based their recall on whether each letter had been presented earlier.

Like storage strategies, retrieval strategies can also be induced. Kobasigawa (1974) developed a paradigm for documenting how children use organizational strategies to enhance retrieval. In this study, children were presented 24 pictures that could be grouped into 8 categories (i.e., 3 pictures per category). Later, children had to recall these pictures naturally, or were shown another picture that would jog or cue their recall. For example, imagine having to learn the pictures—cow, silo, and chicken—and then later presented a picture of a farm.

The results of this study, and others contrived with similar methods (Ackerman, 1988), suggest that during free-recall tasks (with no cues), the performance of younger children is less complete than that of older children. However, in the present investigation, the youngest children (first-graders) performed just as well as the older counterparts (sixth-graders) if during the recall task the child was shown a picture cue (e.g., farm), told how many items belonged to the picture, and asked to recall items associated with the cue. These data suggest that the first-graders did in fact store the information; they just needed help in retrieving the information from long-term memory.

There are other paradigms for assessing children's use of retrieval cues (Fivush & Hudson, 1990); we can ask children to recall personal experiences or stories that they have just read. Spontaneous recall can be assessed for some children, whereas others may be given hints on how to get recall better organized as they recall the story. The organizational content of the child's narrative can then be coded. Much of this research supports Kobasigawa's (1974) original conclusion: younger children perform better when organizational hints are suggested, which suggests the information is getting in, but they need assistance in getting it out.

What Do You Think?

In terms of your own life, think about some situations in which retrieval strategies have been handy. For example, how might you remind yourself that you need to mail a letter the next day? What do you do when you lose the remote control or your car keys?

Do you remember that teaching a memory aide does not work if the child does not understand its efficacy? Well, metacognitive awareness regarding effective retrieval strategies is just as important. We need to be aware of *what's* effective and *why* it's effective, and must remind ourselves to actually *use* the strategy. So, what's important to know about retrieval strategies? Well, they can assist us in remembering something that we have to do in the future. For example, I generally put my briefcase by the door so I will not forget it the next morning. In addition, it's good to use retrieval strategies when we have lost something. For example, I lost my wallet the other day and after mentally retracing my steps, realized that my youngest son played with it near the garbage can. I found it right under a damp pizza box!

How can we measure children's knowledge about such retrieval strategies? Beal (1985) assessed beliefs regarding retrieval strategies that could be used to remember *future events* and *object relocation*. In terms of the former strategy, participants (kindergartners and adults) were shown pictures portraying children in different predicaments, such as a little girl who had to remember to wear a certain dress the next day. As detailed in Table 6.3, the children's awareness of what would constitute a relevant, detailed retrieval cue was assessed. For example, using the dress as a cue is going to jog memory better than using a crayon. In addition, knowing where to correctly place a cue is just as important. For example, if you need to remember to take your backpack to school, it does you no good to put your backpack in a place where you cannot see it, such as in a dresser drawer.

TABLE 6.3   *Vignettes Accompanying Beal's (1985) Retrieval-Dilemma Pictures Assessing Knowledge Regarding Retrieval-Cue Information*

Assessment	Example
Cue-association awareness	"Here is a picture of a little girl. Sometimes she likes to play with paper clips. Today, when she gets home from school she has to remember to rake the yard outside. What would help her remember to rake the yard: if she put a leaf on the desk in the bedroom, or if she put a paper clip on her desk, or would they help exactly the same?" (p. 633)
Cue-ambiguity awareness	"This little girl has these three dresses in her closet. Her mother wants her to wear this red, flowered dress to school the next day, so she has to remember to wear that dress. Which picture would help her remember?" *Child is then shown a picture clearly outlining a flower or a picture of a red blob.* (p. 634)
Cue-detail awareness	"Here is a picture of a boy who is going to a birthday party. He has to remember to take a plate of special chocolate cookies to the party. But the party is not for two weeks, and that's a long time to remember just in his head. Which picture would help him remember the best?" *Child is shown two pictures. One picture illustrates a plate of cookies, the other a cookie, a birthday cake, and the boy's friend.* (p. 634)

Beliefs regarding retrieval cues and location were next assessed. Almost all of the first-graders knew that a retrieval cue must be clearly associated with the task and placed in a location that would be easily encountered. However, only about 50 percent of the kindergartners knew this, suggesting that metacognitive awareness shows major development between kindergarten and first grade. However, such awareness is not complete by first grade. For example, third-graders in contrast to the first-graders, were twice as likely to know that retrieval cues must be clear and detailed.

Using a different sample, Beal (1985) developed a simple task for assessing children's metacognitive awareness regarding relocating lost objects. Preschoolers, kindergartners, and third-graders watched the experimenter hide a penny under different cups and then place a paper clip to mark the correct location. Next, in a series of trials, the experimenter placed the penny in different correct and incorrect locations, and the child had to judge whether different paper clip placements would serve as an effective retrieval aide. Only about half of the preschoolers realized that placing the paper clip on top of the correct location would serve as an effective retrieval aid. Almost all of the older children possessed such awareness. For example, third-graders clearly knew that ambiguous retrieval information, such as placing paper clips on a correct and incorrect location, would impede finding the correct location.

Summary of Information-Processing Methods

Much of the information-processing data we have on children is based on simple task performance, such as memorizing a short list of words or quickly hitting a button when a stimulus changes. Relatively simple methods have also been designed to study children's reasoning about storage and retrieval strategies. For example, children may witness hypothetical children using different strategies and then make judgments regarding their efficiency.

These methods are both simple and creative. By simple, I mean that this field is very accessible to student researchers. The authors of these techniques have generated a detailed literature regarding the task materials and procedures required to assess processing speed, storage and retrieval strategies, and the development of metacognitive awareness. Most of these procedures are easy for a novice to conduct and of low financial cost. This entire area is both scientific and highly applied; some of this exciting applied research is described in Box 6.2.

Information-processing research is not without its critics. For example, children's processing abilities have been largely derived from highly structured laboratory research. Thus, how well the results of this research translate to actual processing in real contexts (e.g., schools) is frequently questioned. In addition, the results of training studies have been somewhat disappointing; however, this finding may change as we become more savvy regarding the development of children's metacognitive abilities.

BOX 6.2 • *Assessing Eyewitness Recall in Children*

The use of children as witnesses is a controversial issue, and data on the workings of child memory can provide ammunition for both the people who interview minors and experts who use this testimony in legal cases. However, the laboratory is not typically viewed as a useful tool for eyewitness-recall research. In the real world, children are often asked to recall important information about emotionally arousing events that they have personally experienced or crimes that involve other victims that they have personally witnessed. These highly charged events are thought to affect storage and retrieval very differently than a standard list-learning task, and suggest that laboratory research on this topic might have very little external validity.

Eyewitness research has recently moved out of laboratory environments into more real-world research settings. Although some researchers examine thinking in a time period following major societal events, such as 9/11/01, children can also be interviewed about highly personal experiences, such as routine medical or dental procedures (Schneider & Bjorkland, 1998). For example, routine inoculations and physical examinations are experiences that are highly personal, arousing, and more likely to approximate the circumstances that surround

actual crimes (i.e., personal and arousing) than events staged in a laboratory environment.

Researchers are also sensitive to the realities pertaining to eyewitness recall in children involved in legal cases. For example, in the real world, how is information typically extracted from children who may be victims or witnesses of crimes? *Different-aged* children often are interviewed by *different* people using *different* methods in the days, weeks, and years after the crime was committed (Steward & Steward, 1996). This interview process is important, because it is acknowledged that young children store information well. The problem is that they just are not as good as adults at spontaneously recalling the events in a very complete manner.

With these ideas in mind, what are the some of the key variables that we need to think about when conducting such research?

Age. The recall of young children is less complete than that of their older counterparts. Not surprisingly, most studies suggest that younger children have lower levels of recall regarding eyewitness memories and are more gullible to misleading suggestions by interviewers (Schneider & Bjorkland, 1998). Of course,

(continued)

BOX 6.2 • Continued

some of the variables that follow can lessen or magnify these age differences in recall breadth or accuracy.

Type of Event. Recall of events that are distressing (e.g., 9/11/01) is sharper than for situations that are not. Also, some argue that our memories and how much we are influenced by suggestibility are affected by how personal the event was. This is an important variable to consider. The field once felt that our memories are more accurate and less prone to false information provided by interviewers if the event was personally experienced (e.g., sexual abuse); some believe this particular idea is dated.

Setting. Although some researchers contrive events for children to observe using tapes or live actors, there does seem to be a movement to study children's recall accuracy in more real-world contexts. Again, assessing children's recall of events following dental and medical procedures is becoming an increasingly popular paradigm (Bruck et al., 1995).

Time. Even preschoolers' recall can be accurate in the minutes following an event. However, thinking degrades in the hours, days, and weeks following the event, although these declines are more evident in younger children.

Suggestibility. "Well, he touched you right there (pointing to private parts) didn't he?" Ugh, what a leading question, and the dream of defense lawyers who know this literature! Preschoolers, in particular, are gullible to false information presented in such a leading manner (Goodman & Clarke-Stewart, 1991). However, there are certain conditions that induce more false memories than others. Young children are less likely to be fooled by false suggestions in the minutes or hours following an event, and their recall can remain accurate (although it may lack completeness).

Use of props, drawings, and photos. Carefully administered anatomically correct dolls, drawings, and photos can enhance the accuracy or completeness of recall (Steward & Steward, 1996). The idea is that we are turning a free-recall task into a recognition procedure. Use of these materials should make it much easier for young children to provide a more accurate record of what actually happened. However, these techniques have been questioned in terms of validity (Bruck & Ceci, 1996), and thus call for more study.

Are you feeling "hooked" by this research? If so, you should review the referenced material in this section. Perhaps this work can also help you understand why theory and research involving the information-processing perspective is important. The legal community is influenced by this cognitive science. Remember, our field is both scientific and applied!

Chapter Summary

There are common elements to information processing and Piagetian perspectives. Researchers using either perspective traditionally observe children's thinking using contrived tasks in laboratory settings; what separates these traditions is the level of analysis. Piagetian researchers are interested in the broad features of children's thinking, such as whether children are more logical than preschoolers. Information-processing researchers assess more quantifiable data that reflect specific processing features, such as storage.

The research contexts Piagetian and information-processing researchers use have begun coming full circle. For example, Piaget's initial infant studies involved naturalistic assessments of his own children; thereafter, most of his data collection, and that of information-processing researchers, was largely confined to task performance in laboratory settings. Increasingly, though, researchers are documenting how children reason and process information in more naturalistic settings, such as schools and the peer group. Many experts know there are individual differences in terms of what people can mentally do, and these differences largely result from variations in our learning environments. As we will discover in the next chapter, capturing this variability has become a major research angle.

Finally, some suggest that we should not think of Piagetian and information-processing perspectives as separate approaches, and argue that the human mind contains layers of skills that drive the way we think about this world. In these integrative theories, information-processing skills are thought to influence the way we reason (a la Piaget), and reflect general human intelligence (Demetriou et al., 2002). I would expect that cognitive development research would be driven by more integrative theories in the future (Case & Okamoto, 1996).

If intelligence is reflective of information-processing and reasoning skills, then I have set the stage for the next chapter. Whereas Piagetian and information-processing perspectives explain the "process" of knowledge acquisition, psychometric experts are more interested in the outcome, or "product," of such learning. In the next chapter, we will discuss methods of assessing cognitive intellect in children, and describe ways to measure their communication processes.

Research Navigator™ Exercise: Working Memory in Children

The objective of this assignment is to learn more about methods used to assess children's working memory. Go the Research Navigator™ website: http://www.researchnavigator.com. In the "ContentSelect" section, choose the Psychology database, and type *working memory* and *children* using the Advanced Search option (p. 60). After reading an article, answer the following questions:

1. What were the primary research questions and hypotheses?
2. What components of working memory were assessed (e.g., memory span)?
3. Were working-memory abilities considered an independent or dependent variable?
4. What were the primary conclusions?

7

Assessing Child Intellect and Language

In this chapter, you will learn how to assess the "product" of human cognition. *Psychometric,* or testing, experts assess *what* a child knows, and are less concerned about *how* the child arrived at this point. Not all intelligence tests are alike; for example, there are major differences between group and individual tests of intelligence and how they are used. There are also cognitive competencies not "normally" associated with intelligence tests. In this chapter, you will learn about other abilities that may reflect "real world" importance, such as creativity.

We will also discuss how to assess the development of human communication. First, I will describe how to assess language in children. Next, you will learn more about screening and comprehensive language assessments. Finally, social forces also play a role in cognitive and language development. Rather than consider parents or peers as "confounds" that should be controlled for, we can specify how interactions with these social agents constitute stimulating contexts for cognitive and linguistic development. You will also learn about techniques designed to capture the educational quality of the learning environment.

After reading this chapter, you should be able to:

- Describe differences between theoretical perspectives on cognitive development.
- Offer distinctions between group and individual and between achievement and aptitude tests.
- Describe strategies for assessing creativity and practical knowledge.
- Describe methodological issues that language-assessment experts must consider.
- Outline basic linguistic milestones.
- Discuss the differences between screening and comprehensive language tests.
- Explain methods used to assess collaborative learning.

Assessing Child Intellect

The **psychometric approach** describes individual and developmental differences in performance on standardized tests of intelligence (Chen & Siegler, 2000). These tests identify children with achievement difficulties, and states hold schools accountable for student test scores. Why is this an important issue? When asked where the best schools are by potential homebuyers, real estate agents may base their response on whether a school in a particular community is considered "passing" or "failing" by the state based on these test scores. This information may influence where the family eventually purchases their home.

General tests of intellect were developed before the advent of cognitive-developmental and information-processing theories. The general intent of the earliest tests, which eventually evolved into the popular *Weschler Intelligence Scales,* was to identify children who were seriously delayed in achievement. The way the tests are used in practice settings today is similar to their original intent, and the content of the test items have not changed much over the years. However, information-processing research has begun to make a mark on intelligence tests, or at least on those administered at the individual level.

To learn more about the history of intelligence tests, and assessments that are less in vogue (e.g., Stanford-Binet), I urge you to consult the *Handbook of Intelligence* (Sternberg, 2000). I also recommend this book as a starting point for students interested in discovering how experts pinpoint the contribution of biology and environment on intellectual development.

Group-Administered Intelligence Tests

Group tests can be administered to large numbers of children, and can be quickly computer-scored. The data can be used to estimate the cognitive abilities of the general student population and screen children for learning problems. Test developers often set loose parameters regarding the range of test scores that would classify a child as delayed or at risk. The idea is to throw a large net out to identify children that may be delayed. Thus, the spirit of the group test is to identify a pool of children who *may* be at risk. We can conduct a more detailed individual test to determine whether a child is truly suffering major achievement problems.

Intelligence tests have different purposes. If our purpose were to identify cognitive abilities that the child had acquired up to the time of testing, then we would select an **achievement test**. There are two group-administered tests that are widely used in schools across the United States. Generally, states choose between the *Iowa Tests of Basic Skills* or the *Stanford Achievement Test.* These tests have been given to thousands of children, and are standardized, norm-referenced tests. You can contrast data on individual children or entire samples to national, regional, or state norms. These achievement tests assess a variety of areas of knowledge, such as spelling and mathematics; sample evaluation areas are depicted in Table 7.1.

From a research standpoint, these are easy data to collect; achievement-test data are in the school records of children across the country. However, these tests only reflect one form of academic achievement. For example, researchers frequently collect grade-point-average (GPA) data across different school subjects to complement test-score data. Although skeptics may scoff at the accuracy of GPA data, these grades are based on the careful evaluations of teachers who conduct school-required assessments on a daily basis.

Assuming we can obtain permission from parents and school administrators to access achievement data, we can use this information to address important research questions. For

TABLE 7.1 *Sample Evaluation Areas Assessed by Iowa and Stanford Achievement Tests*

Iowa Tests of Basic Skills	Stanford Achievement Test
Spelling (grades 1–12)	Spelling (grades 1–12)
Listening (grades K-2)	Listening (grades K-8)
Word analysis (grades K-2)	Word analysis (grades K-2)
Reading comprehension (grades 1–12)	Reading comprehension (grades K-12)
Mathematics (grades K-12)	Mathematics (grades K-12)
Social studies (grades 1–12)	Social studies (grades K-12)

example, one could conduct a study comparing the test scores of students exposed to different teaching methods or curriculums, or we could look at how family variables, such as homework assistance or parental school involvement, are related to achievement data.

Whereas achievement tests are used to gauge how the child is *currently* performing, **aptitude tests** are used to *predict* the child's potential in a novel or unfamiliar, environment. Aptitude-test items look like the basic verbal and mathematical problems contained in achievement tests, yet have a different purpose. You are probably familiar with the *Scholastic Aptitude Test,* the *ACT,* and the *Graduate Record Exam.* Test performance is used to determine how well students will perform in a new environment, such as graduate school. However, these tests are not used exclusively for adolescents; my 10-year-old recently took a musical aptitude test, and the score was used to gauge how quickly he might learn different musical instruments.

What Do You Think?

What is the difference between achievement and aptitude tests? How are these tests used in practical settings? How might you use these tests for research purposes?

Individual Tests of Intelligence

Like group-administered tests, standardized individual tests of intelligence have been given to large numbers of children, and come with detailed manuals that provide administration instructions, psychometric history (reliability and validity data), and scoring information. The researcher can also contrast the data of one child, or a sample of children, with national norms.

Wechsler Scales of Intelligence.   The most popular, contemporary individual tests are the *Wechsler Scales of Intelligence* (Kaufman, 2000). Practitioners and researchers rely on these scales, and school psychologists often use the Wechsler Scales as the starting point in an evaluation. They have also been standardized in a number of large-scale, national studies. During standardization trials, these tests were administered to thousands of preschoolers, children, adolescents, and adults. Special care was taken to adequately represent different regions of the country, as well as participants from different racial and ethnic groups.

This family of tests includes the *Wechsler Preschool and Primary Scale of Intelligence* (WPPSI-R, Wechsler, 1989; ages 3–7 years), *Wechsler Intelligence Scale for Children*

(WISC-III, Wechsler, 1991; ages 6–16), and the *Wechsler Adult Intelligence Scale* (WAIS-III, Wechsler, 1997). All three scales provide three intelligence scores or quotients (IQ): Full-Scale, Verbal, and Performance intelligence quotient (IQ). IQ scores from all three indexes have a mean of 100 and standard deviation of 15.

Full-Scale or "Total" IQ is derived from scoring a battery of subtests that represent Verbal and Performance IQ. Verbal IQ includes subtests that you would associate with general *acquired* verbal abilities. Some sample items are presented in Figure 7.1. For example, the WISC-III contains subtests that assess factual knowledge (e.g., "What is the shape of a ball?"), vocabulary, verbal comprehension, and mathematics. In this regard, the Wechsler scales have one thing in common with virtually every other group-administered or individual test of intelligence. That is, it is highly unusual for a test of intellect not to include tests of general vocabulary, verbal comprehension (e.g., "What do you if you find an envelope with a stamp on it?"), factual knowledge, and mathematics.

Verbal subtests assess acquired semantic knowledge (see Chapter 6), or **crystallized intelligence** (Horn, 1989). Of course, verbal skills represent only one type of intellect assessed by these tests. For example, Performance IQ is a type of intellect that is distinct from acquired or crystallized abilities. In many areas of life, we are required to quickly and efficiently solve tasks that we *do not* have much experience with. Performance IQ is a measure of **fluid intelligence**, or the ability to quickly solve novel problems. Sample items that assess this ability are also presented in Figure 7.1.

Performance IQ requires us to solve novel, *nonverbal* problems; the subtests that make up Performance IQ on the Wechsler scales require one to quickly complete puzzles (Object Assembly), assemble unorganized cartoon pictures (Picture Arrangement), and organize differently colored blocks into a pattern (Block Design). These tests are often timed, and assess nonverbal abilities such as processing speed, spatial abilities, and motor coordination.

Perhaps because of advances in information-processing theory, Wechsler has added new tasks and supplemental scoring systems to assess general processing abilities. For example, the WISC-III allows examiners to calculate *processing speed* by observing performance during tasks that require the child to rapidly copy different symbols (Coding subtest), complete mazes, and discriminate between similar and different patterns. In addition, the speed at which the child solves math problems (Arithmetic subtest), and repeats back strings of digits (Digit-Span subtest), can be used as an index of attention and working-memory prowess. Although the Processing Speed Index is a relatively new addition to the Wechsler scales, it nevertheless represents a growing sensitivity to information-processing theories of cognitive development.

The Wechsler scales have displayed excellent reliability, are generally a "first choice" when conducting formal intellectual assessments involving children, and are well correlated with academic progress and social adjustment (Kaufman, 1993; 2000). Nevertheless, these instruments have their critics. Because many items are timed, children may be penalized for lengthier, yet highly accurate problem solving (Kaufman,

What Do You Think?

Define and provide examples of crystallized and fluid abilities. Provide some examples from everyday life that might reflect these abilities. Discuss how information-processing research has influenced the development of intelligence-test items.

Sample Verbal Subtests

Information

What has to happen for water to boil?
If you were flying from Los Angeles to New York, what direction would you be flying?
What country is Paris in?

Similarities

In what way are a pen and a piece of chalk alike?
In what way are a cow and a dog alike?
In what way are an inch and a foot alike?

Arithmetic

If I have five pencils and get two more, then how many pencils do I have?
If a 50-dollar coat is 50% off then how much does it cost?
At 20 cents each, how much would eight candy bars cost?

Vocabulary

What does *elated* mean?
What is a *stapler?*
What does *concerned* mean?

Sample Performance Subtests

Coding

KEY: 1 = #; 2 = &; 3 = *; 4 = ^ 5; = $

Copy, as quickly as you can, the symbols from the key into the boxes below:

Sample

3	2	1	4	5	1	3
*	&					

Block design	**Picture completion**	**Object assembly**
The task is to reproduce a figure, such as this one, using red or white blocks	The task is to identify the missing part of the picture	The task is to assemble the puzzle pieces into a meaningful object

FIGURE 7.1 *Typical Items Illustrating Verbal and Performance Subtests.* Note that the items are similar to those found on the Wechsler scales, but not identical.

2000). Also, processing speed is just one component of information processing, and the test items do little to assess reasoning, storage, and retrieval strategies. Finally, the Wechsler scales, and other intelligence tests, often ignore problem-solving abilities, motivation, and social intelligence (Sternberg, 1985). These abilities may be just as important predictors of success in everyday life.

Additional Individual Tests.   The psychometric approach has received criticism for possessing an atheoretical foundation. For example, cognitive-developmental and information-processing perspectives, which explain the process of learning and knowledge, were introduced after the development of the first intelligence tests. Also, theories on the relative contribution of biological and environmental influences on intellectual development emerged after the development of the tests. Finally, intensive debates regarding how to define intelligence, as well as appropriate items to include on the tests, also emerged after initial test development.

Although the Wechsler scales have recently included information-processing tasks in the assessment protocols, some experts feel that the developers of this hugely popular assessment have not gone far enough (Kaufman, 2000). Perhaps in response to this concern, three tests have emerged that place a heavier emphasis on information-processing abilities that are thought to reflect general intelligence (Demetriou et al., 2002; Horn, 1989).

For example, the increasingly popular *Woodcock-Johnson Psycho-Educational Battery-Revised* (WJ-R; Woodcock & Johnson, 1989) is a comprehensive assessment that can be administered to both children (age 2 and older) and adults (90+). This inventory contains a number of subscales, such as mathematical and vocabulary comprehension, that one would expect on any group-administered achievement or individual test of intelligence. However, this assessment instrument also contains items that tap information-processing abilities, such as:

- Short-term memory, which includes items that assess immediate recall of words, sentences, and numbers. These items assess the capacity of the episodic buffer (see Chapter 6).
- Long-term memory, or memory for information that must be recalled seconds or minutes after item presentation.
- Auditory processing, such as understanding word pronunciation.
- Visual processing, such as the ability to mentally rotate objects.
- Fluid reasoning, or the ability to solve novel problems.
- Processing speed, or quick, correct item responses on timed items.

Like the Wechsler scales, the WJ-R has been normed on thousands of people, and yields an overall cognitive ability score with a mean of 100 and a standard deviation of 15. The Wechsler scales and the WJ-R assess different components of intellect, which may explain why a high Weschler total IQ score does not necessarily translate to high scores on the WJ-R (Daniel, 2000). For example, children referred for learning problems may receive similar scores on the WISC-III, yet show considerable variability on the WJ-R. Five children referred for the same difficulty (e.g., reading), who all score below average on WISC-III, may show differential scores on the WJ-R. One student may score low in terms of processing speed, another may score low on auditory processing, and yet another may show difficulties with immediate recall.

Thus, this assessment can identify specific strengths and weaknesses of children with learning problems. A child who scores high on auditory subtests and low on visual processing subtests probably learns best through auditory stimulation. The assessment can inform more individualized treatment of children with special needs, and explains why many states require both WISC-III and WJ-R assessment to guide diagnostic decisions. I am not surprised that graduate students specializing in school, clinical child, and educational psychology now receive almost equal training on the Wechsler scales and WJ-R.

Two additional individual tests of intelligence include the *Kaufman Assessment Scales* (*K-ABC* for 2–12-year-old children, Kaufman & Kaufman, 1983; *KAIT* for adolescents and adults; Kaufman & Kaufman, 1993), and the *Das-Naglieri Cognitive Assessment System* (CAS; Naglieri & Das, 1997). These assessments stand out because they are more heavily devoted to information-processing assessment. The CAS (ages 5–17) contains a large battery of items that assesses how a child develops strategies for problem solving, and a scale to assess different aspects of attention. For example, children are required to sustain attention, and inhibit incidental learning, or the tendency to learn irrelevant task features (see Chapter 6).

The CAS and Kaufman scales contain sub-scales that assess *sequential* and *simultaneous* processing. What's the distinction between these two types of processing? Sequential processing involves encoding and retrieving information in a step-by-step, or sequential, fashion. For example, the child may be presented hand movements portraying first a fist; next a peace sign, next raised index and pinky fingers, and so on, and then asked to repeat these actions in that exact order. In simultaneous processing, the child is expected to integrate different pieces of information at once. For example, if asked to integrate separate pictures of two eyes, a mouth, a chin, and two eyebrows into one term, most people would say the pictures represent a face.

The Woodcock-Johnson R, Kaufman Scales, and CAS represent cognitive tests that have incorporated information-processing theory into item and scale development. Because each assessment measures slightly different aspects of intellect, one should carefully read the background literature and reliability and validity information before selecting one of these tests for an actual research study.

These tests have their critics. One concern rests with how emotional and psychological variables influence scores on these instruments (Kaufman, 2000). For example, individuals suffering from stress or depression may show temporary information-processing deficits that have little to do with intelligence. However, a depressed person is still likely to know how to put a puzzle together, know that Mexico is south of Chicago, and understand why government is necessary; these items reflect what one encounters on the Wechsler scales.

Perhaps one reason the Wechsler scales remain popular is that current mood or stress levels are less likely to affect scores. However, in the real world, these tests are usually not used in isolation from one another. For example, in my sons' school district, test scores on all four of these assessments are required to identify children with learning disabilities. Because these tests tap different aspects of intellect, it is probably wise for researchers interested in a comprehensive achievement assessment to consider using data from more than one test.

Reliability and Validity of Intelligence Tests

The widely used group (e.g., Iowa; SAT; GRE) and individual tests (e.g., Wechsler Scales) of cognitive abilities are reliable and valid. Children who score high or low on these tests generally score the same way during adolescence, tests scores are related to current school performance, and aptitude tests predict later academic performance (Chen & Siegler, 2000). These results are quite strong, well replicated, and partly explain *why* we use these tests.

Why do people criticize methods that have such sound scientific support? Well, these tests do a good, but not a perfect, job. For example, suppose you develop a group-administered aptitude test and want to predict how well elementary school students will perform in middle school. After you conduct your longitudinal study, you discover that the correlation between your test and GPA in middle school is .70. This correlation means that students who scored high on your aptitude test currently perform very well in middle school. However, you would probably like to predict performance 100% of the time. To determine the real effectiveness of your test, predictive power is best estimated by squaring your correlation coefficient (see Chapter 1). Squaring .70 ($.70 \times .70$) equals 49%, which suggests that you are about halfway to reaching your goal of measuring 100% predictive power.

If we rely solely on test scores to make judgments, then we may make two potential errors. A **false positive error** results when a child tests very well, yet the test score does not correlate with everyday academic performance. Thus, a small group of children may score very high on the mathematics section of the Iowa, yet display major mathematical deficiencies in school settings. A **false negative error** occurs when a child scores low on a test, but everyday performance regarding the ability suggests otherwise. An adolescent may score very low on the SAT or ACT, yet may be perfectly capable of achieving solid academic performance in college. Thus, when conducting research, we may also want to collect data beyond these test scores. For example, student GPA in certain subject areas and evaluative data provided by teachers could paint a more complete picture of the child's mental abilities.

Another concern with intelligence tests rests with potential unfairness and cultural bias. I know I was completely mystified by the term "detassling"—an agricultural term related to corn—when I moved to the Midwestern United States. Would it be fair to use this term as a vocabulary word on a standardized test of intelligence that was used nationwide? Some children may not have received any exposure to terms and items that are on these tests. Also, a response that is marked incorrect by an examiner may be viewed as an intelligent, adaptive response in certain communities. For example, what is a person to do with a stamped, addressed envelope lying on the sidewalk? A child who indicates it is acceptable to open it up and look for money would be given a "0" on an intelligence test but may be viewed as a street-smart child within their own community. Although this is a slightly tongue-in-cheek example, the way intelligence experts define intelligence may not be shared by everyone.

Test developers are constantly revising these tests to make them fairer to children from all racial, social class, and ethnic groups. Also, verbal subtests might be more "culturally loaded" than scales that tap performance or fluid intelligence. Thus, many experts consider other data beyond single verbal test scores to guide important decisions about children, and are allowed in some cases to make adjustments in item administration. For example, the Kaufman Assessment Battery for Children allows the examiner to model and practice items that may be unfamiliar to certain groups of children before actual item administration.

Assessing "Total" Intelligence

Some experts view intelligence as more multifaceted than basic "academic smarts." For example, Sternberg's (1985) triarchic theory of intelligence asserts that over all intelligence is composed of Analytic, Creative, and Practical Intelligence. In this theory, *analytical intelligence* is conceptualized as intellectual prowess that is currently captured by traditional tests of intelligence (e.g., crystallized and fluid abilities). Conversely, *creativity* is defined as an ability to solve problems in novel and relevant ways (Sternberg & Lubart, 1999). Finally, *practical intelligence* can be conceptualized as "street smarts," or the ability to relate to others, influence others, and engage in sound everyday problem solving.

Interestingly, these different modes of intelligence are only modestly or weakly correlated (Wagner, 2000). A test of general intellectual abilities, such as the Wechsler, may not tap important cognitive abilities that may be relevant for making predictions about people. Let us now turn to some methods of assessing these sub-components of intelligence.

Assessing Creativity.   What are all of the things you can do with a brick? Researchers who study creative thinking often pose questions like this, and then code responses as either convergent or divergent. **Convergent thinking** involves developing a single, relevant, conventional response, such as, "You can throw the brick in a lake and make a big splash." **Divergent thinking** is the ability to think of multiple, relevant, unusual possibilities when solving a problem, such as, "You can use a brick to save water. For example, you can put it in the toilet basin. The brick displaces the water." Although this idea may help us define creativity, it does not give us much ammunition for assessment. How exactly do we measure such a slippery construct? Sternberg (1999) outlines three basic approaches to measuring creativity:

1. *Psychometric approach.* There are a number of standardized, structured tests that assess creativity. Some tests are designed to assess *creative thinking,* such as, "Tell me all of the things you can do with a pair of pantyhose." However, other tests assess how well one can *create a product,* such as how well a child designs a robot from sticks. In short, we can assess creative processes, creative products, or both. There are also personality tests that allow examiners to probe for creative personality traits, such as curiosity, artistic thinking, and originality (Runco, 1989).

2. *Experimental approaches.* Some experts contrive their own tasks to assess creative thinking in both children and adults; the participant may generate ideas for how to attract tourists to an area that few people would want to visit. In experimental approaches, we manipulate different features of the task or identify significant subject or person variables that may moderate creative thinking. For example, in assessing creative thinking regarding possible story conclusions, we can craft either ambiguous and straightforward plot lines. The researcher may also compare children with

different backgrounds. For example, one could compare children whose parents regularly read them stories filled with paradox and irony to children who were read books of a different nature.

3. *Case study and historiometric perspectives.* When using these methods, experts study the creative thinking and behavior of a single, unusually talented person or a small group of individuals who are viewed as creative. When using a *historiometric perspective,* experts code creative thinking and accomplishments using a careful review (or history) of a person's writings, creative works, and influence on a field or discipline (Simonton, 1999). These methods are used to specify the creative ideas of influential people such as Mary Ainsworth, Jean Piaget, Martin Luther King, and Albert Einstein.

For novice researchers, psychometric tests that tap creativity probably represent the most approachable assessment, simply because these methods include explicit instructions for test administration and data coding. However, such assessments measure creative thinking in limited areas; for example, asking a person to think of ways to use a brick may not tap creative prowess in writing, art, or music. There is evidence that creativity may be domain specific (Gardner, 1983), suggesting that we must be careful in how we assess this complex construct.

Practical Thinking.   You will see in the next chapter that one facet of practical thinking, social "know how" or *social competence,* is highly tied to adjustment in peer and school contexts. Although the assessment of social competence represents the most popular method of assessing practical thinking in children, there are additional methods we can use to tease apart this construct. Unfortunately, many of these assessments have been developed for adults! However, Berg (1989) has crafted a self-report measure of practical thinking that has been used with both children and adolescents. Embedded within the *Everyday Problems Questionnaire* are vignettes that pertain to routine daily hassles, such as:

> "You are in several after-school activities. You have a piano recital in 1 week. You have not been practicing as well as you should have for your recital. Rate how good each answer is in *meeting your piano-recital deadline* (Berg, 1989, p. 618).

For each vignette, the participant rates the efficacy of different responses, such as, "Get your piano teacher to let you out of the recital," or, "Dig in and begin to practice a little each day." How meaningful were the responses on this measure? Teachers and adults who completed the instrument endorsed similar strategies as the older, but not the younger adolescents, suggesting that practical thinking undergoes developmental progression. Higher-level practical thinking was related to the academic achievement (Iowa scores) of the youngest children in the study; thus, using the measure enables us to capture individual differences in practical thinking in young children.

What Do You Think?

Should the definition of intellect include emotional and social abilities? Is it possible to develop a test that assesses these abilities that could be standardized and given to all children? If so, should we give more or less weight to these abilities, than, say, academic intelligence?

The premise that there are specific domains of intellect other than general academic abilities is a well-accepted idea. Unfortunately, the relative associations between traditional measures of cognitive competence and other indices of intellect still need to be linked by research. These associations may change with age, and sometimes may be stronger than expected. For example, children who are liked by their peers—suggesting a high degree of practical intelligence—usually also have excellent academic abilities.

Assessing Child Intellect: A Summary

Intelligence tests are widely accepted in practice settings; test scores heavily guide diagnostic evaluations, and many states require these data to qualify children for state-assisted intervention. However, because these tests primarily assess basic acquired cognitive abilities, other assessments have emerged to assess information-processing abilities and other domains of intellect, such as creativity and practical reasoning. These assessments also have a place in research contexts. For example, researchers have identified environmental variables that predict scores on these intelligence tests, GPA, and general achievement motivation. The results of some of this fascinating work are presented in Box 7.1.

BOX 7.1 • *Does Television-Viewing Warp Thinking?*

There are different theories that explain why television viewing may negatively affect learning. Some worry that a diet of trivial, sexist, or violent television programming directly influences the way we process and acquire knowledge (Huesmann & Miller, 1994). They say that, heavy usage may cause children to internalize cognitive and social expectancies regarding how to treat others and think about the world. Other experts argue that television viewing takes very little mental or physical effort, and that failure to practice thinking skills diminishes our achievement potential. Still others speculate that television viewing "unplugs" or diminishes other important activities, such as family dinnertime conversations and homework (Koolstra & Van der Voort, 1996). Such *displacement hypotheses* are not relevant just for television viewing; recall that the first Music Television (MTV) video was "Video Killed the Radio Star."

Specifying the effects of television viewing on intellect and social behavior is very difficult. Some argue that laboratory research, in which the content of television programming is carefully edited, rarely represents what is happening in the real world, and cannot pinpoint the long-term influences of television exposure. Naturalistic research is also hard to conduct;

television-viewing time may be affected by variables that play a strong role in intellectual development. For example, if children who watch a lot of TV have parents with low education, then it is difficult to determine which variable might "cause" low achievement score. In addition, consider the answer to this question: Does heavy television viewing corrode thinking and achievement, or is it more accurate to say that lower-achieving children watch a lot of television?

How would you design a study to untangle these important methodological issues? If you are considering a longitudinal design, then you have made a good guess. In fact, a number of longitudinal studies have examined how television viewing affects academic and social behavior. Not all of this work assumes the worst; that is, it is possible that educational television viewing may have positive effects on learning and achievement over time (Huston & Wright, 1997). In one study, researchers documented the television-viewing habits of preschoolers and then tracked them into adolescence (Anderson et al., 2001). During preschool, parents completed "viewing diaries" of their children's television viewing. The parents recorded both the *duration* of

(continued)

BOX 7.1 • Continued

television viewing and the *types* of programming their children viewed for at least one year. The researchers were able to quantify both the amount of television viewing and its content (e.g., educational versus violent).

These children were tracked into adolescence, and their present grade point averages, extracurricular involvement, and achievement motivation were monitored. Interestingly, *total viewing time* during the preschool years was a poor predictor of adolescent adjustment. Also, the content of the programs the preschoolers viewed was not strongly related to current television tastes; preschoolers who watched violent television programming were not inclined to watch similar programming as adolescents. This finding contradicts the notion that steady, violent television viewing early in life gives one an addictive "taste" for violent programming.

What about academic performance? The study results documented that preschool children, particularly young boys, who viewed a lot of educational television had higher grades and stronger achievement expectancies as adolescents than their counterparts who did not watch such programming. Also, a diet of violent television programming during preschool was related to weaker academic performance during adolescence, particularly for girls. These findings held true when controlling for important demographic factors, such as parent education.

So, does heavy television-viewing channel one into set pathways of intellectual success or doom? Most likely not, given the fact that the links between early television viewing and later adolescent behavior were quite weak, even when statistically significant. Although these findings could be strengthened by stronger measures or more detailed observations of television-viewing patterns throughout childhood, even the study authors concluded that there are many other variables that have a stronger impact on intellectual development.

In summary, when making predictions about important variables, such as achievement or aggression, it is important to obtain a more complete, multicontextual "picture" of a child's life. For example, consider a child who plays violent video games yet lives in a household and community that disdains violence. Could risk be elevated when the child receives a steady diet of violence through video games, television programming, and domestic-violence encounters? In a related fashion, some caregivers may "police" television and video game involvement better than others. Thus, some parents may eventually take away a video game system if a child becomes overly surly or their grades slip. Such involvement may be another important variable to include when conducting media research.

In addition, cognitive abilities may help us better understand links between variables that seem to have nothing to do with intelligence. For example, although child abuse is related to delays in empathy and prosocial behavior, an unusually bright child may overcome these odds. However, one cannot make such a claim if an intelligence test or some other measure of academic achievement is not integrated into the study protocol.

Intelligence tests can also serve as a useful "yardstick" when using nonstandardized, Piagetian, or information-processing tasks. For example, demonstrating that an information-processing task is moderately related to fluid-intelligence test scores provides two information items. First, the data informs us that something about the information-processing task is *significantly related* to general intelligence. Second, the fact that scores from the standardized test and experimental task are only modestly correlated suggests that *something unique* is assessed by the new procedure that is not measured on the standardized test.

Both this chapter and Chapter 6 discuss methods of assessing cognitive abilities in children. In the next section, we will discuss an ability that helps children bridge their cognitive and social worlds. Language assessment is indeed a fascinating area.

Language Assessment

People who conduct language assessments often have different theoretical and practical agendas. Professionals interested in assessing cognitive competence routinely assess important linguistic abilities, such as vocabulary comprehension. However, others who prize the communicative value of language, are interested in how children use language to relate to people. In this section I will first describe general assessment issues and identify several types of language tests. After outlining the course of language development, we will explore some basic methodological issues involving language assessment. Next, we will cover a variety of methods designed to assess language, ranging from brief screening inventories to highly detailed linguistic samples.

Types of Language Assessments

Like intelligence tests, language assessment can involve brief assessments that can be administered to large groups of children and more detailed tests that can be given to individuals. For example, some experts conduct language assessments for screening purposes; it is possible to administer to large groups of children relatively brief standardized tests that identify a sample who *may be* at risk for speech and hearing difficulties. Thus *screening tests* represent one special form of language assessment.

Linguistic screening tests do not offer a highly detailed picture of the capabilities of children. For this reason, experts often collect comprehensive, detailed language assessments on children. We will discuss two special types of comprehensive language assessment. First, *standardized, comprehensive* tests provide large amounts of information regarding language competence across many different arenas, such as vocabulary comprehension, grammatical development, and pragmatic functioning (i.e., the "social" side of language, such as linguistic turn taking). These data can be utilized strictly for research protocols or, in some cases, for diagnostic purposes.

Comprehensive tests share common features. For example, many standardized language assessments are highly *structured,* and yield highly quantifiable data that can be compared to large, representative results obtained on thousands of children. However, even structured assessments are limited. Because of time constraints and the nature of the structured protocols, detailed information about *particular* aspects of language may not be possible.

For this reason, a second form of comprehensive language assessment has been developed. When using *unstructured or naturalistic methods,* we may audiotape lengthy conversation samples between children and mothers in their homes. In summary, comprehensive language assessments include both standardized tests and more unstructured, naturalistic methods.

In addition to instrument choice, we need to consider who is going to conduct the assessment. A cynic would argue that we should not trust parental input and rely on data collected by a trained linguistic expert; *parents may have poor recall regarding linguistic events or may provide overly optimistic data.* However, parent input might be the only way to gather data about particular types of linguistic abilities that may be difficult to elicit using structured linguistic tasks or that possess very low occurrence rates. Thus, this concern represents a methodological issue that we will discuss throughout this section.

Another issue that you should think about concerns the many children throughout the world who are fluent in several languages. Unfortunately, many standardized language tests, as well as naturalistic assessment paradigms, have been designed for English-speaking children. Thus, when selecting a language assessment, we should be sensitive to this issue. For example, you would not want to administer a test written in English to children who do not understand or speak this language; thus, a central requirement when working with multilingual children is establishing the child's *dominant language.*

There are a variety of ways to establish language dominance; for example, standardized tests, such as the *Assessment Instrument for Multicultural Clients* (Adler, 1991) or the *Teacher Language Observation Report* (American Speech-Language Hearing Association, 1982), are commonly used to make such an evaluation. Alternatively (or additionally), one could observe the child's linguistic skills across several environments and tabulate how frequently a particular language was used. Heavy use of one language across several contexts (e.g., play ground, classroom) would answer this question.

Another consideration regarding language assessment is that research contexts may have different meanings in different cultures. For example, observing adolescent peers heatedly debate family rules may constitute a wonderful setting for uncovering linguistic social rules. However, such a setting may be meaningless for adolescents from cultures that do not debate family rules or are not allowed much access to the adolescent peer group! This issue becomes very important when we directly compare children from different cultures on a language assessment.

Language Development: A Very Brief Landscape

Although the exact ordering of linguistic milestones is sometimes debated, there are a number of major abilities that most language experts would designate as important. For example, in prelinguistic infants and toddlers, there are important communicative markers among the seemingly random grunts, gestures, and noises that babies make. These markers would include *babbling, intentional communication,* and *vocabulary comprehension.*

Each of these prelinguistic abilities develops along a predictable course; competency in these areas is known to predict later language development. For example, babbling begins as vowel sounds, but by 5 months of age progresses to redundant consonant-vowel syllables (e.g., *ma-ma; da-da*), which gradually evolves into more varied consonant-vowel babbles (e.g., *mo-da; ga-di*). Later language development can be predicted by assessing the frequency or amount of babbling and heavy consonant-vowel use in vocalizations (Mitchell, 1997).

Intentional communication involves the infant's attempts to influence another person's attention (e.g., mother directs her attention to a toy as the baby gestures toward toy), *as well as* behavior (e.g., playing "peekaboo") (Bates, 1979; Bruner, Roy, & Ratner, 1982). The key to prelinguistic intentional communication is that the infant is playing an active role in its own linguistic and cognitive development; that is, the baby uses gestures, vocalizations, and gaze as a communicative vehicle to influence another's attention and behavior. The use of such intentional communication increases rapidly during infancy, and doubles from 6 to 13 months of age (Mosier & Rogoff, 1994). Like babbling, the shear frequency of intentional behaviors has been shown to predict later language acquisition (Tomasello, 1990).

Infants *comprehend* language before they can *produce* it; prelinguistic infants are highly capable of pointing to people, pets, and objects during "show me" games, and can exhibit or inhibit behavior upon request (e.g., "No no, don't pull doggie's tail"). Because early vocabulary comprehension is tied to later word production, almost every standardized, prelinguistic communication assessment includes strategies for measuring this ability.

Around age 1, infants utter their first word, slowly begin adding words to their vocabularies during the early toddler years, and then rapidly acquire 10–20 new words per week between ages 18 and 24 months (Reznick & Goldfield, 1992). During this time period, we can assess both vocabulary production and comprehension. The assessment of vocabulary production and comprehension in children is not just a research agenda. Our ability to understand and produce words is viewed as a major marker of intelligence, and these skills are commonly assessed on achievement and aptitude tests (e.g., SAT, ACT).

In addition to *understanding* words, the child must correctly *pronounce* word segments to provide meaning. In **phonological assessment**, the expert carefully pinpoints how well a child articulates words and word segments. In this section we will examine additional important linguistic abilities; for example, by 2 years of age, children begin combining words in grammatically correct ways (e.g., subject before verb). When conducting a grammatical assessment, experts frequently study competence in **morphology** and **syntax**.

An expert interested in identifying the development of morphological rules scrutinizes grammatical morphemes, which include the child's mastery of suffixes, prefixes, prepositions, and verb tense. These language units, or *morphemes*, are more than just utterances, because they communicate meaning. For example, the grammatical morpheme "*s*," when added to the word, *dog*, changes the word meaning from singular to plural. Gradually, children master the morphological complexities of their native language and use morphemes in correct ways. Thus, *went* replaces *goed, mice* replaces *mouses*, and "*I went to the store*" substitutes "*Me 'went to the store*." Although we gradually get better at morphological capabilities, I once heard a TV announcer indicate that a race-car driver's engine had "blowed up."

In addition to learning these rules, children begin to master *syntax*, or rules for organizing words into sentences. They move from using one phrase ("Uh-oh"), to putting words and phrases into meaningful order and learning to construct questions (Brown, 1973). When analyzing language samples, we can focus on either the morphological or syntactical (or both) components of language.

There is a social side to language development; young children learn culturally acceptable conversational techniques, such as turn taking and the downside of conversational interruptions. The rules that we develop to master the art of linguistic communication are termed **pragmatics**. As you might guess, the assessment of pragmatics is much more slippery than measuring a child's vocabulary comprehension or grammatical competence.

To keep the terms straight, you can review them in Table 7.2. To also help, think about how there are three main components to language (Bloom & Lahey, 1978):

1. Form, which includes phonology, syntax, and morphology.
2. Content, or vocabulary knowledge.
3. Use, or the social goals of language, including pragmatics.

TABLE 7.2 *Fundamental Linguistic Abilities*

Ability	Description
Phonology	Accuracy and constancy of sound production and articulation. For example, "wayne" gradually becomes pronounced as "rain," "dis" becomes "this."
Grammatical morphology	Brief word units that have meaning, such as prefixes, suffixes, pronouns, possessives, and tense forms. For example, the plural *-s* changes *car* to *cars,* or adding the prefix *un-* changes the meaning of the word *dress* to *undress.*
Grammatical syntax	Rules for establishing order in phrases and sentences. For example, " I ran to the store" versus "The store ran to I."
Pragmatics	The social side of language. Culturally acceptable "rules" for conversational turn taking, interruptions, speech intensity, etc.

Major Considerations Regarding Language Assessment

The choices we have at our disposal for assessing the prelinguistic capabilities of infants and the linguistic competencies of older children, are simply dizzying. Although I may be oversimplifying matters, our choice of linguistic methods depends on how we answer five major questions:

1. *What type of prelinguistic or linguistic competency do you wish to assess?* When assessing prelinguistic infants, do you want to assess babbling, intentional communication, vocabulary comprehension, *or all three abilities?* Your answer will guide assessment selection. In the case of prelinguistic communication, some methods cover all three abilities, whereas others focus on one (e.g., vocabulary comprehension). When assessing older children, both grammar and pragmatics are multifaceted, linguistic constructs. Thus, like prelinguistic markers of competence, we must decide on whether we want a complete picture of the construct (grammar) or a detailed account of one facet (e.g., syntax).

2. *How detailed a record do you want regarding the child's linguistic abilities?* For example, a researcher interested in providing a detailed record of different forms of infant babbling or the narrative discourse of classroom peer conversations would probably favor highly concentrated naturalistic observations of this behavior across different time periods. Conversely, an investigator interested in quickly identifying a group of children at risk for language problems would consider a screening inventory.

3. *Whom do you trust as an informant?* Although some argue that only trained experts should collect linguistic data, other experts rely on parents and teachers as informants. Parents witness children's language abilities across multiple contexts and have the opportunity to observe children at their top linguistic potential. Also, teachers are

required to routinely test the vocabulary, grammatical, and pronunciation (phonology) skills of their students. Thus, it is possible that children exhibit their top linguistic performance with familiar people.

Do parents tell the truth? Actually, individuals in my field often interview a parent first when we suspect a child has a developmental or medical problem. However, if an instrument requires a parent informant, it is important to read the reliability and validity work regarding the assessment. Still, some studies have found that parent reports more strongly predict later language functioning than do detailed laboratory assessments (Bates, Bretherton, & Snyder, 1988).

4. *What is an appropriate context for language assessment?* Individuals using screening or structured comprehensive tests may not need to worry about setting effects if parents or teachers are providing the data. However, researchers who assess linguistic competence via direct observation must consider how settings influence language abilities. Although some argue that language should be assessed in "social" free settings (e.g., laboratory without parental presence), having a parent present may elicit the child's top linguistic performance.

This debate can be addressed by considering what competency we want to measure. For example, imagine two adolescent-development experts; one is interested in vocabulary comprehension, whereas the other is intrigued with the way adolescents use pragmatic functioning. The expert interested in vocabulary comprehension would worry less about setting effects than the pragmatic researcher; a trained examiner in a quiet room could easily assess the former ability. Conversely, because pragmatics represents the social side of language, the second researcher might want to observe adolescents in the midst of conversation with their friends.

There are other examples I can provide regarding the importance of setting. For example, scholars with interests in cognitive development argue that language helps organize thought during challenging intellectual tasks. For instance, have you ever noticed that young children talk to themselves or whisper when trying to solve problems or read? In this example, the child is really not trying to communicate but rather is using language as a way to organize thought. An accurate assessment of such "self talk" or **private speech** is often directly related to the way the research setting is structured. This issue is further explored in Box 7.2.

5. *Comprehension, production, or both?* When selecting a language assessment, it is important to assess what the child can understand (comprehension) and what he can produce. Although we can solely assess expressive or receptive language, experts who diagnose language-delayed children often assess both capabilities. In fact, identifying unnaturally large gaps between comprehension and production may inform diagnosis and subsequent treatment plans.

In summary, there are many important considerations regarding language assessment. We must determine *what* type of language competency (or competencies) we desire to assess, and delineate *how detailed* a record we want of

What Do You Think?

Describe some major considerations that language researchers grapple with. What role should parents and teachers play in the language-assessment process? Should their opinions be considered more valid than data gathered by a trained professional?

BOX 7.2 • *Talking to Myself: The Assessment of Private Speech*

Have you noticed that young children talk to themselves when nobody is around? Some experts assumed that such *private speech,* or vocalizations addressed to nobody, in particular, was a sign of cognitive immaturity (Piaget, 1926). However, others stipulate that this behavior serves a more glamorous role. Vygotsky (1934, 1986) theorized that private speech serves as a self-regulating mechanism and helps children organize behavior and cognitive activity in mentally demanding situations. If private speech plays such a role, one might question the wisdom of a teacher uttering, "Shush!" as young children whisper during assignments!

Laura Berk has conducted studies that have yielded fascinating data on this topic. In her earliest work, research assistants observed different forms of speech utterances in young children residing in Appalachia. Berk theorized that private speech during problem-solving tasks, such as describing one's activity ("I need a blue crayon to paint the sky"), self-answered questions ("How do you do this problem, oh, I know, you have to add the numbers"), and reading aloud *should be differentiated* from utterances that do not serve such a regulatory purpose (Berk & Garvin, 1984). For example, speech acts communicating emotions ("Wow, a neat crayon!"), and repetitive word play ("Merry, merry, la la la"), though technically private speech acts, would also be considered low-level forms of this construct (Berk & Garvin, 1984).

Next, children were observed in different types of activities (e.g., playground, classroom) during the school day. Interestingly, children exhibited the most private speech during *specific classroom assignments.*

Thus, to obtain a private speech sample in children, this work suggests that more complex classroom tasks, such as mathematics assignments, serve as a natural elicitor for this type of behavior (Berk & Garvin, 1984).

Berk's research program has spawned a number of major advancements in this field. For example, she has developed a sophisticated coding system for identifying different levels of private speech, ranging from simple word play (Level 1), to reading aloud or self-guiding comments (Level 2), to quiet muttering and lip movements (Level 3). In addition to private speech, Berk recommends that researchers examine other coping behaviors during problem-solving tasks, such as chewing on a pencil (tension reduction) or finger counting (task-facilitator behavior) that may assist the child in self-regulation (Berk, 1986).

Berk has conducted other studies that have provided validity for this coding system, supported Vygotsky's theory of private speech, and identified individual differences in the rate of private speech in children. For example, in a series of studies involving cross-sectional and longitudinal designs, she has documented a development course for private speech. In general, younger children (e.g., first-graders) use lower levels of private speech than their older counterparts (e.g., third-graders), suggesting that this activity shifts from somewhat random utterances to constructive vocalizations (e.g., self-guided comments), to the inaudible whispers and lip movements of older children (Berk, 1986). This research indicates that self-guided private speech becomes internalized with cognitive maturity (Bivens & Berk, 1990).

the ability. Also, we must ascertain *who* will provide the data, and determine *where* the data collection will take place. Finally, children may differ on how well they receive (comprehend) or express (produce) language.

Screening Infants and Children for Communicative Abilities

Screening tests are used to provide a brief sample of the child's language capacity. These tests can identify children who *may* be experiencing language delay and thus need special attention. In a perfect world within applied settings, the child would be designated for individual testing to determine whether he or she truly has some form of delay. Again, this ideology parallels the way professionals use group-administered intelligence-test data.

Screening children for linguistic difficulties is important, considering that the identification of children for communication disorders prior to school entry is a matter of federal law (Sturner et al., 1994). However, these tools serve an important role in research. For example, we might want to identify a group of children who are linguistically delayed or prone to a particular language disorder. Thus, the researcher may administer a screening test to a large pool of children to help *identify* this study population. However, just like a speech-and-hearing specialist, the researcher would eventually want to conduct a more comprehensive, individual language assessment to ensure that the screened children truly fall within designated groups.

Before rushing to conduct mass screenings of children for possible language delay, consider that school districts may require routine screening before school entry and throughout a child's educational process. Thus, it is possible that important information regarding the child's language development, like intelligence, could be neatly tucked away in school records. Of course, accessing school records regarding language, developmental, and intelligence test scores usually requires written parental and school permission.

Linguistic screening tests should be brief, not time consuming, and norm referenced. That is, the results for an individual child, or group of children, can be contrasted to that for a wider, representative population (Lund & Duchan, 1993). As with any test or method, the screening test should be reliable and valid. I would also distrust a screening test that does not consistently predict performance on well-established, comprehensive language tests that are routinely used to diagnosis speech and language disorders.

I have provided a brief sampling of screening tests available for infants, children, and adolescents in Table 7.3. Please keep in mind that it is beyond the scope of the book to provide an exhaustive account of every tool for speech and language screening; however, there are some experts who have assembled comprehensive lists (see Paul, 2001; Sturner et al., 1994). The tests I have suggested meet a number of the suggested criteria in the preceding paragraph.

Comprehensive, Standardized Language Tests

I must admit some difficulty with the term *comprehensive* when considering this family of language-assessment techniques. Some language experts may view a comprehensive assessment as a highly detailed record of *all* language competencies for a particular developmental period. For example, an individual working with lower-primary-school children may select a language test that assesses vocabulary knowledge, phonology, syntax, and pragmatics. In this instance, "comprehensive" seems to be synonymous with "breadth" and indicates that we are assessing linguistic competency across a wide variety of modalities.

However, someone who wants a highly detailed record of vocabulary comprehension or morphological development may express dissatisfaction with such test. Such a comprehensive test may assess some abilities that we are not interested in testing, and may not provide a very complete or deep picture of linguistic functioning within a particular area. For example, there are comprehensive language assessments that measure some features of pragmatic functioning in conjunction with other abilities, and there are others that *only*

TABLE 7.3 *A Sampling of Speech- and Language-Screening Tests*

Name of Test	Ages	Comments
Clinical Linguistic and Auditory Milestone Scale (Capute et al., 1986).	<2	Parent estimates approximate ages for babbling, intentional communication ("When did your baby first wave bye-bye?"), first word utterance, and 50-word vocabulary. Parent recall deemed accurate, and synchronous with independent evaluation of these abilities assessed via the Bayley scales of infant development.
Language Development Survey (Rescorla, 1989).	1–2	Parent checks off vocabulary words the child can actually say, including people, places, actions ("hug"), and modifiers ("all gone"). Limited vocabulary knowledge at age 2, using this sceening instrument, forecasts language delay on more comprehensive preschool language tests.
Joliet 3-minute Speech and Language Screen (Kinzler & Johnson, 1993).	K, 2nd & 5th grades	3-minute screen that identifies children with problems in grammar, word meaning, and phonology (e.g., articulation problems). Predicts performance on comprehensive language assessments, and includes a computer program for quick scoring and evaluation.
Clinical Evaluation of Language Fundamentals— Screening Test (Semel, Wiig, & Secord, 1998).	5–16	30–35 minute test that assesses a broad range of language competencies, including word meaning, pragmatics, morphology (e.g., proper use of tense), and syntax (or grammatical word arrangements). Performance on this screening instrument has been shown to predict competencies on standardized comprehensive language tests.
Speech and Language Evaluation Scale (Fressola et al., 1990)	4.5–18+	20-minute test includes speech and language scale for assessing sentence structure, pragmatics, and word articulation. Test completed with teacher input. Includes computerized scoring software.

assess pragmatic functioning. A researcher interested specifically in measuring pragmatic functioning should carefully shop for an assessment that provides a highly detailed record of this particular ability.

However, there are unifying themes regarding these assessments. First, these assessments are usually *structured* and accompanied with a standardized protocol that examiners use to collect the linguistic data. For example, a typical protocol may mandate that the examiner receive assessment training, collect the data in a special setting (e.g., laboratory), administer items in a set order, and score the results in a particular manner. Second, linguistic experts often view structured comprehensive linguistic assessments as the "gold standard." For example, in order to receive state-assisted funding for speech and hearing interventions, a child may have to fall below a certain cut-off score in order to receive such treatment. Following this logic, the validity of a screening test is frequently judged by how well it predicts performance on a highly valid, comprehensive language assessment.

TABLE 7.4 *A Sampling of Structured, Comprehensive Prelinguistic and Linguistic Assessments*

Name of Test	Ages	Comments
MacArthur Communicative Developmental Inventory (Fenson et al., 1993)	8–24 months	CDI contains instruments that assess prelinguistic communication, such as early intentional communication and vocabulary comprehension, as well as more sophisticated language competencies in older children, such as vocabulary production and grammar. Possesses strong reliability and validity (Fenson et al., 1994); data on CDI are *solely provided by parent.*
Reynell Developmental Language Scales III (Reynell & Gruber, 1990).	1–7	30–40 minute assessment that requires trained examiner. The scales assess vocabulary comprehension, grammatical syntax and morphology. Can be administered to handicapped and hearing impaired children, normed on large representative sample.
Clinical Evaluation of Language Fundamentals (Semel, Wiig, & Secord, 1998).	5–16	Very comprehensive test that assesses virtually all aspects of language including pragmatics, syntax, morphology, and vocabulary comprehension. Normed on large sample, contains computer scoring package.
Comprehensive Assessment of Spoken Language (Carrow-Woolfolk, 1999).	3–21	25–45 minute language test that constitutes "an in-depth assessment of oral language" (author). Includes extensive vocabulary assessment, as well as syntax and pragmatic functioning competence. Test includes age-based norms and excellent validity.
Test of Adolescent and Adult Language (Hammill et al., 1997).	12–25	Standardized test that assesses a number of major areas of language including speaking, vocabulary comprehension, advanced grammar, and listening skills. Requires trained examiner.

Structured comprehensive language assessments can also be used for research. For example, what if you could identify variables that predicted performance on one of these tests 5 years in the future! A brief description of some of these tests is contained in Table 7.4.

Like linguistic screening tests, many comprehensive language-assessment tools have been norm referenced on large representative samples, possess structured protocols that require a trained examiner, and include reliability and validity data. Like intelligence tests, some of these assessments are expensive and may have training requirements that go beyond simply reading the protocol. You can read about many of these tests using the Internet. The companies that sell these language tools frequently post information, such as validity and standardization data, sample items and test scales, and the feasibility of using the test with special populations.

What Do You Think?

Briefly describe similarities and differences between screening and structured, comprehensive language tests. How might you use these tests for research purposes?

Comprehensive Assessment of Language in Naturalistic Settings

I often point students in the direction of structured assessments when they are in pursuit of a "good language test"; the data are easy to quantify, and there are structured tests that can be easily completed by the child's parent or teacher (Rescorla, 1989). However, in such structured assessments, we still may lack a detailed, representative sample of the child's optimal performance. Also, very young children display their peak performance when they are actually encouraged to guide a conversation with an adult (Fenson et al., 1994). A structured assessment might not allow such latitude; for example, traditional assessments often require examiners to ask children to produce or pronounce words or sentences without context. Finally, there may be some aspects of language, such as pragmatics, that simply are too complex to adequately assess using the brief exemplars on standardized tests. Thus, it appears that one could generate an argument for the use of naturalistic assessments in certain situations.

There are two types of naturalistic language assessments. When obtaining *representative language samples,* the researcher typically records utterances as the child plays with toys, is taking a bath, or converses with parents at mealtime. Although we could spend hours recording the speech utterances of children, most experts ask parents to lend assistance in data collection. For example, the parents may be given a tape recorder and asked to record language samples in settings that elicit language (e.g., play- or mealtime). Researchers have also supplied parents with diaries in which to record the language production of children.

Although this may seem to be a "pure" way to assess language, these particular naturalistic assessments are difficult to conduct. As with structured assessments, somebody has to be trained to conduct the assessment and interpret the data. Also, like behavior observational coding, analyzing linguistic processes via audiotape frequently requires a lengthy transcription record. Thus, representative language samples, though likely to produce a more representative record of the child's language capabilities, are frequently very time consuming in nature.

A second naturalistic method can be loosely termed *elicitation language sampling.* There are certain linguistic capabilities, such as language comprehension, that are very difficult to assess in completely naturalistic settings. Thus, researchers often contrive tasks and methods that provoke or elicit linguistic expression in children. For example, a researcher interested in language comprehension may construct a large battery of questions that start with the stem, "Show me your _____" (e.g., nose, shoes, hair).

Let us next turn to how researchers naturalistically assess prelinguistic communication in babies and more advanced linguistic capabilities in older children. For just about every method I describe, there is a standardized language test that assesses the same competency. It is perfectly permissible to use more than one method. There is no harm in using both naturalistic methods and standardized tests to obtain converging evidence on a particular linguistic ability.

Naturalistic Assessment of Prelinguistic Communication.   Infant prelinguistic communication consists of babbling, intentional communication (e.g., gesturing), and vocabulary comprehension. Although there are parent-completed, standardized tests that can be used to assess these abilities, data garnered from these instruments are quite limited. For example, data gleaned from such measures frequently indexes when the baby acquired the ability (e.g., 8 months), or simply whether the baby can do it or not. For example, "When did your baby say his or her first word?" or "If you say bottle, does your baby know what that means?" might represent typical items on a parent-completed, standardized test.

You, of course, want a highly detailed record of infant prelinguistic communication. To conduct such an assessment, the research setting is an important consideration. For example, routine settings, such as bath time, feeding, and diaper changing encourage a lot of communication between babies and caregivers. Unfortunately, the primary mode of communication during these interactions is babbling, so, capturing intentional communication and verbal comprehension may be very difficult in these settings.

Of course, because babbling frequency, as well as content, predicts later language development, these settings provide a valid assessment context. Thus, it is not surprising that some researchers only observe babbling within these setting events (e.g., bath time), and assess incidental communication and verbal comprehension using other methods. Although some experts sample babbling over long periods of time, a valid "babbling sample" can be obtained from observing just 20 minutes of interaction between infant and caregiver (Mitchell, 1997).

Babbling represents only one form of prelinguistic communication; infants use gestures, vocalizations, and body movements to influence caregiver attention and behavior. Such intentional communicative behavior might be quite difficult to observe in an unstructured, naturalistic environment. Hence, paradigms exist that provoke or elicit such behavior in the baby. In one study, investigators observed 6- to 13-month-old infants and their mothers in a laboratory setting. In order to elicit intentional communicative behavior, the researchers contrived a number of manipulations that required the mother to delay assistance to the infant. For example, in one scenario, a set of toys was sneakily toppled from the infant's high-chair tray. During this "accident," mothers were instructed to casually read a magazine as if nothing had happened; even 6-month-old babies were not happy with this response!

In this study, observers noted infant facial expressions, body movements and gestures, and vocalizations. The coders noted the effects of these behaviors on the mothers and on the infant's behavior after a goal was achieved. Thus, gazing at a toy was not directly coded as intentional communication, but such behavior was considered in the context of its effect on the mother. For example, in one dyad, a baby smiled at a toy, thrust her body toward the object, and extended her hand as if to say, "Gimme." The mother subsequently gave the baby the toy; the baby then hugged the toy *and* smiled at her mother. Such behavior signifies that the baby was not simply satisfied that she had obtained the toy; rather, she was clearly happy that she influenced her mother to give her the toy! The researchers noted that even the youngest infants could engage in such communication; however, 1-year-old babies successfully used intentional communication about twice as much as 6-month-olds (Mosier & Rogoff, 1994).

The third form of prelingusitic communication is vocabulary comprehension. Do you think this ability is easy to assess in naturalistic settings? Although possible (Wetherby & Prizant, 1993), an extremely large sample of caregiver-infant interactions must be recorded to assess the complete vocabulary comprehension of an infant! Thus, investigators often rely on parental reports using structured comprehensive tests to assess this particular construct. For example, vocabulary-comprehension measures, like the *MacArthur Communicative Developmental Inventories* (Fenson et al., 1993), include an extensive catalogue of common words that cover a broad vocabulary breadth (e.g., animals, people, and action words).

Although a caregiver can be asked to recall whether the baby understands these words, some experts familiarize caregivers with these structured measures, and then conduct later interviews to trace the infant's language development (Tamis-LeMonda, Bornstein, & Baumwell, 2001). Similar methods can be used when working with older children; however, there is no denying that researchers more frequently use standardized tests to assess both vocabulary comprehension and production with more linguistically advanced children (e.g., older preschoolers).

Individuals interested in combining the best elements of comprehensive tests and naturalistic language assessments in infants, toddlers, and preschoolers should review the *Communication and Symbolic Behavior Scales* (CSBS; Wetherby & Prizant, 1993). In this assessment, a trained examiner observes how young children use gestures, sounds, and vocabulary words to communicate goals and intentions. The examiner records these behaviors as the child plays naturally with toys, and in play bouts. The parent also rates his or her impressions of the child's linguistic capabilities; these results can be compared to the data collected during the linguistic-observation period. Although this assessment requires a trained examiner, it shares some common features with standardized tests. For example, the CSBS has a structured protocol and a standardized sample to which the researcher can compare results. In addition, this method quantifies how effectively the child uses words, in combination with other communicative tools, to communicate goals and intentions in seminaturalistic settings. However, the parent also evaluates the child's abilities using a structured questionnaire.

Thus, the CSBS incorporates a method typically used by researchers who study language samples of older children in naturalistic environments. For example, when working with older children, we often use a parent or teacher as an informant to obtain a good-faith estimate of the child's linguistic capabilities. Then in a less-structured environment, we obtain a representative sample of the child's capabilities in a target setting (e.g., mealtime). The CSBS shares a similar format, although it measures linguistic functioning in much younger children.

Naturalistic Assessment of Language in Children.   Assessing the linguistic skills of older children is easy because of the large number of standardized tests that can be completed by trained raters, parents, or teachers. However, some argue that the most accurate language assessment is best achieved in more naturalistic contexts (Lund & Duchan, 1993); we achieve our top linguistic potential when spontaneously using phrases and sentences in a familiar, meaningful context. Put yourself in the research environment of the subject. Isn't it easier to master complex grammar when talking about people, places, or events that are familiar?

There are other reasons we may want to use a naturalistic assessment of language. Although both standardized tests and naturalistic assessments can be used to assess fundamental aspects of language, such as vocabulary comprehension or grammatical development, structured tests unfortunately do not tell us a lot about the process of language. For example, when producing language, children often start and restart, make mistakes and then self-correct, veer off topic and then return, and develop themes for their stories. Thus, assessing language in less-structured contexts allows researchers to study the deep structure and form of language.

How can we obtain the most *complete* picture of a child's language abilities when using more naturalistic assessments? Perhaps one model would be to use several methods to obtain a representative language assessment. For example, in favor of, or perhaps in addition to, a comprehensive standardized test, the language expert may collect the following data:

1. Information about the child's linguistic capacities (e.g., vocabulary, grammar, and pragmatics) that is supplied by a reliable informant (e.g., parent or teacher).
2. A representative speech sample—that is, a relatively free-flowing language assessment that is collected in a familiar context.
3. Linguistic data that is collected through structured elicitation procedures.

Let us think about each recommendation. First, because it is often impossible to obtain a complete picture of the child's linguistic capabilities in naturalistic settings, using the parent or teacher as an informant can be valuable in obtaining information regarding language processes that are hard to elicit or possess low base rates. Although there are standardized tests parents can complete (Dale, 1996), some researchers have developed comprehensive interviews that allow us to estimate vocabulary comprehension and production, simple grammatical development (e.g., using language to talk about the past), and the acquisition of a 50-word vocabulary (Tamis-LeMonda et al., 2001). Also, parents can be supplied diaries to record the emergence and use of advanced linguistic competencies (Bennett-Kastor, 1988). Thus, the first step when conducting less structured language assessments would be to obtain some initial picture of the child's capabilities using a reliable informant.

Once you have a baseline measure of the child's language abilities, you next obtain a **representative language sample**. In this naturalistic assessment, we may audiotape a lengthy sample of spontaneous speech that is contextually relevant and *developmentally appropriate*. For example, the speech of young preschoolers can be recorded as they are playing with their toys. When collecting speech samples of older children and adolescents, we can have them recount a personal experience or produce a description of a favorite book. Also, because one goal of a representative speech sample is to record socially meaningful, context-dependent language, we can record the conversations of children, parents, and other family members at mealtime (Pan, Perlmann, & Snow, 2000) or during peer interactions (Ervin-Tripp, 2000).

The recording length of the session and eventual analysis of the language sample is dependent, as usual, on the nature of the research question. For example, it is recommended that 50 utterances constitute an appropriate sampling for a phonological assessment, whereas 50 to 100 utterances are viewed as an adequate measure of syntax. Although a 30-minute language sample may be viewed as quite adequate for most linguistic areas, individuals interested in assessing pragmatics and narrative discourse processes may desire more lengthy samples across a variety of contexts (Bloom & Lahey, 1978). Of course, after these samples are transcribed, the nature of the research questions and linguistic constructs of interest (e.g., grammar versus pragmatics) also dictates what units of language will be analyzed (Bennett-Kastor, 1988).

Recall that representational language sampling constitutes one naturalistic method used by experts interested in tapping the linguistic prowess of children. *Elicitation paradigms* represent another special form of naturalistic language assessment that can be used in addition to, or in place of, a language sample. Elicitation methods can be used to assess language comprehension and production. In terms of *language comprehension,* there are three ways that we can assess this ability in children. In each case, you basically observe how well the child comprehends simple directions or responds to a task that requires language comprehension (Paul, 2001):

1. **Behavioral-compliance linguistic paradigms** require subjects to respond to simple examiner *directives* or *questions.* We can assess vocabulary comprehension by asking the child to touch their nose or point to an object, or assess grammatical development by observing responses to select phrases, such as, "Show me your sister's doll," or "What did you eat yesterday?" These assessments have been used with children as young as 1 year of age, are very simple to conduct, and generally do not require task materials.

2. In **contrived-comprehension linguistic paradigms**, we ask the child to perform some type of task, often using materials that serve as natural elicitors. For example, asking one to point to different pictures in a book can serve as a measure for assessing simple word comprehension ("I spy a bird; can you point to the bird?") (Rice & Watkins, 1996), or more complex sentence structure and meaning. For instance, using a toy dog, cat, and mouse, one could assess the child's understanding of sentence structure by saying, "The dog bit the cat, who was chasing the mouse. Can you show me this story?"

3. With older preschoolers and children, we can use **judgment-comprehension linguistic paradigms** to assess more complex forms of grammatical comprehension. In this method, the child is shown two side-by-side pictures. For example, as Paul (2001) suggests, the child may be shown a picture of a woman dressed conventionally, as well as a woman "acting silly." Next, the child is asked to point to the woman who would most likely say, "The boy ran down the street," or the one who would indicate, "The street ran down the boy." We can infer that a child who indicates that the silly woman would utter the ungrammatical sentence understands or comprehends proper sentence structure.

The assessment of language comprehension in older children often requires one to set up contrived tasks and scenarios, simply because it is difficult to assess comprehension in naturalistic settings. Why would a researcher go to so much trouble to assess comprehension, given the variety of structured tests that assess the same capability? To review, standardized tests may have only a few items or tasks that tap specific features of language development. Experts who want a detailed picture of a competency, such as grammatical development, often administer a number of elicitation tasks to obtain a larger linguistic sample of this ability.

Remember, comprehension is just one side of language; there is also an expressive, or production, side. We can use a number of naturalistic procedures to assess language production in children. In most of the paradigms that assess production, some form of elicitation stimuli is required (Lund & Duchan, 1993; Paul, 2001; Ritchie & Bhatia, 1999):

1. **Elicited-Imitation linguistic production paradigms** represent one of simplest methods, but they have been frequently criticized for external validity difficulties (Lund & Duchan, 1993). As the term suggests, one simply asks the child to repeat a sentence or story in the same format in which they heard it (Lust, Flynn, & Foley, 1996). Why might such a technique have low external validity? As you might have guessed, people are rarely asked to repeat phrases or sentences back in the same way they heard it. Thus, this method is probably most effective when used to assess simple word pronunciation (i.e., phonology) and is less valid for measuring complex grammatical development.

2. **Patterned-Elicitation linguistic production paradigms** involve modeling a series of phrases and then asking the child to produce a novel, analogous response. For example, using a puppet as a prop, the researcher might say:

   "Here's a sad puppet. Whatever we say, he says the opposite. If I say, sick, he'll say well. If I say up, he'll say down. Now you be the puppet, If I say stop, what does the puppet say?" (Paul, 1992).

   We can test a variety of linguistic abilities in children using such a procedure. For example, we can assess a syntactical ability, such as negation abilities, by saying:

   "The puppet is bad; he always says no to his mother. If his mother says, Come in here, he says _____" *(correct answer: "No, I won't")* (Lund & Duchan, 1993, p. 237).

3. In **pretending or role-playing linguistic production paradigms**, one may ask the child to help a doll who is "lost," interview a "new friend" regarding his family, or help a dog better understand a cat. For example, morphological abilities can be assessed by asking the child to describe what mommy does at work to a puppet. Next, the researchers can carefully analyze the use of suffixes, prefixes, pronouns, and proper tense (e.g., "Mommy went to her boss" versus "Mommy goed to he"). In addition, in the same task, more complex syntactical grammar could be assessed.

4. **Narrative-elicitation linguistic production paradigms** represent an excellent way to examine a broad range of linguistic production abilities. For example, the child can be asked to describe a summer vacation, or in more structured situations, all children could be read the same story and then asked to describe it. This technique may be useful with children with certain communication disorders, who could retell the story through reenactment, using gestures and props.

What Do You Think?

What are some common ways to assess language production and comprehension in more naturalistic ways? Why should one go to such trouble to assess language capabilities when there are standardized tests that allow for more rapid assessment?

Summary of Language Assessment

Language-development experts frequently use standardized screening, standardized comprehensive tests, and more naturalistic methods to assess the linguistic skills of children. Screening tests provide a quick picture regarding these skills and can be used to identify a group of children who have unusually low (or high) linguistic abilities. Comprehensive tests are lengthier in nature, may cover a broad range of linguistic abilities (e.g., vocabulary comprehension, grammar), and are often used to diagnose children with serious communication problems. Both screening and comprehensive tests often have structured protocols, require a trained examiner, and yield data that can be compared to a large representative sample.

Because of concerns that these structured tests may not provide a representative or highly detailed picture of certain linguistic capabilities, researchers have developed naturalistic assessments to address these concerns. We can interview parents or teachers about the linguistic abilities of children or ask them to complete diaries detailing linguistic behavior over the course of a week. Additionally, researchers can record linguistic behavior across time samples to obtain a representative language assessment. Finally, we can assess both language comprehension and production using a variety of methods that elicit these abilities.

The choice of our language-assessment tool and how we analyze the subsequent data are dependent on the original research questions. We can use these assessments for a variety of purposes; however, many researchers are interested in identifying variables that predict individual differences in linguistic abilities. Like those who study cognitive development, language experts often argue that a child's cognitive and linguistic environment can facilitate or undermine language potential. Let us next examine some exciting theory and methodologies that researchers commonly use when assessing the cognitive and linguistic environments of children.

Assessing the Cognitive and Linguistic Environments of Children

Some linguistic experts, as well as cognitive-developmental theorists, such as Jean Piaget, view learning as a child-centered process, and feel that linguistic and cognitive assessments are best obtaining by viewing the child's activities in isolation from other social agents. However, sociocultural theorists argue that cognitive and language development primarily takes place in the context of child-partner interactions (Rogoff, 1990; Vygotsky, 1978). In this case, the pinnacle of cognitive and linguistic performance is reached in the context of social interactions between children and other members of their community. These *sociocultural theorists* argue that children can only achieve their top level of cognitive or linguistic performance through assistance. Once mentored, these children will eventually acquire the learning and communicative strategies of their culture or community (Wertsch, Tulviste, & Hagstrom, 1993).

In this section, we discuss how adult and peer behavior can facilitate learning in children. Assessments in this area are unified by some themes. First, most sociocultural experts assess the child's linguistic and cognitive abilities during solitary activities and in collaboration with others. This strategy allows us to study both children's solitary performances and their ultimate performance during collaboration. The child's peak level of cognitive or linguistic performance is termed the **zone of proximal development**, or **executive capacity** (see Chapter 4).

Second, because these theorists systematically document changes in children's thinking over time, experts who embrace this perspective often use *microgenetic methods* (Kuhn et al., 1995). Experts may carefully observe the interactions between children and other important social agents (e.g., parents, siblings, teachers) as they negotiate learning tasks. By using a microgenetic method, we can capture sudden changes in thinking and the gradual integration of newly acquired strategies that support such changes. This analysis allows us to document precise analyses of change that cannot be uncovered using traditional developmental designs (i.e., cross-sectional, longitudinal) (Chen & Siegler, 2000) (see Chapter 1).

Assessing Adult Mentorship Behavior

How do adults support and facilitate the cognitive and linguistic abilities of children? Some experts monitor how parents or teachers structure the child's environment over time and then assess subsequent cognitive or linguistic changes. Adult mentorship behavior may include scheduling specific learning activities for children, such as chess club, or encouraging the child's own interests, such as pretend play (Gauvain, 2001).

Other sociocultural researchers use laboratory and microgenetic methods to assess such learning. In the typical paradigm, a child in the presence of an adult is instructed to complete some simple tasks, such as completing puzzles or creating an object. Next, researchers record the quality of adult-child interactions within the confines of the learning task. Using microgenetic methods, the researcher carefully traces shifts in child cognitive and linguistic functioning and specifies whether there was anything, in particular, during the interaction that provoked such change. Typically, the researcher examines how adult mentorship behavior bolsters child intellectual and linguistic functioning and documents whether the child, over time, begins adopting learning strategies that were used by the adult.

These assessments routinely measure **scaffolding**, or *guided participation* (Rogoff, 1990), as the adult completes the task with the child. To assess this construct, we code the following behaviors (Wood, Bruner, & Ross, 1976):

1. How efficiently the adult attracts the child's attention to task and materials.
2. How well the adult maintains and supports the child's pursuit of a goal.
3. How clearly the adult communicates to the child differences between his initial performance and ideal performance.
4. How effective the adult's efforts to reduce frustration are.
5. How well the adult models and demonstrates ideal task performance.
6. How well the adult simplifies the task, rearranges task materials, or adjusts directions.

Perhaps you can see why scaffolding is not just simple modeling. The adult's behavior is consistently monitored as the child solves a problem, with a specific focus on how the adult *makes adjustments* to the motivation, attention, failures, and successes of the child. Theoretically, a parent who is really good at this will have high-achieving children. That is, the child will learn how to operate at their top performance level, and will internalize important learning skills in the process (Rogoff, 1998).

Although there are different ways you can assess scaffolding, Rogoff and colleagues have developed a very nice coding system to capture this important mentoring behavior (Rogoff et al., 1993). This scheme was based on lengthy observations of parent-child interactions across a variety of cultures, and a number of mentoring or scaffolding behaviors have been consistently observed across all societies. A sample of her scheme is depicted in Table 7.5.

Note that Rogoff's complete coding system allows for the rating of caregiver, child, and dyadic behavior. By carefully coding behavior over time, we can examine the rise and fall of caregiver and child behavior, examine child behaviors that antecede caregiver behavior (and vice versa), and document the process of a child taking over a task and beginning to operate in a higher zone of cognitive development. The great feature of the system is that it can be adjusted to incorporate scaffolding techniques that are relevant to a particular culture.

What Do You Think?

> Suppose you are interested in documenting how parental behavior influences children's learning. How would you assess scaffolding? How might you document that the child has internalized the learning strategies offered by the parent?

Beyond the Parent-Child Dyad

Although sociocultural researchers frequently study how parent-child interactions influence cognition and language acquisition, there are also other methods at our disposal. For example, some researchers have developed methods for evaluating the tutoring efforts of

TABLE 7.5 *Assessing Scaffolding: Sample Coding Form (Adapted from Rogoff et al., 1993, p. 40)*

Sample Items/Codes

Caregiver introduces/orients nature of activity:	Verbally	Nonverbally	Neither	
Caregiver simplifies:	Verbal	Adjusts object	Gestures	Gaze/Touch/Posture

Caregivers' explanation: extends to other situations?

	Extensive	Moderate	Brief	None
Caregiver demonstration efforts				
Before child participates	_____	_____	_____	_____
During child participation	_____	_____	_____	_____
Caregiver directs attention to process?	_____			
Caregiver turns task over to child?	_____			
Caregiver acts as playmate?	_____			
Uses excitement to motivate child?	_____			
Caregiver poised to help?	_____			
Child seeks clarification?	_____			
Child refuses/insists?	_____			

adults (McArthur, Stasz, & Zmuidzinas, 1990). In addition, because teachers are natural learning partners, there are numerous ways of assessing how teacher instruction and communication influence the learning environments of children (Mercer, 1995).

Adults, of course, are not the only members of the community who can enhance the cognitive and linguistic environments of children. For example, sociodramatic play with peers offers a rich context for cognitive, language, and social development (Creasey & Jarvis, 2003). Also, there are methods of assessing interactions between peers that facilitate cognitive development in cooperative learning environments (Rogoff, 1998). Finally, we can compare the relative effectiveness of various different social agents. For example, delineating how different social agents, such as teachers and slightly older peers, differentially facilitate the learning of young children represents another interesting research direction.

Assessing Learning and Cognitive Environments: A Summary

Rather than view social agents as a nuisance, sociocultural experts stipulate that we should examine how interactions among children, parents, siblings, peers, and teachers help foster cognitive and linguistic growth. Sensitivity to environmental context is a concern not only in the field of human development but in other scientific disciplines as well. Also, the cross-cultural focus of this work is fascinating, and makes us realize that the way we think, process information, and use communication is dependent on the culture in which we live.

Chapter Summary

In this chapter you learned more about how to assess the results of human cognition. We made distinctions among different types of intelligence tests; for example, these assessments can be given to large groups of children or to a single child. The format we choose often depends on our purpose. We can use group-administered intelligence tests to screen children for possible learning problems, to evaluate teacher and curriculum effectiveness, and to compare children in different schools or school districts. In addition, group-administered tests can be used for both current (achievement tests) and predictive (aptitude tests) purposes.

Individual tests of intelligence are used to guide the diagnosis of children with ability delays. Researchers often use these tests as predictor variables, and document how well these tests predict future developmental outcomes. Also, the tests can be used as dependent variables; we can study how factors such as family educational practices, television, and schooling affect intellectual growth. There are also experts who assess more than just traditional academic intellect; accordingly, we discussed ways of assessing creative and practical intelligence.

In this chapter, you learned three broad approaches to linguistic assessment. Screening tests, like group-administered intelligence tests, are frequently used to identify a pool of children who may be at risk for developmental delay. Comprehensive, structured language tests, like individual tests of intelligence, are used to help diagnose children with learning problems and offer guidance for intervention.

When conducting naturalistic language assessments, representative language samples can be obtained by observing child utterances in everyday settings. Although we can record the information ourselves, experts often ask parents to audiotape their child's language or to complete detailed diaries. Because some linguistic abilities have low base rates in everyday naturalistic settings, some contrive experimental procedures to elicit such difficult-to-obtain information.

Many experts feel strongly that cognitive, intellectual, and linguistic processes should not be studied in isolated, stimulus-free environments. Rather, because cognitive and linguistic growth is a collaborative process, it follows that we should focus more on how social agents, such as parents, siblings, peers, and teachers contribute to this process. In this chapter, we discussed a number of ways to better capture the cognitive and linguistic environments of children.

Research Navigator™ Exercise: Intelligence in Children

The objective is to learn about methods used to assess children's intelligence. Go the Research Navigator™ website: http://www.researchnavigator.com. In the "ContentSelect" section, choose the Psychology database, and type *intelligence* and *children* using the Advanced Search option (Page 60). After reading an article, answer the following questions:

1. What were the primary research questions and hypotheses?
2. What intelligence test(s) was (were) used? What specific abilities were viewed as particularly important in this study (e.g., verbal, performance, linguistic, etc.)?
3. Was intelligence viewed as an achievement or aptitude variable?
4. What were the primary conclusions?

8

Assessing Social Development in Children

Debbie knows that her peers dislike her, yet cannot tell her parents because she feels they would not understand her problem. She feels bad about herself, and is not liked because she makes ugly comments without considering how they affect people. She is an unhelpful person who does not seem to care about the plights of others.

Although a sad case, Debbie can nevertheless consider the perspective of others, and can provide us with data about her emotional health. In this chapter, you will learn about techniques that assess such self-worth and perspective taking, and discover how we can study moral, prosocial, and gender-related thinking. All of these mental processes pertain to **social cognition**, or our thinking about our social position, and that of others, in our collective world.

In addition to the development of impressive social-cognitive competencies, youth also experience major advancements in their interpersonal world. Note that Debbie also seems to have relationship problems with her parents and peers. In this chapter, we will examine how experts specify attachment processes in older children, and how adjustment in the peer group is measured. After reading this chapter, you should be able to:

1. Describe techniques for obtaining the best social-cognitive data from children.
2. Identify methods used to assess self-representation and self-esteem.
3. Identify ways to specify gender-related attitudes, preferences, identity, and behavior.
4. Discuss how to assess perspective taking, moral reasoning, distributive justice, social conventional thought, empathy, and sympathy.
5. Discuss how to measure attachment processes in preschoolers and children.
6. Describe methods for measuring friendship, friendship quality, and peer acceptance.

Obtaining Consistent, Accurate Data from Children

When asked to provide information about themselves or others, how confident are you that the child will give you an *honest, meaningful answer*? We must ensure that children provide us social-cognitive data that is both consistent (reliable) and relevant (valid). Reliability and validity are both important considerations, that is, we want the data to represent a stable way of thinking (reliability), and an ability that is developmentally important (validity).

Are Children Good Informants?

We can gain access to their private thoughts of children and adolescents using question-naires, interviews, or laboratory tasks. Should we trust such data? The following should be considered when conducting assessments that require the child to function as an informant.

1. *Consider the cognitive and linguistic abilities of your sample.* When considering an instrument, you must read its instructions regarding mental and linguistic requirements. Social-cognition assessments often have different versions of the same measure for different age groups. The versions for younger children may include easily understood directions and vocabulary, allow the use of pictures and cartoons to prompt thinking, and provide directions on how to get the best data. For instance, the protocol may call for practice sessions to ensure that the young child "gets" the task, or understands questionnaire and interview items.

2. *Target populations, reliability, and validity.* You should be familiar with the population the measure was designed for. The instrument should also be reliable and predict something important, such as achievement or mental-health problems (i.e., good predictive validity).

3. *Multiple informants, multiple contexts.* Social-cognitive abilities in children may not be consistent in every context; some may have low self-esteem at school but not at home. Thus data can be collected from people who witness the child's abilities in different environments. For example, Achenbach (1991) has developed a series of scales that assess child behavior problems via different informants (e.g., youth, parent, and teacher reports).

4. *Stuck with one informant?* If you had to choose only one informant, would you rely on the child, parent, or teacher? The answer is *it depends!* Children and adolescents are sometimes not forthcoming regarding academic and achievement problems, so, when assessing perceptions regarding school performance, I would want the teacher's impression. This informant consistently observes the child's thinking and behavior in this setting.

However, parents can provide a comprehensive picture of a child's abilities across a variety of contexts. If I could choose, I would usually pursue the mother's opinions; even distressed mothers can rate their child's feelings and behavior quite accurately—even in cases in which the mother is clinically depressed (Richters & Pellegrini, 1989). I would not view the child as the last possible resort as an informant; matters depend on the nature of the assessment. Children have access to private thoughts

What Do You Think?

Suppose you are interested in assessing children's thinking about terrorism. In constructing an interview, how would the age of the child influence your item selection? Would you rely exclusively on the self-reports of your participants or use multiple data sources?

and feelings a parent may not be aware of; for example, it is impossible to assess the self-esteem of children without input from the children themselves!

5. *Child reactivity.* Because social-cognition experts frequently interview children after they have been read social or moral dilemmas, the social and linguistic competence of the researcher becomes a paramount concern. Competent, well-trained interviewers are required to study the topics that follow. Box 8.1 contains some more tips on how to interview children.

BOX 8.1 • *How to Interview Children*

The starting place for "interviewer technique" is the *interview protocol*; this document gives us instructions on how to administer the method and train the interviewers. Of paramount importance is that interviewer behavior and demeanor must be standardized; that is, each interviewer should be interchangeable and not unduly influence the participant's behavior.

It is common knowledge that the interviewer should make the participant as comfortable as possible from the beginning. In part, rapport establishment is dependent on the developmental status of the participant. For example, a colleague of mine has a video-game system and attractive toys in her child-development laboratory. She usually invites the child to play with the toys while she is organizing the interview materials. Before she begins the interview process, she establishes rapport by asking the child about their favorite toys, activities, and so on. With older children, we can establish similar rapport by asking them about their favorite movies, music groups, and CDs.

Boggs and Eyberg (1990) also offer advice for researchers interested in conducting interviews with children. First, the interview should begin with very easy, nonthreatening questions. In addition, they make some wonderful recommendations regarding resistance during the interview process. For instance, if a participant becomes upset, or even begins to cry, the temptation may arise to quickly move on to other questions. What would *you* do?

First of all, it is not uncommon for clinical interviews to contain questions that are emotionally arousing! The first thing to ascertain is whether the participant's emotional reaction is atypical. For example, gentle crying during the discussion of a parental loss would be expected; a head-banging episode would not! In the former case, a comment such as, "I see that you might not want to talk about this right now; however, I think it's important, so I might come back to this question later," would be deemed appropriate (Boggs & Eyberg, 1990).

Another methodological consideration rests with how the interview (or questionnaire, experimental task, etc.) is initially presented. Children and adolescents often view research projects as some type of "test," whereas adults worry that "I'm going to be analyzed." To combat such evaluation apprehension, it is often wise to present the data-collection measures as a fun game for younger participants or to ensure adolescents and adults that one is not interested in individual responses. Older participants are often worried not just about appearing "dumb," but also about the confidentiality their of responses. This is particularly true of adolescents, who may worry that reports of substance use or sexual behavior may be shared with others (e.g., parents). Thus, for research involving the collection of such sensitive data, I usually recommend that researchers go beyond the informed-consent document and verbally assure participants that their responses are private and will be held in the strictest confidence.

Finally, when protocols call for us to project a warm and friendly demeanor during the interview, usually the participant's performance is praised *after* they have provided a response to interview queries. One of the first rules new interviewers must learn is that positive statements should not be made *while* the participant is giving us interview data. Injecting positive statements or nodding the head as the subjects respond may signify to them that they have provided enough information and may actually discourage them from providing complete accounts of their thinking on the matter (George, Kaplan, & Main, 1996).

The Use of Child Informants: A Summary

Because the thinking of children is a private event, we must design methods to get this information "out." Data quality can be improved if we use methods that have a strong reliability and validity history, are developmentally appropriate, and are sensitive to the cognitive and linguistic skills of our sample. The use of multiple informants who observe the child's abilities across multiple settings offers converging data on the child's performance. Of course, there are some constructs (e.g., self-esteem, gender identity) that can only be assessed with a single child informant. In such cases, a sound interview protocol and a trained interviewer are mandatory.

Assessing Self-Representation and Self-Esteem

Self-representation and *self-esteem* are two important cognitive appraisals that develop across childhood and adolescence. We will define **self-representation** as one's general description of themselves. Think for a moment how you would describe yourself to someone you just met. **Self-esteem** is how *you feel*—good or bad—about your self-representation.

Assessing Self-Representation

The fact that self-representations predict psychological health is a testament to the validity of the construct and the need for proper assessment (Harter, 1999). How do you measure self-representations? One idea would be to supply a person a rating scale in which they simply endorsed interests, abilities, and personality traits, such as "warm" or "friendly." Do you see problems with such a simple evaluation method? The child does not really have to produce a mental self-representation; they just evaluate attributes designated by you as important. Beyond concerns regarding social desirability and response sets, one might wonder whether we could develop a checklist method that would be easily understood by different developmental populations; consider how preschoolers would struggle with the term *introverted* (Eder, 1990).

In response to these methodological concerns, short, open-ended interview protocols have been used to assess self-representations (Livesay & Bromley, 1973). In one such interview script, the opening items are questions such as, "What are you like?" and "What kind of person are you?" (Damon & Hart, 1988). The initial interview thus doubles as a self-esteem measure; other items are questions such as, "What are you especially proud of about yourself?" The interview data are next classified into different self-understanding codes. Let's now consider some hypothetical responses to a typical "Who are you?" query.

Leatrice (Age 6): I am a girl and have a bike. I like big trucks and math. I am six.

Tabatha (Age 11): I'm in fifth grade. Art is absolutely my favorite subject. I am smart, and I always get my way. Except around my parents; they think I'm a brat. I'm not sure what will happen next year; I'm going to middle school.

Trina (Age 16): Most people think I'm friendly, but I can get pretty moody, especially when I have homework. I need to get stable; people think I'm crazy when I'm like that! However, I'm not as moody as my best friend; I hope I'm *never* like her. I wish I could get closer to guys. I like guys, but they think I'm sort of cold. It bothers me that I just freeze when I'm around guys, you know, except at my job; then I'm totally comfortable around them.

Jot down the similarities and differences in these self-representations. As mentioned earlier, coders must be trained to identify self-representational *content areas* that are deemed theoretically important. For example, appearance, possessions, activities, general information, personality attributes, interpersonal style, and ideological beliefs are just a few of the content areas that can be coded using these assessments. The descriptions listed above support some common developmental findings. As we mature, we are less likely to mention appearance ("I have brown hair"), general information ("I am in third grade"), and possessions ("I have a bike"), and more likely to mention psychological traits ("I am shy") and beliefs ("I am liberal").

The narrative data we gather from these interviews often goes beyond simple self-descriptions involving general information and psychological traits. Notice that the older adolescent shows more evidence of perspective taking, or how other people view her (Harter, 1999). Indeed the older adolescent also indicates who she *really* is, how people view her, who she would *like* to be, and who she does *not* want to be. Through it all, she includes multiple contexts (parents, teachers, friends, romantic partners) in her self-description. In particular, during adolescence, we see the evolution of an *actual self* (who we *think* we are) and *ideal self* (who we would *like* to be) (Higgins, 1991). In addition, when adolescents indicate that they see themselves one way ("I really am an outgoing person"), yet perceives that others view them differently ("Most people see me as a shy person") then they are articulating a *false self.*

There are other ways the more complex psychological self-descriptions of older children and adolescents can be coded. Harter and Monsour (1992) have created a simple method that provides a wealth of information about children's self-representations. In this method, depicted in Figure 8.1, children provide self-descriptions across multiple domains and indicate how they see themselves with their parents, friends, romantic partner, and at school. In each domain, the participant provides six descriptors. This is an activity you can try right now.

After placing a plus or minus beside each descriptor, the descriptors are transferred to gummed labels which are placed into the categories, ranging from least to most important, as outlined on the self-portrait wheel illustrated in Figure 8.1. The child also identifies descriptors that appear to be contradictive (denoted by the arrows). In the hypothetical self-representation presented earlier, the 16-year-old was concerned with just such conflicts ("I need to get more consistent; people think I'm crazy when I'm like that!").

Note that we have not discussed the self-descriptions of preschoolers; they may consider themselves shy, but cannot put the concept into words. However, Eder (1989; 1990) has developed a self-representation measure that has been used with children as young as 3. In this method, the child is presented two puppets controlled by the researcher in a "puppet theater." One puppet will utter a statement, such as, "I usually play with friends," while the other puppet will say, "I usually play by myself." The researcher then turns to the child and asks, "How about you?" The responses are coded into different self-categories, such

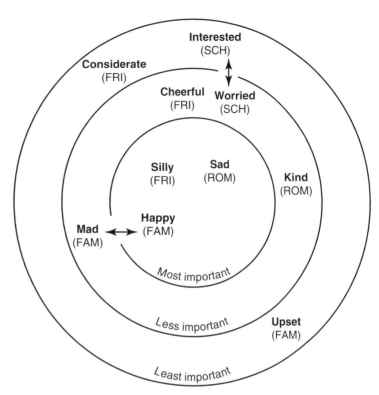

FIGURE 8.1 *Sample Self-Portrait Wheel (adapted from Harter & Monsour, 1992).* Subject affixes self-descriptors to wheel ranging from "most" to "least" important. Abbreviations under self-descriptors refer to context—for example, FAM, family; SCH, school FRI, friend; ROM, romantic partner. Subject notes self-representational contradictions by affixing arrows to conflicting descriptors.

as well-being ("I like myself"), achievement beliefs ("I mostly do things that are hard"), and social closeness ("It's more fun to do things with other people than by myself"). The results of this work indicate that very young children can make accurate judgments about self-representations. Further, the responses of the children are consistent over time, indicating that the self-representations of preschoolers may be more stable than originally thought (Eder, 1990).

Having covered some self-representation measures, let's think about some important conclusions. First, simple checklists in which children endorse activities, behaviors, or traits that apply to themselves do not supply as rich an account of self-representational thought as open-ended interviews that require them to *produce* such thinking. Second, we can garner a richer perspective of such thinking if children are asked to consider the way they represent themselves around different people or in different places (e.g., church versus school). Third, methods such as Damon and Hart's interview protocol, or Harter's self-portrait grid, are valid; highly developed self-representational thought indexed by these assessments is tied to positive mental health (Harter, 1999). Readers might note that some have cataloged a listing of self-representation measures that includes reliability and validity information for each instrument (Davis-Kean & Sandler, 2001). Finally, although simpler methods have been developed for younger children, more reliability data is needed to judge the stability of their self-representations, and the clinical and developmental meaning (or validity) of their responses on such measures.

Assessing Self-Esteem

Self-esteem research has closely paralleled self-representation work; it is easy to collect data on both constructs. For example, after children have given us a self-representation, we can ask them to evaluate this description. As I mentioned earlier, a number of self-representation assessments double as self-esteem measures (Damon & Hart, 1988).

We can use two methods to measure self-esteem. First, one could measure *global self-esteem* or self-worth. In this assessment, we rate the child's general or overall self-evaluation. Rosenberg's (1965) ten-item *Self-Esteem Scale* is the most widely used measure of general self-esteem for school-aged children, adolescents, and adults. This scale contains items such as, "On the whole, I feel satisfied with myself," and, "At times I think I am no good at all." This measure is short, and measures one's *overall perception of self-worth*. A good global self-esteem measure must include context-free items, such as, "Most of the time I feel good about myself," and not tap abilities within select areas (e.g., school, peer group) (Harter, 1999). A global self-esteem measure that contains items such as "I am usually good at school work" suffers from two problems: it doesn't reveal general thinking about self-worth, and it would not be appropriate for use across widely spaced age groups. A measure assessing school performance would not be appropriate for preschool children or older adults.

The Rosenberg inventory is useful for students interested in a quick assessment of general self-esteem. The reliability and validity work on this instrument is extensive, and low general-self-esteem scores have been consistently associated with psychological problems (see Rosenberg, 1989, for scale items and psychometric history). Developmentally, most research has suggested that general self-esteem rises throughout childhood and adolescence, stabilizes during adulthood, and possibly declines in later life (Trzesniewski et al., 2003). However, the fact that not all people show this developmental pattern suggests there are different self-esteem trajectories, and more research is needed to determine why some do not fit this profile.

Children and adolescents are capable of making evaluative judgments in competencies across different contexts; we all possess a general self-esteem and feelings of self-worth in different environments (e.g., school, family, peer group) (Shavelson, Hubner, & Stanton, 1976). Like self-description research findings, the self-esteem of older children (e.g., fifth-graders) and adolescents is more differentiated than younger children (e.g., third-graders) (Byrne & Shavelson, 1996; Harter, 1999; Marsh, Carven, & Debus, 1991). Although it is easy to locate domain-specific self-esteem measures that can be used with different age groups, I am impressed with the *Perceived Competence Scales* designed by Harter and the *Self-Description Questionnaires* developed by Marsh. Let's discuss Harter's assessments first, because they have a more extensive history.

Harter has created inventories that tap self-evaluative processes in young children (preschool–second grade), older children (third grade–preadolescence), and adolescents; these methods are sensitive to the cognitive-linguistic abilities of these different age groups. When administered the *Pictorial Scale of Perceived Competence and Social Acceptance Scale for Young Children* (Harter & Pike, 1984), children are shown side-by-side pictures. In one, a child is portrayed as behaving in a competent way, whereas the counterpart in the other picture is not. As depicted in Figure 8.2, children point to the circle that they believe is most like them.

FIGURE 8.2 *Sample Item from Harter's Pictorial Scale of Perceived Competence for Young Children.* Child is instructed to mark the picture that most applies to her. From, Harter, S., & Pike, R. (1984). The Pictorial Scale of Perceived Competence and Social Acceptance for Young Children. *Child Development, 55*, p. 1973. Reprinted by permission of the Society for Research in Child Development.

Although the child is asked to make self-evaluations across five areas (e.g., physical appearance, social acceptance, cognitive and physical competence, and behavioral conduct), the finding is that children younger than 8 can only make distinctions between general competence (cognitive and physical competence) and feelings of social acceptance (physical appearance, social acceptance, behavior conduct). Despite these limitations, these broad indicators of self-worth are tied to actual competence; that is, children who feel poorly about social acceptance are usually similarly rated by teachers (Harter & Pike, 1984; Harter, 1999).

Harter has found that older children can provide self-esteem ratings using a questionnaire format. The *Self-Perception Profile for Children* (Harter, 1985) and *Self-Perception Profile for Adolescents* (Harter, 1988) are both easy to administer, yet these self-report measures tap different domains. The child version taps feelings of self-worth across one general and five specific domains (scholastic competence, athletic competence, peer likability, physical appearance, and behavioral conduct). The adolescent version contains these same scales but also taps perceptions of self-worth in close friendships, romantic appeal, and job competence. Both of these inventories possess impressive reliability and validity data (Harter, 1999).

Marsh has developed self-esteem measures that can be used with children and preadolescents (kindergarten–grade 6), early and middle adolescents (grades 7–11), and late adolescents and adults (Marsh, 1990). These assessments are all self-report questionnaires, requiring the participant to evaluate overall competency, and feelings of self-worth across different academic (e.g., reading, math) and nonacademic domains (e.g., physical appearance, peer relationships). Researchers should *read* the questionnaire items to children between kindergarten and second grade (Marsh, Carven, & Debus, 1991). When read self-esteem questions in "practice sessions" children seem to "get the hang" of the measure. This finding suggests that preschoolers do not need to be shown pictures or cartoons of the behavior of other children (as in Harter's pictorial assessment). Rather, with a carefully trained interviewer, young children could be directly asked their perceptions of self-worth without prompts or aids.

To test these ideas, Marsh and colleagues administered the 64-item *Self-Description Questionnaire-I* (Marsh, 1988) to kindergartners, first-, and second-graders across multiple times of measurement (Marsh, Carven, & Debus, 1998). Interviewers administered a number of practice items until each child understood the intent of the task. Once this "training session" was over, the interviewer administered the assessment, and noted considerable variation in the self-evaluations of even the kindergartners; even these young children varied their responses when questioned about their feelings of self-worth about school, about school subjects (e.g., math versus reading), parents, and peers. These data suggest that self-esteem may become more "compartmentalized" earlier than originally believed. However, the accuracy of these feelings may get better with maturity; associations between the self-esteem ratings of the children and other informants (parents, teachers) were stronger with the older children (Marsh et al., 1998).

Summary of Self-Assessment

We have covered instruments that assess self-esteem during childhood and adolescence; additional evaluations measure self-variables in adulthood (see Harter, 1999, for a sampling). Experts in this area continue to argue definitional and measurement issues (e.g., Marsh versus Harter). Indeed, some argue that self-esteem may not be a distinct concept. In one study, participants evaluated their general self-esteem (using Rosenberg's assessment) and other constructs, such as confidence, perceptions of control, and emotional stability. The study results revealed the assessments were *highly* correlated, suggesting these concepts are not distinct, and measure one grand, personality trait (Judge et al., 2002)!

What Do You Think?

Suppose you want to do a longitudinal study that begins with self-representation and self-esteem assessments in 8-year-olds. In terms of self-esteem, you want to assess both global and situation-specific feelings of self-worth. How would you assess these study variables at the first time of measurement? How might you change this strategy as your sample matures?

Assessing Gender-Related Thinking and Behavior in Children

When he was 3, my son told me, "Daddy, we are strong, because we are both mens." It is compelling that at very young ages, children understand their sex and begin to develop gender-related thinking about themselves and others. In this section, you will learn about methods researchers use to assess such fascinating gender-related thinking and behavior.

Gender-Schema Theory

A number of theories (e.g., psychoanalytic) explain the development of gender-related thinking and behavior; **gender-schema theory** (Martin & Halverson, 1981) currently guides most work in this area. What is a gender schema? These mental schemes represent a mind-set that we use to apply gender-related information to our social worlds and ourselves. You can understand social-cognition experts are interested in this concept!

The beliefs and expectancies that make up our gender schemas encompass three major constructs. *Gender-related attitudes*, *preferences*, and *identity* are assessed at the cognitive level. Each form of thinking is thought to represent a distinct construct. **Gender-related attitudes** reflect the child's thinking on how males and females should act. These gender-related attitudes are often measured by asking the child to consider gender-based stereotypes, such as, "Boys should never play with dolls," or "Its OK for girls to say bad words."

Gender-related preferences tap desires regarding toys, activities, and role models (Ruble & Martin, 1998). Children select masculine or feminine activities they identify with, or endorse characteristics or occupations that they aspire to obtain, that are stereotypically associated with one gender or the other. **Gender identity** focuses on our self-perception—that is, how masculine, feminine, or androgynous we view ourselves. Androgynous people believe they possess a mix of masculine and feminine traits or characteristics.

Gender-schema theorists believe that these belief systems develop as a result of socialization and maturational forces. Gender-related messages set forth by parents, peers, teachers, and the media encourage individual differences in these schemes, and reconfirm existing thinking. For instance, it is presumed that a child who holds traditional views of one gender or another will attend to information that is consistent with its belief system and ignore or reject data that is not (Martin & Halverson, 1981). Thus, a child who endorses traditionally masculine preferences and attitudes may not remember that the doctor in a television show was a woman. Gender-schema experts assert that maturational forces also play a role in the development of these schemas. The flexibility with which we view gender (e.g., both men and women can be doctors) depends on cognitive development (Martin, 1993).

Sex As an Independent Variable

A common question I hear from students is "Well, in my study, should I *look* for sex differences?" It seems unfortunate to "explore" sex differences without theory or hypotheses. In reality, the field has assembled an arsenal of theory and research that would point to sex differences (as well as cultural and ethnic differences) in some areas but not in others (Ruble & Martin, 1998). This past work allows us to make concrete hypotheses, so it is important to consider diversity issues *before*, as opposed to *after*, conducting a study.

When sex differences are documented, the overall power or magnitude of the findings is often debated. Some argue that sex differences on certain abilities are large, whereas others assert that even when statistically significant, such findings have little clinical meaning because of overlap between the outcome scores for males and females. Because the power of a statistical effect can be measured, it is recommended that you estimate such effects when reporting statistically significant sex differences (Eagly, 1995; Ruble & Martin, 1998). Another idea is to consider how sex, culture, and ethnicity may interact with other variables to explain abilities. A researcher who fails to consider such possibilities would miss the finding that males are more at risk for depression before puberty; however, this syndrome is more common in females after that (Compas et al., 1997). Thus, the impact of sex on an outcome variable might be enhanced when coupled with other variables (e.g., age, gender identity, ethnicity).

The participant's sex should be assessed, regardless of whether we want to consider it a study variable, We want to describe our sample, and lack of data regarding the participants' sex, age, race, ethnicity, and socioeconomic status raises questions about how well the results generalize to a target population (i.e., external validity). Students interested in recommendations for how to assess demographic variables, such as ethnicity or socioeconomic status, should consult the guidelines suggested by Entwisle and Astone (1994).

Assessing Gender-Related Attitudes and Preferences

Gender-related attitudes encompass general concepts and beliefs about gender. To assess these attitudes, we measure whether the child endorses characteristics, such as activities, objects, colors, psychological traits, or occupations, that are stereotypically associated with one sex or the other. An individual who utters, "Only girls play with dolls," or "Only men can be bankers" would receive a high "masculine" attitude score. In contrast, asking children to express their *own* wishes or desires pertaining to gender-stereotypical behaviors, traits, or activities constitutes a gender-preference assessment. To assess preferences, a child may be asked what color they like or what occupation they would like to pursue during adulthood. Thus, a child who indicates that he prefers the color pink, wants to play with dolls, and wishes to pursue a career in fashion design would receive a high feminine-preference score. Having distinguished between gender-related attitudes and preferences, let's now turn to some methods.

FIGURE 8.3   *Examples from Adult Figures, Child Figures, and Objects Section of the Sex Role Learning Index.* When shown figures from the Objects section, the child is asked, "Here is a hammer. Who would use a hammer to hammer nails, boys or girls?"

From Edelbrock, C., & Sugawara, A. (1978). Acquisition of sex-typed preferences in preschool children. *Developmental Psychology, 14*, p. 616. Reprinted by permission of the American Psychological Association.

Sex Role Learning Index.   Historically, the most popular assessment for measuring gender-related attitudes and preferences in children is the *Sex Role Learning Index* (SERLI; Edelbrock & Sugawara, 1978). To assess thinking, children are presented a variety of pictures, depicted in Figure 8.3. The pictures are contained in three sections: Objects, Child Figures, and Adult Figures. In the Objects section, the child is shown a picture of an object and asked, "Here is a hammer. Who would use a hammer to hammer nails, boys or girls?" There are a total of 20 pictures; 10 represent objects (e.g., shovels, boxing gloves) that are stereotypically masculine in nature, and 10 are stereotypically associated with feminine characteristics (dishes, baby bottle). The researcher creates an attitude score by noting the number of objects assigned "for boys" or "for girls." Thus, a boy who endorses a large number of objects stereotypically associated with males—"for boys"—would receive a high masculine-attitude score.

The Objects section measures gender-related attitudes, whereas the other sections assess preferences. In the Child Figures section, the child is shown a picture series of children participating in different activities (e.g., playing baseball, combing hair), and asked to select the activity they would most want to participate in. This first picture is removed, and the child then selects their next preference; this strategy allows one to rank-order their gender preferences.

In the Adult Figures section, the child is asked, "Which one of these things would you like to do when you grow up?" (e.g., different occupations). As with the Child Figures section, the rank-ordering of preferences is noted. In terms of scoring, a girl who selects lots of activities stereotypically associated with females would receive a high feminine-preference score.

This measure was initially designed to assess gender-related thinking and behavior in preschoolers, and may not be applicable for older children (Beere, 1990). Also, the domains assessed in measures such as the SERLI have been questioned. For example, the masculine items focus more on play activities and objects (e.g., baseball, play with soldiers), whereas the feminine items pertain more to housework (e.g., brooms, cooking). A concern with such items focuses on the desirability of the depicted behaviors to young children, and on whether the masculine and feminine items are equal in desirability. Are items such as baseball and playing with soldiers—masculine items that mostly appeal to children—comparable to sweeping and cooking (i.e., feminine items that may not be appealing for *either* boys or girls)? Such discrepancies may explain why young girls display less consistent same-sexed preferences on such measures (Ruble & Martin, 1998).

OATS and COATS. Liben and Bigler (2002) have assembled measures of gender-related thinking that can be administered to school-aged children, adolescents, and adults. In these assessments, participants are asked to think about gender issues regarding occupations, activities, and traits (*OAT*). These investigators have crafted an assessment for older adolescents and adults (OAT Scale), as well as for children (COAT scale). The best way to appreciate these measures is to see some of the items. As you can see in Table 8.1, these

TABLE 8.1 *Sample Items from OATS (Adults) and COATS (Children)*

Gender-Related Attitudes (OATS)	*Preferences (OATS)*	*Gender Identity (OATS)*
Who should:	**How much would you want to be:**	**Is this like you?**
be emotional	an airline pilot	strong
enjoy math	a birth attendant	enjoys geography
be brave	an architect	tries to look good
Gender-Related Attitudes (COATS)	*Preferences (COATS)*	*Gender Identity (COATS)*
Who should:	**How much would you want to be:**	**Is this like you?**
misbehave	a cheerleader	good at math
enjoy art	a ship captain	aggressive
study hard	a spy	loving

Source: Liben & Bigler, 2002.

assessments measure gender-related attitudes, preferences, and identity (i.e., how the subjects see themselves). Note how the "masculine" and "feminine" items that assess the
gender-related attitudes of children are more age appropriate and equal in desirability. For
example, rather than considering whether ironing or housecleaning is more appropriate for
boys or girls, children are encouraged to consider horseback riding, shopping, and cookie
baking (more age appropriate feminine items). In short, *both* the masculine and feminine
items are equivalent in desirability.

When completing this measure, the correlations between the gender attitudes, preferences, and identity scores were stronger for young adults and adolescents than for children; perhaps gender-related thinking becomes more integrated as we mature (Liben &
Bigler, 2002). Thus, an adult who endorses masculine stereotypes (e.g., "Men should be
doctors") is likely to hold stronger masculine preferences (e.g., "I like car racing"), which
corresponds to a masculine gender identity (e.g., "I see myself as aggressive"). Young children are less likely to display such highly connected, integrated thinking. In theory, strong
concordance between gender-related attitudes, beliefs, and identity may better predict
gender-typed behavior than in cases of less integrated thinking. Perhaps this is why stereotypical gender-related attitudes among young children *do not* strongly forecast masculine
or feminine behavior. In any case, the OATS and COATS appear to be very intriguing assessments, and the authors promise us a pictorial version for preschoolers in coming years
(the POATS!) (Liben & Bigler, 2002, p. 102).

Assessing Gender Constancy and Gender Identity

Tapping gender-related self-awareness can be accomplished in young children. In this section, we will discuss how to assess gender constancy and identity.

Gender Constancy.   **Gender constancy** is the belief that one's sex is permanent and will
not change, even if one chooses to wear an article of clothing or engage in an activity not traditionally associated with their sex (Kohlberg, 1966). Although cognitive maturity predicts the
development of gender constancy, individual differences in gender constancy have been reported among similarly aged children. Thus, some younger children have completely developed this ability, whereas some older children have not (De Lisi & Gallagher, 1991)!

These discrepant findings could result from methodological issues (Ruble & Martin,
1998). Even preschoolers can think logically when given tasks that they have done before
or have been given practice sessions on. Unfortunately, many gender-constancy assessment methods require the child to respond to hypothetical questions (e.g., "If you put on a
dress, would you be a boy or girl?") or consider drawings of children as real children (e.g.,
"This is a drawing of Sally. If she cut her hair, would she be a boy?") (Emmerich et al.,
1977). A young child might think if you simply erase the hair then you could also erase
anatomical features of sex and transform the girl into a boy! When preschoolers are shown
actual pictures of boys and girls with clearly defined anatomical features (i.e., penis for
boys, vagina for girls), even 3–5-year-olds (40%) will indicate that putting a dress on a boy
will not turn him into a girl (Bem, 1989).

However, even methodological advances have not eliminated the individual differences we routinely observe among children at different age levels. This finding suggests

that cognitive development alone does not explain the development of gender constancy. We suspect that socialization processes, coupled with advances in cognitive development, play a role in the development of this competency, as well as in other aspects of gender-related thinking.

Gender Identity.   *Gender identity* pertains to how masculine or feminine people view themselves in terms of behaviors and personality characteristics. In such an assessment, a participant is not asked, "Are you masculine or feminine?" Rather, the individual considers whether they possess characteristics (e.g., assertiveness, empathy) that are stereotypically associated with one sex or the other. I believe a good starting point is a description of two excellent assessments, the *Bem Sex Role Inventory* (BSRI; Bem, 1974) and the *Personal Attributes Questionnaire* (PAQ: Spence & Helmreich, 1978). The inventories possess a number of similarities. First, both inventories encourage respondents to rate themselves across a number of psychological and interpersonal characteristics, such as aggression, interpersonal understanding, and dominance. Second, both inventories tend not to contain traits that are considered undesirable, such as "greedy," or "whiny." This strategy is to ensure that people not rate themselves high on items that are simply socially desirable. Another strength is that the instrument developers do not view masculinity and femininity as either/or dispositions. Rather, the scoring protocols allow one to identify individuals as possessing highly masculine, highly feminine, both masculine and feminine, or neither masculine nor feminine characteristics. Possessing a mix of masculine and feminine characteristics is termed *androgyny.*

Experts interested in identifying gender identity in adolescents and adults primarily use the aforementioned methods. Young children may not understand such psychological labels as "theatrical," or "individualistic," but some gender-identity inventories can be completed by children; the most widely used assessment of this type is the BSRI-based, *Children's Sex Role Inventory* (CSRI; Boldizar, 1991). Sample items for this measure are given in Table 8.2. Children are not required to endorse difficult concepts, such as empathy and dominance; rather, these traits are illustrated using simple, easy-to-understand sentences.

TABLE 8.2   *Sample Items from the Children's Sex Role Inventory*

Masculine Items	*Feminine Items*	*Neutral Items*
I can take care of myself.	I am a gentle person.	I am an honest person.
I am sure of my abilities.	I like babies and small children a lot.	I like to keep secrets.
I am willing to take risks.	I like to do things with girls and women.	I have many friends.
I am good at sports.	I am faithful to my friends.	I try to tell the truth.
I get pretty angry if someone gets in my way.	It makes me feel bad when someone else is feeling bad.	I'm always losing things.

Source: Boldizar, 1991.

Although school-aged children become more flexible in their self-perceptions as they mature, over the course of puberty, early adolescents suddenly endorse masculine and feminine traits on the CSRI that are consistent with their own sex (Boldizar, 1991), supporting current theoretical musing regarding the development of gender identity during adolescence. It is theorized that males and females tend to display "gender intensification" and subscribe more to traditional gender roles during early adolescence (Crouter, Manke, & McHale, 1995). Perhaps stressors associated with puberty, and anxieties over sexuality and dating, influence boys and girls to briefly, albeit temporarily, subscribe to more traditional gender roles.

Given all this fine theory and these measurement strategies, is there any need for more research regarding gender identity? I believe the field is still unsettled. The longitudinal course of gender identity is debatable, and some have challenged the notion that youth adhere more to traditional gender-related thinking during early adolescence (Galambos, Almeida, & Petersen, 1990). Also, the relationship between gender identity and healthy psychological functioning may be moderated by both age and gender. Androgyny seems to be related to good psychosocial outcomes during childhood. However, during adolescence, highly masculine males show better adjustment than their androgynous counterparts (Massad, 1981). Thus, more longitudinal research is needed to explain how gender identity is related to adjustment during all stages of life.

Assessing Gender-Related Behavior

Some researchers prefer to observe the behaviors of young children in order to make estimates regarding gender-related attitudes and preferences. For example, one might assume that a little boy who likes the color blue, plays with trucks, and constantly wrestles with his siblings holds more masculine preferences and attitudes. As you might guess, there are a plethora of studies that have identified toy and activity preferences in children, as well as contrasted boys and girls on psychological and social abilities. Students interested in the experimental procedures used in these studies should begin by reading the excellent reviews compiled by Huston (1983) and Ruble and Martin (1998). I do caution that one should not assume that a little girl who likes to play with dolls automatically believes that boys cannot play with dolls or desires to become a hair dresser when she grows up! There are no strong associations between gender-related attitudes, preferences, and behavior in younger children.

One of the easiest ways to assess gender-related behavior in children is to ask parents or teachers for their perceptions. For example, the *Preschool Activities Inventory* (PSAI; Golombok & Rust, 1993) consists of 24 items that assess object and activity preferences, as well as personality characteristics. The informant is asked to rate how often the child uses objects as guns, plays house, and shows interest in spiders, snakes, and insects. Based on the PSAI scoring system, children are given a single gender-preference score; a low score signifies higher femininity, and a high score equals more masculinity. Research involving this method confirms that boys display more masculine preferences (e.g., rough-and-tumble play) and girls show more feminine characteristics (e.g., prefer to play with dolls) at very young ages (18–23 months); however, it has been noted that gender preferences are stronger in older children. Also, ratings by the children's parents and their day-care teachers were correlated only modestly (Golombok & Rust, 1993). One might ask whether discrepancies between the parent and teachers ratings resulted from differences of opinion or whether gender-typed preferences are encouraged (or expressed) in one context (e.g., family) but not in others (e.g., day care).

The PSAI is a good behavior inventory that taps gender-related behavior preferences in young children. Future researchers should examine similarities and discrepancies between different raters, similarities or differences between ratings and actual behavior observations, and better establishment of links between gender-related thinking and behavior.

Summary of Gender-Related Assessments

In this section, we discussed strategies for assessing different components of our gender schemata: gender-related attitudes, preferences, and identity. As in many fields, many issues remain unresolved regarding theoretical, conceptual, and measurement concerns. Although I have covered a number of them, consider how socialization practices contribute to individual differences in gender-related thinking and behavior. Some exciting research has been conducted to identify how parenting practices, peer involvement, and media exposure contribute to the development of stereotypical thinking and behavior in children (Ruble & Martin, 1998).

What Do You Think?

Suppose you want to explore the idea that associations between gender-related attitudes, preferences, identity, and behavior are dependent on both age and context. That is, you hypothesize that the relationship between these variables might be stronger in some environments (e.g., peer group) than in others, and are dependent on age. How would you design this study?

Assessing Prosocial Reasoning and Behavior

When does prosocial thinking and behavior develop? During the early preschool years, children form **social perspective-taking** skills, and develop the ability to put themselves in the shoes of important social agents, such as parents and peers. In this section, we will discuss ways of assessing the degree to which children consider the thinking and emotions of others. Also, you will learn about methods used to assess cognitive abilities that emerge after the development of perspective-taking skills. In particular, we will examine how to assess the development of moral reasoning, the understanding of societal rules and norms, and beliefs regarding fairness. Finally, if helpful behavior and empathy result from this advanced thinking (Eisenberg & Fabes, 1998), then a discussion of how to assess these competencies is warranted.

Assessing Perspective Taking

Perspective taking is multifaceted. Even young preschoolers can point to or locate an object from the point of view of another person. In addition to such *perceptual* perspective taking, we can consider the thoughts and emotions of another person, or *social perspective taking*. However, social perspective taking is a multidimensional construct; for instance, answering the question, "What is Johnny thinking?" is conceptually different from the query, "What is Johnny feeling?" Thus, people are capable of considering both the thinking and emotions of another person; each ability is a component of social perspective taking (Eisenberg & Fabes, 1998).

Cognitive Perspective Taking.   **Cognitive perspective taking**, or how we consider other people's thinking or thought processes, can be assessed via a variety of methods. Flavell (1968) developed a series of ingenious perspective-taking tasks that can be used with preschoolers and young school-aged children. In one task, children are shown a "store" that contains gifts such as toys, neckties, and books and asked to select a "gift" for both himself or herself and a variety of other people (e.g., teachers, peers, parents). The children's choices are then recorded, along with their reasoning behind the responses.

In a similar vein, both the "*Secret Task*" (Marvin, Greenberg, & Mossler, 1976) and "*Syllogisms Game*" (Greenberg, Marvin, & Mossler, 1977) are also neat perspective-taking tasks. In the "Secret Task," the child, among other things, is shown a toy that is witnessed by one research assistant but not another (who covers her eyes). The child has to then articulate who would know the location of the toy and who would not. In the "Syllogisms Game" the child is presented very brief problems, such as, "This little girl does not want to get dirty. Should she read a book or play outside in the rain?" Again the participants must consider the thought processes of the character in the story.

These simple perspective-taking tasks can help us understand the thinking of very young preschoolers (e.g., 2–3 years). We once believed that preschoolers had limited perspective-taking abilities (Underwood & Moore, 1982); however, newer research using these methods has demonstrated that *some* preschoolers (through not all) show advanced perspective-taking skills. Such advanced thinking predicts how well these young children treat others, such as siblings (Howe & Ross, 1990). Not only are these methods valid but also the results of research using these methods have changed the field's thinking about the development of perspective taking.

Because older children can easily master the tasks crafted for preschoolers, more difficult tasks must be given to these children (e.g., Chandler, 1973). In particular, researchers have presented children longer, more complicated dilemmas of people experiencing diverse problems. Selman (1976) has developed a series of social dilemmas for children to ponder. One such hypothetical dilemma is as follows (Selman, 1980, p. 36):

> Holly is an 8-year-old girl who likes to climb trees. She is the best tree climber in the neighborhood. One day while climbing down from a tall tree she falls off the bottom branch but does not hurt herself. Her father sees her fall. He is upset, and asks her to promise not to climb trees anymore. Holly promises. Later that day, Holly and her friends meet Sean. Sean's kitten is caught up in a tree and cannot get down. Something has to be done right away or the kitten may fall. Holly is the only one who climbs trees well enough to reach the kitten and get it down, but she remembers her promise to her father.

After reading the dilemma, you ask the child to consider the thinking of Holly's father, Holly's thinking, and that of her friend. For example, should Sean know why Holly

TABLE 8.3 *Selman's (1976) Levels of Social Perspective Taking*

Stage	Age Range	Description
Stage 0 **Egocentric viewpoint**	about 3–6 years	Cannot take the social perspective of another, although can point to the location of an object another may be looking at (perceptual role taking). Can understand own feelings, but perceive the emotions of others as similar to their own across all contexts.
Stage 1 **Social informational role taking**	about 6–8 years	Can understand that others may have emotions in the same situation that are different from own. However, may have difficult time coordinating social information—for example, difficulty understanding that a person who is smiling may not necessarily be happy.
Stage 2 **Self-reflective role taking**	about 8–10 years	Can step outside self and understand another's social perspective, and is aware that others can do the same back (e.g., "I know that she knows that I know that she knows") (Selman, 1980). Has difficulties translating information regarding self and others into action. For example, may be aware self is happy and friend is not, yet not know how to resolve this discrepancy.
Stage 3 **Mutual role taking**	about 10–12 years	Can engage in third-party perspective taking. For example, can step outside of both parties and resolve discrepancies in emotions and feelings using objective compromise. May not be able to justify *rationale* for compromise.
Stage 4 **Social and conventional system role taking**	about 12 to 15+ years	Better understanding of the moral, legal, familial, and economic reasons that underlie the social thinking and behavior of self and others. Can use these different reasons to rationalize third-party compromise (unlike Stage 3).

might decide not to climb up the tree (Selman, 1980)? Once the interview is completed, the child's responses are coded into the categories outlined in Table 8.3.

Most who use dilemmas to assess role taking and moral reasoning in children, including Selman, do not expect children to provide 100% consistent responses across the social dilemmas. Some children may provide responses that could be coded Stage 3, yet other responses may fit Stage 2 better. In such cases, the rater can average the responses to provide a quantitative score (e.g., 2.88) and provide the child a modal stage score. For instance, more Stage 3 responses would garner the child a Stage 3 rating (Gurucharri & Selman, 1982).

Selman and others have documented consistent developmental differences in the perspective-taking skills of children (Flavell, 1968; Selman, 1980). For example, although even preschoolers can tell when Mommy or Daddy is mad, they cannot understand why different people might experience different emotions in response to the same event. Thus some preschoolers may respond to the "Holly" dilemma by saying, "Holly would feel sad," because *they* feel sad.

School-aged children can understand that people have different perspectives on an issue yet cannot articulate the motives or reasoning behind the other person's thinking. Thus, a child might say that Holly's father would be mad (even though the child wouldn't think this way) but may not be able to reason why there is a discrepancy in thinking between the two parties (i.e., respondent and Holly's father). During adolescence, individuals begin to understand the *motives* behind social reasoning (e.g., familial, economic, moral, legal) that drive such thinking. For example, an adolescent might indicate that Holly's father would place the value of the kitten's life below concerns about being sued if Sean were to climb the tree and fall out!

You should note some methodological issues at this point. Thus far, the methods we have described would be considered *production methods*; the child is presented a task and required to produce a response in their own words. Although this type of method provides a rich account of the child's thinking, considerable training is required to accurately probe this thought and then code the responses into perspective-taking categories.

Assessing Affective Perspective Taking.   The methodologies designed to assess **affective perspective taking** are similar to strategies used to assess more general role-taking abilities. For example, when using social perspective-taking dilemmas or vignettes, we can ask children to discuss the *thoughts and feelings* of a character (Harris et al., 1989). However, a long vignette portraying the emotional plight of another person can present problems for preschool children, who typically have difficulty comprehending *long* stories that involve *hypothetical* people.

What assessments might be suitable for younger children? Just like assessments designed to measure cognitive role-taking abilities in preschoolers, researchers have developed very simple instruments for assessing affective perspective taking in young children. In one such assessment, young children witness puppets enacting a variety of scenarios, such as going to the doctor, coming in to dinner from outdoor play, or receiving a favorite food. In some cases, the puppet portrays emotions that a child would typically feel, such as apprehension about going to the doctor. In other scenarios, the puppet displays an emotion that would not be consistent, such as anger over receiving an ice-cream cone. After each scenario, the child is asked to affix a happy, sad, angry, or scared face to the puppet (Denham, 1986; Denham, Zooler, Couchourd, 1994). In addition, these researchers assess the child's interpretations of the puppet's general thinking; thus the assessment also measures cognitive role-taking abilities.

Perhaps the key issue is to determine whether the young child can understand that the puppet may have an emotion the research subject may not necessarily possess. The results of this fascinating work clearly indicate that a substantial percentage of preschoolers can consider the thinking and emotions of another—even when these young children do not share those views! For example, most of these children could understand that the puppet going to day care might actually experience happiness over this event, even though these same children were reported as being unhappy when they were taken to day care by their caregivers (Denham,

What Do You Think?

Suppose you are interested in assessing role-taking skills in preschoolers, school-aged children, and adolescents. How would you measure these skills in such different age groups? How would you ensure that your methods were understandable and fair for each age group?

1986). The results of this work suggest that like Piaget, perspective-taking experts may have underestimated the depth of preschoolers' thought. Although earlier research failed to make consistent connections between the affective role-taking skills of young children and prosocial behavior, work using these more modern methods has found rather strong correlations (Bosacki, 2003; Denham et al., 2003).

Assessing Moral Reasoning, Distributive Justice, and Social Conventions

The development of perspective taking allows us to comprehend the moral plights experienced by self and others. Research on such **moral reasoning** has been greatly influenced by the work of Lawrence Kohlberg (Kohlberg, 1969; 1978), who developed moral-dilemmas scenarios to assess this ability. In one such dilemma, a man has to decide whether to steal a drug to save his wife's life. When assessing one's moral reasoning in such conflicts, we are not as interested in whether the subject says "yes" or "no" to such dilemmas. Rather, the individual's *rationale* behind the response is coded. Higher moral-reasoning scores are based on the ability of the person to separate from personal motivations and feelings and engage in advanced perspective taking that considers the problem from a legal or societal position (Kohlberg, 1976).

However, presenting children with long stories that involve unfamiliar topics or people creates a situation in which reasoning skills are often underestimated. For example, Kohlberg (1969) documented that individuals typically do not justify their moral decisions using empathy or sympathy—two important abilities that involve perspective taking—until adolescence. However, when using more "child friendly" stories that involve familiar activities, it is not uncommon for a child to justify their moral reasoning using statements such as, "I'd feel bad if I didn't help him, because he'd be in pain" (Eisenberg, 1982). This would suggest that Kohlberg might have underestimated the moral-reasoning abilities of younger children.

Such methodological concerns may explain why early studies involving young children often yielded weak links between moral reasoning and prosocial behavior (Eisenberg & Fabes, 1998). To combat this problem, researchers have adapted Kohlberg's methods to include simple stories on helping behavior, involving common real-life dilemmas (Eisenberg, 1982).

What do we mean by a "real life" dilemma? Let's consider the plight of the child in the following vignette:

> One day a girl named Mary was going to a friend's birthday party. On her way she saw a girl who had fallen down and hurt her leg. The girl asked Mary to go to her house and get her parents so the parents could come and take her to the doctor. But if Mary did run and get the child's parents, she would be late for the birthday party and miss the ice cream, cake, and all the games. What should Mary do? Why? (Eisenberg, 1982, p. 231).

Can you see how this vignette is more "kid friendly" than a story involving the moral plight of a man who must consider stealing a drug to save his wife's life? Once the child has been read such dilemmas, their responses are coded according to the stages outlined in Table 8.4.

TABLE 8.4 *Prosocial Moral-Reasoning Stages*

1. Hedonistic, pragmatic orientation.	Reasoning regarding goodness is guided by physical consequences. For example, "I would help, because I'd get spanked if I didn't." Alternatively, reasoning may be primarily guided by own needs. For example, "I would help, because I would get a lot of ice cream."
2. "Needs of others" orientation.	Concern for others' physical, material, or psychological needs. For instance, "She should go to the party, because she might be hungry."
3. Approval and interpersonal orientation or stereotyped orientation.	Realization that others are human, living people. For example, "She should help her, because she is hurt and feels bad." Alternatively, reasoning based on the stereotyped impression of what is good or bad; for example, "She should help her, because it is the nice thing to do."
4a. Empathetic orientation.	Reasoning guided by expressions of sympathy or role taking; for example, "She should help because she would feel sorry for her," or, "She should help; I know I would."
4b. Transitional stage.	Justification for helping behavior based on internalized values, though these ideas may not be well rationalized; For example, "She should help: it is something I've learned and think is important."
5. Internalized stage.	Beliefs guided by highly developed internal beliefs and principles that are based on well-reasoned individual and societal obligations. For example, "She should help; if more people did that, we'd all be better off." Positive or negative affect related to maintenance of self-respect for living up to one's own values is clearly stated.

Adapted from Eisenberg-Berg, 1979; Eisenberg, 1982.

Several points regarding the validity of this scheme should be overviewed. First, Eisenberg and colleagues (1983; 1991; 1995) have noted that preschoolers often offer responses relevant to the earliest stages of this theory, school-aged children usually fall within the middle stages, and adolescents are more likely to have more internalized beliefs. However, because even young children sometimes offer well-reasoned responses and adolescents occasionally show low levels of moral reasoning, this theory does acknowledge individual differences in such thinking.

Second, when using simpler, more "real-world" stories, the responses of preschoolers and school-aged children are more sophisticated than those offered in response to hypothetical people involved in adultlike moral conflicts. Older preschoolers and young, school-aged children often justify their moral reasoning using a "needs of others" approach (Eisenberg, Lennon, & Roth, 1983), which is inconsistent with what others have found using more complicated, hypothetical dilemmas (Kohlberg, 1969). This work demonstrates that young children can take the emotional perspective of others, even when it may contradict their own beliefs about the dilemma.

A final point rests with associations between moral reasoning and prosocial behavior. In a series of studies, Eisenberg and colleagues have documented, under certain conditions, that moral reasoning is related to actual prosocial behavior. This seems to be particularly true in cases in which the child is asked to respond to the *emotional* needs of another, or in situations in which there is actually some cost to the helper, such as having to volunteer an hour of time after school (Eisenberg & Fabes, 1998). Eisenberg speculates that engaging in helpful behavior that involves some cost to the helper creates a context that provokes moral conflict, and is the type of scenario in which one is more likely to see an association between moral reasoning and behavior.

Although the dilemma method seems to be a favorite among moral-reasoning researchers, Eisenberg's laboratory has developed a self-report measure for use with older children and adolescents (Carlo, Eisenberg, & Knight, 1992). This *Prosocial Moral-Reasoning Scale* contains six stories similar to Eisenberg's original dilemmas. The respondent is asked to read the stories, and then evaluate the importance of different reasons for why the main story character should help the needy person in the story. Each rationale directly parallels Eisenberg's stages of moral development; when presented the "Mary dilemma" presented earlier, the person can rate the importance of responses ranging from a hedonistic response such as, *"It depends on how much fun Mary expects the party to be, and what sorts of things are happening at the party"* (Hedonistic, Stage 1) to a more sophisticated, internalized response, such as, *"It depends on how Mary would feel about herself if she helped or not"* (Internalized Affect, Stage 5).

What might be the drawbacks to such a self-report measure? Recall that we frequently assess perspective-taking and prosocial reasoning using *production methods*—that is, the child is asked to create or produce a response after hearing a dilemma. When using *evaluation methods*, such as in this case, children do not provide spontaneous thinking on such scales; they simply endorse one of the responses presented to them. One might wonder whether children are prone to give us the responses we want here, and may not actually reason in this manner. How might you test the validity of this measure? Adolescent endorsements on this measure are consistent with what they produce on the open-ended moral dilemmas. In addition, scores from the self-report measure have been related to self-reported measures of prosocial behavior and maternal reports of adolescent helping behavior (Eisenberg et al., 1995). Thus, it seems this evaluation measure of moral reasoning could be considered a practical, potentially valid measure that can be used with older populations (e.g., adolescents and adults).

Assessing Distributive Justice. **Distributive justice** is a facet of moral reasoning that involves how we think about fairness and allocation of resources. This issue plays out in many arenas of life, ranging from the arguments among children over who deserves the best birthday presents to committee members who must decide whether to give a student award based on need or merit. Indeed, "It's not fair!" is a cry not just emitted by children!

Damon (1977), like many who study social-cognitive thinking in children, has developed both hypothetical and real-world dilemmas in which children must consider resource allocation (see also Enright et al., 1980). These dilemmas are followed by an interview that taps children's thinking regarding distributive justice. With the aid of pictures, the child is read a short story involving four children; one is younger than the other three. The children are asked to make bracelets, which turn out to be of varying quality; for example, the youngest child makes an ugly one and an older peer happens to make a beautiful one. The children then are given 10 candy bars and asked to divide them up as they see fit (Damon, 1977, p. 64–65).

After the story is read, the interviewer asks such questions as, "Should the little girl who made the prettiest one get extra candy?" or "Should the youngest child, who made the ugliest bracelet, get less?" Next, the child's responses are coded and the respondent is placed in a distributive justice "stage." Children who receive lower justice scores often want to distribute the candy bars based on physical characteristics, so that the most attractive person gets the most. Older children are better at this game, and base their decisions on equality ("everyone gets the same"), merit, or special needs. The most sophisticated reasoning is based on advanced perspective taking; the child can consider both the individual qualities and accomplishments of each person, and balance this thinking with the demands of the situation (Damon, 1977).

Damon has documented a number of compelling findings from this program of research. First, associations between perceptions of fairness in hypothetical and "real life" dilemmas are highly correlated with age. In others words, adolescents provide similar types of reasoning in response to hypothetical and real-world stories, whereas the more advanced reasoning in younger children is usually tapped in response to more familiar dilemmas. This finding again points to the methodological drawbacks to using hypothetical stories for very young children.

Another question is whether "fair thinkers" identified in this method treat others fairly. Damon has documented that *self-interest* interferes more with the association between fair thinking and behavior in younger children. In situations in which self-interest is less of a concern, Damon has found that children who receive higher justice scores are more likely to allocate resources based on need and less likely to devote resources based on physical appearances or merit, when compared to their counterparts with lower scores (Damon, 1977; 1980).

These findings suggest that personal and situational factors interact with distributive justice thinking in predicting behavior. For example, young children (e.g., kindergartners) distribute resources the same way for strangers and friends. However, older children are more discriminating, and will help needy friends more than needy strangers. Thus, character familiarity is another situational factor that must be considered when developing dilemmas for assessing distributive-justice reasoning (McGillicuddy-De Lisi, Watkins, & Vinchur, 1994).

The content of the social-moral dilemmas that we present to subjects seems to be a very pressing methodological concern; children and adolescents select different aspects of the situation to guide their eventual decisions. Also, dilemmas that contain attachment figures, such as friends, siblings, or parents, raise a thorny issue. In such cases, the participant must balance concerns for fairness (distributive justice) with their feelings for the person (Hoffman, 2000). Dilemmas involving strangers and attachment figures signify that we are assessing *more* than perceptions of fairness; the individual is also assessing the person's empathetic regard for the participants. Although one might want to separate out such "noise" and focus just on distributive justice per se, many of the dilemmas that we face on a day-to-day basis are quite complicated. A teacher who likes a student who turns in a late assignment must balance his feelings for the student with fair treatment of the others (Hoffman, 2000).

Finally, students interested in dilemma methods that require a skilled interviewer often express concerns about training. However, Enright et al. (1980) have developed the *Distributive Justice*

What Do You Think?

What's the difference between moral thinking and distributive justice? How would you test the idea that they are interrelated? What dilemmas would you create to test your hypotheses?

Scale, in which children (ages 5–11) are presented Damonlike dilemmas and then shown drawings of possible outcomes representing each stage of his theory. This measure is easy to score, takes only about 15 minutes to administer, and appears to have good psychometric properties (i.e., reliability and validity).

Assessing Social Conventions. **Social conventions** can be conceptualized as social knowledge about customs within a particular society. Through social experience, we learn social-conventional acts, such as how to treat others (e.g., how to address people as Mr. or Mrs.) and behave in different contexts (e.g., church versus concert hall). Can you distinguish between moral reasoning and social conventions? Moral thinking tends to transcend cultures; for example, stealing, killing others, and damaging property would probably not be tolerated in most societies. However, social-conventional reasoning taps a mode of thinking that is heavily dependent on the customs of one's culture; the way we address elders, dress, and behave in a park are more influenced by cultural expectancies (Turiel, 2002).

In a series of studies, Elliot Turiel interviewed people regarding their reasoning on moral (hitting others) and social-convention violations. Consider a boy who addresses his teachers by their first names or an individual eating with his hands rather than with a fork and knife. Like those who conduct research on moral reasoning, the primary methodology used in social-convention studies employs a short dilemma followed by an interview to tap reasoning. The following represents an interview clip involving a story about a boy who took his clothes off at school because it was warm (adapted from Turiel, 1983, p. 62):

Interviewer: Was it all right to do this?

Child: No, because it's a school, and other people don't like to see you without your clothes on. It looks silly.

Interviewer: I know a school where there is no rule about this. Is it OK for that school to say it's OK if the children want to do it?

Child: Yes, because it's their rule.

Interviewer: Why can they have that rule?

Child: If that's what the boss says, then it's OK.

Interviewer: How come?

Child: Because he is the boss; he is in charge of the school.

Interviewer: The little boy who took off his clothes, he goes to that school. Is it OK then?

Child: Yes, if he wants; it's the rule.

Turiel (1978) has a coding system that allows researchers to categorize respondents into social-conventional stages. One important marker of advanced social-conventional thought is how well the respondent understands that the issue is embedded within a larger social context. For example, when asked if it is OK to call a teacher by her first name, an individual in the lowest stages would say it is wrong simply because the teacher said it was wrong. A more advanced person might go beyond an individual authority figure and think of the rule embedded in a larger context (e.g., "It's against school rules"). In the highest levels, the individual considers the social-conventional transgression as a major societal rule or custom. For example, an older participant might say it's wrong to call a teacher by a first name, because one should show respect for anyone who is older in such an important position (Turiel, 1978). Now, if I could just get my students thinking like that when it comes to handing assignments in on time!

Turiel and others (Prencipe & Helwig, 2002; Smetana, 1985) have noted consistent developmental trends when using this system; school-aged children are more advanced than preschoolers, and adolescents and adults are rated as more sophisticated in thought than children (Turiel, 1978). Turiel has also examined whether children's social-conventional reasoning predicts their actual behavior in school settings. Children who score higher in social-conventional thought often display fewer social-conventional transgressions (e.g., talking in class, refusing to wear gym clothes during physical education) than their less-advanced counterparts (Turiel, 1983). Thus, there appears to be predictive validity for his classification system.

Assessing Prosocial Behavior

Prosocial behavior is voluntary behavior intended to help another (Eisenberg & Fabes, 1998). Most who study such behavior have assessed comforting, altruistic acts, cooperation, or sharing behaviors (Radke-Yarrow, Zahn-Waxler, & Chapman, 1983); however, most experts assess prosocial behavior under different conditions for preschoolers, school-aged youth, and adolescents (Eisenberg & Fabes, 1998). Researchers often observe the sharing and helping behavior of young children in *naturalistic settings*, such as day care (Zahn-Waxler et al., 1995). In contrast, the behavior of older children is often assessed using *structured laboratory tasks*, in which the child is asked to engage in helping behavior with either real (adults or other children) or hypothetical people. Although there is some consistency between laboratory and naturalistic assessments of different aspects of prosocial behavior (e.g., sharing, comfort), high rates of such behavior in the lab *do not* automatically forecast it at home or at school (Yarrow & Waxler, 1976).

These methodological difficulties make it hard to conclude whether children become more prosocial with age, because both younger and older children are often observed in different contexts (i.e., lab versus field). For example, people are more likely to engage in more prosocial behavior in structured laboratory contexts (Eisenberg & Fabes, 1998). Because laboratory assessments are usually designed for older children, one might wonder whether the more frequent prosocial acts of older children result from maturity or are affected by the experimental context.

When considering the research setting, laboratory assessments *are* tempting to use, because we can study children under carefully controlled conditions. Indeed, prosocial behaviors, like aggression, might be difficult to capture in naturalistic settings because of low occurrence or "opportunity" rates. However, I am much more comfortable with laboratory experiments that assess behavior that is easily verifiable by other informants. For example, a child who cooperates with other peers in the lab should receive high "cooperation" scores by parents and teachers who witness these prosocial acts on a more consistent basis. However, consistency across ratings supplied by multiple informants is sometimes spotty, and these ratings do not always predict direct observations of prosocial behavior (Eisenberg et al., 1991).

Why might there be a lack of connectedness between laboratory and field assessments of prosocial behavior? Perhaps it is time to consider the meaning of direct observations of prosocial behavior. Although I often tell my students that behavior observations reflect an assessment "gold standard," I sometimes question the external validity of some classic assessment techniques. Should a child who gives seven poker chips to a peer be viewed as more "prosocial" than one who gives only five? Is a child who does not readily share necessarily immoral, and does this refusal actually forecast helping behavior during a crisis in the real-world? Thus, when conducting assessments of prosocial or antisocial behavior, we have to consider it in context, a point that is stressed in Box 8.2.

Partly because of these concerns, and partly to save time, we can use a variety of self-report measures to tap global perceptions of prosocial behavior across most situations (e.g., Green et al., 1994; Rushton, Chrisjohn, & Fekken, 1981). However, keep in mind that there are certain types of prosocial behavior (e.g., helping, cooperation) that may be context specific. Assessments tapping prosocial behavior "in most situations" is limited, because such measures ignore the different domains of this behavior. To address this concern, Carlo and Randall (2002) have developed a domain-specific self-report measure of prosocial behaviors. This measure is well grounded theoretically, and the items tap different domains of prosocial behavior (e.g., helping versus comforting behavior) across different contexts. For example, items such as, "I often make anonymous donations, because they make me feel good," tap a different context than "I can help others best when people are watching me." Evidently, some people are more likely to engage in helping behavior when they know others will be aware of their benevolent acts!

Although this new measure has only been used with adolescents, people often report fairly consistent levels of prosocial behavior over short periods of time (i.e., good test-retest reliability). In addition, scores on this measure are related to prosocial reasoning skills. For example, individuals who report high rates of anonymous helping behavior also show strong perspective-taking skills. Conversely, individuals who need a high degree of public awareness in order to exhibit prosocial behaviors tend to score low on moral reasoning (e.g., hedonistic thinking) (Carlo & Randall, 2002). I am excited about the future of this particular assessment.

Assessing Empathy and Sympathy

Some theorists believe that some people are motivated to engage in prosocial behavior, because they have a high degree of empathy for others. However, considerable disagreement exists regarding how to define empathy. Eisenberg (1986) asserts that **empathy** is emotion sharing, or the ability to experience emotions similar to those of the person in trouble. Further, **sympathy** has less to do with "emotional matching," and more to do with showing concern for the *welfare of another* (Eisenberg, 1986). If one accepts these definitions, it would seem that sympathy should predict prosocial behavior better than pure empathy. Unfortunately, researchers tend to use these terms interchangeably!

It would make sense to theorize that empathy-related responding should be related to advances in moral reasoning and perspective-taking skills, and should predict certain aspects of prosocial behavior (Hoffman, 2000). In particular, we would expect a sympathetic person to help others experiencing distress. However, this association is somewhat

BOX 8.2 • *Assessing Aggression in Context*

One reason that prosocial behavior is a popular area of study is that it is often difficult to experimentally study antisocial behavior and aggression in an externally valid way. Research of this nature also raises ethical concerns; it is one thing to contrive settings to elicit good behavior in children, and it is another to set up a situation that encourages negative activities! Even researchers who naturalistically study the development of antisocial behavior in children admit that it is often difficult to get human subjects' approval for their work, and it may be hard to get parental permission to study the most aggressive children in a school or community.

I would like to overview some recent paradigm shifts in the study of children's aggression. First, although there are some highly valid behavioral inventories, such as the *Child Behavior Checklist* (Achenbach, 1991), that can be completed by parents and teachers to provide frequency estimates of aggressive and antisocial behavior, there is a growing trend to study such behavior in context. Although one could study a child's rate of "overall aggression," it is far more meaningful to determine where—family, neighborhood, school— the behavior is occurring. Second, although the family has been a traditional context in which to study aggression and violence in children (Cummings & Davies, 1994), increasingly, researchers are concentrating their attention on aggression and victimization in the peer group (Bierman, 2004).

Serious acts of aggressive behavior toward peers are referred to as "bullying behavior." The presence of bullying behavior can be estimated by teachers (Crick, 1996; Ladd & Burgess, 1999), peers (Swearer et al., 2001) or by the bullies themselves (Espelage & Asidao, 2001), using behavior checklists. Alternatively, children can nominate the most aggressive children by simply pointing to names on a class roster (Crick & Grotpeter, 1995; Schwartz et al., 1997).

Sample questions might include items such as "Hits, shoves, or pushes peers."

When using peer-aggression measures such as these, it is useful to also gather data on peer rejection; the outcomes for bullies are much poorer when accompanied by serious rejection (Bierman, 2004). Also, I believe Crick's (1996) teacher-completed measure of peer aggression has exciting potential. First, it includes items that tap both physical and *relational aggression*; the latter behavior is more likely exhibited by girls, and includes activities such as malicious gossiping. Second, teacher ratings of peer aggression are valid, in the sense that they correlate well with peer data and predict later adjustment in these children (Crick, 1996). However, these findings are weaker for relational aggression; perhaps peers have greater insight into this activity. In any case, if teacher data is as reliable as that of peers, then perhaps we can circumvent the ethical dilemma of asking children to nominate aggressive and disliked peers.

There do exist observational coding systems to index naturally occurring aggressive behavior in playgroups or classroom settings. One such system allows the rater to code different types of aggression. For example, *reactive aggression* would be an aggressive response to the actions of another child, whereas *instrumental aggression* consists of an aggressive behavior to reach a goal, such as grabbing a toy from another child. *Bullying behavior* is coded as unprovoked assaults or taunting where there is no explicit goal other than to harm another (Coie et al., 1991). The system is valid, in that peers dislike children who use bullying behavior more than children who use other forms of aggression. However, not all bullies are disliked, and it is the co-occurrence of these variables that most strongly forecasts problematic outcomes.

dependent on the way we attempt to measure empathy or sympathy. For example, children who display high rates of empathy or sympathy via self-reports, or in response to hypothetical stories *do not* show much prosocial behavior when given the opportunity (Eisenberg & Miller, 1987).

Eisenberg and colleagues have developed a battery of methods for better measuring these constructs (Eisenberg et al., 1988). As a child watches a video portraying a child actor with a disability, researchers monitor the participant's heart rate and facial sadness. Children are also asked to report on their emotional experiences (e.g., sadness) during this video. This research group proposes that this battery of measures provides converging data for *empathy*—that is, an emotional response to another's distress.

The researchers assess *sympathy* by surveying the child's appraisals regarding concern, such as, "Do you feel concerned for the other child?" or "Do you feel sorry for the other child?" These assessments can be used in a number of ways. For example, one can use them to predict related cognitive processes (e.g., perspective taking) or prosocial behavior. In a number of studies, these researchers, and others (Zahn-Waxler et al., 1995) have noted that sympathetic responses, in particular, are related to certain aspects of prosocial behavior in the laboratory (Eisenberg et al., 1989) and in naturalistic settings (e.g., classrooms) (Eisenberg et al., 1990).

Physiological measures of empathy and facial expressions of concern are much stronger predictors of prosocial behavior than self-reports. However, is there a way to more economically measure empathy and sympathy? Strayer (1993) has developed an assessment in which children view videotapes of people experiencing different emotions (e.g., sadness, anger) in response to various events, such as a little boy receiving punishment. Using an interview, children are next asked to describe their reactions to the different events and provide a rationale for each response. When coding the responses, raters analyze how well the child's emotions match those of the distressed person and then evaluate the reasoning behind their reactions. Children receive higher scores if their emotional experiences are similar to those of the object character, *and* if their rationale is more sympathetic than empathetic. A child who says, "I would feel sad too if I got punished like that" would receive a higher score than one who utters, "I was sad because he was sad."

Children's responses are then rated on a sixteen-point scale. Low scores would indicate very little empathetic responding, emotional understanding, or emotional matching, whereas moderate scores (e.g., 5–10) would indicate some emotional matching, yet with more focus on the subject's own emotions than those of the characters portrayed (e.g., "I feel really sad that she's sad"). Children who receive the highest scores show the ability to display sympathetic concern, and exhibit sophisticated role taking (e.g., "I would be concerned if she felt like that.") (Strayer, 1993).

I believe that Strayer's system is very promising, because it is easy to use and allows the researcher to simultaneously focus on the child's emotional responses to, and reasoning about, the plights of other people. The fact that children are awarded the highest scores for simultaneous empathetic and sympathetic responses makes sense. Subsequent research using this system has noted that children who receive the highest empathy and sympathy scores demonstrate prosocial behavior in laboratory tasks and receive high ratings by parents, teachers, and peers regarding certain components of this behavior (e.g., comforting, cooperation) (Roberts & Strayer, 1996).

Also, awarding higher empathy and sympathy scores to children who show *both* empathetic and sympathetic responses (as opposed to just empathetic) taps a process that one typically observes in the real-world. That is, empathy typically precedes sympathy; however, having empathy, or emotional understanding, does not always guarantee a sympathetic response! I believe that most of the research results in this area suggest that there are "triggers" that move an empathetic response to a sympathetic one, and discovering those triggers (e.g., socialization experiences, situation factors) holds exciting implications for intervention.

Thus far, we have discussed fairly sophisticated ways of assessing empathy and sympathy in children and adolescents. As you might have guessed, there are self-report measures that tap this construct (e.g., Bryant, 1982); however, the bulk of the research suggests that self-report measures of empathy do not consistently predict prosocial behavior (Eisenberg & Fabes, 1998). This finding probably results from a number of factors; however, my guess is that simply asking people to think about issues such as, "Seeing a person who is crying makes me cry as well," is not the best context in which to assess empathy and sympathy. In such cases, one is assessing perceptions of emotions and cognitions during such events, which can be clouded by poor recall.

However, self-report measures of empathy and sympathy nevertheless have a place. For example, when considering the child's typical responses in different settings (e.g., home, schools), it may be useful to allow *other* people to complete such measures on a target child or adolescent. Indeed, intensive laboratory assessments of child empathy and sympathy do predict other people's (e.g., parents, teachers, peers) impressions of the child's emotional responses in a variety of contexts (Roberts & Strayer, 1996). These data would suggest that the validity of self-reports measures of this type might very well depend on the informant (i.e., child or another person).

What Do You Think?

Suppose you are interested in determining whether certain elements of prosocial reasoning, such as perspective taking, predict empathy, sympathy, and prosocial behavior. How would you design a study to support this theory? In formulating your answer, consider how you might assess each construct and how developmental status may influence the association between these variables.

Assessing Prosocial Reasoning and Behavior: A Summary

Although we discussed a variety of methods in this section, it is quite apparent that most researchers use stories or videos that communicate the plights of others to research participants to assess prosocial and moral reasoning. After these story presentations, researchers conduct interviews and then code the participant's responses into different reasoning categories. One could pursue many research angles in this area; however, I recommend that students think about variables that may influence this process (e.g., parenting behavior), and to consider how social-cognitive reasoning might predict important developmental outcomes down the road. Because the association between prosocial reasoning and behavior is not always consistent, it is important to identify developmental and situational variables that might better explain this relationship.

Assessing Relationships with Others

In this section, we will continue our discussion from Chapter 5 regarding how to assess attachment relationships between children and their caregivers, and also examine methods of assessing competency in the peer group. These factors are, of course, interconnected, and both are predictive of long-term adjustment.

Assessing Child-Caregiver Attachment

Commonly used attachment methods for children are outlined in Table 8.5. In Chapter 5, you learned about the Strange Situation and Attachment Behavior Q-set. As you recall, in the *Strange Situation*, the infant and caregiver are observed in a laboratory setting marked by brief separations and the occasional presence of a stranger. Some researchers have modified the Strange Situation to make it more appropriate for older children.

Modified Strange Situations for Older Children. Researchers have developed techniques similar to the Strange Situation to assess attachment processes in older preschoolers and young school-aged children (e.g., 6–7 years). To elicit arousal, researchers may create lengthy separation periods, use a variety of different strangers, or ask the child to complete difficult tasks when separated from their caregiver. As in the Strange Situation,

TABLE 8.5 *Popular Attachment Assessments*

Name	Description
Strange Situation (Ainsworth et al., 1978)	Infants (12–20 months) observed in lab setting with caregiver. Four attachment classifications—secure, avoidant, anxious-resistant, and disorganized—derive from observing infant's behavior during brief separations from caregivers, interactions with a stranger, and ability to receive comfort from caregiver during times of duress.
Attachment Behavior Q-set (Waters, 1987)	Rater (parent or observer) sorts 90 cards containing classic attachment behaviors or emotions (e.g., easily comforted by caregiver) into categories that are like or unlike child (1–5 years). Child receives an overall, continuous security score.
Modified Strange Situations (see Solomon & George, 1999, for review)	Children (preschool/young school-aged) observed with parent in a lab setting. Parent routinely asked to leave the room while child performs different tasks with experimenter. Raters carefully observe attachment behaviors during these segments, and also note quality of reunion behavior. Classifications parallel infant attachment classifications, although the attachment behavior patterns for older secure or insecure children may not be exactly the same as those witnessed in younger children (e.g., Main & Cassidy, 1988).
Story or picture response assessments (Jacobsen, Edelstein, & Hofmann, 1994)	Children are read stories, accompanied by pictures or enacted by dolls that contain attachment-relevant themes (e.g., prolonged caregiver separation). Attachment classifications, which parallel infant categories, are determined from coding the quality of the child's story interpretation as it relates to attachment.
Adult Attachment Interview (George, Kaplan, & Main, 1996)	Interview that probes adolescent or adult state of mind regarding caregiving experiences. Attachment classifications—secure, dismissing, preoccupied, and unresolved due to loss or trauma—are based on coherence of responses during interview. Attachment classifications parallel infant-attachment categories.

we rate the behavior of the child when the caregiver reappears in the room ("reunion be-havior") (e.g., Cassidy, 1988; Main & Cassidy, 1988; Stevenson-Hinde & Shouldice, 1995).

Researchers have developed rating systems to classify children into different attach-ment categories (Cassidy & Marvin, 1992; Crittenden, 1994; Main & Cassidy, 1988). Al-though the child's behavior during separations and reunions continues to be a strong focus of inquiry, the classifications systems used with older children also place a strong empha-sis on the child's verbalizations (or lack thereof) during these observations. In the spirit of the original Strange Situation classification system, children can be rated as secure, avoidant, or anxious-resistant (or ambivalent) (Cassidy & Marvin, 1992; Main & Cassidy, 1988). The classifications designed for children show similarities to, and differences from, those developed for infants. Unlike secure infants, older secure children tend *not* to be-come distressed when separated from their caregivers, and display relaxed and confident behavior during separations, reunions, and interactions with strangers. Like anxious-resistant infants, ambivalent children often strongly protest when separated from care-givers, yet might not display the same angry behavior during reunions displayed by their infant counterparts. For instance, ambivalent children may show babyish, immature be-havior when reunited with their parent (Main & Cassidy, 1988).

Recall that in addition to the classic secure, avoidant, and anxious-resistant attach-ment patterns, some infants show symptoms of attachment disorganization, leading at-tachment experts to develop a fourth infant classification—disorganized attachment status (Main & Solomon, 1990). Disorganized infants show contradictory (e.g., approach and avoidant), disoriented (e.g., freezing), and bizarre (e.g., suddenly falling down) attachment behavior during the Strange Situation. Disorganized attachment behavior evolves into a new constellation of behaviors during childhood (Lyons-Ruth & Jacobvitz, 1999); they often display controlling behavior toward caregivers during the separation-reunion assess-ments designed for older children. A child might say, "Mom, sit down NOW!" or "Oh, mommy, sit down and let me take care of mum-mum."

Exactly how and why seemingly confused, fearful, disorganized infants develop such controlling behavior during childhood is open to debate; some theorists have sug-gested that over time, these children somehow discover that overly controlling or solici-tous behavior toward caregivers elicits some form of desirable caregiver behavior (Lyons-Ruth & Jacobvitz, 1999). Perhaps a confused and hostile caregiver becomes less so when a child acts overly sweet and maternal, or exhibits commanding behavior. With this idea in mind, attachment classification experts have added a fourth attachment category, *controlling* (Main & Cassidy, 1998) or *controlling/disorganized* (Cassidy & Marvin, 1992) to capture these bizarre, yet fascinating, attachment patterns.

The attachment classification systems developed for older children have shown very interesting promise. Infants rated as secure or insecure in the Strange Situation often show parallel attachment classifications during childhood (Main & Cassidy, 1988). In addition, the insecure childhood attachment classifications predict unique forms of child maladjust-ment (e.g., peer problems, conduct disorders) (Solomon & George, 1999). However, al-though such systematic behavioral analysis represents a very powerful method of assessing attachment processes in children, it does take considerable training to master the coding systems. Keep in mind, for new researchers, the Attachment Behavior Q-set is easy to use, yields a continuous insecure-secure score, and can be used with older preschoolers (Chapter 5; also see Table 8.5).

Generalized Attachment Representation. As thought becomes more internalized, it becomes difficult to use behavioral assessments to measure attachment processes in older children and adolescents. Indeed, we discussed in Chapter 5, the Adult Attachment Interview (AAI), an assessment that is especially designed to reveal attachment-related thinking. This method allows us to classify adults in much the same way that we categorize infant and child attachment. Although the AAI has been used with adolescents, you might be interested that a parallel interview has been developed for middle- and junior high school-aged adolescents (Ammaniti et al., 2000). In the spirit of the AAI, attachment classifications are derived from the participant's state of mind throughout the interview.

We have not yet discussed attachment methods for young, school-aged children. A tricky population—too old to participate in modified Strange Situation, yet too young to partake in sophisticated attachment interviews. To circumvent this issue, experts have developed attachment-related stories with photographs to induce thinking regarding attachment (Kaplan, 1987; Jacobsen, Edelstein, & Hofmann, 1994). The child might be shown a series of pictures depicting an adult who is departing on a plane as a child looks on, the child returning home, and the child opening up a package delivered by a letter carrier with a toy plane inside.

Similar to the interview methods used with older people, experts code the responses into different attachment categories. Secure children provide empathetic or sympathetic responses to such stories and offer methods of coping with these feelings of distress, such as, "The little girl feels sad because her dad is away; she can go hug her mommy to feel better." In contrast, insecure children may deny that any emotional separation has occurred (avoidant), express strong anger during the story (ambivalent) or express extremely fearful or bizarre responses (disorganized), such as "He's going to die in a plane crash" (Jacobsen, Edelstein, & Hofmann, 1994). Similar methods have been used to tap individual differences in attachment-related thinking in even younger children, although experts often relay stories to preschoolers using dolls rather than pictures (Bretherton, Ridgeway, & Cassidy, 1990). Researchers theorize that these differences in attachment-relevant thinking have strong relevance for mental and interpersonal health (Bowlby, 1988) as thought becomes more internalized with age.

What Do You Think?

What is meant by the concept that thinking regarding attachment is "externalized" during infancy, but become increasingly "internalized" as we get older? What implications does this theory have for instrument development?

Assessing Peer Relationships

In this section, we will overview methodological issues pertaining to two major themes in peer group research. First, I will describe methods of assessing friendship involvement and the quality of these affiliations. Next, I will overview strategies for measuring a child's adjustment in the peer group, or **sociometric methods**. These methods typically focus both on how well the child gets along with others and on general acceptance in the peer group.

Assessing Friendships.   Our approach to friendship assessment is determined by the developmental status of the child. Because preschoolers may not have a good or stable concept of the term *friend*, we commonly poll parents or preschool teachers about a child's friendship network (Howes, 1988). In such schemes, it is advisable that we supply the informant an operational definition of what is meant by "friendship." However, not all believe that young children are limited in friendship reasoning skills. In one study, 4-year-old children could identify a friend and discriminate relationship qualities (e.g., conflict, assistance) among friends, parents, and siblings (Gleason, 2002). I expect that there will be more research of this nature involving preschoolers in the near future.

Unlike younger children, we can simply ask children and adolescents to nominate their best friends. However, because a true friendship should contain reciprocal feelings of closeness and intimacy, it is fairly common to poll a large group of children about their friendship network. In such cases, peers are deemed friends if both members of the dyad report mutual feelings of closeness and affection (or liking) in the relationship (Criss et al., 2002). It is interesting that researchers who evaluate friendship membership in other cultures frequently use the same criteria when assessing this relationship (Shulman & Laursen, 2002).

Beyond determining the mere *presence* of a friendship, we can assess the *quality* of these affiliations by polling children regarding their perceptions of time involvement, satisfaction, conflict, and mutual assistance in these relationships. The *Friendship Quality Questionnaire* (Parker & Asher, 1993) allows children to consider conflict, affection, and intimacy in friendship by endorsing items such as, "We make up easily after a fight," or "We tell each other secrets." Measurement robustness can be tested by asking other informants to complete the same inventory on the target child or by comparing self-report data with observed interaction quality with their friends (Simpkins & Parke, 2001).

Although time-consuming, some researchers use observational methods to assess friendship quality. Research involving preschoolers and kindergartners often focuses on specifying the quality of interactions and emotional behavior during play bouts with friends (Dunn, Cutting, & Fisher, 2002; Youngblade & Belsky, 1992). This tactic changes as children enter school. For example, observational research involving older children and adolescents typically focuses on measuring more complex individual (e.g., conversational quality, positive or negative affect) and dyadic (e.g., gossiping, physical proximity, mutual smiling) behavior (Flyr, Howe, & Parke, 1995).

How children perceive their friendship quality is not always consistent with the quality of dyadic interactions observed in laboratory settings. This could be because the friendship qualities reported on questionnaires (e.g., feelings of closeness, intimate disclosure) are difficult to capture during brief observations (Simpkins & Parke, 2001). Alternatively, questionnaires that poll people on relationship perceptions may tap day-to-day feelings about others that are influenced by temporal events. For example, a child who has just had an argument with a friend may provide very negative ratings on a relationship perception survey, and not consider the overall history of the relationship. However, if allowed to interact with the friend, these feelings might quickly dissipate and result in an observational sequence inconsistent with what was reported on the survey.

Sociometric Assessment.   Sociometric assessment is the measurement of social competence in the peer group and is often assessed using a very simple method. In the

peer-nomination paradigm, children are shown class lists and asked to nominate three children they like and three peers they dislike (Coie, Dodge, & Coppotelli, 1982). These systems give us two important pieces of data. First, **social preference,** or popularity, is based on the difference between liked and disliked nominations. In the peer-nomination paradigm, the researcher can identify five groups of children based on social preference scores:

> *Popular:* Children who receive high rates of liked nominations and few negative ratings.
> *Rejected:* Children who receive few liked nominations and many disliked ratings.
> *Neglected:* Children who receive few liked or disliked nominations.
> *Controversial:* Children who receive many liked and disliked ratings.
> *Average:* Children who receive an average number of liked nominations.

These systems also yield a **social-impact** rating. Social impact refers to visibility in the peer group, and is based on the total number of liked and disliked nominations. Controversial, rejected, and popular children receive high impact ratings, although for different reasons! Thus, social preference measures are a stronger predictor of adjustment.

As you might guess, rejected children often have poorer psychological, interpersonal, and academic outcomes than any of these other groups of children (Kupersmidt, Burchinal, & Patterson, 1995). However, there is considerable diversity within the rejected status group. In order to understand this diversity, researchers typically augment peer-nomination procedures with additional behavioral and academic data collected via observations or other informants (e.g., peers, teachers). In light of these additional data, we can identify three types of peer rejection. **Rejected-aggressive** children bully others, are academically challenged yet athletically strong, show difficulty getting along with others, and have difficulties accurately "reading" social situations. **Rejected aggressive-withdrawn** children are both academically and athletically challenged, are rated as very socially incompetent, and are both hostile and very unsure of their social abilities. Finally, **rejected-withdrawn** youth are socially awkward around peers (but not adults), socially immature, and academically strong, yet viewed as athletically weak (Hymel, Bowker, & Woody, 1993). The latter two groups are also frequent targets of the first one.

Let me summarize some points to ponder. First, the correlates of peer rejection, such as academic difficulties and aggression, in themselves, may not be strong predictors of later adjustment. In making predictions, these correlates must be considered in light of peer acceptance; for example, bullies do not always have bad outcomes; rather, it is the bully who is disliked who experiences the greatest number of future difficulties (Dodge et al., 2003).

Second, aggressive or withdrawn behavior may have different meanings at different ages. Pushing other children around has a different meaning in adolescence than it does in kindergarten (Espelage, Holt, & Henkel, 2003), just as awkward social behavior is more harshly judged during the teen years (Rubin, Rahhal, & Poon, 1998). Thus, the "profiles" of peer rejection may show developmental shifts; for example, Crick and colleagues have noted that during adolescence, there is a group of gossipy, highly disliked teens who spread malicious rumors that undermine the social standing of other peers (Crick, 1996). Although such *relational aggression,* which is correlated with aggressive-withdrawn social standing, tends to be more prominent in females across cultures (French, Jansen, & Pidada, 2002), there are some adolescent males who engage in such behavior.

This finding leads to a third consideration. When conducting peer-acceptance research, it is important to note how gender relates to social standing. Although it has been assumed that boys are more at risk for peer rejection, the aforementioned research would suggest that girls might cope with such rejection in less noticeable ways. In addition, the association between peer rejection and adjustment may also be dependent on gender. Crick (1997) has noted that rejected children who "cross" traditional gender lines in their behavior—that is, disliked boys who spread rumors and girls who bully—often show the worst adjustment outcomes.

Finally, because of potential ethical concerns, some have softened the standard peer-nomination procedures by changing the directions of the assessment. Instead of asking children to nominate peers that they like or dislike, one team polled children on who should be assigned acting parts—ranging from glamorous to unglamorous—in a class play (Luthar & McMahon, 1996). Interestingly, these researchers noted two distinct groups of popular children, one seen as talented socially and the other viewed as strong in leadership qualities. This is an interesting assessment, and I will be interested to see what the future holds for it.

Another alternative is to solely focus on positive ratings. In such systems, children are asked to nominate children they like or rate who they would like to play or work with on a rating scale (1 = No; 5 = Very Much So). Note that the focus of the assessment is for children to identify who they like or want to play with, and there are no direct inquiries regarding who is disliked. In one study, this type of instrument was administered along with the standard procedure for soliciting positive and negative peer nominations. There was a high correspondence between these systems (Asher & Dodge, 1986); thus this assessment allows us to identify the same groups of children without having respondents nominate peers they dislike.

What Do You Think?

Suppose a school superintendent asks you to identify rejected children in her elementary, middle school, and high school. How would you assess general peer rejection and different types of rejection?

Assessing Relationships with Others: A Summary

In this section, you learned about methods of studying attachment processes in children and ways of assessing competence in the peer group. Although qualitative relationships in the family are theoretically tied to peer-group competence, cross-contextual research of this nature is exceedingly rare (Parke & Ladd, 1992). Another research issue to consider pertains to the antecedents or causes of peer rejection. Although attachment researchers have documented infant and family variables that forecast patterns of attachment over time, there is less longitudinal research of this nature involving the evolution of social competence in the peer group.

Chapter Summary

In this chapter, we spent considerable time discussing assessments that measure how children think about themselves and others, as well as how youth relate to parents and peers. Did you stop to consider that many of the important social-cognitive variables that were discussed earlier in the chapter might be a potential root to attachment and peer problems? For example, children with attachment problems often have low self-esteem and bizarre self-concepts and ultimately exhibit major problems in affective perspective taking when administered attachment interviews (Main & Goldwyn, 1994). For example, an insecure adolescent may mutter, "My mom hates me, but I don't know why."

Also, rejected peers show deficits in perspective taking, moral reasoning, and empathy and sympathy. Thus, many concepts presented in this chapter are more integrated or connected then you might suppose they would be. Documenting interrelationships between these variables holds exciting implications for both research and practice.

Research Navigator™ Exercise: Bullies and Victims

The objective of this assignment is to learn about methods used to assess bullying and its victims. Go the Research Navigator™ website: http://www.researchnavigator.com; choose the Psychology database, and type *bullying* and *victims* as keywords using the Advanced Search options (p. 60). After reading a full-length article, try to answer the following questions:

1. What were the primary research questions and hypotheses?
2. How was bullying and victimization assessed?
3. Were attributes of the victims viewed as the consequences of bullying, or did the authors speculate that these attributes might have played a role in the victimization?
4. What were the primary conclusions?

9

Assessing Adolescent Development I: Biological, Cognitive, and Social Changes

When describing the typical teen, many point to the images displayed on music television and daytime talk shows that portray adolescents as drugged-out, sex-obsessed, hedonistic creatures. Unfortunately, this is a dated impression of adolescence; just about every form of adolescent risk behavior has *declined* in recent years. In general, getting adolescents to wear seat belts, for most parents, is often a far greater concern than crack cocaine.

In this chapter, you will learn about a modern framework for understanding adolescent development that can be used for developing research ideas. Next, we will discuss methods that explore biological, mental, and social changes in adolescents. In your reading, stay focused on the second word of the term, adolescent *development*. Although topics like eating disorders, depression, and substance abuse are clinically interesting, most adolescents do not identify with these issues. Rather, as in infancy and childhood, there are important competencies that develop during this time period. Indeed, in the next chapter, we will discuss how to assess these important psychosocial outcomes. After reading this chapter you should be able to:

1. Describe a framework for better understanding adolescent development.
2. Explain how to assess hormonal changes, pubertal development, and pubertal timing.
3. Describe Piagetian methods of assessing formal operational thought, and illustrate how new research on adolescent thought has challenged his theory.
4. Describe how information-processing researchers study adolescent cognition
5. Argue the advantages and disadvantages of using questionnaires, interviews, and observational methods to assess social changes.
6. Describe how researchers study the transition of adolescents into adult roles.

Understanding Adolescent Development: A Brief Overview

Premodern theories of adolescent development posited that this stage was beset by turmoil (Hall, 1904) or overemphasized some contexts (e.g., family) and ignored others (e.g., schools) (Freud, 1938). The latter idea is not surprising; the peer group, secondary schools, and part-time jobs are recent contexts when one considers this population from a historical perspective. You could not grab a cheeseburger at a fast-food establishment during the 1940s!

A Contemporary Framework

Modern frameworks for understanding adolescent development, as depicted in Figure 9.1, converge at several points. First, adolescents undergo three fundamental transitions:

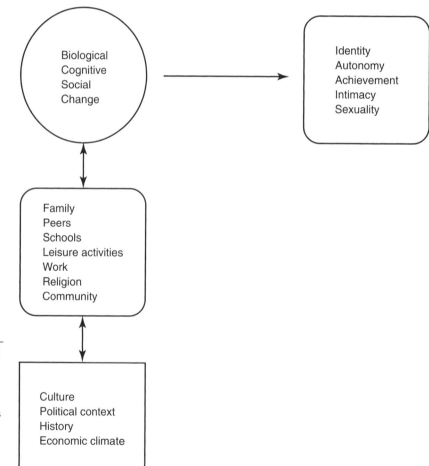

FIGURE 9.1 *Grotevant/Hill Conceptual Framework of Adolescent Development.* Note that the association between fundamental changes and healthy development depends on how changes are handled in different contexts or environments.

Biological
Cognitive
Social
Change

Identity
Autonomy
Achievement
Intimacy
Sexuality

Family
Peers
Schools
Leisure activities
Work
Religion
Community

Culture
Political context
History
Economic climate

biological, cognitive, and *social* (Hill, 1983). Historically, most researchers who have worked with adolescent populations would agree with this position. These fundamental changes do not occur independently; maturation of the brain, sparked by biological changes, spurs cognitive growth, which encourages social changes. An adolescent who begins to think hypothetically may become more of a challenge to his parents, which may create more adolescent-parent conflict. It is not that adolescents really argue more than children; they just become *better* arguers!

Although biological, cognitive, and social changes may co-occur, we also know that a biological → cognitive → social change interpretation of adolescent development is too simplistic. For example, frequent debates in the peer group regarding career choices may provoke changes in how the adolescent thinks (cognition). Also, high levels of family stress have been linked to early pubertal timing in adolescents (Graber, Brooks-Gunn, & Warren, 1995). Thus, when designing adolescent research, keep in mind that biological, cognitive, and social changes are interconnected and reciprocal. How and when these changes are interconnected can best be determined using longitudinal designs. When using such methods, the three major changes can be assessed concurrently and over multiple measurement times.

Adolescent change does not occur in a vacuum. As depicted in Figure 9.1, biological, cognitive, and social changes occur in a variety of contexts, such as the family, peer group, schools, and the part-time work force. Although these four domains represent major contexts for adolescent development, some view other arenas, such as the media and religion, as equally important. Also, there are "higher systems" that affect adolescent interactions and behavior within these contexts, such as cultural and historical trends (Grotevant, 1998). For instance, although the percentage of adolescents involved in the part-time labor force has dropped in recent years, adolescents work more if there is economic downturn. In any case, researchers are sensitive to the role of context on adolescent development.

The framework in Figure 9.1 depicts adolescent milestones or outcomes. We believe that healthy adolescent development is marked by five psychosocial outcomes (Hill, 1983). These outcomes are defined as follows:

> *Autonomy*. The growth of emotional independence, the ability to resist pressure from other parties (e.g., peer pressure) to conform, and the development of an independent moral value system that may not be consistent with one's family or culture.
>
> *Intimacy*. The development of close, interpersonal relationships with attachment figures (e.g., best friends, romantic partners).
>
> *Identity*. An emerging understanding regarding where one has come from, where one is, and where one is going regarding relationships, careers, and ideology.
>
> *Achievement*. Developing competence in school and work settings.
>
> *Sexuality*. More than simple sexual experience, a healthy sense of sexuality requires both knowledge and "comfort level" regarding the topic. For example, a virgin could technically have a healthy sense of sexuality.

We will revisit these adolescent outcomes in the next chapter; however, for now let's consider some theoretical and methodological concerns when working with adolescent populations. First, the framework presented in Figure 9.1, assumes that the association between the three major changes (biological, cognitive, and social) and adolescent development (e.g., sexuality) is *moderated by the contexts for development* (Hill, 1983). So does biological change guarantee that an adolescent will develop a healthy sense of sexuality or will a bright adolescent achieve a doctoral degree? Well, according to the framework, *it depends!* A healthy sense of sexuality or achievement success often depends on how these issues are supported in the aforementioned contexts. Thus, this framework is often merely a *starting point for researchers.* For instance, how does early maturation or pubertal timing affect adolescent development? Although girls who mature early face more risks than boys, these findings are moderated by the individual's broader context (Brooks-Gunn & Reiter, 1990). That is, early pubertal timing does not *guarantee* problems; it depends on how it is negotiated in one's family, school, peer group, and culture.

A second issue is that experts have different theoretical orientations on the importance of context. Some may acknowledge that the peer group, schools, and part-time work experiences influence development yet may argue that the family is *more important.* Thus, some researchers may study developmental processes within certain contexts, without much consideration for the others. I actually believe that this, at least in some cases, is a mistake.

Also, some would argue that although adolescent development is affected by contextual variables we must also consider the role of adolescent personality and intelligence in this process. The framework contained in Figure 9.1 looks awfully deterministic, and suggests that contexts for development automatically influence adolescents in a unidirectional manner. However, could it also be the other way around? For example, adolescents who struggle in school sometimes choose to work very heavy hours in a part-time job (Steinberg, Fegley, & Dornbusch, 1993). In such cases, the adolescents' achievement behaviors are not a *result* of part-time employment but rather more of an *antecedent!* Again, although our framework can guide predictions, only sound methodology can determine the direction of effects.

A final issue pertains to how we define the term *adolescence.* Adolescent researchers broadly define adolescence as a series of stages. Early adolescence roughly encompasses the ages 10–13, middle adolescence 14–18, and late adolescence 19–22 (Arnett, 2000). Whereas scholars in the United States generally agree with these age ranges, these estimates may not pertain to children in other parts of the world, particularly in countries in which children mature later. Keep this idea in mind when designing research and identifying your target population.

Understanding Adolescent Development: A Summary

What Do You Think?

Suppose you hypothesize that bright adolescents will likely obtain good adult jobs. Based on the framework outlined in Figure 9.1, what variables might moderate this process? How would the theory alter your methods and research design—that is, what variables might moderate associations between mental abilities and later work experiences?

In this section, I provided a framework for understanding adolescent development. We understand that adolescents undergo biological, cognitive, and social changes. Further, we theorized that adolescent development—marked by advances in autonomy, identity, achievement, intimacy, and sexuality—is partly dependent on the way these changes are negotiated in important contexts for development, such as the family, peer group, schools, and part-time work force. Adolescent researchers use this framework, and sometimes modify it, to guide empirical questions, hypotheses, and research designs.

Assessing Pubertal Development

One of my friends in graduate school was interested in how the timing of menarche (a female's first menstrual period) influenced her interactions with her parents. He quit his law practice and proposed his study to his doctoral dissertation committee. Next, he received ethical approval from our Institutional Review Board. He then approached the district school board, who approved the study with one exception: he could do the study, but he had to remove the question about the timing of menarche! Unfortunately, he had to propose another dissertation project. Are you surprised at this outcome? Studying certain pubertal events, such as the appearance of pubic hair, involves delving into highly personal topics. Regrettably for this student, he violated one the first rules of research (see also Chapter 2). One should always garner site access to conduct such research *during the initial phases of study planning*.

There are two broad topics involving pubertal development. One group of experts documents how internal biological events, such as hormone release, affect emotional and social behavior; for example, one might examine how hormonal fluctuations affect moodiness—"Oh, those raging hormones!" Of course, beyond hormonal shifts, "outward" signs of maturity mark puberty as well. The development of secondary sex characteristics, such as facial hair and breast development, alert one's social network that an important biological process is in play. Because the development of more observable signs of the pubertal process has an impact on psychological and social functioning, a second camp of research has emerged that focuses on this issue. These experts are interested in how overall pubertal development, or the occurrence of singular events such as menarche or a first ejaculation, affect psychological and social processes.

Assessing Hormonal Concentrations

The study of adolescent hormonal shifts and concentrations is important for two reasons. First, pubertal onset is not observable and can only be assessed via such internal changes. Also, most people expect that hormonal changes during puberty affect emotional and mental functioning. Demonstrating positive correlations between certain hormonal concentrations and, say, more moodiness, provides empirical evidence to support such widespread beliefs.

Most experts rely on a simple blood draw across short time periods (e.g., first draw, second draw at 20 minutes, third at 40 minutes) to assess hormonal concentrations such as estrogen and testosterone, and hormonal fluctuations over this time period (Dorn et al., 1999; Nottelmann et al., 1987). Because concentrations vary over the course of the day, assessments should occur at roughly the *same time* for all subjects in the *same place*. In one study, blood draws from a sample of girls, ages 10–14, were collected at school at about the same time. In this case, the researchers controlled for both the time of day and location (school) of the blood samples (Brooks-Gunn & Warren, 1989).

These hormonal assessments can be obtained in conjunction with other behavioral and emotional data (e.g., moodiness), or tied to the occurrence of other pubertal events, such as menarche. In one study, researchers collected multiple hormonal samples over short periods of time as adolescent girls underwent the process of menarche. These investigators noted that concentrations of key hormones normally associated with the pubertal process *did not* demonstrate major fluctuations during the menarcheal process, suggesting that hormonal fluctuations may not be reliably tied to the exact timing of pubertal events (Dorn et al., 1999).

Although many of us associate hormonal concentrations with crabbiness, a direct hormonal → emotions model is too simplistic. Whereas high hormonal concentrations or uneven fluctuations during early adolescence are associated with moodiness, most of these effects are temporary (Buchanan, Eccles, & Becker, 1992). Indeed, mood changes are more affected by the changing temporal, environmental circumstances encountered by adolescents than by hormonal concentrations. Adolescents often report mood fluctuations when they are engaged in daily events that happen to make them happy (e.g., interactions with peers) or apprehensive or depressed (e.g., an algebra quiz) (Csikszentmihalyi & Larson, 1984). Methods used to document such chronology of daily mood fluctuations are described in Box 9.1.

BOX 9.1 • *An Event-Sampling Method for Documenting Mood Changes*

Recall that earlier chapters described *event-sampling* or *representative sampling methods* that have been crafted to measure behavior change over the course of hours, days, or weeks. To observe such changes, researchers may briefly observe a person at random times of the day within important settings. For example, researchers might assess infant language by asking parents to audiotape such behavior during setting events, such as bath time or diaper changing. Alternatively (or additionally) the parents may be asked to complete diaries at random times of the day to record the linguistic behavior of their babies (Chapter 7).

Would these techniques work well with adolescent samples? Unlike infants and children, parents just do not have as much extended contact with adolescents, and often find themselves in competition with part-time jobs, extracurricular activities, peers, and romantic partners. Additionally, adolescents become increasingly private about their feelings and thought processes around parents, so researchers might question the accuracy of parental reports even in cases in which a parent had some extended contact with a son or daughter.

Diary methods could be viewed as an alternative methodology, but we might question whether the typical adolescent would complete it accurately. Even in cases in which an adolescent writes a diary entry at the end of each day, one might question whether they were accurately recording their thoughts and feelings over the course of the day. Clearly, adolescent-development researchers face some methodological concerns.

Csikszentmihalyi and Larson have used a piece of familiar technology that allowed researchers to capture adolescent mood and behavior using traditional event-sampling methods. Using this approach, adolescents were trained to use electronic beepers, which in this day in age, is probably a very easy task! In such "beeper studies," adolescents were encouraged to write down their thoughts and feelings when they were beeped at different times of the day. They were trained to record their mood, as well as to indicate the environmental circumstances surrounding their mood (e.g., "I'm in school, I feel bad, he's giving a pop quiz"). The adolescents in the study were not just given beepers and beeped at periodic times; rather, the researchers *carefully trained them* on how to use the technology and how best to record their data (Csikszentmihalyi & Larson, 1984; 1987; Larson, 1989).

(continued)

BOX 9.1 • Continued

For example, what if an adolescent is robbing a bank or having sex with their significant other when they are beeped? Because it is doubtful that the subject would be truthful in such circumstances, these experts would suggest in the training session that they could possibly record, "doing some banking" or "making out with my boyfriend," and then assign an appropriate mood to such activities. A review of the lives of some of these adolescents suggested that they are quite honest in their record keeping. For instance, adolescents, upon being beeped, have reported fantasizing about others and sharing drugs with romantic partners (Csikszentmihalyi & Larson, 1984). In addition, when asked to report the typical moods their adolescents experience when encountering daily events, (e.g., homework, or hanging out with friends) parent estimates approximate the actual adolescent reports, which somewhat bolsters the validity of this method (Larson, 1989).

Research using this method challenges the notion that adolescents are more moody or emotional than young children (Larson, 1989). Rather, adolescent emotional stability is largely dependent on the social context; thus, adolescents who report extreme emotional responses typically do so not because of hormonal concentrations but because they are upset over problems at school, in the peer group, or in the family (Larson & Ham, 1993). Adolescents may seem moodier than children because they experience more adult like stressors than their younger counterparts do; this may be particularly a problem for young adolescents, because they are coping with more "grown up" stressors for the first time. In other words, life can be pretty simple and carefree for a 7-year-old, whereas an 11-year-old must deal with biological changes, the rise of cliques and crowds, different teachers, and more responsibilities in the classroom.

These methods have been successfully used in other cultures and with different populations. For example, this research team has used beeper event-sampling methods in a variety of populations ranging from Korean adolescents coping with severe academic stress (Lee & Larson, 2000) to adult men rating different emotional experiences at work and home (Larson, Verma, & Dworkin, 2001). Students interested in the reliability and validity work on this method should consult some of the earlier work of this research group (e.g., Csikszentmihalyi & Larson, 1984; 1987; Larson, 1989).

Thus, the influence of hormonal concentrations on adolescent adjustment is either minimal or has a stronger effect when measured in conjunction with other potentially arousing events in the adolescent's environment (Brooks-Gunn & Warren, 1989; Susman, 1997). Indeed, some even question this particular model, and suggest that changing environmental circumstances might directly influence hormonal concentrations. For instance, it has been suggested that stressful family circumstances, such as parental fighting, influence hormonal concentrations, which in turn, can influence emotional health (Brooks-Gunn, Graber, & Paikoff, 1994). Thus, understanding the connections between hormonal concentrations and socioemotional development entails considerably more than analyzing a blood draw. When conducting such research, one should consider the possible theoretical models offered by Susman and colleagues (1996) outlined in Figure 9.2.

Assessing Pubertal Change and Status

Although the timing and duration of puberty vary from one adolescent to another, average ages and ordering for various pubertal events have been specified. For girls, the first observable sign of puberty is initial breast development (or budding, age 10, average range 8–13), menarche occurs during mid-puberty (average age 12–13, average range 10–15),

1. Hormone levels → Adolescent behavior and mood

2. Environmental demands → Hormone levels
   (e.g., family stress;
   academic problems)

3. Hormone levels ←→ Adolescent behavior and mood

4. Hormone levels + Environmental demands → Adolescent behavior and mood

---

FIGURE 9.2   *Hormone-Behavior Theoretical Models (adapted from Susman et al., 1996).*
There are a number of explanations of how hormones might affect behavior; an astute
researcher could develop a study that tested the efficacy of each model.

whereas adult stature, breast, and pubic-hair completion occur late in the process (average
age 13–15). For boys, initial penis and testes enlargement and pubic-hair development
mark the first observable sign of puberty (average age 11–12), the first ejaculation (or sper-
marche) represents the mid-point (average age 13, range 12–16), whereas voice deepen-
ing, adult stature, and pubic-hair growth completion represent events that occur later in the
process (average age 14–15, upper range 16–17) (Tanner, 1990).

Assessing Normative Pubertal Development.   Health-care professionals who work
with adolescents are trained to use Tanner's (1962) *Sexual Maturation Scale* (SMS), which
contains a series of drawings that depict the normal growth of pubic hair and genitalia, as
well as breast development in females. Each drawing, which represents a different stage of
pubertal development, is accompanied by a brief descriptor for the rater. Some researchers
have trained parents to estimate Tanner stages on their adolescents using these drawings
and scales, and in some cases, have used adolescents as informants (Morris & Udry, 1980).
Although the use of young adolescents as informants may appear to be a questionable
practice (in terms of validity), researchers have noted good consistency between adolescent and health-care professionals' ratings when using the SMS. The self-ratings of adolescents and physician reports are more consistent with one another than ratings provided
by adolescents and their parents (Coleman & Coleman, 2002; Dorn et al., 1990).

Unfortunately, building principals, parents, or even some adolescents might object to
physical examinations and the nude drawings. Because of such concerns, short interviews
have been developed that probe different aspects of pubertal development. The most popular instrument of this kind is the *Pubertal Development Scale* (PDS: Peterson et al.,
1988). This instrument begins with the question, "Now I'm going to ask you some questions about physical development." Next, we inquire about the occurrence of different pubertal events, such as pubic-hair development, growth, breast development, and menarche
in girls, and facial hair and voice changes in boys. For each pubertal marker, adolescents
indicate on a scale their degree of developmental progress (e.g., no development, barely
begun, already completed). Overall pubertal development is determined by summing the
items to form a total score.

By now, you should know how to obtain psychometric information using such instruments. Because physical examinations by physicians trained on the Tanner scales represent

the most accurate assessment of pubertal status, a logical step would be to see whether the adolescents' interview ratings are consistent with those of the health professionals. Brooks-Gunn and colleagues contrasted PDS ratings with estimates provided by physicians and obtained relatively modest correlations (e.g., over .60) (Brooks-Gunn et al., 1987). These data would suggest that this scale could serve as a fairly accurate indicator of pubertal status for research purposes. However, it is a weaker measure than actual physician reports or information supplied by the adolescent using Tanner's SMS.

Recall that some experts study how specific pubertal events, such as menarche or a first ejaculation, affect adolescent mood and social development (Benjet & Hernández-Guzmán, 2002). Unfortunately, the accuracy of an adolescent's recall of these events is very dependent on each pubertal event; thus students who have interests in this area should read the reliability and validity information for individual assessments. For example, the occurrence ratings (*Has it happened or not?*) of pubertal events are more accurate than estimates of actual timing (*When did it happen?*). For instance, females supply more accurate data to the question, "Have you had your first period?", than to "When did you have your first period?" (Brooks-Gunn et al., 1987).

Assessing Early and Late Pubertal Timing.   Because puberty is a "biological roadsign," some researchers have examined how "on" or "off" pubertal timing affects adjustment. Pubertal timing can be assessed in a number of ways, and the more measures, the better. As a starting place, one could estimate pubertal timing by using data provided by the Tanner scales or Peterson's PDS in conjunction with a measure of chronological age. After accounting for age, we then rank youth relative to one another on pubertal development, and establish cutoffs for late (e.g., below 25th percentile) or early (e.g., above 75th percentile) pubertal timing (Craig et al., 2001; Graber, Peterson, & Brooks-Gunn, 1996; Seiffge-Krenke & Stemmler, 2002).

However, use of the aforementioned instruments may not be feasible. Also, older adolescents will have achieved most, if not all, of the pubertal milestones depicted on these measures, rendering these inventories useless as an estimate of pubertal timing for late adolescents. To circumvent these issues, experts have crafted short inventories that query whether the adolescent was an early or late "bloomer." Perceptions of pubertal timing can be assessed using the query, "When you look at yourself now, do you think you are more or less physically mature compared with others (of the same gender) your age?", or in older adolescents, "When you started to mature physically, did this begin earlier or later compared to other females your age?" (Alasker, 1992; Wichstrom, 2001). Alternatively, the parent can be asked the question, "Does your son's/daughter's physical development seem to be earlier or later than most of the other boys/girls his/her age?" (Peterson et al., 1988). Finally, estimates regarding pubertal timing can also be assessed using physician ratings, which have more predictive power than ratings provided by either parents or the adolescents themselves (Dorn, Susman, & Ponirakis, 2003).

Research using these methods suggests that early-maturing females are more at risk for body-image problems, self-esteem difficulties, mood disorders, and earlier sexual activity than their on-time and late-maturing female peers. Also, both early-maturing males and females "grow up faster" (e.g., use alcohol or drugs) than their peers who mature later (Ge, Conger, & Elder, 2001; Graber et al., 1996; Wichstrom, 2001). In our society, early-maturing boys and girls also encounter dissimilar experiences; early-maturing boys are often viewed as attractive and popular, whereas early-maturing girls are more withdrawn and unpopular (Graber et al., 1996; Livson & Peskin, 1980). Although most research suggests that early maturation might be a risk factor for adolescents, there is some evidence that the reverse may be true—that is, it is the late bloomers who may have more adjustment and body-image problems (Dorn et al., 2003).

If you think that early maturation is an automatic determinant of adolescent difficulties, then you are not using the theory presented in Figure 9.1; fundamental changes, such as puberty, do not *directly* affect development. Rather, associations between biological change and developmental outcomes are *moderated by context*. If true, then what environmental factors buffer the early-maturing adolescent from difficulties? Although there are many factors that affect adjustment (e.g., parent and cultural attitudes regarding body image, sexuality, etc.), interactions with peers play a strong moderating role in the process. Early-maturing girls who go to schools in which peer groups strongly identify with "in" and "out" crowds or attend schools that contain peers who are much older suffer more problems than their counterparts who go to schools without these tendencies (Blyth, Simmons, & Zakin, 1985; Richards et al., 1990). These data serve as a reminder to consider contextual variables when conducting lifespan research!

Measuring Pubertal Development: A Summary

As indicated earlier, a thorny issue in this area is that some of the most accurate methods, such as scientific hormonal analyses and unclothed physical examinations, may not be feasible in instances in which adolescents, parents, or school administrators object to the use of these procedures. Although the self-reports obtained by adolescents or their parents are positively correlated with the results gathered by more scientific methods, the accuracy of such reports have been questioned. Finally, it is evident that the association between biological events and development is not a direct one, and is moderated by the contexts outlined in Figure 9.1.

What Do You Think?

Suppose you predict that hormonal concentrations, pubertal timing, and daily stressful events influence moodiness. How would you assess hormonal levels and pubertal timing? Identify all study variables that you would use in this investigation and potential findings.

Measuring Cognitive Changes in Adolescence

A variety of standardized intelligence, achievement, and aptitude tests exist that can be administered to adolescents and used for screening and diagnostic purposes. Most college students are probably all too familiar with the Scholastic Aptitude Test, ACT, or Graduate Record Exam. Because we have already discussed ways of assessing the intellect of children, adolescents, and adults, we will not review these measures in this chapter. In this section, we will primarily investigate methods used to assess the more advanced reasoning and information-processing skills of adolescents.

Go back and look at Figure 9.1 again. It shows that cognitive development does not take place in a vacuum; biological, cognitive, and social changes occur in a reciprocal fashion. In addition, obtaining psychosocial milestones, such as identity and autonomy, largely hinges on cognitive development. An adolescent cannot form an identity and see a vision for her future if she cannot engage in hypothetical reasoning! Figure 9.1 reminds us that cognitive advancements do not guarantee healthy development. Advanced reasoning skills may not be beneficial to an adolescent who is not receiving support from the different contexts for development (e.g., schools, family, peers).

Piaget's Perspective on Adolescent Thought

Recall that Piagetian experts track qualitative differences in thinking across stages of development, or *how* children and adolescents think and reason differently. Chapter 6 described simple Piagetian tasks that assess the differential thinking of preschoolers and school-aged children. Recall that preschoolers have great difficulty solving traditional Piagetian tasks designed to assess logical thinking; for instance, they cannot understand that a round ball of clay that is pressed into a flat piece still possesses the same mass. Thus, we concluded that the growth of logical thought represents a major developmental milestone in school-aged children. Of course, preschoolers *can* exhibit some logical thinking, but only when Piagetian tasks are made simpler and more familiar, or involve training sessions.

Theory of Formal Operations.   Piaget believed that adolescents, like children, are capable of logical thought. However, adolescents acquire specific cognitive competencies that cannot be routinely found in their younger counterparts. These basic changes, which are incorporated into Piaget's **formal-operational stage** of cognitive development, can be summarized as the following interrelated characteristics of adolescent thought (Gallagher & Reid, 1981; Inhelder & Piaget, 1958; Keating, 1991; Piaget, 1972):

1. The ability to isolate the effects of a variable by holding the effects of other variables constant. For instance, to isolate the effects of divorce on adolescent adjustment, one would want to compare the well-being of youth from divorced and nondivorced households while controlling for the rate of inter-parent discord in both groups.
2. The ability to consider how combinations of variables may work together to produce a theorized outcome. For instance, children from divorced households who also have a parent with a mental disorder may have the poorest outcomes, which is similar to positing a statistical interaction among variables in a research project.
3. The ability to combine and order variables in a theoretical, or *hypothetical-deductive framework*. For example, one could posit that divorce may lead to economic problems in the family, which may in turn affect the affordability of college later on for a young adolescent.

Note that developing research studies requires some elements of formal operational thought. When conducting research, we develop a theoretical framework and consider combinations of variables that predict developmental outcomes. Also, when ordering variables to predict development, we are working with ideas rather than with tangible objects. This is

FIGURE 9.3 *Piaget's Pendulum Problem.* The subject is shown a pendulum that has a weight hanging by a string and has at their disposal other weights and pieces of string that vary in length. The subject must determine which variable (e.g., object weight, string length, height from which object is released), or variable combination (e.g., weight and the arc object is dropped from) affects the object's speed.

From, Berk, L. (2003). *Child Development,* 6ᵗʰ Ed., p. 244. Reprinted with permission of Allyn & Bacon, Boston, MA.

where child and adolescent thought differs. When asked to produce "light," and given a verbal list, such as a light bulb, battery, wires, switches, and a light unit, an adolescent can mentally conceptualize the ordering of the objects (e.g., connect wire battery → connect wire → switch → etc.). A young child needs to see these objects, and even then, often will order the objects in an unsystematic, haphazard way. For instance, my 9-year-old almost set our house afire while assembling a "science experiment" without our supervision!

Piagetian Tasks to Assess Formal Operations.   Piaget created tasks for assessing formal-operational skills in adolescents; many look like basic science experiments, such as theorizing the eventual colors of liquids before four different substances are mixed (Gallagher & Reid, 1981). His most well-known experiment for assessing formal operations was the **pendulum problem**, depicted in Figure 9.3. The child is shown a pendulum that has a weight hanging by a string and has at his disposal other weights and pieces of sting that vary in length. His task is to determine which variable (e.g., object weight, string length, force by which the object is dropped), or variable combination (e.g., weight and the height object is released from) affects the object's speed.

Adolescents will often experiment with the different weights independently, and then work with other variables, such as the length of string and the force of the weight push. Gradually, the adolescent will discover, through *systematic* trial and error, that it is string length that makes the ultimate difference. The thinking of younger children is not systematic, and they may not think of testing the effects of one variable (e.g., length) while holding the other variables constant. By contrast, the adolescent can isolate the independent effects of variables, consider the effects of one variable in relation to others, and plan and test a theoretical framework.

The pendulum problem represents one task designed to assess the different elements of formal-operational thought. Piaget also developed other tasks for assessing the *separate* elements of this advanced thought process; thus, one could present tasks for measuring the adolescent's ability to (a) isolate the effects of variables, (b) consider how combining variables produces desired effects, or (c) consider how the interrelationships between variables may affect an outcome. For instance, to solely assess the latter reasoning, one could ask the participant to consider the following (Jacobsen, Edelstein, & Hofmann, 1994):

If I travel to A, I must pass B

Next, the participant is asked a series of questions, ranging from the simple, "If you travel to A, do you pass B?", to the more complex "If you don't pass B, do you tavel to A?" In order to answer the second question, the individual must consider this proposition without concrete evidence (unless you mentally substitute the names of familiar cities for A and B), and must consider the interrelationships between these variables.

How does performance on these tasks translate to data? Like performance on Piaget's conservation tasks, you either get these problems correct or fail. One could administer a series of different tasks and calculate the proportion of tasks passed. Alternatively, one could grade the subject's performance on each task using a continuous scale, such as 1 = simple logic to 4 = formal thought (Jacobsen et al., 1994). Students interested in a comprehensive assessment of formal-operational thought should use a battery of tasks rather than just the pendulum problem.

Modifying Piaget's Theory/Methods.   Piaget asserted that most adolescents should develop formal-operational thought, and they should be able to apply such advanced thinking to most situations. Unfortunately, his theory that formal-operational thought is achieved by most adolescents and can be applied across many contexts is not tenable (Keating, 1990; Keating & Sasse, 1996). Even some adults stumble on Piaget's formal-operational tasks (Danner, 1989), and adolescents in some cultures show little evidence of such advanced thinking (Cole, 1996).

When asked to consider some of the more important aspects of Piaget's theory, such as hypothetical reasoning, most experts believe that there are clear differences in the way children and adolescents reason. Why, then, do we get such inconsistent findings when we put Piaget's theory to test? The answer to this question seems to be *context, context, and more context*! Remember, even young preschoolers display occasion logical reasoning in situations they are familiar with; most are afraid of dragons but know that the furniture will not eat them. Could we apply this same premise to adolescents and formal-operational thinking?

If adolescents are capable of formal operational thought in some areas but not in others, then how would you test this premise? One approach would be to find youth who show considerable talent or expertise in a particular area, and try to discover whether the advanced thinking used in such contexts generalizes to other, less-familiar environments. Such studies show that advanced formal thinking during adolescence is highly dependent on context. Adolescents with a lot of experience with certain activities, such as chess or science, often display hypothetical and propositional thinking in those areas, even though they may not pass Piaget's pendulum-problem test (Chi, Glaser, & Rees, 1982).

One method of studying how well formal-operational thought generalizes across contexts would be to compare the thought process of adolescents who are experts in a particular area to that of nonexperts or to their own thinking in less-familiar tasks. Perhaps a slightly different method for testing the same idea would be to ask an adolescent sample to think about highly routine, everyday dilemmas and compare this thinking to that assessed via standard Piagetian tasks or other unfamiliar problems. In one study, sixth-, nineth-, and twelfth-graders considered problems that were highly relevant to them, such as running in the halls at school or hitting a teacher, as well as problems that were less relevant, such as understanding issues pertaining to retirement. The participants' performance was based on their maturity and task relevance: sixth-graders displayed limited formal-operational thought *under all conditions* (i.e., familiar and unfamiliar), but older adolescents displayed more formal-operational thinking, albeit more often in tasks that dealt with relevant (e.g., school dilemmas) than with less-relevant problems (Ward & Overton, 1990). These data would suggest that there might be some constraints on formal-operational thought during the early parts of adolescence, and that the development of such thought is most likely a function of maturation and environmental experiences.

Although testing the presence of formal-operational thought in familiar and unfamiliar problems represents a very popular method, another tactic would be to examine variables that explain individual differences in such thought within particular age groups. A number of experts have examined how curriculum and instruction influence certain elements of formal-operational thought (Lehman & Nisbitt, 1990; Morris & Sloutsky, 1998). Also, some have examined how differential family experiences spur such cognitive growth. Children with close emotional relationships with parents pass a higher percentage of Piagetian formal-operational tasks than do children experiencing attachment disruptions (Jacobsen et al., 1994). Children with secure attachments to parents are more inclined to develop curiosity, a willingness to explore their environments, and a stronger ability to regulate emotions when challenged than extremely anxious or fearful children (Bowlby, 1988). The results of some of this fascinating research are discussed in Box 9.2.

BOX 9.2 • *Linking Social and Cognitive Development*

Chapters 5 and 8, discussed a considerable amount of material regarding the assessment of infant, child, and adult attachment. Historically, researchers have studied how attachment processes in young children predict both current socioemotional functioning, such as getting along with peers in school, and competencies in later years. For instance, a number of studies have documented strong links between infant attachment processes and the way in which people think about attachment issues during adolescence and adulthood (e.g., Waters et al., 2000). Thus, we strongly assume that *social experiences* with caregivers influence the way we *think* about attachment issues later in life.

Although we have long believed that attachment experiences with family members and other attachment figures (e.g., peers) influence the way we think about relationships, some theorists suggest that attachment processes may influence the way we think *in general*. They theorize that secure relationships with caregivers encourage children to move away from a state of caregiver dependency to one of independence (Bowlby, 1969/1982). Theoretically, a secure, independent child has the capacity to explore her environment, seek challenges, and exhibit strong regulatory processes when confronted with difficult tasks (Bowlby, 1988). Piaget (1981) also acknowledged the connection between social and cognitive development, and suggested that difficulties in relationships and self-regulation processes would only inhibit the quality of thinking and learning.

Unfortunately, experts who study social and cognitive developmental changes in adolescents tend not to consider interconnections between these two important types of changes. However, some scholars have developed fascinating research studies to study how such changes are interrelated (e.g., Sroufe, 1988). In one such study (Jacobsen, Edelstein, & Hofmann, 1994), researchers assessed the attachment representations of children at age 7 using a standard separation story and attachment coding system developed by Kaplan (1987). In this story a child watches an adult figure take off in a plane, waves good-bye, returns home, and then later opens up a present containing a little plane. To assess attachment, children are asked to project what is happening in the story, and coders then rate the quality of their narrative. For instance, a secure child might say that the fictitious child observed a parent taking off on a plane, missed the parent, and then started crying after opening the present because he missed the parent. Conversely, insecure children might not make any emotional connections in the story, or suggest something really bizarre, such as, "The plane crashed and everyone got smashed to pieces."

The researchers followed these children into adolescence and administered a variety of Piagetian tasks to assess the growth of formal-operational thought. The study results confirmed the aforementioned theoretical speculations about the connections between social and cognitive development. Children with secure attachment representations were more likely to show a steady growth of formal-operational thought during adolescence, and the children who displayed more disorganized or bizarre reasoning

(continued)

BOX 9.2 • Continued

during the attachment tasks displayed the most delay in cognitive development. Interestingly, these findings remained strong despite controlling for overall intelligence (Jacobsen et al., 1994).

These findings would not surprise clinicians who work with adolescent and adult populations. In particular, many individuals with relationship problems think very concretely about themselves and others, and make statements such as, "My mother only thinks of herself," or "Dad has never shown one instance of loving behavior toward me." Such dramatic, all-or-none thinking is much more indicative of concrete-operational thinking than of formal-operational thinking. Indeed, the objective of cognitive-behavioral treatment plans is usually to get the client to think about their social world in a formal-operational manner.

I also urge student researchers to consider indirect paths between attachment processes and cognitive development during adolescence. For instance, it has been theorized that close emotional relationships with caregivers spur the development of independence or autonomy during adolescence (Allen & Land,

1999; Hill & Holmbeck, 1986). Because autonomy growth is theorized to spur exploration and deep thinking about identity, we speculate that a secure attachment → autonomy → formal-operational-thought theoretical model could be supported with adolescents. Indeed, consider the theory that secure attachment formations spur a move away from caregiver dependence and a movement toward exploration of the environment, task persistence, and so on.

However, some attachment experts might be skeptical of such a simple model, and argue that attachment problems would primarily inhibit sophisticated, formal-operational thought—but only in attachment relationships. Indeed, adolescents and clients in treatment often think in very limited, concrete ways about their parents or spouses (Slade, 1999), but would be considered very successful people in achievement or occupational environments. It would be interesting to determine whether adolescents with insecure attachment representations show global or contextual (e.g., only in close relationships) deficits in cognitive development.

Piagetian Theory and Methods: A Summary

Many studies using Piagetian tasks that adhere to his protocol have found that different elements of formal-operational thought, such as hypothetico-deductive reasoning, are more prevalent during late adolescence than in early adolescence (Jacobsen et al., 1994; Markovits & Dumas, 1999; Ward & Overton, 1990). However, other research, using different methods, has not supported key elements of his approach. Formal-operational thought is not obtained by all adolescents, and even when it does develop, it does not emerge in such a sudden manner as Piaget originally believed (Keating, 1990). This caveat would explain the "in-out" thinking of my oldest son, who is a hypothetical wizard at planning for chance encounters with romantic interests—as witnessed by his clothing and styled hair—yet, will forget other important steps, such as wearing a coat in the below freezing weather as he runs to the car.

To address the shortcomings of Piaget's theory, experts have developed some interesting methods for assessing this "occasional" formal-operational thought that occurs during adolescence. Adolescents reason in more advanced ways when given problems they are familiar with or have unusual expertise in. In addition, certain contexts facilitate formal-operational thought in adolescence (e.g., family or school variables), and the knowledge acquired through such basic research has tremendous implications for educational curriculums.

What Do You Think?

Suppose you want to study the idea that the best-adjusted adolescents can easily shift between logical (concrete-operational) and hypothetical (formal-operational) thought. How would you design a study to address this premise? In formulating your answer, try to consider social problems or dilemmas that require relatively simple versus more complex thought processes.

Finally an exciting, area of research concerns studying what adolescents are *capable* of in terms of thinking, and then identifying the strategies *they actually use* across different conditions. For instance, formal-operational thought might represent "overkill" in certain situations that require simple solutions in which a basic, logical choice is required. An exciting research direction would be to identify adolescents who show flexibility in productive thinking and are able to adjust their thinking, to the demands of the task (Keating & Sasse, 1996).

Assessing Adolescent Information Processing

Chapter 6 discussed a variety of ways of assessing how people encode, process, store, and retrieve information. Information processing becomes more efficient and quicker during adolescence, and the methods used to assess processing speed, memory span, and storage and retrieval are similar for children and adolescents. For instance, to assess memory span, participants are given an increasingly complex series of numbers and then asked to repeat them back to the experimenter. This method, while widely used with children, is also commonly used with adolescents and adults.

However, there are unique methodological approaches that information-processing experts use when working with adolescents. For example, some identify how changes in attention, memory span, and storage and retrieval processes spur the development of Piagetian competencies, such as analytical reasoning and everyday decision making. Information-processing theorists are now identifying the *mechanisms or processes* that spur formal-operational growth. Once you have read more about this approach, you will better appreciate how Piagetian and information-processing theories are becoming increasingly integrated.

Analytical and Scientific Reasoning.   If adolescents increasingly become critical, scientific thinkers, as Piaget claimed, then what mechanisms spur such development? A number of theorists suggest that improvements in the human information-processing system readily explain such advancement in thought (Keating & Sasse, 1996; Klaczynski, 2000; Kuhn et al., 1995).

Encouraging adolescents to solve scientific and social problems that spur intense debate, such as religion, politics, or the integrity of social-welfare programs, is a method that can test this premise. One can observe how adolescents reason about these problems, and examine whether the processing is different for individuals representing different developmental groups (e.g., early versus late adolescence). From a methods standpoint, rather than looking at whether an adolescent correctly solves a scientific reasoning problem, the information-processing expert is interested in the cognitive steps, if any, the adolescent uses to solve the problem.

One information-processing model of analytical reasoning is depicted in Figure 9.4 (Klaczynski, 2000; 2001). This theorist offers a detailed, step-by-step flow-chart (much

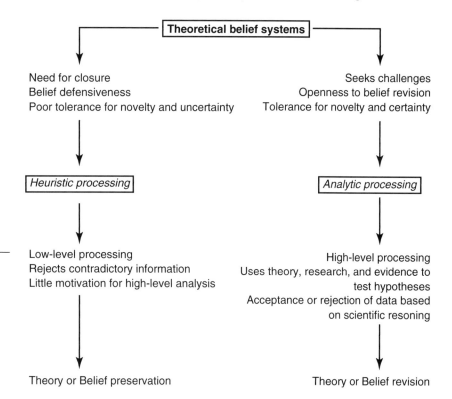

FIGURE 9.4 *Klaczynski's (2000; 2001) Model of Information Processing for Adolescent Analytical Reasoning.* This model explains the conditions that spur either scientific and analytical or low-level reasoning.

like a computer program) on how we process information, and on how this processing is related to the expression of formal-operational thought. In this particular approach, this expert has outlined the conditions that spur advanced analytical reasoning in adolescents.

How would one go about *testing* such an ambitious framework? Note that this model posits that broad, theoretical belief systems provide an important opportunity for analytical reasoning to occur. For instance, some people assume they have "all the answers" (perhaps like some teenagers), whereas others crave the unknown and have a tolerance for uncertainty (Kuhn, Amsel, & O'Loughlin, 1988). These latter individuals will more critically evaluate information that is inconsistent with their own viewpoints, test hypotheses, and consider alternative explanations (i.e., scientific reasoning). Alternatively, individuals who possess a strong need to preserve their own personal theories engage in low-level, heuristic thinking. They quickly reject information that conflicts with their "mind-set," expend little effort in thought, and will not engage in hypothesis testing or analytical thinking. Thus, the starting point regarding assessment is the measurement of these personal belief systems.

To study such belief systems, experts often use short rating scales, which assess the individual's openness to uncertainty, or tendency to feel threatened by opposing viewpoints. Next, they may give subjects certain scenarios, and ask them to consider information that may either confirm or contradict existing thinking. For example, the adolescents may be asked to consider the following:

People who make a lot of money usually have children who are not very bright.

Next, the interviewer carefully probes subjects' reasoning processes, and whether or not the adolescent takes the steps outlined in theory to arrive at a solution (Klaczynski, 2000). Does the model in Figure 9.4 "work"? The answer to this question depends on the age level and belief systems of the participants. For instance, this information-processing theory would be difficult to apply to young children, because when given abstract tasks, they usually do not reflect on their own thinking, which inhibits systematic, scientific thinking (Kuhn, 1999). This is why I reserved this particular discussion for the current section on adolescent cognition.

Research has shown support for the outlined perspective. When presented an idea that conflicts with their own position, adolescents who have a tolerance for uncertainty and are open to differences of opinion engage in more scientific reasoning than adolescents who show little tolerance for different opinions. Likewise, under certain conditions, older adolescents are more likely than younger ones to hold the more flexible views, and to engage in a systematic scientific reasoning process. Further, experts believe that although young adolescents have the *potential* to engage in critical scientific reasoning, their rigid belief systems or lack of metacognitive awareness about the value of scientific reasoning may hinder their thinking and result in a stubborn, "I have all the answers" mode of thinking (Klaczynski, 2001). The fact that the *potential* for advanced scientific reasoning is present during early adolescence has fascinating implications for curriculum development (Kuhn, 1999).

Adolescent Decision Making.   Although some experts are interested in how youth apply advanced critical-thinking skills to scientific problems, others study how adolescents apply such reasoning to everyday problems. These experts have begun to specify the underlying mechanisms that may spur more advanced thinking. For example, the decision-making process is guided by the following steps (Beyth-Marom & Fischoff, 1997; Byrnes, Miller, & Reynolds, 1999):

1. Identify possible options or choices.
2. Think about and identify the consequences of each choice.
3. Evaluate the desirability of each option.
4. Assess the likelihood of the consequences.
5. Review the steps and integrate the information to make a decision.

In order to study this theory, researchers give adolescents everyday problems. For instance, they might present scenarios involving drinking and driving, driving a parent's car without permission, or skipping school. They then interview the adolescents or ask them to complete a survey questionnaire that illuminates each of the steps just outlined. For example, they might ask participants to consider all of the good and bad things that could happen, indicate all of the possible risks and consequences of their behavior, describe what they *might* do, and then discuss what they would *actually* do (i.e., their final decision) (Beyth-Marom et al., 1993). Perhaps you can see the applied value of such research. Uncovering variables that modify steps in the adolescent decision-making process may have important implications for influencing everyday behavior, ranging from studying for an exam to using seat belts.

What Do You Think?

Suppose a teacher remarks that he wants to improve decision-making skills in his students but does not know how to assess this construct. What advice would you offer this teacher regarding assessment strategies? What dilemmas would you use, and how would you assess decision-making processes?

You can see by now that information-processing researchers represent a very diverse group of experts. Some experts who work with adolescents use methods very similar to those used with children to assess processing speed, memory span, and storage-and-retrieval strategies. However, other professionals use an information-processing approach to undercover the mechanisms responsible for the growth of formal-operational thought during adolescence. In this section, I outlined two examples of approaches used to explain the development of scientific reasoning and everyday decision making.

Summary of Cognitive Assessment

Although many believe that adolescents are capable of formal-operational thought, recent research using unique methods has demonstrated that such sophisticated reasoning is limited to domains that are more familiar to adolescents. Researchers have generally measured the presence of formal-operational thought in adolescents in two ways. They can compare adolescents who happen to be "experts" in some topic to age mates who do not hold such expertise, or adolescent thought can be evaluated in familiar (e.g., social dilemmas) or unfamiliar (e.g., retirement planning) situations. Adolescents engage in formal operations in the more familiar situations, although the presence of such thinking is not guaranteed in all youth; both of these findings challenge central components of Piaget's theory.

Information-processing theorists often study adolescent cognitive abilities in two ways. First, they can administer to adolescents information-processing tasks that have been developed for children. Much of the research following this format has demonstrated that adolescents process information more quickly and efficiently than their younger counterparts do. A second approach identifies the information-processing mechanisms responsible for the development of formal-operational thought. In this section, we discussed how different components of the information-processing system underlie the development of scientific reasoning and adolescent decision making. Although I surveyed some strategies for assessing different components of these theories, researchers must often construct rather complex methods to test such perspectives.

Assessing Social Change

In this section, we will discuss methods of assessing social changes in adolescents, with the realization that the research findings in our society may differ from those in other countries. Consistent with the theoretical approach outlined in Figure 9.1, we will discuss approaches to observing adolescent social changes in the family, the peer group, and our broader society. Capturing changes in relationship dynamics among adolescents, family members, and peers is somewhat of an elusive pursuit that *cannot be assessed by studying one particular age group of adolescents during one-time period*. Rather, we must incorporate a longitudinal design into our research plan to assess change, or to at least infer such change using cross-sectional designs. In addition, short-term longitudinal designs might be particularly beneficial for examining social changes in adolescents at particular maturational (e.g., early and mid-point of puberty) or transitional points (e.g., shortly before and after entry into a part-time job or college).

Social Changes in the Family Context

When we suggest there are relationship changes among adolescents, parents, and peers, what exactly is meant by the term *changes?* Collins (1990) suggests that three constructs best capture relationship changes: interactions, affect, and perceptions. *Interactions* refer to changes in relationship patterns over time; for example, interactions with parents become less frequent and intimate during adolescence. *Affect* is the emotional content of relationships. To measure this construct, one could assess the amount of anger or joy experienced by adolescents during interactions with other attachment figures (e.g., parents, peers). Finally, *perceptions* refer to the cognitive appraisals of these interactions; for instance, the adolescent and the parent may view a parent-adolescent conflict encounter differently.

We should consider a couple of important issues at this juncture. Many adolescent researchers use either questionnaires or interviews to "tap" adolescent interactions with parents and peers, affect in relationships, and relationship perceptions. The potential drawbacks to such self-report methods have been raised before. These methods do not really measure interactions, affect, or behavior; rather, they assess *perceptions of these events*. For instance, many of the studies that suggest that conflict intensity increases with parents during early middle adolescence are based on adolescent or parent perceptions of such behavior (Laursen, Coy, & Collins, 1998), rather than on behavioral or affective assessments during actual conflict encounters. Further, most experts assess these perceptions days or weeks after the interaction occurred.

A second issue pertains to theoretical and conceptual concerns. The field of adolescent development enjoys a very rich history, and excellent accounts of this chronology are available as a starting point (Adams & Berzonsky, 2003; Feldman & Elliott, 1990). When it comes to relationship change during adolescence, numerous theoretical accounts exist that discuss all of the potential socioemotional constructs that may contribute to such change. Also, scholars have gone to great lengths to provide operational definitions of such constructs as conflict, intimacy, nurturance, gender intensification, anger, relationship satisfaction, and so on. Be familiar with these theories and definitions before the project is designed, and carefully consider the range of constructs you want to assess. These assessments could represent a highly detailed account of one important construct, such as conflict *(intensity, duration, and frequency)*; or relatively brief measurements of a wide range of relationship variables, such as time commitment, intimacy, and emotional closeness. During such an analysis, it is not uncommon to locate review articles that extensively cover important conceptual and methodological issues regarding a particular relationship construct. For instance, Laursen and colleagues (1998) have provided an excellent article on the definition and measurement of adolescent-parent conflict. Let's now turn to the methods used to study social changes in adolescents.

Questionnaires/Interviews. Although questionnaires and interviews are frequently used to infer changes in adolescent–family-member interaction patterns, these assessments *remain a measure of cognitive appraisals and perceptions of these interactions.* There are numerous self-report measures that have been designed for adolescents that assess perceptions of specific relationship constructs, such as conflict (Laursen, 1995), parent acceptance (Hill et al., 1985), and parent affection (Savin-Williams & Small, 1986).

There exist extensive questionnaire batteries that can be completed by not only the adolescent but also other family members as well. Thus, we can determine how closely the perceptions of an adolescent match those of a parent (or other family members, such as siblings) for the same construct (e.g., adolescent affection directed toward parent). In one study, researchers assessed how parents and adolescents viewed each other's stressors. Adolescent awareness of key parental stressors (e.g., not getting a promotion), as well as vice versa (e.g., a parent knowing that adolescent was upset over a breakup) were markers of a well-connected family system. Both parents and adolescents were more adjusted than their counterparts who were not congruent in stressor perceptions (Lohman & Jarvis, 2000).

When students approach me for method ideas, they frequently indicate that they are interested in some form of global assessment that taps "adolescent-parent relationships." Usually, the student's interest has less to do with a particular relationship quality, such as adolescent-parent conflict, and more to do with locating a measure that will assess the "overall relationship." Although one could piece together separate measures that examine different relationship provisions, such as time commitment, intimacy, and conflict, questionnaires that assess multiple facets of relationships are also available.

One such questionnaire that measures adolescent-parent relationship qualities is the *Network of Relationships Inventory* (NRI; Furman & Buhrmester, 1985), a 33-item survey that polls the adolescent's perception of time commitment and positive-negative relationship qualities (e.g., intimacy, conflict, satisfaction). The beauty of the NRI is that we can point adolescents (as well as children) to multiple relationship targets (e.g., parents, siblings, best friends, and so on), and then, using simple cross-sectional designs, compare how children of different developmental status view different relationship targets (Lempers & Clark-Lempers, 1992). This is a very robust instrument that can be reliably used with both school-aged children and adolescents, and adolescent estimates of dyadic relationship quality with parents correlate well with parent perceptions of the adolescent-parent relationship (Creasey et al., 1989). Sample items are included in Table 9.1

Although more time consuming, interview protocols are available to tap adolescent perceptions of relationship. For instance, both Offer (1969) and Youniss and Smollar (1985) have crafted extensive interviews that allow one to measure adolescent perceptions of different family-relationship domains (e.g., affection, time commitment), as well as perceptions of peer relationships. I might add that Offer's *The Psychological World of the Teenager* and Youniss and Smollar's (1985) *Adolescent Relations with Mothers, Fathers, and Friends* should represent starting points for students interested in assessing adolescent relationships. These works are highly respected, contain entire interview protocols and complementary questionnaires, and provide extensive results from these research programs.

Some interview schedules were designed to tap specific adolescent–family-member relationship domains. For example, in Chapter 5, we discussed the Adult Attachment Interview (George, Kaplan, & Main, 1996), a protocol designed to assess the individual's

TABLE 9.1 *Relationship Provisions Assessed by the Network of Relationships Inventory*

Relationship Provision	Sample Item
Companionship	How much free time do you spend with this person?
Conflict	How much do you and this person get upset or mad at each other?
Instrumental help	How much does this person teach you how to do things that you don't know how to do?
Relationship satisfaction	How satisfied are you with your relationship with this person?
Intimacy	How much do you tell this person?
Nurturance	How much do you help this person with things s/he can't do by (him/her) self?
Affection	How much does this person like or love you?
Punishment	How much does this person punish you?
Admiration	How much does this person admire or respect you?
Relative power	Who tells the other person what to do more often, you or this person?
Reliable alliance	How sure are you that this relationship will last no matter what?

Source: Furman & Buhrmester, 1985.

state of mind regarding attachment relationships with caregivers. Beyond intimacy and attachment, there are interviews designed to assess specific domains of relationships, such as conflict. Smetana has developed a fascinating interview of adolescent-parent conflict that can be administered to both members of this dyad (Smetana, 1989). The interview begins as follows:

> Most children have told us that even when they get along with parents, there may be times when they don't get along or have conflicts or disagreements. These may be about major issues or decisions, or they may feel like everyday responsibilities, such as feeding pets or doing the chores. We would like to talk about the kinds of things that come up in your family. We are interested in all the issues that are really important or that seem to occur over and over again in your relationship with your parents. What kinds of conflicts or disagreements do you have with them? (Smetana, 1989, p. 1054)

As mentioned earlier, researchers interested in assessing a particular relationship dimension, such as adolescent-parent conflict, typically desire a *very detailed* assessment of the construct. Using the system described by Smetana, researchers can code the types of arguments that adolescents and parents routinely get into, their frequency and intensity, and the perceptions that adolescents and parents might hold regarding the underlying reasons for such conflicts. For instance, the possible justifications for conflict can be coded, as outlined in Table 9.2.

Using such methods, Smetana and others found that most adolescent-parent conflicts occur over mundane issues, such as household chores, are not as frequent as once believed, and that parents and adolescents view the meaning of conflict differently (Collins, 1990). For instance, adolescents often indicate that arguments about clothing, hairstyles, and curfews are really unnecessary, because those issues "are really my own business." Conversely, parents often justify their concerns more on moral, societal, or practical levels, such as, "She shouldn't get her tongue pierced because it might get infected." Interestingly, Smetana

TABLE 9.2   *Sample Justification Codes for Adolescent–Parent Conflicts*

For example, in response to question, *"Why do you think it's OK for you to (e.g., get a tattoo) . . ."*

Category	Description
Moral	Appeal to interests of other people; references to feeling of obligation.
Conventional	Appeal to approval of authority figures; appeal to social custom; references to politeness, manners; appeal to be responsible for own behavior in relation to societal expectancies.
Psychological	Appeal to relationship or affective bonds; appeal to unintentional or unconscious nature of act; appeal to child's psychological development.
Personal	Appeal to personal independence, identity exploration, or psychological separation from family.
Prudential/pragmatic	References to health or other potential negative consequences of act.

Source: Smetana, 1989.

and colleagues have noted that many of these same conflicts can be found in adolescent–parent dyads across the world (Yau & Smetana, 1996).

Of course, all of these self-report measures assess relationship *perceptions* rather than the actual quality of the interaction itself. Although "actual behavior" might be the gold standard in relationship assessment, quite frankly, it would be a tall task to assess every relationship quality (e.g., conflict, affection, intimacy) using structured or unstructured observations. Also, some research suggests that how we *think and reason* about relationships may be just as important as the actual relationship behavior itself. Finally, although there are always concerns regarding people's honesty and the accuracy of their memories, some research suggests that perceptions of relationship behavior are tied to actual behavior.

For example, in one study, adolescents and their mothers were polled on relationship conflict and parental support. Next, adolescents and mothers were observed in actual conflict negotiation. These researchers documented that the participants' perceptions of conflict and support in these relationships were tied to the behavior observations of the same constructs. Also, the adolescents' perceptions of conflict and support in these dyads were more strongly tied to the behavioral data than were those of the mothers (Gonzales, Cauce, & Mason, 1996).

The associations between perceptions of relationship behavior and observed behavior are usually significant but often modest (Arellano & Markman, 1995). Although advances in measurement techniques might strengthen associations between relationship perceptions and behavior, some evidence suggests that one's perception of a relationship and its reality can be moderated by other variables. One study (Creasey & Ladd, 2004) noted that associations between perceptions of adolescent relationship conflict and actual conflict behavior were modest, yet moderated by attachment security. For example, adolescents who articulated considerable attachment security in relationships displayed strong correspondence between self-report conflict measures and behavior observations. That is, a secure adolescent who reported high amounts of relationship conflict displayed such conflict during observations. Conversely, insecure adolescents showed major discrepancies between perceptions and behavior; many times, the adolescents who reported the least amount of conflict showed the most difficulties. Thus, specifying congruencies and discrepancies between relationship perceptions and behaviors is a research area in itself!

Behavior Observations.   There are many relationship specialists who feel that "seeing is believing" and that one should exhibit caution relying on self-report data, particularly if from only one informant. Also, conducting observations allows one to assess the affective and behavioral quality of relationships, which were stipulated as two central components of relationship functioning (Collins, 1990). Interestingly, a number of the structured tasks we ask adolescents and parents to engage in (as well as coding systems) parallel the methods used when observing interactions among martial couples, and have been used to assess peer-relationship quality.

A couple of questions that routinely come up when considering observational techniques are "What should we have these people do?" and "What exactly should we code or assess?" Although it is important to use an established coding system when conducting observational research, the first question is frequently the most important to address. The settings that we structure are theorized to elicit certain target behaviors (e.g., encouragement, conflict) and emotional displays (e.g., anger, joy), and asking an adolescent and a parent to resolve an interpersonal conflict may evoke a very different set of emotions and behaviors than asking an adolescent to divulge a personal problem to a caregiver. Again, the systems that we use to code the behavior of the adolescent and family member(s) are important to consider; however, even the best coding system will be rendered useless if careful attention is not given to the observational procedures or tasks that we ask these people to perform.

Indeed, family interaction tasks yield a wealth of data that can be mined using multiple coding systems that assess different adolescent behaviors and parenting constructs. One popular task is to ask the adolescent and a parent (or both parents) to generate a list of possible dyadic interpersonal difficulties (e.g., household chores), and to select one or two disputes that are jointly viewed as difficult to resolve (Gonzales et al., 1996). The adolescent and parent are then videotaped for 15 minutes; these interactions are subsequently coded. This type of task is often also used to assess the relationship quality and conflict tactics of marital couples, and has been used to rate the quality of adolescent dating relationships during conflict (Creasey, 2002).

There are multiple coding systems that can be used to rate behavior and affect during these procedures. Sarason and colleagues (1990) have developed a coding system that allows researchers to rate the intensity of the conflict and the level of parental support and sensitivity offered during the interaction. Also, Gottman (1996) has an excellent coding system that allows one to rate positive (e.g., affection) and negative (e.g., belligerence, contempt) "affective behaviors" during these conflict encounters. The beauty of Gottman's scheme is that it assesses the emotional content of conflict exchanges, which is a stronger indicator of relationship health than whether or not the conflict actually gets resolved (Creasey, 2002).

A method that yields somewhat different data is the *Structured or Planned Family Interaction Task* (Ferreira, 1963; Grotevant & Cooper, 1985; Watzlawick, 1966). In this task, the adolescent and other family members are given a list of issues that are often discussed in families, such as where to go for dinner or possible vacation venues. The researcher asks the family to discuss each issue for a period of five to ten minutes. This procedure taps multiple relationship constructs, such as family decision-making abilities (Steinberg & Hill, 1978); conflict tactics (Holmbeck & Hill, 1991) and parental control and autonomy granting (see Allen et al., 1994; Grotevant & Cooper, 1985 for good coding systems).

At this juncture, let's look at some research ideas involving the procedures just discussed. First, family conflict and decision-making paradigms are not necessarily "either-or" procedures. Rather, there is no harm in assessing families using decision-making *and* conflict tasks; the procedures are not that long and each task yields a wealth of data. In addition, because family interactions may look different in dyadic (e.g., adolescent-mother) versus triadic (e.g., adolescent-mother-father) relationships, one should consider administering decision-making and conflict tasks using different family configurations. Also, the interaction patterns may also look different in families that vary in structure (e.g., two-parent, single parent, divorced parent, etc.), and we need to conduct more research with adolescents and their stepparents in blended families.

Second, longitudinal research can greatly support the validity of family-interaction tasks. Although these tasks are time consuming, the behavior and emotions we witness in them are strongly diagnostic. For instance, during family-decision tasks, parents who support and respect the decisions of young adolescents (e.g., age 14) are more likely to see healthy independence, responsibility, and psychological security in these youth at later ages (Allen et al., 1994). Also, longitudinal research allows us to witness how the *adolescent's status in the family changes*; for instance, because sons increasingly interrupt their mothers in family decision-making tasks, researchers believe that sons gain power in families at the mothers' expense during adolescence (Steinberg & Hill, 1978).

Another question that begs to be answered is *why* adolescents and family members treat each other the way they do. A common (and valid) response relates to the maturational status (e.g., early puberty) and chronological age (e.g., early versus middle adolescence) of the adolescent. A significant percentage of the relationship transformations that we witness during adolescence are influenced by these variables, and clearly suggest that biological, cognitive, and social changes occur in an interconnected, as opposed to isolated, fashion (Grotevant, 1998). However, not all of the variation that we see in family interactions results from adolescent maturational forces, and there are other important variables on both the adolescent (e.g., temperament, attachment history with parents) and parent (e.g., marital functioning, parent midlife concerns) side of these relationship that affect these relationships at any one time or over the course of adolescence. In addition, the broader culture experienced by the family has a bearing on family relationships during adolescence (Grotevant, 1998).

What Do You Think?

If relationships involve *interactions, emotions, and perceptions*, then how can this premise be used to design a study on whether adolescent-parent relationships change over the course of adolescence? In formulating your response, consider both an appropriate design and methods you could use to assess these constructs (i.e., interactions, emotions, perceptions) using conflict as a key study variable.

Assessing Social Changes in the Peer Group

A number of the methods we already covered could be used to assess adolescent-peer dyadic relationships. For instance, the NRI (p. 279; Furman & Buhrmester, 1985) is a great measure for contrasting the time commitment, levels of conflict, intimacy, and affection in adolescent-parent, adolescent—best-friend, and adolescent-romantic-partner dyads. Con-flict-management and decision-making paradigms and coding systems used in family research have also been applied to adolescent peer relationships (Creasey, 2002).

Although these strategies are appropriate procedures for contrasting adolescent-peer and adolescent—family-member associations, there are also differences between these relationships. If one is exclusively interested in gathering a detailed account of adolescent peer relationships, there are other methods that have been specifically designed for these affiliations. Berndt and colleagues (Berndt & Perry, 1986) have developed a 20-item survey that queries adolescents about the level of conflict, intimacy, prosocial behavior, and rivalry in their friendships, and Raffaelli (1997) has developed an interview designed specifically to assess adolescent peer conflict. In terms of behavior observations, McNelles and Connolly (1999) have adapted the traditional family decision-making task and developed a coding system that provides a detailed account of intimacy development in adolescent peer relationships. Similar to research involving children, it is advisable that we provide a definition of the term *friendship* to adolescents, and ensure that this perception is a mutual one between two adolescent friends.

When we consider social changes in the adolescent peer group, it is important to consider that the nature of these relationships is different than that witnessed among children. Although time commitment and intimacy in friendships are obvious differences, the structure of adolescent peer groups also routinely differ from those of children; witness the small groups of adolescents you see at the shopping mall or fast-food restaurant. Most adolescents increasingly find themselves involved with small, intimate groups of close friends, or **cliques**, and also align themselves with a larger group of peers that tend to share a common theme (e.g., clothing styles, achievement orientation, athletic involvement), or **crowds**. Because clique and crowd involvement represent important social changes in the adolescent peer group, it is important for us to think about how to assess these affiliations.

So, how does one go about assessing clique membership? Perhaps you can see why this might be a complex issue. It is one thing to ensure friendship reciprocity among two potential friends, but is quite another to ensure that Susan is friends with Mary, Betty, Rocio, and Yvette *and* that these feelings are mutual among all of these individuals. As you might have guessed, one usually needs access to an entire school population to conduct a proper clique assessment.

Luckily, we have studies that form a methodological precedence for this type of work (Ennett & Bauman, 1996; Urberg et al., 1995). The analysis begins with adolescents in the school context nominating their best friend and their closest friends (see Hallinan, 1981 for one such nomination procedure). It is very important that a large majority of adolescents in the school participate in the nomination procedure to check for friendship reciprocity.

Next, these data are then exposed to **social-network analysis**, which is conducted using a standard computer program developed by Richards and colleagues (Richards, 1989; Richards & Rice, 1981). The computer program provides an analysis that identifies adolescents as belonging to a clique (i.e., a cluster of mutual, yet exclusive, friends), as liaisons or as isolates. A liaison is an individual that seems to belong to more than one clique, a very interesting person who may help bridge relationships between members of different cliques. Once these data are assembled, we can investigate important questions, such as clique demographics, the psychological and developmental correlates of clique (non)membership, and whether clique formation is moderated by other variables (e.g., school size, community characteristics). A configuration of these different friendship patterns is outlined in Figure 9.5.

Crowd membership is assessed differently than clique configurations. In the *Social Type Rating Procedure* (Brown, 1989), school administrators nominate a group of adolescent boys and girls from each grade level who represent a cross section of the student population. Next, observers assemble small groups of students, or **focus groups**, who are demographically similar—that is, group membership is based on sex, gender, race, and grade level. Researchers then give group members a list of the different "crowds" they are aware of (e.g., jocks, skaters, druggies, preps), and ask them to identify adolescents they know who best represent those crowds. The observers then ask these latter adolescents, along with a randomly selected group of youth, to identify everyone they know who is in a particular crowd; these data are important because they allow for the computation of reliability estimates (Brown et al., 1993). That is, the researchers need to ensure that the adolescents are consistent in their views of who belongs to which crowd. The system allows for students to potentially belong to more than one crowd, and also allows researchers to identify crowds that are more potentially influential than others (Brown, Mory, & Kinney, 1994).

In summary, although some measures that are used to assess adolescent–family-member interactions can be adapted for use with adolescents, these modifications often apply only to dyadic interactions. Because the adolescent peer landscape is more complex

FIGURE 9.5 *Clique Network Diagram Using Social-Network Analysis.* Clusters represent clique members; liaisons are adolescents who appear to belong to more than one clique (e.g., F). Isolates are adolescents who do not belong to, or affiliate with, a clique.

From, Ennett, S., & Bauman, K. (1996). Adolescent social networks: School demographic, and longitudinal considerations. *Journal of Adolescent Research, 11*, p. 203. Reprinted by permission of Sage Publications, Thousand Oaks: CA.

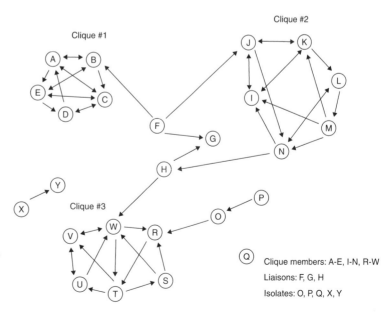

Clique members: A-E, I-N, R-W
Liaisons: F, G, H
Isolates: O, P, Q, X, Y

than that of children, methods have been designed to assess membership in small friendship groups, or cliques, as well as in larger, reputation-based peer groups, or crowds. For the moment, our discussion has involved assessment issues involving adolescent friendships and friendship networks; in the next chapter, we will discuss how to assess adolescent dating and steady romantic relationships.

Assessing Adolescent-Adult Transitions

Beyond assessing how adolescent relationships change in the family and peer contexts, we can also examine how adolescents adjust to new adultlike roles, such as employment, the collegiate experience, marriage, or parenthood. I must admit that terms like *transition period,* and *transition adjustment* can be very difficult to define. For instance, consider two 18-year-olds who choose to work at full-time jobs after graduating from high school. One adolescent moves out of her family house and receives good performance evaluations at work, yet is lonely and depressed living alone. The second adolescent is happy but receives marginal performance evaluations, and still lives with her parents. Which adolescent, in your view, is more adjusted? This example should clarify why it is difficult to study adjustment in a new context; there are innumerable short- and long-term developmental and psychological variables that could be considered in such a study. Indeed, there may be some late adolescents who show short-term adjustment problems in adult roles who later become very productive adults!

When conducting research on adolescent-adult transitions, it is important to define the transition event (e.g., first adult job), the transition period length, relevant adjustment variables, and the contextual variables outlined in Figure 9.1 (e.g., family or peer support) that may make the transition period more or less difficult for the adolescent. It is also important to define a set of variables that adequately captures social and psychological stability or change in the adolescent adult during the transition period. For interested readers, Connell and Furman (1984) offer some sound advice regarding design and data-analytic strategies when conducting transition research.

Next, we will examine methodological issues that face researchers who study social transitions during late adolescence. Most experts in this area stipulate that key adolescent–young adult transition points rest with the collegiate experience, the obtainment of the first job, marriage, and parenthood (Greene, Wheatley, & Aldava, 1992). Because we will cover major assessment issues pertaining to marriage and parenting in subsequent chapters, in this section we will stick to methodological issues involving the transition to college and adult work roles.

Transition to College.   Most adolescent-adult transition research has focused on adjustment to the collegiate experience (Creasey, 2002; Larose & Bernier, 2001). This emphasis is not surprising, because over 65 percent of American teens attend college after graduating from high school (NCES, 1999). Although some may view research with college students as an overdone topic, it is clear that college administrators are interested in why some students adjust well to this experience and others do not. Indeed, professionals who work in student counseling centers are aware of the fact that homesickness, loneliness, and disputes with new roommates constitute major reasons for self-referral.

What variables should be assessed to measure "adjustment to college?" The psychological health of college students, grade point average, retention, and the development of psychosocial variables, such as identity, represent important study variables to consider when tracking the adjustment of adolescents making the transition from high school to college. The very best studies of this nature are longitudinal in nature (Compas et al., 1986; Larose & Boivin, 1998); indeed, cross-sectional methods can yield data that is notoriously confounded. For instance, simply contrasting the psychological adjustment of high school and college students is problematic, because not all of the high school students will go to college. Alternatively, contrasting the health and psychosocial development of first-year college students and seniors is problematic, because some new students will not make it to their senior year! Finally, studying college students at a single time point tells us little about potential causal mechanisms. For instance, simply identifying students who suffer from loneliness sheds little light on *why* they are troubled. It could be that the transition to college has not changed anything in these students; they simply could have had social difficulties well before they enrolled in college.

The question that most people want answered pertains to why some adolescents adjust easily to college and others do not. To address this question, researchers have examined myriad variables, including a number of the contextual variables outlined in Figure 9.1, such as school (e.g., size of high school and current college, involvement in college "transition" programs); family (e.g., attachment to parents); and peer factors (e.g., ability to make new friends) (Larose & Boivin, 1998; Rice, 1992). Such variables are also frequently used to assess major transitions adolescents make earlier in life; for instance, family (e.g., social support) and school variables, such as school size, are factors that are thought to affect the adolescent's adjustment to middle, junior high, and high school. This issue will be explored further in the next chapter when we discuss the assessment of academic achievement.

Assessing Adolescent Work Transitions.   There are two separate camps of researchers who study adolescents' transition to work environments. Clearly, there should be a major distinction between the part-time jobs that many adolescents hold during high school and full-time occupational employment. Let's start with a discussion of part-time employment. Do part-time work experiences "kick start" a smooth transition to adulthood? If so, I would expect to see two results. First, adolescents who participate in the part-time work context should show *increases* in responsible behavior, more autonomy from the family system, and the development of a healthy work ethic. Second, a certain continuity between part-time experiences and later employment; for instance, one might expect an adolescent with a part-time job to make a smoother transition to adult work than an adolescent who has never held a job.

What are some methodological issues that these researchers must face? The following are some of the major issues that researchers examining adolescent part-time workers must consider:

- *Design, design, design.* Caution must be used when interpreting data on adolescent part-time work that is drawn from research lacking a longitudinal focus. A researcher who compares the adjustment of working and nonworking adolescents is going to have a difficult time generating meaningful conclusions from the study results. Documenting that the workers are more or less responsible than the nonworkers does not tell us whether the workers were more or less responsible before they punched their first time card! Also, a portion of the nonworking adolescents might have worked at one time (e.g., summer vacations). Although time consuming, the very best work on this topic is represented by research that has used longitudinal methods (see Steinberg, Fegley, & Dornbusch, 1993 for one example).

- *Type of work and work hours.* Although most adolescents work in the fast-food industry, it has been proposed that certain types of work might be more beneficial than others (Greenberger & Steinberg, 1986). Beyond keeping track of the type of work done by adolescents, we must record the amount of time they work per week. Studies have shown that working long hours (e.g., more than 20 per week) are tied to adolescent adjustment problems (Steinberg et al., 1993).

- *What to Assess?* Experts should be challenged to do more than assess changes in self-esteem or psychological health as youth begin to participate in part-time work environment. If part-time work has an impact on social transitions, then one would expect that over time, youth should become more responsible and build a healthy work ethic. Students interested in locating a battery of instruments that have been used to assess school engagement, independence from parents, self-reliance, spending habits, occupational deviance, and worker cynicism should consult the work of Steinberg and colleagues (Steinberg et al., 1982; Steinberg et al., 1993).

Much of the current research indicates that adolescent part-time work experiences *do not* help "jump start" a smooth transition to adult roles. Adolescents report that their part-time work experiences are boring and repetitive, are often pessimistic regarding the importance of work, and engage in a high proportion of occupational deviance (e.g., stealing) from employers (Ruggiero, Greenberger, & Steinberg, 1982; Steinberg et al., 1982). On the other hand, adolescents who work relatively light hours often balance work and school commitments rather well, and adolescents from low-income communities who have a part-time job are more likely to stay in school and have more successful adult transitions than those who do not work (Leventhal et al., 2001a).

Far fewer studies exist that track adolescents and young adults into the full-time labor force, and the extant research tends to focus on the adjustment patterns of adolescents who seek full-time employment after high school or transitional issues faced by young adults who have had college experience. Methodologically, it is important to make such a distinction, because the employment patterns of youth who do not go to college are frequently very rocky, and are often marked by a series of part-time jobs (sometimes experienced concurrently) before the individual finds some form of steady employment (Kerckhoff, 2002). In short, **educational attainment**, or the amount of education obtained by an adolescent or young adult is almost a mandatory study variable. This educational marker is a more powerful predictor of early occupational success than gender, ethnicity, and family socioeconomic status (Arum & Hout, 1998).

Like adjustment to the part-time work experience, researchers who study the adolescent and young-adult transition to the full-time labor force—defined as the first job an individual accepts after leaving school for the last time (Arum & Hout, 1998)—have studied shifts in psychological and developmental functioning and job satisfaction after a period of employment. However, the employment opportunities for adults are also clearly different from the typical adolescent part-time job in terms of pay and prestige. It is not uncommon for researchers to assess both the amount of money a person makes in their first major job (Arum & Hout, 1998) and occupational prestige (Hollingshead, 1975) as markers of early occupational success.

Finally, experts who study adolescent-adult social transitions have used living arrangements as a marker of success (Raymore, Barber, & Eccles, 2001). Adolescents and young adults who continue to live with their parents after high school or college gradua-tion are at risk for general unhappiness or developmental delay (e.g., lack of autonomy). For instance, older adolescents who live at home with their parents frequently complain that their parents tend to treat them like they were still children (Flanagan, Schulenberg, & Fuligni, 1993), which suggests these youth are suffering from social-transition problems. Thus, living arrangements (e.g., living at home, living with roommates, living alone, etc.) is an important variable to consider in such transition research.

Assessing Social Changes: A Summary

During adolescence, status in the family, peer group, and society changes. When assessing social changes in the family and peer group, researchers have used questionnaires, inter-views, and observational techniques to examine how these relationships undergo interac-tive, affective, and perceptual changes over the course of puberty and adolescence. The overall time commitment in these contexts changes, along with the quality of these re-lationships. The relative structure of the peer group shifts, as well. For this reason, we discussed ways to assess clique and crowd membership in adolescent peer groups. The sta-tus of adolescents also changes within society. As adolescents mature, they begin to explore new roles in occupational settings, and most adolescents today also attend college. Accord-ingly, we discussed methodological issues that confront experts who study adolescent social and psychological adjustment in part-time work settings, the collegiate context, and full-time employment during later adolescence and early adulthood.

What Do You Think?

Suppose you are interested in studying how well adoles-cents who choose not to attend college adjust to adulthood. What type of developmental design would you use to study their transition? What variables would you consider in assessing adolescent "adjustment?" What contextual variables might you assess that might make the adjustment process smoother for these adolescents?

Chapter Summary

Urie Bronfenbrenner, a noted developmental expert, deserves a lot of credit for encourag-ing lifespan experts to consider the effects of context on development (Bronfenbrenner, 1979; 1989). Some time ago Dr. Bronfenbrenner gave an address to a large group of child and adolescent development experts. He applauded our group for studying the impact of context on development, but then added that it had gotten to the point that people were starting to study context *without* development. I believe what he meant was that documenting that teens who work many hours are more depressed than nonworking youth, or discovering that heavy peer involvement is related to self-esteem, does not tell us anything about the development of adolescents.

His words of wisdom remind us that we need to include measures of development in our research if we want to adhere to the perspective depicted in Figure 9.1. In the next chapter, we will discuss how to measure identity, achievement, sexuality, intimacy, and autonomy in adolescents. I believe that most experts strongly believe that these developmental milestones contribute to the overall adjustment of adolescents. For instance, many youth who have serious problems, such as substance abuse or truancy, generally display developmental delays when evaluated for treatment. Thus, accurately assessing these developmental milestones is important for both research and practice.

Research Navigator™ Exercise: Adolescents and Culture

The objective is to learn more about how researchers study cultural influences on adolescent development. Go the Research Navigator™ website: http://www.researchnavigator.com; choose the Psychology database, and type *adolescents* and *culture* as keywords using the Advanced Search option. Select a full-length article that compares adolescents in different cultures or provides an intensive analysis of the behavioral outcomes of youth in a single culture. After reading the article, answer the following questions.

1. What cultures were represented in this paper?
2. How were cultural influences predicted to influence adolescent behavior?
3. How did the authors assess these influences, and how were components of adolescent behavior measured?
4. What were the primary findings and conclusions?

10

Assessing Adolescent Development II: The Developmental Outcomes

Adolescents in our society achieve five psychosocial outcomes: autonomy, identity, intimacy, sexuality, and achievement (Grotevant, 1998; Hill, 1983). In this chapter, there are three ideas that you should consider:

1. Although these milestones are considered healthy psychosocial outcomes in our society, other cultures may not support such development. For example, some societies encourage parenting practices that restrict the development of autonomy or sexuality, and believe these competencies should develop in later adulthood (if at all).

2. Although these psychosocial milestones are referred to as "adolescent outcomes," many people continue to experience such development during adult life.

3. Many adolescents suffering from problem behavior, such as delinquency, substance abuse, or eating disorders, are often seriously delayed regarding one or more of these developmental milestones (Johnson, 1993; Weisz & Hawley, 2002). The idea is that if the adolescent can become directed and achieve these outcomes, then the problem behavior will dissipate.

After reading this chapter, you should be able to:

- Describe how to assess attachment representations, attachment styles, and intimacy.
- Define strategies for assessing different facets of autonomy.
- Illustrate how Erikson's theory has guided instrument development in identity.
- Describe ways of assessing educational achievement while offering distinctions among performance, academic achievement, and educational attainment.
- Indicate what is meant by the phase "psychology of achievement." Describe how researchers assess different facets of achievement motivation.

- Describe different approaches to studying adolescent occupational aspirations.
- Illustrate methodological issues pertaining to adolescent sexuality research.

Attachment and Intimacy

People sometimes interchange the terms *attachment, intimacy,* and *sexuality;* however, these terms represent distinct constructs. When we speak of the term *attachment* we are not referring to how close we feel to a particular person. Rather, most experts believe that an important component of the attachment process involves the development of **generalized attachment representations** and **attachment orientations.** Generalized attachment representations are a *broad* set of conscious and unconscious beliefs and expectancies that one holds for relationships (hence the term *generalized*) (Bretherton & Munholland, 1999). These representations reflect our lengthy history with certain attachment figures. For instance, we develop generalized representations for caregivers, and over time, romantic partners. These representations are stable and quite resistant to change during adolescence (Bowlby, 1988).

In contrast, attachment orientations reflect more specific and transitory relationship expectancies (Waters et al., 2002). When it comes to romantic relationships, do you occasionally feel emotionally distant from your partner? An attachment orientation is more fluid and unstable than a generalized attachment representation, and reflects more day-to-day feelings for a particular relationship or person (Creasey & Ladd, 2004). For instance, your anxiety about romantic relationships might increase temporarily upon learning that your partner is at the same vacation location as his former romantic interest. In such instances, a person who has a very secure generalized attachment representation—which reflects a lengthy and largely positive history—may temporarily show a more anxious attachment orientation but quickly get over these feelings because of her underlying secure generalized representation.

Although attachment representations and orientations reflect attitudes and beliefs about people, **intimacy** refers to the warm emotions and supportive behaviors that we display toward particular attachment figures (and vice versa). However, the two constructs are related, because individuals with secure generalized attachment representations display more intimacy with friends and romantic partners than do insecure adolescents (Fischer, Munsch, & Greene, 1996). Intimacy, in our discussion, does not refer to sexual behavior. It is possible to be intimate with a person but not have a sexual relationship, or to have a sexual relationship and not be intimate, or to experience both behaviors with a person. Having briefly covered some conceptual issues, let's now turn to methodological concerns regarding these constructs.

Attachment

Our section begins with a discussion of how to assess generalized attachment representations and attachment orientations. Although some use these terms interchangeably, they are thought by many attachment experts to reflect different constructs. Because of common confusions regarding this area, some theoretical background will be necessary. In addition, a review of the attachment material in Chapter 5 might be helpful at this point.

Generalized Attachment Representations. Attachment experts propose that repeated experiences with attachment figures become internalized as generalized attachment representations (Bretherton & Munholland, 1999). Consider generalized attachment representations as your "attachment foundation," a brick wall that is relatively resistant to day-to-day perturbations. In Chapter 5, we discussed individual differences in generalized attachment representations. A person who has a lengthy history of positive attachment relationships often develops a *secure* attachment representation, marked by a high value for close relationships, the ability to comfortably pursue new attachment relationships, and adeptness at regulating negative emotions in an autonomous manner (Allen & Land, 1999). An *insecure* adolescent is believed to have a history of neglect, rejection, or even abuse in attachment relationships, which can lead to beliefs that attachment is not an important issue, feelings of anger regarding attachment figures, and difficulties modulating negative emotions in relationships (Hesse, 1999).

A person's attachment history may not necessarily be entirely positive for a secure generalized attachment representation to develop. Plenty of adolescents who have had negative experiences with parents develop secure representations (Creasey, 2002). These adolescents may have also developed close, emotional relationships with others (e.g., peers, romantic partners), so that the support, intimacy, and good feelings in these relationships gradually lead them to value relationships (Main, 2001). Another point is that these representations reflect *conscious and unconscious* processes. Some people are convinced that they have always had great relationships with others, and perceive they have a secure attachment representation. However, a significant number of those who have such perceptions also display negative behavior toward attachment figures.

Some attachment experts posit that the only way to assess generalized attachment representations is to measure an adolescent's *state of mind* regarding attachment using narrative or interview methods (Crowell, Fraley, & Shaver, 1999) (see Chapter 5). When assessing state of mind regarding attachment, one is evaluating not what the subject is *saying* about attachment and relationships, rather what he *shows* you. Consider the partner who says she loves you but always forgets your birthday! Indeed, about 20–25 percent of adolescents possess an insecure, dismissing attachment representation marked by the tendency to ignore or dismiss negative experiences, and interpersonal problems when interviewed (Hesse, 1999). Many adolescents perceive themselves as secure, yet show difficulties in relationships.

We have already discussed the most popular narrative method for assessing state of mind regarding attachment in Chapter 5, the *Adult Attachment Interview* (AAI; George, Kaplan, & Main, 1996). As you recall, individuals who are administered the AAI can be classified into one of four attachment categories. Adolescents can reliably complete the AAI, although there is a new version that has been developed specifically for adolescents (Ammaniti et al., 2000). In general, adolescents with secure generalized attachment representations display the best functioning. Secure adolescents possess better psychological health and better relationship functioning with dating partners, and are likely to achieve a number of psychosocial outcomes (e.g., emotional autonomy) more quickly than their insecure counterparts (Allen & Land, 1999; Allen et al., 2002; Furman et al., 2002). These study results attest to the validity of these narrative-based protocols.

The AAI is primarily an assessment of state of mind regarding experiences with caregivers. Recall that any lengthy history with a person can lead to a stable, internalized attachment representation; the word *internalized* means a representation that is undisturbed by occasional squabbles with that person. Based on this theory, experts have developed interview schedules, such as the AAI, that probe attachment relationships with romantic partners. One such measure, the *Current Relationships Interview,* assesses generalized attachment expectancies about romantic partners (CRI; Crowell & Owens, 1996). Like the AAI, the CRI yields secure and insecure attachment classifications, and the use of both methods predicts romantic couple behavior better than the use of any single method (Crowell, Treboux, & Waters, 2002). However, it is unlikely that this assessment could be used with most adolescents. Dating relationships among adolescents are short-lived and there is often not enough time commitment for a generalized attachment representation to develop. We will revisit the CRI when we discuss committed relationships during adulthood in Chapter 12.

Is there an "easy" way to assess these representations? We have questionnaires that measure attachment relationships between adolescents and their parents, and friends (Armsden & Greenberg, 1987; Brennan, Clark, & Shaver, 1998; Pottharst, 1990). The most widely used instrument of this type is the *Inventory of Parent and Peer Attachment* (IPPA; Armsden & Greenberg, 1987). The IPPA assesses adolescent thinking regarding relationships with mothers, fathers, and peers, and measures the quality of communication, degree of mutual trust, and negative feelings. Curiously, the correlation between parent and peer attachment security is low, which contradicts the idea that a secure generalized attachment representation regarding caregivers should predict similar security in other adolescent relationships (Allen & Land, 1999).

Although this measure was accepted as a good attachment measure at one time, many attachment experts do not currently view this instrument as an acceptable instrument. A self-report measure of attachment assesses what a person *says* rather than *shows* regarding relationships, and it is likely that these surveys only measure surface, conscious perceptions of attachment representations. The aforementioned self-report measures are probably measures of attachment orientations, and reflect more transitory, day-to-day thinking about parents and peers.

Attachment Orientations.   An attachment orientation reflects our day-to-day feelings about attachment figures (Waters et al., 2002), which may not be consistent with our generalized attachment representations. There may be times when we feel anxious about our relationship with a person during a particularly stressful time period (attachment orientation) but hold deep beliefs that everything will turn out OK because of our lengthy, secure relationship with that person (generalized attachment representation). When defined in this fashion, attachment orientations constitute an important assessment. Consider the adolescent who holds a very insecure generalized attachment representation with caregivers but begins to develop some feelings of trust with a romantic partner. Although these feelings may not be permanent, it is possible that such perceptions may be related to positive functioning in that particular relationship at that given time (Creasey & Ladd, 2004).

By and large, most researchers who assess adolescent-attachment orientations or styles rely on questionnaire methods (Bartholomew & Horowitz, 1991; Brennan, Clark, & Shaver, 1998; Hazan & Shaver, 1987), and these measures can be used to assess attachment styles with parents, peers, or people in general. Mostly, these assessments have been used to predict romantic relationship functioning in adolescents, although the bulk of this research has involved college students. Although college students may seem like a population of convenience, the romantic relationships of these late adolescents are more lasting and intimate than those of high schoolers (Creasey & Hesson-McInnis, 2001), and about 30 percent of these couples end up married (Sprecher, 1999). When conducting this type of research, we must define what we mean by "casual dating" or "steady dating," and collect information on length of involvement.

The items and attachment-style constructs reflected on most of these assessments look quite similar; many contain items that reflect perceptions of attachment security (e.g., "I find it relatively easy to get close to others"), avoidance (e.g., "I am nervous when anyone gets close to me"), and anxiety (e.g., "I often worry that my partner does not really love me"). Although some have attempted to classify adolescents into secure, avoidant, and preoccupied or anxious orientations (Hazan & Shaver, 1987), the most popular approach involves tabulating continuous scores for these different orientations. Thus, a person could have a high degree of attachment security but also possess moderate levels of attachment anxiety (Crowell et al., 1999).

Correlations among such attachment measures and self-reports of relationship behavior are robust. People who report high security report better relationship behavior, more satisfaction, and less conflict than adolescents who report more anxiety or avoidance (Bartholomew & Horowitz, 1991; Creasey & Hesson-McInnis, 2001). However, research has failed to show that people who display high avoidance or anxiety display different relationship functioning or a unique way of interacting with others (Crowell et al., 1999). One would think that the outcomes of adolescents who were more anxious or more avoidant would be different.

The correlations between security scores on attachment self-report measures and assessments of generalized attachment representations, such as the Adult Attachment Interview, are weak (Crowell et al., 1999). Also, the convergence between attachment data collected on these self-report measures and behavior observations involving romantic partners are inconsistent (Simpson, Rholes, & Phillips, 1996; Waters et al., 2002). Individuals who report more attachment security may resemble adolescents who report considerable insecurity in terms of how they actually resolve conflicts with their partner. In general, interview methods that assess generalized attachment representations, such as the Adult Attachment Interview, have better predictive power in forecasting behavior observations with parents (Kobak et al., 1993) and romantic partners (Creasey, 2002) than the attachment-orientation questionnaires.

In summary, generalized attachment representations reflect our history with attachment figures (chiefly caregivers), and give adolescents a solid foundation for the development of emerging attachment relationships. These representations are chiefly assessed using interview methods. In contrast, attachment orientations, which are often measured using self-report techniques, reflect more transitory feelings about attachment figures. Although these latter assessments have not compiled a good track record in predicting actual behavior observations, they can be used in conjunction with measures like the Adult Attachment Interview to predict relationship behavior. Creasey and colleagues (2004) documented that adolescents who were insecure on the AAI yet expressed considerable attachment security regarding their romantic partners resolved conflicts with their dating partners just as well as individuals who were secure on both measures. Thus, it is possible that future research may prove these somewhat separate research traditions to be complementary, rather than competing, perspectives on attachment.

Intimacy

Intimacy reflects our emotional, cognitive, and behavioral orientation toward attachment figures, such as parents, best friends, and romantic partners. The emotional component of intimacy refers to positive and negative feelings we have for different people, whereas our cognitive appraisals reflect our intimate knowledge regarding a person. Finally, the behavioral component of intimacy includes our ability to disclose private feelings to another, and how well we engage in problem-solving or conflict management with that person.

Attachment theorists posit that individuals with secure generalized attachment representations should have positive views of parents and peers, possess the ability to comfortably disclose to others, and be good listeners and empathizers as well (Bowlby, 1969/1982). However, attachment processes do not completely explain intimacy development; attachment, temperament, and age, among other variables, are all considered important predictors of adolescent intimacy (Fischer, Munsch, & Greene, 1996). Although it is assumed that even young children show some seeds of intimacy in their behavior toward others, it is not until adolescence that intimacy theoretically becomes an integral part of our relationships with family members and friends (Sullivan, 1953). However, some controversy remains regarding whether adolescent relationships are truly intimate; for instance, some theorists, such as Erik Erikson (1968), claim that an intimate relationship cannot develop until the adolescent has forged an interpersonal identity.

Emotional closeness, openness or *disclosure abilities,* and the *ability to mutually give and receive support* are all markers of an intimate relationship (Fischer, et al., 1996; Prager, 2000; Sullivan, 1953). Like those who conduct attachment-orientation research, most of the work in this area examines whether adolescents score high or low on each of these dimensions with a particular person, and researchers have avoided classifying relationships as intimate or nonintimate. Although this is a popular approach, one might wonder about the meaning of a relationship that is marked by heavy disclosure but low emotional closeness.

Because intimacy represents feelings, perceptions, and behaviors, it is not surprising that most use self-report measures to assess this multidimensional construct. Although we have many short intimacy inventories that provide a brief picture of this construct (Buhrmester & Furman, 1987; Camarena, Sarigiani, & Petersen, 1990; Hunter & Youniss, 1982), the most detailed measure of adolescent intimacy is Sharabany's *Intimacy Scale* (Sharabany, Gershoni, and Hofman (1981). This scale assesses eight possible facets of intimacy; sample items and scale dimensions are listed in Table 10.1.

The validity of the Intimacy Scale is quite impressive. When comparing adolescent ratings of their peers (and vice versa), intimacy scores are more highly correlated among best friends than an adolescent and a casual acquaintance. In Sharabany's original cross-sectional study of adolescents (fifth–eleventh grade), older youth reported more overall intimacy in their relationships with best friends than their younger counterparts did. These research findings are similar to those documented by others using different measures of intimacy (Hunter & Youniss, 1982; Camarena, Sarigiani, & Petersen, 1990). The power of

TABLE 10.1 *Sharabany's (1981) Intimacy Scale: Sample Items and Factors*

Intimacy Factor	Sample Item
Frankness/spontaneity	I feel free to talk with him (her) about almost everything.
Sensitivity/knowing	I know how he (she) feels about things without his (her) telling me.
Attachment	I feel close to him (her).
Exclusiveness	I do things with him (her) that are quite different from what other kids do.
Giving/sharing	If he (she) wants something I let him (her) have it even if I want it, too.
Imposing/taking	I can count on his (her) help whenever I ask for it.
Common activities	Whenever you see me you can be sure that he (she) is also around.
Trust/loyalty	I speak up to defend him (her) when other kids say bad things about him (her).

the Intimacy Scale is that it assesses different facets of intimacy, some of which may show developmental shifts during adolescence (e.g., increase in disclosure), whereas others may not (e.g., friendship loyalty).

We have other ways of assessing adolescent intimacy development. Berndt and colleagues have developed an easy-to-score semistructured interview that illuminates different facets of intimacy (e.g., loyalty, disclosure, emotional closeness) (Berndt & Perry, 1986) as well as intimate knowledge (Diaz & Berndt, 1982). In the latter construct, researchers query the adolescent about a target person's personal characteristics (e.g., birthday), preferences (e.g., favorite sports, television shows, etc.), and personality characteristics (e.g., "What makes this person mad?"). These researchers have documented that intimate knowledge regarding peers increases with age, and that participant knowledge about best friends is often quite accurate (i.e., information can be verified by asking the target subject) (Diaz & Berndt, 1982). Both of these findings attest to the fine psychometric properties of the instrument.

There are studies that have examined intimate behavior using observational methods involving adolescent-parent; adolescent-best friend, and adolescent-romantic-interest relationships. These studies often target specific domains of intimacy, such as disclosure ability or problem-solving strategies (Creasey, 2002). However, there are methods that reveal a number of the important features of intimacy at one time. McNelles and Connolly (1999) have developed one such method. As with the family-interaction tasks surveyed in Chapter 9, these experts ask adolescent friendship dyads to engage in problem-solving tasks, such as how to spend some lottery winnings. Next, coders rate affective (e.g., shared laughter) and behavioral (e.g., disclosure) dimensions of adolescent intimacy. These researchers found that intimate affect and disclosure are more apparent among older adolescents; this finding attests to the validity of this paradigm.

Some Remaining Questions

Although psychological theories of adolescent intimacy have been available for decades, this field is a good example of how measurement development can lag behind theoretical musings. Most research using the instruments described above has found that certain aspects of intimacy, such as disclosure and emotional closeness, increase with adolescent maturity. These results suggests that the self-report and observational techniques described in this section are reasonably valid assessments of intimacy.

However, we need more research on this topic. It is possible that the different contexts for adolescent development (e.g., family, peer group) may moderate the associations between age and intimacy development. For example, adolescents may develop intimacy more quickly if their family system is supportive. In addition, although some have documented that adolescents are more intimate with their friends and romantic partners than with their parents (Buhrmester & Furman, 1987; Hunter & Youniss, 1982), these studies have largely relied on self-reports of intimacy. Does intimacy with parents suffer during adolescence, or is it merely that adolescents think it is not "cool" to admit that they feel close to a parent? Thus, the possibility of self-representation biases remains a methodological concern in this area of research.

Assessing Attachment and Intimacy: A Summary

In this section, we discussed techniques for assessing adolescent attachment and intimacy. Although we have research that has connected attachment processes to intimate behavior in adolescent relationships (Roisman et al., 2002), much of this work focuses on particular dyads (e.g., adolescent–romantic partner), with little work identifying how attachment variables affect intimate behavior across multiple relationship targets (e.g., adolescent–parent versus adolescent–best friend). Finally, research specifying the role of contextual variables in explaining attachment-intimacy connections is virtually non-existent. For instance, might marital conflict or child abuse affect the development of generalized attachment representations and intimacy?

What Do You Think?

Does intimacy with parents suffer at the hands of peers during adolescence? How could you design a study that addresses this question? In formulating your response, consider how you would assess the different facets of intimacy. Would you use more than one method?

Autonomy

Autonomy is a multifaceted concept (Silverberg & Gondoli, 1996; Zimmer-Gembeck & Collins, 2003). **Emotional autonomy** refers to the ability to move away from the emotional dependence that is normally associated with the child-parent bond. In short, adolescents become better at coping with negative emotions on their own. **Behavioral autonomy** is a multifaceted concept in its own right. The behavioral component of this form of autonomy refers to the ability to resist peer or parent pressure and behave in an independent yet competent manner. The cognitive side of this ability guides the behavioral component; adolescents who behave in an independent and competent way have developed decision-making capabilities that encourage such behavior. In fact, there are strong cognitive components to all three forms of autonomy; thus, it is not surprising that autonomy researchers often assess decision-making skills in conjunction with autonomy measures. Finally, **value autonomy** refers to the development of moral, social-conventional, political, and religious belief systems that are outside the thinking of our immediate family system. This is also a multifaceted concept, and develops after emotional and behavioral autonomy (if at all).

Emotional Autonomy

Emotional autonomy refers to changes in our emotional dependence with caregivers. The term encompasses different facets. First, in order to become autonomous, we need to understand that parents have their own flaws and that their suggestions on how to cope with problems may not always be helpful (Smollar & Youniss, 1989). Once they have perceived this, adolescents can move away from the dependence characteristic of child-parent relationships. They are now ready to gradually cope with certain problems on their own. However, emotional autonomy does not signify a severing of attachment relationships with caregivers, nor does such independence mean that they must cope with distress on their own across all contexts. Rather, adolescents gradually achieve the ability to deal independently with the negative emotions associated with day-to-day issues, such as a bad quiz grade (Silverberg & Gondoli, 1996). They will continue to rely on parents for emotional support when coping with more major life events, such as leaving home for college.

There are limited methods for assessing emotional autonomy, because this construct reflects some private thoughts and actions of which the adolescent might be aware. For instance, if an individual copes with stressful events on his own, others would not be able to complete complementary measures on the adolescent, because they would not be privy to this information! Thus, most emotional-autonomy measures are of the self-report, questionnaire variety (Chen & Dornbusch, 1998; Loevinger, Wessler, & Redmore, 1970; Noom, Dekovic, & Meeus, 2001; Steinberg & Silverberg, 1986).

Historically, the measure that has received the most attention is the *Emotional Autonomy Scale* (Steinberg & Silverberg, 1986). This scale is theoretically sound, in that the questionnaire items reflect facets of adolescent thought and behavior that have been posited as major markers of emotional autonomy (Blos, 1967). Some researchers have asked adolescents to complete this inventory twice when thinking about their relationships with parents—once for their mothers, and once for their fathers (Fuhrman & Holmbeck, 1995). Table 10.2 shows the EAS dimensions and sample items.

The EAS dimensions directly reflect theoretical components of emotional autonomy. The *Perceives parents as people* and *Parental deidealization* items reflect two cognitive facets of emotional autonomy; that is, in order to become autonomous, adolescents must develop the realization that their parents are not "all-knowing Gods." Indeed, adolescents and adults who highly *idealize* parents—that is, view them as perfect in every way—have more adjustment problems than their counterparts who can objectively see some faults (Hesse, 1999).

TABLE 10.2 *Dimensions of Emotional Autonomy and Sample Items Reflected on the Emotional Autonomy Scale*

Emotional Autonomy Dimension	*Sample Item*
Perceives parents as people	I might be surprised to see how my parents act at a party.
Parental deidealization	Even when my parents and I disagree, my parents are always right.
Nondependency on parents	I go to my parents for help before trying to solve a problem myself.
Individuation	There are some things about me that my parents do not know.

Source: Steinberg & Silverberg, 1986.

The EAS also contains items that tap dimensions of emotional autonomy that reflect the ability to cope with negative emotions in an independent manner. Adolescents who score high on the *Nondependency on parents* scale represent youth who do not disclose all of their personal problems to their caregivers. This premise is also reflected in the *Individuation scale.* Youth who score high on this scale hold private feelings that are not privy to their caregivers; by now you can see why experts who study emotional autonomy often rely on self-report.

Unfortunately, research using this scale has documented inconsistent findings; in some cases, emotional autonomy, as measured by the EAS, has been associated with good adjustment (Steinberg & Silverberg, 1986), whereas other researchers have yielded contradictory results (Ryan & Lynch, 1989). Perhaps such self-report measures of emotional autonomy are too brief to adequately assess the construct. For instance, questions such as, "If I had a problem with my friends, I would go to my parents before trying to solve the problem myself" could be interpreted in different ways. Coping with a suicidal peer is quite different from negotiating a disagreement over a favorite baseball team; it would be prudent to ask advice from an adult regarding the former issue. Thus, whether emotional autonomy is "good" or "bad" may be dependent on the type of stressor or on whether the adolescent is from a supportive family.

Those who assess emotional attachments using interview techniques are familiar with some youth who claim that they are autonomous from parents yet lace the interview with comments such as "Do you see what I mean?". These attempts at enlisting agreement are not autonomous statements (Main, Goldwyn, & Hesse, 2002), even though the adolescent claims they are completely autonomous! Thus, one would question whether all of the adolescents who claim they are emotionally autonomous on measures such as the EAS are truly independent (Schmitz & Baer, 2001). This may be an area that is ripe for more instrument development.

Behavioral Autonomy

Behavioral autonomy is the ability to resist parent or peer pressure and behave in a manner that may not be consistent with the desires of others. This construct has been assessed using a number of self-report methods. Traditionally, Berndt's (1979) "dilemma method" has represented one of the most popular assessments. When using this method, experts question adolescents regarding their behavior in response to hypothetical events that communicate major acts of antisocial behavior, such as taking drugs, or minor, everyday dilemmas, such as choosing which restaurant to eat at. For example:

> You are with a couple of your best friends on Halloween. They're going to soap windows, but you're not sure whether you should or not. Your friends all say you should, because there's no way you could get caught. What would you *really* do?

The respondent indicates whether they would go along with the peer suggestions, or do something else, which would reflect nonconformity. Berndt has added other manipulations; the peers may be identified as relatively familiar or unfamiliar, and he has vignettes that assess conformity or resistance to parental suggestions in these scenarios. Self-reported conformity to parents using this instrument steadily declines during adolescence, whereas resistance to peer pressure seems to build more slowly (Berndt, 1979; Brown, Clasen, & Eicher, 1986). Further, high behavioral autonomy on this scale correlates well with emotional-autonomy scores derived from the Emotional Autonomy Scale, suggesting that these two forms of independence may develop somewhat concurrently (Steinberg & Silverberg, 1986).

One might question whether adolescents who *report* strong resistance to peer pressure in such dilemmas really *behave* that way. To address this concern, researchers have examined behavioral autonomy to peer and parent pressure using methods that tap current, real events. For instance, the *Decision-Making Questionnaire* (Steinberg, 1987) encourages respondents to consider who makes rules pertaining to issues common to adolescent life, such as curfews and when to do homework. Respondents then indicate whether the adolescent, parent, or both parties make such decisions. Typically, both the adolescent and parent complete this measure, and their responses tend to correlate very well (Holmbeck et al., 2002).

Peer resistance and conformity are more slippery to assess. Beyond determining whether the adolescent and a peer behave in the same way, the sheer number of potential peers to rate can be high. If you were to conduct such an assessment, how would you identify a target friend to evaluate? If you were thinking of a best friend, then you have made a good guess. Think back to your own adolescence for a moment, and consider whether you would more likely conform to the behavior of someone you really liked or to the actions of someone you hardly knew.

Having identified a best friend using a friendship-nomination scale (see Chapter 8), we could poll the adolescent and friend separately about their use of certain drugs, engagement in antisocial behaviors such as stealing, or commitment to school. Next, we could examine the correlations between adolescent and peer responses, with the assumption that behavioral autonomy is more likely present in adolescent peer dyads in which correlation strength is weaker.

In one interesting study using such a measure, researchers examined peer conformity in a sample of youth as they became friends with other adolescents over the year. Of particular interest were cases in which adolescents began to associate with individuals who might constitute a "bad influence" on the youth. These researchers noted that adolescents who became friends with peers who used drugs became more like their friends over time. However, the family context played a role in these findings; for instance, the impact of having a drug-using friend was more negative for adolescents who had unsupportive parents (Mounts & Steinberg, 1995).

These findings illustrate why we should be sensitive to context when designing research. Like emotional autonomy, the association between behavioral autonomy and adjustment is dependent on contextual factors. Behavioral autonomy often occurs in family systems that contain warm, harmonious parent-adolescent relationships (Zimmer-Gembeck & Collins, 2003).

Value Autonomy

Value autonomy is also a multidimensional construct. For example, thinking regarding societal, moral, political, and religious philosophies represents related yet distinct components of value autonomy. Although researchers theorize that value autonomy develops during adolescence—hence, the presence of classes such as political science and government in high school—they also believe that the way younger children consider fairness, the plights of others, and social rules (such as "no running in the hall") provides a foundation for the development of sophisticated moral reasoning during adolescence. We learned about ways of assessing some of these foundation skills (e.g., prosocial reasoning, social conventions) in Chapter 8.

The most studied component of value autonomy is moral development. Unlike social conventions (see Chapter 8), which represent rules and customs that differ across cultures—for example, how to behave at a wedding—moral behavior pertains to acts that are universally viewed as right or wrong across many societies, such as "one should not kill." When considering moral issues, one must simultaneously balance legal, personal, situational, and cultural perspectives to make a moral judgment. For instance, although even young children know that it is wrong to steal, this interpretation may change if we are led to believe that stealing might save someone's life (Turiel, 2002). Such flexibility in thinking is somewhat rare in children; thus, the methods that follow are typically administered only to adolescents and adults.

Kohlberg's Approach.   Lawrence Kohlberg's theory represents the most cited account of adolescent and adult moral development. Like Piaget's theory regarding the growth of child cognition, Kohlberg speculated that moral development progresses through a series of *invariant stages,* as described in Table 10.3. He theorized that once people reach a certain stage of moral development they do not regress, or go back to earlier stages, and they don't skip stages. Like Piaget, Kohlberg postulated that moral development, like cognitive growth, is best facilitated by cognitive conflict. Thus, he speculated that a steady diet of ideas and beliefs that contradict our moral beliefs creates a context for moral development (Kohlberg 1968; 1969).

Like those who study perspective taking, distributive justice, prosocial reasoning, and social conventions (see Chapter 8)—which all fall under the rubric of value autonomy—Kohlberg used hypothetical dilemmas to tease out individual differences in moral reasoning. After considering each dilemma from his *Moral Judgment Interview (MJI),* the subject indicates how the character in the story should behave and then provides a rationale for the decision. Consider some of the moral dilemmas, presented in Table 10.4, and think about how you might respond.

The responses on the dilemmas are coded in the stages of moral development described in Table 10.3. Of particular note is the relation of Kohlberg's stages to Piaget's stages of cognitive development, and Selman's theory of perspective taking (Chapter 8). Indeed, Kohlberg believed that good perspective taking was a major facilitator of moral development, and downplayed the role of emotional development and socialization processes in its growth. Like Piaget, Kohlberg believed that the moral development of children was quite primitive, because they were limited in their perspective-taking skills (Eisenberg & Fabes, 1998). Thus, it comes as no surprise that Kohlberg recommended that his dilemma methods worked best for children older than 10 years of age (Colby & Kohlberg, 1987).

Let's clear up some common misunderstanding's regarding Kohlberg's *MJI:*

1. The interview involves administering three moral dilemmas; thus, how subjects respond to one dilemma may not be indicative of their global stage score. That is, an overall stage score is based on coding the responses to all three dilemmas (Colby & Kohlberg, 1987).

TABLE 10.3 *Kohlberg's Stages of Moral Development*

Stage	Description	Possible Response to Heinz Dilemma
1. Punishment and obedience	Reasoning guided by outcomes of actions; avoids breaking rules because of fear of punishment; avoids damage to property or person.	Heinz should steal the drug; if his wife dies, he could go to jail.
2. Instrumental purpose and fair exchange	Following rules because of self-interest; tit for tat, "eye for eye thinking"	He should not steal the drug; the druggist worked hard to make the drug. If Heinz wants it, he should go out and make some money to buy it.
3. "Good boy, good girl"; mutual personal, relational expectancies	Living up to what other people expect of you, particularly family and friends. *Their* rules are *your* rules.	The druggist is terrible; where I come from, you don't let people die; that is just how I was raised.
4. Law and order; social system and social consciousness	Reasoning guided by formal, legal rules	Can't go around stealing; if everyone did it we would all be in hot water. That's why we *have* laws; it's as simple as that.
5. Morality of social contract	Certain rules can be broken, depending on the situation.	There are laws against stealing, but in this case, stealing the drug is justified; we have a moral obligation to save a life, even if it means breaking a societal law.
6. Universal ethical principles	Following self-chosen ethical principles. Reasoning is internalized rather than guided by external authority.	The druggist, Heinz, and his wife are all probably in conflict here. I believe, unlike my friends, that we all have a responsibility for preserving a human life, no matter what the law says about stealing. However, this is not universally true; for example, I am not sure you would keep the wife alive if she had no decent quality of life.

    2. Whether the respondent, for example, indicates that Heinz should steal the drug or not is irrelevant in the coding system. Rather, the assignment of a moral stage is dependent on the *quality of the reasoning* behind the participant's response to the dilemmas.

    3. Coding the responses using Kohlberg's system can be difficult. Kohlberg and his colleague Anne Colby developed lengthy manuals that describe the complexities of coding moral reasoning. Adolescents and adults sometimes produce long-winded responses that contain reasoning that cuts across different stages of moral development. These systems

TABLE 10.4 *Sample Moral Dilemmas Developed by Kohlberg*

Heinz Dilemma: To Steal or Not to Steal?	*Valjean's Dilemma: Prison Escapee Becomes Hero to Community; Should He be Reported?*
In Europe, a woman was near death from a special type of cancer. There was one drug that the doctors thought might save her. It was a form of radium that a druggist in the same town had recently discovered. The drug was expensive to make, but the druggist was charging 10 times what the drug cost him to make. He paid $200 for the radium and charged $2,000 for a small dose of the drug. The sick woman's husband, Heinz, went to everyone he knew to borrow the money, but he could only get together about $1,000, which is half of what it cost. He told the druggist that his wife was dying and asked him to sell it cheaper or let him pay later. But the druggist said, "No, I discovered the drug, and I'm going to make money from it." So Heinz becomes desperate and considers breaking into the man's store to steal the drug for his wife. Should Heinz steal the drug? Why or why not?	In a country in Europe, a poor man named Valjean could find no work, nor could his sister or brother. Without money, he stole food and medicine when he needed it. He was captured and sentenced to prison for six years. After a couple of years, he escaped from the prison and went to live in another part of the country under a new name. He saved money and slowly built up a big factory. He gave his workers the highest wages and used most of the profits to build a hospital for people who couldn't afford good medical care. Twenty years had passed when a tailor recognized the factory owner as being Valjean, the escaped convict whom the police had been looking for back in his hometown. Should the tailor report Valjean to the police? Would it be right or wrong to keep it quiet? Why?

Source: Colby et al., 1983.

are not for novices, and luckily, simpler methods exist that new researchers can use. In-deed, there are at least 16 steps that the researcher must consider when assigning a stage score to any one dilemma (Colby & Kohlberg, 1987).

In terms of validity, research using Kohlberg's dilemmas has documented that children and adolescents progress through the stages in an orderly, invariant manner (i.e., they do not regress to an earlier stage). Longitudinal research has indicated that moral development demonstrates an orderly progression, people do not appear to skip stages, and there is little evidence of stage regression (Colby et al., 1983; Walker, 1989). However, some have questioned some core tenets of Kohlberg's theory. Moral development does not appear to develop in a sudden, all-or-none manner; rather, its growth seems to be more continuous than originally theorized. In addition, although adolescents are more likely than children to display postconventional thinking, not all adolescents consistently demonstrate such thinking. This finding, as well as data collected on adolescents regarding political and religious thinking, suggests that value autonomy develops after emotional and behavioral autonomy (Smetana & Turiel, 2003).

Alternatives to the Moral-Judgment Interview.   There are alternative methods to Kohlberg's MJI that are easier to use. The *Sociomoral Reflection Measure* (SRM; Gibbs, Basinger, & Fuller, 1992), unlike the MJI, requires subjects to rate the importance of moral issues across a variety of family, legal, and life-or-death moral domains; this measure assesses the *evaluation* rather than the *production*, of moral thinking. Participants do not have to *produce* moral thinking; they merely *evaluate* the moral responses provided to them. On the SRM, each moral issue is introduced with a lead-in question, such as:

How important is it for people to obey the law?
In general, how important is it for people to tell the truth?

Next, participants indicate whether the issue is *very important, important,* or *not important.* Thus, they are not asked to sort out a hypothetical dilemma. At first glance, this method seems too simple, and could yield data that is biased in a positive way. Nevertheless, higher moral evaluations on this scale are related to higher moral reasoning on the MJI (or good *concurrent validity*), and responses on this measure are related to prosocial behavior. Finally, people prone to giving socially desirable responses (and that don't necessarily reflect their honest opinions) do not seem to position themselves favorably on this assessment (Gibbs, Basinger, & Grimes, 2003). Because it is so quick to administer and score, I would look for much more research involving this alternative to the MJI.

There are other methods that tap moral reasoning that adheres to Kohlberg's dilemma approach yet do not require one to code the quality of the responses. One such assessment is the *Defining Issues Test* (DIT; Rest, 1979; Rest et al., 1999). When using this method, subjects are asked to consider dilemmas similar to Kohlberg's, yet are provided response alternatives that reflect thinking in the different stages of his theory. They simply have to read the different alternatives and then rank the responses they consider most important or relevant. As with the SRM, participants do not have to produce anything; they simply evaluate responses that are given to them. The DIT can be administered quickly to large groups of people, and it shows good concurrent validity with the MJI; that is, people who show sophisticated moral reasoning on the MJI endorse similar responses on the DIT (Gibbs, Basinger, & Grimes, 2003).

In summary, longitudinal research has supported Kohlberg's cognitive-developmental approach, although adolescents may not progress through the stages as quickly as he originally theorized that they would. Experts have developed other measures to make the field more accessible; however, the reliability and validity work on these alternative measures is still emerging.

Some Conclusions About Autonomy Assessment

Autonomy, like attachment and intimacy, is a multidimensional construct. Although theorists have made considerable advancements in determining how to assess emotional, behavioral, and value autonomy, more research is needed to identify the antecedents and consequences of these milestones. Indeed, some continue to debate whether autonomy from the family is even *beneficial* to adolescent development, although there is considerable theory that would suggest that it is most healthy when it occurs in a supportive family system.

What Do You Think?

Is there a relationship between attachment and autonomy? Review the material in the "Attachment and Intimacy" section presented earlier and design a study that would address this question. Formulate a hypothesis and indicate how you would test your idea.

Identity

This section is divided into two parts. First, a discussion of adolescent identity is not possible without some theoretical overview of Erik Erikson's perspective. Next, you will learn about identity assessments that have been influenced by his theory.

Erikson's Theory: A Brief Overview

Erik Erikson embraced a psychoanalytic perspective on human development that was different from the most recognizable theorist of the time, Sigmund Freud. Freud believed that personality development occurred through a series of psychosexual stages, that parents primarily influenced development, and that most emotional milestones were achieved during the preschool years. His perspective was pessimistic, in the sense that he argued that personality and behavioral problems that developed early in life could be remedied only through intensive psychotherapy.

Erikson (1950) modified Freud's perspective, and posited that development was influenced by our interactions within society. Thus, because development is influenced by society, his theory is *psychosocial* as opposed to psychosexual. Unlike Freud, Erikson proposed that personality and behavioral development continues to occur throughout the lifespan. However, like Freud, Erikson proposed a stage approach to personality development, and assumed that we progress through these stages in an orderly, invariant manner. He asserted that there are eight psychosocial conflicts that we negotiate over time (see Table 10.5).

TABLE 10.5 *Erikson's Eight Stages of Psychosocial Development*

Stage/Approximate Age	*Positive Resolution*
Trust versus mistrust (First year)	Synonymous with secure attachment; learns to trust that caregivers will reliably meet needs or support when distressed.
Autonomy versus doubt (Second year)	Moves away from dependence characteristic of attachment phase; marked by high exploration and willful behavior.
Initiative versus guilt (3–6 years)	Learns to initiate interactions and attachment relationships with others; beginning of friendship development.
Industry versus inferiority (7 years puberty)	Learns to master activities deemed important by parents, teachers, and other social agents.
Identity versus role confusion (Adolescence)	Develops understanding regarding his role in society, and direction regarding interpersonal and occupational issues.
Intimacy versus isolation (Early adulthood)	Develops close intimate relationships, and makes choices regarding a stable relationship.
Generativity versus stagnation (Middle adulthood)	Productive in work and family contexts; develops the ability to mentor others (e.g., younger coworkers, grandchildren).
Integrity versus despair (Late adulthood)	Able to reflect back on life and objectively determine whether one's life course has been fulfilling and important; should be able to support this decision with evidence.

Erikson proposed that identity concerns represent the core developmental issue facing adolescents. In addition, other developmental milestones, such as intimacy, occur at various stages of the life cycle. Erikson speculated that in order to develop intimate relationships, one must have achieved a proper sense of identity, or some general direction regarding interpersonal goals.

Some identity experts (e.g., Marcia, 1966) posited other theoretical points. Marcia theorized that an unsuccessful resolution of a psychosocial conflict does not guarantee that a person is doomed for life. An adolescent who does not achieve a proper identity may eventually, with support, experience later achievement. Also, identity development represents only one component of self-development during adolescence; for instance, some adolescent developmental specialists view changes in self-esteem and self-representation (see Chapter 9) as additional of identity facets.

Identity achievement involves both *exploration* and *commitment* (Erikson, 1968; Marcia, 1966). Exploration is the search we engage in when it comes to interpersonal, occupational, and ideological issues. An adolescent who "dates around" is exploring different types of relationships. Exploration and experimentation are viewed as healthy and normative adolescent behaviors, and may explain why my son has a different hairstyle every week! However, these theorists also assume that adolescents and adults gradually begin making interpersonal, personal, and career commitments. Thus, an adolescent who undergoes an identity search and then makes a commitment would be defined as *identity achieved.* Of course, society is different than when Erikson developed his original theory (the 1950s). Thus, because of all the options facing adolescents today, many assume that true identity achievement may not occur until well after the adolescent years. For instance, notice how the age of first marriages continues to rise.

Identity: Additional Methodological and Theoretical Issues

James Marcia is given much credit for major theoretical and methodological advances regarding Erikson's theory of identity. Marcia, like Erikson, proposed that exploration is a major component of eventual identity achievement, and theorized that there are three components to such development: *interpersonal, occupational, and ideological.* He proposed four identity classifications (Marcia, 1966; Marcia, 1994):

1. *Achievement.* High exploration and commitment
2. *Moratorium.* High exploration and little commitment
3. *Foreclosure.* High commitment and little exploration
4. *Diffusion.* Little commitment or exploration.

Marcia developed the *Identity Status Interview (ISI)* to assess this construct (ISI; Marcia, 1966; Marcia et al., 1993). This interview takes about 30–60 minutes, and on it subjects indicate their degree of exploration and commitment to interpersonal, ideological, and occupational issues. After completion of the interview, the participant receives an identity classification for each domain, and a "global identity" status. The original reliability and validity studies involving this instrument were quite impressive. Marcia and colleagues noted that coders typically agreed about 80 percent of the time regarding identity classifications, older adolescents were more likely to achieve integrated identity than younger youth, identity achievement was positively related to psychological health, and foreclosure and diffusion were both correlated with adjustment problems.

However, Marcia's approach has some drawbacks. It takes significant training to master such complex interview methods. In addition, some have (see Côté & Levine, 1988; van Hoff, 1999) questioned Marcia's interpretation of Erikson's original theory. For instance, Marcia's technique ignores other stages of Erikson's developmental theory, and does not assess other important dimensions of identity, such as gender and ethnic identity.

In order not to neglect other important features of Erikson's lifespan theory, some experts favor a quicker assessment of identity. Constantinople (1969) developed the *Inventory of Psychosocial Development (IPS)* to measure development or conflict resolution across the first six stages of Erikson's approach, outlined in Table 10.5 (e.g., trust versus mistrust; identity versus role confusion; intimacy versus isolation). This method has also been modified by others to test resolution capacity regarding the remaining two stages of Erikson's theory (Whitbourne et al., 1992).

This method will not tell you whether someone is foreclosed or has achieved identity; rather, the results of the assessment yield *resolution scores* for each stage of his theory (e.g., higher scores are more indicative of overall identity achievement). Some impressive research on this inventory has incorporated very sophisticated developmental designs to untangle the potential effects of age and ongoing historical changes on adolescent and adult psychosocial development. Some of these studies are presented in Box 10.1.

BOX 10.1 • *Is Erikson's Theory Developmentally Valid?*

How do you test the validity of a lifespan theory such as Erikson's? Constantinople (1969) developed the 60-item *IPS* specifically to test the viability of Erikson's perspective. This self-report measure requires the respondent to endorse short phrases that reflect (non)resolution for each developmental stage, such as "comfortable in intimate relationships" (intimacy versus isolation) (1 = uncharacteristic to 7 = characteristic). Summing the scale items allows researchers to compile total resolution scores for each stage. Although Consantinople's original measure assessed resolution of the first six stages of Erikson's theory, other researchers have augmented this assessment with additional items to measure resolution regarding the final two stages of his theory (Whitbourne et al., 1992).

How could we best test Erikson's theory using this method? It might seem that a study using a simple cross-sectional design, in which different cohorts or age groups are assessed at one time, would be just as effective, and much less costly and time consuming than a longitudinal study. However, differences in educational and historical experiences among age groups or cohorts—that is, *cohort differences*—can affect the results of a cross-sectional study. Such a problem could lead to observers overestimating the effects of maturation on development, because age is confounded with history (or cohort).

However, could historical events really influence the personality structure of an entire generation of people and not another? That is, could there have been historical eras in which different percentages of adolescents have achieved identity or remained diffused? I seem to remember the term "slacker" used as a popular expression at one time; could it be true that there are more diffused adolescents and young adults today than during previous eras? If so, then Erikson's theory would predict that these individuals would experience continued struggles with future psychosocial conflicts. When looking at this sample later in life, this theory would suggest that these same individuals would

(continued)

BOX 10.1 • Continued

continue to have resolution problems. Thus, any age differences we noted between this sample and other age groups could have more to do with historical events than with maturation or age.

Of course, a longitudinal design could control for these cohort effects; however, we might not have the time to conduct 60-year studies on personality development. One alternative would be to consider a sequential design, or a design that combines elements of the cross-sectional and longitudinal approaches (see Chapter 1). In one study, researchers sampled 347 college students and administered the IPS in 1966, and augmented this instrument with additional questions to also assess resolution in Erikson's last two stages (Generativity versus Stagnation, Integrity versus Despair). About ten years later (1977), 155 of the original students were located and completed this assessment again. Also, at this time of measurement (1977), 298 new college students completed the IPS. About ten years later (1988), both of these samples were readministered the IPS, and the researchers added a new sample of college students. This *cohort sequential design* can be conceptualized as follows (Whitbourne et al., p. 262):

Year of Testing

Age	1966	1977	1988	
	20	31	42	Cohort 1
	$N = 347$	$N = 155$	$N = 99$	
		20	31	Cohort 2
		$N = 298$	$N = 83$	
			20	Cohort 3
			$N = 292$	

The beauty of sequential designs is that they often include a *time-lag component;* in the present design,

20-year-olds are represented in each time era (1966, 1977, 1988). The design thus allows the researcher to disentangle the effects of age from ongoing historical influences. The results of the study supported a variety of Eriksonian tenets. Successful resolution of more advanced psychosocial conflicts occurred as the respondents matured. For instance, 30-year-olds were more resolved regarding identity issues then they had been ten years earlier. In addition, successful resolution of earlier stages was highly correlated with later resolution of more advanced stages, supporting Erikson's point that resolution success should predict later success. The effects of ongoing historical changes on identity were relatively minimal. The college students at each time of measurement were quite similar regarding identity resolution, which is somewhat surprising, given the increasing number of interpersonal and career options that seem to become available to young adults with each new generation.

Although this study was supportive of Erikson's approach, some thorny issues were raised by the results of this study. For example, individuals at all ages were more likely to have experienced intimacy resolution than either autonomy or identity resolution. These data would suggest that the successful development of intimate relationships, and generalized knowledge regarding the factors that contribute to a successful relationship, occurs earlier than Erikson postulated. This was an important finding, and raises questions about Eriksons' claim that intimacy resolution cannot occur without a coherent identity regarding interpersonal issues. Of course, it is possible that these participants believed that they had resolved intimacy issues, yet lacked a solid interpersonal identity. It would seem that such people might experience rocky committed relationships, particularly if their interpersonal identity development over time made them question their choice of partner.

Of course, some researchers want a detailed description of the adolescents' identity, and are not as interested in how they have resolved other stages in Erikson's theory. Both interview (Grotevant & Cooper, 1985) and questionnaire methods exist that extend Marcia's conceptualization of identity to include broader interpersonal domains, such as dating and friendship, as well as contexts specified by Erikson as important yet not captured by Marcia's system, such as gender identity (Adams, Shea, & Fitch, 1979; Adams, 1999; Bosma, 1992; Dellas & Jerigan, 1990).

The method used most often is the *Objective Measure of Identity Status* (Adams, Shea, & Fitch, 1979; Adams, 1999). This questionnaire contains queries that tap exploration and commitment regarding interpersonal, occupational, and ideological identity, and further subdivides these domains into eight different facets: occupations, religion, politics, philosophic lifestyle, dating, friendship, sex roles, and recreation and leisure (Adams, 1999). The method allows the researchers to determine the magnitude of identity achievement, moratorium, foreclosure, and diffusion in the eight facets, or they can aggregate the scores to determine identity achievement in two major domains: *ideological* (politics, occupations, religion, philosophic lifestyle) and *interpersonal* (dating, friendship, sex roles, recreation and leisure). It's easy to identify the identity domain and identity category assessed by each question:

"I attend the same church my family always attended. I've never really questioned why." (*Religion/Foreclosure*)

"I've tried many different types of friendships, and now I have a clear idea of what I look for in a friend." (*Friendship/Achieved*)

"Opinions on men's and women's roles seem so varied that I don't think much about it." (*Sex Roles/Diffused*)

"My preferences about dating are still in the process, but I'm trying to figure out what I can truly believe in." (*Dating/Moratorium*)

The scoring methods and statistical procedures for data reduction allow us considerable flexibility when considering a subject's identity status. First, we can determine the participant's level of achievement, foreclosure, exploration, and diffusion, for each of the eight identity components or the two major domains (interpersonal and ideological). We can also tabulate identity achievement, exploration, foreclosure, and diffusion scores for the entire instrument, which can lead to an overall identity classification (Berzonsky & Adams, 1999). The choice of strategy depends on our research questions. There is good congruence between identity scores on this instrument and data obtained using interview methods; for example, an individual who receives high achievement scores in the interpersonal domain is likely to achieve similar scores on more detailed interviews (Adams, 1999).

Several reviews of the identity literature using both the interview and questionnaire measures of identity have supported the theoretical speculations of Erikson and Adams (Berzonsky & Adams, 1999; Bosma et al., 1994; Kroger, 2003). In longitudinal studies, adolescents become more achieved over time, and achievement is generally correlated with good functioning. Most adolescents show orderly progression in identity development, and move from diffusion to foreclosure to moratorium, and finally to achievement over time (van Hoff, 1999). However, some studies involving these measures (Meeus et al., 1999) have yielded results not consistent with the conclusions in the preceding paragraph. Also, much of the research has been conducted with college students, and we do not have much data on late adolescents who might be suffering from the most serious identity problems. For instance, consider the number of late adolescents and young adults in our society who cannot find meaningful employment and are forced to continue to live with their parents.

Some Conclusions Regarding Identity Assessment

Why are there such contradictory findings in this area? Well, two studies involving college students that used the same identity measure could yield conflicting data if the participants were drawn from different campuses. Schools and families differ in how well they support adolescent exploration and commitment, and these contextual issues probably explain the differences in identity that we witness between and within study samples (Kroger, 2003).

In addition, some wonder whether identity achievement is the developmental "end-point" for the various identity domains. For instance, sometimes adolescents who are foreclosed in certain domains, such as political or religious issues, are happier than achieved people (Meeus et al., 1999). Perhaps thinking like our parents regarding politics and religion leads to harmony in family relationships, and thus family members avoid the arguments and conflicts that frequently take place when our beliefs begin to differ from those of the rest of the family. In any case, more research is clearly needed in this area to clear up some of these concerns.

What Do You Think?

Is interpersonal, occupational, and ideological identity achievement associated with adjustment? How would you design a study to address this question? In formulating your response, think about how you would measure identity and how developmental status might influence your results.

Achievement

Adolescent achievement is conceptually different from that of younger children. The struggle to successfully join or gain acceptance into the peer group, extracurricular, attractive part-time jobs, and eventually the collegiate or adult occupational world are all concerns that pertain more to adolescents than to younger children. Also, achievement outcomes for adolescents are often more critical; for example, a low standardized test score in grade school might gain a young child special mentoring and a second chance. However, a low test score for an adolescent might slam a door shut (e.g., deny admittance to a preferred college). Adolescents also appraise achievement tasks differently and are more apt to consider how a low exam grade compares to those of their peers. A final consideration rests with the occupational plans of young children and adolescents; the thinking of the latter is more likely to be tied to future educational and occupational attainment. In summary, although one could argue that the methodological and theoretical issues pertaining to achievement could be applied to any age group, adolescent achievement is conceptually different than that of children.

Assessing Educational Achievement

Educational achievement is captured by four variables; three of them reflect the *product*, or outcome, of educational experiences. These three variables are *academic achievement, educational attainment, and school performance.* The fourth variable reflects more the psychological and motivational *process* behind the first three variables. It is believed that our school performance and success are tied to the way we think about achievement issues. Thus, there is a psychology to achievement. Let's first discuss the "products" of educational achievement.

Performance, Academic Achievement, Attainment.   When considering educational achievement, there are important variables at our fingertips if we have access to school records. Perhaps the easiest data to collect involves **school performance**—grade point average or grades within given classes. However, there are some concerns with these data. First, pupils in the same school often take a varied curriculum, and curriculum experiences may vary widely across different school systems. Also, school personnel have been accused of grade inflation, which might have something to do with the following headline obtained from a local newspaper:

Harris Named 1 of 10 Central High Valedictorians

Finally, if researchers do not have access to school records, then they must rely on adolescents or parents to provide these data. Students have been known to occasionally "misrepresent" their academic records; thus, researchers generally insist on actual transcripts or report cards.

Beyond school performance, researchers can obtain information about the adolescent's **academic achievement**, or scores on standardized tests. Chapter 7 discussed a plethora of tests designed to assess the achievement and aptitude of children. **Achievement tests** are often used as dependent variables; in other words, these tests are thought to reflect the achievement history of the individual. In many school systems across the country, adolescents are required to take various achievement tests that reflect required standards of learning (SOL). Although many individual tests of intelligence could also be considered an achievement test, the SOL tests targets adolescent competence in certain subjects, such as social studies or history.

Although *aptitude tests* (e.g., SAT, GRE, ACT) look somewhat similar to achievement assessments in content, they are used as predictor variables, and assess potential in an environment the adolescent has not yet participated in (e.g., college). Because the tests covered in Chapter 7 pertain to adolescents and adults (there are also similar versions for older participants), I will not go into much more detail on these tests. A large amount of research has focused on *how* personal (e.g., gender, ethnicity), family (e.g., social class, achievement expectancies), peer, school (e.g., curriculum, teacher behavior), part-time work, and cultural variables influence academic achievement or nonachievement, such as school drop out (Dornbusch, Herman, & Morley, 1996; Eccles & Roeser, 2003). Thus, most experts are interested in *why* children and adolescents perform the way they do on these assessments.

Another marker of educational achievement pertains to **educational attainment**, or the highest level of education experience obtained by the adolescent. There is great variability in the educational attainment of our adolescents and adults, ranging from the school dropout to individuals completing postbaccalaureate degrees. I have heard many people say, "Well, it's not whether you get a degree or not, it's motivation to succeed that ultimately predicts success." This statement is not valid; educational attainment predicts future occupational success much more accurately than school grades or achievement test scores do (Arum & Hout, 1998).

Academic achievement (i.e., test scores), school performance [grade-point average (GPA)], and educational attainment are attractive variables for study, because they yield understandable, quantitative data. These data can be used to predict later success or used as dependent or outcome measures; the latter seems to be the more popular research use. Although school performance might be the easiest piece of data to collect, many in this area view this variable suspiciously. It should come as no surprise to you that most researchers prefer to measure achievement in adolescents via the norm-referenced, standardized tests. Unfortunately, there may be situations in which such data acquisition is not possible. In such cases, I would recommend that researchers obtain recent adolescent report cards.

Psychology of Achievement. Although some researchers are content to examine how family, peer, school, and cultural variables predict adolescent educational achievement, others concede that the association between these contextual variables and achievement is not direct. Rather, it has been theorized that personal and motivational factors residing in the adolescent mediate the association between the educational environment and educational achievement. One such psychological variable that has been specified is **achievement motivation**. A large volume of research has been devoted to this topic, and in particular, how school structure and teacher behavior influence this competency (Eccles & Roeser, 2003). Achievement motivation encompasses the following questions (Eccles, Wigfield, & Schiefele, 1998):

1. Can I do the task?
2. Do I want to do the task, and why?
3. What do I have to do to succeed on this task?

From reading these questions, this construct reflects *more than just wanting to do well*; most people *desire* to succeed. Rather, achievement motivation is a process that reflects a student's *confidence* in her ability to do the task, her desire to do the task or *goal orientation*, and beliefs regarding what she must accomplish to meet these goals, or *learning strategies*. Although these psychological processes lie within the individual, the task demands, or the learning environment, play a role in explaining this process (Henderson & Dweck, 1990). How confident would you be if your instructor announced that 80 percent of the students would fail a class you were taking?

To better conceptually understand this process, consider how the three aforementioned achievement questions can be schematically represented as follows:

Can I do the task?	Do I want to do the task?	What do I have to do?
Confidence	*Achievement Goals*	*Learning Strategies*

Evaluating the adolescent's task confidence, their goals for success, and the cognitive, behavioral, and emotional strategies (i.e., learning strategies) they use to help them complete the task constitute measures of the achievement-motivation process. To further demystify these competencies, let's consider what they mean. Confidence, of course, refers to how confident they feel about success in the learning environment. Achievement goals pertain to what types of goals or rewards they see emerging from task success. Some are motivated by *performance goals*, such as getting a good grade or making a lot of money, whereas others pursue learning opportunities for the sake of learning. These latter individuals have *mastery goals*. Some adolescents' primary goal is to avoid embarrassment, or "save face," which has been termed performance avoidance (Elliot, 1999). The interplay between confidence and goals is thought to elicit *learning strategies*, such as deciding whether to study and self-directed learning.

There are different methodological approaches to studying achievement motivation. Some researchers have developed measures that provide an in-depth analysis of particular components of the achievement-motivation process (e.g., confidence or goals), whereas others have developed measures that attempt to assess the process in its entirety. Let's first discuss approaches to assessing distinct segments of the achievement-motivation process.

Confidence.   The power of achievement motivation can be appreciated when one considers that expectancies regarding success strongly predict future achievement success in adolescents (Harackiewicz et al., 2002; McGregor & Elliot, 2002). Much of the work on such academic confidence adheres to self-efficacy theory, in that high general self-confidence is tied to development and adjustment across the lifespan (Bandura, 1997). Some researchers feel that efficacy beliefs are so vital to the adaptation process that low self-confidence can lead to very poor outcomes, even if the individual selects an appropriate learning or coping strategy. For example, would you think a student who was concerned about a grade would have a very good interaction with an instructor if he believed that the meeting would hold no benefit?

Bandura and colleagues have developed a short, 15-item questionnaire that assesses the adolescent's confidence in mastering different academic courses, structuring their learning environmental to reduce distractions, and meeting the expectancies of parents and teachers. High confidence in academic abilities, as assessed by this instrument, is related to the development of academic achievement, parent confidence, educational aspirations, and less problem behavior, such as delinquency (Bandura et al., 1996; 2001; 2003). Bandura has documented that the predictive power of such academic confidence increases when other forms of confidence, such as confidence in resisting peer pressure and the ability to regulate negative emotions, are factored in. This work suggests that we need to consider these variables when assessing academic confidence and achievement, simply because the relationship between confidence and academic outcomes is indirect (Bandura et al., 1996).

What Do You Think?

Suppose you believe that academic confidence predicts future achievement success, but your friend argues that it is the other way around. How would you design your study to settle the debate? Consider measures you would use to assess academic self-efficacy and academic achievement.

Achievement Goals.   Another link in the achievement-motivation chain consists of the adolescent's goals in the learning process. Recall that youth can have performance goals, such as wanting good grades, or mastery and learning goals, which have to do with their desire to learn for the sake of learning. Recently, experts have added a third goal, performance avoidance. This is a motivation to do well in order to please others and not appear incompetent.

Some self-report measures assess such achievement goals (Duda & Nicholls, 1992; Elliot & Church, 1997; Harackiewicz et al., 2002; Midgley et al., 1998). The *Achievement*

Goal Questionnaire (Elliot & Church, 1997) contains items that tap each achievement goal:

> Performance Goal: *"It's important for me to do well compared to others in the class."*
> Mastery Goal: *"I desire to completely master the material presented in class."*
> Performance-Avoidance Goal: *"I just want to avoid doing poorly in class."*

An added advantage is that achievement-goal measures are traditionally short. For instance, two of the most well-validated achievement-goals measures, the *Goal Orientation Scale* (Midgley et al., 1998) and the *Achievement Goal Questionnaire* (Elliot & Church, 1997) contain fewer than 20 items, yet possess enough responses to allow measurement of the three different achievement goals.

Although the item and scale construction of the measures just described is excellent, it is disappointing that the different achievement goals do not predict student accomplishments as well as originally hoped. Some well-designed studies have documented that these goals do not predict future collegiate grade point average. Although performance-avoidance goals are negatively related to high aptitude-test scores, performance goals are only weakly related to eventual grades, and mastery goals are primarily associated with task enjoyment and interest in school (Harackiewicz et al., 2002). In each case, the power of these findings is quite weak. However, I do not think that these findings have to do with conceptual or methodological weaknesses regarding these studies. Rather, like Bandura's claims, other achievement beliefs, task persistence, and contextual factors, such as peer behavior, may play a role in shaping goal expectancies, and may help to explain the association between achievement goals and success. These ideas again suggest that we need to consider the role of context when designing research.

Learning Strategies. Finally, a number of scales are available to researchers who want to obtain a reading of the adolescent's task behavior (McCoach & Siegle, 2003; Pintrich et al., 1993). For instance, Pintrich and colleagues have developed the 56-item *Motivated Strategies for Learning Scale* (Pintrich et al., 1993); sample items are reproduced in Table 10.6. This scale also contains items that measure motivational goals, confidence, and perceptions

TABLE 10.6 *Sample Items from the Motivated Strategies for Learning Scale*

Scale	Sample Item
Intrinsic Value	"I prefer class work that is challenging, because I can learn new things."
Self-Efficacy	"I expect to do well in this class."
Test Anxiety	"When I take a test, I think about how poorly I am doing."
Cognitive Strategy Use	"I outline the chapters in my book to help me study."
Self-Regulation	"Even when study materials are dull and uninteresting, I keep working until I finish."
Productive Classroom Work	"Students have some choice over the topics for class reports."
Teacher Effectiveness	"The teacher explains the material well."
Cooperative Work	"I had the opportunity to work with other students in this class."

Source: Pintrich et al., 1993.

of the task environment. Thus, *this instrument represents the most comprehensive measure of the achievement-motivation process.* In studies involving this method, highly confident adolescents who possess a mastery orientation are more likely to engage in task persistence and better self-regulation than individuals who lack these beliefs or goals or possess high test anxiety (Pintrich & De Groot, 1990; Pintrich, Roeser, & De Groot, 1994). The latter findings support Bandura's claim that psychological dispositions, such as mood, should be studied in conjunction with achievement expectancies and behavior.

In summary, a variety of studies using measures that tap academic confidence, achievement goals, and the cognitive and behavioral strategies adolescents use in learning environments have documented modest relationships between these assessments and academic interest, or even success. However, these associations are almost always modest, and in some studies, nonsignificant. Some experts theorize that links between achievement expectancies and success can be strengthened via a more through examination of the learning environment, other contextual variables (e.g., peer behavior), and additional psychological characteristics of the person (e.g., test anxiety, depression).

I believe more work should be undertaken to examine the accuracy of adolescent judgments on self-report measures of achievement motivation. In my own work involving interpersonal relationships, my colleagues and I have identified about 20 percent of adolescents as "extreme optimists" who report robust expectancies regarding their ability to solve conflicts with their romantic partners and regulate emotions during these encounters. However, when observed, these very same adolescents are the very worst at managing these conflicts! I worry that the same finding might hold true for adolescents involved in achievement settings, and that high confidence in academic achievement or mastery "orientation" might not always match reality.

Assessing Occupational Aspirations

Perhaps one of the easiest ways to assess adolescent occupational achievement is to identify their level of exploration regarding careers using an identity assessment, such as the *Objective Measure of Identity Status* (page 310). This inventory contains questions such as, "I'm still trying to decide how capable I am as a person and what work will be right for me." (Adams, 1999). Of course, many adolescents may not have made occupational commitments because theoretically, many youth are still experimenting, and their decisions regarding occupational paths are more speculation than reality (Erikson, 1968; Super, 1967).

Another approach to studying adolescent occupational achievement involves polling youth regarding *occupational aspirations and expectancies.* **Occupational aspirations** pertain to the careers that adolescents are considering pursuing, whereas **occupational expectancies** involve the level of confidence they have that they will pursue a particular occupational track.

Examples of questionnaires that tap into these belief systems are the *Vocational Preference Inventory* (Holland, 1985), *Campbell Interest and Skill Survey* (Campbell, Hyne, & Nilsen, 1992), and the *Strong Interest Inventory* (Harmon et al., 1994). For instance, when completing the 317-item Strong Interest Inventory, the subject rates interests across different occupations that cluster into 25 basic interest scales, such as social services, sales, art, military activities, and public speaking. Although the Strong has an excellent reliability and validity history (Donnay & Borgen, 1996), any closed-ended occupational-interest scale should be critically evaluated to ensure that the measure contains occupations that reflect current career trends.

A number of other questionnaires have been designed to assess occupational expectancies; examples are the *Career Beliefs Inventory* (Krumboltz, 1991) and the *Expanded Skills Confidence Inventory* (Betz et al., 2003). Still others assess variables that might facilitate or impede achievement, such as the *Career Counseling Checklist* (Ward & Bingham, 1993), and the *Career Barriers Scale* (CBS; Swanson & Tokar, 1991). The CBS is probably the most comprehensive assessment of perceived occupational barriers; it examines both personal obstacles (e.g., finances, family obligations) and discrimination concerns regarding gender, sexual orientation, ethnicity, and disability.

Any measure that requires the respondent to simply evaluate aspirations and expectancies can be problematic, because we are feeding the participant choices that we feel are positive or negative. Thus, adolescents may choose attractive responses to which they may not have given much thought. To circumvent this concern, some researchers have developed interview techniques to force the adolescent to produce responses on their own. In such work, researchers poll children and adolescents regarding occupational achievement using questions such as, "If you could have any job when you grow up, what would it be?" (*Aspiration*), and "Of all the jobs there are, which one do you think you will probably get when you grow up?" (*Expectancy*) (Armstrong & Crombie, 2000; Cook et al., 1996).

The results of such work is often very fascinating, particularly if we examine how demographic variables, such as gender or social class, relate to congruency regarding such aspirations and expectancies. Cook and colleagues (1996) noted that African-American preadolescents (fourth-graders) who lived in poor, urban areas aspired to become professional athletes, whereas the majority of European-American youth who reside in middle-class, suburban neighborhoods wanted occupations that required considerable education (e.g., doctors, lawyers). Although older adolescents who resided in the poorer neighborhoods aspired to more realistic occupations than their younger counterparts, only a small percentage (less than 5 percent) expected that they would actually hold such a job one day. The assessment of occupational aspirations and expectancies is a fascinating area for both researchers and applied professionals; many believe these expectancies can be modified among at-risk youth.

Finally, some experts theorize that adolescents' personality style enables them to "match well" with certain occupations. For instance, a shy, introverted adolescent may not function well in an occupational climate that demands heavy social interaction and public speaking. John Holland (1985) developed the *Self-Directed Search Inventory* to help both adolescents and adults better understand the match between their personality and occupational profiles. To complete this measure, adolescents first list "occupational daydreams," which essentially amount to occupational aspirations. Next, they rate an assortment of activities and competencies that cluster into six personality and occupational traits, as listed in Table 10.7. After completing these items, the adolescents then use these data to plot profiles that estimate their potential abilities in a range of occupational domains, such as sales, management, manual labor, science, and music or art. For instance, adolescents who rate themselves as energetic, organized, good debaters, and leaders would receive a very high rating in terms of sales ability.

TABLE 10.7   *Personality Domains of the Self-Directed Search*

Domain	Sample Items
Realistic	"I can read blueprints."
	"Take a shop course."
Investigative	"I can use a microscope."
	"Work on a science project."
Artistic	"Attend plays."
	"I can make pottery."
Social	"I am a good judge of personality."
	"Go to parties."
Enterprising	"I am a good debater."
	"Give talks."
Conventional	"Take business course."
	"I can post credits and debits."

Note: For each item, respondent indicates their *competence or interest* in the issue.
Source: Adapted from Holland, 1985.

It is interesting that adults often "match" their interests and personality traits with their eventual occupational choices. However, what use might this scale have for adolescents? Beyond the concern that adolescents may apply the results too literally to themselves, young people often change in their perceived competencies and interests. In one longitudinal study, only about 20 percent of adolescents showed consistency in the way they viewed their personality and vocational profiles. Indeed, when considering the six personality and vocational dimensions listed in Table 10.7, about 60 percent of adolescents displayed the complete *opposite* profile in at least one of the six dimensions over the course of adolescence (Helwig, 2003)!

In summary, researchers who study adolescent occupational achievement assess occupational exploration, interests, expectancies, and the fit between personality characteristics and career paths. It is not uncommon for vocational counselors to use these instruments; however, most experts use them more as screening tools than as a method for making definitive judgments about adolescent achievement. Because adolescents engage in active occupational exploration during this developmental period, it would seem that data from these instruments can more profitably be used to gently push, rather than shove, adolescents in the direction of careers for which they appear to be well equipped.

Achievement: A Summary

In this section, we discussed methods of assessing achievement. Whereas delineating links between educational and occupational achievement represents a meaningful direction, more work is needed to identify contextual variables, such as family, peer, school, and cultural factors that predict achievement, and to explain why good educational choices do not always translate in, to career development. For example, educational attainment almost always correlates positively with later occupational success to some degree, but this is *most* true of European-American males (Vondracek & Porfeli, 2003).

Sexuality

This section briefly covers some pressing issues that face sexuality researchers who work with adolescents, such as how to locate an appropriate research context and what forms of sexual activity are most frequently assessed. In addition, because sexual attitudes and behavior in this society are often viewed as extremely personal issues, you will learn how researchers have developed methodological strategies to coax the most honest data from their participants.

Locating Research Contexts and Samples

Unlike the other Western countries, people in the U.S. more often view adolescent sexuality in our society as a problem rather than as a normal developmental milestone (Crockett, Raffaelli, & Moilanen, 2003). To state the obvious from the onset, *it is very difficult, if not sometimes impossible, to conduct research on adolescent sexuality in schools.* Consider the educational experiences about this subject that you may have received in school. Any school with a limited sex-education curriculum will not be receptive to sexuality research. You might be thinking that school districts that grapple with high rates of unintended teen pregnancy or sexually transmitted infections would be the most receptive to this type of research. However, researchers have found that schools within these districts are often the toughest to access.

Of course, we must also cope with the local Institutional Review Board (IRB), and access parental permission when working with minors. The IRB will demand an intensive review process for sexuality research, and will want a thorough explanation of how the researcher will guarantee confidentiality and address potential emotional distress. For instance, a researcher interested in assessing sexual abuse would need to have a referral system in place. Although these issues routinely come up when conducting research pertaining to other adolescent psychosocial outcomes, the "war stories" of professionals who collect data on human sexuality are akin to the frustrations experienced by those who study adolescent pubertal development. Also, researchers who *do* obtain access to public schools must admit that they are not obtaining data on high school dropouts and students who are attending alternative schools, and, ironically, these populations are more likely to be sexually active than are those attending conventional schools (Crockett et al., 2003).

However, there are strategies we can use to obtain data pertaining to adolescent sexuality. First, data sets that contain large amounts of information on adolescent sexual behavior do exist; examples are the archives managed by the Centers for Disease Control (CDC, 2000) and the National Survey of Adolescent Health (Add Health; Blum et al., 2000). Researchers who wish to conduct independent data analysis that has not been conducted by the original investigators can access parts of these data sets with permission. However, adolescent sexual behavior and attitudes are fluid and fluctuate over time. When using archival data sets, we must determine when the data were collected; a ten-year-old data set can sometimes look very dated, and may no longer be useful.

Another tactic for new researchers is use college students as a target population. Although this group represents a select sample, the sexual knowledge, attitudes, and behavior of college students represent important topics in their own right. Indeed, some federal grant programs specifically target niche research areas, such as sexual coercion.

Although you might expect college students to employ safe sexual practices and be generally well educated about sexuality, this is not often the case. I once had a very academically talented student tell me that a certain soft drink could substantially lower sperm counts and therefore could be used as a contraceptive!

Trained health-care professionals often obtain valuable data during routine pediatric checkups. Although adolescents might fabricate such data, particularly regarding sexual activity, these professionals are well versed in how to obtain sensitive information. Thus, in terms of obtaining data on adolescent health, pubertal development, and sexuality, medical settings may represent a more viable research context than the schools.

On a positive note, adolescent and adult attitudes regarding sexuality are firmly entrenched within a changing society. Although teen pregnancy and childbearing have declined in recent years, the United States has a higher teen-pregnancy rate than any other modern, industrialized country (Zabin & Hayward, 1993). Also, sexually transmitted infections, and possible mutation of the human immunodeficiency virus (HIV) into a more easily transmittable infection concern many social scientists, educators, health-care professionals, and parents. Researchers in our field hope that these concerns may spur more federal and state pressure to allow comprehensive sexuality research in schools (Herold & Marshall, 1996).

What to Assess?

Many adolescent sexuality experts focus on some measure of sexual activity as focal data, most often collected using survey methods. Although there are many types of sexual activity that could be accessed—masturbation, mutual petting, anal intercourse, sexual coercion, and oral sex—the benchmark statistic regarding adolescent sexual behavior is an assessment of vaginal intercourse. Some researchers only assess this form of sexual behavior, partly because heterosexual adolescents view intercourse as personally and interpersonally more significant than other sexual behaviors, such as oral sex (Katchadourian, 1990). Many studies have documented the antecedents (e.g., parent-adolescent communication, family stress, age, pubertal timing) and consequences (e.g., mental health, self-esteem) of this sexual milestone (Crockett et al., 2003; Katchadourian, 1990).

How do we measure adolescent sexual behaviors? Perhaps the first step is to ensure that the items that tap these behaviors are easily understood by the adolescents and that *any one item reflects only one behavior.* For instance, some adolescents define "hooking up" as engaging in a simple conversation with a potential romantic interest, whereas others equate the term with intercourse. Based on this concern, some researchers have gone to great lengths to conduct pilot work on sexuality interviews or questionnaires to ensure that the items are easily understandable to adolescents and do not contain dual meanings (Jaccard, Dittus, & Gordon, 1998).

Another step regarding instrument development pertains to assessing the occurrence and frequency of sexual behavior. Occurrence pertains to whether the adolescent has *ever* engaged in the behavior, whereas frequency pertains to *how often.* Occurrence can be assessed using a simple "yes" or "no" item-response format, and frequency can be tapped by asking participants to estimate the amount of activity within a designated time period (Jacobson & Crockett, 2000; Jaccard, Dittus, & Gordon, 1998; Rowe et al., 1989) or rate items using alternative scale anchors (e.g., once, rarely, often) (Buzwell & Rosenthal,

1996). Most assessments are obtained using questionnaires, although such data has also been collected using interview techniques (Capaldi, Crosby, & Stoolmiller, 1996). Adolescent responses on such measures are consistent over time (Rowe et al., 1989), and female adolescents who report high rates of activity are more likely to experience later unintended pregnancies (Jaccard et al., 1998). To increase honest responses, Jaccard and colleagues (1998) recommend the following steps:

1. Be very candid about how responses will be kept confidential.
2. When using interviews, allow the adolescent the opportunity to record their responses on a separate sheet of paper, so that they do not have to verbally reveal their answers.
3. Stress the importance of honest responses and the need to maintain scientific integrity.
4. Ask the more sensitive questions at the end of the survey or interview.
5. Administer a social-desirability measure in conjunction with the sexuality instruments. Individuals who are more prone to giving socially desirable responses could be eliminated from data analyses (Rowe et al., 1989).

Sexual *behavior* is just one facet of adolescent sexuality; there are measures that assess sexual orientation, sexual self-esteem, and adolescent attitudes regarding sexuality (see Buzwell & Rosenthal, 1996 for relatively brief, yet reliable and valid measures for assessing each of these constructs). Many social scientists believe that an accurate assessment of adolescent beliefs and attitudes regarding sexuality is paramount to understanding the development of sexual activity. Indeed, unintended pregnancies, sexual coercion, and contraception misuse (or nonuse) often result from problematic thinking regarding sexuality, such as, "You can't get a sexually transmitted infection the first time you have sex," or "Girls who wear skimpy clothing are just asking for it." Also, because gender and ethnic differences regarding sexual attitudes, beliefs, and behavior are often apparent (Feldman, Turner, & Araujo, 1999), an assessment of these demographic variables would be necessary in any study involving adolescent sexuality.

Some Remaining Methodological and Theoretical Issues

Researchers who are careful about these matters often publish highly consistent findings; for example, almost 90 percent of adolescents who report they have had sexual intercourse in middle school indicate that they engaged in such behavior during this time period when asked about it later in high school (Alexander et al., 1994). Here are some other issues to consider when conducting research on adolescent sexuality:

1. *Sampling.* Although access to large school districts or health-care settings may seem like the ultimate research context, the results obtained from such samples may not generalize to the entire adolescent population. For example, the ethnic and socio-economic makeup of schools and school districts can widely vary, and not all adolescents get routine medical checkups.

2. *Antecedents versus consequences.* Many who study adolescent sexuality desire to document biological and contextual variables that may explain or predict the debut or frequency of adolescent sexual behaviors. However, the use of cross-sectional developmental designs clouds the potential antecedents (predictors) and consequences (or outcomes) of adolescent sexual behavior. Thus, more longitudinal research is needed on this subject (Herold & Marshall, 1996).

3. *Partner versus casual acquaintance.* I once heard a sexuality researcher comment, "It's not what teens are doing, it's whom they are doing it with." Tabulating the occurrence or frequency of sexual activity among adolescents, without some knowledge about their sexual partners, can paint an incomplete picture of the behavior. Adolescents engage in different sexual behaviors and use different strategies for protection when engaged in sexual activity with romantic partners than they use with casual partners. Buzwell and Rosenthal (1996) have created a measure that accurately taps the frequency of sexual behavior and risk taking with both regular and casual partners.

4. *What is "sexually active?"* The term *sexually active* is used loosely. Some dichotomize adolescents as "active" or "not active" based on reports of intercourse occurrence. Adolescents who indicate that they have had intercourse are often lumped into the former group, whereas everyone else is pooled into the latter category. This popular approach has been heavily criticized. Herold and Marshall (1996) indicate that adolescents who are "sexually active" (meaning intercourse) often show very sporadic behavior over time, marked by periods of nonactivity. Because of this finding, more contemporary research on this topic typically includes measures of occurrence and frequency over a designated time period.

Assessing Sexuality: Some Concluding Thoughts

What Do You Think?

Suppose you want to poll adolescents on their sexual behavior, but your colleagues tell you that the data will be meaningless, because adolescents lie about their activity. You want to prove your colleagues wrong on this issue. In order to get the "best" data on this subject, what strategies would you use to encourage honest responses? Can you think of any strategies you could use to ensure that your data are reliable and valid?

Collecting data on this topic can be both rewarding and frustrating. We can empathize with the intervention specialist who develops a comprehensive sex-education program that significantly reduces risky sexual behavior and unintended pregnancies in adolescents, only to see their funding cut because the research is viewed as "too controversial." Unlike research involving the other psychosocial outcomes, such as autonomy and identity, sexuality research is considered sensitive at all political levels (Herold & Marshall, 1996).

Chapter Summary

Go back and look at Figure 9.1 again. In this theoretical framework, fundamental biological, cognitive, and social changes partly account for the development of the five psychosocial outcomes outlined in this chapter. However, this perspective also assumes that major contexts for adolescent development, such as the family, peer group, and schools, moderate associations between these basic changes and the developmental outcomes. It is easy to lose sight of this idea after reading this chapter, because my major objective was to expose you to methods for assessing each developmental milestone. Again, Figure 9.1 includes a beautiful framework to help you select variables that predict these psychosocial outcomes, which can greatly enhance your ultimate research design.

Although I presented identity, achievement, autonomy, intimacy, and sexuality as separate psychosocial outcomes, there is dependency regarding these constructs. For example, it may be impossible to achieve a healthy sense of identity without the development of autonomy. Based on these ideas, I encourage student researchers to consider assessing multiple psychosocial outcomes in cases that are theoretically justifiable.

Research Navigator™ Exercise: Adolescents and Sex

The objective is to learn more about how researchers study adolescent sexual behavior. Go the Research Navigator™ website: http://www.researchnavigator.com; choose the Psychology database, and type *adolescents* and *sexual behavior* as keywords using the Advanced Search option (p. 60). After reading a full-length article, answer the following questions.

1. How were the adolescents recruited for the study?
2. How was sexual behavior measured?
3. What were the primary findings, conclusions, and limitations of the study?

11

Methodological Issues in Adult Development Research I: Biological and Cognitive Changes

"How many questions are on this thing? Is this a test? You know, I'm not stupid." This was the response I, a 20-something graduate student, received when working with my first adult research participant. My first thought was "Wow, this is harder than working with children!"

In this chapter, you will learn that there are some methodological wrinkles (no pun intended) that face adult-development researchers that are less pressing for experts who work with younger populations. You will also come to understand research issues that confront experts who study biological and intellectual processes in adults. You will learn that methodological advancements have led to new thinking about the aging process. For example, some abilities do not decline, and some competencies may actually *develop* during later life. After reading this chapter, you should be able to:

- Describe central methodological issues that face experts who work with adults.
- Indicate how to best study the effects of normal, biological aging on functioning.
- Describe the various methodological approaches to studying disease, health, and health risk.
- Indicate the methodological challenges that face stress and coping researchers.
- Illustrate how the use of sophisticated developmental designs and research paradigms has increased our knowledge about the effects of age on intellectual performance and information-processing abilities.
- Describe how to assess postformal thought, wisdom, and creativity in adults.

Methodological Issues Facing Adult Developmentalists

Some unique methodological issues face adult-development experts. For example, infant specialists may work with babies who were born only a few months apart, whereas adult development experts often work with participants who were born many years apart and experienced very different educational and historical experiences. Let's now consider some of the thorny methodological concerns that face researchers who work with adults.

What Influences Development?

Chapter 1 made distinctions between *normative age-graded*, *normative history-graded*, and *nonnormative influences* on development. Normative age-graded influences are events that happen to most people, usually around the same age, such as graduation, menopause, or having a child, that cause developmental change. Experts who study normative influences are interested in delineating how age and maturity provoke biological, cognitive, and social change. At study culmination, we would like to say, "With age or maturity, we slowly begin to lose our respiratory capacity or we begin to take fewer risks in life."

You have already learned that the popular *cross-sectional developmental design* (see Chapter 1) presents special difficulties for those who study adults. In this design, different-aged people are assessed at the same time. Although quick and inexpensive, the problem with this design is the confounding of age and history. Adults in different age groups have different educational and historical experiences, or *cohort differences*. For example, older people may engage in less sexual activity than younger ones, because they grew up during a time era when sexuality was a closed subject. These individuals may have always engaged in low rates of activity; such behavior has more to do with history-graded influences than with age-normative influence.

A major methodological advancement has been a movement away from cross-sectional methods in favor of short-term longitudinal and sequential designs (Schaie, 2002). Recall that sequential designs often incorporate both cross-sectional and longitudinal components, and thus allow the researcher to discern the effects of both age and historical changes. The results of more recent research using these designs have revolutionized the field of adult development. Unlike research findings involving cross-sectional designs, newer work using longitudinal and sequential methods reveals that declines in behavioral, cognitive, and health functioning involves a very slow, gradual process (Hertzog, 1996; Schaie, 2002; Schaie & Hofer, 2001).

So, are you ready to conduct a six-year sequential study for your thesis? Less-time-consuming, cross-sectional designs involving adults do have a place. However, this particular design presents more problems when we contrast adults who differ significantly in terms of age. A researcher who conducts a study on young adults who are either engaged, newly married, or married for two years or less would probably not need to worry about potential historical confounds.

Also, longitudinal and sequential designs are not immune to problems. Chapter 1 addressed potential methodological problems with these designs, such as the effects of testing and attrition, or non-random dropout. Also, the results of longitudinal designs can be misleading if the researcher limits data collection to two points in time. Studies involving only two times of measurement provide only a narrow picture of development or decline, and a strong correlation between time 1 and time 2 assessments does not preclude the possibility that some form of change took place between the two measurement points (Collins, 1996).

Finally, it is unfortunate that those who use more sophisticated developmental designs often ignore the presence of *nonnormative influences*, such as a rare illness or winning a lottery, that affect the minority, yet dramatically influence developmental change. Polling participants on potential life-altering events can identify the presence of these influences. It is possible that their effects may interact with age in predicting development; that is, younger and older individuals might be affected differently by nonnormative influences.

In summary, the increased use of longitudinal and sequential designs has dramatically affected the way we think about the aging process. Although these designs are not without their problems, they can influence our confidence in how aging and historical forces influence developmental change. I might add that the statistical methods for analyzing such change are quite complicated; students interested in some advanced reading on this topic should consult a number of excellent sources (Little, Schnabel, & Baument, 2000; Nesselroade & Molenaar, 2003).

Sampling

Two potentially problematic methodological issues emerge in developmental research conducted with adults. First, older and younger adult samples are often not drawn from the community; rather, they are recruited from contexts that allow researchers convenient access to participants, such as colleges, health clinics, and adult organizations. Second, the contexts that participants are sampled from vary by age group. That is, young adults are most frequently accessed in collegiate settings, whereas older participants are sampled from community organizations, health practices, or through word of mouth. Thus, the sampling environments are different, and older adults are accessed through more varied means than are younger people (Salthouse, 2000).

Indeed, even sophisticated sampling techniques can raise methodological concerns when working with different-aged adults. For instance, let's say we sampled adults 20–80 years of age from the community. How could we ensure that the different age groups are comparable on major demographic variables yet are also representative of the community? Our age groups may be comparable regarding education, ethnicity, and income level, yet in achieving this quest, one particular cohort may not be representative of people in the community at large.

Salthouse (2000) offers some suggestions on how to address such sampling concerns.

- Researchers should assess a full gamut of demographic variables, such as income level, education, ethnicity, and gender. Also, brief intelligence tests should be administered to tap verbal and nonverbal intelligence. Although this sounds like a daunting task, one could administer a brief subtest, such as a short vocabulary subtest, to measure intelligence.
- They should conduct statistical analyses to determine whether the age groups differ on the demographic and health measures. The demographic information for the

different age groups could also be compared to the demographics for each age
group in the community.

- They could compare the age groups on the ability test, and contrast the test scores
for each age group with national norms.

All of these strategies can be used to bolster the researchers' claims that they have recruited
a sample that is somewhat similar to the community, and that the participants in the different age groups are comparable on variables other than age alone.

Maximizing Data Quality

Working with adults can be challenging because, unlike research involving children and
adolescents, the participants are frequently older than the researchers! Also, although
many of us are comfortable with computer technology, Op-scan forms, and a general "testing environment," this is not generally true of older adults. Participants who are anxious
about these issues or are worried about appearing incompetent may provide data that does
not reflect their true ability. Carp (1989) offered some recommendations for researchers
who work with adults, with the notion that some of these tips could be used with almost
any developmental population (e.g., adolescents):

***Watch Vocabulary Level and Reading Comprehension of Interviews and Question-
naires.***   Older participants are often less educated than their younger counterparts and
may be prone to difficulties with understanding certain words or directions. When possible, format items and directions in easy-to-understand language.

Watch Instrument Format.   Older individuals are less familiar with structured, multiple-
choice questions than younger adults, yet are also more likely to complain about surveys or
interviews that require simple yes–no or true–false responses. Rather than abandon a more
complex response format, Carp (1989) recommends that the experimenter occasionally clarify the requirements of the task and encourage the respondent to answer as best they can.

Perceived Threat Produces "I Don't Know" or "Rosy Response."   Although a person may really not know an answer to the question, older folks often provide ambiguous
or noncommittal responses when threatened. Indeed, confusion over items, directions, or
response formats would all be candidates for such responses. Also, questionnaire or interview items that are perceived as threatening, such as queries regarding income level, sexual impotence, or intellectual abilities, could result in noncommittal answers or so-called
"*rosy responses.*" That is, it has been shown that older participants are more likely than
younger people to provide positive responses, such as "Everything is OK," even if they are
currently experiencing adverse conditions (Carp, 1989).

How do researchers cope with this problem? Although it is possible to alter task items,
one must be careful in changing the format or item structure of measures that contain standardized protocols. In such cases, we must consider whether such alterations would seriously compromise the integrity of the test. For example, one popular mental-status exam
contains items requiring the subject to identify certain items, such as a pen and a watch.

Older participants frequently become upset when asked to complete this task, because they feel they are being treated like children. To address this issue, I have altered somewhat the nature of the task, and present the items as a vision test. Thus, rather than asking, "Do you know what this is?," when holding up a watch, I will query, "I need to test your vision for a second: Can you see this? What is it?" It is doubtful that such a subtle change in directions would affect the accuracy of the response, but the alteration preserves the integrity of the participant.

Of course, sometimes we must ask questions that unavoidably threaten the participant. In such cases, it is wise to ask such questions at the end of the survey or interview. Carp (1989) indicates that older adults are particularly prone to "rosy responding" when asked *general* questions, such as "How would you describe your living conditions?" yet are more direct when asked more *specific* question, such as, "How satisfied are you with the temperature in your apartment or house?" With older adults, general questions tend to lead to general responses!

Perception and Fatigue.   Older adults can also be prone to perceptual difficulties. Thus, we must ensure that survey items are readable and that subjects can comprehend verbal queries and directions. Also, although some older adults have good stamina, individuals older than 75 are most susceptible to fatigue, particularly in cases in which the procedures run more than an hour (Gibson & Aitkenhead, 1983). This suggests we should keep our procedures reasonably short, consider multiple sessions, and vary task difficulty over the course of the study. In addition, there may be cases in which the researcher desires to screen or control for perceptual difficulties in participants, particularly when making age comparisons regarding mental abilities (Schaie, 1994a).

The Research Assistants.   Research assistants are often younger than the participants when conducting such research. Although people connect better with researchers and therapists who share common characteristics (e.g., age, gender, ethnicity), it is not always possible to have research assistants that demographically match up with our participants. In such cases, it is possible to "legitimize" the research assistant with advanced introductions (Carp, 1989). For instance, when conducting research with middle-aged adults, the person who initially schedules a study session (by phone) should be an adult who is similar in age to the participant. When discussing the study procedures, this contact person could provide the name of the research assistant, explain her role in the study, and stress the importance of providing honest responses to the assistant. Carp (1989) noted that in one study, this particular strategy worked very well, in the sense that there was no subject attrition, rapport was established between the young research assistants and participants, and there was very little resistance during data collection.

Summary

The use of sophisticated developmental designs, representative sampling methods, and better knowledge about how to work with older research participants has resulted in some excellent empirical work in recent years. This research clearly demonstrates that many adults "age" gracefully, and there is even room for development in adulthood! Although this research has advanced the knowledge of professionals who work with adults, it is also important to emphasize that this information is often disseminated to the public at large.

Assessing Biological and Health Ramifications of Aging

We will discuss different, yet related, research areas in this section. Some experts specify how basic, fundamental aging processes lead to normal, age-related organ- and perceptual-system changes. These researchers typically recruit *healthy adults* who lead rather risk-free lifestyles, and view external contributions to aging, such as smoking, as something that should be controlled for. Some researchers also identify how primary aging and secondary variables, such as smoking, affect *adverse health outcomes* in adults. In this section, we will delineate methods researchers use to determine adult health.

Associations between risky lifestyle choices, aging, and health are not direct; rather, we theorize that these variables are mediated by psychological and cognitive functioning (Schaie, 2002). Although it may seem like a stretch to claim that a poor attitude might mediate associations between heavy smoking and lung cancer, it is true that a state of mind might explain associations between certain risk factors and physical and mental health. Therefore, this section will discuss how researchers have created methods of studying the connections between stress and health.

The Biology of Aging: Methodological Considerations

The biology of aging refers to the genetic and biological processes that affect the development and decline of major organ systems, such as the cardiovascular system, and perceptual systems, such as vision and hearing. A major question is how much organ system decline results from "pure aging," rather than from secondary factors, such as exercise or diet. This field is complex, because methodological concerns facing researchers interested in aging and the nervous system are not always the same as those that face the perception experts. Let's now examine some common methodological issues that face researchers in this field.

Recruitment of Healthy Adults.   One primary method of ascertaining the effects of primary aging on various organ systems is to limit a research sample to well-functioning, healthy adults. When recruiting a sample, the researcher limits participation to adults who are disease free and lead lifestyles relatively free of risk. Thus, the researcher interested in the effects of aging on the nervous system would exclude participants who were smokers, clinically depressed, or exhibited signs of Alzheimer's disease. During recruitment, the researcher may carefully interview potential participants regarding health and lifestyle, ask them to complete a health inventory, and administer a short cognitive screening inventory, such as the *Mini-Mental Status Exam* (MMSE; Folstein, Folstein, & McHugh, 1975). The MMSE is a short, norm-referenced memory and orientation measure that includes cut-off scores for probable dementias, such as Alzheimer's disease. This instrument requires participants to answer simple orientation queries ("What day is it?") and perform simple tasks, such as folding a piece of paper in half and handing it to the experimenter. Potential participants who score below the cut-off—designed to identify those with possible Alzheimer's—are excluded from the study.

"Matching Up" Healthy Older and Younger Participants. If one is conducting a cross-sectional study on the functioning of older and younger adults, we must do more than just ensure that the adults are all disease free and lead similar healthy lifestyles. It is important to equate the younger and older participants on social class, educational experiences, ethnicity, and so on.

Using Modern Science. Advances in medical technology have enhanced our understanding of normal, biological aging; researchers who study the effects of aging on different organ systems often have specific instruments for detecting age-related changes. For example, when making inferences about the effects of aging on the brain, researchers must possess the technology to study how both brain structure and functioning may change with age.

The development of noninvasive imaging techniques has revolutionized the way we think about age-related changes in various organ systems (Albert & Killiany, 2001). For example, standard X rays of the brain can only detect gross changes in the structure of the brain. However, more modern medical technology, such as Computerized Axial Tomography (CAT Scan) and Magnetic Resonance Imaging (MRI Scan), provide highly detailed images of cross sections of the brain. These technologies allow researchers to ascertain age-related changes in various brain structures, such as the frontal-lobe region, which have been implicated in memory functioning. In addition, devices such as Positron-Emission Tomography (PET scan) provide highly detailed accounts of *brain activity*. Using it, researchers can ask participants to memorize a list of words, and document varying amounts of activity in various regions of their brains.

Behavioral Genetics. To disentangle genetic and environmental influences on the aging process, experts have studied aging in identical, monozygotic twins reared together and apart, the latter sets having had different environmental experiences. Through controlled research one can conduct **heritability estimates**, or the relative impact of genetics, environment, or a combination of the two, on the aging process. This strategy represents one of the few methods that actually allow us to examine the respective effects of biology and environment on aging.

It may be impossible to accurately determine the effects of environmental events, such as family stress, on the aging process without some genetic information about participants and their families. For example, although one could assume that family stress is a straightforward "environmental variable," it is also possible that family dynamics, interactions, and relationships are governed by genetic influences (Finkel & Pedersen, 2001). Thus, you can see why comparative studies of monozygotic twins, dizygotic twins, and ordinary siblings provide naturalistic experiments on the aging process and how genetic and environmental variables contribute to it.

Alternative Measures of Biological Aging. When assessing anatomical or functional changes in the major organ systems, one must possess the technology to assess neuronal loss in the brain, arterial narrowing of the circulatory system, or lung-cell deterioration *and* also have a professional on staff—usually a physician—to evaluate these data. Does this sound like an accessible area for student research? For the newcomer, there are general biobehavioral markers of aging, such as blood pressure, that can be used to infer how aging

TABLE 11.1 *Biobehavioral Markers of Aging*

Biobehavioral Measure	Description
Forced expiratory volume	Assesses respiratory functioning by having participant, with nasal passages blocked, expel as much air as possible into a spirometer, which assesses total respiratory volume.
Mean arterial pressure	Assesses, arterial functioning using both systolic and diastolic blood-pressure data. These data are used together to calculate mean arterial pressure using a simple formula.
Grip strength	Assesses grip strength using a dynamometer, which requires participants to squeeze a handle as hard as they can. Highest grip strength out of six attempts constitutes their scores.
Motor functioning	Assesses motor functioning using a series of simple tasks created by Finkel et al. (2000); participants are asked to perform a series of activities, such as screwing in a lightbulb, pouring water from one glass to another, and touching right toes with left hand.
General "well-being"	Assesses well-being as defined by the participant via a 3-item general health scale, life-satisfaction measure, and self-rating of personality and mental health functioning.

Adapted from Finkel et al., 2003.

affects our overall physical functioning (Finkel et al., 2003). A listing of these markers, which are often assessed concurrently, is given in Table 11.1. As you can see, these data provide a snapshot of an individual's overall aging progress and represent assessments that are easy to conduct.

What Do You Think?

Researchers A and B are debating the influence of genetics and lifestyle choices on biological aging. Researcher A argues that aging is "all genetics," whereas Research B claims that aging results from a combination of genetics and risky lifestyle choices, such as smoking. You step in and claim that you can design a study that can address this issue. How would you design this study?

In sum, experts who study the effects of aging on the human body recruit adults who are free of disease and lead healthy lifestyles. Because many age-related changes are internal, advances in medical technology have enhanced our knowledge regarding normal biological aging. Twin studies have increased our knowledge of the role of genetics and heredity in the aging process. Although some study the effects of aging in specific organ or perceptual systems, we also have ways to assess the aging process using simpler biobehavioral measures.

Health, Disease, and Health Risk

When studying health and disease issues, we adopt a different methodological approach than when we chart the "normal" course of biological aging. Recall that the latter expert screens out adults with significant health problems, as well as individuals that exhibit health risks, such as smokers. In contrast, professionals who study health and disease processes in adults are looking for variability in the health functioning and lifestyles of their participants.

Researchers who study health and disease face a number of methodological issues. First, they must define what they mean by "healthy" or "not healthy" and identify mechanisms for measuring the concept. Also, although theorists in the field acknowledge that genetic factors might be partly responsible for the development of certain physical (e.g., cancer) and mental (e.g., depression) disorders, they are nevertheless engaged in a never-ending race to identify the *health-risk behaviors* that might affect the onset and course of a particular disease.

Disease and Health.   Those who study disease processes often rely on physician diagnoses to determine whether a person is affected by diseases such as breast cancer, cardiovascular disease, or osteoporosis. However, such reports may not provide a complete accounting of a disease's course or severity, and we have methods identifying such progression.

For example, there are different stages of Alzheimer's disease, each of which has predictable levels of cognitive, physical, and daily functioning. Alzheimer's disease is a progressive degenerative disorder that causes extensive brain damage, striking memory problems, and eventual death. Researchers who work with adults with Alzheimer's disease may find "dementia, probable Alzheimer's type" in the medical record, yet may not have any data to estimate disease progression. To better define progression, neuropsychological inventories have been developed, including the *Global Deterioration Scale* (GDS; Reisberg et al., 1982). As you can see in Table 11.2, there are 7 GDS stages, ranging from

TABLE 11.2   *Global Deterioration Scale*

Stage	Description/Characteristics
1 No cognitive decline	No memory deficits, well-oriented, no difficulties in daily functioning (e.g., finances, bathing, dressing).
2 Very mild cognitive decline (age-associated)	Subjective complaints of memory problems, such as occasionally forgetting names or place of objects. No evidence of disruptions regarding daily functioning.
3 Mild cognitive decline	Objective evidence of memory problems based on clinical interview. Declines occasionally interfere with daily living; for example, may have difficulty traveling to new locations or forgets major passage of newspaper article. Decreased performance in demanding environments (e.g., work).
4 Moderate cognitive decline (mild dementia)	Decreased knowledge of recent events. Increased difficulty with daily functioning, such as finances or planning dinner party. Decreased knowledge of some past events, such as personal history.
5 Moderately severe cognitive decline (moderate dementia)	Little knowledge of recent events and major decreased knowledge regarding personal history (e.g., birth date). May have major difficulty with some forms of daily functioning (e.g., choosing clothing, finances).
6 Severe cognitive decline (moderately severe dementia)	Requires assistance in most daily activities, such as dressing, toileting and bathing. Largely unaware of any recent events, sketchy memory of personal history; for example, may not know names of spouse or children.
7 Very severe cognitive decline (severe dementia)	All verbal abilities lost. Motor skills severely diminished. Needs complete assistance with all aspects of daily functioning.

Adapted from Reisberg et al., 1982.

1 (No cognitive decline) to 7 (Very severe cognitive decline). Using a brief interview, one can evaluate the individual's memory, orientation, and daily functioning, and then assign the person a stage score. Thus, we could form early-middle (stages 4 and 5) and later-stage (stages 6 and 7) groups using this information. The methods used to assess disease progression are not unique to Alzheimer's disease; that is, there are also ways to assess the progression of cardiovascular disease and different forms of cancer.

Of course, *disease* and *health* are distinct concepts. Although disease progression is determined via medical technology and standardized tests, the participant often determines health. There are different methods for assessing health; measures are defined as either *self-rated health* or *health-related quality-of-life assessments* (Siegler, Bosworth, & Poon, 2003). **Self-rated health** is very easy to assess; for example, we can ask people to rate their health on a simple rating scale, such as 1 = Excellent, 2 = Very Good, and so on. These ratings are valid, because people with chronic diseases report their health as poorer than disease-free adults, individuals with more serious diseases rate their health as poorer than their counterparts with less serious maladies, people over 65 are more likely to view their health as less good than younger people, and self-ratings of general health are correlated with physician ratings (Siegler, Bosworth, & Poon, 2003).

Simple self-rated health measures do not inform us about the adult's physical or mental problems. Thus more detailed measures of health have been developed that assess **health-related quality of life**. Such an assessment is more comprehensive than single-item measures of self-rated health, and can tap the psychological, mental, and social aspects of health (Sherbourne et al., 2000; Siegler, Bosworth, & Poon, 2003). Like single-item health assessments, health-related quality-of-life measures can be used to study age-related trends in perceived health and to monitor the effects of different diseases and interventions on health perceptions.

Perhaps the best-validated measure of this type is the 36-item *Short-Form Health Survey* (SF-36; Ware, 1993). As shown in Table 11.3, the SF-36 measures perceptions of

TABLE 11.3   *Brief Description of the Short-Form Health Survey*

Dimension	Items	Meaning of Low Scores
Physical functioning	10	Limited in performing physical activities, such as dressing or bathing.
Role limits resulting from physical problems	4	Difficulties performing daily activities, such as work, because of physical health.
Social functioning	2	Major interference with social activities because of physical or emotional problems.
Bodily pain	2	Serious and debilitating pain.
General mental health	5	Feelings of frequent anxiety or depression.
Role limits because of emotional problems	3	Emotional problems severely interfere with daily activities such as work.
Vitality	4	Frequent feelings of fatigue.
General health perceptions	5	Perceives health to be poor and likely to get worse over time.

Adapted from Ware & Sherbourne, 1992.

health functioning, ranging from physical functioning (e.g., walking) and bodily pain to mental health. This method has good *discriminate validity*; that is, it clearly discriminates different groups of people on variables of theoretical importance. For instance, individuals with major medical problems, such as severe cardiovascular disease, often perceive their general physical functioning as poorer and more socially debilitating than adults with more minor ailments. Similarly, adults with diagnosed, clinical depression rate their mental health and its social consequences as more problematic than individuals who have experienced occasional problems with depressive symptoms (i.e., occasionally sad) (McHorney, Ware, & Raczek, 1993). The developers of this scale have recently crafted an even shorter, 12-item version of this instrument (Ware, 1999).

In sum, self-ratings of health have great utility in research and practice settings. The reliability and validity work on such measures is quite impressive, yet there are problems to consider. Although self-ratings of health are often correlated with physician ratings of disease, these ratings should not be used to diagnosis disease. That is, not everyone who rates their health as poor has a diagnosable disorder, and some adults who rate their health as excellent have terminal diseases! On the other hand, incongruence between self-ratings of health and physician ratings of health and disease would be an interesting research area to explore in itself.

Health Risk. There have been innumerable *risk factors* associated with developmental, physical, or mental health problems in infants, children, adolescents, and adults. Researchers who study relationships between environmental, psychosocial risk factors and health and development indicate that it is often impossible to offer firm conclusions regarding the causal role of, say, heavy smoking, on the development of lung cancer. Put simply, because of ethical and legal ramifications, one cannot randomly assign adults to different risk categories, leaving us with only nonexperimental methods for studying associations between risk, health, and development.

The simplest way to study the relationship between health risks and the development of disease processes is to poll adults on the occurrence or frequency of health-risk behaviors and healthy lifestyle choices. It is important to make these assessments *before* a person has developed a disease; a chronic disease may influence the way people choose to lead their lives. There are many surveys we can use to assess the presence of health risk and promotion variables. Some sample items from one such self-report measure are given in Table 11.4.

There are methodological concerns with this research. Beyond the lack of experimental control and concerns regarding memory and honesty, it is often difficult to isolate the effects of a single risk factor, such as smoking, on health outcomes because people often exhibit **risk comorbidity**. That is, a heavy alcohol consumer may also be a heavy smoker, be overweight, and possess an extremely stressful job. Another consideration is that the relationship between health risk and disease is often dependent on the individual. A person's age, weight, and organ-system resiliency can affect such associations. Adults are built differently and may react differently to certain lifestyle choices. These differences could explain why two heavy smokers of the same age and gender may have different health outcomes.

TABLE 11.4   *Sample Items from a Health-Risk or Promotion Assessment*

Risk or Promotion Dimension	Sample Items
Weight/Nutrition	What is your weight?
	Has there been a significant change in your weight (i.e., 10 or more lbs. in either direction) over the past year? (yes or no)
	Do you limit foods high in sodium, such as luncheon meats, bacon, canned foods, and potato chips? (usually/sometimes/rarely/never)
Fitness	Do you participate in a regular exercise program, such as walking, calisthenics, swimming, or biking at least three times a week, for 20 minutes or more each time? (yes/no)
Stress	Do you feel anxious or tense? (every day almost every day/sometimes/rarely/never)
	Are you widowed less than 1 year, more than 1 year, or never widowed?
Habits/Medications	Do you currently smoke? (yes/no)
	Do you drink alcohol? (yes/no)
	If you do drink alcohol, have you ever felt the need to cut down on your drinking? (yes/no)
General health	How would you rate your own overall health at the present time? (poor/fair/good/excellent)

Adapted from Haber, 2003.

However, there is nothing wrong with promoting health! It is perfectly acceptable to conduct controlled interventions to examine the effects of diet, exercise, or psychological stress reduction on health and development. Although there are assumed benefits to healthy behaviors, such as exercise, and the reduction of health risks, such as smoking, few controlled experiments have confirmed these ideas (Leventhal, Rabin, Leventhal, & Burns, 2001).

Summary

Those who study the effects of normal aging on the body recruit different participants than those who study health and disease in adults. That is, the former researcher desires participants who are disease free, whereas the latter researcher wants their adults to display variability. Although much of this work is open to methodological concerns, our understanding of aging, health, and disease has made a significant impact both on the field and on the public at large, and has undoubtedly played a role in expanding the longevity of adults in our society.

What Do You Think?

Suppose you feel that there is one major variable that adversely affects health, and there is one variable that strongly promotes it. How would you design a study to support your ideas? Select two variables (one healthy, one unhealthy) for your design, and explain how you would develop a study with as many controls as possible. Consider also your criteria for sample selection.

Stress and Coping: Methodological Issues

This section will cover methodological, conceptual, and theoretical issues that face "stress and coping" researchers. It will discuss how to assess the stress and coping process, as well as overview ways to measure so-called stress outcomes.

Stress: Definitional and Methodological Issues

Stress is a process in which environmental demands tax or exceed a person's adaptive capacity, resulting in psychological and physical changes that place him at risk for injury, physical illness, or mental-health problems (Cohen, Kessler, & Gordon, 1997). Pioneering stress researchers assumed that the presence of demanding environmental circumstances almost automatically produced deleterious effects on the human mind and body (Holmes & Rahe, 1967; Selye, 1956). For example, adults who experience major life events, such as the death of a spouse, are at risk for significant health problems; thus, it is not surprising that it was originally believed that stressors automatically forecasted problems in adults, adolescents, and children.

Major Life Events.   Holmes and Rahe (1967) developed one of the first stress measures. When completing the 43-item *Social Readjustment Rating Scale* (SRRS) participants simply note whether certain major life events, such as job loss, divorce, or financial problems have occurred over a short period of time. Researchers then weight each event using a "life change unit" (LCU). For example, death of a spouse contains a LCU of 100, whereas the gain of a new family member is weighted at 39. This latter item shows that even *positive* major life events may have potential negative influences on adjustment. Consider people who claim that they almost terminated a romantic relationship over wedding plans! When selecting a major-life-events scale for research, one should preview the items to check item relevance; for example, the SRSS contains items such as, "Wife begins or starts work" and "Mortgage over $10,000." My, have times changed! Perhaps a less-dated instrument would be Sarason's 82-item *Life Events Questionnaire* (LEQ; Sarason, Johnson, & Siegel, 1978). You can overview some of the items from the LEQ in Table 11.5.

An added advantage to the LEQ is the inclusion of **cognitive-appraisal** items. Cognitive appraisals are personal perceptions or appraisals of the event. Thus, beyond indicating whether an event happened or not, subjects indicate whether the event was "good" or "bad" and whether it had a major impact on their life. This method has good validity, in that efforts that have included this measure have documented positive correlations between the frequency of major life events and psychological or physical health difficulties (Turner & Wheaton, 1997). Experimental research has indicated that more-stressed people who are randomly exposed to rhinovirus (i.e., common cold virus) develop more cold symptoms than their low-stressed counterparts (Cohen, Tyrell, & Smith, 1993).

There are numerous life-event checklists specifically designed for adults, children, and adolescents (see Turner & Wheaton, 1997, for an extensive review). For those who want a more in-depth picture of how life events are related to changes in health outcomes, we have a variety of interview schedules that allow participants to reflect on the relative impact of these events. For example, when completing the *Life Events and Difficulties Schedule* (Brown & Harris, 1978), the subject is asked to provide a "story" or background

TABLE 11.5 *Sample Items from the Life-Events Questionnaire*

Stress Dimension	Items	Sample Items
Health	9	Major change in sleep habits. Major change in eating habits.
Work	10	Being fired or laid off work. Retirement from work.
School	4	Change in career goal or academic major. Problem in school, college, or training program.
Residence	4	Difficulty finding housing. Moving to different town, city, state, or country.
Love and marriage	15	Divorce. Infidelity.
Family	8	Death of a child. Birth of a grandchild.
Parenting	5	Conflicts with spouse or partner about parenting. Changes in child-care arrangements.
Personal and social	13	Major personal achievement. Acquired or lost a pet.
Financial	5	Credit difficulties. Took on a major purchase or mortgage loan.
Crime and legal matters	6	Involvement in a lawsuit. Being robbed or victim of identity theft.
Other	3	Participant has opportunity to list three events not included on the LEQ.

Adapted from Sarason et al., 1978.

regarding the life event, appraise the significance or threat of the event, and describe the impact the event had on daily life. Thus, interview schedules provide more detail on the circumstances leading up to the event, appraisals as the event took place, and potential consequences of the event. Of course, when using interviews, we must use trained interviewers and code the large amounts of qualitative data generated via such methods. In this sense, checklist methods are quicker to administer and more cost effective.

Beyond the assessment of cumulative life events, some researchers study the impact of one-time major life events, such as natural disasters, criminal victimization, and the untimely loss of a young spouse or child (see Schwarzer & Schultz, 2003, for a review). Others specialize in studying the effects of *chronic stress*, such as ongoing poverty, marital conflict, or severe occupational stress. Thus, we have a variety of approaches to studying the influence of significant stress on developmental and psychological functioning.

Daily-Hassles Measures. In recent years, social scientists have attempted to specify how routine day-to-day issues relate to functioning. These **daily hassles** are more routine irritants, such as costly car repairs, final exams, or squabbles with friends. Experts agree that a buildup of hassles contributes to the development of psychological and physical health symptoms.

The most common way of assessing daily hassles is to ask study subjects to note the occurrence of various irritants. The most popular measure of this type is the *Daily Hassles Scale—Revised* (DHS-R; DeLongis, Folkman, & Lazarus, 1988), a 53-item inventory that includes a variety of hassles encountered by adults residing in a given community, including occupational, marital, and child-related difficulties. Research using this method has documented that hassle frequency is modestly tied to the occurrence of psychological and physical health symptoms (DeLongis, Folkman, & Lazarus Delongis et al., 1988). Although self-report measures are open to methodological criticisms, such as validity of recall, researchers have replicated these findings via other methods, such as intensive interview protocols (Bolger et al., 1989); thus, the DHS-R is both valid and economical.

Stress researchers have documented other interesting findings when using life-event and daily-hassles measures:

1. The presence of daily hassles is more predictive of health problems than is a history of stressful life events. However, most of this work consists of correlational studies that used only one assessment. It is possible that the presence of a major life event, such as loss of a parent, could provoke an eventual buildup of hassles because of missed time at work, and inattentiveness to daily details, such as forgetting to mail a bill that is due (Eckenrode & Bolger, 1997). We need more longitudinal work in this area, because, the association between major life events and health may be indirect in nature and mediated (or even caused) by a build-up of daily hassles.

2. People react in very different ways to stressful events; adults who worry a lot display more distress by daily hassles than their more easygoing counterparts. Thus, researchers have devoted much attention to how personality plays a role in stress appraisal and to how individuals cope with stressful events (Lazarus, 1991). We will revisit this issue in the next section.

3. The fact that individuals react to stressful events in different ways raises an important methodological issue, particularly in light of the fact that adults with depressive symptoms are more threatened by these events than are psychologically healthy adults (Carver, 2001). When connecting the presence of stressful events to health, it is sometimes difficult to discern the chicken and the egg. Do daily hassles predict the development of depressive symptoms, or do depressed people make a mess of their lives? This issue is exacerbated by the fact that some stress inventories include mental and physical health items, which could lead to a confounding of measures; it would be understandable that an assessment of stress and a measure of depression would be correlated if they contained similar items. Although the Daily Hassles Scale has been revised to address this problem (Holm & Holroyd, 1992), researchers should examine the items on both stress and stress-outcomes measures they are considering to check for possible item redundancy.

What Do You Think?

Reread the material presented in Box 11.1. The *Parenting Hassles Scale* (Crnic & Greenberg, 1990) contains items that pertain to the potential irritants created by young children, such as "Kids' schedules interfere with parent/household needs" or "Kids demand to be entertained or played with." However, suppose you want to create a hassles scale for parents of adolescents. How would you go about developing this scale; for example, how would you arrive at a decision regarding item content? How would you demonstrate the instrument's reliability and validity?

4. Some daily stress inventories may not be relevant to certain populations. Many measures have been developed for community-residing adults only, and would not be applicable to adolescents and children. Also, some people face issues that are not included on traditional hassle measures; for example, college students, caregivers of ill family members, and people in certain occupations face unique stressors. Thus, researchers have developed inventories that specifically assess parenting (Crnic & Greenberg, 1990), family (Rollins, Garrison, & Pierce, 2002), caregiving (Kinney & Stephens, 1989), and children's hassles (Kanner et al., 1987). An example of this work is included in Box 11.1.

Stress Outcomes

Stress outcomes have been traditionally measured using physical- and mental-health questionnaires. These outcome measures often include the assessment of physical symptoms (e.g., headaches, colds), medical diagnosis, physiological symptoms (e.g., hypertension), psychological complaints, and daily functioning (e.g., work absenteeism) (Schwarzer & Schultz, 2003). For researchers interested in the psychological impact of stress, I often recommend the *Brief Symptom Inventory* (BSI; Derogatis & Melisaritos, 1983) or the *Center for the Epidemiological Studies Depression Scale* (CES-D; Radloff, 1977). The 53-item BSI captures a very broad range of psychological symptoms, including anxiety, depression, and paranoid ideation. Although the BSI contains 9 different symptom dimensions, the symptom scales are intercorrelated, indicating that this scale is a better index of the degree, though not the precise nature, of psychological symptoms (Boulet & Boss, 1991).

The 20-item CES-D is one of the most popular methods used to assess depressive symptoms in adults, and encourages respondents to think about their feelings and behaviors over the past week. The CES-D includes such items as "I felt sad," "I had crying spells," and "I talked less than usual." Because depressive symptoms are theorized to be the chief negative psychological symptom of stress, the CES-D would be a good bet as an outcome measure.

Both the CES-D and BSI are easy-to-administer inventories that can be used to identify and screen people experiencing psychological symptoms. The scales are norm-referenced, so we can contrast study results with national norms. However, they should not be used to *diagnose* people with a mental illness; instead, researchers should describe an individual who receives high scores as scoring "high on psychological or depressive symptoms." A person who scores high on depressive symptoms may *not* have a major clinical depression.

The Assessment of Coping

Researchers have tried to explain why people react so differently to shared events (see Cohen, Kessler, & Gordon, 1997; Lazarus, 1991). Look at the conceptual framework presented in Figure 11.1 and think about how it might apply to you. The beginning of the stress-distress process is marked by the presence of some form of "environmental demand," or a potential hassle, major life event, or chronic stressor. Next, we make a series of cognitive appraisals, which include an appraisal of our potential *resources*. These resources might involve thinking about how well we have coped with the issue before (i.e., history), perceptions of confidence and stress controllability, our social support network, and personality (e.g., general hardiness).

Based on these initial appraisals, we can rate the events as threatening, challenging, or benign. In fact, there are various methods we can use to measure the respondent's perceptions

BOX 11.1 • *Parents are Hassled: No Kidding Around*

Researchers are interested in how adults cope with more **domain-specific hassles**, or daily stressors that occur within a particular context or population. Consider the hassle item "occupational demands." An adult who checks this item indicates that something is wrong at work; yet, we are not enlightened as to the exact nature of the difficulty. Such data has little practical value for professionals seeking to conduct workplace interventions.

Domain-specific hassles can include both contextual hassles, such as school or occupational demands, and hassles confined to a particular population. For instance, Dolan (1994) crafted a stress inventory, the *Nurse Aide Hassles Inventory,* specifically for workers in a nursing-home setting. Also, Crnic & Greenberg (1990) developed the 20-item *Parenting Hassles Scale,* which contains hassles that parents of children typically face. When completing this inventory, one must consider a variety of hassles that encompass two major dimensions of parenting: parenting tasks and challenging behavior. A parenting-tasks hassle would include irritants that pertain to the broader parenting context, such as "Having to run errands for the kids." Challenging behavior refers to irritants that pertain more to the child, such as "Being nagged, whined at, or complained to." Crnic and Greenberg (1990) determined that these different hassles pertain to different dimensions or factors; parents who indicate that they are hassled by parenting tasks do not necessarily feel bothered by the child herself.

Anyone creating a new, improved, domain-specific hassles measure must face some key challenges. For example, a parenting-hassles measure should meet the standard reliability criteria that any test or measure must meet, such as two-week test-retest reliability. The researcher will be charged to demonstrate that the instrument predicts something meaningful *in a unique way.* One would expect that parents who endorse frequent,

intense child-related hassles to exhibit more strained interactions with their children than their less-hassled counterparts. This is exactly what Crnic & Greenberg (1990) documented; indeed, the challenging-behavior dimension of this instrument predicted less maternal responsiveness during parent-child interactions, whereas the parenting-task factor did not.

However, to qualify as a legitimate domain-specific hassle scale, one must also demonstrate that these hassles predict an important outcome measure *over and beyond other hassles or stressors.* For instance, what would you think if the Parenting Hassles Scale did not predict parenting behavior any better than the more general Daily Hassles Scale did? If we garnered such a result, one would question the need for a new measure!

To the credit of the Parenting Hassles Scale, Crnic and Greenberg (1990) have demonstrated that this instrument predicts parenting behavior in a unique manner. For instance, this scale is a better predictor of actual parenting behavior than major life events are. In addition, Creasey and Reese (1996) demonstrated that the more general Daily Hassles Scale could predict both mother and father's psychological distress; however, this distress significantly increased if the parent also reported frequent hassles on the Parenting Hassles Scale. Both of these studies demonstrate that the Parenting Hassles Scale predicts both parenting behavior and general distress over and beyond the presence of more general daily hassles or life events.

The Parenting Hassles Scale is a nice inventory to use when working with families with school-aged children. However, the items on this scale do not completely apply to other stages of life; for example, both infants and adolescents may create stressors for caregivers that are different from child-related hassles. I say this from recent personal experience, because my son is now tackling dating and learning to drive at the same time.

---

of threat (Monroe & Kelley, 1997) and initial emotional reactions (Stone, 1997) to the stressful event. Interestingly, some stress experts are specifically interested in this appraisal process. For example, some experts study the role of personality in the appraisal process, whereas others, such as Albert Bandura, strongly focus on confidence or self-efficacy.

It is assumed that coping processes mediate associations between these appraisals and mental and physical health outcomes. Various theoretical accounts explain the coping

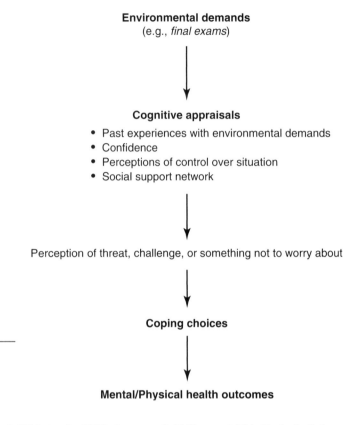

Environmental demands
(e.g., *final exams*)

Cognitive appraisals
- Past experiences with environmental demands
- Confidence
- Perceptions of control over situation
- Social support network

Perception of threat, challenge, or something not to worry about

Coping choices

Mental/Physical health outcomes

FIGURE 11.1   *Model of the Stress, Appraisal, and Coping Process.* The figure explains the relationship between stressful events, cognitive, appraisal and coping behavior.

process (Carver, Schier, & Weintraub, 1989; Lazarus & Folkman, 1984; Roth & Cohen, 1986). One camp argues that coping options can be broken down into *behavioral* or *problem-focused* and *emotional* or *cognitive* choices. When coping with a critical supervisor, we can directly talk with this person (behavioral or problem focused) or calm down by changing the way we think about the situation (emotional or cognitive). However, others theorize that coping options can be *active* or *approach* and *avoidant* (Roth & Cohen, 1986). That is, we can directly confront a stressor or distance ourselves from it. Both of these perspectives can be integrated, as presented in Table 11.6.

Traditionally, the coping process has been studied via self-report measures, such as the *Ways of Coping Checklist* (Folkman & Lazarus, 1980; Folkman et al., 1986) or the *COPE* scale (Carver, *Schier, & Weintraub,* 1989). Essentially, participants identify a recent stressor and indicate how they coped with the event. The *Ways of Coping Checklist* then allows for an analysis of behavioral or problem-focused versus emotional or cognitive strategies used, whereas the *COPE* scale yields dimensions and scales similar to what is presented in Table 11.6. More of the recent stress

What Do You Think?

Traditionally, experts interested in the coping process have asked adults to identify a recent stressful event and indicate how they coped with it. What concerns do you see with this approach? What does such work really tell us about the coping process?

TABLE 11.6 *Integrated Perspective on Coping*
Coping Dimensions

	Active or Approach	Avoidant
Behavioral	*Adaptive confrontation* (e.g., study for exam).	*Engagement in irrelevant activities* (e.g., cleaning apartment rather than studying)
	Instrumental support seeking (e.g., asking teacher for help or direction)	*Drinking or drug use*
Emotional or Cognitive	*Formulating plan of action* (e.g., mentally considering ways to solve the problem)	*Denial*
	Emotional support seeking	*Rumination* (e.g., worrying about stressor without problem-solving attempts)
	Emotion regulation	

Adapted from Carver, Schier, & Weintraub, 1989; Lazarus & Folkman, 1984; Roth & Cohen, 1986.

and coping research appears to incorporate the COPE scale as a primary methodology, perhaps because it yields more coping scales and is better aligned with the theoretical presentation shown in the table. However, this is not to say that the Ways of Coping is an invalid measure, and more research that includes both instruments is needed.

Let's consider the question just posed. What happens when you give out a coping inventory to 100 different adults and ask them to indicate how they coped with a recent stressful event? Generally, people are going to rate a wide range of events. I recently had one research participant indicate how he coped with a faulty cell phone, whereas another rated coping strategies after losing a good friend who perished in the World Trade Center on 9/11/01.

We could cope (no pun intended) with this concern in different ways:

- We could ask respondents to rate certain appraisals regarding the event (Monroe & Kelley, 1997) and evaluate the coping strategies used by adults who endorse mildly, moderately, or highly threatening events.
- We could ask them to focus on a particular event, such as coping with relationship conflict. When using this strategy, everyone is evaluating a coping repertoire for the same event.
- We could limit our sample to one population; for example, much research has examined how women cope with breast cancer (Epping-Jordan et al., 1999).

Another concern pertains to the uneasy association between the data that are yielded by coping checklists and the construct, *the coping process*. Most stress and coping theories assume that coping is an active, dynamic process, and that people adjust their coping strategies over time. Thus, a person who indicated that she engaged in high denial might also stipulate that she engaged in active problem solving. A coping checklist may not inform you of the *history of strategy use over time*. In this example, we do not know whether the person engaged in denial or problem solving first (Coyne & Racioppo, 2000).

To provide a better picture of the coping process, experts have used diary methods, such as the *Daily Coping Inventory* (Stone & Neale, 1984) to evaluate daily feelings, stress perceptions, and coping strategies in adults. This method has major advantages. First, respondents can write down their more immediate thoughts, emotions, and coping methods. Also, this method allows us to study the coping process over time, monitor coping changes, and evaluate the relationship between coping methods and healthy functioning in adults (Manne, 2003).

Summary

Although I segregated the concepts of stress and coping in this section, many researchers study stress appraisals, coping, and potential health outcomes in the same study. Unlike some of the other research areas presented in this book, this research context is very new. New researchers should approach even "established" stress and coping measures skeptically, and perhaps engage in some pilot research before conducting a study with adults.

Adult Cognition

This section will discuss methodological issues concerning adult cognition. Some of this discussion will be review; however, there will be some new ideas for you to consider in this section, as well. Like experts who study the biology of aging, it is important to discern and untangle the effects of basic aging and extrinsic secondary aging variables on cognition. In addition, because there is evidence that certain types of thinking improve during adulthood, we need to be aware of the methods researchers use to examine such development.

Intelligence

A large amount of research has focused on the assessment of mental abilities in adults. Much of this work relies on traditional intelligence tests, such as the Wechsler Adult Intelligence Scale (WAIS-III, Wechsler, 1997; see Chapter 7). However, there are major methodological concerns regarding the study of aging and intellect. First, studies using traditional developmental designs can yield somewhat misleading information. In addition, the use of age as the sole study variable can diminish the impact of such research.

Design.   When contrasting the intellects of older and younger adults, researchers who use different developmental designs obtain different results. Research incorporating cross-sectional designs, in which different-aged adults are assessed at the same time point using an intelligence test, indicate that certain mental abilities appear to dramatically decline after middle age. In particular, *fluid intelligence* (see Chapter 7), which pertains to the ability to quickly solve problems, such as solving a jigsaw puzzle, declines faster than *crystallized intellect.* Crystallized intelligence is our general, semantic knowledge base, such as vocabulary.

Research using short-term longitudinal and sequential designs portrays a different picture of aging and intelligence. Recall that the latter design may incorporate cross-sectional

40	→	45	→	50 years of age
45	→	50	→	55 years of age
50	→	55	→	60 years of age

2005	2010	2015

Year of intelligence test

FIGURE 11.2   *Sample Sequential Design.*
Notice how the relationship between age, ongoing history, and IQ can be assessed using this design. For instance, time-of-measurement effects can be analyzed by same-age comparisons over time (i.e., contrasting 50-year-olds IQ scores at each time of measurement).

and longitudinal elements; we may give an IQ test out to 40-, 45-, and 50-years-olds and then reassess the participants twice over five-year intervals. Note in Figure 11.2 that the association between age and intellect can be assessed while controlling for ongoing historical, or time-of-measurement effects (see Chapter 1). Indeed, documenting differences between, say the 50-year-olds, across different times of measurement would be an interesting finding in itself!

These designs are superior to the aforementioned cross-sectional method and long-term longitudinal design. Cross-sectional designs are problematic, they confound age and cohort; the older participants may have received less education than the younger adults, which could account for the significant age differences in intelligence. Longitudinal designs are problematic because of the problems of attrition and cost, and the effects of repeated testing—there are only so many versions of an IQ test that can be administered! In any case, most studies using sequential designs indicate that intellectual growth advances into midlife and then slowly declines. Also, the amount of change detected depends on the facet of intelligence tested. A number of studies suggest that crystallized intelligence shows advancements after middle age, whereas others abilities, such as fluid intellect, show slow declines (Salthouse, 2000; Schaie, 2002).

The newer use of sequential designs has addressed other important issues pertaining to intellectual development. For example, have you noticed that the government, employers, and the insurance industry keep increasing the minimum ages for social service and pension programs? These changes are often done under the mantra, "We have a new breed of older citizens who are functioning much better than previous generations." Newer research using sequential designs has supported this point, in the sense that people between the ages of 60 and 75 today score higher on intelligence tests than the same age group in decades past (Schaie, 2002). Again, neither a cross-sectional, nor a longitudinal study includes provisions to check for such historical and generational effects. Sequential designs with built-in time-lag components can help us disentangle the effects of age and ongoing historical influences (see Chapter 1).

Assessment of Individual Differences.   Although methodological advances have created a new "profile" for intellectual change, this profile does not apply to all adults. Experts have noted substantive *individual differences* in functioning over time; thus, some show the typical pattern of intellectual development described earlier, whereas others display stability, growth, or even steep decline. Also, research suggests that some abilities decline at certain points and then begin increasing again with new skill development or expertise (Fischer, Yan, & Stewart, 2003).

These data suggest that age and intelligence should not be sole study variables, no matter how sophisticated the developmental design. For instance, K. Warner Schaie has discerned associations among age, history, and intellect using sophisticated sequential designs (Schaie, 1994; 1996; 2002). His work suggests that intellectual declines occur much later than originally thought, and a number of personal and environmental variables moderate this process.

What might we want to include as study variables in such research? Using medical-history data, Schaie (1994) noted that adults who reported the presence of certain chronic diseases, measured by medical diagnosis or the presence of multiple chronic diseases, measured by annual illness counts, are more susceptible to intellectual decline than disease-free adults. Which chronic diseases might present the most problems? Aside from diseases such as Alzheimer's disease (potential participants suffering from it are screened out of such studies) cardiovacular disease presents the most difficulties (Schaie, 1996). This finding results from the fact that reduced blood flow to the brain is related to substantive difficulties with memory and information processing. Thus, it appears that both illness diagnosis and frequency represent important study variables to include in such research.

Moderate-to-serious vision and hearing deficits and a slowing of visual and auditory processing speed, have also been consistently linked to intellectual declines (Singer, Lindenberger, & Baltes, 2003). Although the presence of a serious sensory deficit could be ascertained by interviewing participants, most evaluate visual acuity by assessing reading distance, whereas auditory acuity can be assessed via hearing tests (Lindenberger, Scherer, & Baltes, 2001). An accurate assessment of auditory and visual acuity would seem to constitute important study variables, because perceptual difficulties predict large discrepancies in cognitive functioning among older adults, and discrepancies between older and younger participants are significantly reduced when those with sensory problems are screened out (Lindenberger & Baltes, 1994; Singer et al., 2003).

Demographic variables, lifestyle choices, and psychological and personality functioning also affect intellectual functioning during adulthood (see Schaie, 1994; 1996b; Schaie et al., 1994, for a listing of variables and measurement strategies). However, one significant research finding pertains to the functioning of one's spouse or partner. Although better-educated people generally show slower rates of intellectual decline, a well-educated, intelligent spouse provides an additional buffer (Schaie, 1996). When assessing intellectual functioning in adults researchers should take note of the participant's committed-relationship status, and determine whether the abilities of the partner play a role in predicting the participant's functioning. This idea could also be applied to social and emotional development in adults, as well.

In summary, experts who study aging and intellectual functioning in adults have been recently influenced by several methodological advancements. First, they have moved away from traditional cross-sectional and longitudinal designs and increased their use of hybrid, sequential methods. This methodological shift allows for better estimates regarding the influence of age and ongoing history on intellectual functioning. An additional concern pertains to secondary, or extrinsic, factors that may interact with age to predict intellectual functioning. Although this is also an issue facing experts who study age-related changes in health and social functioning, the extrinsic factors that affect intellectual functioning are not always the same variables that affect health and social functioning. Further, the finding that chronic diseases, such as cardiovascular disease, and select aspects of social functioning, such as social engagement, are predictive of intellectual changes (Schaie, 1994) suggests that it is unwise to view cognitive, health, and social and emotional functioning as isolated, unrelated constructs.

The aforementioned research has revolutionized the way we think about aging and intellect. We used to think that intellectual decline was inevitable, nonreversible, and entirely a result of biology. We now believe that the effects of aging on intellectual functioning are only modest at best, and that interindividual differences between adults result from extrinsic factors, such as education, health, and mental activity. This premise has implications for intervention; some of the exciting applied work in this field is described in Box 11.2.

BOX 11.2 • *Can We Reverse Cognitive Decline?*

In the typical cognitive-retraining treatment program, adults who have mild-to-moderate memory difficulties are taught storage-and-retrieval strategies over a period of days or weeks. The adults are screened for major dementing illnesses, such as Alzheimer's disease, so their memory problems are largely nonorganic in nature. In the best studies, impaired and nonimpaired adults are assigned to different experimental conditions. This strategy allows researchers to ascertain whether treatment effects are limited to those experiencing declines or transfer to the more high-functioning adults.

Much of this intervention work has concentrated on training adults to better process spatial information and develop better problem-solving abilities (e.g., Willis & Nesselroade, 1990; Willis & Schaie, 1986; Schaie & Willis, 1986). The results are exciting. A series of studies have documented that older adults, many of whom have been suffering intellectual declines for years, can be trained to think and reason as effectively as they ever had before. These results are not related to the educational level of the participants, and adults who are *not* currently experiencing decline also show improvements! Finally, when assessed years later, the benefits of such training are often still apparent (Willis & Nesselroade, 1990).

Although these results are exciting, there are some important issues to consider. First, although adults show improvements in functioning with training, one might wonder whether the training effects carry over and transfer to the real world. In addition, cognitive-training interventions with children often do not generalize well to the everyday world if the child does not understand how or why such training works. Thus, some argue that interventions designed to increase memory self-efficacy and metacognitive awareness should be conducted *before* training adults on memory strategies or giving them intellectual tips (Dunlosky & Hertzog, 1998).

Students interested in additional methodological issues regarding cognitive and behavioral intervention with older adults should consult Willis's (2001) excellent review. In this review, Willis articulates the need for control groups in such research, and reminds us that intervention work with adults is subject to familiar confounds. That is, without a comparison group, it is difficult to rule out maturational influences. Adults who have difficulties with problem-solving may get better naturally via their own efforts. A control group would allow the researcher to account for various threats to internal validity (see Chapter 1).

Willis (2001) also recommends that researchers understand the power of *transfer:* that is, on a proximal level, the intervention should influence performance involving similar, yet not identical, tasks. For instance, an adult who is allowed to practice mental rotation tasks should not be given the same tasks to perform at a later date. Rather, the researchers should expose the adult to similar, but new, rotation tasks to gauge the effectiveness of the intervention. In addition, Willis recommends that intervention specialists develop mechanisms to delineate exactly *how* and *why* a treatment might work. For instance, consider the logical flaws inherent in a treatment–control group study in which the intervention involves multiple training components. Imagine a case in which researchers present adults in the treatment group with different training modules, and make efforts to improve their memories. At the end of the study, a significant treatment by control group contrast would signify an intervention effect, yet the researcher would be at a loss regarding *which component* of the training package primarily produced the desired effect. The remedy to this concern would be to randomly assign adults to a control group, as well as to *different treatment groups.* Thus, participants would receive different components of the treatment program.

Information Processing and Memory

Like work involving younger populations, information-processing research with adults often involves measures of visual processing that is experimentally assessed in the laboratory context. One of the most popular paradigms that has been used with adults is to ask them to quickly store and retrieve word lists. This technique allows researchers to exert tight experimental control and standardize stimulus presentation. Such work is highly replicable, and stimulus presentation can be controlled via computer technology. Responses can be easily recorded by asking the participant to quickly press the keyboard space bar when they detect a stimulus change or type a list of words that they were instructed to memorize minutes or hours earlier. The data are automatically recorded and stored in a data set for statistical analyses.

The bulk of the research suggests that with age, attention processes can be clouded by perceptual problems (e.g., hearing decline), processing speed slows, and there are selective deficits in working memory and memory retrieval (Lindenberger, Scherer, & Baltes, 2001; Rogers & Fisk, 2001). Older adults use less-sophisticated storage-and-retrieval strategies than their younger counterparts do (Hertzog & Hultsch, 2000); that is, an older participant may not use organizational strategies or mental imagery to help store a word list. Of course, the usual suspects emerge when critically evaluating such research; for example, by now you might be thinking:

> *"How much longitudinal research has been conducted on this topic?"*
> *"Do researchers routinely compare the performance of younger, college-educated participants with that of older participants with less education?"*
> *"Wait a minute; what happens if you screen out older participants who have serious health problems and then make age comparisons?"*

If you are tired of me bringing these issues up, then you've learned something! However, despite controlling for these methodological issues, older adults are slower at processing, less likely to use sophisticated storage-and-retrieval strategies, and display less-accurate retrieval than younger adults do. Although these results have primarily been drawn from studies involving laboratory methods, the results of the scattered longitudinal and naturalistic studies suggest that primary aging does have selective influence on storage-and-retrieval processes (Zelinski & Burnight, 1997). Certain difficulties are not specific to any particular activity; older adults often have greater difficulty remembering isolated events and facts than their younger counterparts across most tasks (Salthouse, 1996; Verhaeghen, Marcoen, & Goosens, 1993).

On the other hand, in the previous section we concluded that associations between age and certain aspects of intellectual functioning *are* task specific. That is, many older adults hold their own at vocabulary knowledge and verbal comprehension when contrasted with younger adults; however, they may "show their age" when presented tasks that are novel or that require quick processing. These findings suggest that the same principle could be applied to the information-processing system; that is, there may be certain abilities that display inevitable and modest declines during adulthood, whereas other abilities may be more resistant to decline and amenable to intervention. This is the research angle I would recommend pursuing.

One of the hottest research areas is memory development during adulthood. Although this area is of great scientific importance, on a practical level this is the very issue that many older adults complain about! However, the term *memory* is a very generic concept, with different components (Zacks, Hasher, & Li, 2000). Let's consider those components, discuss how to assess them, and then illustrate how recall sharpness regarding even our weakest memories can vary as a function of task and experimental context.

Chapter 6 indicated that most scientists believe that there are different facets of permanent, or long-term, memory. Some memories can be easily accessed without really thinking about them. Some examples of such *implicit* (nondeclarative) memories would include simply knowing that you have to put a car in drive or that you put on clothes before going to work; we do not need to consciously think about these issues before engaging in the behavior.

However, we also possess *explicit* (declarative) memories, we often must direct conscious thought processes at certain memories to retrieve them. Broadly speaking, these memories can be *semantic* or *episodic*. Semantic memories, which represent a form of crystallized intelligence, are deeply integrated memories of general knowledge and facts that have been stored after considerable rehearsal. Knowing the names of famous movie stars or articulating the purpose of education would represent some examples of this memory system. Episodic memories, on the other hand, represent a more isolated, less "connected" type of memory, such as the location of car keys or trying to remember the name of a person you just met. *At all ages, recall of episodic memories represents the weakest link in long-term memory.*

Implicit Memory. Let's now think about how to assess each memory system. There are four approaches to studying implicit memory in adults (and they can be used with children and adolescents as well) (Prull, Gabrieli, & Bunge, 2000). In **skill-learning paradigms**, participants are trained to do a very simple task, such as learning to type a series of letters or building a structure out of blocks. They are allowed to practice this skill, and then observers compare their performance to that of younger adults or contrast it with their own performance on a novel skill task.

Using a different approach, researchers who use **repetition-priming** (or **recognition-recall**) **paradigms** give participants a word list to memorize. Later, they review another list of words that contains the original set, as well as distracters, and their task then is to pick out the words they have seen before. Yet another method includes **lexical decision-making tasks**, such as showing the participant two, series of letters, such as *night* and *XDFD,* and asking them to identify the one that is a real word. Finally, in **conditioning paradigms** participants are trained to respond to a stimulus that would not normally evoke a reaction. For instance, when using the *eye-blink method,* the researcher pairs a certain tone (or conditioned stimulus) with a puff of air to the eye (unconditioned stimulus). The air puff, of course, automatically elicits an eye blink (unconditioned response); however, over a period of trials, the tone alone will produce the eye blink (conditioned response). All of these tasks are very easy to learn to perform, and are thought to evoke implicit memory processing.

At one time, experts believed that the effects of age on implicit-memory performance were minimal. Indeed, a number of studies have indicated that the performance of older adults on certain implicit-memory tasks, such as word recognition, are very strong and often equal the performance of younger people. However, the research outcomes in some studies are contradictory; for example, older adults exposed to conditioning paradigms almost always show implicit-memory delays when compared to their younger counterparts (LaVoie & Light, 1994; Prull, Gabrieli, & Bunge, 2000). Indeed, in eye-blink conditioning studies, there are often age differences in implicit-memory performance between even 20- and 30-year-olds.

Adult performance might be related to the nature of the task. Adult performance on implicit-memory tasks is often equal to that of younger adults when there are contextual cues present; for example, their performance is often excellent in cases in which the respondent is asked later to recognize a series of pictures (Smith, 1996). Age differences across implicit-memory paradigms diminish when we control for health status and the possible presence of early-onset dementias, such as Alzheimer's disease. Thus, the study of implicit memory in adults seems to be an area that needs more exploration.

Semantic Memory.   We can access semantic memories in different ways; for instance, verbal tasks on standardized tests of intelligence reflect semantic-memory competence. Semantic-memory capacity can also be assessed experimentally using **semantic priming paradigms**. For example, when using word-association methods, participants must decide whether the *doctor-nurse* word pair is more similar than *newspaper-cat*. Older adults, up till age 70, perform similarly to younger adults on these tasks; some studies have noted that vocabulary knowledge may even *increase* up to late adulthood (Bäckman & Nilsson, 1996).

Remote and **autobiographical memories** represent two memory facets that could be associated with semantic memory. Remote memory pertains to our recall of distant information, whereas autobiographical recall is our ability to remember *personal events* from the distant past. Thus, to assess remote memory, one could poll adults on their recall accuracy for verifiable historical events that occurred in different decades (e.g., 1930–1940, 1940–1950, etc.). However, this method is limited, because we do not know whether particular adults were privy to the events. For example, a recent immigrant may be unaware of Academy Award winners during the 1960s.

To address this methodological issue, respondents can be prompted to spontaneously recall events. We can then ascertain the accuracy of their recall of the event and document whether it actually occurred in the time era reported by the participant. The results of research crafted in this fashion are intriguing. Studies involving older adults (e.g., 60–80) across cultures have revealed that remote memories for such events are more accurate from the period when the participants were 10- to 30-years-olds (Schuman, Rieger, & Gaidys, 1994). This finding has been replicated by researchers using different methods. In one study, adults were given multiple-choice questions regarding different historical and cultural events across different decades, such as "Which Republican candidate lost the 19XX presidential election?." Memory accuracy was sharpest for events that occurred when the participants were between 10 and 30 (Rubin et al., 1998).

Autobiographical memory represents recall for remote but personal events. When using the **cued-recall method**, researchers give respondents certain primes; for example, the experimenter might encourage the adult to think about previous memories in the following manner:

> *"The event you think of does not have to be important; it does not have to be interesting; it can come from any point in your life, even as recently as this morning. The event does need to be very specific, however; by that I mean that it must have happened at a very particular place and point in time. For example, if I were to use the word store, you might think of having gone to the store yesterday"* (Rubin & Schulkind, 1997, p. 527).

The results of such work document that, like remote-memory recall, older adults (e.g., 70 years) often most accurately recall personal memories from the period when they were between the ages of 10 and 30. In addition, when asked to rate their most important memories, younger participants recall more recent events, whereas older people name events that occurred when they were between 10 and 30. This intriguing "bump" in remote, autobiographical recall is illustrated in Figure 11.3. The fact that older adults are more likely to endorse list events as both personal and important may provide diagnostic information regarding why recall of these memories is so good: we are probably more likely to revisit these memories repeatedly over time through reminiscing about them on our own or during later discussions with friends, spouses, children, and grandchildren (Rubin, 1999).

Episodic Memory. Episodic memory is definitely the weak memory unit; if you are constantly misplacing your keys, then you are not alone. Because this system is so vulnerable, it is not surprising that primary aging processes seem to hit this component the hardest, and serious episodic memory loss is often the first major symptom in a number of degenerative memory disorders, such as Alzheimer's disease. However, aging and disease processes are not the only variables that affect episodic memory. For instance, mental activity, general health, and psychological adjustment also affect episodic memory functioning over adulthood.

When given a word list to memorize, both older and younger adults often show considerable differences in **free-recall memory paradigms**. In such a task, the researcher presents a word list, stories, or pictures. The participant commits them to memory and then

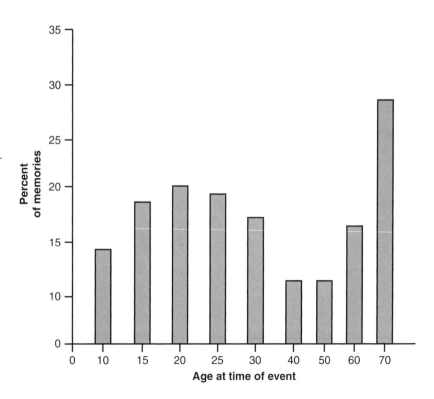

FIGURE 11.3 *"Bump" Phenomenon in Autobiographical Recall.* In a study of older adults, other than sharp recall for most recent memories, participants were most likely to have the most accurate recall for events that occurred when they were between 10 and 30 years of age. This recall phenomenon is apparent in all age groups tested; that is, people have the best recall for events that occurred during this age span.

spontaneously recalls the items minutes, hours, or even days later. Younger adults usually perform better on such tasks than their older counterparts. However, interindividual variability is often large among the older adults; a minority of them perform just as well as the younger adults (Craik, 1999). On the other hand, declines in episodic memory do not seem to be task specific; researchers have noted consistent deficits in such recall in older adults in tasks (e.g., recall of grocery items) contrived to simulate everyday recall in both naturalistic and experimental settings (Allaire & Marsiske, 1999; Kirasic et al., 1996). These recall difficulties are not limited to visual recall, because similar deficits have been noted in auditory, tactile, and olfactory processing (Bäckman, Small, & Wahlin, 2001). These findings raise a very interesting methodological issue; consider the accuracy of self-report data from older adults that includes items that tap episodic-memory processes (e.g., "When did you last feel stressed and how did you specifically cope with the event?") (Craik, 1999).

Arguing for, or against, age differences in episodic memory is not very debatable, given the consistency of these findings. However, occasional results emerge that cause us to rethink these pessimistic findings. For instance, Kirasic (1991) noted that older adults could locate grocery items just as well as younger adults in familiar grocery stores. Perhaps moving to more naturalistic research would be a more meaningful direction for research.

Another fruitful endeavor would be to better specify secondary, extrinsic variables and interventions that might promote episodic-memory functioning. Unfortunately, many studies that associate extrinsic variables with memory functioning incorporate cross-sectional designs; thus, it is difficult to isolate causal mechanisms in this process. Even in carefully controlled longitudinal research, it is often difficult to discern whether lifestyle and health variables affect cognitive functioning or if it is the other way around. For instance, in a six-year longitudinal study, researchers noted that changes in the intellectual activities of older adults predicted parallel changes in cognitive functioning (Hultsch et al., 1999). However, this finding could also mean that cognitively bright adults may lead intellectually challenging lifestyles until cognitive declines discourage such activity (Bäckman et al., 2001).

Working Memory.   Newly acquired information is not always effectively stored in long-term memory. Many times, we must *do* something with new information in order to retrieve it later. The study of adult working memory represents an exciting area, because we could possibly train people in memory-enhancing techniques that might reverse intellectual and memory deficits.

Many aspects of working memory remain preserved; older individuals perform as well as younger adults on simple *memory-span tests*. That is, when presented a series of numbers to hold in working memory, older adults can usually repeat back just as many of them as younger people can. Thus, age differences on simple memory tests are either nonexistent or very mild (Verhaeghen, Marcoen, & Goosens, 1993). However, when using more complicated memory-span tests, such as learning a new series of digits while retaining one learned earlier, older adults consistently have problems. The inability to effectively divide attention in working memory has been tied to performance problems in a number of learning tasks (e.g., reading comprehension) (Hultsch, Hertzog, & Dixon, 1990). Thus, adult memory-span efficiency can be traced to how it is assessed.

Working memory also "works"; that is, we often use strategies or control processes to increase the efficiency of processing. Recall that Chapter 6 discussed how memory strategies, such as the use of rehearsal, organization, and imagery, can enhance the quality of information storage. Starting around middle age, adults use these strategies less often, possibly because of decreases in processing speed and less-effective attention processes (Salthouse & Babcock, 1991). Sometimes, in order to store or retrieve information, we must simultaneously select a memory aid, along with the relevant information that we are attempting to process.

Although these declines are not thought to have a major impact on daily functioning, the fact that older adults often possess mild memory complaints has encouraged experts to develop interventions to bolster functioning. Much of this work involves training older adults to use better strategies in a laboratory setting without checking to see whether the newly learned strategy is used outside the lab or whether the training enhances day-to-day functioning. The few longitudinal intervention studies have yielded contradictory data; some studies have reported treatment benefits listing for years after the training, whereas others report quick "washout" effects (Anschutz et al., 1987; Verhaeghen, Marcoen, & Goosens, 1992; Neely & Bäckman, 1993).

Chapter 6 concluded that teaching children memory strategies could enhance storage and retrieval; however, it is also paramount that children possess *metacognitive awareness,* or *monitoring,* regarding how and why these strategies work. Newer intervention work with older adults supports this theory; that is, simply training an older adult to use rehearsal or retrieval strategies may not be effective unless the participant understands the power of the strategy (see also Box 11.2). Thus, the assessment of adult metacognitive awareness is an important study variable in training studies.

Metacognitive awareness can be compartmentalized into two facets: **memory self-efficacy** and **memory monitoring** (Hertzog & Dixon, 1994; Nelson & Narens, 1990). Memory self-efficacy is defined as our confidence level in our memory and the efficacy of memory strategies. Memory monitoring is our knowledge of memory strategies and how they influence storage-and-retrieval processes (Dunlosky & Hertzog, 1998).

Various intervention techniques have been used to promote memory self-efficacy and monitoring in both children and adults (Best, Hamlett, & Davis, 1992; Caprio-Prevette & Fry, 1996; West, 1989). The underlying assumptions of these efforts make theoretical sense. For example, a person who performs a task well using a certain memory strategy should show increases in self-efficacy; however, people are unlikely to use a particular strategy if they are unaware of the technique or do not understand how or why it works. Memory-improvement programs are unlikely to be effective if certain cognitive appraisals are not modified during the training process.

Self-report checklists that assess memory self-efficacy and monitoring can also be useful. The *Memory Self-Efficacy Questionnaire* (MSEQ; Berry, West, & Dennehey, 1989) represents one way of assessing memory confidence. The MSEQ requires respondents to estimate their degree of confidence in memory functioning across different everyday tasks. To do so, they must assess their confidence in their ability to remember grocery lists, phone numbers, errands, and directions. Studies using this instrument have revealed that high self-efficacy is related to memory performance (Berry, West, & Dennehey, 1989) and self-reports of everyday strategy use (McDougall, 1994).

The *Metamemory Functioning in Adulthood Questionnaire* (MIA: Dixon & Hultsch, 1984) is an economical instrument, because it assesses both self-efficacy and metamemory beliefs. This measure assesses the adult's beliefs about strategy use, such as "For most people, facts that are interesting are easier to remember than facts that are not," as well as beliefs regarding ability change, "The older I get the harder it is to remember things clearly." Similar to findings regarding the MSEQ, adults who possess increased knowledge regarding the effectiveness of memory strategies use more sophisticated strategies and perform well on memory tests (Hertzog, Hultsch, & Dixon, 1989; Jonker, Smits, & Deeg, 1997).

How do researchers tie these belief systems to actual memory performance? Researchers are often compelled to choose between standard laboratory memory tasks, such as word list memorization, and self-reports of memory functioning in everyday life (Hertzog et al., 1989). Although the former technique represents a method that has strong internal validity, some question how well such tasks represent memory challenges encountered outside the lab. Conversely, self-report methods rely on retrospective accounts of strategy use and functioning, which could be faulty if the participant has a bad memory to begin with! In such cases, using an additional informant to augment the self-report data might be useful.

Alternatively, some researchers have developed laboratory methods for assessing adult functioning that are analogous to real-world events. West and colleagues have developed a test battery that assesses memory for grocery items, phone numbers, and news events. In addition, attention processes and reaction time are measured by asking the adult to simultaneously work an accelerator and brake in a computer-simulated car (West, Crook, Barron, 1992). When using such a package, the researcher is balancing both internal and external validity to assess daily memory functioning.

Like intellectual functioning, some facets of the information-processing system are affected by primary aging. However, these declines are selective, are dependent on the memory task, and may be moderated by extrinsic factors, such as mental activity. These findings raise methodological issues; however, we need more research on everyday memory functioning. For instance, how many adults show memory problems in the laboratory, yet "know" they must park their car near a favorite department store so they can quickly relocate it? Are there certain extrinsic factors that predict such thinking and behavior, or does simply forgetting the location of a car once spur use of this strategy? Finally, if we conduct more externally valid research, how can we achieve experimental control in naturalistic settings? All of these issues represent important research concerns.

Qualitative Cognitive Changes

Thus far, we have discussed methodologies that identify the decline or maintenance in cognitive functioning. However, there are components of cognition that actually show improvement over time (Dixon, 1999). People use these abilities to compensate for declines we mentioned earlier; for example, an adult who is good at planning and thinking about hypothetical issues may reason out a plan of action for attending a busy downtown art show. The older adult may ask an adult child to drive to avoid worrying about driving, parking, and re-locating a car. At the same time the individual may reason, "This would also be a good time to visit with my son or daughter." In this section, we will discuss methodological issues facing experts who study how and why such thinking changes with age. We will cover postformal thinking, wisdom, and creativity.

Postformal Thinking.   Advances in thinking beyond Piaget's period of formal operations are referred to as **postformal thinking**. Experts agree that formal-operational thought is a precursor to postformal thinking and that we may not engage in such advanced thinking in all situations. An additional tenet is that postformal-operational thought is a mode of thinking that increases between young adulthood (e.g., age 25) and middle age (e.g., age 35–45), although there is considerable disagreement whether such thought advances, stays stable, or declines thereafter (Commons, Richards, & Armon, 1984; Labouvie-Vief, 1997; Sinnott, 1994).

Just what *is* postformal thought, and how does it differ from formal operations? Recall that the formal-operational thinker is an abstract, scientific thinker who can solve problems by analyzing information, generating theory and hypotheses, testing these predictions, and developing well-thought-out, "bottom-up" solutions. That is, the adolescent and young adult uses data to build a case or an overall solution to a problem. Formal-operational thinkers are often fairly certain of their decision-making processes and conclusions regarding a problem.

Like formal-operational thinkers, postformal adults often carefully considers information and data but also use their lengthy personal experiences or **expertise** regarding the subject to help guide their decisions. The postformal thinker is also more likely to use **relativistic thought** when solving problems or dilemmas; they understand there are multiple causes to problems, and that there may be multiple, yet equally correct, solutions to real-life problems (Sinnott, 1984; 1998). The postformal adult also is likely to engage in **reflective judgment** (King & Kitchener, 1994). That is, after making a decision, they may express uncertainty regarding a solution, understand that solutions sometimes create difficulties of their own, and realize that conclusions must sometimes be reassessed. In contrast, the formal-operational thinker, after analyzing a problem, offers a strong single conclusion but engages in less reflective judgment.

How does one assess the various components of postformal thought? Like researchers who study moral development, experts who specify the structure of adult cognition frequently use dilemmas to provoke thought processes. In the **thinking-aloud paradigm** (Ericsson & Simon, 1984), the experimenter asks the respondent to reason out the dilemma aloud as the experimenter audiotapes the discourse. The experimenter can then code the various components of formal-operational or postformal thought and evaluate the adult's degree of certainty regarding stated solutions or conclusions (see Blanchard-Fields, 1986; Kitchener et al., 1993; Labouvie et al., 1994; Sinnott, 1989 for coding strategies for the thinking-aloud and similar paradigms).

Methodological concerns with this line of research persist. Like researchers who study moral reasoning, experts debate the importance of using hypothetical versus real-world, or everyday, dilemmas. Also, if expertise or past experiences with problems and dilemmas spurs postformal thought, then it is important to craft dilemmas that adults have likely had some experience with, such as marital conflict or occupational dilemmas. A thoughtful researcher might be able to develop a study that would identify the role of maturity and expertise on postformal development. Theoretically, one would expect an interaction between age and expertise in explaining the growth of this cognitive ability; older participants who hold expertise in a particular area should show the strongest evidence of postformal thinking.

Another exciting angle concerns the emotionality, or emotional impact, of the dilemma. Because of their expertise and ability to accept multiple, ambiguous solutions to problems, older adults can effectively offer solutions to problems that have significant emotional ramifications (Labouvie-Vief, 1997). By contrast, adolescents and young adults may be cognitively handicapped. First, these individuals may be used to effectively solving problems that require well-reasoned but simple solutions. Consider the difference between answering exam questions with single correct answers and the plight of a single parent who has a demanding job, young children, and a sick parent. The latter issue demands advanced reasoning skills for a dilemma that has many possible solutions.

Second, because adolescents are encouraged to develop emotional independence, they may focus on a single, problem-focused solution to emotionally- charged dilemmas, without balancing emotion- and problem-focused coping choices. Although these ideas have not been well tested, there is some evidence that older adults are more likely than adolescents and young adults to offer several alternative solutions to emotionally charged dilemmas (Blanchard-Fields, Jahnke, & Camp, 1995). Thus, the emotional salience of real-life dilemmas seems like another methodological and theoretical issue to consider when conducting research on postformal thought.

Wisdom.   Wisdom can be defined as possessing expert knowledge that can be used to correctly and effectively solve fundamental problems in everyday life, such as life planning and management (Staudinger & Leiplod, 2003; Sternberg & Lubart, 2001). Researchers study *implicit* and *explicit* approaches to this construct. Implicit approaches to studying wisdom involve assessing how different people define or conceptualize it; this is an important line of study, because one could argue that people in different occupations, communities, or cultures may have different definitions.

In contrast, explicit approaches to wisdom assume that wise people possess universal, common attributes. Experts who use this approach objectively assess wisdom-related performance, using criteria such as those listed in Table 11.7. Although some characteristics of postformal thought are reflected in these criteria, not every postformal thinking adult is a wise person. Wise people possess the ability to diagnose, define, and solve problems that have a great deal of uncertainty, and has considerable expertise in coping with dilemmas across many life domains. They can consider the past, present, and future to guide their decisions, so people across most cultures believe that aging and wisdom are correlated.

What Do You Think?

How would you define a wise person? What attributes or abilities might a wise person exhibit? How would you measure these abilities?

How can we assess wisdom? Some experts who conducted initial research on postformal thought processes have moved into this area; thus, the *thinking-aloud paradigm* described in the previous section is a popular methodological choice. Wisdom researchers often craft dilemmas that are socially relevant and involve considerable *life planning;* this is an important point, because the wise thinker should be able to use their considerable expertise to offer solutions to complicated problems. Consider the following dilemma:

Michael, a 28-year-old mechanic with two preschool children, has just learned that the factory in which he is working will close in 3 months. At present, there is no possibility for further employment in this area. His wife has recently returned to her well-paid nursing

TABLE 11.7 *Criteria for the Evaluation of Wisdom*
Basic Criteria

Rich factual knowledge	General and specific knowledge about life matters.
Rich procedural knowledge	Good decision-making abilities, self-regulation, and life-planning, uses these abilities to provide sound advice.
Lifespan contextualism	Ability to consider past, current, and future contexts (e.g., family, work) and the many circumstances (e.g., history) in which life is embedded.
Value relativism	Knowledge that there is a core set of universal goals that must be balanced with values and goals within the individual as well as in relation to others.
Awareness and management of uncertainty	Understanding that there are uncertainties and problems in life, and that one must develop strategies for coping with such uncertain or unexpected problems.

Adapted from Staudinger & Baltes, 1994; Staudinger & Pasupathi, 2003.

career. Michael is considering the following options: He can plan to move to another city to seek employment, or he can plan to take responsibility for childcare and household tasks. *Formulate a plan that covers what Michael should do and consider in the next three to five years. What additional information is needed* (Smith, *Staudinger, & Baltes,* 1994).

The dilemma is different than those used by researchers who study the components of postformal thought, such as relativistic thinking (see previous section). Note that there is no simple, short-term solution to the problem; the participant is required to use procedural knowledge to solve a highly contextual dilemma and develop a long-term plan. Also, note the age of the character and that the social problem would more likely be encountered by a younger than by an older adult. Experts who study age differences in wisdom-related thinking often manipulate various components of the dilemma to determine whether such thinking results from age or the relevance of the problem to a particular age group. Why is this type of manipulation important? If younger adults displayed high levels of wisdom-related knowledge in dealing with a familiar dilemma, then one could claim that the development of wisdom is based on expertise rather than age.

An assessment of wisdom involves the following steps, some of which are relevant to the study of standard, postformal thought processes in adults (e.g., reflective judgment) (see Staudinger, Smith, & Baltes, 1994, for one protocol and coding manual):

1. Experts train assistants to conduct probes and familiarize participants with the *thinking-aloud paradigm.*

2. After a series of "warm-up" dilemmas, the administrators present to the participant a battery of dilemmas, in which the age of the character and the nature of the dilemma are manipulated.

3. Researchers give the judgments of the participant a rating based on the wisdom criteria outlined in Table 11.7, and an overall wisdom score.

TABLE 11.8   *Example of a High-Score Wisdom Response*

Dilemma	High-Level Response
A 14-year-old girl absolutely wants to move out of her family home immediately. What should she and her parents do and consider?	First, I would ask why it is that the girl wants to move out. There can be reasons like violence or abuse, but it can also be more emotional reasons resulting from adolescence. If it is the case that there are real problems at home, it depends on their severity. There can be cases in which it is absolutely necessary to help the girl move out right away. . . . But in the case of emotional disturbances on the part of the girl, I would first try to talk to both the girl and the parents. If no compromise can be reached, one could also think about a temporary solution. Often time helps. . . . Any solution to the problem needs to take into account that circumstances and attitudes are likely to change and that modifications after a certain amount of time should be possible. . . . One also has to consider that these things become fads among teenagers. . . . Also, times have changed, and girls at 14 nowadays are more grown up than girls of 14 were twenty years ago. . . .

Staudinger, Lopez, & Baltes, 1997, p. 1212.

A high-level response appears in Table 11.8; notice how the different criteria for wisdom-related knowledge are incorporated into the response. The participant offers specific strategies, articulates the perspectives and goals of involved parties, and uses expertise regarding the changing nature of adolescence from a historical perspective to guide the judgment.

Research using such methods suggests that wisdom-related knowledge develops during late adolescence and young adulthood and then levels off (Staudinger & Pasupathi, 2003), and that both older and younger adults are likely to provide high-level responses to in which dilemmas they have expertise (Baltes et al., 1995; Smith et al., 1994). However, high-level wise responses are still *quite rare* in adults who do have considerable expertise with similar problems. For instance, only a small percentage of clinical psychologists provide high-level solutions to social problems, such as family conflicts. Thus, rather than study simple associations between age and wisdom, experts are now specifying intellectual, lifestyle, and personality correlates of the minority of adults identified as wise (Kunzmann & Baltes, 2003).

Creativity.   Chapter 7 noted that we study creativity in children using different paradigms. We can study the creative thinking of a person, actual creative performance, or examine the intellectual, personality, and social attributes of people identified as unusually creative.

Although it is possible to assess creative thinking and production in adults using laboratory tasks, one of the most popular methods is assessing the creative output of adults in different occupations. When conducting such an assessment, the researcher notes both the *quantity* and *quality* of novel output. Quantity can be recorded by tabulating the frequency of creative work, whereas quality, a much more difficult assessment, involves assessing the innovativeness of the work and the impact it has on a particular occupation or field. For instance, to assess the quality of a particular product or invention in a scientific discipline, we can tabulate how much the creative effort has been cited by other experts in their own work (Sternberg & Lubart, 2001). Using such methods, observers have documented that peak creativity is reached during middle age, and adults are more likely to produce the most qualitative work when they are producing a lot. These results vary across different disciplines; computer programmers reach their creative potential much earlier than experts in other areas, such as psychology or philosophy (Simonton, 1988).

Because creativity, like wisdom, is a rare ability, most experts are moving away from tabulating simple age differences in creative potential. Rather, researchers today try to document how changes in intellect, motivation, and environment affect creative performance over time (Sternberg & Lubart, 2001). These changes could account for both individual and age differences in such performance.

Summary

Using very innovative methods, researchers have determined that age differences regarding these abilities often depend both on the ability and on how it is measured. If you are interested in this work, consider how secondary, environmental, and person (e.g., psychological, personality) variables interact with age to predict these cognitive abilities, and ponder how one could conduct interventions to assist older adults with mild-to-moderate cognitive problems. In formulating such interventions, it is wise to consider how we can use the adult's cognitive strengths to help them overcome these modest declines.

Chapter Summary

So, what's the big picture from this chapter? When designing research, it might be wise to consider how biological, cognitive, and social changes affect adult development in both *independent and interrelated ways*. Of course, only longitudinal research can untangle such chicken-or-egg issues. We can sort out potential effects by conducting more short-term research using sequential designs. These designs allow us to better ascertain age-related changes, and initial assessments of physical, cognitive, and social development can be used to predict individual differences in growth or decline over time. Also, these designs allow us to ascertain the effects of ongoing historical trends. This is important; new, well-publicized research may have major effects on subsequent cohorts of adults. For instance, could 70-year-old adults today be healthier than similar-aged adults 10 years ago because of the increased emphasis on cholesterol screening or exercise?

Those interested in pursuing graduate education in lifespan development should consider an emphasis in adult development and aging! Our population is getting older, and professionals trained in this area are in short supply. In addition, our research knowledge regarding developmental processes in older adults is much more limited than it is for younger populations.

Research Navigator™ Exercise:
Stress and Coping

The objective is to learn more about how researchers study stress and coping processes. Go the Research Navigator™ website: http://www.researchnavigator.com; choose the Psychology database, and type *stress* and *coping* as keywords using the Advanced Search options (p. 60). After reading a full-length article, address the following questions.

1. What was the purpose of the study, and how was stress and coping defined?
2. How were stress and coping processes assessed in the sample?
3. Were the data collected at one time, or was a longitudinal method used?
4. What were the conclusions and possible limitations of the study?

Methodological Issues in Adult Development Research II: Personality and Social Processes

This chapter will discuss methodological issues facing experts who study personality and interpersonal processes in adults. It will first present methodological issues pertaining to personality development. Like most developmental issues, method selection is dependent on one's theoretical perspective. Theoretical orientations of personality development widely differ; some claim that personality structure remains essentially the same during adulthood, whereas others assert that there are vast changes.

The discussion will then take up contexts for adult development, focusing on methods used to assess marriage, parenting, and other contexts for development that occur later in life, such as grandparenthood. The chapter concludes with a section on how best to assess development in occupational environments. After reading this chapter, you should be able to:

- Discuss how best to measure personality structure and change.
- Describe methods used to assess marital behavior, cognitions, and quality.
- Distinguish between parenting styles and practices and methods of assessing them.
- Illustrate the direct and indirect influences that grandparents have on grandchildren, and indicate methodological issues that face intergenerational researchers.
- Describe methodological concerns regarding caregiving research.
- Describe ways of assessing career development and job performance.

Methodological Approaches to Personality Development

Personality research is the study of individual differences in tendencies or traits, goals and motives, emotions and goals, coping processes, self-evaluation, and identity (Ryff, Kwan, &

Singer, 2001). When considering this definition, personality could be viewed as a construct that includes behavioral, emotional, and cognitive components. Let's now discuss methods used by personality researchers who possess different theoretical orientations. *Trait theorists* chart changes in basic personality tendencies, or more outward behavior, across the life course. Another group of scholars focus more inwardly, and examine how adulthood brings changes in self-awareness and identity. These latter theorists adhere to a *stage approach* to personality development, and claim that life events or chronological age itself (e.g., age 50) produce sudden changes in the way we think and act.

Trait Theory and Research

What is meant by the term *trait?* If you associate it with "tendencies" then you are in good company. However, the nature of the term might spark a pessimistic response; it implies that people behave in a similar, consistent way throughout their lives, and that orderly personality development does not occur for most.

Costa and McCrae possess the most widely cited trait theory on personality development. To investigate adult personality development, they have conducted both cross-sectional and longitudinal research to help disentangle the effects of maturity and history on this construct. To increase the validity of their work, they have assessed adult personality using multiple informants; that is, they may poll both target adults and their spouses regarding the personality traits of the target adults. Also, they have assessed personality structure using multiple methods, including questionnaires, interviews, behavior observations, and q-sorts (described later) (Costa & McCrae, 1988; John, 1990; McCrae & Costa, 1987; 1990). Costa and McCrae's research program serves as an exemplar for how to conduct rigorous lifespan-development research.

Based on this work, these experts assert that personality structure is encompassed by five traits—the **Big Five** personality traits. These traits include openness to experience, conscientiousness, extraversion, agreeableness, and neuroticism (hint: think of the acronym *OCEAN* to remember these traits). Examples of these traits are given in Table 12.1.

The *NEO Personality Inventory* (NEO PI-R) and the shorter *NEO Five-Factor Inventory* (NEO-FFI) (Costa & McCrae, 1992) represent the most accessible measures developed by this research team. Sample item content from the NEO scales are shown in Table 12.1; many of the items begin with sentence stems such as, "I usually. . . ." or "I rarely. . . ." Perhaps now you can see a central theme to trait theories of personality is the underlying assumption that these tendencies reflect how the adult *usually* thinks and acts. Although it is acknowledged that contextual variables may influence the display of certain personality tendencies—for instance, a normally outgoing, gregarious person may not behave that way during an opera performance—trait theorists assume that these tendencies are manifested *a majority of time across most contexts.*

The NEO PI-R and the NEO-FFI both assess adult, Big Five personality traits. These instruments are norm referenced, so the results of a sample or an individual can be compared with national norms. The difference between the measures is that the longer NEO PI-R allows researchers to take a deeper look at personality facets within the original Big Five. Consider the trait *Neuroticism;* Although both the NEO PI-R and NEO-FFI assess this trait, the PI-R contains enough items to examine subfacets of this trait, such as

TABLE 12.1 *Examples of Big Five Traits and Corresponding California Adult and Child Q-Set Sample Items*

Big Five Traits and Descriptors	Adult Q-Set Items	Child Q-Set Items
1. Extraversion assertive, outgoing, active	Gregarious Behaves assertively Expressive	Talkative Emotionally expressive Makes social contact easily
2. Agreeableness kind, sympathetic, trusting	Warm, compassionate Basically trustful	Helpful and cooperative Warm and responsive Tends to give, lend, share
3. Conscientiousness organized, reliable	Behaves ethically Not self-indulgent Dependable, responsible	Planful; thinks ahead Persistent in activities Attentive, able to concentrate
4. Neuroticism anxious, tense, worrying	Thin-skinned Anxious Fluctuating moods	Fearful and anxious Goes to pieces under stress Not self-reliant or confident
5. Openness to experience curious, imaginative	Introspective Wide range of interests Values intellectual matters	Has an active fantasy life Curious and exploring Creative in play and work

Source: Adapted from Caspi, 1998.

anxiety, hostility, depression, and vulnerability. Thus, beyond an overall Neuroticism score, we can obtain scores for each subfacet.

The NEO scales do not represent the only personality inventories. John and colleagues have developed the shorter, 44-item *Big Five Inventory* that assesses the same personality traits (John & Srivastava, 1999; scale is free of charge). We can also assess the presence of personality disorders, via various self-report measures, such as the *Minnesota Multiphasic Personality Inventory-II* (MMPI-II; Butcher et al., 1989), as well as social traits (e.g., social poise; self-control), such as the *California Psychological Inventory* (CPI; Gough & Bradley, 1996). Self-report measures, such as the *Hogan Personality Inventory* (HPI; Hogan & Hogan, 1992) match certain personality tendencies, such as sociability, with occupational potential. Finally, methods other than questionnaires, such as q-sort methodologies, can assess personality functioning, and intensive work has investigated the personality structures of children; some of this interesting work is presented in Box 12.1.

Big Five trait scores remain highly consistent over time (McCrae & Costa, 1999). However, their stability depends on the way examiners analyze the data. Although a single adult participant often shows similar, highly correlated trait scores over time, different age groups in adult samples exhibit mean differences in scores. For example, longitudinal research has documented that average scores for conscientiousness and agreeableness increase from young and middle age, and neuroticism scores decline during midlife (at least for women) (Srivastava et al., 2003). These data suggest that a careful, conscientious young adult is likely to remain that way throughout adulthood (a strong positive correlation, suggesting some stability in personality structure), but there may also be times in life when he is less or more so. A good research project would be to study when personality

BOX 12.1 • *Assessing the Personalities of Children*

Most parents can readily describe the personalities or tendencies of their children. Some central questions asked by personality researchers concern the nature of child personality and how it compares to adult personality structure, the stability of this personality, and variables that could be identified as antecedents (e.g., temperament) and consequences (e.g., later delinquency) of child personality structure (Caspi, 1998; Caspi & Silva, 1995).

One of the most interesting child-personality measures is the *California Q-set* (CCQ; Block & Block, 1980). The CCQ consists of 100 items, printed on individual cards, each of which names a behavior or tendency, such as "Initiates humor," "Tends to be self-defensive," "Is calm, relaxed in manner." The adult rater (often a parent) then sorts the cards into piles, ranging from extremely uncharacteristic to extremely characteristic. Requiring the adult to limit the number of cards per pile creates a normal distribution. Because some of the items on the CCQ require advanced vocabulary skills (e.g., "Is fastidious"); Caspi and colleagues (1992) have developed a similar q-set that contains more-common language.

What information does the CCQ provide? The items from this instrument have historically been used to assess *ego resiliency* and *ego control*. Ego resiliency refers to confidence and regulatory skills; thus, CCQ items such as "Is self-reliant, confident," or "Can recoup or recover after stressful experiences" tap this personality dimension. Ego control is somewhat akin to impulse control and the ability to delay gratification; items from the CCQ that reflect this tendency include "Is unable to delay gratification" and "Has rapid shifts in mood." What I like about these constructs is that they have tremendous developmental and clinical ramifications. For instance, it is common knowledge that young children with poor impulse control are at risk for developmental and psychological problems later in life.

In one study, researchers noted that high scores on certain CCQ items obtained in nursery school sorts, such as "Immature behavior under stress" and "Unable to delay gratification" predicted drug use years later during adolescence (Block, Block, & Keyes, 1988)!

Researchers have made some conceptual and methodological advances regarding the CCQ. For instance, the association between ego control and problem behavior is not linear; it is possible to identify children who are under- or over-controlled (Block, 1971; Robins et al., 1996). An over-controlled personality typology reflects a tendency to hold emotions and feelings in; it is not surprising that this trait is a predictor of subsequent depression and anxiety.

The CCQ can be used to identify Big Five traits in children that are similar to those present in adults. John and colleagues (1994), using a sample of early adolescents (ages 11–12) documented that a number of items on the CCQ correspond directly to Big Five traits. A sampling of these items appears in Table 12.1. In one study, adolescents who scored lower on consciousness and agreeableness were more likely to exhibit criminally delinquent behavior; thus, there is good predictive validity for this measure.

Q-sort methods that assess personality structure are not just used with child and adolescent populations; we also have q-sorts that can be used with adults, such as the *California Adult Q-set* (McCrae, Costa, & Busch, 1986); some items from this instrument also appear in Table 12.1. Examiners use this q-sort to identify Big Five personality traits in adults, and the adult participants themselves can sort the cards. An interesting clinical use of the q-sort is to ask an adolescent or adult to conduct a sort that describes their own personality, as well as an "ideal" personality. Theoretically, evaluating how well the two sorts begin to match over time could assess treatment progress.

structure changes, and which life events, such as the transition to parenthood, might provoke such change (Helson et al., 2002).

Stage Theories of Personality

Some trait theorists assume that personality structure remains quite stable. Others take issue with that assertion, and believe that important components of personality structure are added throughout the lifespan. Theorists who assume that development is marked by abrupt changes are *stage theorists*. They assert that when change occurs, there *are dramatic shifts in the way people view themselves, their life priorities, and the people around them.* Stage theorists acknowledge that broad personality dispositions, such as extraversion, remain relatively stable during adulthood, yet they also believe that personality development is related to maturity in the way people view those around them, their own life priorities, and themselves.

Chapter 10 described Erikson's stage theory of personality development. He proposed that adulthood was marked by certain struggles; during early adulthood, the individual must cope with intimacy or isolation (Stage 6). His theory embraced the *epigenetic principle*—that is, resolving a current transition based on successful resolution of previous crises. Erikson theorized that adults could not master the concept of intimacy unless they had previously established trust in relationships (Stage 1) and developed a healthy interpersonal identity (Stage 5).

Other stage theories adhere to the idea that personality structure demonstrates abrupt changes over the life cycle (Levinson, 1978; Levinson & Levinson, 1996; Loevinger, 1976; Vaillant, 1993). Although these theorists disagree on the forces that spur personality development, they all believe that adults change abruptly in the way they view themselves, others, moral obligations, and life priorities. By now, you can see that stage approaches differ substantially from trait theories. Among other things, stage theorists view personality as a much broader construct, and assert that shifts in personality structure are not gradual but quite sudden.

Support for stage theories has been stonewalled somewhat by questionable methods and contradicted by some empirical research. Several major studies involving adult personality development have relied on highly educated samples or have limited participation to either men or women rather than including both (Levinson, 1978; Vaillant, 1977). Also, concepts such as how people view themselves, others, and life priorities are difficult to define and quantify. For the most part, experts have relied on open-ended interviews to assess such complexities in personality structure (see Loevinger, 1985, for an exception). Although this method can lead to rich, qualitative data, researchers other than the original developers, could probably not easily master the interview methods and subjective scoring systems without extensive training.

Although these theorists believe that personality structure displays major changes over the adult life course, few longitudinal studies have tested this belief (see Whitbourne et al., 1992 for an exception). Most of these theories embrace the epigenetic perspective—that is, that early transition resolution serves as a foundation for future transition success. Although this idea makes sense, it lacks support because of the lack of longitudinal data.

The question of whether changes in personality structure are marked by abrupt change or crisis remains open. Recall that trait theorists have documented startling consistency in the disposition, neuroticism, or the tendency to worry, feel anxious, and ruminate. If adult life were marked by personality upheaval, there would be corresponding time periods associated with increases in neuroticism. Indeed, the stability of neuroticism over time argues against major personality transitions during midlife, and casts doubt on a normative "midlife crisis."

Finally, although stage theorists posit that changes in adult personality structure are based on interactions between the person and the environmental context (e.g., career entry, marriage, parenthood, etc.), only limited attempts to demonstrate that this is actually the case have been mounted. For example, documenting that older adults have more capacity for intimacy than younger people does little to explain why this is so. More research is needed to delineate how changing life circumstances, such as marriage, affect personality structure and vice versa.

Summary

Trait theorists often argue that personality dispositions, such as extraversion, solidify during early adulthood and demonstrate little change thereafter. This idea has been supported in many studies using a number of methods, including questionnaire, interview, and observation assessments of the same adults over time. Although scores on personality assessments remain highly correlated over time from one adult to another, mean age differences on certain personality traits have been uncovered. This finding suggests that some aspects of our personality structure do slightly change, and new work has been launched to determine how adult transition points (e.g., marriage, parenting, retirement) predict changes in personality dispositions (or vice versa).

Stage theorists define personality differently, and assert that personality structure is based on how we think about ourselves, others, and life priorities. The methods of stage theorists have been questioned. Some have used select samples (e.g., highly educated men), yielding results based on subjective, open-ended interviews. Although these experts claim that personality structure changes at critical transition points, their research efforts have not associated these changes with contextual events, such as the transition to parenting or marriage.

What Do You Think?

Do you think our personalities change or stay stable during the transition to parenthood? How could you design a study to answer this question? What are some study variables that you would either have to directly measure or control for?

Assessing the Context of Marriage

Marital research is not an area that generates a "so what" attitude. A quick glance in the phone book reveals plenty of experts who specialize in relationship, premarital, marital, and postdivorce counseling. Relationship counselors have lots of clients, and marital research efforts have greatly shaped how these professionals conduct their intervention efforts.

A glance at the framework illustrated in Figure 12.1 indicates that theorists have located important constructs that play a role in the martial process. This conceptual framework posits that certain marital behaviors, such as *secure-base behavior, problem-solving abilities,* and *conflict tactics* represent important constructs that forecast relationship satisfaction and stability (Karney & Bradbury, 1995). This section will discuss how to assess these relationship constructs. These measures are widely-used by professionals that work with both married and nonmarried couples in committed relationships.

A glance at the left side of Figure 12.1 reveals that *distal variables* have some input into the marital process. These variables are labeled distal, because they represent issues that people bring into present relationships from the past. Many researchers find this piece

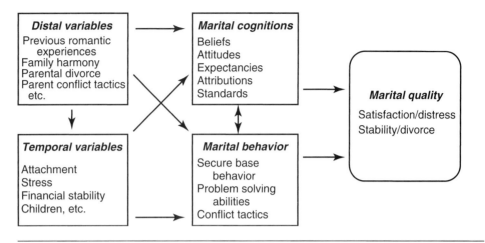

FIGURE 12.1 *Conceptual Framework of Distal and Temporal Variables that Predict Marital Behavior and Satisfaction.*

Adapted from Karney & Bradbury (1995).

of the framework to be the least interesting for research purposes. First, "the past is the past," and one cannot undo exposure to inter-parent conflict, divorce, or child abuse. Second, these variables are notoriously weak predictors of present relationship functioning; many people are surprised to learn that "children of divorce" negotiate conflicts with their partners no differently than children from intact, or nondivorced, family systems (Creasey & Ladd, 2004). Third, retrospective recall of these past events might not be accurate, so it is difficult to isolate the effects of one distal variable (e.g., child abuse) if it co-occurred with other risk factors (e.g., parental marital instability).

An interesting study would be to analyze temporal variables that forecast marital behavior and relationship distress. Some of these constructs have already been discussed. Chapter 5 discussed ways to assess generalized attachment representations regarding caregivers and romantic partners (e.g., *Adult Attachment Interview* and *Current Relationship Inventory*). We can generate a list of other temporal variables that might also affect marital adjustment, such as occupational distress, child characteristics such as temperament, and financial stability. You can probably think of additional items to add to this list.

Finally, theorists group together a cluster of variables labeled *marital cognitions.* These cognitions represent current beliefs, attitudes, and attributions people make regarding their romantic partners. Research identifying the causes and consequences of these cognitions represents an important issue, because these thought processes are amenable to intervention. We will discuss how to assess three important components of the conceptual framework illustrated in Figure 12.1: marital behavior, marital cognitions, and marital quality.

Marital Behavior

It makes sense to posit that marital quality is predicted by the way we actually treat our partners. Perhaps the biggest paradigm shift has been a movement away from using questionnaire or self-report measures of marital behavior to more reliance on behavior observations (Gottman & Notarius, 2002). Some observers have raised concerns regarding the validity of self-report assessments, because respondents' perceptions of marital behavior are not reliably consistent with those witnessed during actual observations (Alexander et al., 1995; Gottman et al., 2002). Respondents find it difficult to remember how they or their partners actually behaved during a problem-solving task or conflict encounter, particularly if the interchange occurred days or weeks earlier.

What makes behavior observations such a gold standard? Such observations are stronger predictors of future relationship stability (including divorce) than data acquired via self-report methods. However, this is not to say that respondents' perceptions of their marital behavior are not worthy of study. If anything, there has been a trend toward using multiple methods—behavior observations, questionnaires, and interviews—to increase our knowledge about how marital behavior influences relationship quality (Johnson, 2001). Also, determining why some couples show discrepancies between their impressions of marital behavior and their actual behavior is an intriguing direction for research.

Two major paradigms are used to study marital behavior. In the social-support, or secure-base paradigm, researchers examine how well partners articulate and empathize with personal problems. In the problem-solving, or conflict encounter, they observe how well the couple resolves an interpersonal conflict or how well the partners treat one another during a disagreement. Other observational methods can also be used to assess marital behavior; however, these particular procedures seem most accurate, because marital interactions observed using these paradigms are the most reliably predictors of relationship quality and stability (Karney & Bradbury, 1995).

Secure-Base Behavior.   Secure-base behavior, or how well a person can give or receive emotional support, is one important marital behavior. Secure-base behavior was first identified by infancy researchers as a marker of attachment; that is, babies who can readily calm down with parental reassurance are typically secure infants. Because marital relationships are also attachment relationships, adults who can readily give and receive effective social support probably have a close and secure relationship with their partner (Crowell, Treboux, & Waters, 2002).

The most straightforward way to assess secure-base behavior would be to observe interactive behavior as a partner discloses a personal problem. In one paradigm, the researcher flips a coin and asks the designated partner to disclose a personally distressing problem (Pasch & Bradbury, 1998). The other partner is asked to listen and respond to this problem as he normally would and observers record the behavior of both the "helper" and "helpee." After a designated time (e.g., 10 min), the partners switch roles and this interaction is duly recorded. Because this procedure is designed to assess supportive, or secure-base behavior, researchers instruct couples to divulge only personal problems, such as work troubles, rather than interpersonal concerns between the two of them. A discussion of an interpersonal problem, such as in-laws, is problematic, because it may generate conflict, which represents another important, yet different, behavioral assessment.

After the couple's behavior is recorded, observers code the behavior of each partner. There are different coding schemes, such as the *Social Support Interaction Coding System* (SSICS; Bradbury & Pasch, 1996) and *Secure Base Scoring System* (Crowell et al., 1996).

These systems allow researchers to code the behavior of both partners. In the SSICS they note the frequency of emotional and instrumental support the helper provides the helpee, and rate how well the helpee articulates the problem and responds to the helper's assistance. Both of these coding systems are valid; couples that score poorly are at high risk for divorce (Treboux, Crowell, & Waters, 2004).

Conflict- and Problem-Solving Tactics. The standard paradigm to elicit conflict exchanges between romantic partners is straightforward. Each partner evaluates, on a self-report measure, relationship issues (e.g., in-laws, sex) that commonly lead to conflict. The inventories are completed separately, and the researcher selects "hot" issues (e.g., those that both partners listed) for the couple to discuss.

Observers next instruct the couple to discuss these interpersonal problems and move toward conflict resolution. This is a key manipulation, because many of these problems cannot be easily resolved in just a few minutes. The researcher then records these interactions for a short period of time (e.g., 15 min). Such an observation should be a final assessment, because a particularly negative interaction could color how the participants respond on other measures.

Researchers can code these data in at least three ways. They can analyze the problem-solving abilities of each partner, and of the couple as a unit, as they attempt conflict resolution. They can also evaluate how well the couple resolved the disagreement. Finally, they can examine how well the partners treated each other emotionally during the interaction.

Examples of coding systems designed to capture this behavior are the *Verbal Tactics Coding System* (Sillars, 1982) and the *Interactional Dimensions Coding System* (Julien, Markman, & Lindahl, 1989). I particularly like John Gottman's (1996) coding systems, because they capture all of the conflict facets described above; that is, problem-solving abilities, conflict resolution, and emotional treatment can all be assessed together. His system is easy to learn, and he includes training tapes that coders can use to achieve better reliability or interrater consistency.

When using Gottman's *Rapid Couple Interaction Scoring System* (RCISS; Gottman, 1996), the coder rates major components of couple problem-solving abilities, such as agenda building. For example, the codes *positive presentation of own views* and *criticism* represent very different ways of presenting an interpersonal problem to a partner. The former code pertains to taking ownership of the problem, such as, "I think we have a problem with the kids." Criticism, on the other hand is more personalized, and marked by a negative emotional tone, such as, "You didn't give the kids a bath last night—*AGAIN*." Why is problem-solving an important skill? Consider how you would personally respond to the aforementioned statements; the latter statement would probably just create conflict escalation. Indeed, the RCISS contains codes that tabulate conflict escalation and de-escalation during these disagreements.

Gottman's *Specific Affect Coding System* (SPAFF; Gottman, 1996) is used to rate positive and negative *emotional behaviors* exhibited during these disagreements; some primary codes are listed in Table 12.2. The SPAFF codes can be used individually or aggregated together using statistical analyses (Katz & Gottman, 1993). Analyses of husband-and-wife SPAFF data reveal two conflict profiles: *Mutually hostile* and *Demand-withdraw.* Mutually hostile couples hurl degrading comments back and forth. In demand-withdraw couples, one partner is highly domineering and critical, whereas the other partner is tense,

TABLE 12.2 *Sample Specific Affect Coding System Codes*

Code	Examples
Humor	Laughing, good-natured teasing, or private humor between couple.
Affection	Concerned emotional expression; direct statement of affection, such as, "I love you."
Validation	Nods head in response to partner comment, or says, "I see what you mean."
Defensiveness	Deflects responsibility or blames partner, such as, "We wouldn't be in this mess if you made more money."
Belligerence	Attempts to provoke partner emotionally, such as, "So what if I date other people; what are you going to do about it?"
Domineering	Attempts to shut partner down, such as, "Just shut up, I don't want to hear it," or incessantly interrupts partner.
Contempt	Attacks partner's personality or utters emotionally abusive comments, such as, "You whine just like your mother, blah blah blah blah."

Source: Gottman, 1996.

defensive, and withdrawn. Both profiles are problematic, and forecast later divorce, marital violence, and child-behavior problems in the family (Holtzworth-Munroe, Smutzler, & Stuart, 1998; Katz & Gottman, 1993).

Problem-solving abilities and the emotional content of the conflict interaction are potent predictors of relationship distress. The way we treat our partners during these disagreements is more important than the actual resolution of the conflict itself (Gottman, 1994). Gottman has found that couples happily married for decades often argue about the same old things over time! Perhaps some conflicts can never be resolved.

In summary, the concern that adults may present inaccurate information on self-reports of marital behavior has led researchers to rely on behavior observations to provide a more accurate index of this behavior. However, we should not abandon self-reports of marital behavior. Poor congruence between perceptions of marital behavior and actual behavior is an interesting avenue of inquiry. Also, certain behaviors have low base rates or are not amenable to visual scrutiny, such as physical violence. These are review papers that provide a summary of measures used to assess these less-observable constructs (Fincham, 1998; Johnson, 2001).

Marital Cognitions

People in distressed relationships view their marriage and partner very differently than their counterparts in nondistressed relationships. For example, when their partner is late, a person in a distressed relationship may think, "She's running late because she does not want to be around me," whereas a person in a nondistressed marriage may muse, "She must have had to work late, the poor thing!" Indeed, the goal of cognitive-behavioral marital therapy is to change these relationship cognitions in a more positive direction.

Because such cognitions are internalized, many questionnaire and interview methods exist to tap these thoughts (Baucom & Epstein, 1990; Fincham, 1998; Johnson, 2001).

However, because these cognitions are routinely verbalized during interactions with partners, we can rate them when conducting observations of marital behavior. The *Leeds Attributional Coding System* (Stratton et al., 1988) represents one observational coding system that allows observers to code spontaneous utterances during interactions that represent relationship cognitions.

Martial cognitions include relationship attributions, expectancies, beliefs or assumptions, and standards (Baucom et al., 1989). Definitions of these various thought processes, as well as some popular measures, are presented in Table 12.3. Consider how you might relate these cognitions to your own romantic relationship or how you might conceptualize an ideal partner. These modes of thinking affect marital behavior. Adults who make unfair or inaccurate attributions about their partner's behavior display more problematic marital behavior than adults who do not hold these views (Baucom et al., 1996; Bradbury & Fincham, 1992; Fincham et al., 1995; Karney et al., 1994).

TABLE 12.3 *Different Marital Cognitions*

Marital Cognition	Description	Sample Measure/Description
Attributions	Inferences about the causes of the partner's behavior. For example, "He is always late because he does not love me."	*Relationship Attribution Measure* (Fincham & Bradbury, 1992): Respondents read various stimulus items, such as, "Your wife is cool and distant." Next, they rate different attribution indexes for the stimulus, such as the likelihood that this partner's behavior is selfishly motivated.
Expectancies	Forecasting how a partner *will* think or behave in a situation, such as, "He won't agree with me on that."	*Marital Agendas Protocol* (Notarius & Vanzetti, 1983): Each partner is presented 10 areas of frequent problems in relationships (e.g., finances). Respondents then rate their degree of confidence in how well the conflict with their partner can be resolved.
Beliefs	Assumptions about how the partner thinks or acts, such as, "I believe that my partner understands why I get so upset," or assumptions about relationships in general.	*Relationship Belief Inventory* (Eidelson & Epstein, 1982): 40-item self-report measure that contains such items as, "Damages done early in a relationship probably cannot be reversed."
Standards	Beliefs about how a partner *should* act as well as assumptions about how romantic relationships should function in general.	*Inventory of Specific Relationship Standards* (Baucom et al., 1996): Scale assesses relationship standards regarding control and power, investment, and boundaries. Contains items such as, "My partner and I should take part in our leisure activities with each other" (*boundaries*), and "Only one of us should have the final say on decisions about money" (*control*).

Because methods used to assess relationship cognitions are often of the self-report variety, some doubt their validity. However, the fact that experts have linked these modes of thinking to actual marital behavior casts doubt on the assumption that people paint unusually rosy or pessimistic portrayals of relationships. These cognitions predict marital behavior when controlling for depression, demographic variables, and marital distress (see Fincham, 1998 for review).

Marital Quality

Marital quality refers to our evaluation of overall marital health. It is often used as an index of marital distress or satisfaction. Marital quality, as a construct, is held in high esteem by relationship experts—so high that it is not uncommon for researchers to create samples of distressed and satisfied couples for comparison purposes. Two of the most commonly used marital-quality measures are the 15-item *Marital Adjustment Test* (MAT; Locke & Wallace, 1959) and the 32-item *Dyadic Adjustment Scale* (DAS; Spanier, 1976). The DAS was developed from the shorter MAT, and has become the most commonly used marital assessment. The DAS assesses general agreement about standard marital issues (e.g., finances, sex, careers), and how often the couple does things together (e.g., household projects, recreation).

Although the DAS has been widely used, some recent concerns have emerged. Items on marital-quality measures, such as the DAS, sometimes overlap with those on other measures of marital functioning (Fincham, 1998). Multiple DAS items inquire about specific types of conflict in the relationship; thus, it would not be surprising to obtain a significant correlation between the DAS and a conflict-tactics measure because of item redundancy.

Also, polling adults about how often they do things together (e.g., laughing, sex, kissing) or how much they agree on issues (e.g., career decisions)— standard DAS items—does not provide us a measure of the *adult's evaluation* of the marriage. Thus, some researchers have concluded that marital quality is best assessed using shorter, *more direct* measures of marital satisfaction (Fincham, 1998). For instance, the *Kansas Marital Satisfaction Scale* (Schumm et al., 1986) contains just three short items that specifically inquire about marital satisfaction, such as "How satisfied are you with your marriage?" The advantages of this instrument are that it is very short and provides the researcher the adult's own direct appraisal or evaluation of overall marital quality.

Summary

In this section, we discussed methods used to assess the context of marriage. Marital cognitions and behavior are important to measure, because they affect overall marital quality and relationship stability. Although space limitations precluded a discussion of the various temporal (e.g., occupational stress) and distal (e.g., child abuse) variables that may influence marital processes, when making such predictions, it is important to assess marital cognitions, behavior, and quality over time in order to identify the mechanisms behind relationship distress. For example, establishing links between occupational stress and marital quality is an inherently uninteresting finding, because it does not allow us to conclude

What Do You Think?

Suppose you and your friend disagree about occupational stress and marital functioning; you cannot agree on what causes what. How would you design a study to better address this question, with the realization that your nonexperimental design will be limited in terms of conclusions? Identify your study variables and how you might measure them.

how such stress disrupted the mechanisms contributing to marital quality (i.e., marital cognitions and behavior). In addition, temporal variables, such as occupational distress, may not automatically impinge on marital relationships in a unidirectional manner. For example, an individual in a bad marriage may allow this disruption to interfere with work performance, which ultimately accounts for occupational stress.

Methodological Issues in Parenting Research

To help understand the landscape of parenting, take a look at the conceptual framework presented in Figure 12.2 (Belsky, 1984; Parke & Buriel, 1998). This figure is akin to the theoretical framework presented earlier regarding marital behavior and quality; as in Figure 12.1, distal and temporal variables affect the way parents think and behave around their children. Examples of distal variables might include the parent's own child-rearing history or cultural background, whereas temporal variables might be marital quality or child characteristics. As any parent of a teenager could attest to parenting, raising an adolescent is much different from raising a toddler!

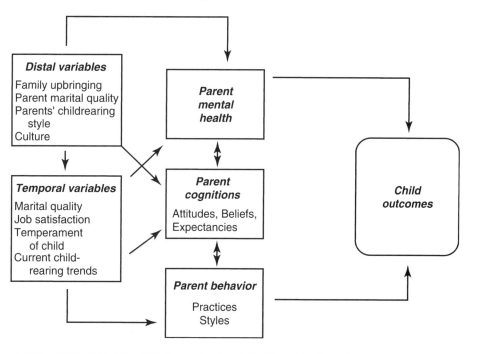

FIGURE 12.2 *Conceptual Framework of Distal and Temporal Variables that Predict Parenting Behavior.*

Adapted from Belsky (1984); Parke & Buriel (1998).

Note that the influence of parents *is not directly confined to parenting behavior.* For example, parents with mental health problems, such as depression, may directly affect the emotional development of their children, even when they raise them in optimal ways (Teti et al., 1995). This section will describe techniques used to assess such affective, cognitive, and behavioral components to parenting, each directly affects the welfare of the child, and they all relate to one another. For example, a depressed parent may display negative affect around their child, exhibit little confidence in their parenting abilities (a cognitive component), and engage in permissive or control-oriented behavior.

What Child Outcomes Should I Predict?

A common question I hear from students is, "I can identify parenting variables, but what should I predict?" This is a good question, because a well-designed, theoretically justified study loses its impact if we choose dependent or outcome variables that are not important for human development. The answer to this question is challenging, because some areas of child functioning are meaningful and easy to assess at all stages of childhood, whereas other developmental processes are more important at particular stages of development. For example, child behavioral problems can be reliably assessed from late toddlerhood through adolescence, and a high frequency of behavioral problems are developmentally and clinically relevant during all stages of development. In addition self-concept, social competence, and intellectual abilities would represent salient outcome variables for children and adolescents alike.

However, special issues arise at particular times of development. The changing dynamics of family interactions during adolescence, or the emergence of identity, sexuality, or emotional autonomy would represent more important outcomes for adolescents than for younger children. Thus, when selecting a dependent measure to associate with parenting processes, we must give special thought to our outcome variable(s) and determine whether they represent an important issue for all children or only for a certain developmental period. If you want a laundry list of infant, child, and adolescent outcomes associated with parenting processes, I encourage you to consult the *Handbook of Parenting* (Vol. 1., Bornstein, 2002).

Parental Emotional Functioning

How does the emotional functioning of the parent affect the developing child? Perhaps the most naturalistic way to answer this question would be to analyze the types of emotions the parent frequently experiences and note corresponding changes in the child. This could be done by observing the spontaneous emotions the parent displays during parent-child interactions or by encouraging the parent to sequentially exhibit contrasting emotions to observe how the child reacts to emotional shifts (e.g., from joy to sadness). Researchers frequently use the latter strategy to determine how young infants react to the emotional displays of parents. From a somewhat different perspective, other researchers study how parents with major affective disturbances, such as clinical depression, influence the socioemotional environment of their children. Finally, another strategy would be to identify how parents help their children when they are experiencing emotional distress. We will discuss each of these strategies in this section.

Spontaneous or Elicited Emotional Expressions.   Some experts have studied and reported on how children respond to the naturally occurring emotional expressions of parents in naturalistic settings (Radke-Yarrow et al., 1985), or have examined how children react to sudden changes in affect when parents are instructed to display various emotions (e.g., anger, fear, happiness) in a structured situation. Chapter 5 discussed how infants and young children readily attend to the emotional expressions of parents, and display sudden changes in their own emotional expressions, behavior, and physiological responses when parents are instructed to "look happy or sad" (Izard et al., 1995). Chapter 5 also discussed the concept of "maternal sensitivity"; the emotional expressions that parents display when responding to infant distress have important implications for socioemotional development (Main & Hesse, 1998).

However, delineating links between the spontaneous emotional expressions of caregivers and child functioning is not a method that is confined to infancy and preschool researchers; parent anger or sadness elicited during problem-solving tasks affects the conflict tactics and emotional expressiveness of the adolescent (Holmbeck & Hill, 1991). Similarly, researchers have noted the spontaneous emotions exhibited by parents during challenging tasks to determine whether they parallel the emotions displayed by a child (Cassidy et al., 1992). It is quite obvious that a parent who displays poor emotional regulation when interacting with their child sets a poor exemplar for their child or adolescent (Cummings & Davies, 1994).

Is there a quicker way to elicit such emotional expressiveness? The 36-item *Family Expressiveness Questionnaire* (FEQ; Cassidy et al., 1992) was designed to assess parents' expressiveness in the family environment. The FEQ is a self-report measure that assesses the tendency of parents to display positive and negative emotions around other family members. Positive items include whether the parent expresses gratitude over a favor or spontaneously hugs family members. In contrast, negative items would include the tendency to become angry at the carelessness of others or put down the accomplishments of a family member.

The validity data on the FEQ are quite impressive. Mothers who reported more positive emotional expressiveness around their children and other family members displayed more positive emotions when their school-aged children played a challenging game in a laboratory context. Parental emotions exhibited during this game correlated well with the same types of emotional expressions displayed by their children. Finally, parental emotional expressiveness recorded on the FES was related to their child's peer acceptance; families that display high amounts of positive emotions have children that are better liked by their peers (Cassidy et al., 1992). This is not surprising, because competent peer interactions require good regulatory skills and the ability to empathize with the plights of others.

Parents with Serious Emotional Disturbances.   Most of the research in this area involves clinically depressed mothers. Historically, the effects of maternal mood disorders have been examined in younger children; however, recent work has associated parental emotional functioning with adolescent adjustment (Brennan et al., 2002; Nelson et al., 2003). We can identify mood disturbance in parents in various ways, but obtaining a clinical diagnosis by a trained professional is a rather rare method. Most researchers who study depression in families ask a parent (almost always the mother) to complete a self-report measure of depressive symptoms, such as the 20-item *Center for Epidemiological Studies— Depression Inventory* (CES-D ; Radloff, 1977). The CES-D requires the respondent to indicate the frequency of events associated with clinical depression, such as appetite problems and crying (see Chapter 11). The CES-D has a cutoff score that may designate possible clinical depression; it is tempting to label adults with this score or higher as clinically depressed, because 99 percent of such diagnosed people score above the cutoff!

When using self-report measures, the researcher should concede that they are assessing depressive symptoms rather than clinical depression; unfortunately, this idea is a rule that is not always followed. However, despite the lack of a diagnosis, researchers who use such self-report measures routinely uncover findings that are consistent with what is found with clinically diagnosed parent samples. That is, parents who report frequent depressive symptoms display disruptions in parenting behavior, and their children display problems in emotion regulation (Elger et al., 2003; Lyons-Ruth et al., 1990; Rosenblum et al., 2002).

Why are mothers the frequent target population in such studies? There is no question that mothers have an important influence on the emotional development of their children (Collins, Madsen, & Susman-Stillman, 2002). However, a strict maternal depression → child outcome interpretation is probably only one of several correct theories (Lovejoy et al., 2000). For example, maternal depression is co-morbid, or co-occurs with other maternal problems, as well as with other disruptions in family functioning. Some adults experience symptoms of both anxiety and depression, whereas others primarily exhibit depressive symptoms. Likewise, paternal alcoholism and maternal depression are frequently correlated (Eiden, Edwards, & Leonard, 2002), and child adjustment problems are made worse when both mothers and fathers experience depression (Brennan et al., 2002). Thus, developing a research design to isolate the effects of maternal depression, per se, is difficult because of other problems pressing on the mother, family, and child.

Also, because certain mental disorders may have a genetic component, it is difficult to tease out whether the child is adversely affected by having a depressed parent around or whether their emotional functioning is driven by genetic input. Although research using identical twins can partly untangle this issue, longitudinal research could allow researchers to estimate whether the emotional functioning of children improves or declines as a result of changes in parental mood. For example, maternal employment is associated with subsequent declines in maternal depression, which in turn predict improvements in children's socioemotional adjustment (Newcombe, 2003). Such research contradicts the notion that mental health problems are "set in stone" and not modifiable due to changing environmental circumstances.

Parent Meta-Emotions.   **Meta-emotions** are akin to metacognition (See Chapter 6), and reflect our ability to think about our emotional abilities, experiences, and expressions. Gottman has broadened this idea to include parents' emotional understanding of their child, and their tendency to "emotionally coach," and provide' "emotional education" to the child. Gottman and colleagues (1996) have developed the *Meta-Emotion Interview,* to capture parental awareness of their own and children's emotions and their emotional coaching abilities. The interview contains questions such as, "How do you feel about being sad?", "What are the subtle signs of anger in your child?", or "How do you help your child feel better when upset?" Note how each question taps important elements of the meta-emotion construct.

Using this interview, Gottman identified three types of parents. Some parents are dismissing or disapproving of their children's emotions; they may discipline the child for displaying anger or sadness, even in cases in which the child is not really misbehaving. Other parents understand the emotions of their children, yet are indecisive regarding how to coach the child through their distress. Finally, a third group of parents understand their own emotions and react appropriately to their child's negative emotions. It is not surprising that their children are socially competent, possess good regulatory skills, and are well liked by their peers. The typologies possess a ring of truth when one casually observes the various ways parents respond to the emotions of children in naturalistic settings. It is not uncommon to witness parents who suppress the negative emotions of children; others smoothly assuage the feelings of their children, whereas others seem somewhat uncertain about how to respond.

What Do You Think?

Suppose you want to determine how parental depression affects emotional expressiveness and parent meta-emotional abilities. How would you assess these constructs? Speculate on what you might find.

Parental Cognitions

Gottman's work suggests that the way we reason about emotions is an important precursor to parenting behavior. This idea is not new, and there have been efforts designed to identify which parent cognitions may forecast parenting behavior. These efforts are similar to the work of marital researchers, who theorize that marital assumptions, expectancies, and attributions ultimately predict marital behavior and quality.

Parenting Knowledge and Assumptions.   Theoretically, a caregiver who is educated regarding developmental issues should display better parenting practices than one who knows little about children. One excellent measure that assesses parental knowledge is the *Concepts of Development Vignettes* (CODV, Sameroff & Feil, 1985). This assessment consists of six stories that depict developmental problems and parenting practices common to all cultures; one of these vignettes is presented below. Read it over and jot down how you would respond.

> Mr. and Mrs. Raymond have two children: Billy, who is 5, and Mary, who is 3. Billy was a very demanding baby, and still asks for a lot of attention from his parents. Billy would get very angry if he didn't get what he wanted from his parents. Lately, Mr. and Mrs. Raymond have had a lot of money problems, because Mr. Raymond was laid off from his job. One evening at bedtime, Mrs. Raymond heard Billy and Mary fighting over a toy. She stormed into the bedroom, began spanking Billy very hard, and wouldn't stop. Mr. Raymond had to pull her away from the boy and had a hard time calming her down.
>   How would you explain Mrs. Raymond's behavior? (Gutierrez & Sameroff, 1990, p. 388).

More complex answers that reflect advanced perspective-taking skills typically receive higher ratings. Two sample responses of varying quality are given in Table 12.4. Note how the second response is deeper in terms of perspective taking and theory building. The respondent considers the parent's behavior from multiple angles, and reasons that characteristics of the

TABLE 12.4 *Sample Responses to Concepts of Development Vignette*

Categorical Response	*Perspectivistic Response*
Mrs. Raymond is obviously bothered by other things; for example, the family is having financial problems. Perhaps they can't make their mortgage payments, so she is just letting her emotions out. So, her behavior really does not have much to do with Billy; the kids fighting over the toy just broke the camel's back. She just seems to be getting her anger out, over the mounting pressure of financial strain.	There are a lot of issues that come in to play here. First, she may have always had a hard time dealing with Billy; he may have been born with colic or simply has a difficult temperament. True, the situation is made worse by the financial problems, and she may have been fighting recently with her husband over these issues. The marital conflict may have shortened her fuse, and also causes Billy to act out more than ever before. Billy might have even more problems if the family cannot get their stress under control. The family may need more support and perhaps should seek some type of family counseling.

Source: Adapted from Gutierrez & Sameroff, 1990.

child and the marital context have exacerbated the situation. Also, note how the respondent considers the long-term implications of the situation.

Sameroff's lab has also developed a parallel questionnaire, the *Concepts of Development Questionnaire* (Sameroff & Feil, 1985), that yields information similar to that of the vignette method. This measure is very easy to administer and can be used by students new to this area of research, who may have concerns about mastering the coding system tied to the vignette methodology.

In addition, these experts have identified variables that predict high knowledge scores on these methods. For instance, immigrants to the United States who are bicultured—that is, who readily accept certain customs and belief systems from both their new and old cultures—often produce perspectivistic thinking on the vignettes (Gutierrez & Sameroff, 1990). These researchers believe that bicultural adults are highly flexible people, and cognitive flexibility may allow them to consider parenting issues from different perspectives. They also note that parental concepts of development predict the development of child intellect over time. Children of perspectivistic parents have better intellectual outcomes than their counterparts with more categorical caregivers (Sameroff et al., 1993). This finding was confirmed while controlling for parent intelligence; thus, parenting expertise predicts child outcomes in a unique manner.

Beyond the assessment of parental knowledge, some researchers have examined how parenting beliefs regarding different child behaviors (misbehavior, academic behavior) and popular child contexts (e.g., peer group, extracurricular activities) affect parenting behavior and child-rearing practices. It is somewhat difficult to provide a comprehensive account of these belief measures, because there are so many. Some of these belief inventories target specific domains of child behavior. For example, some belief inventories tap parental thinking regarding academic behavior (Frome & Eccles, 1998; Halle, Kurtz-Costes, & Mahoney,

1997), misbehavior and discipline (Hastings & Grusec, 1998), emotional development (Gottman et al., 1996), and social behavior (Hastings & Rubin, 1999).

Still other instruments provide a more comprehensive account of parenting beliefs. The *Child-Rearing Practices Report Q-sort* (CRPR; Block, 1981) is a 91-item card-sort procedure that assesses parental attitudes and beliefs about children, as well as actual parenting practices (see Chapter 5 for details on how to administer and score q-sorts). The q-sort assesses a number of parenting beliefs, such as thoughts regarding child independence ("I believe children should not have secrets from their parents"), parental control ("I believe physical punishment is the best way of disciplining"), and achievement ("I think it is good practice for a child to perform in front of others") (Roberts, Block, & Block, 1984). It is interesting that child adjustment is more optimal when both parents share similar belief systems on this measure (Vaughn, Block, & Block, 1988).

What does the validity work on this measure look like? Belief systems assessed on the CRPR have been tied to actual parenting behavior. In one study, researchers administered the CRPR Q-Sort (Block, 1981) with the intent of examining parents' beliefs about child independence and parent control. Links between these beliefs systems and behavioral inhibition, or "social wariness," in Chinese and Canadian children was specified (Chen et al., 1998). Behavioral inhibition reflects the tendency to approach social situations cautiously, and exhibit shy, deferential (yielding) behaviors during social interactions.

The findings garnered from this study support the conceptual framework presented earlier in Figure 12.2; cultural influences strongly predicted parenting beliefs and practices. The Chinese parents viewed social inhibition as a good quality; broader Chinese philosophy views social restraint as a way to preserve good feelings and smooth social interactions. Western parents did not hold these beliefs. Canadian parents viewed behavioral inhibition as a sign of weakness. Also, these belief systems from the CRPR predicted actual child-rearing behavior. The Chinese children were much slower to approach a stranger, but whether this behavior is a sign of strength or a problem seems to be in the eye of the beholder. Notice how such research provides validity data for not only the measure, but also the theory presented in Figure 12.2.

Parental beliefs about their children represent only one important assumption. For instance, researchers have created methods for discovering how parents develop beliefs about their *own parenting competencies* (Sigel & McGillicuddy-De Lisi, 2002). Broadly speaking, this work fits in the realm of parenting self-efficacy, or self-confidence in parenting. Chapter 10 discussed the concept of self-efficacy and pointed out that children and adolescents who hold a high degree of confidence in their academic abilities (or academic self-efficacy) exhibit more positive achievement outcomes than their counterparts with less confidence. Likewise, seminal work with parental self-efficacy measures has yielded parallel findings. In one study of impoverished children, researchers noted that single mothers who reported high parenting self-efficacy were more likely to have loftier academic goals for the children than their counterparts with less confidence (Brody, Flor, & Gibson, 1999). Thus, when assessing parenting belief systems, we can examine the parents' thought processes regarding both themselves and their children.

Parental Expectancies and Attributions.   When assessing parental expectancies, we can ask adults to forecast a possible outcome of an event (e.g., child academic failure) and predict how this outcome will affect *three* possible domains:

1. The parent can conceptualize how the outcome will affect the child; this has been labeled a *child-centered expectancy,* because the focus of the outcome is the child.

2. Parents can be asked to estimate how an outcome will actually affect them, or *parent-centered expectancies.*

3. They can be asked to make predictions about how the outcome will affect the parent-child relationship, or *relationship expectancies* (Dix, 1992; Grusec & Goodnow, 1994).

The strength of this approach is that we can assess the accuracy of parent expectancies and the parent's goals regarding an outcome. When asked to make predictions about reactions to a child's academic failure, a parent who says, "I expect my child will get upset and will need my help" would be viewed differently than a parent who says, "I expect my child will get upset and that will make me really upset." The first parent is focused on the child or relationship, whereas the second adult is focused on how the outcome will affect his or her own well-being.

To assess such expectancies, Hastings and Grusec (1998) created vignettes about difficult interactions between parents and children, such as inappropriate child behavior in a public setting. Parents were asked what types of outcomes they would expect and prefer, noting whether the parent tended to focus on their own needs, the needs of their child, or the relationship in general. The researchers documented that adults who expected and preferred more short-term parenting goals, such as getting the child to be quiet in the public setting to preserve their own comfort level, were more likely to use more power assertion (e.g., commanding words and physical punishment) in their parenting practices than adults who possessed child- or relationship-centered expectancies. The point of this work is that expectancy assessment entails more than asking a parent to predict a simple outcome of an event; rather, this method should include an assessment of the *reasoning behind this prediction.*

Researchers have also developed methods to assess *parent attributions* regarding child behavior or performance. A large amount of work has examined how parenting beliefs, expectancies, and attributions affect the academic cognitions and behavior of children and adolescents (Eccles, Wigfield, & Schiefele, 1998). Of course, many other arenas also seem ripe for attribution assessment; for example, some assess the attributions of parents who have children with disabilities or learning problems. Charlotte Johnston has examined the attributions of parents who have children with attention-deficit hyperactivity disorder (ADHD), a disorder marked by child inattentiveness, impulsivity, and high activity levels.

Johnston and colleagues have developed a battery of measures that assess the attributions parents formulate when reading vignettes involving defiant, oppositional ADHD children, and attributions they make following a recent event involving their own child. They also observed parents interact with their child in structured contexts designed to elicit oppositional behaviors, such as not allowing the child a turn in a game. The children are more likely to act out in such situations, and at the end of the interaction the researchers asked the parents to make attributions regarding the child's behavior (Johnston & Freeman, 1997).

After administering these assessments, observers coded the parent attributions. They noted large individual differences in the parental attributions. Parents of highly oppositional ADHD children often view the more negative behaviors as uncontrollable, not subject to change, and resulting from the basic nature of the disorder (Johnston & Freeman 1997; Johnson, Reynolds, 1998). These attributions are in direct contrast to those of parents with nonproblem children, and these experts believe that for effective parenting interventions to take place, the more rigid thinking must be overcome (Johnston & Freeman, 1997). A parent who believes they cannot control their child's behavior would not directly benefit from parent training until these attributions are modified.

In summary, although researchers have documented associations between parenting cognitions and child developmental outcomes, this is an area that is far from settled. On methodological grounds, researchers continue to improve on methods that assess these different modes of thinking. One research team has developed an intensive coding system to capture parenting beliefs and expectancies that are offered spontaneously during family dinnertime conversations (Fiese et al., 1999). There are other angles that should be pursued. For example, although most theorists view parenting beliefs, expectancies, and attributions as separate constructs, few have examined how these cognitions are interrelated (Miller, 1995). Also, we still do not know how these parental cognitions develop, are maintained, or change over time.

Parenting Styles and Practices

What parenting styles ultimately predict optimal child and adolescent outcomes? In perhaps one of the most famous parenting studies of all time, Baumrind gathered a sample of families with young children and rated parent-child interactions (spanning 20–30 hours) using home-based observations when the children were 4 years of age, and repeated these observations when the children were 9 and 15 (Baumrind, 1971; 1991; Baumrind & Black, 1967). These observations were conducted at a time when all family members were home, and allowed the researchers to note parent-child interactions during routine setting events, such as dinner-, bath-, and bedtime. Besides the observational data, they polled the parents regarding their customary parenting practices and assessed the behavioral functioning of the child over time.

The researchers coded 75 parenting behaviors, such as "Provides an intellectually stimulating environment," "Many rules and regulations," "Lacks empathetic understanding," and "Encourages independent actions." Using statistical techniques, they identified two broad dimensions of parenting behavior—*demandingness* and *responsiveness*. Because parents can score high or low on both dimensions, Baumrind proposed the four parenting prototypes depicted in Table 12.5. In the vast majority of cases, both parents were classified identically.

Many studies have validated this system; children and adolescents reared in authoritative households have better developmental outcomes than their counterparts raised in nonauthoritative families (Collins, Madsen, & Susman-Stillman, 2002; Steinberg & Silk, 2002). Children reared in households that contain cold and neglectful parents are at high risk for problematic developmental and mental-health outcomes (Repetti, Taylor, & Seeman, 2002). These characteristics, of course, are major facets of the rejecting or neglectful

TABLE 12.5   *Baumrind's Parenting Styles*

Parenting Style/Description	*Modal Child Outcomes*
Authoritative: Sets limits for child; however, adjusts limits depending on developmental status or temperament of child. Warm, emotionally responsive caregiver.	Healthy psychological adjustment, few behavior problems. Socially and cognitively competent, predicts healthy identity, autonomy, intimacy, and achievement outcomes during adolescence.
Authoritarian: Rigid, power-assertive parent who demands compliance, order, and strict adherence to rules. Scores low on emotional responsiveness, although may score high on parental monitoring.	Conforming and dependent; thus, may have difficulties with identity and autonomy during adolescence. Likely to be well behaved, and parenting style seems to discourage substance abuse during adolescence.
Permissive/Indulgent: Lenient and avoids confrontation or parent-child conflict. Responsive to the emotional needs of the child.	Displays difficulties coping with the demands of social institutions, such as schools. Likely to be irresponsible and dependent. Likely to have identity problems during adolescence, and susceptible to peer pressure.
Rejecting/Neglecting: Neither demanding nor responsive. Little limit setting or parental monitoring; not emotionally responsive to the needs of the child.	More likely to have behavioral and psychological problems than children with nonrejecting parents. Associated with major psychosocial problems during adolescence.

parenting style in Baumrind's typology. Interestingly, the benefits of an authoritative style are not confined to the parenting domain. Teachers who are demanding yet emotionally responsive have higher-achieving students than their nonauthoritative counterparts (Roeser & Eccles, 1998)

Alternative Methods.   Having read about Baumrind's research program, are you now ready to observe parent-child interactions over a 20-hour time period per family? Perhaps one of the biggest methodological contributions involves the development of parenting measures that make this research arena more accessible. What are some good methods for assessing parenting styles? One of the most respected measures is the *CRPR Q-sort* (CRPR; Block, 1981), which was described earlier in this chapter. As you recall, the CRPR assesses parental attitudes, expectancies, and child-rearing practices; parents (or observers) are required to sort a variety of cards into stacks ranging from most to least descriptive of the parent. Q-sort methods give us an added edge over traditional questionnaire methods, because the respondent can place only a limited number of cards in each stack. This strategy forces respondents to discriminate among the various items (Chapter 5).

One question that arises about the CRPR pertains to its construct validity; it contains items that assess both parenting beliefs (cognitions) and perceptions of child-rearing practices. The fact that the CRPR assesses multiple constructs creates contradictory messages; some researchers claim that this instrument assesses child-rearing *attitudes* (Chen et al., 1998), whereas others report it as a child-rearing-*practices* measure (Kochanska et al., 1989). The scoring instructions do not allow for segregation of these belief and behavior items; thus, a parent who scores high on independence would strongly endorse both belief

("I believe that children should not have secrets from their parents") and practice ("I let my child make many decisions for himself/herself") items. This issue causes one to wonder just what this instrument is measuring, and how scores could be affected if a parent's belief system does not correlate with their practices.

Despite this concern, researchers have tied data from this instrument to parenting behavior and important child outcomes. In one study, mothers were observed interacting with their young children after completing the CRPR. There were modest correlations between certain CRPR dimensions and parenting behavior. Caregivers who endorsed more restrictive parenting beliefs and practices made more direct commands, reprimands, and physical enforcements (e.g., arm pulling) than parents who endorsed more autonomy-granting practices (Kochanska et al., 1989). As you know by now, demonstrating that data from a self-report measure correlates well with behavior observations is an important step in the validity process.

There have been other important contributions made by researchers using the CRPR. For example, certain CRPR items can be clustered to create parenting typology categories in the spirit of Baumrind's original theoretical and empirical work (e.g., authoritative versus authoritarian) (Kochanska et al., 1989; McNally, Eisenberg, & Harris, 1991). In addition, numerous studies have linked CRPR parenting styles to child and adolescent functioning, including socioemotional adjustment, academic functioning, and delinquent behavior and drug use (e.g., Block, Block, & Keyes, 1988).

We also have many parenting questionnaires that are potentially useful. Some instruments allow researchers to evaluate the parent's stance regarding Baumrind's original parenting typologies (authoritative, authoritarian, etc.) (Hinshaw et al., 1997), whereas others provide an in-depth analysis of select parenting practices (e.g., parent involvement) (Shelton, Frick, & Wooton, 1996). When considering a measure, it is important to note whether the developer has tied the questionnaire data to parenting or child behavior in theoretically meaningful ways (Hinshaw, 2002).

Other instruments allow older children and adolescents to evaluate their parents' childrearing practices. They may contain scoring instructions that allow one to formulate continuous scores that reflect Baumrindlike parenting dimensions (e.g., acceptance, behavior control, etc.) (Dornbusch et al., 1987; Steinberg, Elmen, & Mounts, 1989) or instructions for categorizing parents into the parenting typologies (e.g., authoritative, authoritarian, etc.) (Steinberg et al., 1994). I like the parenting-style assessments developed by Steinberg and colleagues. These instruments were specifically developed with Baumrind's theory in mind, and these experts have consistently replicated her original findings using the self-report measures.

Are there short, observational procedures that can be used to identify Baumrind's parenting styles? In general, researchers have stayed away from observational methods and coding systems that categorize parents into the four parenting types; rather, they have attempted to create methods that estimate the parent's stance on her two major dimensions of parenting, responsiveness and demandingness. For example, researchers working with younger children may observe caregiving practices as the parent prepares meals, attempts to put the child down for a nap, or handles child demands while engaged in other activities, such as talking on the phone. Although this method is similar to Baumrind's, it is not as time intensive. For instance, arrangements can be made to observe the family during time periods that elicit a series of setting events in a relatively short time period, such as meal preparation, mealtime, and cleanup (Kochanska et al., 1989). Alternatively, the researcher may create laboratory tasks that elicit individual differences in responsiveness and demandingness, such as a series of difficult child-parent problem-solving exercises (Allen et al., 1994; Denham, Renwick, & Holt, 1991).

As mentioned earlier, researchers who use these methods focus more on identifying a range of scores on the parenting dimensions (demandingness, responsiveness) than on categorizing parents into specific parenting styles. There is validity for this approach; for example, caregivers who score high on parenting facets that reflect responsiveness, such as providing helpful suggestions during task performance, are more likely to be categorized as authoritative on alternative measures (e.g., CRPR Q-sort) (Kochanska et al., 1989). In addition, studies using coding systems that capture these parenting dimensions often demonstrate results that are consistent with Baumrind's work. For example, Hauser's *Constraining-Enabling Coding System* (Hauser, Powers, & Noam, 1991) allows researchers to rate parental responsiveness during problem-solving tasks with adolescents. Parents who support the decision-making abilities of their adolescents during these procedures are more likely to see healthy autonomy development in their children over time than parents who project more of an authoritarian demeanor (Allen et al., 1994).

Thus, we have many methods of assessing Baumrind's parenting typologies and dimensions of these categories. However, some have raised theoretical and statistical arguments regarding whether to use a category approach or use continuous scores on the parenting dimensions (i.e., responsiveness or demandingness) (Steinberg & Silk, 2002). Although it is tempting to categorize parents in the spirit of Baumrind's original work, it is well known that we lose statistical power when we move from continuous to categorical treatment of our data. Likewise, it is sometimes very difficult to classify people when using typology approaches; for example, what do we do with individuals who do not score either high or low on the parenting dimensions? In any case, students interested in assessing parenting styles would be safe using the measures described in this section, all of which possess good reliability and validity data.

Parenting Styles or Practices?   You may have noticed that I have made distinctions between parenting styles and parenting practices. Although the terms parenting styles and parenting practices are used somewhat interchangeably, they are nevertheless distinct constructs. Parenting practices are *behaviors* that parents engage in, whereas parenting styles reflect the *way* the parent carries out these practices (Darling & Steinberg, 1993). Thus, two different parents could be heavily involved in their children's academic work, and routinely check schoolwork, set rules regarding homework time, volunteer to help teachers, and so on, but using different styles. These behaviors are parenting practices. However, authoritative and authoritarian parents display different styles of involvement. For example, under special circumstances, the authoritative parent may alter a rule regarding curfew, whereas the authoritarian parent may rigidly expect their child to adhere to this rule.

We can use innumerable methods to assess different parenting practices, such as parental warmth (Dunifon & Kowaleski-Jones, 2002), disciplinary techniques (Kelley, Power, & Wimbusch, 1992), child time management (Ladd & Golter, 1988), school involvement (Steinberg et al., 1992), and parental monitoring (Smetana & Daddis, 2002).

There are also techniques that allow us to simultaneously assess a broad range of parenting practices (e.g., monitoring, involvement, disciplinary techniques) such as the aforementioned *CRPR Q-sort* or the *Alabama Parenting Questionnaire* (Shelton, Frick, & Wooton, 1996). The beauty of CRPR is that it can function as an assessment of both parenting practices and style methodology.

I made a distinction between parenting styles and practices, because researchers rarely study both constructs in conjunction. This is unfortunate, because there is evidence that parents can engage in similar practices, yet exhibit different styles in doing so. For example, parental achievement expectancies and school involvement are unrelated to student academic achievement in nonauthoritative families (Steinberg et al., 1992).

Summary

A host of measures have been developed to assess parenting cognitions, styles, and practices. To generate research ideas, you might revisit Figure 12.2 and think about how the variables could be considered jointly in a study. Too often, researchers study important parenting variables separately, without considering how they might work together (e.g., cognitions and parenting practices) to predict child functioning. Another neglected area of research is how temporal variables (e.g., occupational stress) affect parenting beliefs and practices; this is an important avenue of inquiry. Although one's culture shapes initial parenting beliefs and practices, characteristics of the child and the immediate environment (e.g., marital quality, parent mental health) may play a stronger role over time.

What Do You Think?

Suppose you are interested in determining associations among parenting styles, parenting practices, and child adjustment. Think about how you could best assess each construct? Determine a theoretical ordering of the variables to make predictions, and design a study that would test your predictions.

Grandparenting and Intergenerational Relationships

Relationships with parents, siblings, and friends remain important during mid- and late life; however, there is a relationship that is added to our social network. In this section we will discuss the role of grandparents in families and examine how experts conduct research on grandparent-grandchild relationships. Although grandparenthood might be one of the few new relationship roles that older adults assume, existing family relationships may undergo transformations in later life. An intriguing line of study pertains to family caregiving, and how adult adjustment is affected by caring for a spouse or parent. In this section, we will discuss methodological issues that face professionals who conduct such research.

The Theoretical Influence of Grandparents

Figure 12.3 presents an account of how grandparents exert an influence in the family system. The arrows are double-headed, because we recognize that younger family

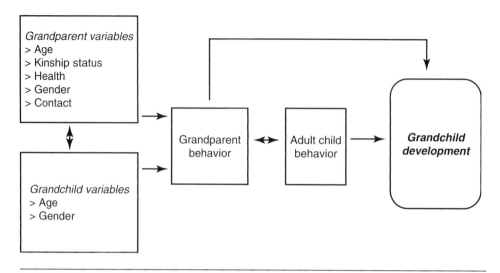

FIGURE 12.3 *Theoretical Framework Denoting the Direct and Indirect Effects of Grandparenting.*

members can also affect the grandparent's development. For instance, a grandparent can tell grandchildren stories about money worries during the Great Depression, whereas grandchildren can introduce grandparents to the world of videogames, roller-blading, and MP3 players.

Grandparents can affect the development of grandchildren in several ways. The grandparent → grandchild model assumes that grandparents can have a direct effect on their grandchildren's development; for instance, a grandparent may teach the child how to do a task or help the grandchild learn more about their identity by recalling stories or historical events that relate to the family's heritage. Also, the mere presence of a healthy, older grandparent shows the grandchild important evidence of a successful aging process.

The grandparent → adult child → grandchild model is also important to consider. Grandparents can influence their grandchildren in *indirect* ways. The grandparent might help the grandchild's own parents resolve a marital dispute or financial problem. In fact, the grandparent's presence in the family may affect the child without the grandparent lifting a finger! Consider a family deciding to buy a house it can barely afford in a safe neighborhood with excellent schools. The child's parents may not ask their own parents for money, but just knowing they could *potentially* contact this person if they needed assistance leads them to make a purchase that ultimately benefits the child.

Grandparents can also have a lasting effect on grandchildren if they are no longer living. For instance, grandparents have projected a model of parenting beliefs and practices on their own children for years. Although you hear new parents swear they will not parent as they were parented, some things are easier said than done. The results of research efforts that have explored this particular idea are presented in Box 12.2.

BOX 12.2 • *The Intergenerational Effects of Parenting and Attachment*

"_____ runs in families, you know." Fill in the blank; you probably know of a lot of variables that have been mentioned as candidates, including mental illness, substance-abuse problems, and child abuse. How exactly do you determine whether a particular trait or characteristic "runs" in families across generations? In the realm of parenting, one could assess the child-rearing practices of a group of parents, wait until their children began having children of their own, and repeat the same assessments. Of course, such longitudinal research is exceedingly rare; you may not live to see your results!

Another methodological angle would be to conduct multigenerational assessments of the same construct. For example, you could contrast the cognitive, linguistic, and emotional environment provided for the child by younger and older adults. In many cases, there are startling similarities. For example, grandmothers who value close emotional relationships tend to have daughters who do, as well. In turn, the infants of these people develop close emotional relationships with their parents (Benoit & Parker, 1994). Voilá, intergenerational continuity!

Methodological controls are necessary (although rarely followed) in such intergenerational research. For example, one would expect mothers and their own mothers to parent a child more similarly than a mother-in-law would. If they all parented in the same way, then evidence of intergenerational continuity has not been provided. In addition, demonstrating evidence of intergenerational continuity does not always provide us with theory for why such continuity exists. Some assume that intergenerational similarity in thinking or behavior reflects broader cultural influences. For example, families who all live in the same community decade after decade may embrace a similar cultural ideal regarding parenting practices. Thus, similar parenting behavior between a maternal grandmother and her own adult daughter may

have more to do with similar cultural ideology than with the way the daughter was parented. This may be why parenting beliefs change when a parent moves to a community that contains an alternative culture (Sigel & McGillicuddy-De Lisi, 2002).

Stability and change in environmental circumstances could also explain the phenomena of intergenerational continuity. In one study, researchers examined the likelihood of children (both sons and daughters) of teen parents becoming teen parents themselves. Contextual variables strongly predicted the likelihood of such continuity. For example, compared to participants who did *not* become teen parents, second-generational teen parents were from unstable families and experienced considerable achievement problems. Because adolescents who become "unplugged" from families and other social contexts, such as schools, are at high risk for early sexual activity and teen pregnancy, it is likely that intergenerational continuity in teen parenthood has more to do with shared environmental circumstances between younger (second-generation) and older (first-generation) family members than anything else (Hardy et al., 1998).

One exciting research angle consists of identifying contextual variables that may alter risky patterns of intergenerational behavior. For example, we have all heard that child maltreatment "runs in families," which implies that such behavior is unavoidable. However, using longitudinal methods, researchers have noted that not all adults abused as children engage in maltreatment of their own children. For example, parents who were abused as children were less likely to abuse their own children if they had a history of close emotional relationships or possessed a stable, supportive relationship with a romantic partner (Egeland, Jacobvitz, & Sroufe, 1988). Identifying variables that break "cycles" of undesirable cross-generational behavior in families would seem to constitute an important research agenda.

Variables That Influence Grandparent–Grandchild Relationships

A host of variables influence interactions and relationships between grandparents and grandchildren. Some of these variables are easy to assess, and omitting any of them could constitute a fatal flaw for a novice researcher. On the grandparent side of the relationship, it is important to assess the grandparent's age, gender, and ethnicity. For example, grandmothers generally have better relationships with grandchildren than grandfathers do, younger grandparents often have more direct contact with grandchildren than older grandparents, and African-American and Latino grandparents are more involved with their grandchildren than White, European-American grandparents (Szinovacz, 1998). It is also important to assess the nature of the grandparent's involvement; for example, a considerable percentage of grandparents function as primary caregivers to their grandchildren (Ehrle, 2001). Finally, the kinship status of the grandparent and grandchild must be assessed as well; traditionally, grandchildren experience better relationships with maternal grandparents, perhaps because these grandmothers are more involved in their lives then other grandparents.

Another important grandparent variable that has major implications for grandparent-grandchild relationships pertains to health status. Debilitating illnesses, such as Alzheimer's disease, dramatically affect contact and relationships between grandparents and grandchildren (Creasey et al., 1989). Although it might be impossible to conduct an intensive health survey on grandparents, some simple assessments of self-perceived health quality could be administered to explore associations between grandparent health and relationships with grandchildren (see Chapter 11). Investigating this relationship would be useful, because grandparent health status does affect these relationships and could partly explain why grandchildren have better relationships with grandmothers than grandfathers: men tend to develop health problems sooner than women (Creasey & Kaliher, 1994).

Variables on the grandchild side of the relationship are also important to assess. A study would be seriously amiss if the ages of the grandchildren were not assessed. Just as relationships between children and their own parents do, relationships between grandchildren and grandparents undergo important transformations during adolescence. Adolescent grandchildren often report less contact, more conflict, and less intimacy with grandparents than their younger counterparts (Creasey & Kaliher, 1994), yet report that they still feel close to their grandparents.

Other variables are important to consider when designing this research. The amount of contact between grandparents and grandchildren has a potent influence on relationship quality (and may represent a bidirectional association). What is missing are research efforts that specify the role of phone and Internet contact between grandparents and grandchildren; with families living further from their extended families, such contact might represent an important connection.

Variables associated more with the child's own parents also need to be considered in planning intergenerational research. Grandchildren have more contact with maternal grandparents in single-parent households, and relationships between grandchildren and paternal grandparents can be particularly strained in cases of parental divorce, at least in mother-custody households (Cherlin & Furstenberg, 1986). However, when considering variables that moderate relationships between grandparents and grandchildren, think about how these variables work together to affect these affiliations. For example, paternal grandparents who are allowed contact with grandchildren in divorced households have relationships with their grandchildren similar to those of paternal grandparents of grandchildren residing in intact households (Creasey, 1993).

In examining Figure 12.3, you may have noticed that the influence of grandparents is partly mediated by the adult children; access to the grandchild is governed in large part by the child's own parents. Traditionally, the adult child who governs this contact is the child's mother. It is assumed that this "gatekeeper" plays a large role in influencing interactions between grandchildren and grandparents, but little is known about the mechanisms that drive this role. One could posit that a bad relationship between a mother and mother-in-law might influence the amount of contact between the grandparent and grandchild. Alternatively, the relationship status of the child's parents could play a role in this process. For example, grandparents may find their role diminished in cases in which one spouse is highly controlling or when there is intense marital discord. All of these theories could provide fodder for your future research agendas.

Methodological Issues in Caregiving

Life comes full circle for an adult child who must consider caring for a parent, and it is not uncommon for caregivers, regardless of their relationship with the person, to occasionally report stress-related symptoms. Researchers typically distinguish between *primary* and *secondary* care providers. Primary caregivers provide the majority of daily care, whereas secondary caretakers are people who provide more occasional assistance. Generally, the patient or client and family members can identify a person who assumes the majority of the caregiving duties; however, it is not uncommon to find situations in which several people share different, yet equally demanding, duties in providing assistance. In any case, much of the caregiving research tends to concentrate on the health and development of primary caregivers, with less attention given to individuals less involved in direct care. However, even young children, who may not provide much direct assistance, can be adversely affected in cases in which their own parents are struggling with primary caregiving responsibilities (Creasey et al., 1989).

The relationship of the care provider to the patient or client is another variable to assess. Typically, caregivers are either the spouse or adult child of the patient or client. The researcher must consider that the caregiving experience may evoke different responses, partly because observing a loved one die of an illness will be appraised differently by a daughter or son than by a spouse. However, other factors also influence these differential appraisals. Spouse caregivers may be older and have fewer resources than adult-child caregivers, whereas the latter caregivers may have other responsibilities, such as their own children and careers, that hamper their efforts. Thus, it is not surprising that both spouse and adult-child caregivers report elevated mental and physical health symptoms during the caregiving process, but probably for different reasons; this is an area that is ripe for future research.

People frequently need such assistance because they have a physical or mental illness. It is very important to assess the nature of the illness; in fact, it is not uncommon for researchers to examine caregiving issues in older people with specific problems, such as cancer, stroke, clinical depression, or Alzheimer's disease. This is a very important consideration, because each condition evokes both common and different demands; caregiving stress is highest in cases in which people are assisting a relative with a mentally debilitating illness, such as Alzheimer's disease (Schultz & Williamson, 1991). This is not to say that taking care of a cancer patient is easy, its just that Alzheimer's-disease presents special challenges, because these individuals are losing their mental faculties.

It is also important to assess the patient's illness duration and severity; researchers should not necessarily expect a linear association between these variables and caregiver problems. Some studies have shown that caregivers may actually show *improvements* in health functioning over time (Zarit & Zarit, 1998), suggesting that it is important to include control groups or waiting-list groups of caregivers in intervention studies. This type of maturational effect could be mistaken for a treatment effect if the investigator only evaluates changes in caregiver health and coping skills in adults receiving interventions (e.g., support-group treatments).

Perhaps one of the most common methodological problems in caregiver research is the failure of researchers to use "illness control groups" when evaluating the health functioning of care providers. For example, let's say we gather a sample of adult daughters taking care of their parents with Alzheimer's disease. Next, we contrast their stress levels with similar-aged women who are *not* taking care of someone. Let's further assume that we, quite correctly, match these women on important demographic variables, such as socioeconomic status and ethnicity. It would seem like we have crafted a perfect study; the participants are equated on a number of variables that could affect the caregiving process.

So, what's the problem? Well, if we detected group differences in stress levels, then what could we conclude? Is there something especially demanding about caring for a relative with Alzheimer's disease, or would these findings hold true for *any* caregiver providing assistance to an ill relative, regardless of the disease? This is an important issue to consider, because illness status may interact with other variables to predict caregiver strain. In one study, male and female caregivers did not significantly differ in psychological symptoms when caregiving for Parkinson's-disease relatives; however, gender differences in such symptoms were apparent among Alzheimer's-disease caregivers (Hooker et al., 2000).

Researchers have spent considerable time identifying variables that predict why some caregivers are more at risk for psychological and physical problems than others. Much of this work has focused on demographic variables, and for good reason; gender, ethnicity, socioeconomic status, and caregiver age are all associated with adjustment to this role (Sinnott & Shifren, 2001). However, the attachment relationship the caregiver had with the patient should also be considered. Providing care to a close relative does provoke attachment issues, and individuals who have experienced conflicted or abusive associations with the patient might demonstrate more difficulties in this role (George & Solomon, 1999).

What Do You Think?

Suppose a colleague wants to study the health of caregivers over time but is unaware of fundamental methodological issues regarding this type of research. What advice would you provide this colleague? What variables should this investigator study and control for?

On a more optimistic note, we need more research exploring positive aspects of the caregiving process. Not all caregivers have pessimistic appraisals of this responsibility, and some might strongly object if they were not allowed to perform this role. In addition, the finding that many caregivers show improvements in health over time, untouched and unaided by professionals, represents a maturational issue that should be studied in more depth.

Summary

In summary, much of the intergenerational relationship research has focused on grandparenthood and caregiver issues. These, of course, do not represent the only relationship concerns of adults; for example, we need more research on marital and parenting processes during later life. In addition, we know little about how relationships with siblings and friends change during later life, in terms of both contact and quality. Finally, although we discussed parenting, marital, and other important relationships in a separate fashion, the quality of any one attachment relationship has important implications for the health of other attachment bonds. This issue represents another important research angle.

Career Development: Methodological and Assessment Issues

This section will cover three primary issues. First, it will examine methodological issues that face experts who study the adult worker. Next, it will describe theoretical approaches to career development and how one can assess such progress. Finally, if career development is associated with occupational adjustment, then we need to identify a set of work-related variables that could be used to assess such adjustment.

The Adult Worker: Methodological Issues

Occupational specialists delineate associations among age, career development, and some type of outcome measure, such as job performance. In terms of a theoretical ordering of these constructs, they speculate that age predicts career development, which in turn forecasts job competencies that comprise job performance, such as occupational knowledge and expertise. This idea is akin to the framework presented in Figure 12.4 (Salthouse & Maurer, 1996).

Salthouse and Maurer (1996) theorize that associations among these variables can be weakened if important methodological issues are not considered. These experts conclude that one or more of the following difficulties often affect studies on career development:

1. *Restricted age ranges.* Many studies on adult career development involve participants under the age of 40. In such cases, restricted age ranges or heavily skewed age-range distributions in one direction or the other make it difficult to detect developmental differences in career development or job performance among adults.
2. *Biased assessment.* Employees, co-workers, and supervisors may not see eye to eye regarding the performance of younger and older workers. To increase accuracy, one should conduct **360-degree assessments**, which rely on the target adult's impression of their own job performance, as well as appraisals by supervisors and co-workers.
3. *Nonequivalent samples.* Older and younger workers differ in more ways than just age and experience. Some younger workers will achieve an orderly career development and strong job performance within a company, whereas others may fail. The older workers, on the other hand, may remain in a company because they are doing well and have historically exhibited strong job performance. Comparisons of younger

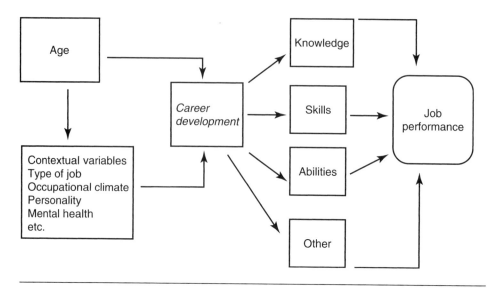

FIGURE 12.4   *Framework of Variables that Predict Career Development and Job Performance.*
Adapted from Salthouse & Maurer (1996).

and older workers on job motivation or competence could be compared to the problems inherent in contrasting high school and college students on achievement motivation. That is, a proportion of the high school students will not go on to college; thus, differences in motivation may have more to do with nonequivalent sampling than with age or maturity.

4. *Job type*. Associations among age, career development, and job performance may vary by job type. For instance, some jobs simply do not allow for occupational development. In addition, there may be situational or contextual factors that vary within certain occupations that may explain associations between age and career development. In other words, two entry-level lawyers may experience very different paths regarding career development based on the occupational climate (e.g., presence of mentors, occupational stress, time demands) of their respective law firms.

5. *Too many college students*. We can't necessarily conclude that older workers have experienced more "career consolidation" or better job performance than younger workers if the younger people are college students working part-time jobs. There are two problems here: First, not all of the older workers even attended college, and their current work experiences are not equivalent. That is, adolescent and young-adult part-time work differs from full-time adult employment in terms of pay, hours, and commitment. Another disturbing trend is that career-development and job-performance measures have primarily been done using college students as subjects. Can such measures be readily used with older adults? When possible, read the reliability and validity information on these assessments. If most of the psychometric information is based on college students, this same information should be obtained on older samples (e.g., 2-week test-retest reliability, predictive validity studies, etc.).

Because of these methodological concerns, it's difficult to locate studies on adult career development, even of the cross-sectional variety. Longitudinal research is very scattered and short-term in nature. For example, many studies have examined how adults initially adapt to their first jobs or retirement, but more lengthy studies of career development are quite rare.

Theories of Career Development

Super's theory of occupational self-concept represents the most widely cited perspective on adult career development. Super theorized that adults reconceptualize their occupational concerns at different stages of life, and that such advancement predicts occupational behavior and performance (Super, 1990). The stages of Super's theory are outlined in Table 12.6; note how these stages explain changes in occupational concerns from adolescence through retirement. These stages make sense. For instance, concerns over career exploration weigh heavily on the minds of adolescents (e.g., see Erikson's theory), whereas young adults are more often concerned with career establishment than with exploration.

However, the theory is open to criticism. The age ranges assigned to each stage may not fit the profile of workers in different jobs; in some occupations, concerns regarding career establishment are over fairly quickly. Also, some adults may not begin to balance work concerns with other societal issues (e.g., family, marriage) until later in life. Thus, the theory may not fit well with today's diverse work force. Finally, the later stages, "maintenance" and "deceleration" conjure negative images, and suggest that decreased job motivation and performance are normative outcomes for older adults.

TABLE 12.6 *Super's (1990) Stages of Adult Career Development*

Stage	Age Range	Description
Exploration	Adolescence–mid-20's	Concerns over career exploration. Concerns shift in this stage with development. For example, adolescents may initially be concerned with choosing a career path and later become concerned with how to actually implement it.
Establishment	Mid-20's–mid-40's	Having explored career options, the adult is now concerned with how to obtain career goals. In this stage, concern shifts from how to obtain a job to the steps in becoming a good worker. Once this concern has been addressed, the adult then develops concerns regarding advancement.
Maintenance	Middle age	The adult becomes concerned with how to maintain career status without compromising other adult roles. He or she may initially be concerned with "holding one's own" and then develop concerns about how to update skills.
Disengagement	Middle age–retirement	Adult concerns shift from work-related concerns to retirement planning.

On a positive note, Super theorized that adults with considerable career maturity develop concerns for how to cope with the different stages. For example, in the *Maintenance Stage,* an older work might consider how to "hold one's own" for a period of time, and then become concerned with new skill acquisition to address this goal (i.e., maintenance). Theoretically, a change in concerns should translate to actual "Reinvention of Onself" (Super et al., 1992). In the previous example, the older worker might move from inaction ("holding one's own") to the pursuit of educational or training opportunities that lead to new skill acquisition. This older worker is not necessarily "working harder," but rather is pursuing opportunities that may make his or her career more stimulating and interesting.

Assessing Career Development

A number of self-report measures have been used to assess different components of Super's stage theory. For instance, the *Strong Interest Inventory* (Harmon et al., 1994) and *Career Development Inventory* (Super et al., 1988) are used to assess career knowledge, exploration, and planning. Because these are concerns typically expressed by adolescents and young adults, researchers and practitioners who work with younger populations routinely use these scales.

Of course, such inventories only test pieces of Super's theory and do not provide a comprehensive assessment of adult career development (as depicted in Figure 12.4). In order to address this issue, Super and colleagues have developed the *Adult Career Concerns Inventory* (ACCI; Super et al., 1988), a self-administered questionnaire that assesses adult concerns over career development and adaptability. The test is norm-referenced, in the sense that the researcher or participant can tally scores and then compare them to national norms. The national norms have been computed for the age groups listed in Super's original theory (see Table 12.6).

The ACCI contains items that reflect adult concerns with career exploration, establishment, maintenance, and disengagement; it has 15 items that tap concerns within each stage of career development. There are also different subscales that reflect the adults' concerns over adaptability within each stage. For example, the establishment scale contains 3 subscales that reflect concerns regarding career stability, consolidation, and advancement. Theoretically, an adult who scored higher on advancement should display more career progress than an adult who scored higher on career stability. In a similar fashion, the maintenance scale contains three subscales that reflect concerns with "holding one's own," updating, and innovating.

In terms of instrument validity, as they age, adult workers report less concern with exploration and increased concern with career establishment. Likewise, researchers have noted developmental patterns in stage adaptation. For example, adults in the maintenance phase initially express concerns on how to simply maintain job performance and then develop concerns regarding skill updating and career innovation when completing this inventory (Super et al., 1992). This is an optimistic finding, and reaffirms the idea that accomplished older workers are not content to "hold their own" but rather strive for increased career excellence and skill development. Also, there is evidence that adults who show development in career concerns display increases in job performance and satisfaction (Smart, 1998).

Career-development experts remark that career development is simply one component of a broader construct referred to as **career maturity**. For example, Super originally proposed that with age, adults increasingly develop concerns regarding select facets of career development (i.e., exploration, establishment, maintenance, and deceleration) and also develop corresponding concerns regarding how best to adapt to the different stages. For example, in the maintenance phase, the adult may query, "Should I be concerned with retraining or with developing more skills?"

These concerns, however, may or may not translate into coping behavior. Thus, career maturity reflects career concerns (Super's theory) and how *adults actually cope with these concerns*. Also, career maturity reflects a trilogy of other career appraisals, such as career knowledge, values, and the relevance of careers to other life goals (also known as *career salience*) (Super et al., 1992; Levinson et al., 1998). As you might guess, many self-report measures have been developed to assess each of these facets; Super and colleagues have developed a comprehensive questionnaire battery that assesses each one. Thus, Super's original theory of career development touches on only one component of the broader construct of career maturity. An assessment of this global construct requires researchers to use multiple measures.

Assessing Career-Development Outcomes

If career development predicts success, then how do we measure such accomplishments? Although job satisfaction and motivation could be viewed as good candidates for study variables, many occupational experts consider *job performance* as the "gold standard" outcome variable. Institutions often develop performance-appraisal methods to assess job performance for specific occupations. For instance, college professors are annually evaluated on the quality of their teaching, research, and service to the university, community, and profession. Unfortunately, such information may not be particularly useful if one is to broaden a study sample to include workers from different professions. The performance appraisals of professors would be difficult to compare to those of lawyers. Also, the manner in which colleges and universities weight teaching, research, and service can be different across institutions. Such disparities make it difficult to reliably assess job performance, because the standards for optimal ratings are so different.

However, some general job-performance assessments could be completed by adults across a variety of occupations. The 116-item *Management Skills Profile* (MSP; Sevy et al., 1985) assesses leadership skills, job motivation, communicative skills, occupational knowledge, and problem-solving abilities. Similarly, the 106-item *Benchmarks Scale* (Lombardo & McCauley, 1994) assesses the adult worker's career-capstone experiences and lessons learned from these accomplishments. Respondents indicate how well they have learned to master the nuances of their occupation, get along with co-workers, and balance work and family life. This would appear to be a good assessment to use when studying career development, because a person with considerable career maturity should have learned how to juggle important adult responsibilities, such as work and family (Super et al., 1992).

These scales measure more than whether a person is "producing" or not. Job performance is a multidimensional construct, and encompasses such factors as task performance, administrative and technical skill development, interpersonal abilities, leadership potential, and professional citizenship (McCauley et al., 1994). Although one could argue that employees and supervisors may not view these job performance facets as equal in importance, empirical research suggests otherwise (Scullen, Mount, & Judge, 2003).

What Do You Think?

Disparities across performance ratings (e.g., worker, peer, supervisor) can range from nonexistent to huge, depending on a number of factors. Suppose you want to see whether the adult worker's career maturity predicts convergence or divergence in these ratings. How would you design a study to test this premise? Based on your reading, what would be one of your central hypotheses?

Thus, job performance is a multidimensional construct. Beyond simply assessing job productivity, experts in this area theorize that occupational knowledge, job skills, leadership abilities, and the civil treatment of co-workers reflect career accomplishments. However, although workers and supervisors alike agree with this idea, a supervisor and employee may not agree on ratings for an individual employee! Because of potential disparities in ratings, it is not uncommon for researchers to use 360-degree assessments to assess job performance.

Summary

In this section we discussed career development and how best to assess it. Although adult career development is thought to predict career success and performance, only a handful of studies have tested this premise. Of equal importance would be the identification of personal (e.g., gender, ethnicity, career motivation) and contextual (e.g., occupational climate, spousal support) variables that predict orderly career development or barriers. This might be the best direction to pursue in terms of research, because for today's diverse workforce, it is unlikely that the route to career development or success is either orderly or consistent.

Chapter Summary

What further adult-development research is needed? Unfortunately, we still lack important data on how adults *develop in their primary roles.* We would like to think that people get better at marriage, parenting, and careers, and that such development is normative in most adults. In addition, improvements in these roles should be associated with adjustment in our children, productivity in our careers, and more satisfaction in our marriages. Unfortunately, much of this discussion is speculative, and can only be supported through your research efforts.

I hope that you have found your journey through this book an enjoyable one. At this point, you should be able to see why we consider lifespan development, as a field, to be scientific, multidisciplinary, and applied. Throughout the book, I have attempted to show close connections between research and practice; these contexts should not be viewed as mutually exclusive.

Research Navigator™ *Exercise: Marital Satisfaction*

The objective is to learn more about how researchers study marital satisfaction. Go the Research Navigator™ website: http://www.researchnavigator.com; and type *marital satisfaction* as a keyword. After reading a full-length article, address the following questions.

1. What was the purpose of the study, and how was marital satisfaction defined?
2. How was marital satisfaction assessed in the sample?
3. Was marital satisfaction viewed as a predictor or as an outcome variable?
4. What were the conclusions and limitations of the study?

References

Achenbach, T. (1991). *Manual for the Child Behavior Checklist/4-18 and 1991 profile*. Burlington, VT: University of Vermont, Department of Psychiatry.

Ackerman, B. (1988). Search set access problems in retrieving episodic information from memory in children and adults. *Journal of Experimental Child Psychology, 45,* 234–261.

Acredolo, L. (1978). Development of spatial orientation in infancy. *Developmental Psychology, 14,* 224–234.

Acredolo, L., & Evans, D. (1980). Developmental changes in the effects of landmarks on infant spatial behavior. *Developmental Psychology, 16,* 312–318.

Adams, G. (1999). *The objective measure of ego identity status: A manual on theory and test construction*. Unpublished manuscript. Ontario, Canada : University of Guelph.

Adams, G., & Berzonsky, M. (2003). *Blackwell handbook of adolescence*. Malden, MA: Blackwell Science.

Adams, G., Shea, J., & Fitch, S. (1979). Toward the development of an objective assessment of ego-identity status. *Journal of Youth and Adolescence, 8,* 223–237.

Adler, S. (1991). Assessment of language proficiency of limited English speakers: Implications for the speech-language specialist. *Language, Speech, and Hearing Services in Schools, 22,* 12–18.

Ainsworth, M. (1967). *Infancy in Uganda: Infant care and the growth of attachment*. Baltimore, MD: The John Hopkins University Press.

Ainsworth, M. (1989). Attachments beyond infancy. *American Psychologist, 44,* 709–716.

Ainsworth, M., Bell, S., & Stayton, D. (1971). Individual differences in strange situation behavior of one-year-olds. In B. Foss (Ed.), *Determinants of infant behavior* (Vol. 4). London: Methuen and Co.

Ainsworth, M., Bell, S., & Stayton, D. (1974). Infant-mother attachment and social development: Socialization as a product of reciprocal responsiveness to signals. In M. Richards (Ed.), *The integration of a child into a social world* (pp. 99–135). London: Cambridge University Press.

Ainsworth, M., Blehar, M., Waters, E., & Wall, S. (1978). *Patterns of attachment: A psychological study of the strange situation*. Hillsdale, NJ: Lawrence Erlbaum Associates.

Alasker, F. (1992). Pubertal timing, weight, and psychological adjustment. *Journal of Early Adolescence, 12,* 396–419.

Albert, M., & Killiany, R. (2001). Age-related cognitive change and brain-behavior relationships. In J. Birren, & K.W. Schaie (Eds.), *Handbook of the psychology of aging* (5th Ed., pp. 161–185). San Diego, CA: Academic Press.

Aldridge, M., Stillman, R., & Bower, T. (2001). Newborn categorization of vowel-like sounds. *Developmental Science, 4,* 220–232.

Alexander, J., Newell, R., Robbins, M., & Turner, C. (1995). Observational coding in family therapy process research. *Journal of Family Psychology, 9,* 1–11.

Alexander, C., Somerfield, M., Ensminger, E., Johnson, K., & Kim, Y. (1994). Consistency of adolescent self-report of sexual behavior in a longitudinal study. *Journal of Youth and Adolescence, 22,* 455–471.

Allaire, J., & Marsiske, M. (1999). Everyday cognition: Age and intellectual ability correlates. *Psychology and Aging, 14,* 627–644.

Allen, J., Hauser, S., Bell, K., & O'Connor, T. (1994). Longitudinal assessment of autonomy and relatedness in adolescent-family interactions as predictors of adolescent ego development and self-esteem. *Child Development, 65,* 179–194.

Allen, J., & Land, D. (1999). Attachment in adolescence. In J. Cassidy, & P. Shaver (Eds.), *Handbook of attachment* (pp. 319–335). New York: Guilford Press.

Allen, J., Marsh, P., McFarland, C., McElhaney, K., Land, D., Jodl, K., & Peck, S. (2002). Attachment and autonomy as predictors of the development of social skills and delinquency during midadolescence. *Journal of Consulting and Clinical Psychology, 70,* 56–66.

Als, H., Lester, B., Tronick, E., & Brazelton, T. (1982). Towards a research instrument for the assessment of preterm infants' behavior (A.P.I.B.). In H. Fitzgeral, B. Lester, & M. Yogman (Eds.), *Theory and research in behavioral pediatrics* (pp. 85–132). New York: Plenum Publishing.

American Speech-Language Hearing Association. (1982). Urban and ethnic perspectives. *American Speech-Language Hearing Association, 26,* 9–10.

American Psychiatric Association. (1994). *Diagnostic and statistical manual of mental disorders* (4th Ed.). Washington, DC: American Psychiatric Association .

Ammaniti, M., van IJzendoorn, MH, Speranza, A., & Tambelli, R. (2000). Internal working models of attachment during late childhood and adolescence: An exploration of stability and change. *Attachment and Human Development, 2*, 328–346.

Anderson, D., Huston, A., Schmitt, K., Linebarger, D., & Wright, J. (2001). Early childhood television viewing and adolescent behavior. *Monographs of the Society for Research in Child Development, Vol. 66* (1, Serial No. 264). Chicago, IL: University of Chicago Press.

Anderson, D., & Levin, S. (1976). Young children's attention to Sesame Street. *Child Development, 47*, 806–811.

Anschutz, L., Camp, C., Markley, R., & Kramer, J. (1987). Remembering mnemonics: A three-year follow-up on the effects of mnemonics training in elderly adults. *Experimental Aging Research, 13*, 141–143.

Apgar, V. (1953). A proposal for a new method of evaluation of the newborn infant. *Current Researches in Anesthesia & Analgesia, 32*, 260–267.

Arellano, C., & Markman, H. (1995). The Managing Affect and Differences Scale (MADS): A self-report measure assessing conflict management in couples. *Journal of Family Psychology, 9*, 319–334.

Arendt, R., Angelopoulos, J., Salvator, A., & Singer, L. (1999). Cocaine-exposed infants: Motor development at age two. *Pediatrics, 103*, 86–92.

Armsden, G., & Greenberg, M. (1987). The Inventory of Parent and Peer Attachment. Individual differences and their relationship to well-being in adolescence. *Journal of Youth and Adolescence, 16*, 427–454.

Armstrong, P., & Crombie, G. (2000). Compromises in adolescents' occupational aspirations and expectations from grades 8 to 10. *Journal of Vocational Behavior, 56*, 82–98.

Arnett, J. (2000). Emerging adulthood: A theory of development from the late teens through the twenties. *American Psychologist, 55*, 469–480.

Arum, R., & Hout, M. (1998). The early returns: The transition from school to work in the United States. In Y. Shavit, & W. Mueller (Eds.), *From school to work: A comparative study of educational qualifications and occupational destinations* (pp. 471–510). Oxford, England: Clarendon Press.

Asher, S., & Dodge, K. (1986). Identifying children who are rejected by their peers. *Developmental Psychology, 22*, 444–449.

Atkinson, J. (1998). The "where" and "what" or "who" and "how" of visual development. In F. Simion, & G. Butterworth (Eds.), *The development of sensory, motor, and cognitive capacities in early infancy: From sensation to cognition* (pp. 3–24). Hove, UK: Psychology Press.

Aylward, G. (2002). Methodological advances in outcome studies of at-risk infants. *Journal of Pediatric Psychology, 27*, 37–45.

Bäckman, L., & Nilsson, L. (1996). Semantic memory functioning across the lifespan. *European Psychologist, 1*, 27–33.

Bäckman, L., Small, B., & Wahlin, A. (2001). Aging and memory: Cognitive and biological perspectives. In J. Birren, & K.W. Schaie (Eds.), *Handbook of the psychology of aging* (5th Ed., pp. 349–377). San Diego, CA: Academic Press.

Baddeley, A. (1993). Working memory or working attention? In A. Baddeley, & L. Weiskrantz (Eds.), *Attention, selection, awareness, and control: A tribute to Donald Broadbent* (pp. 152–170). Oxford, England: Clarendon Press.

Baddeley, A., & Hitch, G. (2000). Development of working memory: Should the Pascual-Leone and the Baddeley and Hitch models be merged? *Journal of Experimental Child Psychology, 77*, 128–137.

Bai, D., & Bertenthal, B. (1992). Locomotor status and the development of spatial search skills. *Child Development, 63*, 215–226.

Baillargeon, R. (1987). Object permanence in 3.5-and 4.5-month-old infants. *Developmental Psychology, 23*, 655–664.

Baillargeon, R., & DeVos, J. (1991). Object permanence in young infants: Further evidence. *Child Development, 62*, 1227–1246.

Baltes, P. (1979). Life-span developmental psychology: Some converging observations on history and theory. In. P. Baltes & O. Brim Jr. (Eds.), *Life-span development and behavior* (Vol. 2, pp. 255–279). New York: Academic Press.

Baltes, P., Cornelius, S., & Nesselroade, J. (1979). Cohort effects in developmental psychology. In J. Nesselroade & P. Baltes (Eds.), *Longitudinal research in the study of behavior and development* (pp. 61–87). New York: Academic Press.

Baltes, P., & Nesselroade, J. (1979). History and rationale of longitudinal research. In J. Nesselroade & P. Baltes (Eds.), *Longitudinal research in the study of behavior and development* (pp. 1–39). New York: Academic Press.

Baltes, P., Reese, H., & Lipsitt, L. (1980). Life-span developmental psychology. *Annual Review of Psychology, 31*, 65–110.

Baltes, P., Staudinger, U., Maercker, A., & Smith, J. (1995). People nominated as wise: A comparative study of wisdom-related knowledge. *Psychology and Aging, 10*, 155–166.

Bandura, A. (1997). *Self-efficacy: The exercise of control.* New York: Freeman.

Bandura, A., Barbaranelli, C., Caprara, G., & Pastorelli, C. (1996). Multifaceted impact of self-efficacy beliefs on academic functioning. *Child Development, 67*, 1206–1222.

Bandura, A., Barbaranelli, C., Caprara, G., & Pastorelli, C. (2001). Self-efficacy beliefs as shapers of children's aspirations and career trajectories. *Child Development, 72*, 187–206.

Bandura, A., Caprara, G., Barbaranelli, C., Gerbini, M., & Pastorelli, C. (2003). Role of affective self-regulatory efficacy in diverse spheres of psychosocial functioning. *Child Development, 74*, 769–782.

Barber, T., & Silver, M. (1968). Fact, fiction, and the experimenter bias effect. *Psychological Bulletin Monograph Supplement, 70*, 1–29.

Barnat, S., Klein, P., & Meltzoff, A. (1996). Deferred imitation across changes in context and object: Memory and generalization in 14-month-old infants. *Infant Behavior and Development, 19*, 241–251.

Baron, J., & Siepmann, M. (2000). Techniques for creating and using Web questionnaires in research and training. In M. Birnbaum (Ed.), *Psychological experiments on the Internet* (pp. 235–265). San Diego, CA: Academic Press.

Barr, R., Pantel, M., Young, S., Wright, J., Hendricks, L., & Gravel, R. (1999). The response of crying newborns to sucrose: Is it a "sweetness" effect? *Physiology & Behavior, 66*, 409–417.

Barrett, K., & Campos, J. (1987). Perspectives on emotional development II: A functionalist approach to emotions. In J. Osofsky (Ed.), *Handbook of infant development* (2nd Ed., pp. 555–578). New York: Wiley.

Bartholomew, K., & Horowitz, L. (1991). Attachment styles among young adults: A test of a four-category model. *Journal of Personality and Social Psychology, 61*, 226–244.

Bates, E. (1979). *The emergence of symbols: Cognition and communication in infancy*. New York: Academic Press.

Bates, E., Bretherton, I., & Snyder, L. (1988). *From first words to grammar: Individual differences and dissociable mechanisms*. New York: Cambridge University Press.

Bates, J., Freeland, C., & Lounsbury, M. (1979). Measurement of infant difficultness. *Child Development, 50*, 794–803.

Baucom, D., & Epstein, N. (1990). *Cognitive-behavioral marital therapy*. New York: Brunner/Mazel Publishers.

Baucom, D., Epstein, N., Rankin, L., & Burnett, C. (1996). Assessing relationship standards: The inventory of specific relationship standards. *Journal of Family Psychology, 10*, 72–88.

Baucom, D., Epstein, N., Sayers, S., & Sher, T. (1989). The role of cognition in marital relationships: Definitional, methodological, and conceptual issues. *Journal of Consulting and Clinical Psychology, 57*, 31–38.

Bauer, P., Hertsgaard, L., & Dow, G. (1994). After 8 months have passed: Long-term recall of events by 1-to 2-year-old children. *Memory, 2*, 353–382.

Bauer, P., & Mandler, B. (1992). Putting the horse before the cart: The use of temporal order in the recall of events by 1-year-old children. *Developmental Psychology, 28*, 441–452.

Baumrind, D. (1971). Current patterns of parental authority. *Developmental Psychology Monographs, 4*(1, Pt. 2).

Baumrind, D. (1991). The influence of parenting style on adolescent competence and substance abuse. *Journal of Early Adolescence, 11*, 56–95.

Baumrind, D., & Black, A. (1967). Socialization processes associated with dimensions of competence in preschool boys and girls. *Child Development, 38*, 291–327.

Bayley, N. (1993). *Manual for the Bayley Scales of Infant Development* (2nd Ed.). San Antonio, TX: Psychological Corporation.

Beal, C. (1985). Development of knowledge about the use of cues to aid prospective recall. *Child Development, 56*, 631–642.

Beere, C. (1990). *Gender roles: A handbook of tests and measures*. San Francisco, CA: Jossey-Bass.

Bell, S., & Ainsworth, M. (1972). Infant crying and maternal responsiveness. *Child Development, 43*, 1171–1190.

Belsky, J. (1984). The determinants of parenting: A process model. *Developmental Psychology, 55*, 83–96.

Belsky, J. (1985). Experimenting with the family in the newborn period. *Child Development, 56*, 404–414.

Belsky, J., Garduque, L., & Hrncir, E. (1984). Assessing performance, competence, and executive capacity in infant play: Relations to home environment and security of attachment. *Developmental Psychology, 20*, 406–417.

Belsky, J., & Most, R. (1981). From exploration to play: A cross-sectional study of infant free play behavior. *Developmental Psychology, 17*, 630–639.

Bem, S. (1989). Genital knowledge and gender constancy in preschool children. *Child Development, 60*, 649–662.

Bem., S. (1974). The measurement of psychological androgyny. *Journal of Consulting and Clinical Psychology, 42*, 155–162.

Bendersky, M., & Lewis, M. (2001). The Bayley Scales of Infant Development: Is there a role in biobehavioral assessment? In L. Singer & P. Zeskind (Eds.), *Biobehavioral assessment of the infant* (pp. 443–462). New York: Guilford Press.

Benjet, C., & Hernández-Guzmán, L. (2002). Sociocultural variations in the body image perceptions of urban adolescent females. *Journal of Youth and Adolescence, 31*, 429–442.

Bennett-Kastor, T. (1988). *Analyzing children's language*. New York: Basil Blackwell.

Benoit, D., & Parker, K. (1994). Stability and transmission of attachment across three generations. *Child Development, 65*, 1444–1456.

Berg, C. (1989). Knowledge of strategies for dealing with everyday problems from childhood through adolescence. *Developmental Psychology, 25*, 607–618.

Berk, L. (1986). Relationship of elementary school children's private speech to behavioral accompaniment to task, attention, and task performance. *Developmental Psychology, 22*, 671–680.

Berk, L., & Garvin, R. (1984). Development of private speech among low-income Appalachian children. *Developmental Psychology, 20,* 271–286.

Berkowitz, L. (1993). *Aggression: Its courses, consequences, and control.* New York: McGraw-Hill.

Berndt, T. (1979). Developmental changes in conformity to parents and peers. *Developmental Psychology, 15,* 608–616.

Berndt, T., & Perry, T. (1986). Children's perceptions of friendships as supportive relationships. *Developmental Psychology, 22,* 640–648.

Berry, J., West, R., & Dennehey, D. (1989). Reliability and validity of the memory self-efficacy questionnaire. *Developmental Psychology, 25,* 701–713.

Bertenthal, B., & Campos, J. (1990). A systematic approach to the organizing effects of self-produced locomotion during infancy. In C. Rovee-Collier & L. Lipsett (Eds.), *Advances in infancy research* (Vol. 6, pp. 1–60). Norwood, NJ: Ablex Publishing.

Bertenthal, B., Proffitt, D., Kramer, S., & Spetner, N. (1987). Infants' encoding of kinetic displays varying in relative coherence. *Developmental Psychology, 23,* 171–178.

Berzonsky, M., & Adams, G. (1999). Reevaluating the identity status paradigm: Still useful after 35 years. *Developmental Review, 19,* 557–590.

Best, D., Hamlett, K., & Davis, S. (1992). Memory complaint and memory performance in the elderly: The effects of memory-skills training and expectancy change. *Applied Cognitive Psychology, 6,* 405–416.

Betz, N., Borgen, F., Rottinghaus, P., Paulsen, A., Halper, C., & Harmon, L. (2003). The Expanded Skills Confidence Inventory: Measuring basic dimensions of vocational activity. *Journal of Vocational Behavior, 62,* 76–100.

Beyth-Marom, R., Austin, L., Fischoff, B., Palmgren, C., & Jacobs-Quadrel, M. (1993). Perceived consequences of risky behaviors: Adults and adolescents. *Developmental Psychology, 29,* 549–563.

Beyth-Marom, R., & Fischoff, B. (1997). Adolescents' decisions about risks: A cognitive perspective. In J. Schulenberg & J. Maggs (Eds.), *Health risks and developmental transitions during adolescence* (pp. 110–135). New York: Cambridge University Press.

Bierman, K. (2004). *Peer rejection: Developmental processes and intervention strategies.* New York : Guilford Press.

Birnbaum, M. (2000). *Psychological experiments on the Internet.* San Diego, CA: Academic Press.

Bivens, J., & Berk, L. (1990). A longitudinal study of the development of elementary school children's private speech. *Merrill-Palmer Quarterly, 36,* 443–463.

Bjorklund, D., & Muir, J. (1988). Children's development of free recall memory: Remembering on their own. In R. Vasta (Ed.), *Annals of child development* (Vol. 5, pp. 79–123). Greenwich, CT: JAI Press.

Blanchard-Fields, F. (1986). Reasoning on social dilemmas varying in emotional saliency: An adult developmental perspective. *Psychology and Aging, 1,* 325–333.

Blanchard-Fields, F., Jahnke, H., & Camp, C. (1995). Age differences in problem-solving style: The role of emotional salience. *Psychology and Aging, 10,* 173–180.

Blass, E., & Ciaramitaro, V. (1994). A new look at some old mechanisms in human newborns: Taste and tactile determinants of state, affect, and action. *Monographs for the Society for Research in Child Development, 59*(1, Serial No. 239).

Block, J. (1971). *Lives through time.* Berkeley, CA: Bancroft Books.

Block, J. (1981). *The Child-Rearing Practices Report (CRPR): A set of Q-items for the description of parental socialization attitudes and values.* Berkeley, CA: University of California; Institute of Human Development.

Block, J., & Block, J. (1980). *The California Child Q-set.* Palo Alto, CA: Consulting Psychologists Press.

Block, J.H., Block, J., & Gjerde, P. (1986). The personality of children prior to divorce. *Child Development, 57,* 827–840.

Block, J., Block, J., & Keyes, S. (1988). Longitudinally foretelling drug usage in adolescence: Early childhood personality and environmental precursors. *Child Development, 59,* 336–355.

Bloom, L., & Lahey, M. (1978). *Language development and language disorders.* New York: Wiley.

Blos, P. (1967). The second individuation process. *Psychoanalytic Study of the Child, 22,* 162–186.

Blum, R., Beuhring, T., Shew, M., Bearinger, L., Sieving, R., & Resnick, M. (2000). The effects of race-ethnicity, income, and family structure on adolescent risk behaviors. *American Journal of Public Health, 90,* 1879–1884.

Blyth, D., Simmons, R., & Zakin, D. (1985). Satisfaction with body image for early adolescent females: The impact of pubertal timing within different school environments. *Journal of Youth and Adolescence, 14,* 227–236.

Boggs, S., & Eyberg, S. (1990). Interview techniques and establishing rapport. In A. La Greca (Ed.), *Through the eyes of the child: Obtaining self-reports from children and adolescents* (pp. 85–108). Boston, MA: Allyn & Bacon.

Boldizar, J. (1991). Assessing sex typing and androgyny in children: The Children's Sex Role Inventory. *Developmental Psychology, 27,* 505–515.

Bolger, N., DeLongis, A., Kessler, R., & Schilling, E. (1989). Effects of daily stress on mood. *Journal of Personality and Social Psychology, 57,* 808–818.

Bond, L., Creasey, G., & Abrams, C. (1990). Play assessment: Reflecting and promoting cognitive competence. In E. Gibbs & D. Teti (Eds.), *Interdisciplinary assessment of infants: A guide for early intervention professionals* (pp. 113–128). Baltimore, MD: Paul Brookes.

Borke, H. (1975). Piaget's mountains revisited: Changes in the egocentric landscape. *Developmental Psychology, 11,* 240–243.

Bornstein, M. (2002). *Handbook of parenting: Children and parenting* (Vol. 1, 2nd Ed). Mahwah, NJ: Lawrence Erlbaum Associates.

Bornstein, M., & Suess, P. (2000). Physiological self-regulation and information processing in infancy: Cardiac vagal tone and habituation. *Child Development, 71,* 273–287.

Bosacki, S. (2003). Psychological pragmatics in preadolescents: Sociomoral understanding, self-worth, and school behavior. *Journal of Youth and Adolescence, 32,* 141–155.

Bosma, H. (1992). Identity in adolescence: Managing commitment. In G. Adams, T. Gullota, & R. Montemayor (Eds.), *Adolescent identity formation: Advances in adolescent development* (Vol. 4, pp. 91–121). Newbury Park, CA: Sage Publications.

Bosma, H., Graafsma, T., Grotevant, H., & de Devita, D. (1994). *Identity and development: An interdisciplinary approach.* Thousand Oaks, CA: Sage Publications.

Boulet, J., & Boss, M. (1991). Reliability and validity of the Brief Symptom Inventory. *Psychological Assessment, 3,* 433–437.

Bowlby, J. (1969/1982). *Attachment and loss, Vol. 1: Attachment* (2nd Ed.). New York: Basic Books.

Bowlby, J. (1988). *A secure base: Clinical applications of attachment theory.* London: Routledge.

Bradbury, T., & Fincham, F. (1992). Attributions and behavior in marital interaction. *Journal of Personality and Social Psychology, 63,* 613–628.

Bradbury, T., & Pasch, L. (1996). *Social support interaction coding system.* Los Angeles, CA: Psychology Department, University of California.

Bradley, R., Corwyn, R., Caldwell, B., Whiteside-Mansell, L., Wasserman, G., & Mink, I. (2000). Measuring the home environments of children in early adolescence. *Journal of Research on Adolescence, 10,* 247–288.

Braungart-Rieker, J., Garwood, M., Powers, B., & Wang, X. (2001). Parental sensitivity, infant affect, and affect regulation: Predictors of later attachment. *Child Development, 72,* 252–270.

Brazelton, T. (1973/1984). *Neonatal behavioral assessment scale.* Philadelphia, PA: JB Lippincott Co.

Brazelton, T. (1990). Saving the bathwater. *Child Development, 61,* 1661–1671.

Brazelton, T., Nugent, K., & Lester, B. (1987). Neonatal behavioral assessment scale. In J. Osofsky (Ed.), *Handbook of infant development* (2nd Ed., pp. 780–817). New York: Wiley.

Brennan, K., Clark, C., & Shaver, P. (1998). Self-report measurement of adult attachment: An integrative overview. In J. Simpson & W. Rholes (Eds.), *Attachment theory and close relationships* (pp. 46–76). New York: Guilford Press.

Brennan, P., Hammen, C., Katz, A., & Le Brocque, R. (2002). Maternal depression, paternal psychopathology, and adolescent diagnostic outcomes. *Journal of Consulting and Clinical Psychology, 70,* 1075–1085.

Bretherton, I., & Munholland, K. (1999). Internal working models in attachment relationships: A construct revisited. In J. Cassidy & P. Shaver (Eds.), *Handbook of attachment: Theory, research, and clinical applications* (pp. 89–111). New York: Guilford Press.

Bretherton, I., Ridgeway, D., & Cassidy, J. (1990). Assessing internal working models of the attachment relationship: An attachment story completion task for 3-year-olds. In M. Greenberg, D. Cicchetti, & E.M. Cummings (Eds.), *Attachment in the preschool years* (pp. 273–308). Chicago, Ill: University of Chicago Press.

Britt, G., & Myers, B. (1994). Testing the effectiveness of NBAS intervention with a substance-using population. *Infant Mental Health Journal, 15,* 293–304.

Brody, G., Flor, D., & Gibson, N. (1999). Linking maternal efficacy beliefs, developmental goals, parenting practices, and child competence in rural single-parent African American families. *Child Development, 70,* 1197–1208.

Bronfenbrenner, U. (1979). *The ecology of human development.* Cambridge, MA: Harvard University Press.

Bronfenbrenner, U. (1989). Ecological systems theory. In R. Vasta (Ed.), *Annals of child development* (Vol. 6, pp. 187–251). Greenwich, CT: JAI Press. ,

Brooks-Gunn, J., Graber, J., & Paikoff, R. (1994). Studying links between hormones and negative affect: Models and measures. *Journal of Research on Adolescence, 4,* 469–486.

Brooks-Gunn, J., & Reiter, E. (1990). The role of pubertal processes. In S. Feldman & G. Elliott (Eds.), *At the threshold: The developing adolescent* (pp. 16–53). Cambridge, MA: Harvard University Press.

Brooks-Gunn, J., & Warren, M. (1989). Biological and social contributions to negative affect in young adolescent girls. *Child Development, 60,* 40–55.

Brooks-Gunn, J., Warren, M., Rosso, J., & Gargiulo, J. (1987). Validity of self-report measures of girls' pubertal status. *Child Development, 58,* 829–841.

Broussard, E., & Hartner, M. (1971). Further considerations regarding maternal perceptions of the firstborn. In J. Hellmuth (Ed.), *The exceptional infant: Studies in abnormalities.* New York: Brunner/Mazel.

Brown, A., Bransford, J., Ferrara, R., & Campione, J. (1983). Learning, remembering, and understanding. In J. Flavell & E. Markman (Eds.), *Handbook of child psychology, Vol 3. Cognitive development* (pp. 77–166). New York: Wiley.

Brown, B. (1989). *The social type rating manual.* Madison, MT: National Center on Effective Secondary Schools, University of Wisconsin.

Brown, B., Clasen, D., & Eicher, S. (1986). Perceptions of peer pressure, peer conformity dispositions, and self-reported behavior among adolescents. *Developmental Psychology, 22*, 521–530.

Brown, B., Mory, M., & Kinney, D. (1994). Casting crowds in a relational perspective: Caricature, channel, and context. In R. Montemayor, G. Adams, & T. Gullotta (Eds.), *Advances in adolescent development, Vol 5: Personal relationships during adolescence* (pp. 123–167). Newbury Park, CA: Sage Publications.

Brown, B., Mounts, N., Lamborn, S., & Steinberg, L. (1993). Parenting practices and peer group affiliation in adolescence. *Child Development, 64*, 467–482.

Brown, D., Pryzwansky, W., & Schulte, A. (1987). *Psychological consultation: Introduction to theory and practice.* Boston, MA: Allyn & Bacon.

Brown, G., & Harris, T. (1978). *Social origins of depression: A study of psychiatric disorders in women.* London: Tavistock.

Brown, R. (1973). *A first language: The early stages.* Cambridge, MA: Harvard University Press.

Bruck, M., & Ceci, S. (1996). Issues in the scientific validation of interviews with young children. In M. Steward & D. Steward (Eds.), Interviewing young children about body touch and handling. *Monographs for the Society for Research in Child Development, Vol. 61*, (4-5, Serial No. 248).

Bruck, M., Ceci, S., Francoeur, E., & Barr, R. (1995). "I hardly cried when I got my shot!" Influencing children's reports about a visit to the pediatrican. *Child Development, 66*, 193–208.

Bruner, J., Roy, C., & Ratner, N. (1982). The beginnings of request. In K. Nelson (Ed.), *Children's language* (Vol. 3, pp. 41–56). New York: Gardner Publications.

Bryant, B. (1982). An index of empathy for children and adolescents. *Child Development, 53*, 412–425.

Bryant, B. (1985). The neighborhood walk: Sources of support in middle childhood. *Monographs of the Society for Research in Child Development, Vol. 50* (3, Serial No. 210).

Buchanan, C., Eccles, J., & Becker, J. (1992). Are adolescents the victims of raging hormones?: Evidence for activational effects of hormones on moods and behaviors at adolescence. *Psychological Bulletin, 111*, 62–107.

Buhrmester, D., & Furman, W. (1987). The development of companionship and intimacy. *Child Development, 58*, 1101–1113.

Butcher, J., Dahlstrom, W., Graham, J., Tellegen, A., & Kaemmer, B. (1989). *The Minneapolis Multiphasic Personality Inventory-2 (MMPI-2); Manual for administration and scoring.* Minneapolis, MN: University of Minnesota Press.

Buzwell, S., & Rosenthal, D. (1996). Constructing the sexual self: Adolescents' sexual self perceptions and sexual risk-taking. *Journal of Research on Adolescence, 6*, 489–513.

Byrne, B., & Shavelson, R. (1996). On the structure of social self-concept for pre-, early, and late adolescents: A test of the Shavelson, Hubner, and Stanton (1976) Model. *Journal of Personality and Social Psychology, 70*, 599–613.

Byrnes, J., Miller, D., & Reynolds, M. (1999). Learning to make good decisions: A self-regulation perspective. *Child Development, 70*, 1121–1140.

Cacioppo, J., Berntson, G., Larsen, J., Poehlmann, K., & Ito, T. (2000). The psychophyioslogy of emotion. In M. Lewis & J. Haviland-Jones (Eds.), *Handbook of emotions* (2nd Ed., pp. 173–202). New York: Guilford Press.

Calkins, S. (1994). Origins and outcomes of individual differences in emotion regulation. In N. Fox (Ed.), The development of emotion regulation: Biological and behavioral considerations *Monographs of the Society for Research in Child Development, Vol. 59* (2-3, Serial No. 240). (pp. 53–72). Chicago, IL: University of Chicago Press.

Camarena, P., Sarigiani, P., & Petersen, A. (1990). Gender-specific pathways to intimacy in early adolescence. *Journal of Youth and Adolescence, 19*, 19–32.

Camp, C., West, R., & Poon, L. (1989). Recruitment practices for psychological research in gerontology. In M. Lawton & A. Herzog (Eds.), *Special research methods for gerontology* (pp. 163–198). Amityville, NY: Baywood Publishing .

Campbell, D., Hyne, S., & Nilsen, D. (1992). *Manual for the Campbell Interest and Skill Survey.* Minneapolis, MN: National Computer Systems.

Campbell, S., Kolobe, T., Osten, E., Girolami, G., & Lenki, M. (1994). *Test of Infant Motor Performance.* Chicago, IL: University of Illinois, Department of Physical Therapy.

Campos, J., Hiatt, S., Ramsay, D., Henderson, C., & Svejda, C. (1983). The emergence of fear on the visual cliff. In M. Lewis & L. Rosenblaum (Eds.), *The origins of affect.* New York: Plenum Publishing.

Campos, J., Kermoain, R., & Zumbahlen, M. (1992). Socioemotional transformations in the family system following infant crawling onset. In N. Eisenberg & R. Fabes (Eds.), *Emotion and its regulation in early development* (New Directions in Child Development, No. 55). San Francisco, CA: Jossey-Bass.

Campos, J., Langer, A., & Krowitz, A. (1970). Cardiac responses on the visual cliff in pre-motor human infants. *Science, 170*, 195–196.

Camras, L., Oster, H., Campos, J., Campos, R., Ujiie, T., Miyake, K., Wang, L., & Meng, Z. (1998). Production of emotional facial expressions in European American, Japanese, and Chinese infants. *Developmental Psychology, 34*, 616–628.

Camras, L., Oster, H., Campos, J., Miyake, K., & Bradshaw, D. (1992). Japanese and American infants' responses to arm restraint. *Developmental Psychology, 28*, 578–583.

Canfield, R., & Haith, M. (1991). Active expectations in 2-and 3-month old infants: Complex event sequences. *Developmental Psychology, 27,* 198–208.

Canfield, R., & Smith, E. (1996). Number-based expectations and sequential enumeration by 5-month-old infants. *Developmental Psychology, 32,* 269–279.

Capaldi, D., Crosby, L., & Stoolmiller, M. (1996). Predicting the timing of first sexual intercourse for at-risk adolescent males. *Child Development, 67,* 344–359.

Caprio-Prevette, M., & Fry, P. (1996). Memory enhancement program for community-based older adults. *Experimental Aging Research, 22,* 281–303.

Capute, A., Palmer, F., Shapiro, B., Wachtel, R., Schmidt, S., & Ross, A. (1986). Clinical linguistic and auditory milestone scale: Prediction of cognition in infancy. *Developmental Medicine and Child Neurology, 28,* 762–771.

Carey, S., & Gelman, R. (1991). *The epigenesis of mind: Essays on biology and cognition.* Hillsdale, NJ: Lawrence Erlbaum Associates.

Carey, W., & McDevitt, S. (1978). Revision of the infant temperament questionnaire. *Pediatrics, 61,* 735–739.

Carlo, G., Eisenberg, N., & Knight, G. (1992). An objective measure of adolescents' prosocial moral reasoning. *Journal of Research on Adolescence, 2,* 331–349.

Carlo, G., & Randall, B. (2002). The development of a measure of prosocial behaviors for late adolescents. *Journal of Youth and Adolescence, 31,* 31–44.

Carlson, S., & Moses, L. (2001). Individual differences in inhibitory control and children's theory of mind. *Child Development, 72,* 1032–1053.

Carlson, S., Moses, L., & Hix, H. (1998). The role of inhibitory control in young children's difficulties in deception and false belief. *Child Development, 69,* 672–691.

Carmichael Olson, H., Grant, T., Martin, J., & Streissguth, A. (1995). A cohort study of prenatal cocaine exposure: Addressing methodological concerns. In M. Lewis & M. Bendersky (Eds.), *Mothers, babies, and cocaine: The role of toxins in development* (pp. 129–162). Hillsdale, NJ: Lawrence Erlbaum Associates.

Carp, L. (1989). Maximizing data quality in community studies of older people. In M. Lawton & A. Herzog (Eds.), *Special research methods for gerontology* (pp. 93–122). Amityville, NY: Baywood Publishing.

Carr, M., Kurtz, B., Schneider, W., Turner, L., & Borkowski, J. (1989). Strategy acquisition and transfer among American and German children: Environmental influences on metacognitive development. *Developmental Psychology, 25,* 765–771.

Carrow-Woolfolk, E. (1999). *Comprehensive Assessment of Spoken Language.* Circle Pines, MN: American Guidance Service.

Carver, C. (2001). Depression, hopelessness, optimism, and health. In J. Smelser & P. Baltes (Eds.), *The international encyclopedia of the social and behavioral sciences* (Vol. 5, pp. 3516–3522). Oxford, England: Elsevier.

Carver, C., Schier, M., & Weintraub, J. (1989). Assessing coping strategies: A theoretically based approach. *Journal of Personality and Social Psychology, 56,* 267–283.

Case, R. (1998). The development of conceptual structures. In D. Kuhn & R. Siegler (Eds.), W. Damon (Series Editor), *Handbook of child psychology, Vol. 2, Cognition, perception, and language* (5th Ed., pp. 745–800). New York: Wiley.

Case, R., Marini, Z., McKeough, A., Dennis, S., & Goldberg, J. (1986). Horizontal structure in middle childhood: Cross domain parallels in the course of cognitive growth. In I. Levin (Ed.), *Stage and structure: Reopening the debate.* Norwood, NJ: Ablex Publishing.

Case, R., & Okamoto, Y. (1996). The role of central conceptual structures in the development of children's thought. *Monographs for the Society for Research in Child Development, 61*(1-2, Serial No. 246).

Case-Smith, J., & Bigsby, R. (2001). Motor assessment. In L. Singer & P. Zeskind (Eds.), *Biobehavioral assessment of the infant* (pp. 423–442). New York: Guilford Press.

Caspi, A. (1998). Personality development across the life course. In W. Damon (Series Editor) & N. Eisenberg (Volume Editor), *Handbook of child psychology, Vol. 3: Social, emotional, and personality development* (5th Ed., pp. 311–388). New York: Wiley.

Caspi, A., Block, J., Block, J., Klopp, B., Lynham, D., Moffitt, T., & Stouthamer-Loeber, M. (1992). A "common language" version of the California Q-set for personality assessment. *Psychological Assessment, 4,* 512–523.

Caspi, A., & Silva, P. (1995). Temperamental qualities at age 3 predict personality traits in young adulthood: Longitudinal evidence from a birth cohort. *Child Development, 66,* 486–498.

Cassidy, J. (1988). Child-mother attachment and the self in six-year-olds. *Child Development, 59,* 121–134.

Cassidy, J. (1999). The nature of the child's ties. In J. Cassidy & P. Shaver (Eds.), *Handbook of attachment: Theory, research, and clinical applications* (pp. 3–20). New York: Guilford Press.

Cassidy, J., & Marvin, R. (1992). *Attachment organization in preschool children: Coding guidelines.* Unpublished manuscript. Seattle, WA: MacArthur Working Group on Attachment.

Cassidy, J., Parke, R., Butkovsky, L., & Braungart, J. (1992). Family-peer connections: The role of emotional expressiveness within the family and children's understanding of emotions. *Child Development, 63,* 603–618.

Cassidy, J., & Shaver, P. (1999). *Handbook of attachment: Theory, research, and clinical applications.* New York: Guilford Press.

Centers for Disease Control and Prevention (CDC). (2000). Youth risk behavior surveillance—United States, 1999. *Morbidity and Mortality Weekly Report, 49*(SS-5).

Cernoch, J., & Porter, R. (1985). Recognition of maternal anxillary odors by infants. *Child Development, 56,* 1593–1598.

Chandler, M. (1973). Egocentrism and antisocial behavior: The assessment and training of social-perspective taking skills. *Developmental Psychology, 9,* 326–332.

Chen, X., Hastings, P., Rubin, K., Chen, H., Cen, G., & Stewart, S. (1998). Child-rearing attitudes and behavioral inhibition in Chinese and Canadian toddles: A cross-cultural study. *Developmental Psychology, 34,* 677–686.

Chen, Z., & Dornbusch, S. (1998). Relating aspects of adolescent emotional autonomy to academic achievement and deviant behavior. *Journal of Adolescent Research, 13,* 293–319.

Chen, Z., & Siegler, R. (2000). Intellectual development during childhood. In R. Sternberg (Ed.), *Handbook of intelligence* (pp. 92–116). Cambridge, UK: Cambridge University Press.

Cherlin, A., & Furstenberg, F. (1986). *The new American grandparent.* New York: Basic Books.

Chi, M., Glaser, R., & Rees, E. (1982). Expertise in problem-solving. In R. Sternberg (Ed.), *Advances in the psychology of human intelligence* (pp. 7–71). Hillsdale, NJ: Lawrence Erlbaum Associates.

Chi, M., Hutchinson, J., & Robin, A. (1989). How inferences about novel domain-related concepts can be constrained by structural knowledge. *Merrill-Palmer Quarterly, 35,* 27–61.

Chi, M., & Koeske, R. (1983). Network representation of a child's dinosaur knowledge. *Developmental Psychology, 19,* 29–39.

Cobo-Lewis, A., & Eilers, R. (2001). Auditory assessment in infancy. In L. Singer & P. Zeskind (Eds.), *Biobehavioral assessment of the infant* (pp. 95–106). New York: Guilford Press.

Code of Federal Regulations. (2001). *Part 46—Protection of human subjects.* Washington, DC: National Archives and Records Administration.

Cohen, L., & Younger, B. (1984). Infant perception of angular relations. *Infant Behavior and Development, 7,* 37–47.

Cohen, S., Kessler, R., & Gordon, L. (1997). Strategies for measuring stress in studies of psychiatric and physical disorders. In S. Cohen, R. Kessler, & L. Gordon (Eds.), *Measuring stress: A guide for health and social scientists* (2nd Ed., pp. 3–26). New York: Oxford University Press.

Cohen, S., Tyrell, D., & Smith, A. (1993). Negative life events, perceived stress, negative affect, and susceptibility to the common cold. *Journal of Personality and Social Psychology, 64,* 131–140.

Cohn, J., & Tronick, E. (1983). Three-month-old infants' reaction to simulated maternal depression. *Child Development, 54,* 185–193.

Coie, J., Dodge, K., & Coppotelli, H. (1982). Dimensions and types of social status: A cross-age perspective. *Developmental Psychology, 18,* 557–570.

Coie, J., Dodge, K., Terry, R., & Wright, V. (1991). The role of aggression in peer relations: An analysis of aggressive episodes in boys' play groups. *Child Development, 62,* 812–826.

Colby, A., & Kohlberg, L. (1987). *The measurement of moral judgment: Theoretical foundations and research validation.* Cambridge: Cambridge University Press.

Colby, A., Kohlberg, K., Gibbs, J., & Lieberman, M. (1983). A longitudinal study of moral judgment. *Monographs for the Society for Research in Child Development, 48*(1-2, Serial No. 200).

Cole, M. (1996). *Cultural psychology: A once and future discipline.* Cambridge, MA: Harvard University Press.

Cole, P., Barrett, K., & Zahn-Waxler, C. (1992). Emotion displays in two-year-olds during mishaps. *Child Development, 63,* 314–324.

Coleman, L., & Coleman, J. (2002). The measurement of puberty: A review. *Journal of Adolescence, 25,* 535–550.

Collins, L. (1996). Measurement of change in research on aging: Old and new issues from an individual growth perspective. In J. Birren & K.W. Schaie (Eds.), *Handbook of the psychology of aging* (4th Ed., pp. 38–56). San Diego, CA: Academic Press.

Collins, W. (1990). Parent-child relationships in the transition to adolescence: Continuity and change in interactions, affect, and cognitions. In R. Montemayor, G. Adams, & T. Gullota (Eds.), *From childhood to adolescence* (pp. 103–110). Newbury Park, CA: Sage Publications.

Collins, W., Madsen, S., & Susman-Stillman, A. (2002). Parenting during middle childhood. In M. Bornstein (Ed.), *Handbook of parenting: Children and parenting* (Vol. 1, 2nd Ed., pp. 73–101). Mahwah, NJ: Lawrence Erlbaum Associates.

Colombo, J. (1995). On the neural mechanism underlying developmental and individual differences in visual fixation in infancy. *Developmental Review, 15,* 97–135.

Colombo, J., & Mitchell, D. (1990). Individual differences in early visual attention: Fixation time and information processing. In J. Colombo, & J. Fagen (Eds.), *Individual differences in infancy: Reliability, stability, and prediction* (pp. 193–227). Hillsdale, NJ: Lawrence Erlbaum Associates.

Commons, M., Richards, F., & Armon, C. (1984). *Beyond formal operations: Late adolescent and adult cognitive development.* New York: Praeger.

Compas, B., Oppedisano, G., Connor, J., Gerhardt, C., Hinden, B., Achenbach, T., & Hammen, C. (1997). Gender differences in depressive symptoms in adolescence: Comparison of national samples of clinically referred and nonreferred youths. *Journal of Consulting and Clinical Psychology, 65,* 617–626.

Compas, B., Wagner, B., Slavin, L., & Vannatta, K. (1986). A prospective study of life events, social support, and psychological symptomatology during the transition from high school to college. *American Journal of Community Psychology, 14,* 241–257.

Connell, J., & Furman, W. (1984). The study of transitions: Conceptual and methodological issues. In R. Emde & R. Harmon (Eds.), *Continuities and discontinuities in development* (pp. 153–173). New York: Plenum Publishing .

Constantinople, A. (1969). An Eriksonian measure of personality development in college students. *Developmental Psychology, 1,* 357–372.

Cook, T., & Campbell, D. (1979). *Quasi-experimentation: Design and analysis issues for field settings.* Boston, MA: Houghton Mifflin.

Cook, T., Church, M., Ajanaku, S., Shadish, W., Kim, J., & Cohen, R. (1996). The development of occupational aspirations and expectations among inner-city boys. *Child Development, 67,* 3368–3385.

Costa, P., & McCrae, R. (1988). Personality development during adulthood: A six-year longitudinal study of self-reports and spouse ratings on the NEO Personality Inventory. *Journal of Personality and Social Psychology, 54,* 853–863.

Costa, P., & McCrae, R. (1992). *NEO PI-R: Professional manual.* Odessa, FL: Psychological Assessment Resources, Inc.

Côté, J., & Levine, C. (1988). A critical examination of the ego identity status paradigm. *Developmental Review, 8,* 147–184.

Cox, B., Ornstein, P., Naus, M., Maxfield, D., & Zimler, J. (1989). Children's concurrent use of rehearsal and organizational strategies. *Developmental Psychology, 25,* 619–627.

Coyne, J., & Racioppo, M. (2000). Never the twain shall meet? Closing the gap between coping research and clinical intervention research. *American Psychologist, 55,* 655–664.

Craig, W., Pepler, D., Connolly, J., & Henderson, K. (2001). Developmental context of peer harassment in early adolescence: The role of puberty and the peer group. In J. Juvonen & S. Graham (Eds.), *Peer harassment in school: The plight of the vulnerable and victimized* (pp. 242–261). New York: Guilford Press.

Craik, F. (1999). Memory, aging, and survey measurement. In N. Schwartz, D. Park, B. Knäuper, & S. Sudman (Eds.), *Cognition, aging, and self-reports* (pp. 95–115). Philadelphia, PA: Taylor & Francis, Psychology Press.

Creasey, G. (1993). Associations between divorce and late adolescent grandchildren's relations with grandparents. *Journal of Youth and Adolescence, 22,* 513–529.

Creasey, G. (2002). Associations between working models of attachment and conflict management behavior in romantic couples. *Journal of Counseling Psychology, 49,* 365–375.

Creasey, G., & Hesson-McInnis, M. (2001). Affective responses, cognitive appraisals, and conflict tactics in late adolescent romantic relationships: Associations with attachment orientations. *Journal of Counseling Psychology, 48,* 85–96.

Creasey, G., & Jarvis, P. (2003). Play in children: An attachment perspective. In O. Saracho & B. Spodek (Eds.), *Contemporary perspectives on play in early childhood education* (pp. 133–151). New York: Information Age Publishers.

Creasey, G., Jarvis, P., & Berk, L. (1998). Play and social competence. In O. Saracho & B. Spodek (Eds.), *Multiple perspectives on play in early childhood education* (pp. 116–143). Albany, NY: SUNY Press.

Creasey, G., & Kaliher, G. (1994). Age differences in grandchildren's perceptions of relations with grandparents. *Journal of Adolescence, 17,* 411–426.

Creasey, G., & Ladd, A. (2004). Negative mood regulation expectancies and conflict behaviors in late adolescent college student romantic relationships: The moderating role of generalized attachment representations. *Journal of Research on Adolescence, 14,* 235–255.

Creasey, G., & Myers, B. (1986). Video games and children: Effects on leisure activities, schoolwork, and peer involvement. *Merrill-Palmer Quarterly, 32,* 251–262.

Creasey, G., Myers, B., Epperson, M., & Taylor, J. (1989). Grandchildren with grandparents with Alzheimer's disease: Perceptions of grandparent, family environment and the elderly. *Merrill-Palmer Quarterly, 35,* 227–237.

Crick, N. (1996). The role of overt aggression, relational aggression, and prosocial behavior in the prediction of children's future school adjustment. *Child Development, 67,* 2317–2327.

Crick, N. (1997). Engagement of gender normative versus nonnormative forms of aggression: Links to social-psychological adjustment. *Developmental Psychology, 33,* 610–617.

Crick, N., & Grotpeter, J. (1995). Relational aggression, gender, and social-psychological adjustment. *Child Development, 66,* 710–722.

Criss, M., Pettit, G., Bates, J., Dodge, K., & Lapp, A. (2002). Family adversity, positive peer relationships, and children's externalizing behavior: A longitudinal perspective on risk and resilience. *Child Development, 73,* 1220–1237.

Crittenden, P. (1994). *Preschool assessment of attachment* (2nd ed.) Unpublished manuscript. Miami, FL: Family Relations Institute.

Crnic, K., & Greenberg, M. (1990). Minor parenting stresses with young children. *Child Development, 61,* 1628–1637.

Crockett, L., Raffaelli, M., & Moilanen, K. (2003). Adolescent sexuality: Behavior and meaning. In G. Adams & M.

Berzonsky (Eds.), *Blackwell handbook of adolescence* (pp. 371–392). Malden, MA: Blackwell Science.

Crouter, A., Manke, B., & McHale, S. (1995). The family context of gender intensification in early adolescence. *Child Development, 66*, 317–329.

Crowell, J., Fraley, C., & Shaver, P. (1999). Measurement of individual differences in adolescent and adult attachment. In J. Cassidy & P. Shaver (Eds.), *Handbook of attachment: Theory, research, and clinical applications* (pp. 434–465). New York: Guilford Press.

Crowell, J., & Owens, G. (1996). *Current Relationship Interview and scoring system*. Unpublished manuscript. Stony Brook: State University of New York.

Crowell, J., Pan, H., Gao, Y., Treboux, D., O'Conner, E., & Waters, W. (1996). *The secure base scoring system for adults*. Unpublished manuscript. Stony Brook: State University of New York.

Crowell, J., Treboux, D., & Waters, E. (2002). Stability of attachment representations: The transition to marriage. *Developmental Psychology, 38*, 467–479.

Crowley, K., & Jacobs, M. (2002). Building islands of expertise in everyday family activity. In G. Leinhardt, K. Crowley, & K. Knutson (Eds.), *Learning conversations in museums* (pp. 333–356). Mahwah, NJ: Lawrence Erlbaum Associates.

Csikszentmihalyi, M., & Larson, R. (1984). *Being adolescent*. New York: Basic Books.

Csikszentmihalyi, M., & Larson, R. (1987). The experience sampling method. *Journal of Nervous and Mental Disease, 175*, 537–544.

Cummings, E.M., & Davies, P. (1994). *Children and marital conflict: The impact of family dispute and resolution*. New York: Guilford Press.

Dale, P. (1996). Parent report assessment of language and communication. In K. Cole, P. Dale, & D. Thal (Eds.), *Assessment of communication and language* (Vol. 6, pp. 161–182). Baltimore, MD: Paul Brookes.

Damon, W. (1977). *The social world of the child*. San Francisco, CA: Jossey-Bass.

Damon, W. (1980). Patterns of change in children' social reasoning: A two-year longitudinal study. *Child Development, 51*, 1010–1017.

Damon, W., & Hart, D. (1988). *Self-understanding in childhood and adolescence*. New York: Cambridge University Press.

Daniel, M. (2000). Interpretation of test scores. In R. Sternberg (Ed.), *Handbook of intelligence* (pp. 477–491). Cambridge, UK: Cambridge University Press.

Danner, F. (1989). Cognitive development during adolescence. In J. Worell & F. Danner (Eds.), *The adolescent decision-maker: Applications to development and education* (pp. 51–81). San Diego, CA: Academic Press.

Darling, N., & Steinberg, L. (1993). Parenting style in context: An integrative model. *Psychological Bulletin, 113*, 487–496.

Das Eiden, R., & Reifman, A. (1996). Effects of Brazelton demonstrations on later parenting: A meta-analysis. *Journal of Pediatric Psychology, 21*, 857–868.

Davis, R. (1999). Web-based administration of personality questionnaire: Comparison with traditional methods. *Behavior Research Methods, Instruments, and Computers, 31*, 572–577.

Davis-Kean, P., & Sandler, H. (2001). A meta-analysis of measures of self-esteem for young children: A framework for future measures. *Child Development, 72*, 887–906.

de Haan, M., & Nelson, C. (1997). Recognition of the mother's face by six-month-old infants: A neurobehavioral study. *Child Development, 68*, 187–210.

De Lisi, R., & Gallagher, A. (1991). Understanding of gender stability and constancy in Argentinean children. *Merrill-Palmer Quarterly, 37*, 483–502.

Deary, I. (1995). Auditory inspection time and intelligence: What is the direction of causation? *Developmental Psychology, 31*, 237–250.

Deary, I., Head, B., & Egan, V. (1989). Auditory inspection time, intelligence, and pitch discrimination. *Intelligence, 13*, 135–147.

DeCasper, A., & Fifer, W. (1980). Of human bonding: Newborns prefer their mothers' voice. *Science, 208*, 1174–1176.

DeCasper, A., Lecanuet, J., Busnel, M., Granier-Deferre, C., & Maugeais, R. (1994). Fetal reactions to maternal speech. *Infant Behavior and Development, 17*, 159–164.

Dellas, M., & Jerigan, L. (1990). Affective personality characteristics associated with undergraduate ego identity formation. *Journal of Adolescent Research, 5*, 306–324.

DeLongis, A., Folkman, S., & Lazarus, R. (1988). The impact of daily stress on health and mood: Psychological and social resources as mediators. *Journal of Personality and Social Psychology, 54*, 486–495.

Demetriou, A., Christou, C., Spanoudis, G., & Platsidou, M. (2002). The development of mental processing: Efficiency, working memory, and thinking. *Monographs for the Society for Research in Child Development, 67*(1, Serial No. 268).

Dempster, F. (1981). Memory span: Sources of individual and developmental differences. *Psychological Bulletin, 89*, 63–100.

Denham, S. (1986). Social cognition, prosocial behavior, and emotion in preschoolers: Contextual validation. *Child Development, 57*, 194–201.

Denham, S., Blair, K., DeMulder, E., Levitas, J., Sawyer, K., Auerbach-Major, S., & Queenan, P. (2003). Preschool emotional competence: Pathway to social competence? *Child Development, 74*, 238–256.

Denham, S., Renwick, S., & Holt, R. (1991). Working and playing together: Prediction of preschool social-emotional competence from mother-child interaction. *Child Development, 62*, 242–249.

Denham, S., Zoller, D., & Couchoud, E. (1994). Preschoolers' causal understanding of emotion and its socialization. *Developmental Psychology, 30,* 928–936.

Derogatis, L., & Melisaritos, N. (1983). The Brief Symptom Inventory: An introductory report. *Psychological Medicine, 13,* 595–605.

DeWolff, M., & IJzendoorn, M. (1997). Sensitivity and attachment: A meta-analysis on parental antecedents of infant attachment. *Child Development, 68,* 571–591. van

Diaz, R., & Berndt, T. (1982). Children's knowledge of a best friend: Fact of fancy. *Developmental Psychology, 18,* 787–794.

DiLalla, L., Thompson, L., Plomin, R., Phillips, K., Fagan, J., Haith, M., Cyphers, L., & Fulker, D. (1990). Infant predictors of preschool and adult IQ: A study of infant twins and their parents. *Developmental Psychology, 26,* 759–769.

Dillman, D. (2000). *Mail and Internet surveys: The tailored design method.* New York: John Wiley & Sons.

Dix, T. (1992). Parenting on behalf of the child: Empathetic goals in the regulation of responsive parenting. In I. Sigel, A. McGillicuddy-De Lisi, & J. Goodnow (Eds.), *Parental belief systems: The psychological consequences for children* (Vol. 2, pp. 319–346). Hillsdale, NJ: Lawrence Erlbaum Associates.

Dixon, R. (1999). The concepts of gain in cognitive aging. In N. Schwartz, D. Park, B. Knäuper, & S. Sudman (Eds.), *Cognition, aging, and self-reports* (pp. 71–92). Philadelphia, PA: Taylor & Francis, Psychology Press.

Dixon, R., & Hultsch, D. (1984). The Metamemory in Adulthood (MIA) instrument. *Psychological Documents, 14,* 3.

Dodge, K., Lansford, J., Burks, V., Bates, J., Pettit, G., Fontaine, R., & Price, J. (2003). Peer rejection and social information-processing factors in the development of aggressive behavior problems in children. *Child Development, 74,* 374–393.

Dolan, M. (1994). *An assessment of the daily hassles of nurse aides: Development of the nurse aide hassles scale.* Unpublished Master's Thesis. Illinois State University, Normal, IL.

Donnay, D., & Borgen, F. (1996). Validity, structure, and content of the 1994 Strong Interest Inventory. *Journal of Counseling Psychology, 43,* 275–291.

Donohue, R., & Berg, W. (1991). Infant heart-rate responses to temporally predictable and unpredictable events. *Developmental Psychology, 27,* 59–66.

Dorn, L., Nottelmann, E., Susman, E., Inoff-Germain, G., Cutler, G., & Chrousos, G. (1999). Variability in hormonal concentrations and self-reported menstrual histories in young adolescents: Menarche as an integral part of a developmental process. *Journal of Youth and Adolescence, 28,* 283–304.

Dorn, L., Susman, E., Nottelmann, E., Inoff-Germain, G., & Chrousos, G. (1990). Perceptions of puberty: Adolescent, parent and health care personnel. *Developmental Psychology, 26,* 322–329.

Dorn, L., Susman, E., & Ponirakis, A. (2003). Pubertal timing and adolescent adjustment and behavior: Conclusions vary by rater. *Journal of Youth and Adolescence, 32,* 157–167.

Dornbusch, S., Herman, M., & Morley, J. (1996). Domains of adolescent achievement. In G. Adams, R. Montemayor, & T. Gullotta (Eds.), *Psychosocial development in adolescence* (pp. 181–231). Thousand Oaks, CA: Sage Publications.

Dornbusch, S., Ritter, P., Leiderman, P., Roberts, D., & Fraleigh, M. (1987). The relation of parenting style to academic performance. *Child Development, 58,* 1244–1257.

Doyle, A., Doehring, P., Tessier, O., de Lorimier, S., & Shapiro, S. (1992). Transitions in children's play: A sequential analysis of states preceding and following social pretense. *Developmental Psychology, 28,* 137–144.

Dubowitz, L., & Dubowitz, V. (1981). The neurological assessment of the preterm and full-term newborn infant, *Clinics in Developmental Medicine, Vol. 79.* Philadelphia, PA: JB Lippincott Co.

Duda, J., & Nicholls, J. (1992). Dimensions of achievement motivation in schoolwork and sport. *Journal of Educational Psychology, 84,* 290–299.

Dunifon, R., & Kowaleski-Jones, L. (2002). Who's in the house? Race differences in cohabitation, single parenthood, and child development. *Child Development, 73,* 1249–1264.

Dunlosky, J., & Hertzog, C. (1998). Training programs to improve learning in later adulthood: Helping older adults educate themselves. In D. Hacker, J. Dunlosky, & A. Graesser (Eds.), *Metacognition in educational theory and practice* (pp. 249–275). Mahwah, NJ: Lawrence Erlbaum Associates.

Dunn, J., Cutting, A., & Fisher, N. (2002). Old friends, new friends: Predictors of children's perspective on their friends at school. *Child Development, 73,* 621–635.

Eagly, A. (1995). The science and politics of comparing men and women. *American Psychologist, 50,* 145–158.

Eccles, J., & Roeser, R. (2003). Schools as developmental contexts. In G. Adams & M. Berzonsky (Eds.), *Blackwell handbook of adolescence* (pp. 129–148). Malden, MA: Blackwell Science.

Eccles, J., Wigfield, A., & Schiefele, U. (1998). Motivation to succeed. In W. Damon (Series Editor) & N. Eisenberg (Volume Editor), *Handbook of child psychology, Vol. 3: Social, emotional, and personality development* (5th Ed., pp. 1017–1095). New York: Wiley.

Eckenrode, J., & Bolger, N. (1997). Daily and within-day event measurement. In S. Cohen, R. Kessler, & L. Gordon (Eds.), *Measuring stress: A guide for health and social scientists* (2nd Ed., pp. 80–101). New York: Oxford University Press.

Edelbrock, C., & Sugawara, A. (1978). Acquisition of sex-typed preferences in preschool children. *Developmental Psychology, 14*, 614–623.

Eder, R. (1989). The emergent personologist: The structure and content of $3^{1/2}$-, $5^{1/2}$- and $7^{1/2}$-year-olds concepts of themselves and other persons. *Child Development, 60*, 1218–1228.

Eder, R. (1990). Uncovering young children's psychological selves: Individual and developmental differences. *Child Development, 61*, 849–863.

Egeland, B., Jacobvitz, D., & Sroufe, L. (1988). Breaking the cycle of abuse. *Child Development, 59*, 1080–1088.

Ehrle, G. (2001). Grandchildren as moderator variables in the family: Social, physiological, and intellectual development of grandparents who are raising them. In E. Grigorenko & L. Sternberg (Eds.), *Family and intellectual functioning: A life-span perspective* (pp. 223–241). Mahwah, NJ: Lawrence Erlbaum Associates.

Eidelson, R., & Epstein, N. (1982). Cognition and relationship maladjustment: Development of a measure of dysfunctional relationship beliefs. *Journal of Consulting and Clinical Psychology, 50*, 715–720.

Eiden, R., Edwards, E., & Leonard, K. (2002). Mother-infant and father-infant attachment among alcoholic families. *Development and Psychopathology, 14*, 253–278.

Eimas, P., Siqueland, E., Jusczyk, P., & Vigorito, J. (1971). Speech perception in infants. *Science, 171*, 303–306.

Eisenberg, N. (1982). The development of reasoning regarding prosocial behavior. In N. Eisenberg (Ed.), *The development of prosocial behavior* (pp. 219–249). New York: Academic Press.

Eisenberg, N. (1986). *Altruistic emotion, cognition, and behavior.* Hillsdale, NJ: Lawrence Erlbaum Associates.

Eisenberg, N., Carlo, G., Murphy, B., & Van Court, P. (1995). Prosocial development in late adolescence: A longitudinal study. *Child Development, 66*, 1179–1197.

Eisenberg, N., & Fabes, R. (1998). Prosocial development. In W. Damon (Series Editor) & N. Eisenberg (Volume Editor), *Handbook of child psychology, Vol. 3: Social, emotional, and personality development* (5th Ed., pp. 701–778). New York: Wiley.

Eisenberg, N., Fabes, R., Miller, P., Fultz, J., Mathy, R., Shell, R., & Reno, R. (1989). The relations of sympathy and emotional distress to prosocial behavior: A multi-method study. *Journal of Personality and Social Psychology, 57*, 55–66.

Eisenberg, N., Fabes, R., Miller, P., Shell, C., Shea, R., & May-Plumee, T. (1990). Preschoolers' vicarious emotional responding and their situational and dispositional prosocial behavior. *Merrill-Palmer Quarterly, 36*, 507–529.

Eisenberg, N., Lennon, R., & Roth, K. (1983). Prosocial development: A longitudinal study. *Developmental Psychology, 19*, 846–855.

Eisenberg, N., & Miller, P. (1987). The relation of empathy to prosocial behavior. *Psychological Bulletin, 101*, 91–119.

Eisenberg, N., Miller, P., Shell, R., McNally, S., & Shea, C. (1991). Prosocial development in adolescence: A longitudinal study. *Developmental Psychology, 27*, 849–857.

Eisenberg, N., Schaller, M., Fabes, R., Bustamante, D., Mathy, R., Shell, R., & Rhodes, K. (1988). The differentiation of personal distress and sympathy in children and adults. *Developmental Psychology, 24*, 766–775.

Eisenberg-Berg, N. (1979). Development of children's prosocial moral judgment. *Developmental Psychology, 15*, 128–137.

Elger, F., Curtis, L., McGrath, P., Waschbusch, D., & Stewart, S. (2003). Antecedent-Consequence conditions in maternal mood and child adjustment: A four-year cross-lagged study. *Journal of Clinical Child and Adolescent Psychology, 32*, 362–374.

Elias, C., & Berk, L. (2002). Self-regulation in young children: Is there a role for sociodramatic play? *Early Childhood Research Quarterly, 17*, 216–238.

Elliot, A. (1999). Approach and avoidance motivation and achievement goals. *Educational Psychologist, 34*, 169–189.

Elliot, A., & Church, M. (1997). A hierarchical model of approach and avoidance achievement motivation. *Journal of Personality and Social Psychology, 72*, 218–232.

Emmerich, W., Goldman, K., Kirsh, B., & Sharabany, R. (1977). Evidence for a transitional phase in the development of gender constancy. *Child Development, 48*, 930–936.

Ennett, S., & Bauman, K. (1996). Adolescent social networks: School demographic, and longitudinal considerations. *Journal of Adolescent Research, 11*, 194–215.

Enright, R., Enright, W., Mannheim, L., & Harris, B. (1980). Distributive justice development and social class. *Developmental Psychology, 16*, 555–563.

Enright, R., Franklin, C., & Mannheim, L. (1980). Children's distributive justice: A standardized and objective scale. *Developmental Psychology, 16*, 193–202.

Entwisle, D., & Astone, N. (1994). Some practical guidelines for measuring youth's race/ethnicity and socioeconomic status. *Child Development, 65*, 1521–1540.

Epping-Jordan, J., Compas, B., Osowiecki, D., Oppedisano, G., Gerhardt, C., et al. (1999). Psychological adjustment in breast cancer: Processes of emotional distress. *Health Psychology, 18*, 315–326.

Epstein, J., Klinkenberg, W., Wiley, W., & McKinley, L. (2001). Ensuring sample equivalence across internet and paper-and-pencil assessments. *Computers in Human Behavior, 17*, 339–356.

Ericsson, K., & Simon, H. (1984). *Protocol analysis: Verbal reports as data.* Cambridge, MA: MIT Press.

Erikson, E. (1950). *Childhood and society.* New York: Norton.

Erikson, E. (1968). *Identity: Youth and crisis.* New York: Norton.

Ervin-Tripp, S. (2000). Studying conversation: How to get natural peer interaction. In L. Menn & N. Ratner (Eds.), *Methods for studying language production* (pp. 271–288). Mahwah, NJ: Lawrence Erlbaum Associates.

Esbensen, F., Deschenes, E., Vogel, R., West, J., Arboit, K., & Harris, L. (1996). Active parental consent in school-based research: An examination of ethical and methodological issues. *Evaluation Research, 20*, 737–753.

Espelage, D., & Asidao, C. (2001). Conversations with middle school students about bullying and victimization: Should we be concerned? In R. Geffner, M. Loring, & C. Young (Eds.), *Bullying behavior: Current issues, research and interventions* (pp. 49–62). New York: Haworth Press.

Espelage, D., Holt, M., & Henkel, R. (2003). Examination of peer-group contextual effects on aggression during early adolescence. *Child Development, 74*, 205–220.

Fagan, J., & Shepherd, P. (1986). *The Fagan Test of Infant Intelligence: Training Manual*. Cleveland, OH: Infantest Corporation.

Fagan, J., & Singer, L. (1983). Infant recognition memory as a measure of intelligence. In L. Lipsett (Ed.), *Advances in infancy research* (Vol. 2, pp. 31–79). Norwood, NJ: Ablex Publishing.

Fagen, J., & Ohr, P. (2001). Learning and memory in infancy: Habituation, instrumental conditioning, and expectancy formation. In L. Singer & P. Zeskind (Eds.), *Biobehavioral assessment of the infant* (pp. 233–273). New York: Guilford Press.

Feinman, S., & Lewis, M. (1983). Social referencing at ten months: A second-order effect on infants' responses to strangers. *Child Development, 54*, 878–887.

Feldman, S., & Elliott, G. (1990). *At the threshold: The developing adolescent*. Cambridge, MA: Harvard University Press.

Feldman, S., Turner, R., & Araujo, K. (1999). Interpersonal context as an influence on sexual timetables of youth: Gender and ethnic effects. *Journal of Research on Adolescence, 9*, 25–52.

Fenson, L., Dale, P., Reznick, S., Bates, E., Thal, D., & Pethick, S. (1994). Variability in early communicative development. *Monographs of the Society for Research in Child Development, Vol. 59* (5, Serial No. 242). Chicago, IL: University of Chicago Press.

Fenson, L., Dale, P., Reznick, S., Thal, D., Bates, E., Hartung, P., Pethick, S., & Reilly, S. (1993). *The MacArthur Communicative Developmental Inventories: User's guide and technical manual*. San Diego, CA: Singular Publishing.

Ferreira, A. (1963). Decision-making in normal and pathological families. *Archives of General Psychiatry, 8*, 68–73.

Field, T. (1979). Interaction patterns of high-risk and normal infants. In T. Field, A. Sostek, S. Goldberg, & H. Schuman (Eds.), *Infants born at risk*. New York: Spectrum.

Field, T. (1994). The effects of mother's physical and emotional unavailability on emotion regulation. In N. Fox (Ed.),

The development of emotion regulation: Biological and behavioral considerations. *Monographs of the society for research in child development, Vol. 59* (2-3, Serial No. 240). (pp. 208–227). Chicago, IL: University of Chicago Press.

Field, T. (1995). Infants of depressed mothers. *Infant Behavior & Development, 18*, 1–13.

Field, T. (1999). Infant massage therapy. In E. Goldson (Ed.), *Nurturing the premature infant* (pp. 102–110). New York: Oxford University Press.

Field, T., Hernandez-Reif, M., & Freedman, J. (2004). Stimulation programs for preterm infants. *Social Policy Report: Giving Child and Youth Development Knowledge Away, 18*, 3–19.

Field, T., Schanberg, S., Scafidi, F., Bower, C., Vega-Lahr, N., Garcia, R., Nystrom, J., & Kuhn, C. (1986). Tactile/kinesthetic stimulation effects on preterm neonates. *Pediatrics, 77*, 654–658.

Fiese, B., Sameroff, A., Grotevant, H., Wamboldt, F., Dickstein, S., & Fravel, D. (1999). The stories that families tell: Narrative coherence, narrative interaction, and relationship beliefs. *Monographs for the Society for Research in Child Development, 64*(2, Serial No. 257).

Fincham, F. (1998). Child development and marital relations. *Child Development, 69*, 543–574.

Fincham, F., & Bradbury, T. (1992). Assessing attributions in marriage: The relationship attribution measure. *Journal of Personality and Social Psychology, 62*, 457–468.

Fincham, F., Garnier, P., Gano-Phillips, S., & Osborne, L. (1995). Preinteraction expectancies, marital satisfaction, and accessibility: A new look at sentiment override. *Journal of Family Psychology, 9*, 3–14.

Finkel, D., & Pedersen, N. (2001). Sources of environmental influence on cognitive abilities in adulthood. In E. Grigorenko & R. Sternberg (Eds.), *Family environment and intellectual functioning* (pp. 173–194). Mahwah, NJ: Lawrence Erlbaum Associates.

Finkel, D., Pedersen, N., Reynolds, C., Berg, S., de Faire, U., & Svartengren, M. (2003). Genetic and environmental influences on decline in biobehavioral markers of aging. *Behavior Genetics, 33*, 107–123.

First, M., Spitzer, R., Gibbon, M., & Williams, B. (1995). *Structured clinical interview for DSM-IV Axis I disorders*. Patient Edition (SCID-I/P, Version 2.0). New York: Biometrics Research Development, New York State Psychiatric Institute.

Fischer, K. (1980). A theory of cognitive development: The control and construction of hierarchies of skills. *Psychological Bulletin, 87*, 477–531.

Fischer, J., Munsch, J., & Greene, S. (1996). Adolescence and intimacy. In G. Adams, R. Montemayor, & T. Gullotta (Eds.), *Psychosocial development in adolescence* (pp. 95–129). Thousand Oaks, CA: Sage Publications.

Fischer, K., Yan, Z., & Stewart, J. (2003). Adult cognitive development: Dynamics in the developmental web. In J.

Valsiner & K. Connolly (Eds.), *Handbook of developmental psychology* (pp. 491–516). London: Sage Publications.

Fivush, R., & Hudson, J. (1990). *Knowing and remembering in young children.* Cambridge, UK: Cambridge University Press.

Flanagan, C., Schulenberg, J., & Fuligni, A. (1993). Residential setting and parent-adolescent relationships during the college years. *Journal of Youth and Adolescence, 22,* 171–189.

Flavell, J. (1968). *The development of role-taking and communication skills in children.* New York: Wiley.

Flavell, J. (1985). *Cognitive development* (2nd Ed). Englewood Cliffs, NJ: Prentice Hall.

Flavell, J., Beach, D., & Chinsky, J. (1966). Spontaneous verbal rehearsal in a memory task as a function of age. *Child Development, 37,* 283–299.

Flavell, J., Green, F., & Flavell, E. (1986). Development of knowledge about the appearance-reality distinction. *Monographs for the Society for Research in Child Development, 51*(1, Serial No. 212).

Flavell, J., & Miller, P. (1998). Social cognition. In D. Kuhn & R. Siegler (Eds.), W. Damon (Series Editor), *Handbook of child psychology, Vol. 2, Cognition, perception, and language* (5th Ed., pp. 851–898). New York: Wiley.

Flyr, M., Howe, T., & Parke, R. (1995). *Observed friendship quality scale.* Unpublished coding system. Riverside, CA: University of California.

Fogel, A., Stevenson, M., & Messinger, D. (1992). A comparison of the parent-child relationship in Japan and the United States. In J. Roopnarine & D. Carter (Eds.), *Parent-child relations in diverse settings* (pp. 35–51). Norwood, NJ: Ablex Publishing.

Folkman, S., & Lazarus, R. (1980). Analysis of coping in a middle-aged sample. *Journal of Health and Social Behavior, 21,* 219–239.

Folkman, S., Lazarus, R., Dunkel-Schetter, C., DeLongis, A., & Gruen, R. (1986). Dynamics of a stressful encounter: Cognitive appraisal, coping, and encounter outcomes. *Journal of Personality and Social Psychology, 50,* 992–1003.

Folstein, M., Folstein, S., & McHugh, P. (1975). Mini-Mental State: A practical method for grading the cognitive state of patients for the clinician. *Journal of Psychiatric Research, 12,* 189–198.

Fox, N. (1989). Psychophysiological correlates of emotional reactivity during the first year of life. *Developmental Psychology, 25,* 364–372.

Fox, N., & Davidson, R. (1987). Electroencephalogram asymmetry in response to the approach of a stranger and maternal separation. *Developmental Psychology, 23,* 233–240.

Fox, N., & Davidson, R. (1991). Hemispheric asymmetry and attachment behaviors: Developmental processes and individual differences in separation protest. In J. Gewirtz & W. Kurtines (Eds.), *Intersections in attachment* (pp. 147–164). Hillsdale, NJ: Lawrence Erlbaum Associates.

Fox, N., & Porges, S. (1985). The relationship between developmental outcome and neonatal heart period patterns. *Child Development, 56,* 28–37.

Francis, G., Neath, I., & Surprenant, A. (2000). The cognitive psychology online laboratory. In M. Birnbaum (Ed.), *Psychological experiments on the Internet* (pp. 267–283). San Diego, CA: Academic Press.

Francis, P., Self, P., & Horowitz, F. (1987). The behavioral assessment of the neonate: An overview. In J. Osofsky (Ed.), *Handbook of infant development* (2nd Ed., pp. 723–779). New York: Wiley.

French, D., Jansen, E., & Pidada, S. (2002). United States and Indonesian children's and adolescent's reports of relational aggression by disliked peers. *Child Development, 73,* 1143–1150.

Fressola, D., Hoerchler, S., Hagan, J., McDannold, S., & Meyer, J. (1990). *Speech and language evaluation scale.* Melbourne, FL: Psych Press.

Freud, S. (1938). *An outline of psychoanalysis.* London: Hogarth Press.

Freud, S. (1957). Five lectures on psycho-analysis. In J. Strachey (Ed. And Trans.), *The standard edition of the complete psychological works of Sigmund Freud* (Vol. 11, pp. 3–56). London: Hogarth Press.

Freud, S. (1963). *An outline of psychoanalysis* (J. Strachey, Trans.). New York: Norton. (Original work published 1940).

Freudigman, K., & Thoman, E. (1993). Infant's sleep during the first postnatal day: An opportunity for assessment of vulnerability. *Pediatrics, 92,* 373–379.

Frijda, N. (1994). Emotions are functional most of the time. In P. Ekman & R. Davidson (Eds.), *The nature of emotions: Fundamental questions* (pp. 112–122). New York: Oxford University Press.

Frijda, N., Kuipers, P., & Schure, E. (1989). Relations among emotion, appraisal, and emotional action readiness. *Journal of Personality and Social Psychology, 57,* 212–228. ter

Frijda, N., & Tcherkassof, A. (1997). Facial expression as modes of action readiness. In J. Russell & J. Fernández-Dols (Eds.), *The psychology of facial expression* (pp. 78–102). Paris, France: Cambridge University Press.

Frome, P., & Eccles, J. (1998). Parents' influence on children's achievement-related perceptions. *Journal of Personality and Social Psychology, 74,* 435–452.

Fuhrman, T., & Holmbeck, G. (1995). A contextual moderator analysis of emotional autonomy and adjustment in adolescence. *Child Development, 66,* 793–811.

Furman, W., & Buhrmester, D. (1985). Children's perceptions of the personal relationships in their social networks. *Developmental Psychology, 21,* 1016–1024.

Furman, W., Simon, V., Shaffer, L., & Bouchey, H. (2002). Adolescents' working models and styles of relationships with parents, friends, and romantic partners. *Child Development, 73,* 241–255.

Galambos, N., Almeida, D., & Petersen, A. (1990). Masculinity, femininity, and sex role attitudes in early adolescence: Exploring gender intensification. *Child Development, 61,* 1905–1914.

Gallagher, J., & Reid, D. (1981). *The learning theory of Piaget and Inhelder.* Monterey, CA: Brooks/Cole.

Gardner, H. (1983). *Frames of mind.* New York: Basic Books.

Gauvain, M. (2001). *The social context of cognitive development.* New York: Guilford Press.

Gauvain, M., & Rogoff, B. (1989). Collaborative problem solving and children's planning skills. *Developmental Psychology, 25,* 139–151.

Ge, X., Conger, R., & Elder, G. (2001). Pubertal transition, stressful live events, and the emergence of gender differences in adolescent depressive symptoms. *Developmental Psychology, 37,* 404–417.

Gelman, R., & Baillargeon, R. (1983). A review of some Piagetian concepts. In P. Mussen (Ed.), *Handbook of child psychology, Vol. 3, Cognitive development* (4th Ed., pp. 167–230). New York: Wiley.

Gelman, S., & Markman, E. (1986). Categories and induction in young children. *Cognition, 23,* 183–209.

George, C., & Solomon, J. (1999). Attachment and caregiving: The caregiving behavioral system. In J. Cassidy & P. Shaver (Eds.), *Handbook of attachment: Theory, research, and clinical applications* (pp. 649–670). New York: Guilford Press.

George, C., Kaplan, N., & Main, M. (1996). *Adult Attachment Interview* (3rd Ed.). Unpublished manuscript, Berkeley, CA: Department of Psychology, University of Califronia.

Gibbs, E. (1990). Assessment of infant mental ability: Conventional tests and issues or prediction. In E. Gibbs & D. Teti (Eds.), *Interdisciplinary assessment of infants: A guide for early intervention professionals* (pp. 77–89). Baltimore, MD: Paul Brookes.

Gibbs, J., Basinger, K., & Fuller, D. (1992). *Moral maturity: Measuring the development of sociomoral reflection.* Hillsdale, NJ: Erlbaum.

Gibbs, J., Basinger, K., & Grimes, R. (2003). Moral judgment maturity: From clinical to standard measures. In S. Lopez & C. Snyder (Eds.), *Positive psychological assessment: A handbook of models and measures* (pp. 361–373). Washington, DC: American Psychological Association.

Gibson, D., & Aitkenhead, W. (1983). The elderly respondent: Experiences from a large-scale survey of the aged. *Journal of the Market Research Society, 25,* 283–296.

Gibson, E., & Walk, R. (1960). The "visual cliff". *Scientific American, 202,* 64–71.

Gjerde, P., & Onishi, M. (2000). In search of theory: The study of "ethnic groups" in developmental psychology. *Journal of Research on Adolescence, 10,* 289–298.

Gleason, T. (2002). Social provisions of real and imaginary relationships in early childhood. *Developmental Psychology, 38,* 979–992.

Golombok, S., & Rust, J. (1993). The Pre-school Activities Inventory: A standardized assessment of gender role in children. *Psychological Assessment, 5,* 131–136.

Gonzales, N., Cauce, A., & Mason, C. (1996). Interobserver agreement in the assessment of parental behavior and parent-adolescent conflict: African American mothers, daughters, and independent observers. *Child Development, 67,* 1483–1498.

Goodman, G., & Clarke-Stewart, A. (1991). Suggestibility in children's testimony: Implications for sexual abuse investigations. In J. Doris (Ed.), *The suggestibility of children's recollections: Implications for eyewitness testimony.* Washington, DC: American Psychological Association.

Gopnik, A., & Astington, J. (1988). Children's understanding of representational change and its relation to the understanding of false belief and the appearance-reality distinction. *Child Development, 59,* 26–37.

Gopnik, A., & Astington, J. (2000). Children's understanding of representational change and its relation to the understanding of false belief and the appearance-reality distinction. In K. Lee (Ed.), *Childhood cognitive development* (pp. 177–199). Oxford, UK: Blackwell Science.

Gordan, M. (1999). *Writing a grant proposal.* Unpublished manuscript: National Institute of Mental Health.

Gottman, J. (1994). *What predicts divorce? The relationship between marital processes and marital outcome.* Hillsdale, NJ: Lawrence Erlbaum Associates.

Gottman, J. (1996). *What predicts divorce? The measures.* Mahwah, NJ: Lawrence Erlbaum Associates.

Gottman, J., Kahen, V., & Goldstein, D. (1996). Rapid Couples Interaction Scoring System: A manual for coders. In J. Gottman (Ed.), *What predicts divorce? The measures.* Mahwah, NJ: Lawrence Erlbaum Associates.

Gottman, J., Katz, L., & Hooven, C. (1996). *Meta-emotion: How families communicate emotionally.* Mahwah, NJ: Lawrence Erlbaum Associates.

Gottman, J., McCoy, K., Coan, J., & Collier, H. (1996). The Specific Affect Coding System (SPAFF) for observing emotional communication in marital and family interaction. In J. Gottman (Ed.), *What predicts divorce? The measures.* Mahwah, NJ: Lawrence Erlbaum Associates.

Gottman, J., Murray, J., Swanson, C., Tyson, R., & Swanson, K. (2002). *The mathematics of marriage: Dynamic linear models.* Cambridge, MA: MIT Press.

Gottman, J., & Notarius, C. (2002). Marital research in the 20th century and a research agenda for the 21st century. *Family Process, 41,* 159–197.

Gough, H., & Bradley, P. (1996). *California Psychological Inventory Manual.* Palo Alto, CA: Consulting Psychologists Press.

Graber, J., Brooks-Gunn, J., & Warren, M. (1995). The antecedents of menarcheal age: Heredity, family environment, and stressful events. *Child Development, 66,* 346–359.

Graber, J., Peterson, A., & Brooks-Gunn, J. (1996). Pubertal processes: Methods, measures, and models. In J. Graber, J. Brooks-Gunn, & A. Petersen (Eds.), *Transitions through adolescence: Interpersonal domains and context* (pp. 23–53).Mahwah, NJ: Lawrence Erlbaum Associates.

Green, J., & Gustafson, G. (1983). Individual recognition of human infants on the basis of cry alone. *Developmental Psychobiology, 16*, 485–493.

Green, J., Gustafson, G., & McGhie, A. (1998). Changes in infants' cries as a function of time in a cry bout. *Child Development, 69*, 271–279.

Green, B., Shirk, S., Hanze, D., & Wanstrath, J. (1994). The Children's Global Assessment Scale in clinical practice: An empirical evaluation. *Journal of the Academy of Child and Adolescent Psychiatry, 33*, 1158–1164.

Greenberg, M., Marvin, R., & Mossler, D. (1977). The development of conditional reasoning skills. *Developmental Psychology, 13*, 527–528.

Greenberger, E., & Steinberg, L. (1986). *When teenagers work: The psychological and social costs of adolescent employment.* New York: Basic Books.

Greene, A., Wheatley, S., & Aldava, J. (1992). Stages of life's way: Adolescent's implicit theories of the life course. *Journal of Adolescent Research, 7*, 364–381.

Grotevant, H. (1998). Adolescent development in family contexts. In W. Damon (Series Editor) & N. Eisenberg (Volume Editor), *Handbook of child psychology, Vol. 3: Social, emotional, and personality development* (5th Ed., pp. 1097–1149). New York: Wiley.

Grotevant, H., & Cooper, C. (1985). Patterns of interaction in family relationships and the development of identity exploration in adolescence. *Child Development, 56*, 415–428.

Grusec, J., & Goodnow, J. (1994). The impact of parental discipline methods on the child's internalization of values: A reconceptualization of current points of views. *Developmental Psychology, 30*, 4–19.

Gunnar, M., Brodersen, L., Krueger, K., & Rigatuso, J. (1996). Dampening of adrenocoritcal responses during infancy: Normative changes and individual differences. *Child Development, 67*, 877–889.

Gunnar, M., Larson, B., Hertsgaard, L., Harris, M., & Broderson, L. (1992). The stressfulness of separation among nine-month-old infants: Effects of social context variables and infant temperament. *Child Development, 63*, 290–303.

Gunnar, M., Mangelsdorf, S., Larson, M., & Hertsgaard, L. (1989). Attachment, temperament and andrenocortical activity in infancy: A study of psychoendocrine regulation. *Developmental Psychology, 25*, 355–363.

Gunnar, M., Porter, F., Wolf, J., Rigatuso, J., & Larson, M. (1995). Neonatal stress reactivity: Predictions to later emotional temperament. *Child Development, 66*, 1–13.

Gunnar, M., & Nelson, C. (1994). Event-related potentials in year-old infants predict negative emotionality and hormonal responses to separation. *Child Development, 65*, 80–94.

Gunnar, M., & White, B. (2001). Salivary cortisol measures in infant and child assessment. In L. Singer & P. Zeskind (Eds.), *Biobehavioral assessment of the infant* (pp. 167–189). New York: Guilford Press.

Gurucharri, C., & Selman, R. (1982). The development of interpersonal understanding during childhood, preadolescence, and adolescence: A longitudinal follow-up study. *Child Development, 53*, 924–927.

Gutierrez, J., & Sameroff, A. (1990). Determinants of complexity in Mexican-American and Anglo-American mothers' conceptions of child development. *Child Development, 61*, 384–394.

Haber, D. (2003). *Health promotion and aging* (3rd Ed.). New York: Springer.

Haight, W., & Miller, P. (1993). *Pretending at home: Early development in a sociocultural context.* Albany, NY: State University of New York Press.

Haith, M., & Benson, J. (1998). Infant cognition. In W. Damon (Ed.), *Handbook of child psychology* (5th Ed.), *Cognition, perception, and language* (pp. 199–254). New York: Wiley.

Haith, M., Hazan, C., & Goodman, G. (1988). Expectation and anticipation of dynamic visual events by 3.5-month-old babies. *Child Development, 59*, 467–479.

Haith, M., & McCarty, M. (1990). Stability of visual expectations at 3.0 months of age. *Developmental Psychology, 26*, 68–74.

Hall, G.S. (1904). *Adolescence.* New York: Appleton.

Halle, T., Kurtz-Costes, B., & Mahoney, J. (1997). Family influences on school achievement in low-income, African-American children. *Journal of Educational Psychology, 89*, 527–537.

Hallinan, M. (1981). Recent advances in sociometry. In S. Asher, & J. Gottman (Eds.), *The development of children's friendships*(pp. 91–115).New York: Cambridge University Press.

Hammill, D., Brown, W., Larsen, S., & Wiederholt, J. (1997). *Test of Adolescent and Adult Language (III).* Austin, TX: Pro-Ed.

Harackiewicz, J., Barron, K., Tauer, J., & Elliot, A. (2002). Predicting success in college: A longitudinal study of achievement goals and ability measures as predictors of interest and performance from freshman year through graduation. *Journal of Educational Psychology, 94*, 562–575.

Hardy, J., Astone, N., Brooks-Gunn, J., Shapiro, S., & Miller, T. (1998). Like mother, like child: Intergenerational patterns of age at first birth and associations with childhood and adolescent characteristics and adult outcomes in the second generation. *Developmental Psychology, 34*, 1220–1232.

Harmon, L., Hansen, J., Borgen, F., & Hammer, A. (1994). *Strong Interest Survey applications and technical guide.* Palo Alto, CA: Consulting Psychologists Press.

Harris, G., Thomas, A., & Booth, D. (1990). Development of salt taste in infancy. *Developmental Psychology, 26,* 534–538.

Harris, P., Johnson, C., Hutton, D., Andrews, G., & Cooke, T. (1989). Young children's theory of mind and emotion. *Cognition and Emotion, 3,* 379–400.

Harter, S. (1985). *The Self-Perception Profile for Children.* Unpublished manual. Denver, CO: University of Denver.

Harter, S. (1988). *The Self-Perception Profile for Adolescents.* Unpublished manual. Denver, CO: University of Denver.

Harter, S. (1999). *The construction of the self: A developmental perspective.* New York: Guildford Press.

Harter, S., & Monsour, A. (1992). Developmental analysis of conflict caused by opposing attributes in the adolescent self-portrait. *Developmental Psychology, 28,* 251–260.

Harter, S., & Pike, R. (1984). The Pictoral Scale of Perceived Competence and Social Acceptance for Young Children. *Child Development, 55,* 1969–1982.

Hastings, P., & Grusec, J. (1998). Parenting goals as organizers of responses to parent-child disagreement. *Developmental Psychology, 34,* 465–479.

Hastings, P., & Rubin, K. (1999). Predicting mothers' beliefs about preschool-aged children's social behavior: Evidence for maternal attitudes moderating child effects. *Child Development, 70,* 722–741.

Hauser, S., Powers, S., & Noam, G. (1991). *Adolescents and their families: Paths of ego development.* New York: Free Press.

Hayes, R., Slater, A., & Brown, E. (2001). Infants' ability to categorize on the basis of rhyme. *Cognitive Development, 15,* 405–419.

Hayne, H., Rovee-Collier, C., & Perris, E. (1987). Categorization and memory retrieval by three-month-old infants. *Child Development, 58,* 750–767.

Hayvren, M., & Hymel, S. (1984). Ethical issues in sociometric testing: Impact of sociometric measures on interactive behavior. *Developmental Psychology, 20,* 844–849.

Hazan, C., & Shaver, P. (1987). Romantic love conceptualized as an attachment process. *Journal of Personality and Social Psychology, 52,* 511–524.

Helson, R., Kwan, V., John, O., & Jones, C. (2002). The growing evidence for personality change in adulthood: Findings from research with personality inventories. *Journal of Research in Personality, 36,* 287–306.

Helwig, A. (2003). The measurement of Holland types in a 10-year longitudinal study of a sample of students. *Journal of Employment Counseling, 40,* 24–32.

Henderson, V., & Dweck, C. (1990). Motivation and achievement. In S. Feldman & G. Elliott (Eds.), *At the threshold: The developing adolescent* (pp. 308–329). Cambridge, MA: Harvard University Press.

Herold, E., & Marshall, S. (1996). Adolescent sexual development. In G. Adams, R. Montemayor, & T. Gullotta (Eds.), *Psychosocial development in adolescence* (pp. 62–94). Thousand Oaks, CA: Sage Publications.

Hertzog, C. (1996). Research design in studies of aging and cognition. In J. Birren & K.W. Schaie (Eds.), *Handbook of the psychology of aging* (4th Ed., pp. 24–37). San Diego, CA: Academic Press.

Hertzog, C., & Dixon, R. (1994). Metacognitive development in adulthood and old age. In J. Metcalfe & A. Shimanura (Eds.), *Metacognition: knowledge about knowing* (pp. 227–251). Cambridge, MA: MIT Press.

Hertzog, C., & Hultsch, D. (2000). Metacognition in adulthood and old age. In F. Craik & T. Salthouse (Eds.), *The handbook of aging and cognition* (2nd Ed., pp. 417–466). Mahwah, NJ: Lawrence Erlbaum Associates.

Hertzog, C., Hultsch, D., & Dixon, R. (1989). Evidence for the convergent validity of two self-report metamemory questionnaires. *Developmental Psychology, 25,* 687–700.

Hesse, E. (1996). Discourse, memory and the Adult Attachment Interview: A note with emphasis on the emerging cannot classify category. *Infant Mental Health Journal, 17,* 4–11.

Hesse, E. (1999). The Adult Attachment Interview. In J. Cassidy & P. Shaver (Eds.), *Handbook of attachment: Theory, research, and clinical applications* (pp. 395–433). New York: Guilford Press.

Higgins, E. (1991). Development of self-regulatory and self-evaluative processes: Costs benefits, and tradeoffs. In M. Gunnar & L. Sroufe (Eds.), *Self processes and development: The Minneapolis symposia on child development* (Vol. 23, pp. 125–166). Hillsdale, NJ: Lawrence Erlbaum Associates.

Hill, J. (1983). Early adolescence: A framework. *Journal of Early Adolescence, 3,* 1–21.

Hill, J., & Holmbeck, G. (1986). Attachment and autonomy during adolescence. In G. Whitehurst (Ed.), *Annals of child development* (Vol. 3, pp. 145–189). Greenwich, CT: JAI Press.

Hill, J., Holmbeck, G., Marlow, L., Green, T., & Lynch, M. (1985). Pubertal status and parent-child relations in families of seventh-grade boys. *Journal of Early Adolescence, 5,* 31–44.

Hinshaw, S. (2002). Preadolescent girls with attention-deficit/hyperactivity disorder: I. Background characteristics, comobordity, cognitive and social functioning, and parenting practices. *Journal of Consulting and Clinical Psychology, 70,* 1086–1098.

Hinshaw, S., Zupan, B., Simmel, C., Nigg, J., & Melnick, S. (1997). Peer status in boys with and without attention-deficit-hyperactivity disorder: Predictions from overt and covert antisocial behavior, social isolation, and authoritative parenting beliefs. *Child Development, 64,* 880–896.

Hirshberg, L., & Svejda, M. (1990). When infants look to their parents: I. Infants' social referencing of mothers compared to fathers. *Child Development, 61,* 1175–1186.

Hoffman, M. (2000). *Empathy and moral development*. Cambridge, England: Cambridge University Press.

Hofstadter, M., & Reznick, J. (1996). Response modality affects human infant delayed-response performance. *Child Development, 67*, 646–658.

Hogan, R., & Hogan, J. (1992). *Hogan Personality Inventory Manual (Revised)*. Tulsa, OK: Hogan Assessment Systems.

Hogrefe, G., Wimmer, H., & Perner, J. (1986). Ignorance versus false belief: A developmental lag in attribution of epistemic states. *Child Development, 57*, 567–582.

Holcomb, W., Stromer, R., & Mackay, H. (1997). Transitivity and emergent seqeuence performances in young children. *Journal of Experimental Child Psychology, 65*, 96–124.

Holditch-Davis, D. (1990). The development of sleeping and waking states in preterm infants. *Infant Behavior and Development, 13*, 513–531.

Holland, J. (1985). *Making vocational choices: A theory of careers*. Englewood Cliffs, NJ: Prentice Hall.

Hollingshead, A. (1975). *Four-factor index of social status*. New Haven, CT: Yale University, Department of Sociology.

Holm, J., & Holroyd, K. (1992). The Daily Hassles Scale-Revised: Does it measure stress or symptoms? *Behavioral Assessment, 14*, 465–482.

Holmbeck, G., & Hill, J. (1991). Conflictive engagement, positive affect, and menarche in families with seventh-grade girls. *Child Development, 62*, 1030–1048.

Holmbeck, G., Johnson, S., Wills, K., McKernon, W., Rose, B., Erklin, S., & Kemper, T. (2002). Observed and perceived parental overprotection in relation to psychosocial adjustment in preadolescents with a physical disability: The mediational role of behavioral autonomy. *Journal of Consulting and Clinical Psychology, 70*, 96–110.

Holmbeck, G., Paikoff, R., & Brooks-Gunn, J. (1995). Parenting adolescents. In M. Bornstein (Ed.), *Handbook of parenting* (Vol. 1, pp. 91–118). Mahwah, NJ: Lawrence Erlbaum Associates.

Holmes, T., & Rahe, R. (1967). The Social Readjustment Scale. *Journal of Psychosomatic Research, 11*, 213–218.

Holtzworth-Munroe, A., Smutzler, N., & Stuart, G. (1998). Demand and withdraw among couples experiencing husband violence. *Journal of Consulting and Clinical Psychology, 66*, 731–743.

Hooker, K., Manoogian-O'Dell, M., Monahan, D., Frazier, L., & Shifren, K. (2000). Does type of disease matter? Gender differences among Alzheimer's and Parkinson's disease spouse caregivers. *The Gerontologist, 40*, 568–573.

Horn, J. (1989). Cognitive diversity: A framework for learning. In P. Ackerman, R. Sternberg, & R. Glaser (Eds.), *Learning and individual differences* (pp. 61–116). New York: Freeman.

Houde, O. (1997). Numerical development: From infant to the child. Wynn's (1992) paradign for 2- and 3-year olds. *Cognitive Development, 12*, 373–391.

Howe, G., & Reiss, D. (1993). Simulation and experimentation in family research. In P. Boss, W. Doherty, R. LaRossa, W. Schumm, & S. Steinmetz (Eds.), *Sourcebook of family theories and methods: A contextual approach* (pp. 303–321). New York: Plenum Press.

Howe, N., & Ross, H. (1990). Socialization, perspective-taking, and the sibling relationship. *Developmental Psychology, 26*, 160–165.

Howes, C. (1988). Peer interaction of young children. *Monographs of the Society for Research in Child Development, 53*(1, Serial No. 217).

Howes, C., & Matheson, C. (1992). Sequences in development of competent play with peers: Social and social pretend play. *Developmental Psychology, 28*, 961–974.

Howes, C., Unger, O., & Seidner, L. (1989). Social pretend play in toddlers: Parallels with social play and with solitary pretend. *Child Development, 60*, 77–84.

Hrncir, E., Speller, G., & West, M. (1985). What are we testing? *Developmental Psychology, 21*, 226–232.

Huesmann, L., & Miller, L. (1994). Long-term effects of repeated exposure to media violence in childhood. In L. Huesmann (Ed.), *Aggressive behavior: Current perspectives*. New York: Plenum Press.

Huffman, L., Bryan, Y., del Carmen, R., Pedersen, F., Doussard-Roosevelt, J., & Porges, S. (1998). Infant temperament and cardiac vagal tone: Assessments at twelve weeks of age. *Child Development, 69*, 624–635.

Hultsch, D., Hertzog, C., & Dixon, R. (1990). Ability correlates of memory performance in adulthood and aging. *Psychology of Aging, 5*, 356–368.

Hultsch, D., Hertzog, C., Small, B., & Dixon, R. (1999). Use it or lose it: Engaged lifestyle as a buffer of cognitive decline in aging? *Psychology and Aging, 14*, 245–263.

Hunter, F., & Youniss, J. (1982). Changes in functions of three relations during adolescence. *Developmental Psychology, 18*, 806–811.

Huston, A. (1983). Sex-typing. In E.M. Hetherington (Ed.), *Handbook of child psychology: Socialization, personality, and social development* (Vol. 4, pp. 388–467). New York: Wiley.

Huston, A., & Wright, J. (1997). Mass media and children's development. In W. Damon (Series Editor), I. Sigel, & K. Renninger (Eds.), *Child psychology in practice: Handbook of child psychology* (5th Ed.). New York: Wiley.

Hymel, S., Bowker, A., & Woody, E. (1993). Aggressive versus withdrawn unpopular children: Variations in peer and self-perceptions in multiple domains. *Child Development, 64*, 879–896.

Ingersoll, E., & Thoman, E. (1999). Sleep/wake states of preterm infants: Stability, developmental change, diurnal variation, and relation with caregiving activity. *Child Development, 70*, 1–10.

Inhelder, B., & Piaget, J. (1958). *The growth of logical thinking from childhood to adolescence: An essay on the construction of formal operational structures.* New York: Basic Books.

Inhelder, B., & Piaget, J. (1964). *The early growth of logic in the child.* New York: Norton.

Izard, C. (1977). *Human emotion.* New York: Plenum Press.

Izard, C. (1989). *The Maximally Discriminative Facial Movement coding system (MAX).* (rev. Ed.). Newark: University of Delaware, Information Technologies and University Media Services.

Izard, C., & Ackerman, B. (2000). Motivational, organizational, and regulatory functions of discrete emotions. In M. Lewis & J. Haviland-Jones (Eds.), *Handbook of emotions* (2nd Ed., pp. 253–264). New York: Guilford Press.

Izard, C., & Dougherty, L. (1982). Two complimentary systems for measuring facial expressions in infants and children. In C. Izard (Ed.), *Measuring emotions in infants and children.* New York: Cambridge University Press.

Izard, C., Dougherty, L., & Hembree, E. (1983). *A system for identifying affect expressions by holistic judgments (Affex).* Newark: University of Delaware, Computer Network Services and University Media Services.

Izard, C., Fantauzzo, C., Castle, J., Haynes, O., Rayias, M., & Putman, P. (1995). The ontogeny and significance of infants' facial expression in the first 9 months of life. *Developmental Psychology, 31,* 997–1013.

Izard, C., & Malatesta, C. (1987). Perspectives on emotional development I: Differential emotions theory of early emotional development. In J. Osofsky (Ed.), *Handbook of infant development* (2nd Ed., pp. 494–554). New York: Wiley.

Jaccard, J., Dittus, P., & Gordon, V. (1998). Parent-adolescent congruency in reports of adolescent sexual behavior and in communication about sexual behavior. *Child Development, 69,* 247–261.

Jackson, Y., & Warren, J. (2000). Appraisal, social support, and life events: Predicting outcome behavior in school-aged children. *Child Development, 71,* 1441–1457.

Jacobsen, R., Edelstein, W., & Hofmann, V. (1994). A longitudinal study of the relation between representations of attachment in childhood and cognitive functioning in childhood and adolescence. *Developmental Psychology, 30,* 11–124.

Jacobson, J., & Jacobson, S. (1995). Strategies for detecting the effects of prenatal drug exposure: Lessons from research on alcohol. In M. Lewis & M. Bendersky (Eds.), *Mothers, babies, and cocaine: The role of toxins in development* (pp. 111–127). Hillsdale, NJ: Lawrence Erlbaum Associates.

Jacobson, K., & Crockett, L. (2000). Parental monitoring and adolescent adjustment: An ecological perspective. *Journal of Research on Adolescence, 10,* 65–97.

Jacob-Timm, S. (1995). Rural School Psychology. In A. Thomas & J. Grimes (Eds.), *Best practices in school psychology-III* (pp. 301–310). Washington, DC: NASP.

Jacobvitz, D., Hazen, N., & Riggs, S. (1997, April). Disorganized mental processes in mothers, frightening/ frightened caregiving, and disoriented/disorganized behavior in infants. In D. Jacobvitz (Chair), *Caregiving correlates and longitudinal outcomes of disorganized attachments in infants. Symposium conducted at the biennial meeting of the Society for Research in Child Development,* Washington, DC.

Jaffe, J., Beebe, B., Feldstein, S., Crown, C., & Jasnow, M. (2001). Rhythms of dialogue in infancy. *Monographs of the Society for Research in Child Development Vol. 66* (2, Serial No. 265). Chicago, IL: University of Chicago Press.

Jennings, K., Harmon, R., Morgan, G., Gaiter, J., & Yarrow, L. (1979). Exploratory play as an index of mastery motivation: Relationships to persistence, cognitive functioning, and environmental measures. *Developmental Psychology, 15,* 386–394.

John, O. (1990). The "Big Five" factor taxonomy: Dimensions of personality in the natural language and in questionnaires. In L. Pervin (Ed.), *Handbook of personality: Theory and research* (pp. 66–100). New York: Guildford Press.

John, O., Caspi, A., Robins, R., Moffitt, T., & Stouthamer-Loeber, M. (1994). The "Little Five": Exploring the five-factor model of personality development in adolescent boys. *Child Development, 65,* 160–178.

John, O., & Srivastava, S. (1999). The Big Five trait taxonomy: History, measurement, and theoretical perspectives. In L. Pervin, & O. John (Eds.), *Handbook of personality: Theory and research* (2nd Ed., pp. 102–138).New York: Guilford Press.

Johnson, D. (2001). Measuring marital relations. In J. Touliatos, B. Perlmutter, & G. Holden (Eds.), *Handbook of family measurement techniques* (Vol. 2, pp. 73–86). Thousand Oaks, CA: Sage Publications.

Johnson, J. (1993). Relationships between psychosocial development and personality disorder symptomatology in late adolescents. *Journal of Youth and Adolescence, 22,* 33–42.

Johnston, C., & Freeman, W. (1997). Attributions for child behavior in parents of children without behavioral disorders and children with attention-deficit hyperactivity disorder. *Journal of Consulting and Clinical Psychology, 65,* 636–645.

Johnston, C., Reynolds, S., Freeman, W., & Geller, J. (1998). Assessing parent attributions for child behavior using open-ended questions. *Journal of Clinical Child Psychology, 27,* 87–97.

Jonker, C., Smits, C., & Deeg, D. (1997). Affect-related metamemory and memory performance in a population-based sample of older adults. *Educational Gerontology, 23,* 115–128.

Judge, T., Erez, A., Bono, J., & Thorsen, C. (2002). Are measures of self-esteem, neuroticism, locus of control, and generalized self-efficacy indicators of a common core construct? *Journal of Personality and Social Psychology, 83*, 693–710.

Julien, D., Markman, H., & Lindahl, K. (1989). A comparison of a global and a microanalytic coding system: Implications for future trends in studying interactions. *Behavioral Assessment, 11*, 81–100.

Jusczyk, P. (1985). The High-Amplitude Sucking Technique as a methodological tool in speech perception research. In G. Gottlieb & N. Krasnegor (Eds.), *Measurement of vision and audition in the first year* (pp. 195–222). Norwood, NJ: Ablex Publishing.

Kagan, J. (1994). *Galen's prophecy: Temperament in human nature.* New York: Basic Books.

Kagan, J., Reznick, J., & Snidman, N. (1987). The physiology and psychology of behavioral inhibition in children. *Child Development, 58*, 1459–1473.

Kagan, J., Snidman, N., & Arcus, D. (1998). Childhood derivatives of high and low reactivity in infancy. *Child Development, 69*, 1483–1493.

Kail, R. (1986). Sources of age differences in speed of processing. *Child Development, 57*, 969–987.

Kanner, A., Feldman, S., Weinberger, D., & Ford, M. (1987). Uplifts, hassles, and adaptational outcomes in early adolescents. *Journal of Early Adolescence, 7*, 371–394.

Kaplan, N. (1987). *Individual differences in six-year-olds' thoughts about separation: Predicted from attachment to mother at one year of age.* Unpublished doctoral dissertation, University of California, Berkeley, CA.

Karney, B., & Bradbury, T. (1995). The longitudinal course of marital quality and stability: A review of theory, method, and research. *Psychological Bulletin, 118*, 3–34.

Karney, B., Bradbury, T., Fincham, F., & Sullivan, K. (1994). The role of negative affectivity in the association between attributions and marital satisfaction. *Journal of Personality and Social Psychology, 66*, 413–424.

Katchadourian, H. (1990). Sexuality. In S. Feldman & G. Elliott (Eds.), *At the threshold: The developing adolescent* (pp. 330–351). Cambridge, MA: Harvard University Press.

Katz, L., & Gottman, J. (1993). Patterns of marital conflict predict children's internalizing and externalizing behaviors. *Developmental Psychology, 29*, 940–950.

Kaufman, A. (1993). King WISC the third assumes the throne. *Journal of School Psychology, 31*, 345–354.

Kaufman, A. (2000). Tests of intelligence. In R. Sternberg (Ed.), *Handbook of intelligence* (pp. 445–476). Cambridge, UK: Cambridge University Press.

Kaufman, A., & Kaufman, N. (1983). *Administration and scoring manual for the Kaufman Assessment Battery for Children (K-ABC).* Circle Pines, MN: American Guidance Service.

Kaufman, A., & Kaufman, N. (1993). *Manual for Kaufman Adolescent and Adult Intelligence Test (KAIT).* Circle Pines, MN: American Guidance Service.

Keating, D. (1990). Adolescent thinking. In S. Feldman & G. Elliott (Eds.), *At the threshold: The developing adolescent* (pp. 54–89). Cambridge, MA: Cambridge University Press.

Keating, D. (1991). Cognition, adolescent. In R. Lerner, A. Peterson, & J. Brooks-Gunn (Eds.), *Encyclopedia of adolescence* (Vol.1, pp. 119–129). New York: Garland.

Keating, D., & Sasse, D. (1996). Cognitive socialization in adolescence: Critical period for a critical habit of mind. In G. Adams, R. Montemayor, & T. Gullotta (Eds.), *Psychosocial development during adolescence* (pp. 232–258). Thousand Oaks, CA: Sage Publications.

Kelley, M., Power, T., & Wimbusch, D. (1992). Determinants of disciplinary practices in low-income black mothers. *Child Development, 63*, 573–582.

Kellman, P., & Banks, M. (1998). Infant visual perception. In W. Damon (Ed.), *Handbook of child psychology* (5th Ed.), *Cognition, perception, and language* (pp. 103–146). New York: Wiley.

Keniston, A., & Flavell, J. (1979). A developmental study of intelligence retrieval. *Child Development, 50*, 1144–1152.

Kerckhoff, A. (2002). The transition from school to work. In J. Mortimer & R. Larson (Eds.), *The changing adolescent experience: Societal trends and the transition to adulthood* (pp. 52–87). New York: Cambridge University Press.

Kerlinger, F. (1986). *Foundations of behavioral research* (2nd Ed.). New York: Holt, Rinehart, and Winston, Inc.

Kessler, D., & Dawson, P. (1999). *Failure to thrive and pediatric undernutrition: A transdisciplinary approach.* Baltimore, MD: Paul Brookes.

Kimmel, A. (1996). *Ethical issues in behavioral research.* Cambridge, MA: Blackwell Science.

King, P., & Kitchener, K. (1994). *Developing reflective judgment: Understanding and promoting intellectual growth and critical thinking in adolescents and adults.* San Francisco, CA: Jossey-Bass.

Kinney, J., & Stephens, M. (1989). Caregiving Hassles Scale: Assessing the daily hassles of caring for a family member with dementia. *The Gerontologist, 29*, 328–332.

Kinzler, M., & Johnson, C. (1993). *Joliet 3-minute speech and language screen.* San Antonio, TX: Psychological Corporation.

Kirasic, K. (1991). Spatial cognition and behavior in young and elderly adults: Implications for learning new environments. *Psychology and Aging, 6*, 10–18.

Kirasic, K., Allen, G., Dobson, S., & Binder, K. (1996). Aging, cognitive resources, and declarative learning. *Psychology and Aging, 11*, 658–670.

Kirk, R. (1995). *Experimental design: Procedures for the behavioral sciences.* New York: Brooks/Cole.

Kitchener, K., Lynch, C., Fischer, K., & Wood, P. (1993). Developmental range of reflective judgment: The effect of contextual support and practice on developmental stage. *Developmental Psychology, 29*, 893–906.

Klaczynski, P. (2000). Motivated scientific reasoning biases, epistemological beliefs, and theory polarization: A two-process approach to adolescent cognition. *Child Development, 71,* 1347–1366.

Klaczynski, P. (2001). Analytic and heuristic processing influences on adolescent reasoning and decision-making. *Child Development, 72,* 844–861.

Klahr, D., Fay, A., & Dunbar, K. (1993). Heuristics for scientific experimentation: A developmental study. *Cognitive Psychology, 25,* 111–146.

Kleinman, J. (1992). The epidemiology of low birthweight. In S. Friedman & M. Sigman (Eds.), *Annual advances in applied developmental psychology: The psychological development of low birth weight children* (Vol. 6, pp. 21–36). Norwood, NJ: Ablex Publishing.

Kobak, R., Cole, H., Ferenz-Gilles, R., Fleming, W., & Gamble, W. (1993). Attachment and emotional regulation during mother-teen problem solving: A control theory analysis. *Child Development, 64,* 231–245.

Kobasigawa, A. (1974). Utilization of retrieval cues by children in recall. *Child Development, 45,* 127–134.

Kochanska, G., Gross, J., Lin, M., & Nichols, K. (2002). Guilt in young children: Development, determinants, and relations with a broader system of standards. *Child Development, 73,* 461–482.

Kochanska, G., Kucznski, L., & Radke-Yarrow, M. (1989). Correspondence between mothers' self-reported and observed child-rearing practices. *Child Development, 60,* 56–64.

Kohlberg, L. (1966). A cognitive-developmental analysis of children's sex role concepts and attitudes. In E. Maccoby (Ed.), *The development of sex differences* (pp. 82–173). Stanford, CA: Stanford University Press.

Kohlberg, L. (1968). Stages of moral growth. *International Journal of Religious Studies, 44,* 8–9.

Kohlberg, L. (1969). Stage and sequence: The cognitive-developmental approach to socialization. In D. Goslin (Ed.), *Handbook of socialization theory and research* (pp. 325–480). New York: Rand McNally.

Kohlberg, L. (1976). Moral stages and moralization: The cognitive-developmental approach. In T. Lickona (Ed.), *Moral development and behavior.* New York: Holt, Rinehart, & Winston.

Kohlberg, L. (1978). Revisions in the theory and practice of moral development. In W. Damon (Ed.), *Moral development* (New Directions for Child Development, No. 2). San Francisco, CA: Jossey-Bass.

Koolstra, C., & Van der Voort, T. (1996). Longitudinal effects of television on children's leisure time reading: A test of three explanatory models. *Human Communication Research, 23,* 4–35.

Kopp, C. (1994). Trends and directions in studies of developmental risk. In C. Nelson (Ed.), *Threats to optimal development The Minnesota Symposia on Child Psycholgy,*

Vol. 27 (pp. 1–33).Mahwah, NJ: Lawrence Erlbaum Associates.

Korner, A., & Thom, V. (1990). *Neurobehavioral assessment of the preterm infant.* New York: Psychological Corporation.

Krafft, K., & Berk, L. (1998). Private speech in two preschools: Significance of open-ended activities and make-believe play for verbal regulation. *Early Childhood Research Quarterly, 13,* 637–658.

Krantz, J., & Dalal, R. (2000). Validity of Web-based and psychological research. In M. Birnbaum (Ed.), *Psychological experiments on the Internet* (pp. 35–60). San Diego, CA: Academic Press.

Kroger, J. (2003). Identity development during adolescence. In G. Adams & M. Berzonsky (Eds.), *Blackwell handbook of adolescence* (pp. 205–226). Malden, MA: Blackwell Science.

Krumboltz, J. (1991). *Career Beliefs Inventory.* Palo Alto, CA: Consulting Psychologists Press.

Kuhn, D. (1999). Metacognitive development. *Current Directions in Psychological Science, 9,* 178–181.

Kuhn, D., Amsel, E., & O'Loughlin, M. (1988). *The development of scientific thinking skills.* Orlando, FL: Academic Press.

Kuhn, D., Garcia-Mila, M., Zohar, A., & Andersen, C. (1995). Strategies of knowledge acquisition. *Monographs of the Society for Research in Child Development, 60*(245, Serial No. 4).

Kunzmann, U., & Baltes, P. (2003). Wisdom-related knowledge: Affective, motivational, and interpersonal correlates. *Personality and Social Psychology Bulletin, 29,* 1104–1119.

Kupersmidt, J., Burchinal, M., & Patterson, C. (1995). Developmental patterns of childhood peer rejection as predictors of externalizing behavior problems. *Development and Psychopathology, 7,* 649–668.

Kupersmidt, J., & Coie, J. (1990). Preadolescent peer status, aggression, and school adjustment as predictors of externalizing problems in adolescents. *Child Development, 61,* 1350–1362.

La Greca, A., & Silverman, W. (1993). Parent reports of child behavior problems: Bias in participation. *Journal of Abnormal Child Psychology, 21,* 89–101.

Labouvie-Vief, G. (1997). Cognitive-emotional integration in adulthood. In K. Schaie & M. Lawton (Eds.), *Annual review of gerontology and geriatrics* (Vol. 17, pp. 206–237). New York: Springer.

Labouvie-Vief, G., Orwell, L., Murphey, D., Chiordo, L., Krueger, C., Goguen, L., Coyle, N., & Schriber, S. (1994). *Self and other in emotional development: A coding manual,* (revised). Unpublished coding manual, Department of Psychology, Wayne State University.

Ladd, G., & Burgess, K. (1999). Charting the relationship trajectories of aggressive, withdrawn, aggressive/withdrawn children during early grade school. *Child Development, 70,* 910–929.

Ladd, G., & Golter, B. (1988). Parents' management of preschoolers' peer relations: Is it related to children's social competence? *Developmental Psychology, 24,* 109–117.

Lange, G., & Pierce, S. (1992). Memory-strategy learning and maintenance in preschool children. *Developmental Psychology, 28,* 453–462.

Larose, S., & Bernier, A. (2001). Social support processes: Mediators of attachment state of mind and adjustment in late adolescence. *Attachment and Human Development, 3,* 96–120.

Larose, S., & Boivin, M. (1998). Attachment to parents, social support expectations, and socioemotional adjustment during the high-school to college transition. *Journal of Research on Adolescence, 8,* 1–27.

Larson, R. (1989). Beeping children and adolescents: A method for studying time use and daily experience. *Journal of Youth and Adolescence, 18,* 511–530.

Larson, M., Gunnar, M., & Hertsgaard, L. (1991). The effects of morning naps, car trips, and maternal separation on adrenocortical activity in human infants. *Child Development, 62,* 362–373.

Larson, R., & Ham, M. (1993). Stress and "storm and stress" in early adolescence: The relationship of negative events with dysphoric affect. *Developmental Psychology, 29,* 130–140.

Larson, R., Verma, S., & Dworkin, J. (2001). Mens' work and family lives in India: The daily organization of time and emotion. *Journal of Family Psychology, 15,* 206–224.

Laursen, B. (1995). Conflict and social interaction in adolescent relationships. *Journal of Research on Adolescence, 5,* 55–70.

Laursen, B., Coy, K., & Collins, W. (1998). Reconsidering changes in parent-child conflict across adolescence: A meta-analysis. *Child Development, 69,* 817–832.

LaVoie, D., & Light, L. (1994). Adult age differences in repetition priming: A meta-analysis. *Psychology and Aging, 9,* 539–553.

Lazarus, R. (1991). *Emotion and adaptation.* London: Oxford University Press.

Lazarus, R., & Folkman, S. (1984). *Stress, appraisal, and coping.* New York: Springer.

Lee, M., & Larson, R. (2000). The Korean "Examination Hell": Long hours of studying, distress, and depression. *Journal of Youth and Adolescence, 29,* 249–271.

Lehman, D., & Nisbett, R. (1990). A longitudinal study of the effects of undergraduate training on reasoning. *Developmental Psychology, 26,* 952–960.

Lempers, J., & Clark-Lempers, D. (1992). Young, middle, and late adolescents' comparisons of the functional importance of five significant relationships. *Journal of Youth and Adolescence, 21,* 53–96.

Lester, B. (1998). The maternal life styles study. *Annals of the New York Academy of Science, 846,* 296–306.

Lester, B., Als, H., & Brazelton, T. (1982). Regional obstetric anesthesia and newborn behavior: A reanalysis toward synergistic effects. *Child Development, 53,* 687–692.

Lester, B., Freier, K., & LaGasse, L. (1995). Prenatal cocaine exposure and child outcome: What do we really know? In M. Lewis & M. Bendersky (Eds.), *Mothers, babies, and cocaine: The role of toxins in development* (pp. 19–39). Hillsdale, NJ: Lawrence Erlbaum Associates.

Lester, B., & Tronick, E. (2001). Behavioral assessment scales: The NICU Network Neurobehavioral Scale, the Neonatal Behavioral Assessment Scale, and the Assessment of Preterm Infant's Behavior. In L. Singer & P. Zeskind (Eds.), *Biobehavioral assessment of the infant* (pp. 363–380). New York: Guilford Press.

Leventhal, T., Graber, J., & Brooks-Gunn, J. (2001a). Adolescent transitions to young adulthood: Antecedents, correlates, and consequences of adolescent employment. *Journal of Research on Adolescence, 11,* 297–323.

Leventhal, H., & Patrick-Miller, L. (2000). Emotions and physical illness: Causes and indicators of vulnerability. In M. Lewis & J. Haviland-Jones (Eds.), *Handbook of emotions* (2nd Ed., pp. 523–537). New York: Guilford Press.

Leventhal, H., Rabin, C., Leventhal, E., & Burns, E. (2001b). Health risk behaviors and aging. In J. Birren & K.W. Schaie (Eds.), *Handbook of the psychology of aging* (5th Ed., pp. 186–214). San Diego, CA: Academic Press.

Levinson, D. (1978). *The season's of a man's life.* New York: Alfred A. Knoph.

Levinson, D., & Levinson, J. (1996). *The season's of a woman's life.* New York: Alfred A. Knoph.

Levinson, E., Ohler, D., Caswell, S., & Kiewra, K. (1998). Six approaches to the assessment of career maturity. *Journal of Counseling and Development, 76,* 475–482.

Lewis, M. (2000). The emergence of human emotions. In M. Lewis & J. Haviland-Jones (Eds.), *Handbook of emotions* (2nd Ed., pp. 265–292). New York: Guilford Press.

Lewis, M., Alessandri, S., & Sullivan, M. (1990). Violation of expectancy, loss of control, and anger in young infants. *Developmental Psychology, 26,* 745–751.

Lewis, M., Alessandri, S., & Sullivan M. W. (1992). Differences in shame and pride as a function of children's gender and task difficulty. *Child Development, 63,* 630–638.

Lewis, M., & Michalson, L. (1983). *Children's emotions and moods: Developmental theory and measurement.* New York: Plenum Press.

Lewis, M., & Ramsay, D. (1995). Developmental change in infants' responses to stress. *Child Development, 66,* 657–670.

Lewis, M., Sullivan, M., Stanger, C., & Weiss, M. (1989). Self-development and self-conscious emotions. *Child Development, 60,* 146–156.

Lewis, M., & Thomas, D. (1990). Cortisol release in infants in response to inoculation. *Child Development, 61,* 50–59.

Liben, L., & Bigler, R. (2002). The developmental course of gender differentiation: Conceptualizing, measuring, and evaluating constructs and pathways. *Monographs for the Society for Research in Child Development, 67*(2, Serial No. 269).

Lindenberger, U., & Baltes, P. (1994). Sensory functioning and intelligence in old age: A strong connection. *Psychology and Aging, 9*, 339–355.

Lindenberger, U., Scherer, H., & Baltes, P. (2001). The strong connection between sensory and cognitive performance in old age: Not due to sensory acuity reductions operating during cognitive assessment. *Psychology and Aging, 16*, 196–205.

Linney, J. (1989). Optimizing research strategies in schools. In L. Bond & B. Compas (Eds.), *Primary prevention and promotion in the schools: Primary prevention of psychopathology* (Vol. 12, pp. 50–76). Thousand Oaks, CA: Sage Publications.

Little, T., Schnabel, K., & Baument, J. (2000). *Modeling longitudinal data: Practical and multilevel issues, applied approaches, and specific examples.* Mahwah, NJ: Lawrence Erlbaum Associates.

Littman, G., & Parmelee, A. (1978). Medical correlates of infant development. *Pediatrics, 61*, 470–474.

Livesay, W., & Bromley, D. (1973). *Person perception in childhood and adolescence.* London: Wiley.

Livson, N., & Peskin, H. (1980). Perspectives on adolescence from longitudinal research. In J. Adelson (Ed.), *Handbook of adolescent psychology* (pp. 47–98). New York: Wiley.

Locke, H., & Wallace, K. (1959). Short marital adjustment prediction tests: Their reliability and validity. *Marriage and Family Living, 21*, 251–255.

Loevinger, J. (1976). *Ego development: Concepts and theories.* San Francisco, CA: Jossey-Bass.

Loevinger, J. (1985). Revision of the sentence completion test for ego development. *Journal of Personality & Social Psychology, 48*, 420–427.

Loevinger, J., Wessler, R., & Redmore, C. (1970). *Measuring ego development* (Vol 2). San Francisco, CA: Jossey-Bass.

Lohman, B., & Jarvis, P. (2000). Adolescent stressors, coping strategies, and psychological health studied in the family context. *Journal of Youth & Adolescence, 29*, 15–43.

Lombardo, M., & McCauley, C. (1994). *Benchmarks: A manual and trainer's guide.* Greensboro, NC: Center for Creative Leadership.

Lovejoy, M., Graczyk, P., O'Hare, E., & Neuman, G. (2000). Maternal depression and parenting behavior: A meta-analytic review. *Clinical Psychology Review, 20*, 561–592.

Lowe, M., & Costello, A. (1988). *Symbolic play test* (2nd Ed.). Windsor, Berkshire, England: NFER-Nelson.

Lund, N., & Duchan, J. (1993). *Assessing children's language in naturalistic settings* (3rd Ed.). Englewood Cliffs, NJ: Prentice Hall.

Lust, B., Flynn, S., & Foley, C. (1996). What children know about what they say: Elicited imitation as a research method for assessing children's syntax. In D. McDaniel, C. McKee, & H. Cairns (Eds.), *Methods for assessing children's syntax* (pp. 55–76). Cambridge, MA: MIT Press.

Luthar, S., & McMahon, T. (1996). Peer reputation among inner-city adolescents: Structure and correlates. *Journal of Research on Adolescence, 6*, 581–603.

Lyons-Ruth, K., Connell, D., Grunebaum, H., & Botein, S. (1990). Infants at social risk: Maternal depression and family support as mediators of infant development and security of attachment. *Child Development, 61*, 85–98.

Lyons-Ruth, K., & Jacobvitz, D. (1999). Attachment disorganization: Unresolved loss, relational violence, and lapses in behavioral and attentional strategies. In J. Cassidy & P. Shaver (Eds.), *Handbook of attachment: Theory, research, and clinical applications* (pp. 520–554). New York: Guilford Press.

MacLeod, C. (1991). Half a century of research on the Stroop effect: An integrative review. *Psychological Bulletin, 109*, 163–203.

MacTurk, R., Vietze, P., McCarthy, M., McQuiston, S., & Yarrow, L. (1985). The organization of exploratory behavior in Down syndome and nondelayed infants. *Child Development, 56*, 573–581.

Mahoney, J., & Cairns, R. (1997). Do extracurricular activities protect against early school dropout?. *Developmental Psychology, 33*, 241–253.

Main, M. (2001). An introduction to attachment theory. In J. Sroufe (Chair), *Adult Attachment Interview Preconference. Preconference conducted at the Biennial Meeting for the Society for Research in Child Development,* Minneaplois, MN.

Main, M., & Cassidy, J. (1988). Categories of response to reunion with the parent at age 6: Predictable from infant attachment classifications and stable over a 1-month-period. *Developmental Psychology, 24*, 415–426.

Main, M., & George, C. (1985). Responses of abused and disadvantaged toddlers to distress in agemates: A study in the day care setting. *Developmental Psychology, 21*, 407–412.

Main, M., & Goldwyn, R. (1994). *Adult Attachment Interview scoring and classification system.* Unpublished manuscript. Berkeley, CA: University of California.

Main, M., Goldwyn, R., & Hesse, E. (2002). *Adult Attachment Interview scoring and classification systems (Version 7.1).* Unpublished manuscript. Berkeley, CA: University of California.

Main, M., & Hesse, E. (1990). Parents' unresolved traumatic experiences are related to infant disorganization attachment status: Is frightened and/or frightening parental behavior the linking mechanism?. In M. Greenberg, D. Cicchetti, & E. Cummings (Eds.), *Attachment in the preschool years: Theory, research, and intervention* (pp. 161–182). Chicago, Ill: University of Chicago Press.

Main, M., & Hesse, E. (1998). *Frightening, frightened, dissociated, deferential, sexualized, and disorganized parental behavior: A coding system for parent-infant interactions.* Unpublished coding manual. Berkeley, CA: University of California.

Main, M., & Solomon, J. (1990). Procedures for identifying infants as disorganized/disoriented during the Ainsworth strange situation. In M. Greenberg, D. Cicchetti, & E. Cummings (Eds.), *Attachment in the preschool years: Theory, research, and intervention* (pp. 121–160). Chicago, Ill: University of Chicago Press.

Makin, J., & Porter, R. (1989). Attractiveness of lactating females' breast odors to newborns. *Child Development, 60,* 803–810.

Malatesta, C., Grigoryev, P., Lamb, C., Albin, M., & Culver, C. (1986). Emotion socialization and expressive development in preterm and full term infants. *Child Development, 57,* 316–330.

Mandler, B., Bauer, P., & McDonough, L. (1991). Separating the sheep from the goats: Differentiating global categories. *Cognitive Psychology, 23,* 263–298.

Mandler, B., Fivush, R., & Reznick, J. (1987). The development of cognitive contextual categories. *Cognitive Development, 2,* 339–354.

Manne, S. (2003). Coping and social support. In A. Nezu, C. Nezu & P. Geller (Eds.), *Handbook of psychology: Health psychology* (Vol. 9, pp. 51–74). New York: Wiley.

Marcia, J. (1966). Development and measurement of ego identity status. *Journal of Personality and Social Psychology, 3,* 551–558.

Marcia, J. (1994). The empirical study of ego identity. In H. Bosma, T. Graafsma, H. Grotevant, & D. de Levita (Eds.), *Identity and development: An interdisciplinary approach* (pp. 67–80). Thousand Oaks, CA: Sage Publications.

Marcia, J., Waterman, A., Matteson, D., Archer, S., & Orlofsky, J. (1993). *Ego identity: A handbook for psychosocial research.* New York: Springer-Verlag.

Markovits, H., & Dumas, C. (1999). Developmental patterns in the understanding of social and physical transitivity. *Journal of Experimental Child Psychology, 73,* 95–114.

Markovits, H., Fleury, M., Quinn, S., & Venet, M. (1998). The development of conditional reasoning and the structure of semantic memory. *Child Development, 69,* 742–755.

Marsh, H. (1988). *Self Description Questionnaire: A theoretical and empirical basis for the measurement of multiple dimensions of self-concept: A test manual and a research monograph.* San Antonio, TX: Psychological Corporation.

Marsh, H. (1990). A multidimensional, hierarchical model of self-concept: Theoretical and empirical justification. *Educational Psychology Review, 2,* 77–172.

Marsh, H., Carven, R., & Debus, R. (1991). Self-concepts of young children 5 to 8 of age: Measurement and multidimensional structure. *Journal of Educational Psychology, 83,* 377–392.

Marsh, H., Carven, R., & Debus, R. (1998). Structure, stability, and development of young children's self-concepts: A multi-cohort-multioccasion study. *Child Development, 69,* 1030–1053.

Martin, C. (1993). New directions for investigating children's gender knowledge. *Developmental Review, 13,* 184–204.

Martin, C., & Halverson, C. (1981). A schematic process-model of sex typing and stereotyping in children. *Child Development, 52,* 1119–1134.

Marvin, R., Greenberg, M., & Mossler, D. (1976). The early development of conceptual perspetive-taking: Distinguishing among multiple perspectives. *Child Development, 49,* 511–514.

Massad, C. (1981). Sex role identity and adjustment during adolescence. *Child Development, 52,* 1290–1298.

McArthur, D., Stasz, C., & Zmuidzinas, M. (1990). Tutoring techniques in algebra. *Cognitive and Instruction, 7,* 197–244.

McCall, R., & Carriger, M. (1993). A meta-analysis of infant habituation and recognition memory performance as predictors of later IQ. *Child Development, 64,* 57–79.

McCauley, C., Ruderman, M., Ohlott, P., & Morrow, J. (1994). Assessing the developmental components of managerial jobs. *The Journal of Applied Psychology, 79,* 544–560.

McCoach, D., & Siegle, D. (2003). The School Attitude Assessment Survey-Revised: A new instrument to identify academically able students who underachieve. *Educational and Psychological Measurement, 63,* 414–429.

McCrae, R., & Costa, P. (1987). Validation of the five-factor model of personality across instruments and observers. *Journal of Personality and Social Psychology, 54,* 81–90.

McCrae, R., & Costa, P. (1990). *Personality in adulthood.* New York: Guilford Press.

McCrae, R., & Costa, P. (1999). A five-factor theory of personality. In L. Pervin & O. John (Eds.), *Handbook of personality: Theory and research* (pp. 139–153). New York: Guilford Press.

McCrae, R., Costa, P., & Busch, C. (1986). Evaluating comprehensiveness in personality systems: The California Q-set and the five-factor model. *Journal of Personality, 54,* 430–446.

McCune-Nicolich, L. (1983). *A manual for analyzing free play.* New Brunswick, NJ: Department of Educational Psychology, Rutgers University.

McDougall, G. (1994). Memory self-efficacy and strategy use in successful elders. *Educational Gerontology, 21,* 357–373.

McGillicuddy-De Lisi, A., Watkins, C., & Vinchur, A. (1994). The effect of relationship on children's distributive justice reasoning. *Child Development, 65,* 1694–1700.

McGraw, K., Tew, M., & Williams, J. (2000). The integrity of web-delivered experiments: Can you trust the data? *Psychological Science, 11*, 502–506.

McGregor, H., & Elliot, A. (2002). Achievement goals as predictors of achievement-relevant processes prior to task engagement. *Journal of Educational Psychology, 94*, 381–395.

McHorney, C., Ware, J., & Raczek, A. (1993). The MOS 36-item health survey (SF-36): 11. Psychometric and clinical tests of validity in measuring physical and mental health constructs. *Medical Care, 31*, 247–263.

McNally, S., Eisenberg, N., & Harris, J. (1991). Consistency and change in maternal child-rearing practices and values: A longitudinal study. *Child Development, 62*, 190–198.

McNelles, L., & Connolly, J. (1999). Intimacy between adolescent friends: Age and gender differences in intimate affect and intimate behaviors. *Journal of Research on Adolescence, 9*, 143–159.

Meeus, W., Iedema, J., Helsen, M., & Vollebergh, W. (1999). Patterns of adolescent identity development: Review of literature and longitudinal analysis. *Developmental Review, 19*, 419–461.

Meltzoff, A., & Borton, R. (1979). Intermodal matching by human neonates. *Nature, 282*, 403–404.

Meltzoff, A., & Moore, M. (1992). Early imitation within a functional framework: The importance of person identity, movement, and development. *Infant Behavior and Development, 15*, 479–505.

Mercer, N. (1995). *The guided construction of knowledge: Talk amongst teachers and learners.* Clevedon, England: Multilingual Matters.

Midgley, C., Kaplan, A., Middleton, M., Maehr, M., Urdan, T., Anderman, L., Anderman, E., & Roeser, R. (1998). The development and validation of scales assessing students' achievement goal orientations. *Contemporary Educational Psychology, 23*, 113–131.

Miller, L., & Roid, R. (1994). *The T.I.M.E.: Toddler and Infant Motor Evaluation—A standardized assessment.* Tuscan, AZ: Therapy Skill Builders.

Miller, S. (1995). Parents' attributions for their children's behavior. *Child Development, 66*, 1557–1584.

Mitchell, P. (1997). Prelinguistic vocal development: A clinical primer. *Contemporary Issues in Communication Science and Disorders (CICSD), 24*, 87–92.

Molfese, V. (1989). *Perinatal risk and infant development.* New York: Guilford Press.

Monroe, S., & Kelley, J. (1997). Measurement of stress appraisal. In S. Cohen, R. Kessler & L. Gordon (Eds.), *Measuring stress: A guide for health and social scientists* (2nd Ed., pp. 122–147). New York: Oxford University Press.

Moore, J., Thompson, G., & Thompson, M. (1975). Visual reinforcement of head-turn responses in infants under 12 months of age. *Journal of Speech and Hearing Disorders, 42*, 328–334.

Morgan, G., & Harmon, R. (1984). Developmental transformations in mastery motivation: Measurement and validation. In R. Emde & R. Harmon (Eds.), *Continuities and discontinuities in development* (pp. 263–291). New York: Plenum Publishing.

Morgan, G., Harmon, R., & Bennett, C. (1976). A system for coding and scoring infants' spontaneous play with objects. *JSAS Catalog of Selected Documents in Psychology, 6*, 105 (Ms. No. 1355).

Morris, A., & Sloutsky, V. (1998). Understanding of logical necessity: Developmental antecedents and cognitive consequences. *Child Development, 69*, 721–741.

Morris, N., & Udry, J. (1980). Validation of a self-administered instrument to assess stage of adolescent development. *Journal of Youth and Adolescence, 9*, 271–280.

Morrongiello, B. (1986). Infants' perception of multiple-group auditory patterns. *Infant Behavior and Development, 9*, 307–320.

Mosier, C., & Rogoff, B. (1994). Infants' instrumental use of their mothers to achieve their goals. *Child Development, 65*, 70–79.

Mounts, N., & Steinberg, L. (1995). An ecological analysis of peer influence on adolescent grade point average and drug use. *Developmental Psychology, 31*, 915–922.

Munakata, Y. (2001). Task dependency in infant behavior: Toward an understanding of the processes underlying cognitive development. In F. Lacerda & C. von Hofsten (Eds.), *Emerging cognitive abilities in early infancy* (pp. 29–52). Mahwah, NJ.

Musch, J., & Reips, U. (2000). A brief history of web experimenting. In M. Birnbaum (Ed.), *Psychological experiments on the Internet* (pp. 61–88). San Diego, CA: Academic Press.

Muuss, R. (1996). *Theories of adolescence* (6th Ed.). Boston, MA: McGraw-Hill.

Myers, B. (1982). Early intervention using Brazelton training with middle class mothers and fathers of newborns. *Child Development, 53*, 462–471.

Myers, B., Jarvis, P., Creasey, G., Kerkering, K., & Markowitz, P. (1992). Prematurity and respiratory illness: Brazelton scale (NBAS) performance of three groups of premature infants. *Infant Behavior and Development, 15*, 27–41.

Naglieri, J., & Das, J. (1997). *Das-Naglieri Cognitive Assessment System.* Itasca, IL, Riverside.

National Center for Health Statistics, Centers for Disease Control. (2000). *NCHS growth curves for children birth to 36 months.* Washington, DC: U.S. Government Printing Office.

Naus, M., Ornstein, P., & Aivano, S. (1977). Developmental changes in memory: The effects of processing time and rehearsal instructions. *Journal of Experimental Child Psychology, 23*, 237–251.

NCES. (1999). *The condition of education, 1999.* Washington, DC: National Center for Educational Statistics.

Neely, A., & Bäckman, L. (1993). Long-term maintenance of gains from memory training in older adults: Two 3 1/2 follow-up studies. *Journal of Gerontology: Psychological Sciences, 48,* P233–P237.

Nelson, C., & Collins, P. (1992). Neural and behavioral correlates of recognition memory in 4- and 8-month-old infants. *Brain and Cognition, 19,* 105–121.

Nelson, C., Henschel, M., & Collins, P. (1993). Neural correlates of cross-modal recognition memory by 8-month-old human infants. *Developmental Psychology, 29,* 411–420.

Nelson, D., Hammen, C., Brennan, P., & Ullman, J. (2003). The impact of maternal depression on adolescent adjustment: The role of expressed emotion. *Journal of Consulting and Clinical Psychology, 71,* 935–944.

Nelson, T., & Narens, L. (1990). Metamemory: A theoretical framework and new findings. In G. Bower (Ed.), *The psychology of learning and motivation* (pp. 125–173). New York: Academic Press.

Nesselroade, J., & Molenaar, P. (2003). Quantitative models for developmental processes. In J. Valsiner & K. Connolly (Eds.), *Handbook of developmental psychology* (pp. 622–639). London: Sage Publications.

Newborg, J., Stock, J., Wnek, L., Guidubaldi, J., & Svinck, J. (1984). *Battelle Developmental Inventory.* Allen, TX: DLM Teaching Resources.

Newcombe, N., & Huttenlocher, J. (1992). Children's early ability to solve perspective-taking problems. *Developmental Psychology, 28,* 635–643.

NICHD Early Child Care Research Network. (2003). Does amount of time spent in child care predict socioemotional adjustment during the transition to kindergarten? *Child Development, 74,* 976–1005.

Noll, R., Zeller, M., Vannatta, K., Bukowski, W., & Davies, H. (1997). Potential bias in classroom research: Comparison of children with permission and those who do not receive permission to participate. *Journal of Clinical Child Psychology, 26,* 36–42.

Noom, M., Dekovic, M., & Meeus, W. (2001). Conceptual analysis and measurement of adolescent autonomy. *Journal of Youth and Adolescence, 30,* 577–595.

Notarius, C., & Vanzetti, N. (1983). The marital agendas protocol. In E. Filsinger (Ed.), *Marriage and family assessment: A sourcebook for family therapy* (pp. 209–227). Beverly Hills, CA: Sage Publications.

Nottelmann, E., Susman, E., Inoff-Germain, G., Cutler, G., Loriaux, D., & Chrousos, G. (1987). Developmental processes in American early adolescence: Relations among chronological age, pubertal stage, height, weight, and serum levels of gonadotropins, sex steroids, and adrenal androgens. *Journal of Adolescent Health Care, 8,* 246–260.

Nugent, J., & Steposki, C. (1984). The training of NBAS examiners. In T. Brazelton (Ed.), *Neonatal behavioral assessment scale* (2ⁿᵈ Ed.). Philadelphia, PA: Blackwell Science, Spastics International Medical Publication.

Offer, D. (1969). *The psychological world of the teen-ager: A study of normal adolescent boys.* New York: Basic Books.

Olsho, L., Koch, E., Halpin, C., & Carter, E. (1987). An observer-based psychoacoustic procedure for use with young infants. *Developmental Psychology, 23,* 627–640.

O'Neil, K., & Penrod, S. (2001). Methodological variables in web-based research that may affect results: Sample type, monetary incentives, and personal information. *Behavior Research Methods, 33,* 226–233.

Ornstein, P., Baker-Ward, L., & Naus, M. (1988). The development of mnemonic skill. In F. Weinert & M. Perlmutter (Eds.), *Memory development: universal changes and individual differences* (pp. 31–50). Hillsdale, NJ: Lawrence Erlbaum Associates.

Ornstein, P., Naus, M., & Liberty, C. (1975). Rehearsal and organizational processes in children's memory. *Child Development, 46,* 818–830.

Oster, H., Hegley, D., & Nagel, L. (1992). Adult judgments and fine-grained analysis of infant facial expressions: Testing the validity of a priori coding formulas. *Developmental Psychology, 28,* 1115–1131.

Oster, H., & Rosenstein, D. (1988). *Baby FACS: Measuring facial movements in infants and young children,* Unpublished manuscript: Derner Institute, Adelphi University.

Oster, H., & Rosenstein, D. (1996). *Baby FACS: Analyzing facial movement in infants,* Unpublished manuscript.

Pan, B., Perlmann, R., & Snow, C. (2000). Food for thought: Dinner table as a context for observing parent-child discourse. In L. Menn & N. Ratner (Eds.), *Methods for studying language production* (pp. 205–223). Mahwah, NJ: Lawrence Erlbaum Associates.

Park, S., Belsky, J., Putnam, S., & Crnic, K. (1997). Infant emotionality, parenting, and three year inhibition: Exploring stability and lawful discontinuity in a male sample. *Developmental Psychology, 33,* 218–227.

Parke, R. (1979). Interactional designs. In R. Cairns (Ed.), *The analysis of social interactions: Methods, issues, and illustrations* (pp. 15–35). Hillsdale, NJ: Lawrence Erlbaum Associates.

Parke, R., & Buriel, R. (1998). Socialization in the family: Ethnic and ecological perspectives. In W. Damon (Series Editor) & N. Eisenberg (Volume Editor), *Handbook of child psychology, Vol. 3: Social, emotional, and personality development,* (5ᵗʰ Ed., pp. 463–552). New York: Wiley.

Parke, R., & Ladd, G. (1992). *Family-peer relationships: Modes of linkage.* Hillsdale, NJ: Lawrence Erlbaum Associates.

Parker, J., & Asher, S. (1993). Friendship and friendship quality in middle childhood: Links with peer group acceptance and feelings of loneliness and social dissatisfaction. *Developmental Psychology, 29,* 611–621.

Parkin, A. (1993). *Memory: Phenomena, experiment, and theory.* Oxford, UK: Blackwell Science.

Parsons, R., & Meyers, J. (1984). *Developing consultation skills.* San Francisco, CA: Jossey-Bass.

Pasch, L., & Bradbury, T. (1998). Social support, conflict, and the development of marital dysfunction. *Journal of Consulting and Clinical Psychology, 66,* 219–230.

Patterson, G. (1982). *A social learning approach to family intervention, Vol. 3. Coercive family process.*Eugene, OR: Castalia.

Paul, R. (1992). *Pragmatic activities for language intervention: Semantics, syntax, and emerging literacy.* Tucson, AZ: Communication Skill Builders.

Paul, R. (2001). *Language disorders from infancy through adolescence: Assessment and intervention* (2nd Ed.). St. Louis, MO: Mosby.

Pederson, D., Gleason, K., Moran, G., & Bento, S. (1998). Maternal attachment representations, maternal sensitivity, and the infant-mother attachment relationship. *Developmental Psychology, 34,* 925–933.

Pederson, D., & Moran, G. (1995). A categorical description of infant-mother relationships in the home and its relation to Q-sort measures of infant-mother interactions. In E. Waters, B. Vaughn, G. Posada & K. Kondo-Ikemura (Eds.), Caregiving, cultural, and cognitive perspectives on secure-base behavior and working models. *Monographs of the society for research in child development, Vol. 60* (2-3, Serial No. 244) (pp. 111–174). Chicago, IL: University of Chicago Press.

Pederson, D., Moran, G., Stiko, C., Campbell, K., Ghesquire, K., & Acton, H. (1990). Maternal sensitivity and the security of infant-mother attachment. *Child Development, 61,* 1974–1983.

Perry, J. (1995). Facilities services in urban settings. In A. Thomas & J. Grimes (Eds.), *Best Practices in School Psychology-III* (pp. 289–299).Washington DC: NASP.

Peterson, A., Crockett, L., Richards, M., & Boxer, A. (1988). A self-report measure of pubertal status: Reliability, validity, and initial norms. *Journal of Youth and Adolescence, 17,* 117–133.

Piaget, J. (1926). *The language and thought of the child.* London: Kegan, Paul, Trench, & Trubner.

Piaget, J. (1929/1979). *The child's conception of the world.* New York: Harcourt Brace.

Piaget, J. (1951). *Play, dreams, and imitation in childhood.* New York: Harcourt, Brace, & World, (Originally published 1945).

Piaget, J. (1954). *The construction of reality in the child.* New York: Basic Books.

Piaget, J. (1972). Intellectual evolution from adolescence to adulthood. *Human Development, 15,* 1–12.

Piaget, J. (1981). *Intelligence and affectivity: Their relationship during child development.* Palo Alto, CA: Annual Reviews.

Piaget, J., & Inhelder, B. (1941/1974). *From conservation to atomism.* In J. Piaget & B. Inhelder (Eds.), *The child's construction of quantities* (pp. 67–116). London: Routledge & Kegan Paul.

Piaget, J., & Inhelder, B. (1948/1956). *The child's conception of space.* London: Routledge & Kegan Paul.

Piaget, J., & Inhelder, B. (1969). *The psychology of the child.* New York: Basic Books.

Pickens, J. (1994). Perception of auditory-visual distance relations by 5-month-olds. *Developmental Psychology, 30,* 537–544.

Pintrich, P., & De Groot, E. (1990). Motivational and self-regulated learning components of classroom academic performance. *Journal of Educational Psychology, 82,* 33–40.

Pintrich, P., Roeser, R., & De Groot, E. (1994). Classroom and individual differences in early adolescent's motivation and self-regulated learning. *Journal of Early Adolescence, 14,* 139–161.

Pintrich, P., Smith, D., Garcia, T., & McKeachie, W. (1993). Reliability and predictive validity of the Motivated Strategies for Learning Questionnaire (MSLQ). *Educational and Psychological Measurement, 53,* 810–813.

Piper, M., & Darrah, J. (1994). *Motor assessment of the developing infant.* Philadelphia, PA: W. B. Saunders.

Porges, S. (1991). Vagal tone: An autonomic mediator of affect. In J. Garber & K. Dodge (Eds.), *The development of emotional regulation and dysregulation.* Cambridge, UK: Cambridge University Press.

Porges, S., Doussard-Roosevelt, J., & Maiti, A. (1994). Vagal tone and the physiological regulation of emotion. In N. Fox (Ed.), The development of emotion regulation: Biological and behavioral consideration. *Monographs of the society for research in child development,Vol.* 59 (2-3, Serial No. 240).

Porter, F. (2001). Vagal tone. In L. Singer & P. Zeskind (Eds.), *Biobehavioral assessment of the infant* (pp. 109–124). New York: Guilford Press.

Posada, G., Gao, Y., Wu, F., Posada, R., Tascon, M., Schöelmerich, A., Sagi, S., Kondo-Ikemura, K., Haaland, W., & Synnevaag, B. (1995). The secure-base phenomenon across cultures: Children's behavior, mothers' preferences, and experts' concepts. In E. Waters, B. Vaughn, G. Posada & K. Kondo-Ikemura (Eds.), Caregiving, cultural, and cognitive perspectives on secure-base behavior and working models. *Monographs of the society for research in child development, Vol. 60* (2-3, Serial No. 244) (pp. 27–48), Chicago, IL: University of Chicago Press.

Pottharst, K. (1990). *Explorations in adult attachment.* New York: Peter Lang.

Power, T., & Radcliffe, J. (1989). The relationship of play behavior to cognitive ability in developmentally disabled preschoolers. *Journal of Autism and Developmental Disorders, 19,* 97–107.

Prager, K. (2000). Intimacy in personal relationships. In C. Hendrick & S. Hendrick (Eds.), *Close relationships: A sourcebook* (pp. 229–242).Thousand Oaks, CA: Sage Publications.

Prechtl, H. (1982). Assessment methods for the newborn infant: A critical evaluation. In P. Stratton (Ed.), *Psychobiology of the human newborn*. New York: Wiley.

Prencipe, A., & Helwig, C. (2002). The development of reasoning about the teaching of values in school and family contexts. *Child Development, 73*, 841–856.

Prinstein, M., & La Greca, A. (2002). Peer crowd affiliation and internalizing distress in childhood and adolescence: A longitudinal follow-back study. *Journal of Research on Adolescence, 12*, 325–351.

Prull, M., Gabrieli, J., & Bunge, S. (2000). Age-related changes in memory: A cognitive neuroscience perspective. In F. Craik & T. Salthouse (Eds.), *The handbook of aging and cognition* (2nd Ed., pp. 91–153). Mahwah, NJ: Lawrence Erlbaum Associates.

Quinn, P., Eimas, P., & Rosenkrantz, S. (1993). Evidence for representations of perceptually similar natural categories by 3-month-old and 4-month-old infants. *Perception, 22*, 463–475.

Radke-Yarrow, M., Cummings, E., Kuczynski, L., & Chapman, M. (1985). Patterns of attachment in two- and three-year-olds in normal families and families with parental depression. *Child Development, 56*, 884–893.

Radke-Yarrow, M., Zahn-Waxler, C., & Chapman, M. (1983). Children's prosocial dispositions and behavior. In E.M. Hetherington (Ed.), *Handbook of child psychology: Socialization, personality, and social development* (Vol. 4, pp. 469–545). New York: Wiley.

Radloff, L. (1977). The CES-D Scale: A self-report depression scale for research in the general population. *Applied Psychological Measurement, 1*, 385–401.

Raffaelli, M. (1997). Young adolescents' conflicts with siblings and friends. *Journal of Youth and Adolescence, 26*, 539–558.

Ramey, C., & Shearer, D. (1999). A conceptual framework for interventions with low birthweight premature children and their families. In E. Goldson (Ed.), *Nurturing the premature infant* (pp. 86–101). New York: Oxford University Press.

Rauh, V., Achenbach, T., Nurcombe, B., Howell, C., & Teti, D. (1988). Minimizing adverse effects of low birthweight: Four year results of an early intervention program. *Child Development, 88*, 544–553.

Rausch, P. (1990). Effect of tactile and kinesthetic stimulation on weight gain in premature infants. In K. Barnard & T. Brazelton (Eds.), *Touch: The foundation of experience* (pp. 253–268). Madison, CT: International Universities Press.

Ray, W. (1997). *Methods toward a science of behavior and experience* (5th Ed.). Pacific Grove, CA: Brookes/Cole.

Raymore, L., Barber, B., & Eccles, J. (2001). Leaving home, attending college, partnership, and parenthood: The role of life transition events in leisure pattern stability from adolescence to young adulthood. *Journal of Youth and Adolescence, 30*, 197–223.

Reips, U. (2000). The Web experiment method: Advantages, disadvantages, and solutions. In M. Birnbaum (Ed.), *Psychological experiments on the Internet* (pp. 89–117). San Diego, CA: Academic Press.

Reisberg, B., Ferris, S., de Leon, M., & Crook, T. (1982). The Global Deterioration Scale for assessment of primary degenerative dementia. *American Journal of Psychiatry, 139*, 1136–1139.

Reisman, J. (1987). Touch, motion, and proprioception. In P. Salapatek & L. Cohen (Eds.), *Handbook of infant perception: From sensation to perception* (Vol. 1, pp. 265–303). New York: Academic Press.

Repetti, R., Taylor, S., & Seeman, T. (2002). Risky families: Family social environments and the mental and physical health of offspring. *Psychological Bulletin, 128*, 330–336.

Rescorla, L. (1989). The Language Development Survey: A screening tool for delayed language in toddlers. *Journal of Speech and Hearing Disorders, 54*, 587–599.

Rest, J. (1979). *Development in judging moral issues.* Minneapolis, MN: University of Minnesota Press.

Rest, J., Narvaez, D., Bebeau, M., & Thoma, S. (1999). *Postconventional moral thinking: A Neo-Kohlbergian approach.* Mahwah, NJ: Lawrence Erlbaum Associates.

Reynell, J., & Gruber, C. (1990). *Reynell Developmental Language Scales* (American Edition). Los Angeles, CA: Western Psychological Corporation.

Reznick, S., Chawarska, K., & Betts, S. (2000). The development of visual expectations in the first year. *Child Development, 71*, 1191–1204.

Reznick, S., & Goldfield, A. (1992). Rapid change in lexical development in comprehension and production. *Developmental Psychology, 28*, 406–413.

Rice, K. (1992). Separation-individuation and adjustment to college: A longitudinal study. *Journal of Counseling Psychology, 39*, 203–213.

Rice, M., & Watkins, R. (1996). "Show Me X": New views of an old assessment technique. In K. Cole, P. Dale & D. Thal (Eds.), *Assessment of communication and language* (Vol. 6, pp. 183–206). Baltimore, Maryland: Paul Brookes.

Richards, M., Boxer, A., Petersen, A., & Albrecht, R. (1990). Relation of weight to body image in pubertal girls and boys from two communities. *Developmental Psychology, 26*, 313–321.

Richards, W. (1989). *The NEGOPY Network Analysis Program.* Burnaby, BC, Canada: Department of Communications, Simon Fraser University.

Richards, W., & Rice, R. (1981). The NEGOPY network analysis program. *Social Networks, 3*, 215–223.

Richters, J., & Pellegrini, D. (1989). Depressed mothers' judgments about their children: An examination of the depression-distortion hypothesis. *Child Development, 60*, 1068–1075.

Ritchie, W., & Bhatia, T. (1999). *Handbook of child language acquisition*. San Diego, CA: Academic Press.

Roberts, G., Block, J., & Block, J. (1984). Continuity and change in parent's child-rearing. *Child Development, 55,* 586–597.

Roberts, W., & Strayer, J. (1996). Empathy, emotional expressiveness, and prosocial behavior. *Child Development, 67,* 449–470.

Robins, R., John, O., Caspi, A., Moffitt, T., & Stouthamer-Loeber, M. (1996). Resilient, overcontrolled, and undercontrolled boys: Three replicable personality types. *Journal of Personality and Social Psychology, 70,* 157–171.

Robinson, W., Ruch-Ross, H., Watkins-Ferrell, P., & Lightfoot, S. (1993). Risk behavior in adolescence: Methodological challenges in school-based research. *School Psychology Quarterly, 8,* 241–254.

Roeser, R., & Eccles, J. (1998). Adolescents' perceptions of middle school: Relation to longitudinal changes in academic and psychological adjustment. *Journal of Research on Adolescence, 8,* 123–158.

Rogers, W., & Fisk, A. (2001). Understanding the role of attention in cognitive aging research. In J. Birren & K.W. Schaie (Eds.), *Handbook of the psychology of aging* (5th Ed., pp. 267–287).San Diego, CA: Academic Press.

Rogoff, B. (1990). *Apprenticeship in thinking: Cognitive development in social context*. New York: Oxford University Press.

Rogoff, B. (1998). Cognition as a collaborative process. In D. Kuhn & R. Siegler (Eds.), W. Damon (Series Editor), *Handbook of child psychology, Vol. 2, Cognition, perception, and language* (5th Ed., pp. 679–744).New York: Wiley.

Rogoff, B., Mistry, J., Goncu, A., & Mosier, C. (1993). Guided participation in cultural activity by toddlers and caregivers. *Monographs of the Society for Research in Child Development, 58*(7, Serial No. 236).

Roisman, G., Padron, E., Sroufe, L., & Egeland, B. (2002). Earned-secure attachment in retrospect and prospect. *Child Development, 73,* 1204–1219.

Rollins, S., Garrison, M., & Pierce, S. (2002). The Family Daily Hassles Inventory: A preliminary investigation of reliability and validity. *Family and Consumer Sciences Research Journal, 31,* 135–154.

Rose, S. (1990). Perception and cognition in preterm infants: The sense of touch. In K. Barnard & T. Brazelton (Eds.), *Touch: The foundation of experience* (pp. 299–323). Madison, CT: International Universities Press.

Rose, S., & Feldman, J. (1995). Prediction of IQ and specific cognitive abilities at 11 years from infancy measures. *Developmental Psychology, 31,* 685–696.

Rose, S., Feldman, J., & Wallace, I. (1988). Individual differences in infant information processing in seven-month-old infants as a function of risk status. *Child Development, 59,* 1177–1197.

Rose, S., & Orlian, E. (2001). Visual information processing. In L. Singer & P. Zeskind (Eds.), *Biobehavioral assessment of the infant* (pp. 274–292). New York: Guilford Press.

Rosen, A., & Rozin, P. (1993). Now you see it, now you don't: The preschool child's conception of invisible particles in the context of dissolving. *Developmental Psychology, 29,* 300–311.

Rosenberg, M. (1965). *Society and the adolescent self-image*. Princeton, NJ: Princeton University Press.

Rosenberg, M. (1989). *Society and the adolescent self-image* (2nd Ed.). Middletown, CT: Wesleyan University Press.

Rosenblum, K., McDonough, S., Muzik, M., Miller, A., & Sameroff, A. (2002). Maternal representations of the infant: Associations with infant response to the still face. *Child Development, 73,* 999–1015.

Rosenstein, D., & Oster, H. (1988). Differential facial responses to four basic tastes in newborns. *Child Development, 59,* 1555–1568.

Rosenthal, R., & Rosnow, R. (1975). *The volunteer subject*. New York: Wiley.

Rosenthal, R., & Rosnow, R. (1991). *Essentials of behavioral research* (2nd Ed.). New York: McGraw-Hill.

Ross, G., & Lawson, K. (1997). Using the Bayley II: Unresolved issues in assessing the development of prematurely born children. *Journal of Developmental and Behavioral Pediatrics, 18,* 109–111.

Roth, S., & Cohen, L. (1986). Approach, avoidance, and coping with stress. *American Psychologist, 41,* 813–819.

Rothbart, M., & Derryberry, D. (1981). Development of individual differences in temperament. In M. Lamb & M. Bornstein (Eds.), *Advances in developmental psychology* (Vol. 1, pp. 37–86). Hillsdale, NJ: Lawrence Erlbaum Associates.

Rothbart, M. (1981). Measurement of temperament in infancy. *Child Development, 52,* 569–578.

Rothbart, M., Chew, K., & Gartstein, M. (2001). Assessment of temperament in early development. In L. Singer & P. Zeskind (Eds.), *Biobehavioral assessment of the infant* (pp. 190–208). New York: Guilford Press.

Rothbaum, F., Weisz, J., Pott, M., Miyake, K., & Morelli, G. (2000). Attachment and culture: Security in the United States and Japan. *American Psychologist, 55,* 1093–1104.

Rovee, C., & Rovee, D. (1969). Conjugate reinforcement of infant exploratory behavior. *Journal of Experimental Child Psychology, 8,* 33–39.

Rovee-Collier, C., Earley, L., & Stafford, S. (1989). Ontogeny of early event memory: III. Attentional determinants of retrieval at 2 and 3 months. *Infant Behavior and Development, 12,* 147–161.

Rowe, D., Rodgers, J., Mescek-Bushey, S., & St. John, C. (1989). Sexual behavior and nonsexual deviance: A sibling study of their relationship. *Developmental Psychology, 25,* 61–69.

Rubenstein, J., & Howes, C. (1976). The effects of peers on toddler interaction with mothers and toys. *Child Development, 47*, 597–605.

Rubin, D. (1999). Autobiographical memory and aging: Distributions of memories across the life-span and their implications for survey research. In N. Schwartz, D. Park, B. Knäuper & S. Sudman (Eds.), *Cognition, aging, and self-reports* (pp. 163–183).Philadelphia, PA: Taylor & Francis, Psychology Press.

Ruble, D., & Martin, C. (1998). Gender development. In W. Damon (Series Ed.) & N. Eisenberg (Vol. Ed.), *Handbook of child psychology, Vol. 3: Social, emotional, and personality development* (5th Ed., pp. 933–1016). New York: Wiley.

Rubin, D., Rahhal, T., & Poon, L. (1998). Things learned in early adulthood are remembered best. *Memory and Cognition, 26*, 3–19.

Rubin, D., & Schulkind, M. (1997). Distribution of important and word-cued autobiographical memories in 20-, 35-, and 70-year-old adults. *Psychology and Aging, 12*, 524–535.

Rubin, K., Bukowski, W., & Parker, J. (1998). Peer interactions, relationships, and groups. In W. Damon (Series Ed.) & N. Eisenberg (Vol. Ed.), *Handbook of child psychology, Vol. 3: Social, emotional, and personality development* (5th Ed., pp. 619–700).New York: Wiley.

Ruggiero, M., Greenberger, E., & Steinberg, L. (1982). Occupational deviance among first-time workers. *Youth and Society, 13*, 423–448.

Runco, M. (1989). Parents' and teachers' ratings of the creativity of children. *Journal of Social Behavior and Personality, 4*, 73–83.

Rushton, J., Chrisjohn, R., & Fekken, G. (1981). The altruistic personality and the self-report altruism scale. *Personality and Individual Differences, 2*, 1–11.

Ryan, R., & Lynch, J. (1989). Emotional autonomy versus detachment: Revisiting the vicissitudes of adolescence and early adulthood. *Child Development, 60*, 340–356.

Ryff, C., Kwan, C., & Singer, B. (2001). Personality and aging: Flourishing agendas and future challenges. In J. Birren & K.W. Schaie (Eds.), *Handbook of the psychology of aging* (5th Ed., pp. 477–499).San Diego, CA: Academic Press.

Saarni, C., Mumme, D., & Campos, J. (1998). Emotional development: Action communication, and understanding. In W. Damon (Editor In Chief), N. Eisenberg (Series Editor), *Handbook of Child Psychology, Vol. 3: Social, emotional, and personality development* (pp. 237–309). New York: Wiley.

Sagi, A. (1990). Attachment theory and research from a cross-cultural perspective. *Human Development, 33*, 10–22.

Salapatek, P., & Nelson, C. (1985). Event-related potentials and visual development. In G. Gottlieb & N. Krasnegor (Eds.), *Measurement of vision and audition in the first year* (pp. 419–453). Norwood, NJ: Ablex Publishing.

Salisbury, A., Minard, K., Hunsley, M., & Thoman, E. (2001). Audio recording of infant crying: Comparison with maternal cry logs. *International Journal of Behavioral Development, 25*, 458–465.

Salthouse, T. (1996). The processing speed theory of adult age differences in cognition. *Psychological Review, 103*, 403–428.

Salthouse, T. (2000). Methodological assumptions in cognitive aging research. In F. Craik & T. Salthouse (Eds.), *The handbook of aging and cognition* (2nd Ed., pp. 467–498). Mahwah, NJ: Lawrence Erlbaum Associates.

Salthouse, T., & Babcock, R. (1991). Decomposing adult age differences in working memory. *Developmental Psychology, 27*, 763–776.

Salthouse, T., & Maurer, T. (1996). Aging, job performance, and career development. In J. Birren & K.W. Schaie (Eds.), *Handbook of the psychology of aging* (4th Ed., pp. 353–364).San Diego, CA: Academic Press.

Sameroff, A., & Feil, L. (1985). Parent concepts of development. In I. Sigel (Ed.), *Parental belief systems* (pp. 83–105). Hillsdale, NJ: Lawrence Erlbaum Associates.

Sameroff, A., Seifer, R., Baldwin, A., & Baldwin, C. (1993). Stability of intelligence from preschool to adolescence: The influence of social and family risk factors. *Child Development, 64*, 80–97.

Sarason, B., Pierce, G., & Sarason, I. (1990). *Parent-child relationships: Social support, conflict, and sensitivity.* Unpublished manuscript.

Sarason, I., Johnson, J., & Siegel, J. (1978). Assessing the impact of life changes: Development of the Life Experiences Survey. *Journal of Consulting and Clinical Psychology, 46*, 932–946.

Savin-Williams, R., & Small, S. (1986). The timing of puberty and its relationship to adolescent and parent perceptions of family interactions. *Developmental Psychology, 22*, 342–347.

Schaie, K.W. (1994a). Developmental designs revisited. In S. Cohen & H. Reese (Eds.), *Life-span developmental psychology: Methodological contributions* (pp. 45–64). Hillsdale, NJ: Lawrence Erlbaum Associates.

Schaie, K.W. (1994b). The course of adult intellectual development. *American Psychologist, 49*, 304–313.

Schaie, K.W. (1996a). *Intellectual development in adulthood: The Seattle Longitudinal Study.* New York: Cambridge University Press.

Schaie, K.W. (1996b). Intellectual development in adulthood. In F. Craik & T. Salthouse (Eds.), *The handbook of aging and cognition* (2nd Ed., pp. 467–498).Mahwah, NJ: Lawrence Erlbaum Associates.

Schaie, K.W. (2002). The impact of longitudinal studies on understanding development from young adulthood to old age. In W. Hartup & R. Silbereisen (Eds.), *Growing points in developmental science: An introduction* (pp. 307–328). New York: Psychology Press.

Schaie, K.W., & Hofer, S. (2001). Longitudinal studies in research on aging. In J. Birren, & K.W. Schaie (Eds.), *Handbook of the psychology of aging* (5th Ed., pp. 24–37). San Diego, CA: Academic Press.

Schaie, K.W., & Willis, S. (1986). Can decline in adult intellectual functioning be reversed? *Developmental Psychology, 22,* 223–232.

Schaie, K.W., Willis, S., & O'Hanlon, A. (1994). Perceived intellectual performance change over seven years. *Journal of Gerontology; Psychological Sciences, 49,* P108–P118.

Schauble, L., et al. (2002). Supporting science learning in museums. In G. Leinhardt, K. Crowley & K. Knutson (Eds.), *Learning conversations in museums* (pp. 425–452). Mahwah, NJ: Lawrence Erlbaum Associates.

Schmitz, M., & Baer, J. (2001). The vicissitudes of measurement: A confirmatory factor analysis of the emotional autonomy scale. *Child Development, 72,* 207–219.

Schneider, W. (1986). The role of conceptual knowledge and metamemory in the development of organizational processes in memory. *Journal of Experimental Child Psychology, 42,* 218–236.

Schneider, W., & Bjorklund, D. (1998). Memory. In D. Kuhn & R. Siegler (Eds.), W. Damon (Series Editor), *Handbook of Child Psychology, Vol. 2, Cognition, perception, and language* (5th Ed., pp. 467–521).New York: Wiley.

Schneider, W., & Pressley, M. (1997). *Memory development between ages 2 and 20* (2nd Ed.). Mahwah, NJ: Lawrence Erlbaum Associates.

Schuengel, C., Bakermans-Kranenburg, M., & van IJzendoorn, M. (1999). Frightening maternal behavior linking unresolved loss and disorganized infant attachment. *Journal of Consulting and Clinical Psychology, 67,* 54–63.

Schultz, R., & Williamson, G. (1991). A two-year longitudinal study of depression among Alzheimer's caregivers. *Psychology and Aging, 6,* 569–578.

Schuman, H., Rieger, C., & Gaidys, V. (1994). Collective memories in the United States and Lithuania. In N. Schwartz & S. Sudman (Eds.), *Autobiographical memory and the validity of retrospective reports* (pp. 313–333). New York: Springer-Verlag.

Schumm, W., Paff-Bergen, L., Hatch, R., Obiorah, F., Copeland, J., Meens, L., & Bugaighis, M. (1986). Concurrent and discriminate validity of the Kansas marital satisfaction scale. *Journal of Marriage and the Family, 48,* 381–387.

Schwartz, D., Dodge, K., Pettit, G., & Bates, J. (1997). The early socialization of aggressive victims of bullies. *Child Development, 68,* 665–675.

Schwarzer, R., & Schultz, U. (2003). Stressful life events. In A. Nezu, C. Nezu & P. Geller (Eds.), *Handbook of psychology: Health psychology* (Vol. 9, pp. 27–49). New York: Wiley.

Scullen, S., Mount, M., & Judge, T. (2003). Evidence of the construct validity of developmental ratings of managerial performance. *Journal of Applied Psychology, 88,* 50–66.

Sears, R., Maccoby, E., & Levin, H. (1957). *Patterns of child rearing.* Evanston, IL: Row, Peterson.

Segal, L., Oster, H., Cohen, M., Caspi, B., Myers, M., & Brown, D. (1995). Smiling and fussing in seven-month-old preterm and full-term black infants in still-face situation. *Child Development, 66,* 1829–1843.

Seifer, R. (2001). Conceptual and methodological basis for understanding development and risk in infants. In L. Singer & P. Zeskind (Eds.), *Biobehavioral assessment of the infant* (pp. 18–39). New York: Guilford Press.

Seiffge-Krenke, I., & Stemmler, M. (2002). Factors contributing to gender differences in depressive symptoms: A test of three developmental models. *Journal of Youth and Adolescence, 31,* 405–417.

Selman, R. (1976). Social-cognitive understanding: A guide to educational and clinical practice. In T. Lickona (Ed.), *Moral development and behavior* (pp. 299–316). New York: Holt, Rineholt, and Winston.

Selman, R. (1980). *The growth of interpersonal understanding: Developmental and clinical analysis.* New York: Academic Press.

Semel, E., Wiig, E., & Secord, W. (1995). *Clinical Evaluation of Language Fundamentals—Screening Test.* San Antonio, TX: Psychological Corporation.

Semel, E., Wiig, W., & Secord, W. (1998). *Clinical Evaluation of Language Fundamentals (III).* San Antonio, TX: Psychological Corporation.

Seranno-Garcia, I. (1990). Implementing research: Putting our values at work. In P. Tolan, C. Keys, F. Chertok & L. Jason (Eds.), *Researching community psychology* (pp. 171–182). Washington, DC: American Psychological Associations.

Sevy, B., Olson, R., McGuire, D., Frazier, M., & Paajanen, G. (1985). *Management Skills Profile technical manual.* Minneapolis, MN: Personnel Decisions.

Selye, H. (1956). *The stress of life.* New York: McGraw-Hill.

Sharabany, R., Gershoni, R., & Hofman, J. (1981). Girlfriend, boyfriend: Age and sex differences in intimate friendship. *Developmental Psychology, 17,* 800–808.

Shavelson, R., Hubner, J., & Stanton, G. (1976). Self-concept: Validation of construct interpretations. *Review of Educational Research, 46,* 407–441.

Shelton, K., Frick, P., & Wooton, S. (1996). Assessing the parenting practices in families of elementary school-age children. *Journal of Clinical Child Psychology, 25,* 317–329.

Sherbourne, C., Hays, R., Fleishman, J., Vitiello, B., Magruder, K., Bing, E., McCaffrey, D., Burnam, A., Longshore, D., Eggan, F., Bozzette, S., Shapiro, M. (2000). Impact of psychiatric conditions on health-related quality of life in persons with HIV infection. *American Journal of Psychiatry, 157,* 248–254.

Shi, R., Werker, J., & Morgan, J. (1999). Newborn infants' sensitivity to perceptual cues to lexical and grammatical words. *Cognition, 72*, B11–B12.

Shiller, V., Izard, C., & Hembree, E. (1986). Patterns of emotion expression during separation in the Strange Situation procedure. *Developmental Psychology, 22*, 378–382.

Shulman, S., & Laursen, B. (2002). Adolescent perceptions of conflict in interdependent and disengaged friendships. *Journal of Research on Adolescence, 12*, 353–372.

Siegler, I., Bosworth, H., & Poon, L. (2003). Disease, health, and aging. In R. Lerner, A. Easterbrooks & J. Mistry (Eds.), *Handbook of psychology: Developmental psychology* (Vol. 6, pp. 423–442). New York: Wiley.

Siegler, R. (1996). *Emerging minds: The process of change in children's thinking.* Oxford, UK: Oxford University Press.

Sigel, I., & McGillicuddy-De Lisi, A. (2002). Parental belief systems are cognitions: The dynamic belief systems model. In M. Bornstein (Ed.), *Handbook of parenting: Children and parenting* (Vol. 3, 2nd Ed., pp. 485–508). Mahwah, NJ: Lawrence Erlbaum Associates.

Sillars, A. (1982). *Verbal tactics coding scheme: Coding manual.* Ohio State University.

Silverberg, S., & Gondoli, D. (1996). Autonomy in adolescence: A contextualized perspective. In G. Adams, R. Montemayor & T. Gullotta (Eds.), *Psychosocial development during adolescence* (pp. 12–61). Thousand Oaks, CA: Sage Publications.

Simion, F., Valenza, E., & Umilta, C. (1998). Mechanisms underlying face preference at birth. In F. Simion & G. Butterworth (Eds.), *The development of sensory, motor, and cognitive capacities in early infancy: From sensation to cognition* (pp. 87–101). Hove, UK: Psychology Press.

Simonton, D. (1988). Age and outstanding achievement: What do we know after a century of research? *Psychological Bulletin, 104*, 251–267.

Simonton, D. (1999). Creativity from a historiometric perspective. In R. Sternberg (Ed.), *Handbook of creativity* (pp. 116–133). Cambridge, UK: Cambridge University Press.

Simpkins, S., & Parke, R. (2001). The relations between parental friendships and children's friendships: Self-report and observational analysis. *Child Development, 72*, 569–582.

Simpson, J., Rholes, W., & Phillips, D. (1996). Conflict in close relationships: An attachment perspective. *Journal of Personality and Social Psychology, 71*, 899–914.

Singer, D., & Singer, D. (1990). *The house of make-believe.* Cambridge, MA: Harvard University Press.

Singer, T., Lindenberger, U., & Baltes, P. (2003). Plasticity and memory for new learning in very old age: A story of major loss? *Psychology and Aging, 18*, 306–317.

Sinnott, J. (1984). Postformal reasoning: The relativistic stage. In M. Commons, F. Richards & C. Armon (Eds.), *Beyond formal operations: Late adolescent and adult cognitive development* (pp. 298–325). New York: Praeger Publishers.

Sinnott, J. (1989). A model for solution of ill-structured problems: Implications for everyday and abstract problem-solving. In J. Sinnott (Ed.), *Everyday problem solving: Theory and application* (pp. 72–99). New York: Praeger Publishers.

Sinnott, J. (1994). The relationship of postformal thought, adult learning, and lifespan development. In J. Sinnott (Ed.), *Interdisciplinary handbook of adult lifespan learning* (pp. 105–199). Westport, CT: Greenwood Press.

Sinnott, J. (1998). *The development of logic in adulthood: Postformal thought and its applications.* New York: Plenum Publishing.

Sinnott, J., & Shifren, K. (2001). Gender and aging: Gender differences and gender roles. In J. Birren & K.W. Schaie (Eds.), *Handbook of the psychology of aging* (5th Ed., pp. 454–476). San Diego, CA: Academic Press.

Slade, A. (1999). Attachment theory and research: Implications for the theory and practice of individual psychotherapy with adults. In J. Cassidy & P. Shaver (Eds.), *Handbook of attachment* (pp. 575–594). New York: Guilford Press.

Smart, R. (1998). Career changes in Australian professional women: A test of Super's model. *Journal of Vocational Behavior, 52*, 379–395.

Smetana, J. (1985). Preschool children's conceptions of transgressions: Effects of varying moral and conventional domain-related attributes. *Developmental Psychology, 21*, 18–29.

Smetana, J. (1989). Adolescents' and parents' reasoning about actual family conflict. *Child Development, 60*, 1052–1067.

Smetana, J.G., & Daddis, C. (2002). Domain-specific antecedents of parental psychological control and monitoring: The role of parenting beliefs and practices. *Child Development, 73*, 563–580.

Smetana, J., & Turiel, E. (2003). Moral development during adolescence. In G. Adams & M. Berzonsky (Eds.), *Blackwell handbook of adolescence* (pp. 247–268). Malden, MA: Blackwell Science.

Smilansky, S., & Shefatya, L. (1990). *Facilitating play: A medium for promoting cognitive, socioemotional, and academic development in young children.* Gaithersburg, MD: Psychosocial and Educational Publications.

Smith, A. (1996). Memory. In F. Craik & T. Salthouse (Eds.), *The handbook of aging and cognition* (2nd Ed., pp. 236–250). Mahwah, NJ: Lawrence Erlbaum Associates.

Smith, J., Staudinger, U., & Baltes, P. (1994). Occupational settings facilitate wisdom-related knowledge: The sample case of clinical psychologists. *Journal of Consulting and Clinical Psychology, 5*, 989–999.

Smith, P., & Pederson, D. (1988). Maternal sensitivity and patterns of infant-mother attachment. *Child Development, 59*, 1097–1101.

Smollar, J., & Youniss, J. (1989). Transformations in adolescents' perceptions of parents. *International Journal of Behavioral Development, 12*, 71–84.

Solomon, J., & George, C. (1999). The measurement of attachment security in infancy and childhood. In J. Cassidy & P. Shaver (Eds.), *Handbook of attachment: Theory, research and clinical applications* (pp. 287–316). New York, NY: Guilford Press.

Sorce, J., Emde, R., Campos, J., & Klinnert, M. (1985). Maternal emotional signaling: Its effects on the visual cliff behavior of 1-year-olds. *Developmental Psychology, 21*, 195–200.

Sostek, A., & Anders, T. (1981). The biosocial importance and environmental sensitivity of infant sleep-wake cycles. In K. Bloom (Ed.), *Prospective issues in infancy research* (pp. 99–118). Hillsdale, NJ: Lawrence Erlbaum Associates.

Spanier, G. (1976). Measuring dyadic adjustment: New scales for assessing the quality of marriage and similar dyads. *Journal of Marriage and the Family, 38*, 15–28.

Spence, J., & Helmreich, R. (1978). *Masculinity and femininity: Their psychological dimensions, correlates, and antecedents.* Austin, TX: University of Texas Press.

Sprecher, S. (1999). "I love you more today than yesterday": Romantic partners' perceptions of change and love and related affect over time. *Journal of Personality and Social Psychology, 76*, 46–53.

Srivastava, S., John, O., Gosling, S., & Potter, J. (2003). Development of personality in early and middle adulthood: Set like plaster or persistent change? *Journal of Personality and Social Psychology, 84*, 1041–1053.

Sroufe, L. (1988). The role of the infant-caregiver attachment in development. In J. Belsky & T. Nezworski (Eds.), *Clinical implications of attachment* (pp. 18–38) Hillsdale, NJ: Lawrence Erlbaum Associates.

Starkey, P., Spelke, E., & Gelman, R. (1990). Numerical abstraction by human infants. *Cognition, 36*, 97–128.

Staudinger, U., & Leiplod, B. (2003). The assessment of wisdom-related performance. In S. Lopez & C. Snyder (Eds.), *Positive psychological assessment: A handbook of models and measures* (pp. 171–184) Washington, DC: American Psychological Association.

Staudinger, U., Lopez, D., & Baltes, B. (1997). The psychometric location of wisdon-related performance: Intelligence, personality, and more? *Personality and Social Psychology Bulletin, 23*, 1200–1214.

Staudinger, U., & Pasupathi, M. (2003). Correlates of wisdom-related performance in adolescence and adulthood: Age-graded differences in "paths" towards desirable development. *Journal of Research on Adolescence, 13*, 239–268.

Staudinger, U., Smith, J., & Baltes, P. (1994). *Manual for the assessment of wisdom-related knowledge* (Technical Report No. 46). Berlin, Germany: Max Planck Institute for Human Development and Education.

Steinberg, L. (1987). The impact of puberty on family relations: Effects of pubertal status and pubertal timing. *Developmental Psychology, 23*, 451–460.

Steinberg, L., Dornbusch, S., & Brown, B. (1992). Ethnic differences in adolescent achievement: An ecological perspective. *American Psychologist, 47*, 723–729.

Steinberg, L., Elmen, J., & Mounts, N. (1989). Authoritative parenting, psychosocial maturity, and academic success among adolescents. *Child Development, 60*, 1424–1436.

Steinberg, L., Fegley, S., & Dornbusch, S. (1993). Negative impact of part-time work on adolescent adjustment: Evidence from a longitudinal study. *Developmental Psychology, 29*, 171–180.

Steinberg, L., Greenberger, E., Garduque, L., Ruggiero, M., & Vaux, A. (1982). Effects of working on adolescent development. *Developmental Psychology, 18*, 385–395.

Steinberg, L., & Hill, J. (1978). Patterns of family interaction as a function of age, the onset of puberty, and formal thinking. *Developmental Psychology, 14*, 683–684.

Steinberg, L., Lamborn, S., Darling, N., Mounts, N., & Dornbusch, S. (1994). Over-time change in adjustment and competence among adolescents from authoritative, authoritarian, indulgent, and neglectful families. *Child Development, 65*, 754–770.

Steinberg, L., Lamborn, S., Dornbusch, S., & Darling, N. (1992). Impact of parenting practices on adolescent achievement: Authoritative parenting, school involvement, and encouragement to succeed. *Child Development, 63*, 1266–1281.

Steinberg, L., & Silk, J. (2002). Parenting adolescents. In M. Bornstein (Ed.), *Handbook of parenting: Children and parenting* (Vol. 1, 2nd Ed., pp. 103–133). Mahwah, NJ: Lawrence Erlbaum Associates.

Steinberg, L., & Silverberg, S. (1986). The vicissitudes of autonomy in early adolescence. *Child Development, 57*, 841–851.

Stenberg, C., Campos, J., & Emde, R. (1983). The facial expression of anger in seven-month-old infants. *Child Development, 54*, 178–184.

Sternberg, R. (1985). *Beyond IQ: A triarchic theory of intelligence.* New York: Cambridge University Press.

Sternberg, R. (1999). *Handbook of creativity.* Cambridge, UK: Cambridge University Press.

Sternberg, R. (2000). *Handbook of intelligence.* Cambridge, UK: Cambridge University Press.

Sternberg, R., & Lubart, T. (1999). The concept of creativity: Prospects and paradigms. In R. Sternberg (Ed.), *Handbook of creativity* (pp. 3–15). Cambridge, UK: Cambridge University Press.

Sternberg, R., & Lubart, T. (2001). Wisdom and creativity. In J. Birren & K.W. Schaie (Eds.), *Handbook of the psychology of aging* (5th Ed., pp. 500–522).San Diego, CA: Academic Press.

Stevenson-Hinde, J., & Shouldice, A. (1995). Maternal interactions and self-reports related to attachment classifications at 4.5 years. *Child Development, 66,* 583–596.

Steward, M., & Steward, D. (1996). Interviewing young children about body touch and handling. *Monographs for the Society for Research in Child Development, 61*(4-5 Serial No. 248).

Stifter, C., & Fox, N. (1990). Infant reactivity: Physiological correlates of newborn and 5-month temperament. *Developmental Psychology, 26,* 582–588.

Stipek, D., Recchia, S., & McClintic, S. (1992). Self-evaluation in young children. *Monographs of the Society for Research in Child Development,* Vol. 57(1, Serial No. 226) Chicago, IL: University of Chicago Press.

Stone, A. (1997). Measurement of affective response. In S. Cohen, R. Kessler & L. Gordon (Eds.), *Measuring stress: A guide for health and social scientists* (2ⁿᵈ Ed., pp. 148–171). New York: Oxford University Press.

Stone, A., & Neale, J. (1984). The effects of severe daily events on mood. *Journal of Personality and Social Psychology, 46,* 137–144.

Stratton, P., Munton, T., Hanks, H., Heard, D., & Davidson, C. (1988). *Leads Attributional Coding System Manual.* Leeds, Great Britain: Leeds Family Therapy and Research Center.

Strayer, J. (1993). Children's concordant emotions and cognitions in response to observed emotion. *Child Development, 64,* 188–201.

Sturner, R., Layton, T., Evans, A., Heller, J., Funk, S., & Machon, M. (1994). Preschool speech and language screening: A review of currently available tests. *American Journal of Speech-Language Pathology, 3,* 25–36.

Sullivan, H. (1953). *The interpersonal theory of psychiatry.* New York: Norton Publishers.

Super, D. (1967). *The psychology of careers.* New York: Harper & Row.

Super, D. (1990). A life-span, life space approach to career development. In D. Brown & L. Brooks (Eds.), *Career choice and development* (2ⁿᵈ Ed., pp. 197–261). San Francisco, CA: Jossey-Bass.

Super, D., Osborne, L., Walsh, D., Brown, S., & Niles, S. (1992). Developmental career assessment and counseling: The C-DAC Model. *Journal of Counseling and Development, 71,* 74–82.

Super, D., Thompson, A., Lindeman, R., Jordaan, J., & Myers, R. (1988). *Manual for the Adult Career Choices Inventory and the Career Development Inventory.* Palo Alto, CA: Consulting Psychologists Press.

Susman, E. (1997). Modeling developmental complexity in adolescence: Hormones and behavior in context. *Journal of Research on Adolescence, 7,* 283–306.

Susman, E., Worrall, E., Murowchick, C., Frobose, C., & Schwab, J. (1996). Experience and neuroendocrine parameters of development: Aggressive behavior and competencies. In D. Stoff & R. Cairns (Eds.), *Neurobiological approaches to clinical aggression research* (pp. 267–289). Mahwah, NJ: Lawrence Erlbaum Associates.

Swanson, J., & Tokar, D. (1991). College students' perceptions of barriers to career development. *Journal of Vocational Behavior, 38,* 92–106.

Swearer, S., Song, S., Cary, P., Eagle, J., & Mickelson, W. (2001). Psychosocial correlates in bullying and victimization: The relationship between depression, anxiety, and bully/victim status. *Journal of Emotional Abuse, 2,* 95–121.

Szinovacz, M. (1998). Grandparents today: A demographic profile. *The Gerontologist, 38,* 37–52.

Tamis-LeMonda, C., Borstein, M., & Baumwell, L. (2001). Maternal responsiveness and children's achievement of language milestones. *Child Development, 72,* 748–767.

Tanner, J. (1962). *Growth at adolescence.* Springfield, IL: Thomas.

Tanner, J. (1990). *Foetus into man* (2ⁿᵈ Ed.). Cambridge, MA: Harvard University Press.

Teller, D. (1979). The forced-choice preferential looking procedure: A psychophysical technique for use with human infants. *Infant Behavior and Development, 2,* 135–153.

Teller, D., McDonald, M., Preston, K., Sebris, S., & Dobson, V. (1986). Assessment of visual acuity in infants and children: The acuity card procedure. *Developmental Medicine and Child Neurology, 28,* 779–789.

Teti, D., Gelfand, D., Messinger, D., & Isabella, R. (1995). Maternal depression and the quality of early attachment: An examination of infants, preschoolers, and their mothers. *Developmental Psychology, 31,* 395–405.

Teti, D., & McGourty, S. (1996). Using mothers versus trained observers in assessing children's secure base behavior: Theoretical and methodological considerations. *Child Development, 67,* 597–605.

Teti, D., Nakagawa, M., Das, R., & Wirth, O. (1991). Security of attachment between preschoolers and their mothers: Relations among social interactions, parenting stress, and mothers' sorts of the Attachment Q-set. *Developmental Psychology, 27,* 440–447.

Thoman, E. (1999). The breathing bear and the remarkable premature infant. In E. Goldson (Ed.), *Nurturing the premature infant* (pp. 161–181). New York: Oxford University Press.

Thoman, E. (2001). Sleep-wake cycles as context for assessment, as components of assessment, and as assessment. In L. Singer & P. Zeskind (Eds.), *Biobehavioral assessment of the infant* (pp. 125–148). New York: Guilford Press.

Thoman, E., & Graham, S. (1986). Self-regulation of stimulation by premature infants. *Pediatrics, 78,* 855–860.

Thoman, E., & Whitney, M. (1989). Sleep states of infants monitored in the home: Individual differences, developmental trends, and origins of diurnal cyclicity. *Infant Behavior and Development, 12*, 59–75.

Thoman, E., & Whitney, M. (1990). Behavioral states in infants: Individual differences and individual analyses. In J. Columbo & J. Fagen (Eds.), *Individual differences in infancy: Reliability, stability, and prediction* (pp. 113–135). Hillsdale, NJ: Lawrence Erlbaum Associates.

Thompson, R. (1990). Vulnerability in research: A developmental perspective on research risk. *Child Development, 61*, 1–16.

Thompson, R. (1994). Emotion regulation: A theme in search of definition. In N. Fox (Ed.), The development of emotion regulation: biological and behavioral considerations, *Monographs of the society for research in child development, Vol. 59* (2-3, Serial No. 240) (pp. 25–52). Chicago, IL: University of Chicago Press.

Thompson, R. (1999). Early attachment and later development. In J. Cassidy & P. Shaver (Eds.), *Handbook of attachment: Theory, research, and clinical applications* (pp. 265–286). New York: Guilford Press.

Tomasello, M. (1990). The role of joint attentional processes in early language development. *Language Sciences, 10*, 69–88.

Treboux, D., Crowell, J., & Waters, E. (2004). When "New" meets "Old": Configurations of adult attachment representations and their implications for marital functioning. *Developmental Psychology, 40*, 295–314.

Tronick, E. (1989). Emotions and emotional communication in infants. *American Psychologist, 44*, 112–119.

Tronick, E., & Cohn, J. (1987). *Revised Monadic Phases Manual*. Unpublished manuscript.

True, M., Pisani, L., & Oumar, F. (2001). Infant-mother attachment among the Dogon of Mali. *Child Development, 72*, 1451–1466.

Trzesniewski, K., Donnellan, M., & Robins, R. (2003). Stability of self-esteem across the life span. *Journal of Personality and Social Psychology, 84*, 205–220.

Turiel, E. (1978). Social regulation and domains of social concepts. In W. Damon (Ed.), *Social cognition: New directions for child development* (pp. 45–74). San Francisco, CA: Jossey-Bass.

Turiel, E. (1983). *The development of social knowledge: Morality and convention*. Cambridge: Cambridge University Press.

Turiel, E. (2002). *The culture of morality: Social development, context, and conflict*. Cambridge: Cambridge University Press.

Turner, R., & Wheaton, B. (1997). Checklist measurement of stressful life events. In S. Cohen, R. Kessler, & L. Gordon (Eds.), *Measuring stress: A guide for health and social scientists* (2nd ed., pp. 29–58). New York: Oxford University Press.

Underwood, B., & Moore, B. (1982). Perspetive-taking and altruism. *Psychological Bulletin, 91*, 143–173.

Urberg, K., Degirmencioglu, S., Tolson, J., & Halliday-Scher, K. (1995). The structure of adolescent peer networks. *Developmental Psychology, 31*, 540–547.

Vaillant, G. (1977). *Adaptation of life*. Boston, MA: Little Brown.

Vaillant, G. (1993). *The wisdom of the ego*. Cambridge, MA: Harvard University Press.

van Hoff, A. (1999). The identity status field re-reviewed: An update of unresolved and neglected issues with a view on some alternative approaches. *Developmental Review, 19*, 497–556.

van IJzendoorn, M. (1995). Adult attachment representations, parental responsiveness, and infant attachment: A meta-analysis on the predictive validity of the Adult Attachment Interview. *Psychological Bulletin, 117*, 387–403.

van IJzendoorn, M., Vereijken, C., Bakermans-Kranenburg, M., & Riksen-Walraven, J. (2004). Assessing attachment security with the Attachment Q Sort: Meta-analytic evidence for the validity of the observer AQS. *Child Development, 75*, 1188–1213.

Vaughn, B., Block, J., & Block, J. (1988). Parental agreement on child rearing during early childhood and the psychological characteristics of adolescents. *Child Development, 59*, 1020–1033.

Verhaeghen, P., Marcoen, A., & Goosens, L. (1992). Improving memory performance in the aged through mnemonic training: A meta-analytic study. *Psychology and Aging, 7*, 242–251.

Verhaeghen, P., Marcoen, A., & Goosens, L. (1993). Facts and fiction about memory aging: A quantitative integration of research findings. *Journal of Gerontology: Psychological Sciences, 48*, P157–P171.

Vondracek, F., & Porfeli, E. (2003). The world of work and careers. In G. Adams & M. Berzonsky (Eds.), *Blackwell handbook of adolescence* (pp. 109–128). Malden, MA: Blackwell Science.

Vygotsky, L. (1966). Play and its role in the mental development of the child. *Soviet Psychology, 12*, 62–76.

Vygotsky, L. (1978). *Mind in society: The development of higher mental processes*. Cambridge, MA: Harvard University Press.

Vygotsky, L. (1986). *Thought and language* (A. Kozulin, Trans.) Cambridge, MA: MIT Press. (1934 original publication).

Wagner, R. (2000). Practical intelligence. In R. Sternberg (Ed.), *Handbook of intelligence* (pp. 380–395). Cambridge, UK: Cambridge University Press.

Wakeley, A., Rivera, S., & Langer, J. (2000). Can young infants add and subtract? *Child Development, 71*, 1525–1534.

Walk, R., & Gibson, E. (1961). A comparative and analytic study of visual depth perception. *Psychological Monographs, 75*(15 Whole No. 519).

Walker, L. (1989). A longitudinal study of moral reasoning. *Child Development, 60*, 157–166.

Ward, C., & Bingham, R. (1993). Career assessment of ethnic minority women. *Journal of Career Assessment, 1,* 246–257.

Ward, M., Brazelton, T., & Wust, M. (1999). Toward understanding the role of attachment in malnutrition. In D. Kessler & P. Dawson (Eds.), *Failure to thrive and pediatric undernutrition: A transdisciplinary approach* (pp. 411–423). Baltimore, MD: Paul Brookes.

Ward, S., & Overton, W. (1990). Semantic familiarity, relevance, and the development of deductive reasoning. *Developmental Psychology, 26,* 488–493.

Ware, J. (1993). *SF-36 Health Survey: Manual and interpretation guide.* Boston, MA: The Health Institute, The New England Medical Center.

Ware, J. (1999). SF-36 health survey. In M. Maruish (Ed.), *The use of psychological testing for treatment planning and outcomes assessment* (2nd ed., pp. 1227–1246).

Wasik, B. (1993). Staffing issues for home visiting programs. In R. Behrman (Ed.), *The future of children: Home visiting* (Vol. 3, pp. 140–157). Center for the Future of Children, The David and Lucile Packard Foundation.

Waters, E. (1978). The reliability and stability of individual differences in infant-mother attachment. *Child Development, 49,* 483–494.

Waters, E. (1987). *Attachment Behavior Q-Set* (Revision 3.0). Unpublished instrument. Stony Brook: State University of New York, Department of Psychology.

Waters, E., Crowell, J., Elliott, M., Corcoran, D., & Treboux, D. (2002). Bowlby's secure base theory and the social/personality psychology of attachment styles: Work(s) in progress. *Attachment and Human Development, 4,* 230–242.

Waters, E., & Deane, K. (1985). Defining and assessing individual differences in attachment relationships: Q-methodology and the organization of behavior in infancy and early childhood. In I. Bretherton & E. Waters (Eds.), *Growing points of attachment theory and research, Monographs of the society for research in child development, Vol. 50* (1-2, Serial No. 209). Chicago, IL: University of Chicago Press.

Waters, E., Merrick, S., Treboux, D., Crowell, J., & Albersheim, L. (2000). Attachment security in infancy and early adulthood: A twenty-year longitudinal study. *Child Development, 71,* 684–689.

Waters, E., Vaughn, B., Posada, G., & Kondo-Ikemura, K. (1995). Caregiving, cultural, and cognitive perspectives on secure-base behavior and working models. *Monographs of the society for research in child development, Vol. 60* (2-3, Serial No. 244). Chicago, IL: University of Chicago Press.

Watzlawick, P. (1966). A structured family interview. *Family Process, 5,* 256–271.

Wechsler, D. (1989). *Manual for the Wechsler Preschool and Primary Scale of Intelligence—Revised (WPSSI-R).* San Antonio, TX: Psychological Corporation.

Wechsler, D. (1991). *Manual for the Wechsler Intelligence Scale for Children—Third Edition (WISC-III).* San Antonio, TX: Psychological Corporation.

Wechsler, D. (1997). *Manual for the Wechsler Adult Intelligence Scale—Third Edition (WAIS-III).* San Antonio, TX: Psychological Corporation.

Weinberg, K., & Tronick, E. (1990). *The Infant Regulatory Scoring System (IRSS)* Unpublished manuscript Boston: Children's Hospital/Harvard Medical School.

Weinberg, K., & Tronick, E. (1994). Beyond the face: An empirical study of infant affective configurations of facial, vocal, gestural, and regulatory behaviors. *Child Development, 65,* 1503–1515.

Weinberg, K., Tronick, E., Cohn, J., & Olson, K. (1999). Gender differences in emotional expressivity and self-regulation during early infancy. *Developmental Psychology, 35,* 175–188.

Weisz, J., & Hawley, K. (2002). Developmental factors in the treatment of adolescents. *Journal of Consulting and Clinical Psychology, 70,* 21–43.

Wellman, H., & Bartsch, K. (1988). Young children's reasoning and beliefs. *Cognition, 30,* 239–277.

Wellman, H., & Gelman, S. (1998). Knowledge acquisition in foundational domains. In D. Kuhn, R. Siegler & W. Damon (Series Editor), *Handbook of child psychology: Vol. 2, cognition, perception, and language* (5th ed., pp. 523–574). New York: Wiley.

Werker, J. (2000). Becoming a native listener. In D. Muir & A. Slater (Eds.), *Infant development: The essential readings in developmental psychology* (pp. 149–162). Malden, MA: Blackwell Science.

Werner, L., & Bargones, J. (1992). Psychoacoustic development of human infants. In L. Lipsett & C. Rovee-Collier (Eds.), *Advances in infancy research* (Vol 7, pp. 103–145). Norwood, NJ: Ablex.

Wertsch, J., Tulviste, P., & Hagstrom, F. (1993). A sociocultural approach to agency. In E. Forman, N. Minick, & C. Stone (Eds.), *Contexts for learning* (pp. 336–356). New York: Oxford University Press.

West, R. (1989). Planning practical memory training for the aged. In L. Poon, D. Rubin, & B. Wilson (Eds.), *Everyday cognition in adulthood and later life* (pp. 573–597). New York: Cambridge University Press.

West, R., Crook, T., & Barron, K. (1992). Everyday memory performance across the life-span: Effects of age and noncognitive individual differences. *Developmental Psychology, 7,* 72–82.

Westby, C. (2000). A scale for assessing development of children's play. In K. Gitlin-Weiner, A. Sandgrund, & C. Schaefer (Eds.), *Play diagnosis and assessment* (pp. 15–57). New York: Wiley.

Wetherby, A., & Prizant, B. (1993). *Communication and symbolic behavior scales.* Chicago, IL: Riverside Publishers.

Whitbourne, S., Zuschlag, M., Elliot, L., & Waterman, A. (1992). Psychosocial development in adulthood: A 20-year sequential study. *Journal of Personality and Social Psychology, 63*, 260–271.

White, R. (1959). Motivation reconsidered: The concept of competence. *Psychological Review, 66*, 297–333.

Whitley, B. (1996). *Principles of research in behavioral science*. Mountain View, CA: Mayfield Publishing.

Wichstrom, L. (2001). The impact of pubertal timing on adolescents' alcohol use. *Journal of Research on Adolescence, 11*, 131–150.

Willis, S. (2001). Methodological issues in behavioral intervention research with the elderly. In J. Birren & K.W. Schaie (Eds.), *Handbook of the psychology of aging* (5th ed., pp. 78–108). San Diego, CA: Academic Press.

Willis, S., & Nesselroade, J. (1990). Long term effects of fluid ability training in old age. *Developmental Psychology, 26*, 905–910.

Willis, S., & Schaie, K. (1986). Training the elderly on the ability factors of spatial orientation and inductive reasoning. *Psychology and Aging, 1*, 129–147.

Wimmer, H., & Perner, J. (1983). Beliefs about beliefs: Representation and constraining function of wrong beliefs in young children's understanding of deception. *Cognition, 13*, 103–128.

Wood, D., Bruner, J., & Ross, G. (1976). The role of tutoring in problem-solving. *Journal of Child Psychology and Psychiatry, 17*, 89–100.

Wood, R., & Gustafson, G. (2001). Infant crying and adults' anticipated caregiving responses: Acoustic and contextual influences. *Child Development, 72*, 1287–1300.

Woodcock, R., & Johnson, M. (1989). *Woodcock-Johnson—Revised, tests of cognitive ability: Standard and supplemental batteries*. Chicago, IL: Riverside Publishers.

Worobey, J. (1990). Behavioral assessment of the neonate. In J. Columbo & J. Fagen (Eds.), *Individual differences in infancy: Reliability, stability, and prediction* (pp. 137–154). Hillsdale, NJ: Lawrence Erlbaum Associates.

Worobey, J., & Brazelton, T. (1986). Experimenting with the family in the newborn period: A commentary. *Child Development, 57*, 1298–1300.

Worobey, J., & Lewis, M. (1989). Individual differences in the reactivity of young infants. *Developmental Psychology, 25*, 663–667.

Wyly, M. (1997). *Infant assessment*. Boulder, CO: Westview Press.

Wynn, K. (1992). Addition and subtraction in human infants. *Nature, 358*, 749–750.

Yaniv, I., & Shatz, M. (1990). Heuristics of reasoning and analogy in children's perspective taking. *Child Development, 61*, 1491–1501.

Yarrow, M., & Waxler, C. (1976). Dimensions and correlates of prosocial behavior in young children. *Child Development, 47*, 118–125.

Yau, J., & Smetana, J. (1996). Adolescent-parent conflict among Chinese adolescents living in Hong Long. *Developmental Psychology, 67*, 1262–1275.

Yonas, A., Granrud, E., Arterberry, M., & Hanson, B. (1986). Infants' distance perception from linear perspective and texture gradients. *Infant Behavior and Development, 9*, 247–256.

Youngblade, L., & Belsky, J. (1992). Parent-child acceptance of 5-year-olds' close friendships: A longitudinal analysis. *Developmental Psychology, 28*, 700–713.

Youniss, J., & Smollar, J. (1985). *Adolescent relations with mothers, fathers, and friends*. Chicago, IL: University of Chicago Press.

Zabin, L., & Hayward, S. (1993). *Adolescent sexual behavior and childbearing*. Newbury Park, CA: Sage.

Zacks, R., Hasher, L., & Li, K. (2000). Human memory. In F. Craik & T. Salthouse (Eds.), *The handbook of aging and cognition* (2nd ed., pp. 293–357). Mahwah, NJ: Lawrence Erlbaum Associates.

Zahn-Waxler, C., Cole, P., Welsh, J., & Fox, N. (1995). Psychophysiological correlates of empathy and prosocial behaviors in preschool children with problem behaviors. *Development and Psychopathology, 7*, 27–48.

Zahn-Waxler, C., Radke-Yarrow, M., Wagner, E., & Chapman, M. (1992). Development of concern for others. *Developmental Psychology, 28*, 126–136.

Zarit, S., & Zarit, J. (1998). *Mental disorders in older adults: Fundamentals of assessment and treatment*. New York: Guilford Press.

Zelinski, E., & Burnight, K. (1997). Sixteen-year longitudinal study and time lag changes in memory and cognition in older adults. *Psychology and Aging, 12*, 503–513.

Zeskind, S., & Barr, R. (1997). Acoustic characteristics of the naturally occurring cries of infants with colic. *Child Development, 68*, 394–403.

Zeskind, S., & Lester, B. (2001). Analysis of infant crying. In L. Singer & P. Zeskind (Eds.), *Biobehavioral assessment of the infant* (pp. 149–166). New York: Guilford Press.

Zeskind, S., Marshall, T., & Goff, D. (1996). Cry threshold predicts regulatory disorder in newborn infants. *Pediatric Psychology, 21*, 803–819.

Zimmer-Gembeck, M., & Collins, W. (2003). Autonomy development during adolescence. In G. Adams & M. Berzonsky (Eds.), *Blackwell handbook of adolescence* (pp. 175–204). Malden, MA: Blackwell Science.

Zuschlag, M., & Whitbourne, S. (1994). Psychosocial development in three generations of college students. *Journal of Youth and Adolescence, 23*, 567–577.

Glossary

AB search errors These errors, because of constraints on object-concern learning, occur when infants are presented with an object that is then hidden in one location and moved to a second location. The infant will search for the object in the original location while failing to search the second location.

academic achievement Scores on standardized tests or assessment of school performance.

accommodation Modifying an idea based on new experiences that conflict with the existing scheme.

achievement motivation The confidence in one's ability to do a task, the desire to do a task, and the beliefs regarding what must be done to meet these goals.

achievement test A test that identifies the abilities that a person has acquired up to the time of testing.

active parental consent Signed parental-consent form allowing a minor to participate in the research.

affective perspective taking The ability to imagine what another person is feeling.

aptitude test A test used to predict a person's potential in a novel, unfamiliar environment.

area populations Populations defined by geographic area or location, such as a community, state, or nation.

assimilation The active integration of new information into previously existing schemes or ideas.

attachment behaviors Actions the infant directs toward the caregiver, which usually result in comfort or reassurance for the infant.

attachment orientations Fluid, day-to-day feelings about a particular relationship or person.

attachment relationship Affectional tie between the infant and the caregiver.

attunement The emotional synchrony between an infant and caregiver during interactions.

autobiographical memory The ability to recall personal events from the distant past.

behavioral autonomy The ability to resist peer or parent pressure and behave in an independent yet competent manner.

behavioral-compliance linguistic paradigms A type of naturalistic language assessment that requires a child to respond to simple examiner directives or questions.

Big Five Five traits of personality structure: openness to experience, neuroticism, conscientiousness, extraversion, agreeableness.

career maturity How well an adult copes with various career concerns and appraises other factors such as career knowledge, values, and the relevance of career to other life goals.

caregiver sensitivity The ability to respond appropriately to the emotional signals of an infant.

centration The inability to focus attention on more than one feature of a task.

class-inclusion tasks Tasks used to determine the classification abilities of a child. The child is presented with a global class and its subclasses, and then must make associations between the two.

cliques Small, intimate groups of close friends.

cognitive appraisal Personal perceptions of an event as stressful or benign.

cognitive perspective taking The ability to imagine what another person might be thinking.

cohort differences Differences in historical experiences between age groups.

cohort effects Major historical events that occur during a study which influence participant behavior. AKA *time-of-measurement effects*.

concrete-operational stage Piaget's third cognitive-developmental stage, in which children begin to use more organized and logical thought patterns.

concurrent validity A significant correlation between the measure (or predictor) and an outcome measure assessed at the same point in time.

conditioning paradigms A form of implicit memory measure in which a participant is trained to respond to a stimulus that would not normally evoke a reaction.

conservation tasks Tasks in which the child is shown objects with altered properties, and the child must determine whether the object itself has been changed.

construct validity The researcher's confidence that the measure truly assesses the hypothetical construct in the study.

content validity The assumption that items on a measure adequately represent the construct.

contrived-comprehension linguistic paradigms A type of naturalistic language assessment that asks a child to perform simple tasks, often using materials that serve as natural elicitors, such as pictures.

control group A group that contains individuals not exposed to the independent variable.

control processes Strategies used, such as rehearsal, to get information in and out of long-term memory quickly and efficiently.

convergent thinking Developing a single relevant conventional response to solving a problem.

correlational design Research design in which the experimenter does not have direct control over the independent variable, because the participants have already experienced the condition or the variable cannot be manipulated. AKA *nonexperimental design.*

cortisol A stress hormone that is released when aroused; mobilizes bodily defenses.

criterion-based habituation procedures Habituation paradigm in which the infant's interest in an object determines its length of presentation; infant behavior drives stimulus presentation.

cross-modal transfer When an object that had stimulated one modality or sense, such as touch, is perceived by another modality, such as vision.

cross-sectional design A developmental design in which participants representing different age groups are studied at one time of measurement.

cross-sectional sequences design A design in which similar cross-sectional studies are conducted over time.

crowds A large peer group that shares a common theme, such as clothing style or athletic involvement.

crystallized intelligence Acquired knowledge and abilities.

cued-recall method An autobiographical memory method in which the participant is provided with certain prompts or primes to encourage recall of personal, remote events.

daily hassles Routine, day-to-day irritants or problems.

deferred imitation The phenomenon of an infant imitating behaviors that it witnessed at an earlier time.

dependent variable (DV) The variable influenced by the independent variable. AKA *the outcome variable.*

dishabituation Renewal of an infant's interest when a new stimulus is presented to it.

distal variable A variable representing an event that theoretically took place some time in the past.

distributive justice How a person thinks about fairness and the allocation of resources.

divergent thinking The ability to think of multiple relevant and unusual possibilities when solving a problem.

educational attainment The highest level of education or schooling obtained by a person.

elaboration A memory strategy using imagery to create associations between related and unrelated information.

elicited imitation Encouraging an infant to repeat a specific series of actions.

elicited-imitation paradigms An experiment in which infants are allowed to practice behaviors before testing and are later prompted to perform the practiced tasks.

elicited-imitation linguistic-production paradigms A type of language assessment that asks a child to repeat a sentence or story in the same format they heard it.

emotional autonomy The ability to move away from the emotional dependence that is normally associated with the child-parent bond; becoming more adept at coping with negative emotions on one's own.

emotional elicitors Events used to trigger an emotional expression.

emotional experience An individual's subjective emotional impressions.

emotional expression An individual's outward appearance.

emotional state An individual's physiological response to an emotionally arousing event.

empathy Emotion sharing; the ability to experience emotions similar to those of another person.

episodic buffer A brain function that represents information that is in conscious awareness.

episodic memories Specific memories regarding past experiences.

ethnographic approach A qualitative approach in which researchers conduct careful observations and interviews to provide a record or description of the behavior of the target sample.

event potentials Electrical activity in specific parts of the brain as a result of specific experiences or stimuli presented to the subject.

event sampling Sampling in which the researcher simply counts the frequency of behaviors or events over a designated period of time.

executive capacity The difference between performance and competence, or a person's peak potential of cognitive or linguistic performance. AKA *zone of proximal development.*

experimenter bias Bias resulting from behavior on the part of the researcher that results in a change in the subject's responses.

expertise Lengthy personal experience regarding a certain subject.

explicit memories Memories that require conscious recall.

external validity The confidence that the results of the study will generalize to the broader population.

failure to thrive (FTT) Condition in which child growth and weight gain is seriously impaired.

false-belief tasks Tasks used to determine whether a child can understand that individuals have different beliefs and emotions.

false-negative error Test result in which a person receives a low test score, yet has the ability or motivation to perform at a high level.

false-positive error Test result in which a person receives a high test score, yet may not have the ability or motivation to perform at a high level.

fine motor abilities Precise motor actions involving small movements.

fixed-trial habituation procedures Repeatedly presenting the same stimulus to a subject over a predetermined time period; the subject has no control over stimulus presentation.

fluid intelligence The ability to quickly solve novel problems.

focus groups Small discussion groups formed to provide qualitative input to the researcher; they allow one to gain insight regarding a particular issue that may not be achieved via a simple survey.

forced-choice paradigm Research approach in which observers records an infant's head-turn and eye movements to two side-by-side stimuli and calculate the infant's orienting response and interest in each stimulus.

formal-operational stage The stage in Piaget's cognitive-developmental theory that pertains to the thinking of adolescents and young adults. Advanced scientific and hypothetical reasoning marks such thinking.

free-recall memory paradigms Research method in which the participant commits the items to memory and then is asked to recall them minutes, hours, or days later without prompts or priming methods.

gender constancy The belief that one's sex is permanent and will not change.

gender identity People's internal image of themselves as androgynous, masculine, or feminine.

gender-schema theory A mental scheme that is used to apply gender-related information to our social world and ourselves.

gender-related attitudes How a person thinks males and females "should" act.

gender-related preference A person's preference for activities, role models, occupations, or characteristics that are stereotypically associated with one gender or the other.

generalized attachment representations A broad set of both conscious and unconscious beliefs and expectancies that one holds for relationships.

gestational age Age, usually calculated in weeks, after conception.

gross motor abilities Broad motor actions, including crawling, walking, and sitting up.

habituation The gradual reduction of attentional processes resulting from the repeated or continued presence of a stimulus.

health-related quality of life Assessment of health that taps the psychological, mental, and social aspects of health.

heritability estimates The relative impact of genetics, environment, or a combination of the two on development and behavior.

High-Amplitude Sucking (HAS) Paradigm Paradigm in which infants are trained to suck on a pacifier to trigger changes in auditory stimulation; used to assess auditory perception.

historical effects The influence of the unique past experiences of participants on the results of the experiment.

implicit memories Recollections that require no conscious effort.

incidental learning tasks A research method used to test the attention control of a child. The researcher gives the child a task that contains distracting features and then assesses the recall frequency of task-irrelevant and task relevant features.

independent variable (IV) Variable that is hypothesized to have an effect on a person's behavior, thinking, or emotions.

infant reactivity How the infant responds to different levels of stimulation.

infant state Stages in an infant's sleep-wake cycle.

information-processing approach A contemporary perspective used to study cognitive processes. Views mental processes much like the workings of a computer.

Institutional Review Board   An institutional oversight committee for research involving human and animal subjects.

instrumental-conditioning paradigm   A research method in which the experimenter presents a stimulus hypothesized to increase a desired response; when the observer see a response, she gives the subject a reinforcer.

instrumentation confounds   Confounds that occur when researchers make mistakes or malfunctions in equipment.

intentional communication   An infant's attempts to use vocalizations, gaze, and gestures to attract another person's attention and alter their behavior.

interaction   Occurs when the relationship between the independent variable and the dependent variable depends on the level of another independent variable.

internal validity   The confidence that the manipulation of the independent variable actually is the cause of a systemic change in the dependent variable.

item reliability   The correlation of a particular item with the total score of the scale.

judgment-comprehension linguistic paradigms   A type of language assessment used for older children, in which the child must decide whether complex sentences are grammatical.

lexical decision-making tasks   An implicit memory assessment in which a participant is simply asked to identify sets of letters as either words or nonwords.

longitudinal design   A design in which the researcher samples individuals constituting a single age group and tracks the developmental progress of the participants over time.

longitudinal-sequences design   A design in which a series of longitudinal studies, using different samples, are completed over time.

main effect   The effect of one independent variable on the dependent variable.

marital quality   A person's evaluation of their overall marital health.

mastery motivation paradigm   Research method in which experimenters model for an infant play behaviors across tasks of varying complexity and later observe the infant during free play for each modeled task.

maturation   Occurs when participants over the course of the study experience naturally occurring intraindividual changes.

memory monitoring   A person's knowledge of memory strategies and how they influence storage-and-retrieval processes.

memory self-efficacy   The confidence people have in their memory abilities and in the efficacy of memory strategies.

memory-span tasks   Tasks used to test the child's ability to recall, in exact order, items presented quickly.

meta-emotions   The ability to think about our emotional abilities, experiences, and expressions.

meta-analysis   Method used to group together studies that contain similar designs, methods, and study populations and then statistically examine the combined effects of the studies on an outcome measure.

metacognitive awareness   Thinking about our own thought processes. For instance, awareness of environmental factors that may facilitate or impede learning. AKA *theory of mind*

microgenetic method   Research method in which observers study subjects intensively over time in order to detect sudden changes in behavior or development.

moral reasoning   The ability to comprehend moral plights experienced by the self and others.

morphology   The study of grammatical morphemes and the mastery of suffixes, prefixes, prepositions, and verb tense.

multivariate correlational design   A design in which the researcher diagrams the theoretical relationships among all study variables.

narrative-elicitation linguistic-production paradigms   A type of language assessment in which a child is asked to describe an event that happened to him or a story he read.

neonates   Newborn infants in their first 28 days of life.

neonatology   The study and treatment of newborn infants.

nonexperimental design   A research design in which the experimenter does not have direct control over the independent variable, because the participants have already experienced the condition or the variable cannot be manipulated. AKA *correlational design*.

nonnormative influences   Rare random or off-time events that affect development.

nonprobability sampling   A sampling method in which the subjects who are most easily accessed are recruited.

normative age-graded influences   Age-related biological, cognitive, or social influences experienced by most people.

normative history-graded influences   Major social or economic events that can influence a generation of people.

object permanence   A child's understanding that when an object leaves the visual field the object remains intact.

object-hiding paradigm   A research method in which the experimenter gives an infant an object, hides it, and records how effectively the infant searches for it.

Observer-based Psychoacoustical Procedure   A research method in which the experimenter presents with an infant continuous and changing sounds. During the presentation, an observer records very subtle changes in infant attention and behavior to determine whether the infant can detect the sound changes.

occupational aspirations Careers and career tracks that adolescents are thinking about pursuing.

occupational expectancies The level of confidence one has about pursuing a particular occupational track.

operational definition A definition assigned to each variable that allows for concrete hypothesis and logical choices of measures to assess the study variables.

orienting response An initial response used by the infant to maximize attention to the stimulus.

organization A memory strategy in which we group together objects or ideas with common features to make them easier to store.

passive parental consent A research approach that assumes that if the form sent to the parent is *not* returned to the experimenter, the parents consent to allow their child to participate in a study.

patterned-elicitation linguistic-production paradigm A type of language assessment in which the researcher involves models a series of phrases, and then asks the child to produce a novel, analogous response.

peer-nomination procedure A method in which children are asked to nominate peers they like of dislike.

pendulum problem A Piagetian task for assessing formal operations, in which the researcher asks the subject to simultaneously consider how an object's speed is affected by various features of the task, such as the size of the object and the lengths of different strings that can attach the object to the pendulum device.

perinatal period The time shortly before and after infant delivery.

phonological assessment Assessing how well a child articulates words and word segments.

postformal thinking Advances in thinking beyond Piaget's period of formal operations.

pragmatics Culturally acceptable conversational techniques, such as turn taking, interruptions, and adjustments in speech intensity.

predictive validity A significant correlation between the measure and an outcome measure that is assessed at a later date.

preoperational stage Piaget's second cognitive-developmental stage, in which older toddlers and preschoolers continue to represent reality using mental images, language, and solitary pretend play. However, thinking is constrained in unfamiliar situations, and the child may lack perspective-taking skills.

pretending or role-playing linguistic-production paradigm A type of language assessment in which the researcher asks a child to act out a role or story and assesses different types of language abilities as the child verbalizes in the role.

private speech Self-talk; talking or whispering to oneself to help organize thought.

probability estimate An estimate used to determine the likelihood of a behavior occurring as a result of a previous behavior.

probability sampling Sampling technique that gives each member of the population the same probability of being selected.

prosocial behavior Voluntary behavior intended to help another person

proximal variable Variable used to reflect a current or recent event.

psychometric approach The assessment of intellect using structured, standardized tests.

psychometric properties Scientific properties, such as reliability and validity, used to determine the adequacy of a research measure.

qualitative approach Holistic method in which the researcher notes global trends in observations or interview behavior; human behavior is not reduced to numbers.

quantitative approach A method in which data is best represented in numerical form; lends itself well to statistical analyses.

quasi-experimental design A design in which *some* of the independent variables cannot be manipulated, and participants cannot be randomly assigned to a particular condition.

quota sampling A sampling technique in which a researcher limits the number of participants included in a study who share a certain characteristic, such as middle-aged, white man.

random selection A method in which the researcher identifies a large potential subject pool that represents the demographic makeup of the target population and then randomly selects participants from this subject pool.

randomized experiment An experimental design in which participants are randomly assigned to experimental conditions.

reactivity Infant responses to different levels of stimulation; a dimension of temperament.

recall memory The ability to spontaneously remember something without the presence of cues.

recognition memory A form of memory in which the subject determines whether an experience is the same or similar to a previous experience.

reflective judgment The understanding that solutions to problems can sometimes create problems in their own right.

rehearsal Simple repetition of information embedded within a task until the data is transferred into long-term memory.

reinforcer A stimulus that increases the occurrence of a behavior.

rejected-aggressive Highly disliked children who bully others, possess limited social and academic skills, and suffer from social information-processing deficits.

rejected-aggressive withdrawn Highly disliked children with limited academic and social skills who display aggression in indirect ways, such as gossiping about others.

rejected-withdrawn Disliked children who typically display silly, immature social behavior.

relational aggression The intentional spreading of rumors to emotionally harm or undermine the social standing of peers.

relativistic thought An understanding that there may be multiple causes and solutions for a problem.

reliability The consistency of a measure in producing the same or similar outcomes over repeated testing.

remote memory The ability to recall events from the distant past.

repetition-priming paradigm An implicit memory method in which subjects must recognize whether they have seen an item or object before; used to assess recognition recall.

representative language sample A sample of spontaneous speech that occurs in a naturalistic setting, such as the child's home.

research sample A group of participants recruited for a study that represents the larger population.

response sets Occurs when participants fall into a pattern of endorsing the same response for every question.

risk comorbidity Exhibiting or experiencing multiple risk factors at the same time.

sampling plan A scheme for defining a population of interest and identifying or recruiting participants who fit this description.

scaffolding How an adult makes adjustments to the motivation, attention, failures, and successes of a child as she guides the child through the task or activity.

scale reliability The interrelatedness of the items in a study. High scale reliability means that items are highly correlated with one another.

scheme Structured knowledge regarding actions and thoughts that allow us to cope with, and learn about, the environment.

school performance Grade point average of grades earned in classes.

secure-base behavior The ability to effectively receive support from an attachment figure and be comforted.

selection bias Bias that occurs when participants are selected from nonequivalent settings, such as recruiting adolescents from colleges and senior citizens from nursing homes.

selective dropout Nonrandom termination of participation in a study.

self-representation A person's general description of his or her self.

self-esteem A person's general feelings about himself and his self-description.

self-rated health An individual's self-report of his or her own health.

self-regulation An infant's attempt to cope with stimuli and how well arousal is inhibited; a dimension of temperament.

semantic memories Broad knowledge regarding important concepts, rules, and general events.

semantic priming paradigm A method to assess a subject's understanding of general rules and concepts, such as understanding that the words *cat* and *dog* are more similar than *flower* and *box*.

sequential analysis A research method that consists of analyzing behavior sequences between two or more individuals.

sequential-touching task Procedure used to determine whether an infant possesses categorization skills; observer notes whether the infant touches objects of a similar category.

setting events Specific behaviors or patterns of social interaction that naturally occur within an environment.

simple random sampling Selecting subjects from the larger population using a specific random method, such as selecting every fifth person.

skill-learning paradigm An implicit memory assessment in which a researcher trains participants to do a very simple task, such as building a tower of blocks. Performance later timed and compared to that of other subjects.

social cognition How we think about our social world.

social conventions Social knowledge about customs within a particular society.

social impact Peer-group visibility; a child may be highly liked or disliked in the peer group.

social-network analysis A detailed peer-group analysis in which researchers document the presence of cliques, crowds, and peers that have multiple or no peer-group affiliations.

social perspective taking   The ability to see the point of view of important social agents, such as parents and peers.

social preference   Popularity, or how much a person is liked by her peers.

social referencing   Imitating and appropriately reacting to the emotional expressions of others.

sociometric methods   Strategies to assess a person's adjustment in the peer group, and how well the person gets along with others.

special populations   Populations that might include people who experience low base rates of a condition, such as clinical depression.

standardization   Uniformity or reliability in procedures across research tasks.

standardized scales   Norm-referenced measures of intellect, growth, or development.

statistical regression   A trend in which participants who score extremely high or low on a measure often begin to score closer to the statistical mean over the course of repeated testing.

Strange Situation   Used to assess infant attachment; the procedure involves a series of brief separations of infant and caregiver.

stratified random sampling   A sampling method used to ensure that a representative number of demographic subgroups exist within the study population.

structural-equation modeling   A technique used to assess all hypothesized relationships simultaneously; the researcher provides statistics regarding how well the data fit into the hypothesized model.

structured observation   An observation in which the researcher manipulates the context and observes the corresponding changes in the behavior of the participants.

study population   All possible subjects available for a study of the target population.

subject matching   Manipulating the participant groups to ensure that equal numbers of participants with similar histories are assigned to each condition group.

subject reactivity   When the research setting causes the participant to behave or think in ways that are not typical.

sympathy   Displaying concern for the welfare of another person.

syntax   The rules for organizing words in sentences.

target population   A hypothetical population with definable labels, such as "early adolescents."

temperament   Individual differences in reactivity and self-regulation resulting from heredity, maturational processes or environmental experiences.

testing effects   Occur when participants are given the same test repeatedly. Participants begin to base their performance upon how they performed on previous assessments.

test-retest reliability study   A study in which participants are asked to complete a measure in two or more trials over a short period of time.

theory   A philosophical assumption about probable associations between different variables or constructs.

theory of mind   Awareness regarding our own thought processes and our beliefs regarding the way the mind operates. AKA *metacognitive awareness.*

thinking-aloud paradigm   Used to assess postformal thought and wisdom-related thinking. The subject is simply asked to verbally reason out dilemmas aloud, and his reasoning is later coded for cognitive complexity.

three-mountain task   Piagetian task in which the subject is asked to consider whether another person can see objects that to you and I, are blocked by a mountain.

360-degree assessment   A work-performance assessment that includes targets' impression of their own performance and supervisor and co-worker appraisals.

time-of-measurement effects   Occurs when major historical events occur during a study. These events then may influence participant behavior. AKA *historical, or cohort, effect.*

time sampling   A method in which the researcher counts the frequency of behavior within periodic time segments over a designated period of time.

time-lag design   A design in which the researcher holds age constant by assessing people of the same age group over time.

transitivity   The ability to apply different ideas or schemes to understand logical conclusions, such as whether pushing a domino over will cause dominos much later in the chain to fall over.

unstructured observation   Observation in which the researcher does not manipulate or alter the subject's behavior.

vagal tone   Variability or patterning of heart beats; a measure of nervous-system integrity.

value autonomy   The development of moral, social-conventional, political, or religious beliefs outside of the thinking of the immediate family system.

visual acuity   How accurately we perceive visual information.

visual cliff   A table is covered with a glass surface, so that it appears to the infant that crawling past a certain point would result in a sudden drop-off; infants that refuse to crawl across are assumed to possess depth perception.

visual-reinforcement audiometry (VRF)   Conditioned head-turning procedures used to study infant auditory processing; can only be used with older infants that are capable of co-ordinated head turns.

working memory   An active mental system that helps us store and retrieve information more effectively.

zone of proximal development   A person's peak cognitive or linguistic performance. AKA *executive capacity.*

Index

Page numbers followed by *f* indicate figures; page numbers followed by *t* indicate tables